PENGUIN BOOKS

# JEFFREY ARCHER
## *Stranger Than Fiction*

Michael Crick was born in Northampton in 1958. He was educated at Manchester Grammar School and New College, Oxford, where he read Philosophy, Politics and Economics. He was also President of the Union, editor of *Cherwell* and founder editor of the *Oxford Handbook*. In 1980 he joined ITN, where he became Washington Correspondent for Channel 4 News and won a Royal Television Society award in 1989. In 1990 he moved to BBC's *Panorama*, and is currently a reporter on *Newsnight*, where he enjoys following Lord Archer in by-election campaigns. His other books include *Militant* (1984); *Scargill and the Miners* (1985); *Manchester United: The Betrayal of a Legend* (with David Smith, 1989); *The Complete Manchester United Trivia Fact Book*; and *Michael Heseltine: A Biography*, recently published by Hamish Hamilton.

Michael Crick divides his time between London, Oxfordshire and Old Trafford. He is married to a former television journalist and they have one daughter.

D0301237

# JEFFREY ARCHER

*Stranger Than Fiction*

## MICHAEL CRICK

PENGUIN BOOKS

PENGUIN BOOKS

Published by the Penguin Group
Penguin Books Ltd, 27 Wrights Lane, London w8 5tz, England
Penguin Books USA Inc., 375 Hudson Street, New York, New York 10014, USA
Penguin Books Australia Ltd, Ringwood, Victoria, Australia
Penguin Books Canada Ltd, 10 Alcorn Avenue, Toronto, Ontario, Canada m4v 3b2
Penguin Books (NZ) Ltd, 182–190 Wairau Road, Auckland 10, New Zealand

Penguin Books Ltd, Registered Offices: Harmondsworth, Middlesex, England

First published by Hamish Hamilton 1995
This revised edition published by Penguin Books 1996
1 3 5 7 9 10 8 6 4 2

Set in 9.5/11.75 pt Monotype Bembo
Typeset by Datix International Limited, Bungay, Suffolk
Printed in England by Clays Ltd, St Ives plc

*To Catherine*

# Contents

CONTENTS

# Illustrations

**17** Jeffrey with Harold Macmillan and a cheque for Oxfam, 1964

**18** With the Beatles in Sir Noel Hall's lodgings at Brasenose College, Oxford, 1964 (© Associated Newspapers)

**19** Jeffrey with President Lyndon Johnson, in the White House, 1964 (Frank Wolfe, LBJ Library Collection)

**20** Jeffrey on the hurdling track, 1966 (© Billett Potter)

**21** Jeffrey and Mary's wedding, 1966 (© Billett Potter)

**22** Jeffrey campaigning with Chris Chataway during the 1967 GLC elections (© Billett Potter)

**23** Mary in her laboratory (© Billett Potter)

**24** Jeffrey with Edward Heath and Leon Underwood at the opening of the Archer Gallery, 1969 (© Billett Potter)

**25** On the steps of Louth Town Hall after winning the 1969 by-election (© Billett Potter)

**26** Jeffrey and Lord Mountbatten at Noël Coward's sickbed, 1970 (© Billett Potter)

**27** Mary during a charity swim in Louth, 1970

**28** Jeffrey on the golf course

**29** Mary with sons William and James (© Billett Potter)

*Third plate section*

**30** Jeffrey with his former personal assistant Andrina Colquhoun (© Alan Davidson)

**31** Monica Coghlan being offered a packet of £50 notes by Jeffrey's emissary, Michael Stacpoole, Victoria station, 1986 (© *News of the World*)

**32** Jeffrey with coffee for journalists outside The Old Vicarage, Grantchester, when the Monica Coghlan story broke (© Press Association)

**33** Jeffrey in front of the Playhouse theatre, which he bought in 1988 (© Associated Newspapers)

**34** Jeffrey's long-lost brother, David Brown, at his wedding in 1988

**35** The cartoonist Jak's response to the news of Jeffrey having a brother (© Jak and the *Mail on Sunday*)

**36** Margaret Thatcher at the Archers' silver-wedding celebrations in 1991 (© Billett Potter)

**37** Jeffrey coaching schoolboy rugby (© Billett Potter)

**38** Jeffrey and Mary with the grotesque she gave him as a silver-wedding present in 1991 (© Billett Potter)

39 Mary *décolletée* in television cabaret, 1992 (© Alan Davidson)

40 Jeffrey with Broosk Saib and others on a visit to Kurdistan, 1992 (© Bob Collier, Times Newspapers Ltd)

41 Jeffrey in the robes of Lord Archer of Weston-super-Mare of Mark in the County of Somerset, with his mother, 1993 (© Bob Bowen)

42 Jeffrey with the author during the 1993 Newbury by-election (Jane Bonham-Carter)

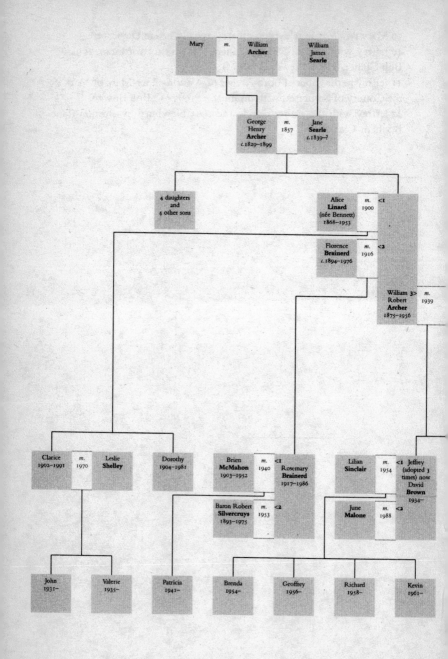

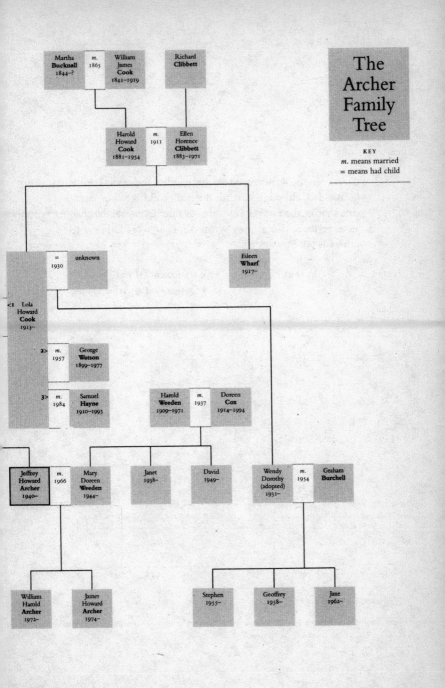

The Archer Family Tree

KEY
*m.* means married
= means had child

Coincidences, writers are told (usually by the critics), must be avoided, although in truth the real world is full of incidents that in themselves are unbelievable. Everyone has had an experience that if they wrote about it would appear to others as pure fiction.

JEFFREY ARCHER, 'THE HUNGARIAN PROFESSOR',
*A Quiver Full of Arrows*, 1980

# Prologue

Writing this book has been an immensely enjoyable experience. Perhaps the most regrettable thing, in fact, has been having to finish it. At times, I find it hard to imagine that I will ever find another subject that is quite as interesting to explore. Whereas most lives are confined to one or two areas of activity, my journey, in contrast, has made me feel almost like another anatomist of modern Britain. There's scarcely an area of public life that Jeffrey Archer's career has not touched at one time or another: politics, both local and national; books and publishing; sport and charities; newspapers and television; theatre and cinema; the law and the City; even the army and the police. The story stretches from the higher reaches of art, academe and government, down to those of financial fraud, prostitution and tabloid journalism.

This rich tapestry is embellished by the great puzzles and mysteries about Jeffrey Archer, the many episodes he has elaborated and the others he never talks about; the strange story of his father, and of his recently discovered long-lost brother. And the great challenge for any Archer biographer is hacking one's way through a formidable jungle of inaccuracies, myths and disinformation.

What follows is the story of the most colourful character in British public life: 'the extrovert's extrovert', as Margaret Thatcher has called him.[1] Like his novels, it's a tale of ambition and power, money and sexual intrigue. His own life is a more compelling story than his own fiction, overflowing with coincidences and twists at almost every stage. Ultimately, I suppose, the story is a tragedy: of how a man with many outstanding qualities is repeatedly brought down by the serious flaws in his character.

The widespread fascination with Jeffrey Archer is more than enough to justify a new biography (this is the second[2]). For more than a decade he has been one of the world's best-selling authors, and one of the most popular Englishmen overseas. At home, Lord Archer is among the few figures to have enjoyed good friendships with the last two Prime Ministers, but it is more than a question of proximity. A self-made millionaire from a lower-middle-class background who hauled himself out of adversity by his enterprise and effort – despite the evident dislike of sections of the British Establishment and intelligentsia – Jeffrey Archer embodies much of the spirit of the Thatcher–Major era, both good and bad. In the words of the Tory MP Julian Critchley, 'The very words "a Jeffrey Archer" came to define a genre: the opium of the striving classes of the Thatcher years.'[3]

This is an independent biography. Others might call it 'unauthorized' or 'unofficial', but I dislike such terms since they provoke all sorts of misleading assumptions. The term 'unauthorized' has come to imply that a work is hostile to its subject, holding out the promise of juicy, sensational revelations. On the other hand, adjectives such as 'authorized' or 'official' suggest that public figures have a right of veto over who writes about them, or what writers say. Yet nobody ever refers to 'authorized' or 'unauthorized' newspaper profiles, or to 'official' or 'unofficial' television portraits.

'It is impossible,' Mary Archer told me, 'to write a serious biography without the cooperation of one's subject.'[4] This seems an uncharacteristically rash judgement. Many of the finest biographies of recent years have been produced without their subjects' cooperation. Among political works, one only has to consider Hugo Young's celebrated portrait of Margaret Thatcher, Ben Pimlott's masterful life of Harold Wilson, or John Campbell's award-winning book about Ted Heath.[5] Was Joe Haines's 'official' biography of Robert Maxwell really superior to the 'unauthorized' account by Tom Bower (which Maxwell tried to stop through the courts and by putting pressure on booksellers)?[6] There are, of course, numerous first-rate 'official' biographies, and many 'unauthorized' lives are truly appalling, but there is no correlation. The crucial factors are an author's skill, diligence, and fair-mindedness. Whatever defects this book has are the result of my shortcomings, rather than because Lord Archer has not cooperated.

Over the years, I have concluded, in fact, that the ideal relationship between a biographer and a living subject is that described by John Campbell in his biography of Heath: no direct help, but no obstacles either.[7] During the course of making several television profiles, I have seen the dangers of getting too close. Subjects who go out of their way to help inevitably create a sense of obligation. Isn't it rather unfair, ungrateful perhaps, after they've spent their free weekends searching out old photos, to dwell upon the more unfortunate aspects of their lives? In the case of Jeffrey Archer, the problems of cooperation would have been particularly acute. What would one do when he insisted on retelling his fanciful claims about his past? Professionally, one cannot ignore them. Yet, if one tried to challenge his assertions, then the 'authorized' biographer might soon become 'unauthorized'.

Nevertheless it was only right that, as soon as I was commissioned to write this book, I should write and tell Lord Archer. My letter suggested a meeting to explain what I planned to do, and I reminded him that I had interviewed him on several occasions for television, including once for a *Panorama* programme about John Major. His response was firm but friendly. My *Panorama*, he felt, had been 'excellent and more to the point fair', but he declined to see me for the book. His tone, and the 'Yours Jeffrey' with which he concluded, suggested, though, that he was not entirely hostile to the project.[8]

Over the past three years, relations between us seem to have swung back and forth. Archer has on occasion written to my publishers complaining about my research methods and threatening legal action. We have been warned how he has been accumulating reports from people I have approached – including, intriguingly, at least one taped report. Many of his friends, apparently, have been ready to swear affidavits.

Yet his attitude towards people talking to me has varied over time. It was some months before I began to approach any of his friends, and, when I did, many said he had asked them not to speak. Educational establishments, for some reason, seemed particularly hostile, and his old Oxford college, Brasenose, was notably unhelpful. So too was Dover College, which once employed Archer as a PE teacher; the headmaster said he had been told to cooperate only with his 'official biographer', though I have yet to encounter this mysterious rival. Archer's old school, Wellington in Somerset, was almost equally uncooperative at first, but for totally the opposite reason, it transpired. Many staff at Wellington are not great fans of their distinguished old boy, and feared I might be working closely with him. When the school discovered my book was independent, it quickly opened up.

Around the middle of 1994 the whole climate began to change, coinciding (and it may be pure coincidence) with the controversy over Archer's involvement in buying Anglia Television shares. Since then I have had little difficulty in seeing almost everyone I wanted; indeed, as my deadline hurtled towards me, I was almost overwhelmed by the sudden new access. People who had previously said 'no' or had ignored my letters were now willing to say their bit, and their contributions were most valuable. As a result, I have now talked to the majority of Lord Archer's closest friends.

Regrettably, one can only thank a small fraction of the many, many people who helped in the writing of this book. I hope those not mentioned here will forgive me.

Over the last three years my wife and I have spoken to well over a thousand people. Many of them asked to remain anonymous, and I am grateful for their help in what were often difficult circumstances. Among those people I can thank publicly are: John Adams, Colin Adamson, Tariq Ali, Bert Allen, Willie Anderson, Don Andrews, Michael Archer, Nicholas Archer, Michael Attenborough, Philip Attenborough, Eddie Bell, Richard Benson, Tom Benyon, the late Humphry Berkeley, Jean Blackbourn, Janet Blackman, Jim Bolton, Derick Bostridge, Terry Bown, Sir Ashley Bramall, Tom Brennand, Ed Breslin, Peter Brewer, Bruce Briggs, David Bromfield, John Bromley, Bernard Brook-Partridge, Michael Brotherton, Brenda Brown, David and June Brown, Gerry Brown, Janet Brown, John Bryant, Kathleen Burnett, Ronald Burrows, Menzies Campbell, Craig Carle, David Carter, Stephen Catt, Chris Chalker, Don Chapman, Peter Chapman, Ray Chapman, Sir Christopher Chataway, Elspeth Chowdharay-Best, Susannah Clapp, John Clare, Colin Clark, Jonathan Coleman, Joyce Collins, Ray Cooney, John Creber, Susan Crosland, Joan Czarnowski, Bruce Dakowski, Julian Dakowski, Marshall Dale, Daniel Dane, Trevor Deaves, Brian Donnelly, Cyril Dowzell, Peter Duke, Ray Dwerryhouse, Ray Edbroke, Bryan Edgell, Janet Eldershaw, Colin Emson, David Ennals, Joni Evans, Richard Exley, Cynthia Farrar, Peter Fawcett, Jill Fisher, John FitzSimons, Clixby Fitzwilliams, Alan Fleming, Jo Fletcher, the late Charlie Ford, Mike Fox, Sir Paul Fox, Ted Francis, Peter Fridlington, Dick Frost, Tudor Gates, Nancy Gee, Philip Gilbert, Sir Arthur Gold, John Golding, Janet Goodyer, Alan Gordon Walker, Maureen Gough, John Gray, Graham C. Greene, Thomas Guinzburg, Lady Elinor Hall, Tom Hardie-Forsyth, Mike Harvey, Valerie Haynes, Martin Henderson, Harvey Hinds, Michael Hogan, John Holt, Hugh Horrex, David Howard, Brian Hulls, Doug Hunt, Robert Hutchison, Derek Ingram, Leonard Isaac, Donald Isles, Bill Johnstone, Tim Jones, Frank Keating, John Kennedy, Peter Killmister, Mig Kimpton, Damien Knight, Trevor

Knight, Rick Kwiatowski, Paul Lamberth, Peter and Carol Lawford, Mort Leavy, David Lewin, Harry Linard, John Lisners, Sir Nicholas Lloyd, John Lovesey, Simon Lytle, Euan MacAlpine, Gordon McBride, David McCall, James McClarnon, Pat Macnaughton, Hugh MacPherson, Jill Makinson-Sanders, Alex Manson, Graham Marks, Jonathan Martin, Tom Maschler, Derek Matthews, George and Penny Matthews, Dave Mattrick, Lee Menzies, Adrian Metcalfe, Evelyn Miller-Barstow, Sir Roger Moate, Tom Mori, Brian Morris, Mike Morris, Jack Moultrie, Alan Mouncer, Mary Mountain, Sally Mountain, Patrick Mullins, John Nash, Charles Neel, Christian Neffe, Leona Nevler, John Nicolson, Philip Norton, Robert Oakley, Michael O'Flaherty, Chris Ogden, Robert Opekar, Andrew Orgill, Pat Otter, Deborah Owen, Paul Oxley, Paul Packer, Larry Park, Geoffrey Parkhouse, John Parsons, Anthony Patten, Sir Geoffrey Pattie, Corinna Peterson, James Philbrick, Richard Platts, Ian Posgate, Billett Potter, Howard Preece, Hope Preminger, Alan Quilter, Alvin Rakoff, J. K. Randle, Adam Raphael, Latif Rashid, Jacqueline Redfern, Sandy Richardson, Bruce Ronaldson, Andrew Ronay, John Roper, Richard Rottenbury, Hilary Rubinstein, Gordon Rudlin, Mike Runswick, Neil Russell, Nigel Ryan, Jack Saltman, Dennis Selinger, John Sellick, Henry Sharpley, Clifford Smith, Cork Smith, Brian Sommerville, Neil Speakes, Michael Stacpoole, Nick Stames, John Steadman, Stewart Steven, Michael Stevens, Jonathan Stockland, David Stockton, John Sunley, Michael Taudevin, Philippa Taylor, Tim Taylor, Harvey Thomas, Mike Thomas, Sir Neil Thorne, Jane Thornton, Gertie Tidball, Henry Togna, Martin Tomkinson, Adrian Twiner, Garth Underwood, Jocelyn Underwood, John Vance, Sam Vaughan, Mike Vincent, Peter Walker, Louise Walsh, Raymond Walters, Peter Wareham, Mel Watman, Susan Watt, Gordon Webb, Michael Webb, Joe West, Phyllis West, Natalie Wexler, Rosemary Whitley, Franklin Wilson, Gordon Wiltsher, Ernest Wistrich, John Woods, George Wool, Duncan Worsley and Nadhim Zahawi.

I have also received valuable help from: Brian Austin, David Bailey, John Bailey, David Bauckham, Reginald Beevers, Maggie Black, Tony Brown, Nick Brunger, Michael Carrington-Wood, Terry Coleman, Tom Crone, Ann Cullen, Rohan Daft, Ian Docherty, Ed Donner, Philip Dutton, Philomena Dwyer, Ruth Escritt, Maureen Ferrier, Paul Flather, Alastair Fyfe, David Gentle, Matthew Gilmore, Sarah Goddard, Tim Godfray, Peter Golds, Anthony Gorringe, Victor Glynn, Sir Peter Hall, Richard Hall, Paul Henderson, Peter Hildreth, Mark Hollingsworth,

Chris Horrie, Steve Humphries, Ian Jack, 'Jak', Oliver James, Tom Kelly, Judi Kisiel, Geoffrey Levy, Anne Lonsdale, Jim Lyttle, George Mackie, Jonathan Margolis, Jean May, Sheridan Morley, Gary Newbon, Richard Northedge, Daksha Patel, Richard Pring, Jim Railton, Jean Richardson, Jean Scott Rogers, Paul Rossi, Mary Rowsell, Philip Sankey, Alison Sergeant, David Sheppard, Bob Sparks, Nigel Spencer Knott, Elizabeth Stamp, John Stapleton, Kenneth Stephenson, Joe Storr, Graham Terrell, John Thompson, Harry Thompson, Matty Townsend, Janet Watson, Sir David Wills, Peter Wilson, Graham Witham and John Withington.

One of the most surprising aspects of the research is how much documentary material about Archer is available in archives. Professor Geoffrey Chamberlain and Shirley Dixon kindly let us consult the files of the National Birthday Trust held at the Wellcome Institute; Gina Dobbs of Random House and Michael Bott at Reading University granted access to the Jonathan Cape archives; Malcolm Harper and Angela Raspin helped me examine the UNA papers at the London School of Economics; while Jeff Walden came up with several interesting documents from the BBC Written Archives Centre at Caversham. I am also grateful for access to the archives of Hodder & Stoughton; Oxfam; the Oxford Union; and the Oxford University Athletics Club. Michael Parrish sent copies of material from the LBJ Library at Austin, in Texas; Christopher Woolgar provided items from the Mountbatten archive at Southampton University; and the Theatres Trust supplied material about the Playhouse theatre. Barry Purkis, Adam Gotch and Anna Pim helped with numerous items from the BBC film and video library. Fazila Shaw and Monica Zeller of the Ontario Securities Commission, and Ruth Maillard and Angela Slazak of the Ontario Attorney-General's office, all demonstrated the value of Canada's freedom of information law. I am also indebted to the Public Records Office in both Chancery Lane and Kew; St Catherine's House; Somerset House; and the local records offices of Bristol, Essex, Gloucestershire, Greater London, Somerset and Wiltshire.

Bryan Rostron and Paul Foot generously lent me a lot of Archer material they have gathered over the years. Christopher Wilson and Danny Gittings also passed on important information from their Archer files. Andrew Huxtable of the Association of Track and Field Statisticians and Malcolm Warburton both helped with details of Archer's athletics career, and John Bromhead welcomed me to the Centre for Athletics

Literature at Birmingham University. Chris Capron supplied useful material from the Louth by-election. Deborah Hoffmann of the *New York Times* and Morgan Roberts of *Publishers Weekly* both compiled data on their bestseller lists. Colin Randall of the *Bookseller* and Suzanne Collier of the Society of Young Publishers also did much to help.

I received assistance, too, from the following media outlets: *Ariel*, Associated Newspapers, the *Bristol Evening Post* and *Western Daily Press*, *Cherwell*, *Dover Express*, *Evesham Journal*, *Grimsby Evening Telegraph*, *Iron Duke*, ITN, *The Job*, *London Police Pensioner*, *Louth Leader*, *Louth Standard*, *Lymington Times*, *One Lime Street*, *Oxford Mail and Times*, *Oxford Today*, Press Association, *Wellington Weekly News* and the *Weston Mercury*. The most valuable of all was News Information at the BBC.

Without librarians, any researcher would be lost. I must acknowledge help from staff at the British Museum; the British Newspaper Library at Colindale; the Bodleian Library, Oxford; the City of London Guildhall Library; the Library of Congress and the National Archives, Washington DC; the local history libraries in Bristol, Dover, Glasgow, Gloucester, Grimsby, Louth, Southwark, Tower Hamlets, Washington DC and Weston-super-Mare; and the reference libraries of Birmingham, Chipping Norton, Manchester, New York, Oxford, Romford, Toronto, Vancouver, Wandsworth and Westminster.

David Hawkings helped investigate Jeffrey's father; my sister, Anne Bellingham, researched William Archer's political career; Anne Cronin discovered the amazing story of his American daughter; and John McGinnis skilfully gained access to valuable legal archives.

It was Bill Hamilton, my agent, who originally suggested the idea while chatting on the steps of the Tate Gallery, within sight of Archer's flat. At Hamish Hamilton, Andrew Franklin was steadfast, encouraging and enthusiastic; Keith Taylor, Kate Jones and the hawk-eyed Bob Davenport all suggested great improvements to the manuscript. Ruth Salazar proved an excellent negotiator, while Cecily Engle and Andrew Stephenson offered wise advice.

The committee of Swerford Village Hall again lent me a peaceful place to spread out my papers and work without interruption. My colleagues at *Newsnight*, particularly my editors, Tim Gardam and Peter Horrocks, have shown remarkable understanding.

Andrew Curry did a wonderful job knocking my original text into shape. John Crick and Pat Crick also read early drafts and proposed numerous adjustments.

Above all, I am grateful to my wife, Margaret, for her great research, and for conducting many hundreds of interviews. She traced every single one of Archer's surviving colleagues from the 1967 GLC, and found more than a hundred people who did the DipEd with him at Oxford. She also compiled the photographs.

Finally, thank you to Catherine for being so patient.

Michael Crick
Swerford, Oxfordshire

# I

# In Search of William Archer

The old cemetery rests on a hillside overlooking the town. Nowadays the dead of Weston-super-Mare are usually buried or cremated at the new cemetery and crematorium, two miles away on the outskirts. But the former burial-ground is still well-maintained, its grass, trees and pathways all tended for the occasional visitor.

'Walk down to the upper section of plot "T",' the official had explained, pointing to the photocopied map he'd given me. 'It should be twenty-six graves up, and two in from the left-hand side.'

A casual passer-by would never notice the site: there's no headstone, just a rectangle of plain kerb-stones worn by the Atlantic weather. The inscription is so illegible one has to kneel down and slowly trace out the letters with a finger:

> In loving memory of William Archer died February 17th 1956
> Rest In Peace

Judging from its appearance, I was probably the first in a very long time to visit the grave. There are no dead flowers drooping from an old vase, no signs that anyone still remembers him.

According to the report in the *Weston Mercury*, only fourteen people came to William Archer's funeral service at the local Holy Trinity Church.[1] Archer's widow, Lola, and her mother, Ellen Cook, were the two principal mourners that winter day. None of William Archer's blood relatives attended the ceremony. Even his fifteen-year-old son Jeffrey was told to remain at his boarding-school, thirty-five miles away. 'He was very, very distressed about his father's death,' his mother, Lola, explained years later. 'The headmaster advised me not to let Jeffrey go to the funeral.' Jeffrey has never once discussed his father's death with her, she said. More surprising still, the small, forgotten grave on the hillside above Weston is totally unfamiliar to him. 'He has never seen his father's grave,' she added.[2]

1

'I was very close to my father,' Jeffrey Archer said recently.[3] Yet, judging from the few fragments of detail he's given the world about William Archer over the years, he cannot have known him well. Indeed, so much that Jeffrey has said about his father has turned out to be mistaken that a great mystery has built up about who William Archer really was. At times this author began to wonder if William Archer ever actually existed. The grave in the Weston cemetery plot provides one of the few remaining pieces of tangible evidence.

The first problem is the name, which had several variations. His death certificate records him as Archibald William Archer, yet on his birth certificate eighty years earlier he was William Robert Archer. At times in between he was just plain William. And, as we shall see, on occasion he was not averse to giving completely false names.

The second difficulty is that William Archer – as I shall call him – had a terrible tendency to invent whole aspects of his life. Often the motive seems simply to have been romantic embellishment and self-aggrandizement. But occasionally there seems to have been a more sinister motive: to cover up the darker, unsavoury aspects of his past.

William Archer's funeral report in the *Weston Mercury* says he served in France as 'a captain in the Royal Engineers during the First World War'.[4] One would expect this information to be fairly reliable, since his widow, Lola Archer, worked as a journalist on the newspaper at that time.

Talk to those who knew him in Somerset in the 1940s and early 1950s, and they too remember him as Captain Archer. Yet the Royal Engineers have no record from that period of any Captain William Robert Archer or Archibald William Archer. Perhaps his obituary got the wrong corps? No, for there is no record of any such Archer serving as an officer anywhere in the British army during the First World War, or for the whole of the period from 1900 to 1940.[5] Jeffrey Archer has sometimes referred to his family's living on his father's army pension, yet for the years after 1940 there is no record of any relevant Archer receiving an officer's pension. So, William Archer's claims to have been an officer in the British army were bogus.

But Jeffrey Archer himself has greatly contributed to the confusion. His version is slightly different. 'My father was a colonel in the Somerset Light Infantry,' he has said.[6] Again one ends up chasing wild geese: that regiment has no trace of his father either.

Strangest of all is the story of the Distinguished Conduct Medal

(DCM) which William Archer was supposed to have won, and which has occasionally been mentioned in profiles.[7] When approached by a representative of the DCM League on one occasion, Jeffrey said, 'I never talk about my father and the DCM,' but he happily agreed to join the organization. League membership is confined to medal-winners and their offspring, and officials seem to have been confused by the fact that a William Archer from the Somerset Light Infantry was recorded as winning the DCM in 1915. But then a man came forward to say that that particular soldier was his grandfather, and definitely not related to Jeffrey Archer, and so in 1992 the novelist was politely asked to resign.

And there is not just William Archer's supposed military career to contend with, but a diplomatic one too. In 1973 Jeffrey told Terry Coleman of *The Guardian* that his father once served as British Consul in Singapore.[8] This is a particularly strange claim, since Singapore was a British colony, and therefore had no British consul. Is it possible that William Archer served as a consul in Singapore for some other country? No. The *Colonial Office Lists* for 1920 to 1940 show no foreign consul in Singapore with Archer's name.[9]

Some of these inaccurate stories stem no doubt from the efforts of a sad, elderly man to polish up a rather lacklustre, unglamorous life for the benefit of his wife and son. But some of William Archer's false claims were more serious; in the case of some official documents he was guilty of perjury. When Archer married Lola in 1939, for instance, their marriage certificate stated that he was fifty-four years old; in fact he was sixty-three. He also claimed, quite incorrectly, that his father had been a farmer.[10] There is good reason to suspect that the falsification of such details and his significant name-changes were both designed to conceal highly embarrassing aspects of his past.

So what is the truth? Who was Jeffrey Archer's father?

Any exploration of the Archer family background is made all the harder by the extraordinary time-span covered by just three generations. Between them, Jeffrey, his father and his paternal grandfather bridge the last 165 years. Neither the inscription on the grave in Weston cemetery nor the obituary in the *Weston Mercury* mentions that William Archer was eighty years old when he died in 1956, having been born way back in 1875. And to find the birth of Jeffrey Archer's paternal grandfather we have to leap all the way back to the reign of King George IV.

Our line of Archers hailed originally from Cricklade, in Wiltshire, where Jeffrey Archer's grandfather, George, was born around 1829, the son of William Archer, a local farmer, and his wife, Mary.

In November 1821, eight years before George Archer was born, Cricklade was briefly visited by the journalist and social reformer William Cobbett. He judged it a 'corrupt' and 'villainous hole' despite his wide, hard-bitten experience of rural England:

A more rascally looking place I never set my eyes on ... The labourers seem miserably poor. Their dwellings are little better than pig-beds, and their looks indicate that their food is not nearly equal to that of a pig ... In my whole life I never saw human wretchedness equal to this ... everything had the air of the most deplorable want.[11]

Like much of the English population in the early nineteenth century, the Archer family worked on the land. William Cobbett argued that Cricklade's farming community gained little from its toil, even though the area boasted 'some of the very finest pastures in all England, and some of the finest dairies of cows'.[12] Instead, he said, most of the profit went to those who sold their produce in London. As farmers, the Archer family would have been better off than local agricultural labourers, but they nevertheless seem to have reached much the same conclusion as William Cobbett. When George Archer was still a boy, his family set out to try their luck in the East End of London.

By the time George Archer married Jeffrey Archer's grandmother, Jane Searle, in Stepney in 1857, he had begun running his own cheesemonger's shop in Islington, where the couple lived for a short period before moving back to the East End. Despite his rural upbringing, it is clear that George Archer knew how to write – unlike a large part of the British population at that time – for both he and his wife signed their own names in the parish marriage register.[13]

The commercial East End of his father and grandfather is the setting for Jeffrey Archer's seventh novel, As the Crow Flies, published in 1991. Intriguingly, it's not clear how much Archer realized when he wrote the story that this was his own family background. If he did, one would have expected him to trumpet the fact while he was promoting the book; yet he doesn't appear to have mentioned it. The novel's hero, Charlie Trumper, is born, and later pitches his vegetable barrow, in the Whitechapel Road, only a few hundred yards from the Archer family home in Stepney Green. If Archer wasn't overtly aware of the connection when he wrote the book, was he subconsciously influenced, perhaps, by tales he'd heard as a young boy sitting on his father's knee?

> Granpa – who was a costermonger by trade – worked the pitch on the corner of Whitechapel Road . . . I quickly discovered that he was reckoned by the locals to be the finest trader in the East End.[14]

But George Archer enjoyed nothing of the success of the fictitious Charlie Trumper's Granpa. For while Trumper's barrow eventually grew into a great department store, George Archer's business lasted only a few years. His cheesemonger's shop appears in the Post Office directories for 1858 and 1862, but disappears with the 1864 edition.[15] By the time of the 1871 census George Archer is merely listed as a 'cheese-monger's assistant'.[16]

According to the records, George and Jane Archer had at least nine children. Their eighth, William Robert, was born in Mile End in May 1875. This was Jeffrey Archer's mysterious father. By now, George had abandoned the cheese trade to become a caretaker with one of the new local board schools springing up with the advent of universal education. Though it would not have been a particularly well-paid job, it was more secure than selling cheese, and the family were provided with a house by the education board.

George Archer died at the age of sixty-nine in 1899, and so just missed seeing his son William get married the following year. William was a clerk to a solicitor in the City, and had already left the East End, moving out along the Eastern Railway into Essex, to the rapidly grow-ing village of Ilford. According to the marriage certificate, William Archer's bride was a widow called Alice Linard, the daughter of a publican from Plaistow. At thirty-two she was seven years older than her new husband, and she brought with her two children, a girl and a boy, from her previous marriage. Although Alice Linard was a devout Roman Catholic, the wedding took place in the local Anglican church.

Within four years the Archers had produced two daughters of their own. Clarice arrived in 1902, and Dorothy was born two years later. He may not have been aware of it until recently, but these were Jeffrey's half-sisters.

The Archers remained in Ilford for almost ten years, though they regularly moved house. Then in 1907, at the age of thirty-two, William Archer took a dramatic step into politics, contesting a council by-election not in Ilford but in Stepney. He stood as the Conservative and Municipal Reform candidate.

'I am a local man, was born in the neighbourhood,' William Archer declared to the voters, 'and having been in your midst all my life, am well acquainted with the needs and requirements of the District.'[17] This was rather misleading, for Archer failed to mention that he actually lived in Ilford, six miles from Stepney. He was entitled to stand for Stepney only because he worked in the area.

Though he fought on a Conservative ticket, and his campaign was run by the party's local agent, Archer's manifesto reads today more like that of a Labour candidate. 'I am in favour of, and will at all times support the payment of Trade Union rates of wages, and Trade Union Conditions,' he asserted, promising 'to enforce vigorously the various Acts relating to Public Health, Sanitation and the Adulteration of Food ... Much illness can be prevented in a district like ours by improved sanitary conditions.' And Archer condemned 'the injustice' whereby 'the wealthier areas are enabled to escape a large portion of their obligations to the community of London as a whole'.[18] In other words, the richer outer London suburbs should contribute more to poorer, inner-city boroughs such as Stepney.

The election was keenly fought, with extensive coverage in the local press. His Labour opponent, Tom Healey, was reported to have the backing of several prominent local Catholics – a significant force in Stepney politics – and to have more posters on display. But on election day, six days before Christmas, it was very close. Archer lost by a margin of six, polling 401 votes to Healey's 407.[19]

Just seven weeks later Archer won a second by-election in the same ward. This time the contest received far less publicity, and in a straight fight he easily overcame his Labour opponent by almost two to one – 677 votes to 385.[20] The ease of his victory may be accounted for partly by the fact that he'd now dropped the Conservative label and stood solely as a 'Municipal Reform' candidate.

Yet William Archer was still a member of the Conservative Party, according to the local press, and both he and his wife, Alice, were active members of the Primrose League, a grass-roots Conservative organization which was active in working-class areas and committed to the memory of Benjamin Disraeli. The local press reported their attendance at several League meetings.

Councillor Archer soon emerged as a vigorous champion of the Stepney borough workforce in their struggles with the council hierarchy. At one of his first meetings he backed a motion to limit the borough treasurer's salary to £600 a year, and then, only a few days later, supported proposals for a minimum council wage of 28s 6d a week – £74 2s a year. He argued that no councillor 'could expect any man with a wife and family to live on less'.[21]

Then suddenly William Archer seems mysteriously to have vanished. After being a diligent attender at council meetings, gaining regular mentions in the local press, no more was heard of him locally. After September 1909 he failed to attend a single meeting of Stepney Borough Council, and he didn't bother to defend his seat in the elections that November. His name came off the electoral roll in Ilford and disappeared from the Post Office directories where once he was mentioned every year.

To find out what next happened to William Archer, I decided to trace the descendants of his 1900 marriage to Alice Linard. When I found a granddaughter, Valerie Haynes, living in south-west London, she was naturally quite surprised to learn she might be closely related to Jeffrey Archer. Mrs Haynes explained that her grandfather, William Archer, did not have a good reputation within her family. The story passed down over the years was that Alice Linard had inherited a good sum of money before she married Archer. But he had quickly spent most of it, and then deserted Alice and her family to go and live with another woman. Alice was forced to pawn or sell many of the remaining family possessions, including fine furniture and individual portraits of the children. One indelible family memory is of the shock one day when one of William's daughters spotted her own picture for sale in a shop window.[22]

As for what became of William Archer, Val Haynes could only remember sketchy stories about him going off to America. It would take another year before I had any confirmation of this. And I stumbled across it almost by accident, during a spare moment in the New York Public Library.

While waiting for a librarian to fetch something else, I came across a biographical index to the *New York Times*. Taking a quick look, I found one reference to an 'Archer, William Robert', though this simply passed me to a separate entry for 'Grimwood, William'. In turn the Grimwood entry referred to an item about a divorce suit, dated 1 April 1919. Things did not look promising: after all, the chances of it being *my* William Robert Archer must be slim. Why would the *New York Times* be interested in a divorce involving an obscure Englishman? But with nothing better to do I ordered up the microfilm. The grainy headline seemed to leap out from the screen:

## WANTS MARRIAGE ANNULLED
### FORMER MISS BRAINARD [*sic*] CHARGES 'WAR HERO'
#### WAS PRETENDER

Instantly I knew the three short paragraphs resolved the mystery of what had happened to Archer. Suddenly the disparate fragments of detail I'd gathered, the unpromising lines of inquiry, all fitted together neatly. And the vital link with my William Archer was clinched by the penultimate line: 'He was married in 1900 to Alice Lenard [*sic*] in Essex, Eng.'[23]

The 1919 article in the *New York Times* led me to several longer reports in the Washington newspapers, though it took another eighteen months to persuade the New York Supreme Court to release its file on the case. Together, these items and court papers from the US National Archives told a quite fascinating story. Jeffrey Archer's father had spent the First World War fighting not in the trenches, but in the courts. He was exposed as a compulsive liar, an imposter and a conman, pursued by the police in three separate countries.

The New York divorce trial had taken evidence from a string of witnesses who'd appeared at special legal hearings in London. One man confirmed how during Archer's marriage to Alice Linard, her husband had indeed spent money liberally, 'originally living in a very large house at Ilford, keeping horses and traps, and playing the part of a man who was possessed of a considerable income'.[24] Alice Linard herself told how Archer had got into such debt that, around 1908, they had been forced to sell their home, and her husband soon deserted her. Alice also provided a fascinating reason as to why Archer may have left. When she had married him in 1900, she had genuinely believed she was a widow, and that her previous husband, William Linard, had disappeared overseas and died. But then, around 1907, Linard dramatically turned up again. Legally, his reappearance nullified Alice's 1900 marriage to William Archer, but Linard made no attempt to re-establish the previous relationship. Indeed, he even furnished Archer with documents to help put Alice's second marriage back on a legal footing.

But William Archer was not interested in legitimizing his marriage to Alice Linard. By now he was living with another woman, a Miss Kingston, with whom he appears to have had at least one child. 'I am positive of one,' Alice Archer told the court, 'but by hearsay two.'[25] In September 1909, Archer had set himself up as a mortgage broker, trading under the name of Williams and Co. The following spring he and Kingston went into catering, and opened the Bristol Restaurant in East Street, Brighton. But neither business lasted very long, and in October 1910, with debts of £356, William Archer was declared bankrupt by the High Court in London.

Apparently undeterred by these failures, and even before the bankruptcy had been formally declared, Archer set sail for New York in search of new business ideas. According to Alice Archer, 'he came home with a chewing gum machine and sold chewing gum'.[26] But this enterprise was a failure too.

Soon William Archer began resorting to increasingly dishonest methods, especially when he resumed work as a mortgage broker in central London. In October 1914, just after the outbreak of the First World War, he appeared at the Old Bailey for a series of fraud offences dating from 1912. The first indictment arose from a cheque for £7 7s, made out to a George Pike, with which Archer had been entrusted. It was alleged that he did 'unlawfully and fraudulently convert the said property to his own use and benefit'.[27]

Second, Archer was accused of obtaining two separate sums of money – £32 and £18 10s – from a man called Walter Speed, 'by false pretences . . . with intent to defraud', and 'unlawfully obtaining credit to an amount of £20 and upwards' from Speed 'without informing him he was an undischarged bankrupt'.[28]

The sums involved were relatively trivial, even by the standards of the time, but the charges were merely those the authorities were confident they could win. Scotland Yard later revealed they actually suspected Archer of far greater deception during his spell as a mortgage broker, and of having obtained almost £600 under false pretences from five other people.[29]

The Old Bailey case was postponed for a month and Archer was released on bail, having persuaded a man called John Austin to guarantee the necessary £200. When the trial reopened, however, Archer had absconded. Amidst the turmoil of war, little effort seems to have been made to trace him.

William Archer had in fact gone to France, and found work as an orderly helping injured soldiers at an American hospital in Neuilly. This might seem an honourable enough war record, were it not that

Archer almost certainly went abroad to escape justice. He had also acquired a false identity, using a passport in the name of William F. G. Grimwood, an Ilford solicitor whom Archer knew through legal business and Masonic circles.

In 1919 the solicitor explained to the New York Supreme Court how Archer had acquired the passport. In 1914 Archer had asked him to go to Paris on a business matter. When the solicitor explained that he had no passport, Archer offered to help obtain one, and got Grimwood to fill in an application form. But then, Grimwood testified, Archer postponed the Paris trip and quickly disappeared.[30] It seems he then simply applied for the passport himself using Grimwood's form but his own photograph.

Around the start of 1916 'William Grimwood', as Archer now called himself, used this fraudulent passport to venture further, returning to New York on the steamer *Rochambeau*. According to later court evidence, he used the voyage to ingratiate himself with as many influential passengers as he could find who might provide useful entrées into American society.

'Grimwood' arrived in New York claiming to be a British army surgeon who had come to America to recuperate from a serious war injury. His story was that his ambulance had been hit by an enemy shell on the battlefield; four colleagues, he claimed, had been killed, while he himself had been badly wounded by shrapnel in the stomach and spent five months confined to a dug-out shelter. 'Grimwood' even showed gullible admirers a scar on his stomach, together with a small album of photos of himself supposedly at the front, dressed both in an officer's uniform and in doctor's clothing. He also carried a small medical case and claimed to have amputated numerous limbs on the battlefield.

At that point the United States had not entered the First World War, but many Americans were sympathetic to the British cause. The man who would later be known around Weston-super-Mare as Captain Archer was soon being celebrated in wealthy east coast circles as a courageous and glamorous war hero. Not for the last time were American audiences captivated by an Archer's clever stories.

His new persona was certainly impressive. After going to Eton, 'William Grimwood' claimed, he'd studied medicine at Oxford University. Often he would proudly show people a silver cigarette-case and explain that the twenty or so signatures engraved upon it belonged to old friends from Oxford, all of whom had been killed in the trenches. The story was that, after qualifying, 'Grimwood' had practised as a physician in

London, and had also stood for Parliament. (The real William Grimwood had, in fact, been a Liberal Parliamentary candidate.) Intriguingly, bogus academic qualifications and an embellished political record will crop up again in this biography.

Americans were also left in no doubt that 'William Grimwood' was a man of considerable wealth and standing. He owned enough property back in England, he told people, to generate an income of $12,000 a year. Not only was his sister married to Sir Charles Cust, equerry to King George V, but 'Grimwood' also boasted a close friendship with Sir John Dewar, the Scotch whisky distiller, claiming that his influence had secured Sir John's knighthood. In reality, Archer had merely been a clerk to Dewar's solicitor, and may also have known him when Dewar served as a Conservative MP in Stepney from 1900 to 1906.

Just as his son, Jeffrey, would later become an enthusiastic charity fund-raiser, in 1916 'William Grimwood' got involved in American organizations raising money for injured allied soldiers. It was through this work, and while staying with a New York couple who had be-friended him, that Archer met Florence Brainerd. Aged twenty-two, she was on a visit from Washington DC, where her father was a prosper-ous estate agent.

As she listened to the English army officer Florence Brainerd was spellbound by his stories of heroic deeds on the Western front, and impressed by his apparent wealth and status. As for his personal circum-stances, he told Florence he was only thirty-two (instead of forty-one), and, she later testified, 'he told me that he had been a widower for eight years'. In one of the few details that was actually true, he also said he had two daughters.[31]

Then, Florence would later allege, 'the glamour which surrounded [Archer] and the sympathy excited by the honourable wounds which he professed to have received on the battlefield, led [her] to listen to his proposals of marriage'. But she was hesitant, not because of any doubts about him, she later explained, but uncertainty about the 'depth and permanency of her love' for him. The Englishman finally persuaded her, it seems, by saying he would soon have to return to England and 'that it was essential to his happiness that [she] should go with him as his wife'.[32]

So, just three weeks after they had first met, the couple married at one of the best-known churches in Manhattan, the Little Church Around the Corner, not far from the famous Flatiron Building. Immediately afterwards 'Grimwood' produced what he said were congratulatory telegrams from both his mother and his sister, Lady Cust. None of Florence's family had attended the ceremony, and her parents didn't even know about it until she phoned them in Washington just beforehand. After the event she sent them a telegram confirming that she was now Mrs Grimwood. The Brainerds were no doubt anxious about what had happened, but when their new son-in-law visited Washington a few days later, they found him 'a man of pleasing manners and personality', and immediately accepted him as a member of the family.[33]

The newly-married couple spent several months on an extended honeymoon in Bronxville, just north of New York City. The bride would later relate how she and her husband were extremely happy at this time. He showed 'apparent affection and generosity' and 'lavished presents upon her', and before long Florence was pregnant.[34] Then, towards the end of 1916, Archer resumed his fund-raising, travelling to several cities on behalf of various war charities.

For one project, 'Grimwood' told potential donors he needed 'money for the purpose of purchasing artificial arms for wounded soldiers of the French army'. The Carnes Artificial Limb Company in New York, he claimed, had already agreed to deliver fourteen false arms to Paris, at a cost of $3,500.[35]

Then suddenly, in January 1917, while having breakfast at the Capital Park Hotel in Washington DC, Archer was arrested, and held in custody on charges of taking money under false pretences. A preliminary police court heard how one man, Harry Wardman, had donated $250 towards 'Grimwood's' limb venture. Two other witnesses said they'd given him $100 and $30. Yet despite 'Grimwood's' claims, the court learned that the Carnes company knew nothing of an order for fourteen artificial limbs.[36]

William Archer pleaded not guilty, but in June 1917, at the Supreme Court in the District of Columbia, he was convicted on the evidence of eleven witnesses. He was sentenced to three years in prison, but first sent to Washington asylum. In November 1917, however, Archer was allowed to withdraw his 'not guilty' plea, and his punishment was reduced to a suspended sentence. Having been incarcerated for almost ten months, William Archer was released on probation.

Archer left America immediately; his wife Florence hadn't seen him since the day he was arrested and never met him again. But rather than return to Britain, he simply slipped across the border into Canada and resumed his criminal career, still in the guise of William Grimwood. In November 1918 he appeared in court in Toronto for an offence committed within days of entering the country. 'Grimwood' had tricked a woman called Dorothy Whittaker into letting him take care of five $100 war bonds she owned. 'He was to put them in a safety vault in the Bank of Montreal for me,' Whittaker explained. 'I asked him several times for the bonds but never got them back.'[37] Archer had instead used them to buy himself a car. He was sentenced to a year's hard labour in the Ontario reformatory, but again the punishment was never carried out; instead he was deported back to Britain.

Having been convicted of serious dishonesty in both the United States and Canada, Archer was arrested on his return to England and at last faced the fraud charges left over from 1914 when he'd jumped bail. Archer urged the Old Bailey judge to deal with the case quickly, and, with a slight variation on his old story, claimed to be suffering from the effects of a serious bullet wound in his abdomen. 'You will receive every attention in the prison infirmary,' the judge assured him.[38]

Yet seven weeks later, he was free again. The prosecution had to drop the case on the grounds that one important witness was now dead, while another was somewhere in France.

Only in reading through the court papers from the 1919 divorce case can one capture the sheer scale of William Archer's criminal activities, the compulsive, incorrigible nature of his dishonesty, the real ingenuity and energy behind his villainous schemes, and the brazen confidence with which he deceived everyone. The charges brought to court represented only a fraction of the many crimes he'd actually committed: witnesses told how he'd passed fake cheques on several occasions, and used his medical 'credentials' to place false orders for drugs on behalf of hospitals and then claimed an agent's commission.

Much of what Archer stole had been donated for charity. One of his activities was to canvass businesses for valuable items that could be sold to raise funds, but there were soon concerns about what actually happened to some of these gifts. The most notable example was the mysterious disappearance of an inlaid piano worth $15,000. Archer explained its absence, according to a police detective, as 'a part of his proceeds'.[39]

During his stay in America scarcely a day seems to have passed without his devising some brilliant new plot to rob someone. Many of his victims were ordinary, trusting people who'd simply fallen for his charm.

And he escaped from all this remarkably lightly. Though William Archer spent several months in custody awaiting trial, he always managed to wriggle out of a proper prison sentence. Many of his more obvious crimes were overlooked: he was never prosecuted for forging 'Grimwood's' passport in 1914, nor for jumping bail. His friend, John Austin, who'd put up the bail, was less fortunate. On Archer's disappearance, the court had demanded that Austin forfeit the £200. When Austin pleaded that he couldn't afford to pay, since he'd already lent all his money to Archer, the poor man was sent to jail.

As for Florence Brainerd, the last she heard of William Archer seems to have been a letter he wrote in August 1919, accusing her of 'doing all you can to blacken my character'. But then he added, 'Please also let me know what has happened to the child.'[40] Their daughter, Rosemary, had been born in June 1917, a few days after Archer's conviction in Washington. She was, of course, yet another of Jeffrey Archer's half-sisters.

Florence's parents, Erwin and Emma Brainerd, had done everything they could to help their distraught daughter, and put great effort into unravelling the real facts about 'William Grimwood'. Having discovered his true name and identity, they managed to contact his first wife, Alice Archer, in England. It was she who told them that her husband was also wanted by Scotland Yard. By now the Brainerds realized that most of his impressive claims were totally bogus: he hadn't, of course, been to Eton or Oxford; he didn't own substantial property; he had never been an army officer; and he wasn't a qualified doctor. And it seems that the 'war wound' Archer had shown people was merely a scar from a stomach operation while working in France.[41]

It was two years before Florence Grimwood, as she was still formally called, applied to the Supreme Court in New York for her marriage to be annulled. Her summons, in March 1919, accused Archer of being 'not only an adventurer but a fraud of the worst type'. He owned 'absolutely nothing', she added, 'but lives on such money as he can dishonestly obtain from other people'.[42]

William Archer refused to answer the summons and, in his absence, the marriage was formally dissolved eight months later. The judge allowed both mother and daughter to drop the name Grimwood and revert to Florence's maiden name, Brainerd.

Also included in the court papers was a letter Florence had received from Archer's first wife in England. 'He is trapped at last,' Alice Archer had written. 'Why does the wretched man not die! . . . Good-bye dear – be brave & all will yet be well with you.'[43]

Yet only two months later Alice Archer met her husband again, with a view to reviving their marriage, and they even spent the night together at a London hotel. But she quickly dropped him, having concluded that William Archer would never mend his ways.

For the previous decade, he had caused Alice and her children considerable hardship and upheaval. From Ilford they had moved out to Southend; then back to East Ham; next down to Brixton. Finally they found some calm in Richmond, in Surrey, where Alice Archer got a job as a live-in housekeeper for an antiques dealer. Her granddaughter, Valerie Haynes, believes that Alice Archer remained in contact with her estranged husband, and that occasionally he even sent the family money. She had dim memories of them receiving funds from William Archer as late as the Second World War, when she herself was a small girl.

The shame and anger over how William Archer treated his first wife and her four children survive down the generations.

Alice Archer died in Mortlake, south London, in 1953, but by then her family were under the impression that her husband was now dead, for her death certificate describes her as the 'widow of William Archer, Solicitor's Clerk'.[44] In fact Archer outlived his first wife by more than three years.

His second daughter, Dorothy Archer, died childless in 1981, while her older sister, Clarice, died ten years later. She had often seen the Tory politician on television during her final years living at home with her daughter's family in Sheen. Clarice died without ever knowing that the millionaire writer and politician was her half-brother.

Of Jeffrey's American half-sister, Rosemary Brainerd, we will hear much more later, and a fascinating story it is too.

Clarice, Dorothy and Rosemary are only three of Jeffrey Archer's long-lost siblings. His father was not the only parent to lead an extraordinary life and leave discarded offspring.

# 2

# The First Jeffrey

Jeffrey Archer may have inherited his creativity as a novelist from his storytelling father, but his energy, ambition and entrepreneurial spirit come from his mother, together with a certain impulsive, reckless streak.

Like the Archers, the Cook family also came from the West Country. Jeffrey's *grandfather* on his mother's side, Harold Howard Cook, was born in Bristol in 1881, six years *after* Jeffrey's father, William Archer. Harold was the twelfth of thirteen children, while his wife, Ellen Florence Clibbett, Jeffrey's maternal grandmother, was the youngest of nine children of a Bristol seaman.

Harold Cook's father, William, had worked as a commercial traveller selling flint glass, while his wife, Martha, ran what was then called a 'refreshment house' in Bristol. Harold followed his father into the wholesale trade, and in the early part of this century went into partnership with an older brother, Arthur. Their business, called Edgar Howard & Co. after the two brothers' respective middle names, sold 'fancy goods' – items such as buttons, clocks and watches – to shops around Gloucestershire, Bristol and Somerset, but it was a small venture.

Jeffrey Archer has often claimed that his grandfather was lord mayor of Bristol. This is not true. Harold Cook was interested in politics, and voted Conservative, but he was never active politically, and he never served on Bristol City Council. However, the family strongly believed that they were cousins of Sir Ernest Cook, Bristol's lord mayor in 1921–2, who sat for forty-five years as a city councillor and alderman. Sir Ernest was one of the most distinguished Bristol figures of the early part of this century: a founder of the university and a prominent freemason, he even played cricket for Somerset in his day. But he and Harold Cook were certainly not first cousins. It is possible there was a more distant relationship, but in any case Jeffrey's mother's family seem never to have had any contact with their supposed relative.

Ellen Cook was remarkably well educated for a woman of her generation, and it's said she spoke six languages. She trained as a teacher in
Swansea, and later worked in a primary school in St Philip's, one of the
poorest parts of Bristol. In those days the local education authority
insisted women teachers give up work when they married, so she and
Harold delayed their wedding until they could afford to live without
Ellen's income. Harold was thirty by that time, and Ellen twenty-eight.

Like Jeffrey Archer, Harold Cook was a workaholic. He left home at
6.30 each morning, cycled or walked to work, and didn't get back until
eight o'clock at night. Ellen was expected to help out with the business,
for example by threading buttons on to cards taken round by the
salesman.

Though Jeffrey Archer has said his grandfather's business was a prosperous one, the Cooks were not well off. They did not employ any
servants, and occupied only a modest terraced house, though in a respectable part of Bristol, high up near the Gloucestershire cricket ground.

Then, in January 1933, Harold and Ellen were enveloped by crisis
when Harold's brother and business partner, Arthur, died suddenly at
the age of fifty-four. He left his wife, Ada, an estate worth more than
£3,000, but most of it was tied up in Edgar Howard & Co., and
consisted largely of his share of the business premises and unsold stock.[1]
Understandably, his widow wanted to realize her inheritance quickly,
and this caused bitter divisions which were settled only after long legal
arguments. Harold Cook very nearly went bust, but like his grandson,
Jeffrey, forty years later, neither he nor his business was actually declared
bankrupt.

If the prospect of financial ruin wasn't bad enough for the Cooks to
contend with in the early 1930s, they also had to worry about their
eldest daughter, Lola. Impulsive, impetuous, immature Lola.

Jeffrey Archer's mother was born in 1913, just before the First World
War, the first of the Cooks' two children; her sister, Eileen, came four
years later. Her mother was a great believer in the virtues of private
education, and Lola was bright enough to win a scholarship to the Red
Maids, a prestigious boarding-school in Bristol, which she attended until
the age of sixteen in 1929. It was then that her problems began.

The 1930s are a period of Lola's life she has often tried to forget, a
time of recklessness which must have been the despair of her parents.
Some years ago she told a friend who'd known her then not to mention
those days. 'I didn't know what I was doing,' she reportedly said.

In 1930, at seventeen, she became pregnant through an affair with a local Somerset boy. The couple were in love, but Lola's parents disapproved of her boyfriend because he came from a lower social class. They wouldn't hear of marriage. In April 1931 Lola gave birth to an illegitimate daughter, Wendy Dorothy. The father's identity was never declared, and it's said that he never saw his child.

Nowadays it's difficult to appreciate the social stigma surrounding illegitimacy during the early part of this century. It brought disgrace on whole families, but, with little sex education, it was hardly surprising that it happened. Many in authority believed that illegitimacy was a hereditary problem or psychological, and, simply because of the 'immoral' act of getting pregnant, unmarried mothers would sometimes be classified as 'mentally subnormal' and be confined to mental institutions. More often, unmarried mothers would be sent to workhouses – or Public Assistance institutions as they were called by the 1930s – or to harsh homes run by the Church Army and the Salvation Army. 'Daughters were constantly reminded that if they brought "trouble" home they would be sent to the workhouse,' says the social historian Steve Humphries. 'The reality was horrific enough but fact became mixed with fiction to create a folklore of fear.'[2]

Unmarried mothers from middle-class homes like the Cooks' might fare a little better. It was common for wealthier parents to pack their daughters off to give birth to their illegitimate child in secret, many miles away from the family home. In Lola's case, she delivered her baby in a pretty cottage some forty miles from Bristol, in the small village of Norton-sub-Hamdon, just outside Yeovil. Strangely enough, the house where Jeffrey Archer's half-sister was born is now the constituency home of the Liberal Democrat leader, Paddy Ashdown.

Wendy was almost immediately put up for adoption, and was subsequently brought up by the Palmers, a working-class couple from South Wales. Leonard Palmer, a van-driver, and his wife, Lilian, were committed members of a gospel church in Cardiff, and Wendy maintained their evangelical fervour after her marriage to an accountant, Graham Burchell. In the early 1960s the Burchells moved to Canada and brought up three children, one of whom they happened to christen Geoffrey. Today, they live in Brantford in Ontario.

In 1988, after the death of her adoptive parents, Wendy and her husband started to trace her blood relatives, and eventually made contact with Lola. She invited Wendy to England for what proved to be an emotional reunion, but the fact that he had a half-sister appears not to have been revealed to Jeffrey. 'I think she was afraid that her son might think badly of her,' Wendy's husband, Graham Burchell, has said.[3]

When the story of 'Archer's Secret Sister' appeared on the front page of the *Daily Mirror* in August 1994, Jeffrey heard for probably the first time about the illegitimate girl his eighteen-year-old mother had given up for adoption. Lola was so angry when the story emerged that she consulted her solicitor about cutting Wendy out of her will – having previously added her name. This was perhaps unfair, since Wendy herself was upset by the coverage; she says she never helped the newspaper, and this was obvious from the *Mirror* articles.[4]

Before the week was out, the world was to learn of another of Lord Archer's many siblings. This relative had both parents in common with him.

Not long after giving away her first child, Lola Cook fell in love with William Archer. It was an unusual match. She was not yet twenty; he was almost sixty. Her 'Bill' was penniless at the time, yet 'He was a charmer,' she has said, and 'looked like an angel'. She adored his blue eyes and shock of silver hair. It's never been publicly revealed how or where the couple came across each other. Both seemed to be leading restless lives. Lola had taken up nursing in Weston-super-Mare, twenty-five miles south of Bristol; yet every now and then she would travel to London, hankering after a career on the stage, and it seems likely that she met Archer in the capital.

It's not clear what happened to William Archer during the years immediately after his American wife divorced him in 1919, or even which side of the Atlantic he lived on – though, given his criminal record, it seems unlikely that the US immigration authorities would have been happy for him to stay in the States. It is possible that in the intervening years before he met Lola he had married for a third or fourth time, and there may still be further children of William Archer yet to surface. By the time he met Lola in the early 1930s, Archer seems to have grown used to his false identity as a retired-injured army officer, and he had acquired a new profession, working as a journalist and in small-time publishing.

It was perhaps not surprising that, in the summer of 1933, Lola Cook fell pregnant for a second time, carrying William Archer's baby. It could not have happened at a worse time, since the Cooks were embroiled in their family dispute over Arthur Cook's estate. Once again

Lola travelled far from the family home – this time hundreds of miles north to the seaside town of Whitley Bay, eight miles east of Newcastle, where she booked into a guest-house at 16 North Parade, just off the seafront. On 24 April 1934, in the Princess Mary Hospital in Newcastle, Lola delivered her second illegitimate child, a baby boy. She called him Jeffrey Neville, the first of two sons who were to be named 'Jeffrey'.

When Lola left hospital with the baby, she fully expected William to be there to meet her. But he had vanished, and she has recently told how she was left with only a few shillings in her pocket. She returned to her landlady and said she would do any work she could to stay there and bring up the boy.

Eight days after her baby was born, Lola visited the local register office. She told the deputy registrar that the boy's father was William Robert Howard, a publisher's agent, and she gave both their addresses as 16 North Parade, the guest-house where she had been staying. She falsely claimed to be Mollie Howard – by implication William Robert Howard's wife. This was perjury, though she did correctly add that her maiden name was Cook.[5]

But within Lola's lies to the registrar of births lay clues to the truth. William and Robert were Archer's first two names, while the name Howard was both her own real middle name and that of her father, Harold Howard Cook. (The name also recurs later in the Archer family tree.)

The boy's birth certificate graphically shows what happened next, for the right-hand margin contains a long, handwritten amendment added six months later, in November 1934. Lola Cook had returned to Tyneside, accompanied by her mother, Ellen Cook. She confessed what she'd done, and the original registration was corrected. She made a statutory declaration to the effect that she, the child's mother, was in fact Lola Howard Cook, though she maintained that she was sometimes known by the name she had previously given, Mollie Howard. Lola also removed all the details she'd provided before about the father, leaving the child officially fatherless. And whereas the effect of the first declaration had been to make the boy Jeffrey Neville Howard, the correction left him with a new name, Jeffrey Neville Cook.[6]

At the time of this confession Lola Cook seems to have been living separately from William Archer – which may explain why she left the father's details blank. Her own father, Harold Cook, was sympathetic to the idea of keeping the baby, but her mother – the more dominant of her parents – insisted she must give him up.

'She was brought up on Victorian values,' Lola has explained, 'and you cannot imagine what the stigma of illegitimacy was like in the thirties, when I was a young woman. My father was a marvellous man, but he wouldn't stand in my mother's way when it came to something like that.'[7]

Lola was heartbroken and wept for weeks. At first the young boy went to live with William Archer in a flat he had just acquired in a new block recently built in Golders Green in north London. Then something even more unusual occurred. On 2 October 1935 a magistrates' court in Middlesex allowed William Archer to adopt the seventeen-month-old boy, after Archer had declared that he was the father. By this act Lola seems to have relinquished custody altogether, and the boy assumed his third name, Jeffrey Neville Archer, thus becoming the first of two Jeffrey Archers.

Today, Lola's first son has almost no recollection of those turbulent early years. His only clear memory is of being taken one day in his pushchair through a city park back to his home, where he heard a couple – William and Lola, he presumes – arguing about what should be done with him.[8] For his new adoption was not to last. When he was about three, it appears that the young boy was taken to live with Lola's parents in Bristol, where she regularly visited him. He still possesses a photograph of himself, aged about four, sitting on his grandmother's knee. But this home too was only temporary.

Lola was finally persuaded that she would have to part with her son permanently, and took the agonizing decision to hand him over to a couple who could bring him up the way she wanted. 'Before I gave him away, [he] was such a lovely little boy,' Lola said recently. 'We had such fun together. But I was only young, and living on nothing. I had no money, and when I went to Dr Barnardo's the people there wouldn't help me. In the end, I had to give him up. It's not that I minded being poor, but I couldn't keep a small boy and not educate him. He went to a middle-class family . . . the sort of family who would bring him up properly.'[9]

In January 1939, before he'd reached the age of five, the young Jeffrey Neville was adopted again, by Samuel and Edith Mayne from Filton, just north of Bristol. The Maynes had no children of their own, and promised Lola's mother to look after her grandson lovingly. They promised to send him one day to Bristol Grammar School and to university – exactly the kind of talk which would have impressed Lola's mother, who'd arranged the adoption. Now he became David Llewellyn Mayne – his fourth name in less than five years. The psychological effect on him must have been traumatic. Edith Mayne's sister recently recalled that when she met the young boy for the first time, around 1939, he told her how he had once been called Jeffrey, but now he was David.

The adoption was settled on 10 January 1939. By coincidence, just two days later, Lola Cook finally married William Archer. She knew he didn't have a penny to his name and that he would regularly disappear for long spells, totally unannounced, without a clue as to where he was going. But she loved him deeply and now says he was the only person who was kind to her. And Lola desperately wanted another child. The only way to ensure she could have a baby and keep it was to be respectably married. She told William he must marry her; he agreed, reluctantly.

The wedding took place in Glasgow, which is strange since neither party seems to have had any connection with Scotland up to that point. One explanation probably lies in the fact that it is much easier to get married north of the border – indeed, the Archers' ceremony seems to have taken place in an ordinary house. William Archer would also have been anxious for as few people as possible to know about the event, which may account for the several false details he gave on the marriage document. These included his incorrect age – fifty-four instead of sixty-three – a wrong occupation for his father – farmer instead of caretaker – and, worst of all, the declaration that he was a 'widower'.[10] In short, William Archer was almost certainly trying to conceal the fact that his first wife, Alice, was still alive in south London, and arguably still married to him. The need to cover things up may also explain why from this point on Archer called himself Archibald William rather than William Robert.

Meanwhile, the sad story of William and Lola's first son had several unhappy chapters to come. From the age of four to six the boy was reasonably happy living with the Maynes, though he felt rather oppressed by some of their efforts to give him a good education: he was forced to have elocution lessons, and do five hours' piano practice every day, thus filling every morning, lunchtime and evening. David Mayne hated this constant practice, though he eventually achieved some success, winning one of the junior contests at the Bristol Eisteddfod. But when the Germans began dropping bombs on the city he was evacuated, first to Caerphilly in South Wales and then to a small village near Looe in

Cornwall, to stay with another set of surrogate parents. Later in the war he returned to the Maynes in Filton, only to be evacuated for a second time when their home was bombed. He was taken to Weston-super-Mare and placed with a couple called Kimberley and Violet Brown, who lived in the centre of the town. By another coincidence, the Browns' home was less than a mile from where his natural parents, William and Lola Archer, were then living.

When the war was over the boy's future was once again settled in court. It was a moment which would be etched in his memory for ever: there he was, forced to choose between two sets of surrogate parents who'd looked after him at one time or other. 'I was in a courtroom, right in the middle of the room. I'm quite sure somebody in the court said, "Who would you prefer to be with – the Browns or the Maynes?" I walked over to the Browns.'[11] He'd made his choice largely on the grounds that they were the family he'd been living with for the past year or two.

With this third and final adoption order, the eleven-year-old boy assumed his fifth name. Having begun as Jeffrey Neville Howard, gone through Jeffrey Neville Cook and then Jeffrey Neville Archer, he'd then become David Llewellyn Mayne, and finally took the name he still bears today – David Llewellyn Mayne Brown, or David Brown.

He probably made the wrong decision, for Brown had a truly miserable time in his teenage years. He always felt that his new mother didn't really love him, and that she showed favour to her own children in petty, inconsiderate ways. Later, serving three years in the army, David always sent his wages home, and asked Violet Brown to save part of them for him. When he returned home, she had spent all the money.

David Brown has lived in the Somerset area almost ever since. And for most of his adult life he's been within just a few miles, sometimes only a few hundred yards, of his natural mother, Lola Archer. In 1955 David Brown got married and began to raise a family of four children. He called one of his sons Geoffrey (with a 'G'), though he says that by then he must have forgotten that he had once been Jeffrey (with a 'J').

It wasn't until 1980 that David Brown came to realize who his true parents were, and that he was not only Jeffrey Archer's brother but in fact the first Jeffrey Archer. He probably would never have found out had it not been for the 1975 Children's Act, which, for the first time, gave adopted people the legal right to discover the identities of their natural parents and to see their original birth certificates. When David's son, Geoffrey, began researching his family tree in the late 1970s, it rekindled his father's interest in finding out about his own origins.

Around the same time, the second Jeffrey Archer was starting to achieve some fame as an author, and the local papers ran stories of a local-boy-makes-good type. Working his way through several sets of court papers, David Brown first spotted that he had the same mother as Jeffrey Archer, and then worked out that he must have the same father too. But perhaps the most poignant moment came while he was watching an edition of the ITV programme *This Is Your Life* in January 1981, featuring Archer. 'That's my mother!' David Brown shouted as Eamonn Andrews introduced Lola Archer to the viewers. He was seeing her face for the first time since the age of four, more than forty years previously.

David Brown didn't see Lola's face again for another thirteen years, partly due to a loss of nerve on his own part, and also because his attempts to make contact through Jeffrey Archer were rebuffed.

Shortly after David Brown realized that Lola Archer was his true mother, he actually drove round to her flat in Weston and rang the doorbell. She was out. Brown was rather relieved, having worried about the effect such a shock might have on a lady who was then nearly seventy. Another concern was that he was having business problems at the time, and didn't want her to think he'd come begging for financial help.

Then, in 1982, David Brown met Jeffrey Archer at a benefit dinner in London for the Somerset batsman Viv Richards – cricket is an interest the two brothers share. Brown says he went up to Archer in the foyer of the hotel. 'I said, "Hello, Jeffrey, I'd like to have a chat with you, because we're related,"' he recalls. 'He just pushed me to one side and didn't want to know, really. He said, "I've got no relations," and just marched away.'[12] Brown's former wife, Lilian, who was with him that night, confirms the story.

It was some years before they spoke again. Around 1984 or 1985, when Archer was becoming a prominent figure in the Conservative Party, David Brown's son Richard approached the *Daily Mail* to see if they'd be interested in Jeffrey's long-lost brother. The reporter who took the call rang Archer to check the story, to be told that it was complete rubbish. So the *Mail* dropped it. But within hours Archer was on the phone to David Brown:

He rang me at home and the first thing he said was: 'It's Jeffrey

Archer, hello. You want to speak to me?' 'Yes.' 'Look, your son's going to the papers. Call him off,' he said, 'because it will only upset mother if the truth comes out.' And I said, 'Well, that's fair enough, but I would like to meet you.' And he said, 'As soon as I get this business over with the Tory Party' – he was in for something like the chairmanship, he said – 'I'll come and see you.'[13]

That was the last he heard from his brother.

By chance, though, Lola nearly bumped into her lost son some years later. David Brown's second wife, June, whom he married in 1988, belonged to the same bridge class as Lola. One afternoon June ended up giving her a lift home, but couldn't pluck up courage to raise the subject. Expecting that she might again give Lola a lift the next time she went to bridge, June Brown put her wedding photos in the car ready to show her what had become of her first son. But, when Lola started complaining about how unwell she was, June had second thoughts: she too was worried that the shock might be too great.

David Brown bears a striking physical resemblance to his younger brother, especially when one allows for the six-year age gap. Jeffrey is fitter and leaner, but they have the same strong nose, their hair is a similar colour and texture, and they have identical hairlines; both give that famous, impish Archer smile, and they possess the same bushy, tufted eyebrows. While David Brown has bifocals, Archer has adopted half-moon spectacles, and both have the same habit of peering rather sternly over the tops of their glasses. Though they both love cricket and debating, the difference comes in their politics. David Brown says he'd love to be a political candidate, but he's always been Labour or Liberal. 'Tory dogma is evil,' he says.[14]

More than once, David Brown has actually been mistaken for his younger brother. On one occasion, a cricket-lovers' tour of the Caribbean, one member of the group refused to talk to him for several days. He'd assumed Brown was the brash politician he disliked so much.

Several people around Weston-super-Mare have known for years that Jeffrey Archer has a brother in the area. Once David Brown had mentioned it to his family and a few friends, word soon spread, though the rumours usually talked about a half-brother, and not many people could actually identify him. Nevertheless, it is astonishing that it took so long for the story of David Brown to become public.

By 1994 David Brown was reconciled to the fact that details would eventually emerge when this book was published. He hoped the news could be broken gently to Lola beforehand, but also felt bitter about the way Jeffrey Archer had rebuffed him and discouraged him from approaching his mother. When the *Daily Mirror* published its story about Jeffrey Archer's half-sister, Wendy, it was obvious that Brown's relationship would not remain quiet much longer. The *Mirror* story led to several tip-offs to tabloid newspapers, and Brown concluded that the best course was to release the story on his own terms to the *Daily Mail*.

The day it was published, Brown wrote to his mother at her nursing home in Weston, apologizing for the way things had turned out. He then telephoned her. 'The first thing she said when I rang her was: "Do you know you were a beautiful baby? I cried for six months when I gave you up. I would like you to come and see me." '[15] Brown said 'No' at first, but changed his mind and nervously rang back to arrange a meeting. It was a highly emotional occasion, of course, seeing his mother for the first time in almost sixty years. They kissed, embraced, and spent two hours talking.

Lola claimed that these two suddenly revealed, long-lost siblings would have been total news to her second son. 'I never told Jeffrey about his sister and brother,' she said. 'He knew nothing until he read it in the newspapers the other day like everyone else. I know I have hurt him.'[16] Archer, who had dismissed the possibility that the two men might be related at their brief encounter at the Viv Richards dinner, was deeply upset about the *Daily Mail* story, and appears to have wanted nothing to do with his long-lost brother. But Lola felt differently. 'He *is* my son, Jeffrey,' she said when he telephoned her from his holiday in Turkey. Archer told people that *Mail* readers were furious at the way the paper had treated his mother. Yet he himself was largely to blame, for not getting back to David Brown, as he had promised, many years before, and arranging a quiet reunion with his mother. By March 1996, more than a year and a half after the relationship was revealed, Jeffrey Archer had still not made contact with his older brother.

'All my adult life,' Lola said, 'I've waited for a knock on the door from those two children. It's a terrible thing for any parent in my position. If you give away your babies, you never know when they will come to find you.'[17] Lola had reacted more as one might expect, at least initially. She was upset to hear of David Brown's highly disrupted and unhappy upbringing. She told the Browns it had been the biggest sacrifice a mother could make, that she was deeply sorry, and that they would never know the full story. Listening to Lola, they couldn't help noticing how she never stopped talking about Jeffrey – 'it was Jeffrey this, and Jeffrey that' – he was 'the apple of her eye', she told them. Quite clearly the love and affection she'd been forced to withdraw from her first Jeffrey had been transferred to her second many times over.

And also to another child. For Lola also told David and June Brown about the foster-daughter that she and her second husband had looked after in the early 1960s. Lola explained how one day she had gone to an orphanage in Weston and asked for all the children to be paraded in front of her. No, the matron insisted, they would bring a child to meet her. Elizabeth ('Liz') Fullerton was half-black and had also had a wretched childhood in Weston. She had been born to a black professional father and a white mother, but her parents had not been married and, just as with Lola more than twenty years earlier, her mother could not look after the child herself. Lola and her husband came to love the girl and fostered her for several years. She would later work as a nanny for Jeffrey and Mary Archer.

After their initial reunion, relations between Lola and David Brown deteriorated badly. Lola was upset at the way the Browns had spoken to the press about their meeting, and was so surprised by the amount of detail that had appeared, that she publicly accused the couple of recording the event. 'He came here swearing undying love for me while his wife secretly tape-recorded our conversion.'[18] It was a ludicrous suggestion; for had they taped the meeting then far more damaging material would have emerged.

'I will never agree to see him again as long as I live' Lola said bitterly. 'I was going to ask the trust to leave him some money in my will, but not now.' More hurtful still was her view on what had become of the son she gave up: 'I find he has wasted his life.'[19] Her private comments were far worse, and mother and son did not see each other again until January 1996, when Lola summoned David to tell him she was leaving Weston, but without saying where she was off to. She moved, in fact, to a smarter, newly-built retirement home near the seafront in Clevedon, about ten miles up the coast.

But perhaps the most poignant moment had occurred during their first reunion in August 1994. The Browns had taken some family photos, to show Lola what David had looked like at various stages of his life. Lola looked at each picture carefully, then chose one and asked to keep it. 'It looks most like Jeffrey,' she explained rather tactlessly.

# 3

# Over the Tea Cups

The validity of Lola's marriage to William Archer may have been open to question, but nobody apart from the groom knew of the tangle behind it. And fifteen months later she got her new baby. It was another boy. Only now she was a respectable wife and could keep him.

She named him Jeffrey – presumably in memory of her first son, and to assuage her conscience about giving him away. (Apparently it is quite common for mothers who have had children adopted to call subsequent babies by the same names.) So arrived the second Jeffrey Archer, only this time his middle name wasn't Neville, but Howard – another name she'd used before.

Jeffrey Howard Archer was born seven months into the Second World War, on 15 April 1940, at the City of London Maternity Hospital. His birth certificate suggests that, even as a newly married couple, William and Lola were still living unorthodox lives. For while her home was given as 18 Nelson Square in Southwark, about half a mile south of Blackfriars Bridge, he was living on the north side of the Thames, five miles away, in a boarding-house in Highbury Grove, Islington. William Archer, who was sixty-four when Jeffrey was born, appeared on the birth certificate as a 'journalist'.[1]

Much of Nelson Square, including Lola Archer's flat, was bombed in 1941. By then, fortunately, she had left with Jeffrey to go to the West Country – within only two or three weeks of his birth. Initially they probably went to stay with Lola's parents in Bristol.

Then, on the third day of Christmas 1941, twenty months after he was born, the young Jeffrey was christened. The ceremony took place not in Bristol, or even northern Somerset, but more than fifty miles away, in a tiny, remote village at the far western end of the county, in Lorna Doone country.

The church of St Mary-the-Virgin at Oare is where the semi-fictitious Lorna Doone was married and then shot by Carver Doone. Only four feet away from a memorial to R. D. Blackmore, the author of *Lorna Doone*, stands the font in which another best-selling popular writer was baptized. In choosing Oare church, with its historic literary connections and its wonderful setting, Lola was displaying a characteristic romantic streak.

It is unclear how much William Archer actually lived with Lola for the first two years of Jeffrey's life. For the early part of the marriage he appears to have carried on behaving much as before, suddenly vanishing without notice, and then turning up again out of the blue several weeks later. Quite what he was doing, or where he stayed, she never knew. In February 1942, for instance, Archer was living in Brockworth, just outside Gloucester. Here he made his short will, leaving 'all I die possessed of . . . to my wife, Lola Archer, née Lola Cook'. Of his other wives and previous children he made no mention. In this document he described himself as a 'publisher'.[2]

In 1942 the Archers moved to the village of Mark in Somerset, about thirty miles south of Bristol. This is the Mark of Jeffrey Archer's rather convoluted title – 'Baron Archer of Weston-super-Mare of Mark in the County of Somerset'. Nowadays Weston is in the redrawn county of Avon, but Archer refused to have the unpopular name of Avon in his new title, and so used his boyhood connection with Mark as a clever way of retaining his beloved Somerset instead.

The Archers lived from 1942 to 1944 at Pack Horse Farm, next to the Pack Horse Hotel where James II is said once to have stayed. The property belonged to Colonel Frederic Mackie, a distinguished doctor, and his second wife, Mary. The Mackies lived most of the time in Bristol, where they knew Lola's parents, and had bought Pack Horse Farm just before the war as an occasional country retreat. They told Lola that she and her husband could borrow the house, at a very reasonable rent, on two conditions. First they had to keep one room for the Mackies to come and stay whenever they wished; second, they had to look after the extensive back garden.

This spell in Mark provides one of the many odd coincidences which pepper Jeffrey Archer's life. The Archers' landlady, Mary Mackie, had once worked as secretary to the MP for the Lincolnshire town of Louth, Margaret Wintringham, who became the first British-born woman to enter the Commons, after winning a by-election in 1921. Almost fifty years later, one of Mrs Mackie's former tenants would be elected at another by-election in Louth.

By allowing the Archers to rent Pack Horse Farm, Mary Mackie may unknowingly have boosted Jeffrey's election prospects. His short stay there, between the ages of one and three, enabled the by-election candidate to boast to Lincolnshire's agricultural community that he had been 'brought up on a farm'.[3]

This was a rather dubious claim, for the Mackies had never been interested in running the property as a farm: the agricultural buildings still stood, but most of the adjoining land had been sold off. All Pack Horse Farm boasted when the Archers were there was a kitchen garden with herbs, asparagus and strawberries, along with several acres of orchard, growing greengages, peaches and nectarines, as well as apples which Lola sold to a local cider-maker.

Lola's two years in Mark seem to have been among the happiest of her life. William Archer at last seems to have settled down to live with his wife and son; she had the child she wanted, and peace and security after her wretched life in the 1930s. Reading her later journalistic reminiscences, one would hardly guess that Britain was fighting for survival. Nostalgically she recalled the 'summer with long, scented days', and 'winter with log fires burning to a fine ash'. Mark's children 'were apple-cheeked, and clear-eyed'.[4] 'Perhaps it was the effect of the war and the fact that other strangers, foreigners from London way, had disordered the even tenor of village life that helped the country folk to accept me,' she wrote.[5]

Gertie Tidball, who still lives in Mark, remembers how, as a young woman, she walked the infant Jeffrey in his pushchair along the local country lanes. Like other locals, she recalls 'Captain' Archer as 'a bent-over man'.[6] John Creber, who used to babysit for the Archers (and was one of Lola's 'apple-cheeked' children), says Jeffrey was 'a happy sort of kiddy', and that Lola and William appeared to be 'a very devoted couple', with 'never any harsh words'. William Archer already looked an old man, however, and would walk slowly down the street with the help of sticks.[7] Mary Wall recalls that her mother sometimes helped out round the Archer home and got cross with William for dipping his finger into her food to taste it.[8]

The fact the Archers could employ somebody suggests that they weren't completely destitute. But their income came mainly from Lola, who was now trying her hand at journalism, presumably at her husband's suggestion. Former neighbours recall seeing her in a back room writing articles for women's magazines, though she also did occasional nursing shifts at the general hospital in Weston-super-Mare eleven miles away.

It wasn't until 1944, around the age of four, that Jeffrey Archer and his parents moved to the place he calls his home town. Weston-super-Mare, twenty-one miles south-west of Bristol, is a rather old-fashioned, out-of-the-way kind of place, which sprang up as a seaside resort in the late eighteenth and early nineteenth centuries. Its interesting features – the sweep of Weston Bay, the craggy Anchor Head and Worlebury Hill – have always given Weston an edge over other beaches along the Somerset coast. The construction of two piers and development of the seafront meant that by the 1920s Weston was greeting 80,000 visitors on some bank holidays.

When the Archers arrived there, towards the end of the war, the population was about 40,000 – compared with around 70,000 today. As a seaside town, there was no shortage of entertainment; its four theatres, three cinemas and numerous sporting facilities would provide an important backdrop to a young boy who grew up amid small-town show business and acquired a lifelong yearning to perform in public.

Weston's electoral registers for the immediate postwar period show that for the next five years the Archers rarely occupied any property for more than a year. They started out in 1944 in a flat in Birnbeck Road below Anchor Head, in the middle of a tall Victorian stone crescent which faces out to sea. For a four-year-old it must have been ideal, situated just above the promenade and the sandy beach and rock-pools below.

Then, just before the war ended, in the spring of 1945, the family moved to a flat at 21 Grove Park Road, a quiet street high up the hillside, not far from the limestone quarry from which much of Victorian Weston was built. A year later they were down below, sharing a house at 8 Trevelyan Road, just off the main route into Weston, Locking Road. But by the time Jeffrey was eight they had moved back up the hill again to Silvercraig Mansions. Hidden by trees, it was a large house divided into flats, perched precariously on a rocky outcrop, with a superb view over the town and Weston Sands. But again the accommodation was only temporary.

In 1949 the Archers settled down for a while, living in a much more mundane terraced house back in a busier part of town, not far from the station. Nowadays visitors to the Venis guest-house at 51 Locking Road may have the honour of sleeping in Jeffrey Archer's old bedroom.

These regular changes may simply reflect the difficulties of finding long-term accommodation, but one suspects that the moves up and down the hill also reflect the family's changing financial fortunes. In appearance the flats suggest varying levels of prosperity. Those at the top of the hill – Grove Park Road (1945) and Silvercraig Mansions (1948) – were in quiet residential areas, and would have been more expensive to rent than those in the town – Trevelyan Road (1947–8) and Locking Road (1949–53).

Initially William Archer got a job with the Bristol Haulage Co., which had a fleet of lorries transporting prefabricated homes then being manufactured on an old airfield just outside Weston. Archer was company welfare officer. 'You'd go to him for help,' says Cyril Dowzell, a former colleague – 'wife trouble, for instance.' Archer must have been something of an expert on that by now. In practice much of his time was spent on health and safety, and organizing social activities, such as fixtures for the firm's skittles team. Like others who knew him then, Dowzell was always struck by how old 'Captain' Archer looked and by his physical disability. 'The way he was bent over, he was looking at the floor all the time,' he says.[9]

In 1946, however, William and Lola set up their own little publishing business, though with postwar paper rationing it was not the best time to start. They issued *What's On in Weston-super-Mare*, a three-part folded leaflet which they gave out free to local hotels for guest bedrooms. The income came from local advertising. Gradually, with the easing of paper restrictions, and with more ads, the publication expanded to become part of Weston's *Official Entertainments and Holiday Journal*, endorsed by the town council.

The *Journal* was almost entirely advertising, which didn't vary much from one issue to the next; virtually the only editorial matter was a page of 'general information', which also rarely changed, and the occasional photo. In summer it came out fortnightly, with twelve pages, and in winter once a month with just eight. Once it was established, publishing each edition can hardly have been a difficult exercise. In the early stages the Archers' business, West Country Publicity, was run from their small terraced home in Locking Road, which they gave the grand title of Press House. Later they acquired premises on the seafront.

Although the Archers worked on the *Journal* together, William was now into his seventies and, as time passed, his wife had to bear an increasing burden. William would spend much of his time drinking at the Constitutional Club, or playing bridge at the Victoria Bowling Club. One family friend recalls Lola's anger when he raided her purse for funds, then went down to the club to announce that the drinks were on him. This occasional generosity with his wife's money notwithstanding, William Archer doesn't seem to have been a very popular figure. One fellow member of the bowling club says they treated him with suspicion, as a rather dishonest character who couldn't keep his hands off people's property. 'He was an artful fellow,' he says – 'you just couldn't trust him.' He remembers how on one occasion a load of toilet rolls went missing, and how Archer was immediately assumed to be the culprit. Whether guilty or not, it shows the kind of reputation he had.

Bert Allen, who printed the holiday journal, says William Archer was always well behind in paying his bills, and it was difficult to get money out of him.[10]

William Archer took a keen interest in watching local sport: he was one of the many vice-presidents of Weston cricket club, belonged to the Rugby club, and also got involved in boxing tournaments organized by the Weston Sportsmen's Association. Though William was now far too old to take an active part, Jeffrey says his father 'introduced me to cricket and to my love of sports generally. He used to take me down to the cricket ground every Saturday from the time I was very little.'[11]

Everyone who knew the family in those years admires the way in which Lola coped with her difficult circumstances. Always short of money, and with a husband who was almost retired, it was a terrible struggle to bring up her son, but she seems to have had enormous energy. Perhaps racked by the memory of her first two children, she doted on Jeffrey and was determined to do the best she possibly could for him. In particular, she and her mother wanted him to have a private education, just as Lola had enjoyed.

In profiles of Jeffrey Archer it's often mentioned how he attended the state-run primary school in Weston. What doesn't appear to have been revealed before is that, when Jeffrey was only about five or six, Lola sent him away to a private boarding-school. And it would have been largely Lola's decision, rather than her husband's. St David's School occupied an eighteenth-century country house amid its own wooded parkland near Congresbury, about nine miles east of Weston. The school had about fifty to sixty pupils, right across the age-range from five to eighteen, divided into four classes. Quite how Lola managed to pay for this when the family had so little money, her friends are unsure: it seems quite likely that at least some of the fees were met by Lola's parents.

Yet strangely, Jeffrey now denies ever attending St David's. After this book was first published in 1995, a journalist mentioned the school to him, and Archer said he couldn't remember it. And when he phoned his mother to check, she wouldn't confirm it either. Yet Adrienne Griffiths, whose family ran the school and knew the Archers well, is adamant that Jeffrey was a pupil there.

It was only when he was about seven or eight that Archer moved to Christ Church in the centre of Weston, a small Church of England primary school with thirty or forty pupils. Yet even then Jeffrey did not live at home much. From Monday morning to Friday evening he would stay with four or five other children in a large semi-detached house in Gerard Road, only 150 yards from his school. It was a kind of foster home, run for several decades by Ellen Lever, who earned money looking after boys and girls whose parents were too busy working during the week to care for them properly. Mrs Lever was pretty strict, and made each child do chores each day, though the real 'mother' figure seems to have been her more popular Welsh assistant, Rose Hughes. Ann Riseborough, who stayed at Gerard Road with Jeffrey, remembers him one day standing at the top of the long garden, thumbs pulling on his braces, boasting about how his father was 'Captain Archer', whereas hers was a mere sergeant. Eventually, after a year or two, Archer seems to have resumed a normal family life with his parents.

As well as coping with William and Jeffrey, publishing the *Journal* and doing other occasional jobs such as being a Sunday waitress, Lola still had time to be active in local theatre. Weston-super-Mare had a thriving amateur dramatic community. Her dreams of a professional career on the London stage unfulfilled, Lola joined the Weston Operatic Society, singing in the chorus in productions of *The Gondoliers*, *The Mikado* and *A Country Girl*.

However, the amateur theatricals had to be cut back a little when, in May 1949, Lola began the job for which she is still widely remembered in Weston-super-Mare. She became the first woman journalist on the local *Weston Mercury*. A female journalist was something of a novelty at the time – 'The *Mercury* did not even have a toilet for women in those days,' Lola recalled recently.[12] She took over a women's column the paper had recently introduced: 'Over the Tea Cups: News and Jottings for Weston Women'. One wonders whether the editor who chose the title had been inspired by W. H. Auden:

[November 1949] It was Tuppence, my nine-year-old, who first introduced me to Pearl in the days when they were both members of the Junior Arts Club. He told me he was going to marry her even if it did mean having to go out to work when he grew up. Various activities, coupled with a general desire to have nothing whatsoever to do with work, have dimmed this ambition.[21]

Lola never explains the origins of this nickname. It's thought to come from Jeffrey's habit of going into the local sweetshop to ask 'Anything for tuppence?' Not once in her articles does she ever refer to him as Jeffrey.

It is interesting to speculate what effect it had on Jeffrey to be spotlighted in public like this by his own mother. From the age of nine he had no real privacy: every childhood misdemeanour was in danger of full exposure in the local press. Most children hate anything that encourages their schoolmates to tease them, and would be highly embarrassed by this kind of attention; some might even be psychologically scarred by the experience. 'Tuppence' certainly was an object of some ridicule, but he seems to have revelled in the limelight. 'He saw himself as a celebrity even then and was brimful of confidence . . . He actually introduced himself to people as Tuppence,' says a former friend, Michael Taudevin.[22]

My sister and I were walking past the entrance to the Grand Pier when up from behind the sea-wall pops a frantic little figure, with imitation guns blazing, shouting 'Bang, bang, you're dead! You remember me – Tuppence, Junior Arts Club. We were caught together under the stage playing chase.'[23]

Yet the young Archer doesn't seem to have been liked very much by his contemporaries, and Taudevin says he was one of Jeffrey's few friends. 'Ask any of the local youth and they would say, "Oh yes, that bighead!" It was a wrong view because he was a very down-to-earth and likeable chap with a burning zeal for life.'[24]

Archer himself admits that he cannot have been very popular: 'I think as a boy I was pretty intolerable. I always wanted to be number one. I wanted to be a sixer in the cubs, captain of the team.'[25]

Later we learn that Lola and the young actress Pearl Brookman are not the only women in Jeffrey's life.

[March 1950] I remember being considerably shaken when my nine-year-old announced that he wanted to clean his teeth regularly, and that he intended to keep his shoes polished. As he invariably looks like one of the 'dead-end kids' I enquired what it was all about, and found out it was due to a Miss Babs Baker, his cub mistress. Babs is getting married on Saturday to Bill Holley and . . . my son confided in me that not one of the Pack can understand why two nice people like Miss Baker and Mr Holley want to bother with getting married.[26]

In one of her funniest passages Lola describes the trials of the successive hobbies Jeffrey adopts. By the time of his tenth birthday, the latest craze is philately:

[April 1950] Stamps are to be found in every room adhering to chairs, tables, rugs, even walls, and small pieces of sticky paper, though often proving highly inefficient when merely expected to hold one small stamp in the album, grow powers of leech-like pertinacity when coming into contact with one's shoes or clothes.

Every holiday my son throws himself wholeheartedly into a hobby. At Christmas it was trains; he demanded one penny every day for a platform ticket and lived on the station. It wasn't until the dirt became ingrained in him that I suggested even marbles might be an improvement. The time before that he collected cigarette packets. I expect most of you can remember that craze. I do, for one unheard-of brand he particularly wanted and couldn't get either by fair means or foul, caused him to enlist my aid, and I found myself surreptitiously watching the gutters in all my walks in the hope that somebody had dropped one. Somebody did, to my extreme joy (it was by then a point of honour that I didn't let my son down), so I promptly picked it up, a perfectly clean, twenty carton, and then to my everlasting embarrassment came face to face with one of Weston's VIPs. She eyed me kindly, with a faintly astonished sort of 'My dear, if I'd known you were that hard up I would have bought you a packet,' look. Any explanation would, I felt, be quite useless, so I hurried home with my prize, knowing that its reception would amply make up for everything. 'Oh, that,' said Tuppence, ten minutes later when I handed it to him, 'I've had that one for ages, still it might do to swap.' So now

I am quite unmoved by any mention of penny blacks, or special Olympic issues.[27]

Two weeks afterwards Jeffrey achieves top billing. Lola begins her column with the heading 'Tuppence' and a scowling picture of the notorious cigarette-packet collector:

[April 1950] It has been suggested from time to time that I might put a photograph of my son in this column – Tuppence the unruly, who so often invades my thoughts when I am writing – well, here he is with an expression that would do justice to an early Christian martyr. When asked if he would like his photo taken he adopted a belligerent attitude, and later, on being shown six indifferent proofs, muttered 'I couldn't care less.' Why going to the photographer with a small boy should prove such agony I cannot think.[28]

[September 1950] During the holidays I have been teaching Tuppence to cook ... After a particularly energetic bout, which only produced one piece of burnt bread, I asked Tuppence what had happened and he explained that he had broken the egg over the floor instead of in the frying pan. 'However,' he added, 'you needn't worry because I've mopped it up.' It's a glorious combination, mop, egg and lino. After I'd washed the floor and shampooed the mop we got down to some basic bread and cheese. And that is the first egg shampoo I've given my mop.[29]

That, presumably, was the very first Jeffrey Archer scrape ever exposed in public. More followed quickly, though he soon learned that Archer knack of turning adversity to his own advantage.

[March 1951] I am never sure of what my ten-year-old will be up to next, and I don't really rest content until he is safely tucked up in bed. Much to my surprise he came straight home from school one day last week, stood truculently on the doorstep, said he must go to the barber and could he have a shilling. Taking off his cap to see if it were such an urgent matter, I realized that there wasn't much left for the barber to do. Tuppence looked like a Trappist monk on one side and a shaggy dog on the other. He and his pals, I learnt, had spent an exhilarating playtime cutting each other's hair, and whoever trimmed my son's head had done so in a spirit of surrealist abandon. Seeing I was taking the whole thing very calmly, Tuppence smiled broadly and said very virtuously, 'If I've saved you a shilling, can I have 6d of it to spend?'[30]

Jeffrey was quickly acquiring his keen eye for a business opportunity. He has often boasted since of how he developed his entrepreneurial skills bob-a-jobbing for the local cubs. The Archer version is that he raised £3 17s 6d and received a letter from the Chief Scout congratulating him on the highest total in the country. One suspects Lola's contemporaneous account of bob-a-job week is rather nearer the truth, with no mention of any record or of congratulations from the Chief Scout:

[April 1951] He tracked down a drapery store manager, who marked his card 'For a cheerful smile, 2s 6d.' In a baker's, they fed him on chocolate biscuits and put, 'To eating the profits, 2s 6d.' It wasn't all quite as easy as that – someone got him to buy four pounds of potatoes and peel them, and somebody else had him on his hands and knees scrubbing. The entry that time, in Tuppence's handwriting, read 'Scrubing flors', with a little aside to the effect that he was worn out. When he totalled up he had 62s 6d.[31]

Archer has spoken of other money-making ventures too, such as carrying holiday-makers' luggage from the station in an old pram, and cleaning shoes outside Woolworth's for sixpence a time. Another involved collecting Disney lollipop stickers:

If you got four Disney characters then you got one token, and ten tokens got you a pen. I discovered that there were very few Plutos so at 7 p.m. each night I used to go to the back of the store and pick up the three or four Plutos there were in each dustbin. In one week I collected enough pens to sell them in front of Woolworth's – the police tried to move me on . . .[32]

Then, having reached the age of eleven, the capitalist cub achieved promotion:

[May 1951] Tuppence has become a full-blown Scout this week. He pretty nearly burst with pride when he attended his first church parade, and took much longer dressing for it than I do for the Arts Ball. It occurs to me that the child is growing up, for when we went to buy his uniform, for the first time in his life he showed some qualms about the expense, and assured me that he would buy me a fur coat in six years' time. He added that he had already applied for a job as a grocer's errand boy and a newspaper rounds-man, but he had not been considered quite old enough![33]

Lola was clearly guilty of spoiling her son at times, but Jeffrey would have had to perform his fair share of chores round the home – assuming, that is, that his mother did as she told readers in one of her newspaper homilies:

[May 1953] How many of you, I wonder, with growing boys in the home, get them to help with the housework? They should, you know. It is all wrong to let them get out of everything, simply because, in most cases, it is much quicker to do it yourself. From about nine years old they should make their beds, lay and clear the table, and help wash or wipe up. From about 11 they can do simple cooking. If you don't start them at an early age, it is much more difficult to persuade them to do their share of the household chores at, say, the age of 14 or 15.[34]

What must have been embarrassing for the young Jeffrey were those regular occasions when Lola sought readers' advice on how to look after him. What was the right bedtime for a thirteen-year-old? Until he was eleven, the people of Weston were told, he'd gone to bed 'at the latest' by seven o'clock.[35]

Worse still came when Jeffrey began pressing for an increase to his three-shillings-a-week pocket money. Lola threw it open to public opinion:

[July 1951] For many months I have pondered over how to settle the question of pocket money for Tuppence. I should be glad of help. What do you give your children and what does their allow-ance have to cover? My son has the idea that most children get at least ten shillings a week, and that I am very mean. It seems to me that 3s today should adequately take the place of the penny we had on Saturday. What do you think?[36]

The future multimillionaire must have been dismayed by the response. Nobody thought ten shillings was the right amount. 'Your ten-year-old is doing very well indeed,' one reader replied. 'Children are like our-selves, they do not value what comes easily.'[37] 'Three shillings is ample and make the boy undertake some task every week so that he can earn the money,' another proposed; and one reader suggested Lola should make clear that Tuppence's three shillings had to pay for 'Sunday collection, sweets, ices, comic paper or magazine, birthday and Christmas presents.'[38]

By now Jeffrey had fulfilled Lola and his grandmother's hopes by winning a scholarship to Wellington School, an independent school near Taunton. The award freed his parents from the prospect of fees, though they still had to buy his uniform; Lola anticipated his future growth by buying clothes several sizes too big. The following winter, motivated one suspects by a sense of pride as much as any desire to inform, she described the school entrance procedure:

[March 1952] My heart goes out to all of you, parents and children, who are waiting for the scholarship results . . . For those trying for a boarding-school, there is an interview at a university before a panel of about 15 men and women. This is for both parents and the child concerned . . . If you satisfy everyone there, you go for an interview before the headmaster of the chosen boarding-school. Having got so far, the chances of being accepted – and acceptance lies entirely with the headmaster – are about 50–50. These results usually come out about the middle of June. Last year I worried solidly from early February onwards; so, indeed, did many of my friends in the same 'boat'. Our usual opening greeting was: 'Have you heard anything yet?' and I am sure we were all thoroughly boring on the topic of education.[39]

As Jeffrey parted for Wellington he made his mother promise never to call him Tuppence again. But Lola seems to have overlooked her own advice on not spoiling children. As she said goodbye at the start of term, Lola simply couldn't resist his pleas:

[May 1952] We both survived the ordeal of a gentlemanly parting. As we nonchalantly shook hands, I suddenly saw him as a small angel turned out (far too young) into a cruel world. The fact that ten minutes earlier he had stung me for a cricket ball, some extra tuck, and a little ready cash over and above his allowance, was forgotten. Needless to say, I came down to earth the following morning on finding all my immediate financial resources spent.[40]

# 4

# Not *That* Wellington

Wellington School has always had an irritating problem – a tendency for people to confuse it with the generally better-known Wellington College, the military-orientated public school in Berkshire. Indeed, Jeffrey Archer is often accused of making this mistake himself. There seem to be no clear examples of Jeffrey actually claiming to have gone to Wellington College, but many people from his old school have complained that on occasion he has seemed to allow such a misapprehension to go uncorrected. Somehow, Jeffrey Archer has managed to upset both Wellingtons at once.

Archer's relations with his old school are rather cool. True, he returned to present prizes at a speech day in 1986 (and Mary did the same in 1995), and he wrote the foreword to the school history in 1992, but one senses a certain exasperation from the school that he is often cited as its most successful old boy, and irritation that journalists take less interest in the other distinguished alumni (who include the TV chef Keith Floyd and the actor David Suchet).

The town of Wellington is six and a half miles from Taunton, not far from the Black Down Hills and the Exmoor National Park. Jeffrey made the journeys to and from Weston each term by train, and it was while travelling home early on in his school career that he first made a name for himself at Wellington. Changing trains at Taunton, he was so involved in chatting to schoolfriends that he followed them on to the wrong train and suddenly found himself heading for London. Jeffrey reacted as only Jeffrey would, and pulled the communication cord to get off. This early scrape made the local press, though Lola made no mention of it in her column.

Wellington School consists of a cluster of buildings either side of South Street, which runs down from the town's central crossroads. It was founded in 1837, during Thomas Arnold's heyday at Rugby and the great nineteenth-century expansion of the public schools. But

Wellington had always struggled in the lower divisions of the public-school league, and survived during the early years of this century only through subsidies from the headmaster's own pocket. Somerset County Council also helped keep Wellington going by paying the school to provide local boys with technical education.

When Jeffrey Archer arrived, in September 1951, Wellington was a direct-grant grammar school. It was officially an independent public school, but it received a grant from central government to supplement its income from fees. This meant that a quarter of all places had to be provided free, and fees for the rest were graded according to parental income. In addition, for some years in the late 1940s and early 1950s, Somerset Council awarded a number of scholarships for boys who lived in the county but a long way from the school. Jeffrey Archer was given one of these.

At that time there were just under 300 pupils, all boys. Most came from the Somerset area, many from local farming families. They were divided almost equally between day-boys and boarders, and Jeffrey boarded throughout. According to one of Lola's former colleagues, she wanted Jeffrey to go away to school partly because she felt it unhealthy to have him at home when William was so old and unwell.

Jeffrey joined the junior house, The Avenue, under the command of a strict disciplinarian, Victor Finn. It was a largely self-contained building, separate from the senior school, with its own eating facilities and sports field. They slept on small steel beds with old springs and thin mattresses, and every morning the housemaster, his deputy, their wives and about sixteen boys had to share three washbasins, one lavatory and a bath between them. Behind the house was a large garden where the boys could play.

By the standards of today, Wellington imposed a fairly regimented system; indeed, one official inspection in 1952 compared some aspects of school life to a 'barrack'. As the school historian, Leonard Isaac, writes:

> Boarders were not allowed home during term time. They were not allowed to talk to girls. They were allowed down the town only at 'Town Leave' time – 4.45 to 5.30 on Wednesdays and Saturdays. Indeed, they even had to seek their housemaster's permission to visit another boarding house. Boarders had no clothes at school other than their school uniform, and when outside the school precincts they had to wear their caps, even when out for a Sunday afternoon country walk, even when out for a cycle ride.[1]

Indeed caps had to be worn even in the sixth form and Archer says he was once caned for wearing a blazer his mother had bought him, instead of the official school jacket. One concession was that boys were free to cycle as far away from the school as they liked, so long as they got back on time.

Since the premises boasted no phone box, boys were restricted to writing home. Parents would generally visit their sons two or three times a term. Marjorie Nicol, the wife of Archer's housemaster in the senior school, remembers that Lola used to visit Jeffrey frequently but, like others, she has no recollection of William Archer ever visiting him at all. Indeed some people at Wellington were under the impression that Jeffrey didn't have a father.

One early schoolfriend, John Nash, says he thought Archer's father was abroad: 'All I remember hearing about was his mother.' Nash was a local day-boy who came from a Labour background and occasionally used to invite Jeffrey back to his family council house for tea. Archer, in contrast, 'was a Tory at a very young age', a great admirer of the Prime Minister, Winston Churchill, and a committed royalist. 'I seem to remember we talked politics a lot.' It was Archer, Nash recollects, who in 1952 first relayed the news that King George VI had died, long before the school had announced it officially: 'It was a Wednesday morning after woodwork. He took me aside and said, "Something very important's happened. Somebody's died." He made a great mystery about it, but eventually I got it out of him.'[2]

During Coronation year, 1953, the Archers switched homes once again – their sixth move within Weston in less than ten years. This time it was back up the hill to a former school which had been turned into a block of flats called Eastern Mansions. The building was known locally as Butt's flats, after the landlord who owned them. And here we encounter another of those delicious Archer coincidences. William and Lola took over flat six from a couple called Reginald and Muriel Cleese, whose teenage son was also away at school (in his case at Clifton College). When Jeffrey came back home in the holidays, he occupied the very same bedroom – possibly the same bed – which had been vacated by the future star of *Monty Python* and *Fawlty Towers*, John Cleese. Sadly, the two boys never knew each other in Weston, though their mothers later became friends.

In the school holidays Jeffrey kept up with his old acquaintances at home. Michael Taudevin notes how he would often ask Jeffrey round for tea, though the hospitality was not returned: 'I can never remember going to tea at his flat.'[3] This may simply have been because by now William Archer's health was too poor to cope with visitors. Michael's sister Jill remembers Jeffrey's father as a 'semi-invalid': 'Jeffrey never used to talk much about his father. I remember once visiting his flat. The old man shuffled across, didn't say "Hello" or anything. I was never introduced to him. It's almost as though he didn't exist really.'[4]

Michael Taudevin remembers how Lola took Jeffrey to have tea with a local girl called Mary Bignal – the future Olympic gold-medal-winner Mary Rand. Jeffrey didn't seem short of pocket money, but Taudevin says he never seemed to have the possessions other kids had, such as roller-skates, a tennis-racket or a bicycle. So for a while the two boys had to share Michael's bike. Jeffrey would run along the Kewstoke toll road as Michael cycled; then they'd swap over and Jeffrey would pedal along while Michael tried to keep up. On other occasions they frequented a snooker hall where one had to put sixpence in the slot to turn the light on. Soon they learned to play without the light, until the manager discovered them and chased them out.

Another of Taudevin's memories gives an indication of the high regard Archer had for his mother:

> On my mother's birthday Jeffrey took me to a local shop and said, 'What does she like?' I said, 'Ships.' 'Buy this,' he said, picking out a little dish with Nelson and his ship, 'They love this sort of thing, they hang them on the wall.' . . . I thought it a bit expensive. His reaction was: 'She's worth it, isn't she? You owe a lot to your mother, she deserves the best.'[5]

In the summer of 1954 Archer went with the Taudevins and a party of Weston teenagers on a week-long trip to Paris. There, Jeffrey became besotted with Jill Taudevin.

> He was always very keen and used to say he would marry me. I used to laugh at him. He was very much smaller than me. When you're that age you just don't want to know – it's a bit embarrassing . . . I had a lot of boy cousins, so I was never impressed by boys. He found it totally impossible to impress me.[6]

Jeffrey persisted, of course. On their return from France he suddenly abandoned his own church, at the western end of town, and began going to St Saviour's in Locking Road, which the Taudevins attended, even though it was two miles away. Lola never understood why he'd suddenly switched. But it made little impact on Jill, who admits she 'spent a lot of time trying to avoid him'. 'He was always full of himself, always trying to impress. He said he was going to be rich and famous.' And Jill had no doubt that 'Prime Minister is what he'd aim for,' though she can't remember him ever actually voicing that ambition. 'I feel quite sorry for him now – the way we treated him. When you're young you can be quite cruel.'[7]

Forty years later, in March 1994, the *Daily Express* arranged for Jill to have tea at the House of Lords with her former admirer: 'It was like *déjà vu*; he was still trying to impress me. That's how it always used to be – him trying to impress. Meanwhile I would be teasing him.'[8]

At the age of fourteen, after three years at Wellington, Archer was promoted to the senior school, and joined the more spartan Willows house, where boys slept in a large dormitory at the top of the building known as 'The Barn'.

Until this point, Archer had made little impact on Wellington, and for his first three years his name did not appear once in the school magazine. He was 'a person of no account', one fellow pupil observes. In his early days at Wellington, Archer was the victim of bullying – among other discomforts, according to one account, his head was pushed down the lavatory. 'The cruellest thing,' he once said, 'was you would be told in the morning that you would be beaten that evening, so you spent the whole day waiting for it. Looking back, I think it was evil.'[9] According to another:

> He was a loner. He didn't really have any friends. In every school, or class, there's one kid that's picked upon. Unluckily for him he was the sort that people took against. He was not one of the crowd. He was very badly disliked ... There was a fat boy that used to sit on him occasionally. There were a lot of other boys from Weston-super-Mare, and I think he suffered because his mother was looked on as a tedious joke by the readers of the *Weston Mercury*.

The boys quickly called him names; first, 'The Mekon', because, says one former pupil, 'he looked rather weird', like the character from the *Eagle* comic. Then he acquired the even less flattering title, 'The Pune' or 'Pune', a derivate of 'puny', based on his rather feeble physical appearance.

Around 1955 Archer changed dramatically. Some contemporaries, among them Richard Benson, date the change from the time Archer foolishly dived into the shallow end of the school swimming-pool and dislocated his neck when he hit the bottom. 'Being brave and not wishing to look sissy, he did not get diagnosed until he fainted at morning service on the next day,' says Michael Taudevin, who visited him in hospital in Taunton.[10] Jeffrey then spent several weeks in a surgical collar – much to the amusement of friends such as Jill Taudevin, who teased him that he looked like an eggcup. 'Suddenly,' says Benson, 'he became a man with a burning ambition. I always maintain it was because he fell on his head.'[11] Howard Preece, another schoolfriend, agrees: 'Up until then he'd been the total non-athlete, the classical wimp.'[12]

A similar wimpish figure occurs in Archer's novel *First Among Equals*:

'When I was at school they used to laugh at me because I was small,' said Andrew. 'They called me puny.'

'What did you do about it?' asked Clarissa.

'I trained hard and ended up as captain of the school Rugby team and that made them stop laughing.'[13]

Almost overnight, it seems, Archer became a driven man. Immediately he began to improve himself physically – trying to shake off the jibe of 'Pune'. One student, David Bromfield, recalls Jeffrey suddenly declaring he was 'going to be the best gymnast in the school'.[14]

Richard Benson remembers that Archer spent long hours fanatically doing exercises and building up his body. At night he'd walk round the dormitory upside-down on his hands for up to an hour. The other boys thought him crazy. 'Initially people were very sceptical about his desire to build himself into an athlete,' says Nigel Coombes, who's kept in touch with Archer ever since, 'but by the end everybody admired what he'd achieved.'[15]

If Jill Taudevin wasn't to be won over by his promises of wealth and fame, perhaps she'd be attracted to this new hyperfit muscle-man. In August 1955 Archer attended an Outward Bound school at Aberdovey in mid-Wales, where the timetable included thirty-five-mile walks. After one particularly strenuous day, this postcard arrived on the Taudevin mat:

Dear Jill

Note I still have strength to pick up pen (with ink in it). The school motto, smile if you are happy, and if you're not, make yourself.

Love from Mr Universe
(Bluebottle)[16]

Archer was fortunate that, during his time, Wellington began to take a much keener interest in gymnastics and athletics – playing its very first gymnastics match against another school, for instance, in 1954. This was very much due to the efforts of the gym master, Hal Kenny, to whom Archer ascribes his 'love of athletics', and who 'convinced me I should run for my country'.[17] Perhaps the most remarkable thing about Kenny was that he was almost blind because of a gym accident during the war. He was also a strong Christian, but had a reputation as a bit of a sadist.

Archer's other great sporting mentor was a fellow pupil, Geoff Bailey, whose parents owned a pub in Uphill, just outside Weston. Bailey, the school's best gymnast, took Archer under his wing and helped him with training, so much so that Jeffrey surpassed him. To this day he and Archer remain good friends – indeed he is the only close friend Jeffrey seems to retain from his days at Wellington. Bailey later developed multiple sclerosis, and over the years Archer has often helped pay for the equipment Bailey needs to overcome his disability, and some of his damages from the famous 1987 libel case helped buy his friend a sophisticated new wheelchair.

Jeffrey Archer's sudden blossoming was greatly assisted by the much more relaxed attitude that Wellington adopted in direct response to the highly critical 1952 inspectors' report. In the early evenings after lessons, boys were now positively urged to take up the kind of extracurricular activities that Jeffrey thrived on. Following in the spirit of his mother, these naturally included the theatre.

Here Archer was greatly encouraged by his English master, Alan Quilter, who had arrived at Wellington in the same term as Jeffrey, and later became headmaster of Wells Cathedral School. Archer acknowledges Quilter as the other influential teacher of his school career. It was Quilter who inspired his love of English literature, and of drama in particular.

When he was still only fourteen, Archer produced and directed a performance of *The Bishop's Candlesticks*, a one-act play by Norman McKinnel based on a story by Victor Hugo. Quilter remembers the request 'Will you look at it, sir?' But Jeffrey was firm that he didn't want a lot of help, and he made it only too clear when he felt that Quilter was starting to interfere too much.[18]

The school magazine reports on Archer playing two small roles in *Julius Caesar*, and then, at the end of 1955, on a highly ambitious dramatic venture all of his own. The magazine commends Jeffrey's 'great enterprise' in producing an English translation of Molière's comedy *L'Avare*, which he also directed and took the lead role in.[19]

Jeffrey proudly invited the Taudevins to come and see the play – though Jill came with a boyfriend. Both Michael and his sister recall how proud Jeffrey was to have cast two rather timid, effeminate boys in female parts. Everyone was impressed by the play, not least his masters. 'We all thought it would be a disaster,' says one teacher, Geoffrey Matthews. 'He took the lead and he wouldn't allow staff interference. It was a splendid performance. His self-confidence and panache came across very well. It's a very difficult part for a boy to play, and he really made an impression.'[20] He was not yet sixteen.

In February 1956 William Archer finally died, after an operation in Weston Hospital. It was no surprise: he was eighty, and his health had been declining for several years. 'The school chaplain, a man named Lancaster, called me in and told me,' Archer has said. 'I took it badly, it knocked me back for about a year.'[21]

William Archer died as he had lived: dependent on others and in debt. Lola eventually paid off the several hundred pounds that he owed. She carried on writing her column as before, as if nothing had happened. The only mention of her husband's death in 'Over the Tea Cups' came at the end of 1956, when looking back on the previous year: 'Thank You . . . to my son, who grew up suddenly and took his father's place overnight.'[22] Jeffrey himself says:

> I didn't realize it at the time, but I think losing my father triggered off my self-motivation, made me realize 'Now you're on your own, mate.' It would be interesting to know how many achievers, as Americans call them, lost their fathers early.[23]

In fact a 1970 study by Lucille Iremonger shows that an unusually high proportion of leading British politicians have lost a parent in childhood.[24] The explanation is, presumably, that this makes them strive that much harder, and provides an early maturity by forcing them to take on part of the role of the missing parent. John Major, for instance, also lost his father while still in his teens.

Yet William Archer's death does not provide a very satisfactory explanation for the change in Jeffrey's character, for the new maturity, the sudden energy, the driving ambition and overriding obsession with physical fitness. These characteristics had actually begun to emerge *before* his father died in the winter of 1956.

A year after William Archer's death the physical training started to pay off. In February 1957 Jeffrey easily won Wellington's individual gymnastics competition, and that summer he began to distinguish himself on the athletics track. Archer was always going to face difficulties as a sprinter – the fact that he wasn't as tall as most of his rivals, and thus had shorter legs, made it almost impossible for him ever to be a great runner. He simply had to make up for this with extra fitness and training. It makes his success as an athlete all the more commendable.

Archer came second in the 1957 Somerset Amateur Athletics Association (AAA) intermediate-age 100 yards, second again in the Area Schools 100 yards, and then actually won the County Schools 100 yards. But his greatest success that year, and his first on the national stage, came one weekend in mid-July in drizzly Southampton.

The All-England Championships are the annual highlight of schools athletics, and one of the biggest yearly track and field events in the world. In those days they involved around 2,000 competitors, divided into county teams and three different age-ranges, boys and girls. This meant six different contests in the 100 yards alone, for instance, each with several heats. And the whole two-day event was infused with a spirited, yet sporting, inter-county rivalry.

It rained a lot that weekend, and for the events on grass it was like 'running through a paddy field', remembers a Yorkshire runner, Adrian Metcalfe, who was one of Archer's main rivals in the relay:

> We saw the Somerset team all together and I remember the smallest of the team who was obviously the boss. He had a very loud voice, barking orders, and we all thought: 'What a prat!' . . . We thought we were the better team, but they ran like a dream. Jeffrey had marshalled and organized them. I'll never forget this little figure.[25]

Adrian Metcalfe doesn't think he actually spoke to Jeffrey Archer that day – that would have to wait until they met six years later, at Oxford. Thanks to Archer's leadership, encouragement and constant cajoling, Somerset became the first minor county side to win the 4 × 100 yards relay, pipping Essex by inches. Archer says he felt it wasn't that much of an achievement, however, since his headmaster didn't even bother to mention it on speech day.

Yet in conventional school team games Archer was much less successful. It was only in his final year at Wellington, 1957–8, that he made the main Rugby XV, the first time he had played Rugby for the school at any level. Exploiting his natural speed, the team coach put him on the wing, where he reportedly 'outpaced much of the opposition'.[26] But he was not so good with the ball. And, despite Archer's celebrated love of cricket, he admits he never progressed beyond Wellington's third XI.

The period around William Archer's death seems to have given a new lease of life to Lola too. From her column we occasionally get glimpses of a highly ambitious woman who'd been restricted by the responsibility of looking after her two men and by the limitations of a small provincial town. Lola yearned for the big city:

> [March 1956] Occasionally the urge to go up to London and live with a capital 'L' overcomes me, and as I leave Somerset for the Metropolis I am convinced, with a faith that would have done justice to Dick Whittington, that every golden opportunity lies there, merely for the asking.[27]

Lola would travel up to the capital twice a year or more. It was a chance to enjoy the latest West End shows, and catch up with Oxford Street fashion, partly for the benefit of her readers. Just as important, it was also an opportunity to knock on the doors of Fleet Street editors. It must have taken some courage for a woman columnist from an unknown provincial weekly to badger the big guns of London journalism like this, and her approach demonstrates all the confidence and persistence Jeffrey exhibited when getting his foot in the same doorways a decade later.

The BBC archives at Caversham contain several records of Lola Archer's early attempts to work for the Corporation – fragments that show just how much of the striving, imaginative side of Jeffrey Archer's character he inherited from his mother. In 1953 Lola wrote to *Woman's Hour* with an idea for a kind of early radio version of *Jim'll Fix It*, a regular feature where 'listeners would be invited to say the one person they have always wanted to meet'. If the person was willing, then the meeting would be arranged and recorded. Lola wanted 'to be allowed to start the series off by being introduced to Arthur Christiansen, editor of the *Daily Express*'.[28]

Internal memos show that BBC staff were rather tempted by the idea, and they asked her to London to discuss it with the editor of *Woman's Hour*. Never one to miss an opportunity, Lola wrote back to ask for a photograph of the editor, so that she could then 'do a "write-up" of her in my column next week'.[29]

In the end she met only the deputy editor, Joanna Scott-Moncrieff, who didn't take up Lola's idea. Nevertheless, she thought Lola worth recommending to the Head of Talks in the west of England:

> She had a very pretty deep voice and great charm at the microphone . . . I may be wrong, but I really feel she might have possibilities as a reporter on women's subjects and I imagine you have probably even more difficulty than we do in finding these.[30]

During 1955 and 1956 Lola recorded three BBC 'talks', which were broadcast in the West of England Home Service series 'Window on the West'. The first, of about four minutes, was on 'Running a Social Club for the Disabled'. Lola described how, in typical Archer fashion, she found a financial patron for her own club in Weston by first drawing up 'the names of six prominent businessmen on a piece of paper'.[31] Listeners were later treated to Lola's 'Portrait of County Alderman Mrs Evelyn Miller-Barstow MBE, JP', a distinguished Weston councillor.

On another occasion, as winter drew to a close, Lola even offered the BBC a short story entitled 'Spring', and asked whether she might be permitted to narrate it herself. Alas, the BBC replied that it was 'much too short'.[32] The story was a sign of how Lola sometimes fantasized about achieving fame and fortune as a writer – daydreams which she shared with readers of the *Weston Mercury*:

> [August 1957] I was busy with my thoughts, having just sold a fabulous story to an editor who was gazing benevolently and asking for more. Editors never gaze benevolently, but when I do anything, I do it properly, so I had thrown in the film rights, a couple of translations into foreign languages, bought a country cottage and a large car . . .[33].

Years later, when Lola was in her seventies, and Jeffrey had finally achieved her literary ambitions instead, she would in fact write a few novels. They included a romantic adventure and an Agatha Christie-style detective thriller entitled *No Reason for Death*. Lola even went to the trouble of getting them properly typed and bound, but Jeffrey would insist that one writer in the family was enough, and that it was up to her to find a publisher. She never could, and in frustration she tore up one of the manuscripts and threw it away.

Unfortunately Lola's career as a broadcaster was almost as unsuccessful, and soon fizzled out. Instead she decided to join Mrs Miller-Barstow in local government, taking the path her late husband had trodden almost half a century before. Yet her journalism had previously shown very little interest in politics, and references to current affairs were rare.

But no reader could have had any doubt from the tone of her writing that Mrs Archer was a Conservative who believed in people pulling themselves up by their own bootstraps. Though she often expressed great concern for people in need, the remedies were to be found through voluntary efforts and self-help, not through the workings of the state, or organized labour.

Lola Archer secured election to Weston Borough Council in May 1957, winning East Ward with a majority of 112 over Labour. But local citizens hardly saw the poll as a momentous occasion – it was one of only two of the town's six wards to be contested. And, once she'd been returned, Lola's fellow councillors made her promise not to discuss council business in her column – to the relief, no doubt, of every reader.

Later in 1957 Lola remarried. Again her husband was much older: Major George Watson, a widower, was fifty-eight, while she was still only forty-four. But, unlike his predecessor, Watson had a genuine military record, and had served with distinction in both world wars. In the 1914–18 conflict he'd enlisted in the Welch Fusiliers, and then served as a fighter pilot with the Royal Flying Corps – hence the nickname everyone used: 'Wings'. Watson had later worked as an exchange banker in Asia, then briefly as British vice-consul in Indo-China. During the Second World War he served on the military staff at the British Embassy in Washington. One suspects that some of these aspects of his stepfather's military and diplomatic career may help explain the stories told by Jeffrey about his natural father.

Lola continued writing her column for a few months, under her new name, Lola Watson, but then in May 1958 she gave it up, after nine years. She was re-elected to Weston Council in 1960, with a slightly larger majority, but at her third contest, in 1963, she fell victim to the Macmillan government's national unpopularity and came a poor third. Sadly, she just missed the distinction of being mayor of Weston – her turn was due the following year.

Lola and her new husband continued publishing the holiday journal, and now, under the direction of the Watsons, its unofficial title of *What's On in Weston* seemed all the more appropriate. And after moving out to Lympsham, a village five miles south of Weston, in the mid-1960s, the couple began producing another version for two towns further down the coast: *The Burnham-on-Sea and Highbridge Holiday Journal*. Lola would carry on publishing the Weston edition up to the late 1970s, by which time the three-part leaflet had expanded to fifty pages.

In his final year at Wellington, Archer was captain of gym and again won the school gymnastics contest, by a vast margin over the runner-up. The athletics success continued, too: he was Somerset youth champion in the 120-yard hurdles, and runner-up in the 100 yards. Yet, just as in recent times when he has been frustrated by his failure to become a government minister, he felt his activity never got the full acclaim it deserved from the authorities at Wellington. Though he would have loved to have been made head boy, and would probably have filled the post rather well, he wasn't even made a prefect, either by the school or by Willows house. There may be an obvious reason. 'He wasn't very popular with the boys,' says one former master, 'because of his cockiness and bumptiousness . . . he was full of enthusiasm, but so arrogant.'

This lack of official recognition didn't stop Jeffrey busying away until the very end. For speech day in the summer of 1958 – the term he left – the guest of honour was Field Marshal Sir Claude Auchinleck. Traditionally on such occasions, the school held a big gymnastics display, and since the gym master, Hal Kenny, was ill, Archer was put in charge. The result was spectacular. With continual rehearsals, firm discipline and an enormous dollop of imagination, he had synchronized his fellow pupils beautifully. Once again the Wellington audience was highly impressed, and Auchinleck himself was thrilled. At the end Archer's boys suddenly formed themselves into three large letters across the field – AUK, the field marshal's nickname. Buttering up old generals was a skill Jeffrey would put to good use in the years ahead.

He left Wellington with triumphs on the athletics track and the school stage, but not from the examination hall. He'd taken the school reading prize for his rendition of 'The Burial of Sir John Moore at Corunna', but academically, in the words of one contemporary, 'he was a no-no'. He'd remained at Wellington for three years after the school-leaving age, well past his eighteenth birthday, yet he never progressed beyond the lower sixth form. Lola and his grandmother must have been deeply disappointed. They themselves had always dreamed of a university education, yet now, in an era when it should have been much easier for him to go on to higher education, Jeffrey simply hadn't achieved good enough qualifications.

Results published in the Wellington local paper suggest he picked up only a trickle of O-levels – English literature in the summer of 1957, art that winter, and history in his final summer, when many of his contemporaries were passing several A-levels.[34] It seems that in his last year Archer did actually sit an English A-level, only for the examiners to tell the future writer that his work was only worth another O-level pass.

Howard Preece, in contrast, was one of the academic stars of that year. A friend of Jeffrey's both in Weston and at Wellington, he went straight to Oxford and now works as a journalist in South Africa. 'If you'd told me that Jeffrey Archer would become the most successful PR man,' Preece says, 'then I'd have said "OK". If you'd told me that he would write, then I would have said "impossible", because he was as near to illiterate as you can get.'[35]

# 5

# The Missing Years

In October 1965, after he had become a minor celebrity at Oxford, Jeffrey Archer was invited to speak at a prize-day at the local Northway School. 'Do not be tied down to your first job,' he advised his audience:

> Move around and see what suits the talents you have. It may be that the first job is the right one, but what better way to find out than to compare it with others? For there is nothing worse than spending your life in the drudgery of something you can't enjoy.[1]

With hindsight, this seems to reflect exactly the course that Archer himself had taken seven years before, as he began fumbling his way into the outside world.

The years from 1958 to 1961, between leaving Wellington and becoming a PE master at Dover College, are the most mysterious period of Jeffrey Archer's life. It's a time which he himself discusses very little; much of what has been written and said about those three years turns out to be untrue, or at best highly inaccurate.

For many years the story was that, after Wellington, Jeffrey Archer spent time as a student in North America. The details vary, but the most common version has him studying in California.

One account, sent by Dover College to Oxford University in 1963 and still in the university archives, says Archer went to the University of California and 'took a two-year course in anatomy, which qualified him as a Fellow of the International Federation of Physical Culture'. His dates in America are given as 1959–61.[2]

In 1967 Archer told London University that he had 'completed a First Degree in America', though he didn't explain what the subject was or where he studied.[3] Another document, drafted in 1966, told a similar story. A leading recruitment agency, Management Selection Ltd (MSL), conducted a long interview with Archer, and then reported: '1960

– Gained BA at University of California, Berkeley, in Anatomy, Physiology and Psychology.' Note that the graduation date is a year earlier than that given to Oxford.

The MSL report added that Archer's BA in 'California has given him an interesting insight into medical, etc. problems – including the ability to talk professionally'. Moreover, Archer hadn't just spent time studying on the West Coast of America: MSL also appeared to be under the impression that 'whilst in Canada (1959) he raised $500,000 for the YMCA'.[4]

Over the years, the story of Archer's studies in North America has cropped up frequently in newspaper interviews and profiles. In July 1973, for instance, Terry Coleman of *The Guardian* was told: 'he sailed to California via Scotland and the Panama Canal on a tramp steamer'.[5] A much earlier profile, in the Oxford University magazine *Isis*, in November 1964, said that:

> Archer's university career began with a two-year course at California University after the opportunity to go to America had arisen in his last year at Wellington School.[6]

Here *Isis* added some curious detail about his time in the States:

> Whilst in his first year, Archer led a small demonstration against the final quashing of the death sentence appeal made by Carl [*sic*] Chessman. It was a move that brought him his first newspaper interview, and with it a passionate dislike for journalists.[7]

The information about Chessman (Caryl, not Carl) is intriguing, as the journalist Ian Jack has noted.[8] It provides some quite credible supporting evidence for Archer's claim to have studied in America. Chessman spent twelve years on death row, and became a *cause célèbre* for American liberals in the 1950s, especially after writing four books in his prison cell, one a best-seller. Chessman had been convicted not of murder but of seventeen other offences, including attempted rape and kidnapping with bodily harm, which then carried a mandatory death penalty in California. After the failure of his last appeal, he went to the gas chamber in San Quentin prison, San Francisco, on 2 May 1960.

The reference to Chessman suggests that Archer really was in California at the time. On the other hand, the case received worldwide attention and Archer may simply have read about it in the press.

The University of California says it has no record of a Jeffrey Archer being enrolled at any of its seventeen campuses at any time during the relevant period. The YMCA in Canada has no record of an appeal in 1959 which raised $500,000, or of Archer working for it.

Later, while he was at Oxford, Archer's story wasn't always about the University of California, but embraced a whole range of other colleges across the United States, depending on whom he was talking to.

In January 1986 some serious revision of the American university education began. A letter from Archer's lawyers to Bryan Rostron and Paul Foot of the *Daily Mirror* stated that his time in America was merely for a 'summer school': 'Mr Archer attended the Summer School at the University of California, but has at no time claimed any qualifications from that University.' The lawyer added that the International Federation of Physical Culture was 'a society which he joined when he was in America and his membership lapsed in 1967'.[9]

In fact it would have been physically impossible for Archer to have completed a serious university degree in the United States, simply because one can now identify other full-time employment for most of his time during the years from 1958 to 1961. To have included a full-blown academic course on the other side of the Atlantic would have required the timetabling and resources of an American Secretary of State and David Frost combined. So what exactly was he doing?

In later life Archer would claim to have joined the Campaign for Nuclear Disarmament (CND) while at school.[10] Even if this is so, he still took an active part in the school's Combined Cadet Force (CCF), where he was promoted to colour sergeant in his final year, and he played as a drummer in its band. The summer he left Wellington, 1958, Archer went on the school's CCF camp at Catterick in North Yorkshire, and an army career was perhaps a logical next step. After all, his father had served in the army – or so he believed – and so too, more genuinely, had his stepfather, 'Wings' Watson. And military life would provide ample opportunity to pursue his sporting activities.

Archer had missed having to do National Service by only seven months. Just before he left school, in 1957, the government had announced that compulsory military training would be phased out by 1960, and that nobody born after September 1939 would now be called up. Instead, Archer signed on for five years as a 'regular', hoping to become an officer, following in what he thought were his father's footsteps. In September 1958 he began basic military training with the Duke of Wellington's Regiment, at their headquarters in Halifax, in the West Riding of Yorkshire. His basic pay would have been about five pounds a week.

By all accounts Archer was not very comfortable with the raw recruits around him in Halifax: most were from the town itself or the West Riding; some came from Scotland, with only one or two from southern England. And they were a rough crowd: several had spent time in Borstal, says John Golding, a National Serviceman who slept in the bed next to Archer's and probably knew him better than anyone else in the Halifax barracks. Archer, he observes, was the 'only person in our group who was at all academic or with intelligence'.[11]

Basic training wasn't a pleasant experience. The barracks consisted of several large Victorian blocks. Stone flights of stairs led to the sleeping-quarters, where everything was laid out symmetrically over a wooden floor: thirty beds and thirty metal lockers – one per recruit.

The young men were not allowed out for several weeks at a time. Often they would be up until two or three in the morning getting ready for the next day, spitting-and-polishing their kit and equipment. One of Jeffrey's less pleasant duties would have been to clean out the urinals, a task always given to officer cadets.

The course involved weapons work, shooting on the range with rifles and Bren machine-guns, and operating a two-inch mortar. And there was drill, of course – lots and lots of it: marching, left turns, right turns for three-quarters of an hour each day, and then for much longer as the recruits approached the final passing-out parade.

Archer had 'terrible problems in drill', John Golding says. 'It was as though he resented getting orders.' For one of the few times in his life, Archer seemed bewildered:

> He was extremely highly strung. He was always asking questions like 'Do you think the other soldiers like me, John? Do I get on with the soldiers?' I told him just to relax . . . He was immature, there's no question about it. He would not have made a good officer. He was sometimes very morose. Then the next minute he would be galvanized and do everything . . . He lacked confidence in himself. He was unnatural for a young man. 'How am I doing on the course, John?' he'd ask . . . The lads didn't warm to him. They didn't hate him either. They just couldn't place him.[12]

James McClarnon, another colleague in the platoon, had the feeling that Archer didn't really want to be a soldier: 'Obviously, you do get that impression of someone who's not keen to do what they have to do.'[13] John Golding agrees, and wonders whether Archer was hampered by his father's military reputation: 'You almost felt the thought that his father was dead was affecting him. You didn't feel Jeffrey Archer wanted to be on the course other than to prove something.'[14]

He used to mention his father a lot, several colleagues recall, though he may have been anxious not just about matching William Archer's supposed record, but also about not disappointing his stepfather.

Sport was probably the only aspect of army life that Archer enjoyed. John Golding, who later played Rugby Union for Halifax, remembers how he and Archer scored two tries against a team from another platoon which contained four county players. 'He was very good where any speed was involved, but there were no athletics played in winter.'[15]

Just before the recruits were due to pass out in December 1958, colleagues say that Archer suddenly vanished. His bed and locker were empty; he had packed his·belongings and left. 'Virtually for a day we didn't realize he'd gone,' says Golding. 'He left without saying good-bye.'[16] His fellow-recruits assumed Jeffrey had had enough, and that he'd been advised he was never going to make it as an officer.

In fact, Archer had been whisked off for several weeks of intensive cramming at the Army School of Education at Beaconsfield in Buckinghamshire. Then, just after Christmas, on 29 December 1958, he travelled to Westbury in Wiltshire to the offices of the Regular Commissions Board. There he underwent four days of rigorous scrutiny – academic examinations, physical tests and health checks. At the end of it, Archer was awarded one of the highly coveted places at Sandhurst, the Royal Military Academy near Camberley.

A few days into the new year he joined more than a hundred and forty others in the January 1959 entry – intake 26 – and was assigned to Burma company, part of the academy's Victory College. But whereas in Halifax he had stood out by being better educated and more sophisticated than most of his National Service colleagues, at Sandhurst Archer was one of the small minority of 'soldier entrants' from other parts of the army, while most cadets had arrived from top public schools and armed with A-levels. And, unlike him, they had passed the difficult Civil Service Commission exam.

The practice was that after two years at Sandhurst a cadet became a commissioned officer, initially with the rank of second lieutenant. Many from intake 26 were to enjoy long and distinguished army careers, becoming generals and major-generals, collecting medals, honours and knighthoods, and adorning the pages of *Who's Who* with their military achievements. Jeffrey Archer, in contrast, lasted no more than a few months at Sandhurst. When cadets returned for the summer term, they learned he had left.

Archer had no difficulty with the course itself, which in its initial stages was highly physical, with everyone on the move all the time, and lots of running, PT, drill, parades and weapons training. The simple difficulty seems to have been that he didn't fit in. 'He was hugely cocky,' says another member of intake 26.

> He did something that was absolutely unique in my experience, I would say, in that he managed to unite all his fellow cadets, all his NCO warrant-officer instructors, and all the officers in a sort of, I think, personal dislike of the guy ... A most unfortunate young man. He had no ability to understand other people's sensitivities. He was hugely insensitive and amazingly pleased with himself, but he was young and we all were.

A more diplomatic verdict comes from Major-General Simon Lytle, now director of the Army Air Corps, who was also in Burma company and recalls him vividly: 'I think Jeffrey decided after three months that the military life wasn't for him, and I think on balance he was probably right.'[17]

During his famous 1987 libel case, Archer was briefly asked about what he did after leaving school. There was no mention of this unhappy spell in the army, but he did reveal his next job, working 'for a short time at the Lygon Arms in Broadway, Worcestershire'.[18]

The Lygon Arms has long been one of Britain's most prestigious hotels, a favourite spot for Americans visiting the Cotswolds. Archer worked as a barman, preparing drinks for waiters to deliver to the dining-room. Janet Eldershaw, who was a receptionist at the hotel, says some of the older staff felt Archer was 'a bit too friendly with the guests. It wasn't the done thing, really.'[19]

The 1987 trial was next told he 'then went to work in the United States of America, in San Francisco'.[20] From what his lawyer told the *Daily Mirror* in 1986, and from sifting the various things he told people around that period, Jeffrey's spell in San Francisco simply appears to have involved a short course in physical education. This is what seems later to have given rise to the myth of a full-scale university degree course. However, though it quite possibly used the facilities of the campus at Berkeley, the course was not a formal part of the university's teaching. And it can have lasted no more than a few months.

By May 1960 Archer was back in Britain, embarking on what must be the most bizarre move of his entire career. Having failed in one regimented, highly disciplined culture which had little time for individuals, he signed up with another. For five months, between May and October 1960, Jeffrey Archer was a constable with the Metropolitan Police.

He did well to get in. Although the Met were always desperate for new officers, they were strict about whom they'd take. The group of fifteen recruits he joined would have been whittled down from perhaps two hundred applicants who'd been interviewed originally – many of them weeded out for poor health or fitness.

Assigned warrant number 149055, and with a weekly pay packet of about £9 7s, the twenty-year-old Archer was initially sent on a sixteen-week training course at what was then one of the two police colleges – Peel House, a large Victorian building in Regency Street, Westminster. In those days the teaching consisted largely of studying criminal law and the police instruction book – the 'IB'. Raw recruits had to learn word for word all sorts of extracts from important legislation – what were known as 'A Reports' – such as Section 66 of the Metropolitan Police Act, the famous 'sus' law. There was also physical training – unarmed combat, lessons in how to restrain prisoners, judo, swimming and first aid. Once again Archer had to do drill. Then, at monthly intervals, he had to pass written exams.

Bill Johnstone, a colleague from the same class at Peel House, says Archer was 'extremely unpopular' with his fellow trainees and 'didn't mix with the rest of us at all'. He was even more disliked by Tom Wall, the notoriously tough training superintendent:

> Tom Wall didn't half put him – Jeffrey – in his place ... Jeffrey had great ideas for changing the system, the way training was done, the police in general, the way they conducted their jobs, did their work, that sort of thing. He was just a clever Dick. You don't tell people with twenty-five, thirty years' service how to do their job.[21]

The fact that police were expected to take part in regular sport must have been a welcome relief, and Archer's physical-training instructor, Sergeant Eddie Elford, encouraged him to join the Metropolitan Police athletics team. He was allowed time off for training, and quickly excelled. A photograph in *Police Review* from July 1960 shows Archer winning the 100 yards at the National Police Athletic Championships in County Durham.[22]

At the end of his training, in August 1960, PC Archer was put on the beat for the rest of his probation period, which was due to last two years. The Met's practice was to send all the officers who were good at one particular sport to the same part of London. For athletes it was 'L' Division, covering the Brixton area, and Archer was posted to Peckham police station, which can't have been an easy patch for a public-school-boy from Somerset.

The problem wasn't the work itself, however, but the living conditions.

In those days all single men who joined the Met were obliged to live in police accommodation during their probationary period. Archer was put in what was known as a 'section house', above a police station in Carter Street, near the Walworth Road in Kennington. He was living only a few hundred yards from the site where the teenage John Major was manufacturing garden gnomes for his father, and also wondering what to do in life.

The sleeping-quarters were primitive. More than a dozen men slept together in a large dormitory which had been partitioned by curtains or boards into tiny cubicles, each about eight feet by six. Each cubicle contained a bed and a simple wooden wardrobe, and recruits had to share communal washing and toilet facilities. For the young PC Archer, things were little better than at school or in the Halifax barracks. And the rules in the section house were extremely rigid. One had to be back by a certain time each evening, and ask permission to go home at weekends.

Archer hated the section house. There was little privacy. At night it was noisy and difficult to sleep. And the petty rules were bound to infuriate any single-minded individual like him. Brian Morris, a police athlete who ran for England, says Archer would often refer to the cubicles as 'horseboxes'. According to more than one account, he asked his superintendent how he expected anyone to live in 'such a horsebox'. Well, if Archer didn't 'bloody well like it', his boss barked back, he could leave.[23]

So he did. The Met lost the man who would one day bring a Tory conference to its feet by urging the Home Secretary to 'stand and deliver' on crime.

Shedding his constable's uniform can't have been a straightforward decision. Archer 'seemed quite proud at the time to be in the police force', says Morris, who remembers him showing off his passing-out photo from Peel House.[24] Yet, for some reason, it is an episode which Archer never mentions. He has no time for former police colleagues who occasionally approach him about those days: his attitude seems to be that his police career was another failure, best forgotten. A rare acknowledgement that he ever served in the police at all came in the letter from his lawyers in 1986. He completed the course, they said, and then 'in common with very many others who started with him, he decided that it was not a career which he wished to follow'.[25] Scotland Yard confirms that Archer was not unusual in this, and that the drop-out rate then was high.

So, more than two years after leaving Wellington, Archer was still drifting. The two careers to which he'd committed himself – the army and the police – had both been failures. But Archer bounced out of the police into a profession which allowed sufficient scope for his energy and imagination, and where he would be less hindered by petty rules and discipline. He returned to the world where he'd been allowed to shine for several years: private education.

Vicar's Hill was a small, private boarding-school near the village of Walhampton on the edge of the New Forest in Hampshire, overlooking the Solent and the Isle of Wight. It was a coaching establishment – a 'crammer' – but a rather unusual one. Many of the boys were being coached for the Common Entrance exam for public schools, just as in any ordinary preparatory school. But the owner and headmistress, Audrey Brewer – always known as 'Dordie' – specialized in teaching boys with learning and behavioural problems. Some were simply backward and needed intensive tuition; one or two had terrible temper tantrums; and some had been expelled from their previous schools – in a few cases they were paid for by local authorities to stop them being disruptive in the state system.

Vicar's Hill had about forty pupils, ranging in age from seven to eighteen. For ordinary lessons in the three Rs they would often be taught one-to-one or in twos, coming together in larger groups for subjects such as history and Scripture. The school was run on a shoe-string, and everyone was expected to muck in, doing odd jobs such as mowing the grass. Like many prep schools, it was quite happy to take on keen young students who had only just left school, simply because they were cheap. According to one former master, 'Mrs Brewer employed endless people on short-term contracts. People were there for one term, two terms, half a term. The staff change-over was enormous.'[26] Sometimes people were persuaded to work for nothing. Yet, considering how little she paid people, Mrs Brewer assembled a remarkably good staff, and at least three masters from Archer's time later went on to become heads of leading independent schools.

Jeffrey was taken on to teach PE. His pay, one colleague estimates, would have been about £120 a term, plus food and a bedroom in the school. Dordie Brewer wouldn't have cared one jot that he'd left Wellington with only three O-levels: what was important were his obvious enthusiasm and inspirational qualities. 'His taking over of PE and the gym was sensationally successful,' says one of his old colleagues, John Steadman. 'He was the finest PE master I've seen or imagined. His energy was absolutely unlimited. He got small boys doing things I've never seen them do before . . . He had a sort of magic effect on young athletes, and they were prepared to make tremendous efforts.'[27]

Archer was at Vicar's Hill for little more than one and a half terms, but almost thirty-five years later several members of staff can remember vividly how they found themselves fascinated by both his boundless energy and his ability to inspire. His activity never seemed to stop from the moment he woke the school each morning with a bugle-call. If an odd job needed doing, Jeffrey was always there to volunteer. In the gym, even the most unathletic specimens would be climbing ropes, standing on their heads and performing somersaults in mid-air. 'There was something quite extraordinary about the man,' says Euan MacAlpine, who later became headmaster of Mill Hill School.

> He was absolutely brilliant. He got people who were incapable of doing anything to do amazing things. He was an absolute inspiration. . . . Depending on what he was doing you could either say it was aggressive, arrogant, conceited or you could say it was very good, charming or whatever – exactly what you see now.[28]

Mrs Brewer's adopted son, Charles Neel, who was also on the staff, was less enamoured. 'He was an alert, pushy young man – very pushy,' he says. 'He was a pain in the arse, in fact.' But even he concedes Jeffrey did 'his job well'.[29]

Neel remembers how Archer ran after-school keep-fit classes and circuit training for the staff. To maintain his own athletic interests, Archer also persuaded both John Steadman and another colleague, Michael Stevens, to set up the kind of running practice he'd done with Michael Taudevin in Weston. 'I used to ride my bike pacing him as he came thundering through the forest behind, and he would run until he couldn't run any further. He would run until he dropped,' Stevens recalls.[30] Steadman would stand and time Archer's sprint-starts on the running-track.

Steadman, a maths teacher, became something of a surrogate father to the young games master – at forty-seven, he was exactly the same age as Lola. Jeffrey would stay with him in the holidays; they played squash together, and sometimes in the evenings they'd go for dinner and a game of snooker. But Steadman says going to the pub with Jeffrey was usually an 'abortive operation, as he never drank anything'.[31]

Steadman thinks he was probably responsible for first planting the idea in Archer's mind that he might go to Oxford one day – largely as a means of getting in some serious athletics training. Archer also toyed with the idea of doing a correspondence degree with Trinity College, Dublin. To impress the admission authorities, he even wrote what Steadman describes as a 'book', which seems to have been inspired by Archer's brief course in California. The work runs to 127 pages and more than 60,000 words – about a third the length of this book.

'A vague, rambling account of the anatomy and physiology of man,' is how Steadman describes it – 'human evolution and things like that'. It opened with a line from Alexander Pope – 'The proper study of mankind is man' – and each chapter began with further quotations from Pope. He remembers Jeffrey sending his drafts back to Weston to be typed by Lola, whom he suspects played quite a large role in writing it, too. 'I helped him with some aspects of it – the English, and with some of the bits about anatomy. There were grammatical errors sometimes, or a lot of journalese which I think was his mother's.'[32]

Steadman doesn't think the thesis was ever submitted to Trinity College. But he has kept a copy of it to this day, and refuses to release it without Archer's consent. In 1994, however, he decided the book might be of some value, and took steps to make it secure. So today Jeffrey Archer's first substantial piece of writing resides in the safe of a bank in Norwich.

# 6

# Muscles and Dover Soul

During the Easter holidays of 1961, Archer was able to celebrate a new appointment as well as his twenty-first birthday. Charles Neel and Michael Stevens recall how they borrowed Dordie Brewer's car, a Humber Hawk estate, loaded up Jeffrey's belongings, and drove him east along the south coast to new digs in Dover. Their passenger had just been made PE master at one of Britain's minor public schools, Dover College.

The new post would prove to be the first significant foothold in Archer's determined ascent to fame and wealth. It was the job which transformed the boy into a man. And from the respectability of Dover College, and the several valuable contacts it offered, all else followed.

The college had gained the blessing of the Establishment in 1923 with the granting of a royal charter. Originally founded in 1871, it had taken over the remains of the old Dover priory; the monks' refectory, now the school hall, is among the few Norman buildings still in daily use in Britain.

During his interview, Archer had won over Dover's headmaster, Tim Cobb, with his ebullience and drive, despite the fact there was a much better-qualified candidate for the job. Cobb, who'd gone to Cambridge and spent eleven years as a headmaster in Uganda, knew employing Archer was a risk, and hard to justify. He freely admits he ignored the advice of Dordie Brewer at Vicar's Hill, who had warned Cobb not to take him on, though she never explained why.[1]

Another problem was that Archer was so young; indeed, he was barely older than one or two of the boys, and actually looked quite a bit younger than his twenty-one years. The wife of a former Dover housemaster remembers having to correct one mother who assumed he was a boy: 'I said, "He's a master," and she said, "He only looks about sixteen." '[2]

There was also the mystery about his past. 'It was a job finding out

68

where he'd been before he came to us,' says Richard Rottenbury, who was head of Dover's junior school and had originally agreed Archer's appointment with Tim Cobb. 'It was very difficult to pin him down. If you added up all the things that he did it would come to about seven years' work, and he only had two or three years . . . Obscure universities in America appeared suddenly.'[3] Most of the school clearly believed Archer had a degree.

Rottenbury remembers how Archer proudly went round brandishing some kind of certificate he'd obtained in America. The Dover College photograph for 1962 shows the new sports master sitting there alongside his colleagues wearing a graduate gown. One old boy, Stephen Catt, recollects the regular chattering about how Archer had acquired it. 'There was always a great deal of debate about his hood and gown. No one recognized the colours. The school gossip was he'd bought it somewhere.'[4]

According to one account, Archer had his gown and hood made by a tailor in Dover, in the blue colours of the American university from which he was supposed to have graduated. Unfortunately the Dover tailor most likely to have performed this task, if the account is correct, is now dead.

Degree or not, it didn't really matter: everyone quickly learned that Archer was a first-class PE teacher; he was just what Dover needed after a period when the school's sport had been under par. Cobb was delighted. 'The boys adored him. What most struck me about him was his certainty that he could command success,' he later observed. 'I was quite certain that if he set his mind to anything he could do it. He lifted our athletics to a very high level.'[5]

Neither staff nor boys had seen a sports master in a track suit before. He was like 'a little dog on a spring', says another ex-pupil, John Wise-Fone. 'He had incredible dynamism. He was so intense, the "grip" kind of chap – always saying "Get a grip on yourself, lad. A hundred per cent; I want a hundred per cent effort." We called him "The Grip Kid".'[6]

Just as at Vicar's Hill, Archer had an unusual ability to get pupils to do things others would not imagine possible. 'Come on, you horrible little boy!' Archer would bark in his clipped, brisk, military voice, and the boys generally did, lifting their legs higher or running them faster. Yet it wasn't simply an ability to inspire and get the best out of people: from talking to former pupils, it's clear that Archer built up a strange kind of adolescent following; in many cases the boys idolized and wor-shipped him. 'Boys died for Jeffrey – he had that kind of charisma,' says one former pupil, Bruce Dakowski, who is now a social anthropologist. 'It was very easy for boys to fall under his spell and overachieve for him.'[7]

With Archer, boys didn't mind being stretched to the limit. There is a story – no doubt apocryphal – that when returning from a cross-country fixture in Folkestone, for example, Archer drove the seven miles home by van, while the boys were expected to run back. Not everyone was an Archer-worshipper, though, and occasionally the boys got their own back. Once, during a basketball match, says Stephen Catt, they all ganged up on him in the gym 'and had him in a corner'.[8]

Occasionally Archer's enthusiasm got the better of him, and he had to be restrained by his senior colleagues. One such incident occurred in the junior school during the great freeze of 1963. Richard Rottenbury remembers how 'I had to placate a lot of parents who didn't want Jeffrey Archer taking their children out in the snow to do PE in bare feet. Bare feet was typical of him.'[9]

At Christmas 1961 *The Dovorian*, the school magazine, congratulated the new games master on 'qualifying to become a Fellow of the Inter-national Federation of Physical Culture'.[10] People might have been less impressed had they known what the organization was.

The International Federation of Physical Culture (IFPC) has puzzled Archer-watchers for years. The common assumption is that it was an American institution, somehow linked to his mysterious period in Cali-fornia. I too concentrated my initial enquiries on the United States. Then one day, while researching newspapers, my wife suddenly spotted an ad in a 1961 edition of the now defunct weekly tabloid *Tit-bits*:

> You Too, Can Be As Other Men
> Over 100,000 men have developed a
> SUPER PHYSIQUE

There, amid drawings of superhulks flexing their muscles, all was revealed. 'Why be ashamed to strip?' the ad asked, when all readers had to do was adopt the '"Body-Bulk" method of home physical training'. A former Mr Universe, Mark Lewis, told how he was living testimony to the federation's method of home training. 'Now is the time to start building a super physique and get yourself a new body for 1961!'[11]

The International Federation of Physical Culture was quite simply a body-building club, which helped members develop their muscles through home exercises. The man behind it, George Walsh, had founded the federation in the late 1940s, and described himself as 'famous throughout the world as the greatest living authority on body-building'.[12] His federation was run not from an American campus, nor even from some sun-drenched beach in California: the IFPC's 'Empire Headquarters' was an office block in Chancery Lane, central London.

That was the organization from which Jeffrey Archer had acquired his proud fellowship. Dover College seemed to treat it like an academic qualification, to rank alongside the degree they thought Archer possessed. The school's class list for Michaelmas Term 1962 reads: 'J. H. Archer, FIFPC, BSc.'[13] Armed with this 'international' recognition, he began moonlighting from his job at Dover College, and went into business offering men advice on how to improve their bodies. The man who later aspired to be a political heavyweight, and whose physique would one day grace the House of Lords, established his first enterprise after placing this ad in the weekly tabloid *Reveille*:

DIRECT FROM AMERICA
The 'Pal Malviro'
BODYBUILDING
Course

'At last,' Archer told the nation's aspiring hulks, 'the famous course with the amazing results is in GREAT BRITAIN. If you want a Mighty Body, more Strength, better Health and Fitness, write for further details, Pal Malviro, 22 Victoria Park, Dover.'[14] However, despite enquiries to historians of body-building in both Britain and America, nobody seems to have heard of the 'Pal Malviro' technique. It was probably something else Jeffrey picked up in California.

Archer's landlady in Victoria Park, Alice Slaughter, was used to having lodgers with unusual activities. Before the war, Mrs Slaughter had owned a house in East Cliff on the seafront near the Eastern Dock, where Christopher Isherwood and W. H. Auden had briefly been her tenants. 'They used to have the strangest people there,' says her daughter Joan Czarnowski, 'and E. M. Forster used to stay.' Alice Slaughter was rather proud of having been their landlady, so it's likely she would have told Jeffrey about it.[15]

Mrs Slaughter was upset that Archer had set up his business from her home without asking her first. Her daughter Joan remembers how Jeffrey would dash downstairs every morning to grab the post, tear the envelopes open, but then leave the letters lying around. Often, she says, customers got so frustrated with the delays in getting a reply from Archer that they called to complain. 'These people were always knocking at the door saying they hadn't had any response, and I used to get annoyed because it was me who used to answer the door . . . I don't know if he ever sent them anything – he was never there; he just used it as a place to sleep . . . He used to rush in and out like a tornado.'[16] At one stage the complaints got so serious that a colleague advised Archer to consult a solicitor.

Around the beginning of 1962 Archer left Mrs Slaughter and began lodging with the Carruthers family in their large Victorian house in Castle Hill Road. Before long he was going out with the Carruthers' daughter, Diana, an attractive redhead a few months older than him. The Carruthers had a respectable middle-class background: Diana's father spent most of the time living away in India, while her mother, like Lola, had trained as a nurse. Diana herself worked as a secretary in Dover. The relationship grew serious, and soon the couple agreed to get married. According to one of his later contemporaries at Oxford, the engagement occurred in circumstances typical of Jeffrey. One night, while he was driving Diana around, his Hillman Minx was involved in an accident. Archer was so shaken by what had happened that he immediately turned to his girlfriend and proposed to her on the spot. Diana accepted.

A close friend of the Carruthers family says Jeffrey was constantly on the look out for funds and 'sponsorship' for his business and continuing running activity. Diana had inherited several hundred pounds, and, as they were now getting married anyway, she happily agreed to lend it to her fiancé. 'She had some money,' says Daniel Dane, another family friend, who thinks it may have come from a family trust. 'As is often the case, when they were engaged, whether it was officially or unofficially, she thought it was a good idea to help him financially.'[17]

It may have been with Diana Carruthers' money that Archer managed to splash out on a vintage car, a 1926 Bullnose Morris. It was an open two-seater vehicle, which he used only on special occasions and kept until the early 1970s. 'He was terrified of it,' says James Philbrick, a fellow master at Dover, who looked after the car for him. 'Once when he got out of it he was pale and sweating, all white and trembling.'[18] That and the Hillman Minx he had bought earlier must together have cost him about £1,000, at a time when his annual income from Dover College would have been only about £750.

Archer had also joined a local amateur drama group, the Dover Players. He had small parts in *Charley's Aunt*, *Antigone* and *Ring Round the Moon*, as well as *Brief Encounter*, in which he played a soldier. Maureen Gough, who produced *Brief Encounter*, has always been struck by Archer's reaction on reading the synopsis she'd written for the programme: 'He said, "Mo, if I could write like that, I'd make a million one day!"'[19]

His most notable role was Puck in *A Midsummer Night's Dream*, which the players performed in the grounds of nearby Kearsney Abbey. Every night the audience was startled as Puck, clad completely in green, suddenly leapt on to the stage from behind a tall hedge. In fact this leap wasn't quite as agile and spectacular as it looked, since he'd actually taken off from a raised platform on the other side. But, in the opinion of the *Dover Express*, 'Never could Dover audiences have seen a more energetic puckish-Puck than Dover College master Jeffrey Archer who created havoc in the wood as he worked for his fairy king Oberon.'[20]

Dover also gave Archer his first taste for charity fund-raising. After his appointment as house tutor for St Martin's house, Archer sent his boys knocking on every door in the town to beg for old books. Newspapers who'd been tipped off by Jeffrey couldn't resist the sight of Dover boys, dressed in boaters and waistcoats, trundling pram-loads of books around the town. The venture even won coverage in the London *Evening Standard* and one of the national dailies. Lola had obviously given her son useful lessons in how to cultivate the press.

Another element of the fund-raising was an essay competition. The title had Archer written all over it: 'It is typical of the world today that, whereas some parents are prepared to spend £400 a year on their own child's education, no one is ready to spend £1 on the education of somebody else's child.'[21] Dover's fees were £400 a year at the time. Although the charity work involved enormous activity by the boys, the result was perhaps disappointing considering the amount of publicity they'd gained. From the book sale, the essay contest and a raffle, Save the Children received a cheque for 250 guineas.

At the 1962 Dover College speech day, parents were treated to a repeat of the gymnastics spectacle that Archer had organized in his final weeks at Wellington. The climax came when fifty boys joined together in a series of pyramids, each one bigger than the last, 'culminating in a tower of boys that stood some 22 feet high'.[22] Again it ended with the gymnasts forming into the initials of the guest speaker – AC, for Sir Andrew Cohen.

An earlier attempt at the pyramids display for the Dover junior school didn't fare so well. According to Penny Matthews, a housemaster's wife:

> He had all these small boys standing on each other's shoulders making a pyramid, and the parents were gasping with admiration. Until, being Jeffrey, he rather carried it to extremes, and they were getting higher and higher, and the parents were getting paler and paler, and finally the headmaster of the junior school had to call a halt![23]

Archer had more than fulfilled Cobb's initial hopes: Dover College sport had been transformed. 'Whenever he put in a team for anything, they practically always won,' Cobb says.[24] The local newspaper claimed that, since Archer had arrived, the college had 'lost only one of their 157 cross-country run fixtures, have not lost any of their 27 schools' athletics meetings nor any of their 22 basketball matches'.[25] The figures were exaggerated, but the basic point was right: results had improved dramatically, though sometimes Dover teams won only by the most unorthodox of methods.

John Holt was then sports master at Tonbridge School, and went on to become general secretary of the International Amateur Athletics Federation. He remembers Archer with mixed feelings, after the time he took a cross-country team for a match at Dover which also involved two other schools. As the home side, Dover was responsible for organizing the match. Holt says Archer had completely failed to prepare properly: as the runners reached the finishing-line, there was just one 'over-zealous sixth-former' there to hand out position markers as each boy came home. When several finished in a bunch, there was chaos. Dover boys were marked down ahead of runners from rival teams who had actually beaten them. The other schools protested that the scores were wrong, and that the finish should be re-created, but the more they complained the more Archer got upset that they were questioning his organization and integrity.

Officially Dover won the fixture, but the boys from the other three

# STEPNEY BOROUGH COUNCIL
## BYE-ELECTION.

—

### NORTH WARD.

—

Polling Day, February 6, 1908.

## VOTE FOR

# ARCHER

## THE MUNICIPAL REFORM CANDIDATE.

1. Election advertisement for Jeffrey's father, William Robert Archer, who became a Municipal Reform councillor in Stepney in 1908, but served for less than two years.

2. William Archer's first wife, Alice, whom he married in 1900.

3. Jeffrey's maternal grandmother, Ellen Cook, around 1937, holding the first Jeffrey Archer, who was adopted three times and is now David Brown, the last of his five different names.

4. Lola Archer frequently featured her second son Jeffrey in her 'Over the Tea Cups' column in the *Weston Mercury*, where she always called him 'Tuppence'.

## OVER THE TEA CUPS

### News and Jottings For Women.

**"TUPPENCE"**

It has been suggested from time to time that I might put a photograph of my son in this column—Tuppence the unruly, who so often invades my thoughts when I am writing—well, here he is with an expression that would do justice to an early Christian martyr. When  asked if he would like his photo taken he adopted a belligerent attitude, and later, on being shown six indifferent proofs, muttered "I couldn't care less." Why going to the photographer with a small boy should prove such agony I cannot think. I remember listening to Joyce Brooks at an Operatic social, giving four priceless impressions of children going to be photographed. I gathered they had been drawn from real life. I am now well able to supply her with material for a fifth.

5. Nine-year-old Tuppence (fourth from right, peering at the camera) at the wedding of his cub-mistress, Babs Baker, in 1950. Lola credited Miss Baker with getting Jeffrey to brush his teeth regularly and polish his shoes.

6. Jeffrey's half-sister, Rosemary, on the day of her second marriage, to Robert Silvercruys in Washington in 1953. The First Lady, Mamie Eisenhower, is on the right.

7. Jeffrey (circled) setting off on the trip to Paris in 1954 during which he pursued his first sweetheart, Jill Taudevin (standing, eighth from right).

8. Leopard-skinned drummer (circled) and colour sergeant in the Wellington School Combined Cadet Force in 1958. Archer's subsequent military career lasted about seven months.

9. Metropolitan Police Warrant No. 149055. PC Archer became national police 100 yards champion, but spent just five months in the force before resigning voluntarily.

10. Vicar's Hill school, Hampshire, the crammer where Jeffrey, clutching the ball, taught PE from 1960 to 1961, and produced his first substantial piece of writing, a 60,000-word 'thesis'.

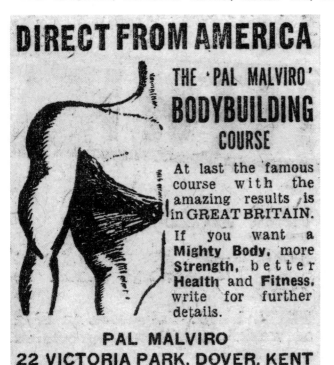

11. When Archer applied to Oxford in 1963, the university was told that he had become a fellow of the International Federation of Physical Culture following a two-year course at the University of California. The federation was in fact based in London and devoted to body-building.

12. A 1961 advertisement for Archer's own body-building course, run from his digs in Dover.

13. Archer (third from left) displays his Thespian skills in *Charley's Aunt*, with the Dover Players, 1961.

14. Wearing a graduate gown in the 1962 Dover College photo. There was much speculation among both staff and boys about how Archer acquired the gown.

**Poor Little Pussy!**

**This kitten nearly died. Now it lives!**

●Mary Weeden (St. Anne's) cradles Priscilla—the cat with eight more lives left! (Photo. by Stephen Fry).

Full details in Oxford Accent on page 4

15. Mary and her lost cat grace the front page of *Cherwell*, the Oxford University newspaper, in 1963.

schools were so angry that they boycotted the tea the college had laid on afterwards, and went to eat in the town. 'It was a scandal really,' says Holt. 'I wrote to the headmaster of Dover and never got an answer. We were so angry about what happened . . . I wouldn't say it was cheating. It was more disorganization, and pride which wouldn't allow the chaps to get together and sort it all out.'[26]

But Archer got results. Indeed, the nearby Duke of York's Military School got so frustrated by Dover College teams beating theirs that they tried to poach him. Even though the academy was willing to pay him more than Tim Cobb could ever afford, Archer remained loyal.

Julian Dakowski, who arrived at Dover while Archer was teaching there, recalls how Jeffrey once confessed that his time at Dover 'was like being the head boy he never was'.[27] Julian's brother Bruce, who later worked for Archer as a personal assistant, believes his impact went well beyond the sports field. 'What Jeffrey brought to Dover College – a very stuffy but very good public school – was he removed the shame from the will to achieve. Endeavour for those that worked with Jeffrey spilled over into the orchestra, the dramatic society, the choir and even academic life, something not usually associated with Dover, or Jeffrey!'[28]

When Archer finally left Dover College, in the summer of 1963, *The Dovorian* delivered a glowing and wonderfully vivid 'obituary':

> Very contemporary, very pukka, with a pronounced taste for Kipling, a voice like a razor-blade, and a 'Henry V' haircut that was never out of character – Mr Archer has made his two-year stay a short and hectic one. He came to spread success and he has spread it . . . It is the sort of success for which all schools are grateful. To achieve it, he has subjected us to many stimuli, ranging from the truly inspiring to the richly comic . . .
>
> In two years he persuaded many of us to take seriously much that we wanted to treat as a joke – including JHA himself. If an Olympics committee does not select him, we advise it to have its reasons ready.[29]

Several Dover colleagues remember how Archer wore some kind of England blazer while he was at the school, though he had not yet represented his country at any significant level. Archer also talked about competing in the Tokyo Olympics in 1964. He'd kept in touch with John Steadman from Vicar's Hill, who'd convinced him that university would give him the opportunity for the necessary training. The *Dover Express* said he would go to Oxford after doing a year on 'a research scholarship at Cologne University'.[30] In fact he went to Oxford immediately, having achieved a place there with considerable help from Tim Cobb. 'My advice was unequivocal,' says Cobb: ' "You've got everything except qualifications. Go off and get some." And of course, that's just what he did.'[31]

Everyone knew Jeffrey was leaving – except his fiancée, Diana Carruthers. Joan Czarnowski couldn't believe how Diana found out about it. 'I was sitting with my mother, and she turned up one day and said, "Is Jeffrey about?" And we said, "Oh, he's gone." And he hadn't told her.'[32]

According to one of her friends, Diana followed Jeffrey to Oxford, and did some secretarial work for Oxfam. Diana herself says they eventually had an amicable parting, and she kept in touch with Lola for many years.

More than thirty years on, now living in rural Gloucestershire, Diana will only confirm that she and Jeffrey Archer were engaged. She harbours no ill-feelings towards her former fiancé. 'That's a part of my past,' she says.[33]

# 7

# A Degree of Uncertainty

Jeffrey Archer's arrival in Oxford in October 1963 is one of the most controversial episodes of his entire career. He came for a one-year course, the Diploma in Education (known as the DipEd), but ended up staying for three years, just as if he were a typical undergraduate. He left Oxford with several of the university's most glittering prizes, and a wife who was regarded as one of the most attractive and intelligent women students of her generation.

The Oxford Department of Education and the DipEd have long been considered a back-door route into the university. About half the department's 280 students were Oxford graduates, and the rest generally had degrees from other universities. While the majority on the education course hoped to become teachers, inevitably there were some who exploited the DipEd as a means of saying they went to Oxford. It was also a way of having a good time at the university – particularly in sport – without having to do a full-blown degree course. Jeffrey Archer seems to have been motivated by all these considerations.

Without Tim Cobb and Dover College, Archer would never have made it. 'He was lucky to get on the course,' says his former tutor, Ronald Burrows, 'but he was very strongly recommended as outstanding by his headmaster.'[1] Archer was particularly fortunate in that the Department of Education was run by Alexander Peterson, Cobb's predecessor at Dover College. And Peterson had been introduced by Cobb to his keen young games master during a return visit to his old school.

In the early 1960s the Oxford Department of Education had much looser ties with the university than today. As Peterson explained in some unpublished memoirs:

> The tutors in the Oxford department were not fellows of colleges,
> though the colleges were happy enough to admit the students to

membership and allow them to play games for the college – like Jeffrey Archer at BNC [Brasenose College].[2]

Alexander Peterson particularly resented the way in which his department was then held in such low regard by the rest of the university. Indeed, despite being director, even he had great difficulty in being accepted as an Oxford fellow.

Today the department is much more closely integrated with the university, but its 'semi-detached' status in the 1960s helps explain why many people are convinced that Archer was never really at Oxford University. This is wrong: education students were, and are, full members of the university, even if their tutors might not have been accepted as Oxford dons. Jeffrey Howard Archer was enrolled into Oxford University – or 'matriculated' as it's officially called – in October 1963, and university membership is something one retains for life. His name appears in the *University Calendar* for 1964 under Brasenose College – though for some reason, in several subsequent years, his name was omitted from the section recording all living matriculated members. His name is also on file at the university offices. Whatever else one might say about Archer, his membership of Oxford University (unlike his father's) cannot be disputed.

What remains contentious is how Jeffrey Archer got into Oxford, and what the university was told about him when he applied. Moreover, how did he manage to spend three years gaining blues and offices in the University Athletics Club when he was only there for a one-year course? Exploring this area is particularly difficult since three separate bodies were involved: the Department of Education, the university and Brasenose, the college he joined. None seems particularly good at keeping records.

The Department of Education appears to have accepted Archer on the basis of a letter of recommendation from Dover College. This is the document which erroneously claimed that from 1959 to 1961 Archer did a two-year anatomy course at the University of California, and then passed the exam which, Oxford was told, qualified him as a fellow of the International Federation of Physical Culture. It is hard to believe that university dons would have been impressed had they known the federation was an organization for muscle-men. The letter from Dover College also said that Archer had six O-levels – in history, English, geography, maths, French and art – and three A-levels – in history,

English and geography.[3] This is rather strange, given that Archer had left Wellington with only three O-levels. But of course this letter was submitted by Dover College, his employer, rather than by Jeffrey himself.

Normally the Department of Education at Oxford takes only graduates, but Ronald Burrows says the rule was usually relaxed for one or two candidates regarded as being of graduate equivalence – older non-graduates who had already been in teaching and had been 'recommended by their headmaster for a course of training'.[4] Sometimes this relaxation was applied to people such as priests, and usually the entrant had to be 'mature' – that is, twenty-five or over. So Archer was not exceptional in not having a degree when he enrolled, though at the age of twenty-three he was really too young for the 'graduate equivalence' rule.

What is most unusual is for any British student to be admitted to Oxford with just three O-levels. Indeed, if Archer did arrive with so few O-levels, he must have been one of the least qualified British students ever to enter the university in modern times. If, on the other hand, Archer had actually acquired the three extra O-levels and the three A-levels cited in the Dover College letter, where and when did he get them?

He could have taken the exams in the same way John Major did after he left school, studying at evening classes and in his spare time, during his spells in the army and the police, during quiet periods at the Lygon Arms, or while teaching at Vicar's Hill and Dover College. If Archer did this, it was very quietly, for nobody from any of these bodies remembers him studying or asking for any tuition. One certainly would expect John Steadman to have known about it, for instance. Unfortunately, there is no way of checking the claim in the Dover College letter. The current political emphasis on rigorous testing in our education system is still outweighed by the British obsession with secrecy. One cannot independently discover what O-levels or A-levels anybody has – as students of John Major's career found some years ago – for the examination boards all refuse to disclose such information. One begins to wonder about the value of O- and A-levels if one cannot verify whether anybody has them.

Years later, in the mid-1980s, when journalists started to ask how he had got into Oxford, Alexander Peterson was shocked to learn that Archer's previous academic record had been so flimsy. Indeed, he felt deceived. Neither he nor anybody else had bothered to ask for proof of the information given by Dover College. It wasn't then the done thing to check. Fortunately, today's Oxford entrance procedures are a little tighter.

In fact, just after he arrived in Oxford, a query was suddenly raised about Archer's qualifications. It wasn't about whether he had a degree, or where he'd obtained his A-levels: typical of the anachronistic way in which the university operated, it arose from the regulation that every student had to have O-level Latin. On 23 October 1963 a university committee met to consider Archer's nakedness in this regard. Fortunately for him, they waived the rule, allowing him to matriculate.

Despite his rather unconventional academic background, Archer swept into Oxford full of confidence that he could repeat his whirlwind achievements at Dover College. Shortly after arriving there, he wrote:

> Oxford, in the first few days is ... a little frightening. There appears to be so much to do, so many things to join and only 56 days to do everything in. I quickly decided that sport, the Union and drama would be my three outside interests and there would be no others, not even on a tiny basis.[5]

Within days, though, this resolution had been abandoned, as Archer resumed the kind of charity fund-raising he'd already begun at Dover College.

That year, 1963, saw the twenty-first birthday of the Oxford-based charity Oxfam. The organization had been founded in 1942 to help the people of war-ravaged Greece, where an estimated 200,000 people had died of famine and disease in the winter of 1941–2. In Trafalgar Square on Sunday 6 October 1963, the day before Archer arrived in the university, Oxfam had launched a 'Hunger £Million' campaign. The actress Susannah York toured the crowd spearing pound notes on the tip of an umbrella, as the start of Oxfam's effort to raise £1 million by the end of that year. It was an ambitious target – the equivalent today of about £12 million.

Archer's involvement with Oxfam initially began with a far less ambitious venture: to raise £25,000 for a hospital in Dehra Dun, in the foothills of the Indian Himalayas. While discussing his fund-raising plans in the Oxfam offices one day, the charity's education officer, Bill Jackson, first alerted him to the Hunger £Million campaign.

Jeffrey's account is that the appeal looked likely to fall well short of its target. Oxfam's internal records, however, suggest that things weren't going badly. After seven and a half weeks, up to 28 November, they'd raised £448,000 – an average of £64,000 a week – and the appeal was gaining momentum.[6] Simply progressing at that rate, Oxfam could have expected to reach £750,000 in the remaining five weeks. With extra push and greater public generosity around Christmas, the £1 million figure might have been attained without Archer's offer to help.

His initial suggestion was to get Oxford students involved; until then undergraduates had rarely taken much interest in the charity, even though many of the founders had been university dons. Jeffrey had heard how the previous Christmas someone from London University had raised £3,000 simply by going round pubs with ten of his friends. So, if a thousand Oxford students toured all the 72,000 pubs in Britain, they ought to be able to raise £300,000 or more.

'He didn't look like a student at all – he was more like a young tycoon,' says Richard Exley, the organizer of the Hunger £Million project.

> He was short, with cropped hair, muscular, bouncing with energy, and had personal pizazz . . . His basic attitude was: 'I'm going to get this thing organized for you. I'm going to get three thousand students with collecting-tins; we're going to do this thing for you.' I jollied him along, and he said, 'Give me three thousand collecting-tins' – which was a bit of an embarrassment, because the organization didn't have as many as that in total! . . . The sheer push of the guy made me take him seriously – the one thing you value above most things in a charity is energy, and he had it in abundance.[7]

Organizing everything as if it were a military operation, Archer assembled a team of lieutenants from around the university. He did this by sending invitations to all thirty-two colleges, inviting each president of the Junior Common Room – the main student body – to a sherry party. They were asked to find a keen volunteer from among their colleagues.

Archer then visited Nicholas Lloyd, that term's editor of *Cherwell*, the university newspaper, at his offices behind the Oxford Union debating chamber. Some weeks later, Lloyd described how he and his staff first reacted when Archer turned up with his scheme:

'He's a nut. He'd believe in fairies.' That's what we all said when on a dirty November day a small bouncy man with ferreting eyes, exploded into the *Cherwell* office. 'I'm going to raise £500,000 for Oxfam by using the undergraduates of this University,' he staccatoed. 'It will be the biggest story you've ever had. But I need your help.'[8]

Attracted by Archer's plans, Lloyd took him for a drink at the Union with Geoffrey Parkhouse, the universities correspondent of the *Daily Mail* – in those days the paper considered such a post worthwhile. Parkhouse was on one of his regular trips to Oxford, where he often picked up good stories from Lloyd. 'They, as Oxford students, were going to launch a campaign to try and pick up the missing half-million,' Parkhouse recalls, 'and would the *Daily Mail* back this campaign? I said, "Very unlikely."'[9] Would it help if they managed to bring in the Beatles, Archer enquired. Yes, of course it would, Parkhouse confirmed – but he warned that the Beatles wouldn't be easy to get.

Parkhouse referred the proposal to his editors in London. At the time the *Daily Mail* was keen on running campaigns, and Oxfam was a good candidate for support. But the paper's policy was not to back any venture unless it was going to be brief and had more than a fifty–fifty chance of success. The latter looked doubtful – unless, of course, the Beatles really could be enlisted.

What happened next, and who exactly was responsible for doing what and when, is a matter of considerable dispute.

Archer's account, written only a few months later, is that, the day after meeting Parkhouse, 'I telegrammed Brian Epstein, the Beatles' manager, and asked for an interview, and signed it on behalf of eight thousand students at Oxford, having of course had the blessing of the Vice-Chancellor and the Proctors.'[10] The alternative version, set out in Maggie Black's official history of Oxfam published in 1992, is that the charity's press officer, Pat Davidson, 'managed to persuade Brian Epstein to allow the Beatles to lend their name to the campaign'.[11]

Archer vehemently refutes this. When he saw Black's book he wrote and complained that it was 'an inaccuracy . . . of farsical [*sic*] proportion', and suggested a correction if the book was reprinted. He insisted Pat Davidson 'had absolutely nothing to do with getting Brian Epstein and I am still in possession of the letters that prove this to be the case'.[12] Archer did not send copies of these letters to Black; nor has she asked to see them.

Support for Archer's contention comes from Oxfam's own bulletin, published in February 1964. 'He roped in the Beatles,' it states simply.[13] Davidson's claim, however, rests on her appointments diary and the address book where she entered Epstein's telephone number – evidence, she says, that she rang the Beatles' manager. In fact it does seem possible to reconcile these apparently conflicting views and that Archer and Davidson can both justifiably claim credit. While Archer appears to have initiated the Beatles idea, it was Davidson who eventually secured formal agreement from Brian Epstein. But that bald conclusion overlooks the two weeks of argument, arm-twisting and downright blackmail that it took to get them.

What is obvious is that Archer and Lloyd jumped the gun. On Saturday 30 November 1963 *Cherwell* ran a front-page splash under the headline 'A Million Pound Beatle Drive' over a stock photo of the four musicians. Yet close reading of the article shows that the group had not yet consented to give their support: 'The Beatles have already been approached to give their help and they are expected to say yes or no within the next few days.'[14]

The following Wednesday Geoffrey Parkhouse ran an even stronger story in the *Daily Mail* in which an Oxfam 'spokesman' was quoted as saying the Beatles had 'agreed'.[15] Yet the group hadn't consented at all. In fact Brian Epstein was extremely reluctant for them to become involved. If they agreed to help Oxfam, he felt, it would make it all the harder to turn down other requests. Epstein clearly didn't know what to think of this odd student whiz-kid who was constantly trying to speak to him. 'He couldn't quite make up his mind if he was a con-man or what,' says Brian Sommerville, the Beatles' press officer.[16] Sommerville himself was rather more sympathetic, and instinctively thought it a good idea. He suggested Archer might get somewhere if he turned up at a forthcoming Beatles concert in Liverpool.

That Saturday, Archer and Lloyd travelled to Merseyside by train, armed with Oxfam posters and collecting-tins. The group was performing at the Empire Theatre, recording both a broadcast for the BBC's *Juke Box Jury* programme and a concert, for transmission later that night, in front of the group's Northern Fan Club. Somehow the two students achieved what hundreds of screaming fans hadn't managed, and talked their way backstage. They then persuaded the group to pose for a photo showing them putting money into the tins, while holding a signed poster saying 'WANTED £1,000,000'. It is the most famous picture of Archer's career. Nick Lloyd, with his longish hair, looks almost like a fifth Beatle; but Archer seems out of place with his short back and sides, tweed jacket and college tie. 'They knew exactly what they were doing,' says Lloyd: '"We'll hold this! Get the camera!" Bang!'[17] Despite Epstein's reservations, the group themselves thought the Oxfam campaign a great idea; Paul McCartney and George Harrison were especially sympathetic since they had various schoolfriends at Oxford University.

Pat Davidson, meanwhile, was tearing her hair out, furious about the premature announcement in the *Mail*. 'The word went round like wild-fire that this was happening and so on, and of course it wasn't. It had never been agreed. All that had happened is that two young lads had gone up and taken their photograph holding some tins. It was a mess, and I really had to try and pick up the pieces.' Davidson found Epstein's ex-directory number and rang to explain how sorry she was about what had been done in Oxfam's name. Epstein was even more upset than she was. 'He was absolutely spitting blood about it. He didn't want to speak to anybody from Oxfam. He was furious.'[18]

The issue was resolved only by an urgent meeting at the *Daily Mail* involving Epstein and Davidson. It was agreed that the Beatles would lend their name to the campaign, but wouldn't do much more. Clearly the group had been railroaded. Nick Lloyd acknowledges that Archer did 'a brilliant job' explaining to Epstein and Sommerville not just how bad it would look if they didn't help, but, worse still, 'that they wouldn't like stories saying that the Beatles had withdrawn'.[19]

Archer finally persuaded the Beatles' manager by telling him that, if the Beatles agreed to come to Oxford, the chancellor of the university, Harold Macmillan, would attend dinner with them.[20] Nowadays, when politicians are far less remote figures, it's perhaps hard to appreciate how much Epstein was tickled by the idea of meeting the man who had only just retired as Prime Minister. 'Macmillan was only a couple down from Churchill really, in terms of charisma and billing,' says Sommer-ville. 'Certainly, at that time, that generation held him in awe.'[21]

It's not clear, however, that Archer had actually booked Macmillan when he made the promise to Epstein. But he was certainly confident that he could. The story is picked up by Bill Jackson's deputy at Oxfam, Jonathan Stockland:

He was in my office and said, 'I need Macmillan to host this lunch.

Of course I can get him.' And he literally picked up the phone and got through to Lady Dorothy, and he got his agreement there and then.[22]

Richard Exley confirms the story, though says the call was made from his office. Macmillan was actually quite a fan of the Beatles, and described them as 'Britain's secret weapon'. 'Let's hope he doesn't cancel us then,' John Lennon is reported to have remarked, 'like he did with Skybolt.'[23]

On Monday 12 December 1963, twelve days after it had been 'announced' in *Cherwell*, the *Daily Mail* launched its Beatle Drive:

> We start today. Three thousand Oxford undergraduates, The Beatles – and the *Daily Mail* . . . We want to help raise £500,000 in 20 days to complete the 'Hunger Million' to save the starving.[24]

The person to collect the most money would meet the Beatles and receive the poster they'd all signed in Liverpool. And every day for the next three weeks the *Mail* pumped the Hunger £Million campaign incessantly, urging its three million readers to contribute half a crown each. Other celebrities were enlisted too – Adam Faith, Jimmy Greaves, Tom Finney, Billy Wright, Harry Secombe, Frankie Vaughan, Bruce Forsyth and Matt Monro.

The paper also did a profile on 'The man behind Britain's biggest pub crawl', which was ironic since Archer rarely visits pubs, and takes pride in never having been drunk. 'Jeffrey Archer probably won't be surprised to learn that three of his friends at Oxford describe him as a nut case, a pain in the neck, and a ball of fire – and all mean the same thing . . . He talks in short, sharp bursts, like an intelligent machine-gun.'[25] The reporter added, rather less perceptively, that Archer didn't 'want a single word written about himself'. Perhaps the writer meant the emphasis to fall on the word 'single'.

More interestingly, the short profile twice touched on Archer's admiration for John F. Kennedy, who had been assassinated in Dallas only a month before. 'Kennedy cared,' Archer was quoted as saying. 'He was so incredibly vital. He may have been a man of *your* generation, but he was also a man of our *age* . . . The worst thing young people today can say is that there's nothing left to do. There's so *much* left to do.'[26]

Day by day the Hunger £Million campaign became the subject of great public interest. On New Year's Day 1964 the *Daily Mail* announced that the Beatle Drive had reached its £500,000 target, and so Oxfam had now raised its million. 'The credit and the congratulations for this fine feat must go to Oxford student Geoffrey [*sic*] Archer, who conceived the crash programme,' proclaimed the *Daily Mail*, before congratulating three thousand Oxford students and the Beatles.[27] Even the *Financial Times* paid tribute to Jeffrey's work.[28]

Jeffrey himself wasn't around at the time – which may be why the *Mail* misspelt his name. He was in Austria on a prearranged skiing trip with boys from Dover College. Just before midnight on New Year's Eve, he says, a telegram brought the news from London.

Like one of those famous *Blue Peter* Christmas appeals, the Hunger £Million project ended up raising rather more than its £1 million target – the total seems to have been about £1.2 million. *Cherwell* later took credit for raising about £700,000 of that. 'That is the total subscribed to the Oxfam crash programme started by *Cherwell* last term,' the paper boasted in late January. It explained that, of this figure, 'approximately £200,000 was collected by the Oxford students' pub crawl. Another £200,000 came from the Beatles' *Daily Mail* Campaign and the rest from the usual Oxfam subscribers.'[29]

That final phrase – 'the rest from the usual Oxfam subscribers' – is revealing. It is an admission that £300,000 of the £700,000 would have been raised anyway. Put another way, the extra push from the Archer–*Cherwell*–*Daily Mail*–Beatles operation raised only an extra £400,000. It is not to be sniffed at, of course – it would be worth almost £5 million in today's money, and without that contribution Oxfam might never have reached its £1 million target – but it is a gross exaggeration to suggest that Archer's efforts raised £1 million for Oxfam. It had also been quite an expensive venture. Oxfam's then finance officer, Gordon Rudlin, says that while most campaigns at that time raised about eight times what they cost, the Hunger £Million appeal achieved only four or five times its outlay.[30]

There remained, of course, the famous meeting between Harold Macmillan and the Beatles. Over the years a myth has developed, repeated ad nauseam in respectable newspapers, that Archer actually introduced SuperMac to the Fab Four. It would have been one of those symbolic moments of the postwar era – the Edwardian Prime Minister, whose tired features seemed to represent the dying gasps of an old-fashioned, class-ridden empire, coming face to face with the men who more than any others reflected the permissive, rebellious 1960s. Sadly, through one of those awful cock-ups of history, the famous meeting never took place.

It had originally been planned for a lunch in late February at a London hotel. When Archer rang a few days in advance to check arrangements, he discovered to his horror that the Beatles were in Florida, relaxing after recording some editions of the *Ed Sullivan Show*. He was furious with Epstein for wrecking his great moment. Epstein was almost as angry – he'd been dying to meet Macmillan – and blamed Brian Sommerville for not taking the diary to America to remind them of the engagement. The lunch went ahead with Macmillan on his own, and he compared the Beatles' absence to '*Hamlet* without the ghost'. He and Jeffrey then posed with a cheque for £500,000.

A new date was fixed for the Beatles to present their autographed Oxfam poster – 5 March 1964, in Oxford. Unfortunately, this time Macmillan couldn't be there. But if the Beatles couldn't meet the distinguished ex-premier, they would get the next best thing – dinner by candlelight in an Oxford college. Epstein punished Sommerville by refusing to let him come.

Archer's principal at Brasenose, Sir Noel Hall, had first been alerted to the Oxfam campaign when his college porters rang to grumble about the crates of collecting-tins which were cluttering up the lodge just as students were taking their luggage home for Christmas. Archer was summoned before him, and apologized for bringing the Oxfam tins into college without permission. But according to his widow, Elinor, Sir Noel Hall was more curious about the way Archer was organizing everything. When Jeffrey later asked to use his lodgings to entertain the Beatles, he was delighted.

'The police were in a terrible state,' says Lady Hall, 'and said they wouldn't be able to control the crowds in Radcliffe Square.'[31] So everything was planned with great secrecy. The Beatles were collected from a train at Didcot and smuggled to Oxford by car.

The Brasenose College dean, David Stockton, was invited in case the secret got out and there were disciplinary problems. His recollection is that John Lennon was 'asleep most of the time' but George Harrison and Paul McCartney 'were full of fun'. In Stockton's view, Paul was so 'quick and intelligent' he could easily have gone to Oxford himself. Ringo was largely 'monosyllabic', but did express great interest in a recent story about an Oxford college servant who'd found a young lady hiding in an undergraduate's wardrobe.[32]

Everyone played up to the occasion. When Paul McCartney asked for milk, a college scout presented it in a tankard on a tray. George Harrison said he'd prefer something else to the smoked salmon. 'Have you any jam butties?' he asked a waiter. 'I'll trade you an autograph for a jam butty.' And a jam sandwich duly appeared.[33]

Earlier in the evening Archer had briefly taken the group to Vincent's, the club for Oxford's sporting élite, to meet several of his athletics chums. It was there, in the gents, that George Harrison is said to have suggested that, given half a chance, Archer would bottle the Beatle's pee and sell it for Oxfam. It seems a pity to spoil a good story, but investigation suggests that the incident didn't happen – or at least not with Archer. The origin of the story seems to be an item in *Cherwell* six days later, telling how another individual, called Tony Maskell, was so taken aback on seeing Harrison in the gents that he nudged a friend next to him. 'Why don't you go and get a bottle, bottle this for Oxfam, and sell it?' Harrison supposedly teased Maskell.[34]

The Beatles' visit to Oxford received extensive coverage in the next day's press, and, to be fair, Jeffrey Archer can still claim that he did at least *arrange* for Harold Macmillan to meet the Beatles. And Brian Sommerville freely admits it was his fault it never happened:

> The buck stopped at me. I was the one who made all the arrangements. I completely forgot. When we'd finished with the last of the Ed Sullivan shows from Miami and were free, we were due to fly home. Somebody said, 'Let's stay – it's fucking marvellous here!' Everybody looked at me and said, 'Why not?'[35]

Perhaps the reason why Jeffrey Archer's role in the Hunger £Million campaign has always proved so controversial is that it's not just a matter of who raised how much, or of who booked the Beatles. The stakes are rather higher – the allocation of credit for a crucial turning-point in the history of Britain's most famous charity. In the view of Oxfam's historian, 'The key thing about the Hunger £Million campaign is that this is the time that Oxfam "took off" and became a nationally visible outfit.'[36] While Archer is certainly guilty of exaggerating his own contribution, there is also, one suspects, an element of many Oxfam people being unable to accept the idea that this future Tory politician played such a decisive role in the charity's history.

Others maintain that the techniques pioneered in the campaign changed the whole nature of charity fund-raising in Britain. 'Jeffrey

Archer's ideas in general sparked off a different attitude in other charities,' says Oxfam's former company secretary, Bruce Ronaldson. 'He
had the imagination that perhaps we lacked by then at Oxfam. And *ipso
facto* he set the trend for other charities. Shelter started round about then
and subsequently used many of the same methods.'[37]

Yet some of those methods were appallingly amateurish. Oxfam was
normally very good at keeping stringent checks on who was collecting
money, but, in the rush and excitement, Archer appears to have kept
scant record of which students had taken collecting-tins, or of what
happened to them afterwards. The following February *Cherwell* revealed
that two thousand tins had never been brought back. Archer appealed
for students to return them to Oxfam, and to pay the money directly
into Barclays Bank.[38]

Once the Hilary term began in January 1964, Archer returned to his
original project, which by now must have seemed tiny in comparison:
raising £25,000 for an Indian hospital. He and other students from the
Department of Education were due to do teaching practice that term.
His plan was to get each student to raise funds in his or her school, and
to ask the same of students doing DipEds at Cambridge. Since many of
his colleagues would be teaching in independent schools, with prosper-
ous pupils, parents and catchment areas, Archer reckoned his total was
fairly reasonable.

Alexander Peterson seems to have been as bowled over by Archer as
Tim Cobb and Sir Noel Hall were. Other DipEd students say he treated
him as a protégé. though most were puzzled as to what Peterson saw in
him.

The two men did share a common idealism. At the end of the previous
term Archer had persuaded Peterson to let him address all his fellow
DipEd students about the fund-raising scheme. Archer bounded up to
the platform and delivered what was by all accounts a brilliant, rousing
speech. Some fellow students still remember it vividly. 'He did put it
across very effectively,' says Mary Dicken – 'playing on people's idealism, saying, "This is really your chance to do something in the Third
World for people who are so much worse off than we are."'[39]

But many of his colleagues remained sceptical. As one student recalls,
somebody asked what he was getting out of it. 'The group of girls near
me all booed because they thought it wasn't proper to ask that, and they
thought he had the best of intentions. He didn't reply. Peterson fielded
it for him and said something to the effect that his motives shouldn't be

questioned.'[40] Others resented the fact that they hadn't been given a chance to discuss the project. Many felt it had more to do with supporting Archer than Oxfam. 'It was a good cause,' says one colleague, 'but the glorification of Jeffrey Archer came first.' Yet, because Peterson was backing the project, many decided they had no choice but to cooperate.

Archer quickly gathered together another committee of assistants. 'I remember he tended to walk through the department like a triumphal procession with his acolytes,' says one student, Stephen Benson. 'We thought of him as a slightly tiresome individual . . . There was an element of self-publicizing about it, but we thought at the same time, "It's in a good cause." '[41] The whole operation took on the air almost of a religious crusade. League tables were drawn up showing which students had collected how much; at departmental meetings people were urged to get up and say how much they'd raised from their school, whereupon they were applauded. And Archer's committee went round checking on people. Adrian Twiner remembers serving as the treasurer of the project, but he says Archer kept a firm personal grip on everything and that he himself never got to handle any money or to see any records. Twiner didn't even know what bank accounts the money was being kept in – 'He saw me just as a nominal treasurer.'[42]

Many DipEd students, however, found it difficult to persuade their schools to endorse Archer's venture, says Mary Dicken. 'They'd already got fund-raising schemes of their own, and they were quite resentful of people coming in from the department and wanting to do something different.'[43] The married DipEd students, who had their own unofficial grouping, met and agreed to boycott the whole scheme. 'There was complete solidarity,' says one of them, John Webster;[44] but they didn't dare tell Archer through fear that Peterson might get to hear about it.

The project culminated that May with a ceremony on the lawn at the Department of Education's premises in Norham Gardens. A car donated by the Cowley factory was awarded to the winner of a raffle, and, to Peterson's delight, the then Education Secretary, Edward Boyle, presented a cheque for £25,000 to Oxfam, although it is not clear whether the DipEd students had actually raised all of this.

Archer meanwhile had been doing his own teaching practice at the Dragon School in Oxford, one of the most prestigious prep schools in the country, where he taught PE and a bit of geography. Teaching locally, of course, enabled him to continue with his other university activities. That summer he easily passed both parts of the DipEd exam, covering subjects such as the history and philosophy of education, psychology, and how to teach. His tutor, Ronald Burrows, recalls that Archer also got a distinction in his teaching practice – something achieved by only 10 per cent of his students. 'He was an outstanding practical teacher, as you might expect. He was a most excellent student,' Burrows observes. 'It's a great tragedy he hasn't taught since.'[45]

The department no longer has any records to confirm Archer's distinction. Moreover, the university offices say that, because Jeffrey never did a further probationary year of proper teaching, officially he never actually acquired his DipEd.

The following autumn, Oxfam, Archer, *Cherwell* and the *Daily Mail* tried to follow up their triumph of the previous year. Instead of collecting cash donations, they asked people to give items of value, in what was called Oxfam's Gift Drive. The target was less ambitious – £250,000 – and once again Archer and his fellow organizers went for star names. Jackie Kennedy agreed to 'lead' the campaign by signing ten copies of the *Kennedy Family Album*. The American civil-rights leader Martin Luther King gave an autographed book; there was a teddy bear from Cilla Black; the new Prime Minister, Harold Wilson, donated one of his famous Gannex raincoats; Sir Alec Douglas-Home gave the cricket bat he'd used when playing for Eton at Lord's; and the Rolling Stones gave an electric guitar. Mary Rand (née Bignal), a colleague of Archer's in the 1957 Somerset schools team, presented the spikes she'd worn to win her gold medal in the 1964 Olympics. Other donors included Clement Attlee, Harold Macmillan and Laurence Olivier. Even the Queen gave some money.

Then Jeffrey conceived an idea just as audacious as enlisting the Beatles and Macmillan had been in 1963. The record company Decca donated an album it had just produced of Churchill's war speeches. Sir Winston himself was too ill to sign the collection – he died a month later – but Archer suggested an ideal alternative. He rang the White House and asked for permission to come and get the records autographed by President Johnson. Amazingly, the White House agreed.

Pan Am agreed to fly him free to Washington and back in time for the auction at the Mansion House the following Monday evening, but then Archer suddenly realized his passport had expired. Fortunately the Passport Office allowed him to jump the queue for renewal, while, untypically, the US Embassy granted a quick visa and waived the fee.

Arriving in Washington on the Saturday afternoon, Archer was met by an official limousine and whisked to the White House.

The Oval Office log shows it was a quiet day for Lyndon Johnson. A meeting with his National Security Advisor, McGeorge Bundy, was followed by a brisk walk round the South Grounds with his communications advisers and the family dog, Blanco. He held discussions with various other aides, a briefing with James Reston of the *New York Times*, and a phone call with his Defense Secretary, Robert McNamara. In the midst of these great duties of state, at 5.40 p.m. the most powerful man in the world spared a few precious minutes for Jeffrey.[46] 'You've come a long way for this,' Johnson apparently said as he shook Archer's hand, before signing the records. 'All through the seven-minute interview,' Archer excitedly told the *Daily Mail*, 'people kept coming and going. The feeling of pressure was fantastic.'[47]

By the New Year he had revised his account a little: 'I was with the President for about twenty minutes,' he told *Cherwell*. 'As I went in, Martin Luther King came out. We had met in London the previous week when he gave a copy of his book to the campaign.'[48] This seems odd, for the President's hour-by-hour logs have no mention of the civil-rights leader visiting the White House that day.[49] Perhaps Archer confused it with a meeting King had with Johnson the day before.

In all, the *Daily Mail* raised 225,000 gifts, which were collected by an army of several thousand Oxford students. Most of the contributions were little better than one would find at a village fête, and were sold off in Oxfam shops. The auction of celebrity items proved to be a disaster, as three days before Christmas the comedian Tommy Trinder tried to entice bids from a sparse gathering at the Mansion House. 'Don't worry,' he joked, 'I am used to playing to small houses.'[50] A second auction, to sell the most precious gifts, including the records, was arranged for a few weeks later, but this was almost as poorly attended. Many of the gifts were bought by the *Daily Mail* editor and his colleagues, who'd been busily bidding all evening to save the paper embarrassment.

Oxford seemed to be nothing but go! go! go! for Archer. One DipEd colleague remembers the day Jeffrey spotted him having tea and muffins in the Union. 'He came storming in and said, "I don't know how you can relax and sit about! There's so much to do!"'[51] Certainly the fund-raising for Oxfam was nothing like enough to absorb his energy, and it accounted for only a fraction of his busy student life. Among other things, he tried for a career in the Union, attempting to emulate his old Wellington friend Howard Preece, who'd served as president of the debating society in 1961.

In March 1965, halfway through his second year at Oxford, Archer was elected to the Union standing committee, its executive body. Immediately he faced his first political crisis. That term's poll had been among the hardest-fought in Union history, with several allegations of cheating. In the battle for president, the left lined up behind the Pakistani Marxist Tariq Ali, while the right supported Quintin Hogg's son, Douglas. Union rules prohibit canvassing or any attempt to organize slates, and the definition of both offences is quite strict. Not surprisingly, the regulations are often broken, but that election was particularly dirty. Some time later several ballot papers for Hogg were found hidden in a book in the library where the count had taken place, though not enough to make up for his defeat by eleven votes.

A number of leading members were hauled before a Union tribunal, including Hogg and Archer, both on charges of canvassing. Jeffrey was accused of writing 'personal letters to a number of Oxfam representatives the main purpose of which was to inform them of Mr Archer's candidature'. The tribunal decided that it hardly mattered, since most of the recipients weren't Union members anyway, and dismissed the charge on the grounds that 'Mr Archer's motive in writing these letters was not sufficiently established'.[52] Douglas Hogg was less fortunate: the future cabinet minister was fined a pound for planning to canvass.

Archer served just one term on the standing committee. His only real mention in the minutes was when he was asked to acquire a new television. The record says he presented his recommendations 'with a clipped urgency which suggested the imminent outbreak of the Third World War'.[53]

The president, Tariq Ali, says the only thing he remembers Archer doing that term is 'trying to persuade me to get Robert Maxwell to come to dinner'.[54] Archer only wanted the publisher to come and eat at the Union, not to debate, but Ali says he resisted the idea.

However, Archer's now-famous organizing skills were enlisted for that autumn's annual recruitment drive, in which the aim was to sign up as many freshers as possible. 'I intend to run it on the same lines as the Oxfam campaign,' he promised, 'with a large committee consisting of dynamic people.'[55]

'It was like a military campaign, like a war-game really,' says Raymond Walters, who has worked at the Union since before Ted Heath's time in the 1930s.[56] Archer erected a blackboard outside the president's office, with a table of targets for each college, and details of how far they'd been met. Walters's recollection is that Archer's operation was successful, but Union membership books suggest he badly failed to meet his aim of increasing membership by 40 per cent. Indeed, fewer people seem to have joined the debating society during the time Jeffrey was running recruitment than they did in the years immediately before or afterwards.

In debates, Archer spoke infrequently – once, twice or at most three times a term. He backed the Conservatives' education policies, defended the power of TV in politics, supported political friendship with America, opposed comprehensive schools, and denied that 'A tired nation is a Tory nation.' It was almost always the right-wing line, except when he agreed that 'Oxford is too fond of its own traditions.'[57] His orations gained mixed reviews in the student press. 'Clearly outclassed,' *Isis* said of one Archer speech, awarding him 'Beta Minus': 'he had easily half a dozen interruptions that he bungled completely, leaving the audience groaning more than once', but 'Mr Archer never lacks confidence, and certainly relishes a struggle.'[58] On an earlier occasion it had been very different: he managed to upset the left, but 'such was his control over the House that they did not interrupt'.[59]

The Union has been tape-recording debates for more than thirty years now, but, regrettably, only one tape from Archer's debates still survives. His floor speech supporting the 'Conservative Philosophy of Life' was witty and extremely well prepared. Archer's voice sounds far plummier – more rounded and much more public school and 'Oxford' than it is today – but then that is also true of other undergraduate recordings from the Oxbridge debating societies, from Tony Benn in the late 1940s, to Kenneth Clarke in the early 1960s.

Most Oxford Union politicians gradually build up support each term as they climb the society's ladder. From the Union's junior committees they run for standing committee, and then try for the coveted officer posts and the presidency itself. Jeffrey's Union career was most untypical. His elevation to standing committee was notable in that it was the first time he'd ever stood in a Union election. Yet, after this promising start, the more he got involved in the society and the more he spoke, the less popular he seemed to become.

By the autumn of 1965, after running the membership drive and meeting lots of new, impressionable members, he should have been well placed to achieve office. Yet Archer came lower down the poll than he had two terms before, and failed even to get back on to the standing committee.[60] After that, he gave up.

The message had been obvious: he was never going to become Union president. In any case, it hardly mattered. Oxford politics is only a rehearsal; Oxford athletics, on the other hand, is the real thing.

Most of his Union contemporaries had been fairly contemptuous of the brash Oxfam fund-raiser, and found it difficult to take him seriously. Many were already planning political careers, and several of his colleagues eventually became MPs and ministers. Yet Jeffrey would be the first from that Oxford generation to reach Westminster.

# 8

# Oxford Blues

In 1963 Oxford was still one of the great centres of British athletics. Many remembered the historic day nine years before when a medical student, Roger Bannister, had broken the four-minute mile on the university sports track at Iffley Road. Bannister had been assisted by two other world-class Oxbridge athletes – Chris Brasher and the future holder of the world 5,000-metres record, Chris Chataway.

When Archer took up the sport, in the mid-1950s, Chataway was one of the great heroes of British athletics: intelligent, articulate and handsome – even dashing – a sporting celebrity. Archer had followed the runner's career with fascination. Chataway had been one of the first newscasters when the commercial television network, ITV, started in 1955, but soon moved into politics. In 1958 Chataway was elected to the then London County Council, and the following year he became a Conservative MP. By 1962, aged only thirty-one, he was a junior minister. Archer would often explain in the 1960s that Chataway was his model, and he was all too aware that his hero's meteoric rise had begun with the presidency of the Oxford University Athletics Club (OUAC).

Despite serving as a minister under Harold Macmillan, Chris Chataway has only just reached retirement age. Yet his political career has long since made way for a lower profile in business and public life. Despite holding office under three Tory leaders, he had to wait until 1995 before even receiving a knighthood. Yet his former acolyte now sits in the House of Lords, having overtaken Chataway long ago in terms of wealth, fame and popularity.

British athletics in the early 1960s was still dominated by people from public and grammar schools, and the universities. The arrival of a generation of inner-city black athletes was fifteen years away. The sport still looked to Oxford and Cambridge for its new stars, though the Oxbridge reputation for athletic excellence was already in slow decline. Today the annual Varsity athletics match is barely reported. In Archer's time, when the fixture was held at White City, the former Olympic stadium in west London, it got the sort of coverage still enjoyed by the Boat Race nowadays. And even minor events in the Oxbridge athletics calendar were covered in the national press.

Oxford's biggest name was the former club president, Adrian Metcalfe, from Magdalen College. Since his confrontation with the Somerset schools relay team in 1957, Metcalfe had become one of the fastest 400-metres runners in the world, and he carried high hopes of a gold medal in Tokyo in 1964. Oxford boasted other stars too – the massive American discus-thrower Stan Sanders, and the Kenyan Olympic hurdler Steve Rotich. Cambridge would later field the sprinter Wendell Mottley, an Olympic silver-medallist from Trinidad.

For all his obsessive body-building at Dover, Archer had maintained an interest in running. Despite the strange England blazer he wore, and reports of him running abroad, official records show he did not participate in any major events. As John Steadman had foreseen, it was only at Oxford that his athletics career blossomed, and he eventually ran for his country.

Within only a few days of arriving at Oxford, Archer had made a surprising impact. In a freshmen's match against the senior team, in the 100 yards he beat the club president, Michael Hogan, who was then one of Britain's top all-round sprinters and hurdlers. Against Cambridge freshmen Jeffrey triumphed in both the 100 and the 220 yards, and also made the national press – but for the wrong reasons. Cheering on competitors in the mile, he was struck by a discus thrown by Stan Sanders. They carried him off on a stretcher, but Archer insisted on watching the final track event, and only then agreed to go for a check-up.

Archer quickly became friends with both Metcalfe and Hogan, and began trying to emulate their performances. They, too, were sprinters (though of a higher calibre), and Hogan had succeeded Metcalfe as club president. Archer invited both men to meet the Beatles in Vincent's, and then to the lunch with Macmillan in London, and the three have remained close ever since.

'I've run against him nineteen times and he's won nineteen times,' Archer says of Metcalfe.[1] It's not strictly true – Archer is often modest about his athletics – for in April 1964, in the Oxford club trials, he inflicted a surprising defeat on his famous friend. Archer again made the national press: it was the first time in four years that Metcalfe had been beaten in a purely university race at Oxford, though he had the excuse of a slight chill. But, as if to show it had been no fluke, Archer beat Metcalfe again in a match against Loughborough nine days later. It was a sign of how good a runner he was becoming.

Metcalfe and Hogan shared digs together at 35 Iffley Road, opposite the athletics stadium, lodging with a local vet, Joe Heather, and his wife, Anne. Before the end of his first year, they had asked Archer to join them. Today Archer describes Metcalfe as his best friend, while Hogan follows closely behind. Metcalfe was best man at Jeffrey's wedding in 1966. Hogan was abroad then; but when Metcalfe couldn't make the twenty-fifth anniversary celebrations in 1991, Hogan spoke in his place. Both men were also to give generous financial help when Archer almost went bust.

Archer won his first athletics blue in the Varsity match of May 1964, running in both the 100 and the 220 yards. In the 100 yards he narrowly finished second to Metcalfe, though Jeffrey was extremely fortunate. Three times he jumped the gun, but he was given only one warning. According to Michael Hogan, Archer was regularly in danger of being disqualified because of his false starts.

That spring, Archer was on the fringes of international recognition, and was picked for the Great Britain 'A' side – a second team – against the Benelux countries. But his Olympic dreams faded – indeed they were never realistic. In the autumn of 1964 he was left to watch events on television as Metcalfe collected a silver medal in Tokyo, and Hogan also ran for his country. The British star of the games was the Somerset girl he'd once been to tea with, Mary Rand, who picked up gold, silver and bronze in separate events.

The Oxford University Athletics Club had recognized Archer, however, by electing him club secretary for 1964–5, though some wanted to know why Jeffrey was staying on at the university when his DipEd was now completed. He assured them he was doing extra research. His tutor, Ronald Burrows, says Archer asked the electors to the Department of Education – its governing body – to let him stay on for this extra work, 'and they approved it and I continued to tutor him'. Burrows's recollection, however, is that this was for only twelve months.

> The research was on 'Educational activities of charitable organizations', particularly Oxfam. He liaised with their education departments – they undertake education overseas, and here too, to some extent – and a large part involved going to schools and talking

about Oxfam. It was a great success and went down very well . . .
He had weekly tutorials and had to account for his movements. At
the end he wrote a long essay for me summing up the whole year's
activities. I returned it to him.[2]

The arrangement was quite unofficial. Alexander Peterson later explained that Archer 'was doing research in an informal capacity. He was
not enrolled in the department or studying for any degree.'[3] Neither
the department nor the university itself has kept any record of his
research.

The whole question of who is or is not at Oxford University is
extremely complicated. It is not a matter of university membership,
which is acquired for life on matriculation: the issue is whether Archer
was *in statu pupillari* – in other words, on the books doing a recognized
course. As far as the official record is concerned, Archer was *in statu
pupillari* for only his first year, 1963–4, after which he is considered to
have left. This is the only period for which he appears in the *University
Calendar* as a resident member of Brasenose.

Archer's extra time in Oxford naturally prompts the question of
how he paid his way. He probably had a grant to do his DipEd, but
it is unlikely that this would have been continued for research that
was so informal. Some think he may have been sponsored by the
*Daily Mail*, but neither Geoffrey Parkhouse, the universities correspondent, nor the deputy editor can remember this. Yet Jeffrey does
not seem to have been particularly poor: indeed he owned two cars
and had bought properties in Oxford, which he rented out. (He took
out mortgages for these totalling about £10,000.) In the university va-
cations he also did a bit of games teaching at Betteshanger prep school
near Dover in Kent. And his finances were sufficiently healthy while
at Oxford for him to acquire an account with Coutts Bank, not
known for its large student clientele.

The secretaryship of the Athletics Club was usually a first step to the
presidency a year later, and Archer made a quick impression by organizing the inter-college athletics finals, according to the *Oxford Mail*:

Unlike many of his predecessors, he had gathered round him a
large number of helpers, and his tight schedule of track and field
events lasting three-and-a-half hours was carried through
efficiently.

In addition, he made frequent announcements to officials,

competitors and spectators, and at the end of a busy day quietly thanked all those who had assisted.[4]

That item was almost certainly written by John Parsons, a sports reporter on the *Oxford Mail*, now tennis correspondent for the *Daily Telegraph*. 'It was unusual,' he says, 'to have somebody announcing results to the public after a race,' but Archer 'brought a bit of public-relations initiative'.[5] In the past, results had simply been written up on boards, and few tracks had public-address systems.

After the Hunger £Million campaign, Archer had become adept at cultivating journalists. John Parsons generated a healthy additional income by selling local stories to the national newsdesks; much of his time was spent collecting results from the university clubs, where Archer was one of the most efficient officials:

> Jeffrey always returned messages you left in college lodges, and, as secretary, got results for you from away matches . . . Getting information from the university tennis club, for example, was twenty times more difficult than athletics under Jeffrey Archer. With some university sports it was impossible.[6]

By now Jeffrey also had his own newspaper outlet. While his mother had once written the weekly 'Over the Tea Cups' for the *Weston Mercury*, he began 'With the Blues', a sports diary column for *Cherwell*. The aim was to keep readers up to date about the latest gossip in the blues sports.

Mike Morris, an editor of *Cherwell* during Archer's second year, saw him as a kind of 'older-brother figure' compared with his fellow students. Whereas undergraduate reporters often forgot commitments, Archer delivered. 'He was incredibly reliable. His copy was immaculately prepared, accurate and always on time.'[7] 'He didn't require much editing, though it wasn't exactly literature,' says another editor, Brian Donnelly, who recalls how Archer went away and privately commissioned his own metal printing block for a regular logo at the top of his column.[8]

And it was through the student newspaper that Jeffrey Archer first came across Mary Weeden, an attractive and highly intelligent young chemistry student from St Anne's College.

Both Jeffrey and Mary say that they met at a party given by the former editor of *Cherwell*, Nick Lloyd, though Lloyd himself isn't certain about this. 'She was stunningly beautiful,' Archer says. 'It was love at first sight for me, but I don't think it was for her.'[9]

'There were so many men who adored Mary,' recalls Michael Hogan, 'that I didn't rate his chances very highly.'[10] But once he knew that Mary Weeden was the one for him, Archer pursued her relentlessly, as if she was a 'trophy'. 'He decided she was the most important woman he'd ever seen,' Adrian Metcalfe says. 'Once Jeffrey had made up his mind, he laid siege in a kind of medieval tryst – he was there all the time. For Mary, who had led such a sheltered life, Jeffrey was so extraordinary. She respected him enormously for the Beatles and the Macmillan thing.'[11]

Above all, Jeffrey was fun. 'She was surrounded by a lot of clever people, but they didn't do anything extraordinary,' Metcalfe suggests. 'Mary knew she'd never meet anybody like this again.'[12]

Jeffrey has often told the story of how, before he invited Mary out, he wrote to her then boyfriend, Jonathan Martin, to say that he intended to do so. He considered it the chivalrous thing to do, though nowadays, of course, it would be considered astonishingly sexist. Their first date was the James Bond film *Dr No*, followed by sausage and chips at a local restaurant.

It doesn't sound like the kind of highbrow activity likely to impress the young Mary, but it worked. Occasionally Mary would turn up to watch Jeffrey training at Iffley Road. One fellow athlete recalls the day that Mary confided that Jeffrey had asked her to marry him. Did he think she should? 'He said he's going to get an Olympic silver medal in the 200 metres,' the athlete remembers her saying, 'and become a millionaire and possibly become Prime Minister.' There was no hope of an Olympic silver, Mary was told. He might possibly make a million. And as for Prime Minister, it was probably best that he didn't.

In May 1965 Archer won his second athletics blue, and this time triumphed in the 100 yards, though strictly speaking it is very doubtful whether he should have been allowed to run. The 1936 rules on Varsity matches said that 'A resident member of the University is eligible to compete in an Inter-University contest . . .' They added that 'For the purpose of this regulation a resident member of the University is defined as any one whose name is on the books of a College . . .' And, to underline matters, 'In principle Inter-University contests are confined to *bona-fide* students resident in the University at the time of participation in the contest'.[13] Only his most loyal friends could argue that this definition applied to Jeffrey.

Years later the *Daily Mirror* began to make enquiries about whether Archer had been qualified to run in the 1965 and 1966 Varsity matches. His lawyer replied that Arthur Selwyn, the university don who looked after the OUAC, had consulted his opposite number at Cambridge, and it was 'agreed that Mr Archer could continue to run for the university until his research was completed'.[14] When approached by the *Mirror* before he died in 1987, Selwyn seemed to agree with this: 'If he says that, I am sure that is what happened.'[15]

As Archer's year as club secretary proceeded, there were mutterings not just about his university status, but also about whether he would make a suitable president. While many admired his energy and imagination, others thought he was too brash – not the kind of figurehead the club wanted. Some felt Archer took competition too far, that the traditions of good sportsmanship and basic courtesy were overridden by his determination to win. 'He was basically a bad sport,' says one critic.

> Not the most gracious of men to his rivals; he didn't present a good image of the university. When he was beaten in races, he'd complain to timekeepers and judges. He'd start berating people, saying that he'd actually won, and that kind of thing. In races, he'd talk to other competitors in a patronizing way – that was something that was not 'done'. We got a feedback from other universities: 'Why doesn't somebody just sit on this guy?'

One of Archer's allies, John Bryant, who also came from Somerset, says this criticism simply reflected an 'Oxford thing' about not being seen to train too hard. 'People resented him because he was so upfront about wanting to win. This got up people's noses. I personally found him very amusing.'[16]

In common with other Oxford sports bodies, the normal OUAC tradition was that as the AGM approached, in May, the outgoing president would nominate a successor on behalf of the committee. Often the nominee was the retiring secretary, and on only four occasions since 1920 had the committee's nomination been contested. Archer let it be known that if he was opposed he wouldn't stand, saying that it would be an indictment of his work as secretary. This looked like a tactical error: he seemed to be encouraging his critics to promote a challenger.

Opposition to Archer was led by two athletes from St Catherine's College: Hugh Fairweather and a British international sprinter, Andrew Ronay. They were quietly supported by the OUAC president, Hugh

Pullan. They nominated Damien Knight, a hurdler from Exeter College, who wasn't even on the committee. Knight had disliked Archer ever since his school had competed against Dover College and the opposing PE master had tried to tell him how to run properly. The club was badly divided, with the president backing Knight, and the rest of the committee supporting Archer.

Archer went round to Damien Knight's room and demanded to know why he was standing. 'I think I told him he was overambitious, that the Oxford University Athletics Club was all part of Jeffrey's career plan; it was all getting too competitive.'[17] When Knight refused to step down, Archer changed his mind and decided to fight for the job.

While Fairweather and Ronay were canvassing support for their nominee, they also began investigating Archer's exact status at the university. Brasenose told Fairweather it had no record of Archer being on the books any more, though the college porters confirmed that he did drop by to pick up his post.

Fairweather raised this discovery at a club meeting. Since Archer was no longer at the university, he argued, his candidature was invalid and there was no need for an election. He pointedly directed his remarks towards the senior member, Arthur Selwyn, on the grounds that it was his duty to uphold club rules. People who were present recall that Selwyn was furious that anyone should raise the issue or question his authority. One member remembers that Damien Knight had to intervene physically between them, and he begged Fairweather not to pursue the question of Archer's credentials any further. Knight wanted to win the contest fairly, not by default.

The ballot was secret. Those allowed to vote included all blues and 'centipedes' – the second team – along with all the presidents and secretaries of college athletics clubs. There was much manoeuvring behind the scenes. Jeffrey was especially good at canvassing the college officials, some of whom didn't even know they had a vote. Many colleges weren't particularly active, but faces now appeared who hadn't been seen at an athletics match all year. Archer worked hard, knocking on doors, taking people to dinner; it was the kind of heavy campaigning familiar to Oxford's political clubs, but not to the sporting fraternity.

His canvassing was probably crucial. No record was kept of the figures, but it is said that Archer scraped home by a single vote.

Over the next twelve months much of the previous ill-feeling towards the new president disappeared. As he so often manages to do, Archer established good relations with his main critics, Hugh Pullan and Andrew Ronay, who now admits Archer 'did a bloody good job' as president.[18] Damien Knight concedes that 'the Oxford University Athletics Club was much better for having Jeffrey than me . . . you have to be astounded by his drive'.[19]

Relatively speaking, Oxford athletics had been going through a bad patch. Between 1961 and 1964 Cambridge had won four Varsity matches in a row, following a period of almost complete domination by Oxford in the 1950s. But at the start of October, Archer set his colleagues a new, highly ambitious target: a clean sweep of the eight major confrontations with Cambridge during the course of a year, something Oxford had never achieved before.

Archer based his strategy on improving club morale and unity. In particular he was keen to heal a rift between the introverted cross-country runners, who generally came from northern grammar schools, and the more explosive, extrovert, track and field men like himself, who more often came from public schools. He stressed that he was president of the whole club, cross-country included. He attended cross-country fixtures and travelled to the match in Cambridge; he sat in the middle of the team photograph, and even appointed himself captain of an imaginary fifth cross-country side. On occasion, if teams were a man short, he ran with them – 'You wouldn't see Adrian Metcalfe doing that,' recalls one member. It promoted a new camaraderie.

'He developed a real sense of excitement,' says Tim Taylor, who succeeded him as president. 'The club moved very much to centre stage in the university. He took an interest in everyone.'[20] Archer would talk to each competitor before a big fixture and tell them exactly what he expected of them. Gordon McBride recalls how, in advance of the Varsity match, Jeffrey skilfully used his powers to award blues. 'I remember him saying to me, "If you're gonna get a blue, you've gotta win on Saturday." '[21]

The example was set in training, where Archer, with few or no academic commitments, had more time to practise than most people. He'd be out on the track every afternoon doing short fifty- or sixty-yard bursts again and again and again, and he worked away in the weight room under the main grandstand. 'He trained his socks off,' says Tim Jones, the club secretary when Archer was president. 'And he was loud in praise of people when they were doing well.'[22]

As he looked forward to that year's Varsity match at White City,

Archer had a personal problem, however: Oxford had a surplus of first-class sprinters. Despite having run at White City for the previous two years, there was now a real danger that he might not be good enough to run for the Varsity team that he was meant to captain. Archer's answer was to try for selection in a new event altogether – the 220-yards hurdles.

He hadn't run a serious hurdles race since Wellington, but he trained himself through the winter, and was soon beating Oxford's more established hurdlers. 'I don't know anything about hurdling but I have worked hard,' he admitted.[23] It's largely a technical event – the runner has to learn how to put his leg up every few yards. Adrian Metcalfe says Archer was never very good at the hurdling aspect, but 'between the hurdles he was quick, so he beat good hurdlers who were not very fast'.[24]

On the day of the big match at White City, Archer knew he had almost fulfilled his ambitious grand slam. Month by month through the autumn, winter and spring, his club had so far won six events out of six against Cambridge. To foster team spirit he equipped the squad with new track suits, and took them to stay overnight at a hotel. In his pre-match talk, the president rallied his men by telling them it was their duty to be magnificent.

And they were. It was a bleak, windy afternoon, with no more than a thousand spectators. As the contest unfolded, the two match announcers (one a former Cambridge blue, Cecil Parkinson) gradually revealed a healthy Oxford victory by 87 points to 66. Archer's 'effervescent leadership', said *The Observer*, 'had brought Oxford not to a pitch where the nerves jangle, but one of confidence at a lower tempo'.[25] It was an impressive change from the early 1960s, when Cambridge had taken four matches in a row.

Three of Oxford's points were won by Archer himself in the 220-yards hurdles, where he finished second, ahead of his Oxford team-mate, though again he made a false start. It wasn't bad for an event he'd barely tried twelve months before. And Oxford's first clean sweep was clinched the following Monday when the second team overcame their Cambridge opponents.

He'd been a first-class leader, but just how talented an athlete was Jeffrey Archer? Good, is the common view, but not outstanding – and not international class.

At 5 feet 10 inches, he wasn't particularly tall, and therefore not blessed with the long legs really great sprinters require. On the other hand, says Tim Taylor, he had good 'stride cadence'.[26]

He didn't have natural running ability in the way that Adrian Metcalfe did. His primary assets were a strong body and the resolve to increase his strength and fitness through incessant body-building and training. 'As an athlete, he had tenacity and determination and a stocky physique,' says Tim Jones. 'He could make his muscles work hard, but beyond 220 yards he'd collapse in a heap.'[27] He had a good torso for a sprinter, and he was helped by being a good gymnast – indeed he won a half-blue for gymnastics in 1965, though his *Who's Who* entries always refer to it as a blue.

'Having people faster than him around helped,' says Adrian Metcalfe – 'me and Andrew Ronay and Mike Hauck. It helped stretch him. He never missed a training session.' And Metcalfe observes how Archer took the same approach to his athletics that he later adopted for his writing: 'He has always pushed the talent he has beyond what people thought was reasonable. He has a fantastic ability to focus on something. He wanted to win.'[28]

What of his statistics? Archer regularly ran 100 yards in under ten seconds, the time then regarded as the main benchmark of a good sprinter. He himself often claims – in *Who's Who* for example – to hold the Oxford record for 100 yards, at 9.6 seconds.[29] This time, achieved twice on a university trip to Canada in 1965, was wind-assisted, and normally such results are not treated as full records. Moreover, Andrew Ronay had already achieved the same time with wind assistance.

Without the help of wind, his best 100 yards was 9.8 seconds in 1964 – a time surpassed by only ten other athletes that year, and matched by ten more.[30] So, at his best, Archer was in Britain's top twenty for the 100 yards, but after 1964 he struggled even to stay in the top hundred.

The 220 yards was Archer's better distance, mainly because the years of body-building had given him a stronger physique than most sprinters. Here he peaked later. Archer's fastest time was 21.6 seconds in 1965, putting him seventh equal in the British rankings with two others.[31] In 1966 he had a slightly faster best time, 21.5 seconds, but was now eleventh equal with two rivals.[32] So at the height of his career Archer was about the tenth-best 220-yards runner in the UK. (Way out on top of the rankings, incidentally, was another future politician, Menzies Campbell, now a Liberal Democrat MP.)

Michael Hogan argues, however, that such statistics don't present the whole picture. 'I would rank him higher on his sheer competitive drive. He delivered the goods when it mattered.'[33] In other words, if Archer had run a hypothetical race against every other top sprinter, he would have finished rather higher than the rankings suggest; he was the kind of athlete who rose to the occasion, and was spurred on by stiff competition.

'He would be about eight or nine yards slower than Linford Christie,' reckons Sir Arthur Gold, who was then in charge of the British team – 'certainly not less than six yards behind him, even if we make allowances for the difference between a cinder track and an all-weather track.'[34]

Throughout the first half of 1966 Archer had high hopes of running in the Empire Games (now the Commonwealth Games) in Jamaica, an easier target than running for Great Britain since it involved being selected only for the England team. In June he was picked to run for England in a match against Ireland, and was sufficiently confident he would be chosen again that he drafted a letter to be posted several days later, saying 'I have been selected to run for England at the Empire Games in Jamaica.'[35] It was not to be.

Archer's disappointment at not going to the West Indies was partially alleviated, however, when Great Britain competed against Sweden that September and Jeffrey won his only full British vest. Many of his rivals were injured or resting after a long summer which involved not just the Empire Games but also the European Championships, and Archer was one of sixteen new internationals taken to Stockholm. 'It was fairly late in the season, and a team is selected from those available,' says Sir Arthur Gold. 'The fact that the Swedes beat us suggests it was not our strongest team.'[36]

Jeffrey ran badly that weekend, and came third with a poor time in the 200 metres, though he was in the successful $4 \times 100$-metres relay team. On the strength of his trip to Stockholm he could say he had run for Great Britain, though his *Who's Who* entry always admits that it was 'never fast enough'.[37]

It had been an exciting summer. The England football team had won the World Cup, and earlier, shortly after the end of term, Jeffrey and Mary had got married. It was a traditional wedding – Mary in white, Jeffrey in morning dress – at the university church, St Mary-the-Virgin, on a hot day.

The choir from Betteshanger prep school, where Archer occasionally taught, were invited to travel up from Kent to perform at the service.

Appropriately, or perhaps not, they sang a William Boyce anthem: 'Examine me, O Lord, and prove me . . . and I will walk in thy truth.'

The reception was held next door at Brasenose, an informal affair with champagne and strawberries on the grass out in the sun. About thirty Oxford blues were there, and Adrian Metcalfe spoke as best man. Sir Noel Hall made a speech too, bringing the house down by remarking that he was the only principal Jeffrey had ever had.

Yet even when filling in the marriage register, Archer seemed to succumb to the same weakness as his father. Under 'rank or profession' Mary put down 'research graduate'. So, too, did Jeffrey.[38] Perhaps on his wedding day he could be forgiven for living in a dream world.

# 9

# Birthday Boy

Andrew Ronay, one of Archer's erstwhile opponents in the Oxford University Athletics Club, later became a friend. He always remembers a piece of advice Jeffrey once gave him: 'The only difference between you and me, Andrew, is that we've both had lots of failures, but I don't tell anyone what they are.'[1] Archer's days in the army and the police have been excised from the record. Also consigned to oblivion is his first job after leaving Oxford.

In December 1965 an advertisement appeared in *The Times* for the job of director-general of an organization called the National Birthday Trust (NBT). 'Candidates must be able to demonstrate successful experience in raising money in excess of £10,000 annually.'[2] For a man of Archer's experience, this was a piffling goal. At university, he claimed to have raised almost fifty times that amount for Oxfam.

The National Birthday Trust had been founded in 1928 to promote the care of mothers and babies in childbirth, and research into perinatal mortality – deaths of babies around the time they are born. In 1958 the charity had carried out a famous survey of nearly all British births in one particular week; it now wanted to make a fresh start with a full-time professional director-general. The trust asked a firm of headhunters, Management Selection Ltd (MSL), to find a money-minded administrator who could drag the organization into the 1960s.

The National Birthday Trust suffered from a dismally low profile. This wasn't helped by its name, which conjured up the idea of children's parties. And it was desperately short of money. The new director-general's primary task would be to build up a fund of capital both to generate a good annual income and to finance a new perinatal study.

The trust envisaged somebody aged 'between the low 40s and the low 50s' but agreed with MSL that this was less important than 'a successful career in fund-raising'. If necessary, it was prepared to pay generously – up to £4,000 a year – the equivalent of about £40,000 today.[3]

Forty applications were narrowed down to a short list of six, and then three. Two of these were retired military officers who'd gone into fund-raising, but the third was a much younger man who 'stood head and shoulders over the others', according to the chairman of the selection panel.[4] 'He has personal letters from leaders in all spheres of life,' the headhunters reported after a ninety-minute interview, 'e.g. Harold Mac-millan, Mr Attlee, Archbishop of Canterbury, Mrs Jacqueline Kennedy; from a very intriguing scrap-book there is evidence to show that he seems "to know everybody".' The headhunters seem to have heard a clever mix of Archer fact and Archer fantasy. They appear to have been told of a BA from Berkeley and his studies of anatomy, physiology and psychology – good qualifications, surely, for someone working for a medical charity. They also learned that he'd raised $500,000 for the YMCA in Canada. When Archer related the story of Oxfam and the Beatles, and showed them pictures of his trip to see LBJ, they were suitably impressed.

> Although he is only 26 he has an immense personality – *vide* President Johnson. He is totally ebullient with enthusiasm, not only did he bring these fascinating scrap-books of his past activities, but also brought a most detailed and carefully thought-out folder setting out the way he would build up the Trust's annual income to £250,000 by 1970.[5]

Adrian Metcalfe remembers Jeffrey putting enormous preparation into the interview, treating it as another Archer campaign. 'He'd decided to think out a policy. He got big sheets of paper and sketched out 125 ideas of what he'd do to invigorate this charity. He had an incredible programme of ideas.'[6]

The charity seemed flattered that such a prominent figure should approach it. 'It was a great compliment to the Trust that he should think of applying,' the chairman reported, 'and the salary offered by the Trust is below that now being received by him.' Quite what salary he meant isn't clear. The panel decided everything should be conducted in secret – at first the executive weren't even told the candidate was Archer: 'If the name "leaked out" there could be press comment, and a most unfortunate situation could arise.'[7]

After meeting him, however, some executive members had doubts about his brashness, and whether he had the right temperament for dealing with the elderly, distinguished medical figures involved in the trust's work. Reassurance came from the Principal's Lodgings at Brasenose. 'Spectacular and public success during his first two years might well have gone to his head in the wrong way,' Sir Noel Hall wrote. 'They seem in fact to have gone the right way.' Sir Noel's reference didn't just glow, it dazzled:

> He is today more considerate of others, more sure in his judgement and more deft in his relationships with people of all types. I feel confident, therefore, that he will be tactful in his dealings with those whom you mention . . . the basis of his touch is a probity of thought and action which has nothing of the Pharisee about it and convinces people of his sincerity when they work with him . . . I have found him increasingly quick to take advice, rigorous in thinking out the implications of his ideas and good humoured in their rejection or modification.[8]

For the first and not the last time, Mary had been summoned to give Jeffrey a certain credibility. 'She is an admirable complement to him,' Hall claimed. 'She is perhaps one of the best female chemists that this University has had . . . very stable in personality and an admirable foil for her husband to be.'[9] Mary herself was about to move to Imperial College, London, to do a PhD, and the couple would move into a flat in Cadogan Place in Belgravia.

Archer was offered the post 'at a salary of £2,000 per annum'.[10] It was only half the advertised figure, but the trust thought it appropriate given his youth and inexperience. Yet when news of the appointment appeared in the press the salary became £4,000.[11] One might think the papers had simply picked up the figure from the original ads, were it not that Archer himself spoke later of earning £4,000 a year.[12] Moreover, Jeffrey was quite happy to justify this salary, even though he wasn't actually getting it. 'In America,' he told *Cherwell*, 'they pay charity organizers three times as much and they get three times the results.'[13]

Archer began making changes even before he officially started. A new secretary was appointed – a woman who had worked for Oxfam. Fresh notepaper was printed featuring the new director-general's name; a Rhodes Scholar friend, Bill Bradley, agreed to pay a cartoonist to design a new NBT logo; and a simpler, more memorable, telephone number was arranged – SLOANE 8000. Finally, on the front door of the offices at 57 Lower Belgravia Street, near Victoria station, a new sign appeared: 'National Birthday Trust Fund, Director-General, J. H. Archer'.

'He perches athletically on the boardroom table,' wrote the diarist of the London *Evening News*, soon after Archer moved in. 'On the walls are solemn portraits of elderly dowagers who were the mainsprings of the fund in the thirties. Behind his desk is a large bronze bust of John Kennedy.'[14]

The pictures of the 'elderly dowager' patrons did not last long: they gave the wrong image. To the dismay of many of the charity's stalwarts, they made way for more recent pictures, such as photographs from Jeffrey's athletics career.

As an administrator, Archer always liked a tidy desk: no loose papers; everything laid out with obsessive neatness. Each morning he began with a fresh sheet of paper, listing ten or so tasks to be tackled that day, and then steadily worked through them one by one. Just as he had bombarded his interviewers with pages of ideas, so executive meetings were dominated by Archer's numbered lists. Once each decision had been reached, the item would be ticked off.

Elspeth Chowdharay-Best is among several trust people Archer soon began to annoy. In particular she disliked the way he quickly asserted his authority over the trust secretary, Doreen Riddick, who had served the charity loyally for thirty years, and was very poorly paid.[15] Another trust member recalls that 'She was very competent and he just sat on her, saying "I'm the director-general." She had a very difficult time.' But others say Riddick was not the kind of woman to be sat on by anybody.

One of Archer's very first fund-raising projects for the trust illustrates the naïvety with which he approached the job – an innocence which probably helped with Oxfam, but which now proved costly. He latched on to a marketing gimmick launched by Shell petrol, called 'Make Money Notes'. Every time drivers filled up with Shell, they got half an imitation banknote, in denominations ranging from ten shillings up to £100. Once somebody had two matching halves, then, bingo, they could redeem the relevant sum. Archer reckoned that it only required good organization to join up the money-note halves on a grand scale. It never occurred to him that there might be a catch in the promotion, or that Shell might have been less than generous.

Archer placed ads in the *Times* personal column asking readers to send the charity any spare half-notes. They rolled in – the equivalent of £25,000, or rather half of that. But to his acute disappointment, not a single pair would match up. Every pound note was a left-hand, while every ten-shilling, five-pound or hundred-pound voucher was a right-hand. Indeed, he had no fewer than twenty-six halves of £100 notes. Desperate to recoup at least his advertising bill on his first money-spinning wheeze for the trust, Archer placed a second notice offering £90 for a left-hand £100 note. None arrived.

In anger Archer wrote to Shell, asking for compensation for the hundred pounds he'd spent on advertising. 'I would of course make a press statement to the effect that the National Birthday Trust had lost nothing because of the generosity of Shell Mex and BP,' he added.[16] But Shell were clearly not impressed by the tone or by the hint of adverse publicity. The company rejected Archer's request because of 'the context of the letter in which it was made'.[17] A lighter approach might have worked; Jeffrey had been too heavy-handed.

What Archer was looking for was one big idea – something that would raise tens of thousands of pounds every year. His answer had echoes of the triumphant Hunger £Million campaign, though it was much more ambitious. The 'Britain's Million Mothers' venture was designed to last twenty years; 1 million mothers would be persuaded to make out covenants of a pound a year. Again Archer sought endorsement from the biggest names. Would the Queen or Princess Margaret be willing to become the 'first British mother'? And Jacqueline Kennedy, having been tapped for the 1964 Oxfam Gift Drive, was invited to become the trust's first 'overseas mother'. But Archer didn't always do his homework. When he asked Barbara Castle, she pointed out that she didn't qualify. And on approaching *Honey* magazine he was told that since '*Honey* is purely a magazine for single girls . . . I don't think we have the kind of reader who would be of much help.'[18]

The actress Britt Ekland became one of his Million Mothers, and so did Chris Chataway's wife, but neither of the British royal mothers, nor America's equivalent regal matriarch, wanted to help. Instead Archer was offered Princess Alexandra, and then only as 'patron' rather than the trust's 'first mother'. But at least the princess had just had a baby.

Kensington Palace asked Archer to keep the news of her becoming patron confidential for a while, to give the princess a chance to recover from giving birth, and time to consider the official announcement. But Jeffrey was so thrilled that he couldn't resist telling people – especially journalists. When the princess's comptroller, Major Peter Clarke, heard of the leaks, he wrote to convey his displeasure:

You will, I am certain, understand why I was rather put out yesterday on hearing that you had informed certain sections of the press about the Princess's patronage, which is still a matter of confidence until the announcement is made. I appreciate your reasons for doing so, but in future would you please consult me before taking such action?[19]

Archer was suffering from inexperience, and from an overconfidence that any project he devised would make money automatically. He attacked the ideas on his lists with gusto, but showed little awareness of the pitfalls. He didn't, for example, understand the importance of the public recognizing his project as a worthwhile cause. It was very different from the days when he could ring up from Oxfam and book Harold Macmillan, the Beatles or President Johnson.

So how would he find his Million Mothers? Archer discovered a commercial operation known as Gift Pax – small parcels of baby products sent out free to every woman who had a baby in hospital. Archer got the promoters of Gift Pax to let him include a small card congratulating the mother and asking her to join his Million Mothers by signing a covenant. He also employed students on commission to scour the birth notices of local newspapers, and to approach new mothers in person.

Archer tried everything. The makers of Stork margarine agreed to sponsor stork-shaped collecting-boxes to be put in shops. He even suggested placing the boxes in betting-shops, but the trust executive ruled this out because of the princess's patronage.

Reading the National Birthday Trust archives, one can only admire the fertility of Archer's imagination, and the persistence with which he pursued each project, at least initially. He wrote begging letters to every conceivable charitable foundation in Britain and the USA; he found out which rich Americans were coming to London and approached them; and he sought the names of a dozen particularly wealthy individuals who might be tapped for several thousand pounds apiece.

He printed National Birthday Trust Christmas cards, and designed a calendar; he sent out appeals through a nappy service, and placed ads on the back cover of Post Office stamp booklets. Some ideas for making money were quite bizarre, such as his design for a new sauce bottle, though it is not clear whether this was actually to benefit the trust, or whether it was in fact his or Mary's invention. He wrote to Heinz:

I have invented a bottle which I thought might be of some interest to you and now that the patent is through I am in a position to consider any suggestions etc.

My wife, who is reading for a Doctorate at Imperial College London, has designed the bottle . . .

One of the problems that manufacturers such as you have is that whatever you are trying to sell, whether it is sauce, cream, jam etc. a small amount gets stuck in the bottom in the corners and either has to be shaken out vigourously [sic], swilled out or got out with a long spoon.[20]

Jeffrey's ingenious answer – or Mary's – was a bottle from which the bottom part could be unscrewed. 'I have, of course, looked into the scientific problems and these are being dealt with by my wife at Imperial College,' he told Heinz. 'It will not be very long before the possessor of this bottle will be "one up" on his rivals,' he advised, suggesting they might like to ring his secretary to arrange a 'consultation'.[21]

Again this betrayed a certain innocence about the ways of the world. Why on earth should sauce manufacturers want customers to use up those last dollops of sauce? Didn't Jeffrey realize that the more sauce is left at the bottom, the sooner people have to buy a new bottle?

Jeffrey and Mary were not to make their fortunes as the brains behind a revolutionary new ketchup jar. He did submit a preliminary patent specification, but neither Heinz nor any of the other four manufacturers he approached were interested.

This seemed to typify Archer's problem: not enough people responded to any of his suggestions. As he came to review his first six months, it was a rather sorry picture. Every promising idea seemed to crumble.

The makers of Stork pulled out – at the last moment – from sponsoring the collecting-boxes. Archer quickly approached several other firms but 'none of them were willing to help'.[22] The Million Mothers idea was going nowhere; by December the total had barely reached 100, and that included Lola and several mothers of his friends.

Worst of all, the Gift Pax scheme collapsed when Archer reported that the Ministry of Health had banned charity appeals in NHS hospitals. His students got nowhere either; they had no response because 'people they approach have never heard of the National Birthday Trust'.[23]

Archer's predicament was summed up when Selfridges allowed a manned collecting-box inside the Oxford Street store just before Christmas. The secretary looking after the box raised just 15s 6d on the first day. 'As she is paid in the region of £3 to £4 a day I withdrew her at speed,' he explained. Again, the problem was lack of public recognition.[24]

At times his set-backs seemed almost comic; yet one has to sympathize, given the effort and ideas he had put in. So far, his fund-raising work had cost about £3,000, including his own salary; he had only £1,374 to show for it.[25]

It was far harder work than raising money for Oxfam. Fighting starvation and disease, of course, was a self-evidently good cause, publicized by dramatic pictures which pricked people's consciences. Few members of the public understood what 'perinatal mortality' was. With Oxfam it was clear how a donation would help the hungry, but with the National Birthday Trust the link between research and saving lives was less apparent.

As he reported on his dismal first six months, Archer refused to admit he was losing heart: 'I am in no way depressed at the moment about the way things are going,' he reassured his colleagues.[26] He clearly was dispirited, however. Jeffrey even suggested he should resign. 'He had other offers,' he told the executive, 'with higher salaries.' Their unanimous view was that their director-general should soldier on.[27]

Archer's problems were internal as well as external. One member of the NBT executive, Anthony Patten, a businessman who had raised funds for the trust in the past, had great sympathy with Archer's position:

> He had enormous energy and tremendous ability but difficulty in communicating on the same level as fuddy-duddy doctors and so on. He was years ahead of his time on the administration side . . . but the NBT committee was ultra-cautious.[28]

Perhaps the best example of this caution was his idea that the trust should run a babysitting bureau. So keen was Archer to go ahead that he placed a series of ads in the London *Evening Standard* appealing for babysitters before raising the matter at a formal committee meeting.

The executive had severe misgivings. What would their scientific advisers think? Surely this wasn't the kind of thing a medical charity should be doing? And did their lease even allow them to run such a business from their offices? Their lack of enthusiasm seemed to mark a turning-point in Archer's attitude to the job. From then on, he appears to have been more concerned to do his own thing.

Archer simply continued with the babysitting idea as a personal business. 'It would not now be run from the office, but by a friend on his behalf,' he told executive members. They were assured that he'd 'formed a company with his own resources', but the trust was nevertheless offered some of the profits.[29]

It was a brilliantly simple idea, and the business Archer set up survives to this day, though in different hands. Parents and babysitters paid ten shillings a year to register, and parents were charged five shillings an hour for a babysitter. Archer quickly abandoned the idea of recruiting sitters from the public, and instead assembled a team of 250 state registered nurses. This notion came from his foster-sister, Liz Fullerton, herself a nurse. She had pointed out that she and her colleagues worked irregular hours and were always looking for extra income; but the real appeal was that nurses were medically trained and trusted by the public.

As Babysitters Unlimited developed as a private enterprise, it ate up more and more of Archer's office time. So too did politics.

During his year as president of the Oxford University Athletics Club, he had finally met his great hero Chris Chataway, at a dinner Archer arranged in honour of Arthur Selwyn, the senior member who had been so helpful in securing the presidency. Archer quickly struck up a good relationship with Chataway, and went to Lewisham for several days to help him fight the 1966 general election. Despite Jeffrey's help, Chataway fell victim to Harold Wilson's ninety-nine-seat landslide. By contrast, Chataway's help to Archer over the next few years was invaluable.

During the summer of 1966 Chataway put Archer in touch with a colleague, Anthony Fletcher, who'd just become a candidate for the following year's elections to the Greater London Council (GLC). Could Fletcher use his contacts at Conservative Central Office to get Archer on to the candidate's list? Fletcher says that it didn't take much to do so:

> It wasn't very difficult, you know. If you'd been a horse they might have had you. To be frank, they were desperate to get people, because the GLC was so demanding – you had day-time meetings. Either you had retired people, or you had bright young or embryo politicians who could get away, but not many people could spare the time.[30]

At that time, GLC councillors weren't elected for individual wards.

Instead, each of the thirty-two London boroughs returned a number of councillors. Archer was one of three Tories chosen to fight Havering – an outer London borough covering the area around Romford, where east London borders Essex.

Havering was only a few miles from the old haunts of Jeffrey Archer's father in the early part of this century. The road from Romford to the City of London passes through Ilford, where William Archer lived with his first wife and two daughters in the 1900s. It then runs through Stepney, where he had briefly served as a councillor. Politicians are prone to exaggerate their local links, and had Jeffrey, who was otherwise a complete outsider, known of this family connection, it is surprising that he made nothing of it.

Whatever identity Havering had once enjoyed had been subsumed by the rapid expansion of London eastwards. Since 1979, Havering's MPs have always been Conservative, but in the late 1960s the area was fiercely contested, with Labour having the edge. The three councillors Havering had elected to the GLC council in 1964 were all Labour, and included the leader, Sir William Fiske.

A swing of just 4.2 per cent would kick Labour out, so Havering was a critical marginal. If the Tories won the borough, they would probably take control of London as well – for the first time in thirty years. Although the Conservative selection meeting was contested, Archer gained one of the three nominations quite easily.

After Labour's victory in the 1966 general election, few thought the Tories were likely to take control of the GLC. But as Harold Wilson's government grew increasingly unpopular towards the end of 1966 and in the early part of 1967 Archer's chances looked brighter. 'We did work jolly hard,' says Bernard Brook-Partridge, one of the other Tory candidates in Havering. 'Between the three of us we didn't miss one single night in that constituency, for the six months right up to the election.' As polling-day approached, the campaign inevitably took more and more of Archer's time. 'He was pretty wet behind the ears, but he was energetic, and got on with it, and was willing to take advice,' Brook-Partridge recalls.[31]

The Tory campaign made much of Archer's sporting background. 'My right-hand adviser has been Chris Chataway,' he claimed. 'He has helped me tremendously.'[32] Chataway, then as much in demand as a Tory 'celebrity' as Archer is today, made one notable appearance with Jeffrey's Bullnose Morris in an early example of a photo opportunity.

The pictures seem to have been seen more in Archer's subsequent career, however, than they ever were at the time.

One of the main policies advocated by Archer and his Tory colleagues was that tenants should be allowed to buy their council homes. Labour adamantly opposed this, but it struck a chord with working-class voters who'd moved to Havering from the East End, as Margaret Thatcher saw when she exploited the right-to-buy issue so successfully a decade later.

The election itself, in April 1967, was a triumph for the Conservatives. They won control of the GLC with a 12 per cent swing from Labour, and the Labour leader, Sir William Fiske, lost his seat in Havering. Archer had polled 43,379 votes, more than 12,000 ahead of him. Subsequently, Archer has often claimed that his victory was boosted because Harold Wilson announced devaluation on the Monday before polling.[33] This is quite wrong: the GLC election was in April 1967, and sterling was not devalued until November 1967.

Almost as soon as Archer had secured his place on the GLC he was off with his old boss, Tim Cobb, on a two-week trip to the Far East. The previous year, Dover College had appointed Jeffrey to its governing body, and Cobb now enlisted his fund-raising skills to rustle up donations in Hong Kong and Singapore. Before setting off, Archer took the opportunity to look for other work while he was out there. 'HONG KONG, Singapore and Kuala Lumpur,' announced yet another small ad in *The Times*. 'Young Director visiting will take commissions. – SLO 8000.'[34]

Archer's election to the GLC was bound to make his position with the National Birthday Trust even more difficult. Since Christmas, he had been concentrating on big projects. In particular, he had tried to set up a football-pools operation with an outside firm. Several other charities ran such schemes, and the venture might have raised all the money the NBT needed. Archer even got to the stage of interviewing possible organizers and pools collectors. But this idea also collapsed, when Jeffrey's contact at the pools company retired suddenly through ill health.

On 1 May 1967 Archer gave three months' notice of his resignation from the trust and promised to find another job sooner if possible. He apologized 'that things have not worked out the way we had hoped'.[35] This time his offer was accepted.

Over the following weeks he kept assuring his employers that he was about to be offered a new job with the BBC. Yet at the same time Archer seemed keen to cushion the embarrassment of his departure by offering to carry on as director-general part-time, on a much-reduced salary of £250 a year. This was swiftly rejected, and the executive suggested, at least initially, that Jeffrey should instead become an unpaid appeals consultant. Archer seemed desperate to continue some kind of paid arrangement to save face – almost anything would do. He even suggested that the trust pay him £125 a year – but that he would repay the money by covenant. The executive even turned this offer down.

It was not an amicable parting. If Archer had not resigned, it is certain that his contract would not have been continued, for the trust simply couldn't afford to keep him; he wasn't even paying his way. In any case, relations had been severely strained by a series of disputes.

First, several executive members were concerned about Archer's election to the GLC. Although he was not to blame, some were upset that they hadn't been told he was standing. Nor did it help when an item appeared in *The Observer* saying Archer was 'paid a large salary . . . by the National Birthday Trust, and so has acquired the freedom to embark upon a political career'.[36] Others objected to election posters which had appeared in Archer's office, though he claimed that these had been put up by colleagues 'rather as a joke' after the poll, while he was in the Far East.[37]

They were also unhappy about Babysitters Unlimited. Archer appeared to have been running the operation from trust premises, during office time. One executive member noticed that the enterprise appeared in the London phone book under the trust's address. Archer said he had put this entry in the directory before the executive had decided not to endorse the business.

These were just small irritations compared with the overriding problem: he simply wasn't raising enough money.

Before leaving, Archer made what he described as 'the eleventh-hour effort that may save our life' – lunch in a private room at the Dorchester with the millionaire publisher and Labour MP Robert Maxwell.[38] He'd made the initial contact through his old principal, Sir Noel Hall – Hall's daughter was a lodger at the publisher's home in Headington, in Oxford. Archer planned to ask Maxwell for a covenant of £3,000 a year, which would yield £7,000 after the tax rebate. 'It really was like a breath of spring to meet you,' he told Maxwell afterwards. 'Your helpful advice and wise words gave me personally great heart about mobilizing support for another attack on the problems of the newborn and unborn baby. This I think is perhaps the greatest reason for loss of life in our time.'[39]

Archer's flattery didn't work. Maxwell gave nothing. Their meeting did produce one spin-off, however: shortly afterwards, the publisher's wife, Betty, joined the NBT executive and later took on some of Archer's role, advising on fund-raising.

As Archer prepared to clear his desk, another major problem surfaced which finally removed any doubts the executive might have had about his departure.

It involved the unsuccessful Gift Pax scheme which Jeffrey had initiated the previous autumn. Archer, it transpired, had ordered 300,000 congratulations cards for the project – instead of the trial run of 50,000 which had been agreed. The trust now faced a printing bill of £2,000 – the equivalent of £20,000 today. Archer felt so guilty about his mistake that he wrote a personal cheque to the trust from his own bank account; when that offer was turned down he found an outside donor to cover the loss.

This final straw prompted the executive to open an enquiry into the whole of Archer's directorship. Anthony Patten was assigned to go through the files.

His report uncovered no wrongdoing, but it was still a damning indictment of Archer's style. For example, executive members learned for the first time how Kensington Palace had been upset over Archer's leaks to the press, and were left wondering how much other damage he might have done to the trust's reputation. 'Quite a lot of goodwill and fund-raising schemes can be salvaged,' Patten reassured them.[40]

The director-general came under particular attack for the crass and tactless nature of his letter-writing. A series of appeals he'd made to union leaders 'could hardly do anything but put the backs of the Trade Unions up', Patten concluded. In another letter, mentioning the trust's distinguished medical advisers, Josephine Barnes and Professor Neville Butler, Archer had suggested it 'would be very easy for you to check on their reputations'. And executive members cannot have been too pleased to read how they had always 'hidden every light possible under every bushel they could find'. The most comic of all was a letter to a leading specialist, acknowledging the 'help given by professional "medicine" men'.[41]

Patten suggested that, towards the end, Archer had been treating his work as a part-time job, using trust resources as a personal office. 'J. Archer appears to spend 50% of his time on non-Trust business,' he declared, adding that, latterly, in the case of his secretary it was as much as '75% of her time'.[42]

Summoned for a final encounter with the executive that June, Archer admitted he had been 'extremely foolish' in several matters – a phrase that would recur in subsequent episodes of his career. The Gift Pax order had been a 'disastrous mistake', he admitted, and he was 'sincerely sorry' for what had gone wrong. However, he had always warned that his fund-raising did not use the 'usual orthodox methods'.[43]

The trust made a clean and immediate break. In effect, Archer was now sacked with four weeks of his contract still to run. The executive decided that 'efforts should be made quietly to restore any damage to the Trust's reputation'.[44]

Over the year Archer had been with them, the whole operation, including his salary and the headhunters' fee, had made a loss of £6,104. He himself claimed to have raised more than £25,000, but this was strongly disputed: his figure included an expected £5,000 from Robert Maxwell which never materialized, and another £10,000 donation which the trust had been negotiating before Archer came.[45]

'Rather an extravagant young man with an extravagant way of raising money,' is how the NBT's long-standing secretary, Doreen Riddick, would remember Archer shortly before she died. 'He certainly was rather expensive as a fund-raiser. He sort of spent money to get money.' Despite the way he treated her, Archer regarded Riddick as an ally in trust politics, affectionately giving her the public-school-style nickname of 'Ridders'. Her opinion was that he simply 'didn't know the line of country at all': that raising funds for a medical charity is not like Oxfam. 'Medical societies, such as ours, are a different sort of thing altogether,' she argued; a matter of 'knowing who you're approaching, not sort of out-of-the-blue in a "cheerio-whistle" style'.[46]

One of the trust's leading medical advisers says Archer 'had big ideas not suited to the scale of the organization, and he didn't raise the money because his ideas – like the Million Mothers campaign – were totally impractical'.

The trust chairman, Walter Gilbey, later wrote to MSL, the headhunters who'd recommended Archer as director-general. He acknowledged Archer's 'drive, initiative, enthusiasm, inventive mind and hard work', but his press contacts and personal approaches had 'not been as good as expected', Gilbey explained.

Unfortunately his manner has been far too brash on many occasions and he has upset a number of people . . . Furthermore, I am afraid

he is considerably lacking in the basic business and social judge-
ments which make the difference to doing things in a manner that
is accepted or in a way that causes offence.[47]

MSL agreed to refund part of their original recruitment fee.

It had been one of the sorriest chapters in Archer's career. He felt
badly that he had let people down, and, to his credit, just before leaving,
he made a positive gesture to show his regret, signing a personal covenant to the trust of £25 a year.[48]

# 10

# Mr 10 Per Cent

Whatever Jeffrey Archer had told the National Birthday Trust, he had not actually been offered a job with the BBC. But his story wasn't entirely without substance.

Ever since he'd left Oxford, Archer had been lobbying hard for a job in television. Adrian Metcalfe had already become a sports commentator with ITV, and television, of course, had been the second area in which Chris Chataway had made his mark. Jeffrey's other model was David Frost. Only a year older than Archer, Frost had rapidly become one of the most famous people in both Britain and America, the first great 'personality' created solely by the new medium.

For several months after Oxford, during his weekends, Archer hung around the BBC sports department doing the odd task here and there, always unpaid. He badgered constantly for a chance to appear on screen. Eventually, BBC producers gave in.

For the England v. France Rugby international in February 1967, the BBC went to the trouble of rigging up a second commentary box at Twickenham with its own line to Television Centre. Alongside the live broadcast on BBC1, Archer's dummy version was recorded back in Shepherd's Bush for sports editors to watch later. 'It wasn't at all bad,' says the BBC's Rugby producer, Alan Mouncer. 'He could have been pretty good, given a bit of practice.' Mouncer was amazed that Archer had managed to get that far; indeed it is the only occasion he remembers so much effort being made to test a potential commentator. 'He had considerable pull,' he says. 'Normally nobody got a nose in the door there.' Archer's vital contact appears to have been the head of sport, Bryan Cowgill, whom he'd met at an international athletics match. The commentary test was rigged up after Cowgill had come complaining about the need to do something about 'this guy on my neck'.[1]

Hence Archer's talk during the spring of 1967 about getting a full-time job in television. 'The BBC does seem to like what it calls "the honest and unfeigned man"',' he advised a friend who was also hoping to join the corporation.² And when he read in the press that David Coleman might be leaving as presenter of the Saturday sports programme *Grandstand*, he quickly pounced. On the day of the GLC elections Archer wrote to Bryan Cowgill:

> I realize you will consider it a colossal nerve . . . to dare presume that I am able to do the job . . . However, I believe I could do this job. If therefore it is in your mind to place someone completely new to the viewers in this position, I would very much like to be considered.
>
> It is not unknown that my ambition follows much the same lines as Christopher Chataway's and that if elected today to the GLC I shall be the youngest ever GLC Councillor. There is only one thing I want as much as reaching the House of Commons and that is the opportunity to do the job such as the one for which your Department is responsible.
>
> You once said to me that you liked people to tell you what they wanted, so at least I have done that. Quite naturally, I would be only too willing to devote my entire time to this one job as I believe it is the most exciting position that can be held in BBC Sport. I can only hope you have had more outrageous ideas suggested and, what is more, seen them work.³

Cowgill replied almost at once, declining Archer's proposal, though he proffered friendly advice on how he might pursue his TV ambitions.

Archer also lobbied other parts of the corporation. 'He desperately wanted to be on screen,' says Sir Paul Fox, then head of BBC Current Affairs. 'He was straight out of Oxford and came for a job as a reporter on *Panorama*. He tried very, very hard.'⁴ In those days, *Panorama* was home to only the most experienced of the BBC reporting corps – distinguished correspondents such as Robin Day, Michael Charlton, Alan Hart and Robert Kee. The idea that *Panorama* might take on a young pup, just down from university, with next to no experience of either television or journalism, was far-fetched.

Yet Paul Fox found him 'engaging', and says he was quite tempted. 'There was something about Jeffrey that was deeply, deeply attractive.' However, there was also 'something about him I didn't quite like', though it wasn't anything nasty. In the end Fox decided it was too much of a risk, and in any case 'there just wasn't a vacancy'.⁵

Since then, however, Archer has often said that immediately after leaving Oxford he worked for the BBC.[6] The corporation has no record of this, and nobody remembers him being on staff. The Archer version even claims that he had to leave the corporation because of his election to the GLC. Yet it was in the spring of 1967 – *after* his elevation to the council – that he was actually telling the National Birthday Trust that the BBC was about to give him a job – 'either for *24 Hours* or the sports programmes at the weekends'.[7] Later the trust was told how the job had fallen through because the man Archer 'was to work with was now leaving to go to Independent Television and he had been asked to wait 6 months'.[8]

No job ever came up. In October 1967, however, Archer was asked to do a match commentary for *Rugby Special*, the Saturday-evening programme on BBC2 which broadcast half an hour's highlights from one of the day's fixtures. Archer went to Richmond for a game between London Scottish and Northampton. He got twenty-five guineas for his performance, and he can't have done badly, for twelve weeks later he did a second match, between Waterloo and Gosforth. The games are stored in the BBC archives on a couple of old-fashioned two-inch videotapes, testimony to Archer's brief career as a television sports commentator.

On his election to the GLC, Archer appeared at County Hall with the reputation of being the man who had toppled Sir William Fiske. He sent Fiske a personal note immediately afterwards: 'May I say what a pleasure it was to fight such a courteous opponent. You were an example to everyone . . . It would be childish to imagine that I have as much to offer the GLC as you had.'[9]

Archer's proud boast – made not only to Bryan Cowgill, but repeated regularly ever since – is that he was the youngest ever GLC councillor. The claim simply seems to have been plucked out of the air because it sounds plausible, but in fact it was not even true for those elected in 1967. Archer was now twenty-seven, but his Tory colleague from Wandsworth, Anthony Bradbury, was only twenty-five. Another Tory, Gordon Dixon from Enfield, had been twenty-six when he was elected to the council in 1964.

Archer was appointed to several GLC committees, only to resign from them straight away when he was appointed to the Inner London Education Authority (ILEA). On the surface, this was an odd appointment, since Havering was an outer-London borough, responsible for its own schools, not part of the ILEA. The reason was that the ILEA's new leader was Chris Chataway.

Chataway was not an elected councillor, but, after losing his seat in Parliament in 1966, he was made a GLC alderman and put in charge of the ILEA. This was done on the instructions of the Conservative Party leader, Edward Heath, to block a right-wing councillor, Seton Forbes-Cockell, who was keen on the job. Heath was concerned that the new ILEA leadership should not confront the Labour government over comprehensive schools, but instead consider each proposed scheme on its merits.

'I only wish I were able to serve you in some capacity,' Archer quickly wrote to Chataway.[10] When his hero indicated that he'd welcome any help, Jeffrey moved himself into the ILEA leader's large office in County Hall, and commandeered a desk on which he placed his bust of John Kennedy. Archer gave himself the title of 'personal assistant', but Chataway can't recall whether he agreed to this. 'I asked Chris Chataway why he'd appointed Jeffrey Archer,' says a colleague, Michael Wheeler. 'Chris said, "I didn't: he appointed himself!"'[11]

Archer saw himself as providing Chataway with political intelligence, particularly on the activities of the Fulham Caucus, a group of Tory right-wingers led by Forbes-Cockell. 'You and I are very much ... "Pink Tories" in their eyes,' he had warned Chataway.[12] However, Archer's 'pinkishness' didn't stop him joining Forbes-Cockell for lunch parties at the Carlton Tower Hotel.

The new ILEA leadership immediately faced a problem to which it had given no thought. The Conservatives were now entitled to appoint a majority of the governors for each of the authority's several hundred schools and colleges in inner London, in Labour Tower Hamlets as much as in Tory Westminster. These had to be found quickly, however, to vote when each governing body chose a new chairman in a few weeks' time. Archer got the job of dragooning several hundred Tories into service.

It was a formidable task. The Conservatives, naturally, were weakest in the inner-London boroughs, and party organization barely existed in some constituencies. Even the most diplomatic person would have had difficulty recruiting so many volunteers so quickly; Jeffrey inevitably got people's backs up. 'People were being chased, and Jeffrey Archer upset nearly every agent in London,' recalls the Tories' then deputy chief whip on the GLC, Geoffrey Seaton.[13] Says another colleague,

'Chairmen and agents all over London were ringing and saying "Get this lunatic off our backs!"'

Archer doesn't appear to have done much else for the ILEA leader. Chataway says Archer's assistance 'didn't really last more than a few weeks. There wasn't a great deal he could do in that role, or I could delegate.'[14]

In his early days on the GLC, Archer intervened in council debates regularly, making long, vitriolic speeches, usually designed to bait the Labour opposition, with whom he made himself deeply unpopular. 'Jeffrey at that time had energy and vitality to offer but not a great deal else initially,' says his colleague from Havering, Bernard Brook-Partridge. 'At 26 you don't know it all but you can give a very good impression of believing that you do. So I think that used to get up people's noses.'[15] 'He was a good speaker,' says another colleague, 'but a bit brash and had a tendency to be overpersonal.' Archer was always to the fore in heckling Labour and cheering contributions from the Tory benches. Few GLC councillors took the young member for Havering seriously; they saw him as a bumptious young whippersnapper desperate for the next stage: a seat in Parliament.

There were some who found Archer impressive, however. Conservative councillor Norman Munday says he felt so inadequate in comparison that he 'gave up politics because Archer was such a brilliant speaker. He had tremendous potential as a politician.'[16]

One of Archer's few GLC achievements was to help bring about the artificial 'tartan track' at Crystal Palace athletics stadium, so called because the cork it was made of looked like tartan. He also took a keen interest in arts issues, anticipating government policy by more than twenty-five years in advocating a lottery to pay for the new National Theatre. And for a time Archer also sat on the so-called 'Sexy Films Committee', and later related how he was sacked by its chairman, the Countess of Dartmouth (later to become Countess Spencer, stepmother of the Princess of Wales):

> I arrived on the first day, never having seen the whole of one of these films, desperately keen to enjoy them on Tuesday afternoons from 4.30 to 7 or 8 o'clock in the evening. Three films were to be shown. I confess that Lady Dartmouth removed me from the committee for sleeping during the second film, making it impossible for me to give an opinion whether it should be X, AA, A, or U.[17]

Perhaps the thing for which Jeffrey Archer is best remembered by many fellow councillors is helping them to claim allowances and expenses. In those days the paperwork for obtaining compensation was so elaborate and forbidding that some of the busier, wealthier Tories simply couldn't be bothered to claim their entitlement. Archer offered to assist.

It probably started quite naturally when he helped Chris Chataway to complete his expense and allowance sheets, as one of his few duties as the ILEA leader's PA. 'It was an extremely complicated form,' Chataway recalls; 'a hell of a sweat to fill them up.'[18] But once Archer had mastered it he let it be known that he was willing to do the same for other councillors too. Mostly it involved checking the minutes to see which meetings people had attended. In return he collected 10 per cent.

Neil Thorne, one of seven Tory councillors who later became MPs, was delighted to use Archer. He simply hadn't got time to do the job himself, since he worked as a chartered surveyor in the mornings and served as chairman of the Central Board Committee in the afternoon, handling planning for central London. Unlike the House of Commons, there was no deadline for claims, so they inevitably got postponed. 'When I heard somebody was willing to do it for me I thought, "Yippee!" I had a two-year backlog.'[19] Thorne reckons that as a leading chairman his claims would have been worth far more than most councillors' – about £1,000 a year, and so £100 to Archer. Christopher Chalker, a solicitor who chaired an important roads committee, also used Archer: 'I was too busy to fill in my claim form. He did it for one or two others too, and got 10 per cent.'[20]

Archer's earnings from doing colleagues' claim forms were undoubtedly modest: at most, a few hundred pounds a year – the equivalent of a few thousand now. But while this service may have helped him make contacts among the council élite, equally it meant that they took him less seriously. In the words of one fellow councillor, 'It put him in a lower position with those he was serving . . . I think it rather diminished him.'

Nowadays Jeffrey Archer denies ever completing fellow councillors' expense forms for commission. 'At no time did I fill in Members' expenses and claim 10%,' he wrote to the publishers of this book after we had asked questions about it. 'If this question is asked again to any person I shall place the matter in the hands of solicitors.'[21] However, no fewer than twenty-four former councillors recall Archer providing this service, and six of them confirm he did it for them.

Quite why Archer should deny this is curious. There was nothing illegal or wrong about it. It was, however, politically unwise, and not likely to be understood by the general public, most of whom believe politicians make too much money anyway. 'He was warned off, of course,' says Geoffrey Seaton. 'He didn't do mine but those of about six to eight people – they couldn't be bothered to claim. It wasn't against the rules.'[22]     .

Archer clearly couldn't rely solely on commission from GLC expense claims for a living, or live in hope that a job with the BBC would come up. At one stage he misleadingly told one firm, 'I am naturally willing to take a drop in salary from my present £4,000.'[23]

He even tried to return to academic life, inspired no doubt by the example of his wife, Mary, who was still doing her PhD at Imperial College. Archer applied to do an MPhil at London University's Institute of Education, only to be asked why no previous degree was mentioned on his application form. He said he had in fact done a degree in America (without giving details), 'and the reason I did not put it on the form was because Oxford never recognizes First Degrees in the US'.[24]

When a job did turn up, it was through Chris Chataway, who had suggested his name to a former parliamentary colleague, Humphry Berkeley.

Berkeley was one of the most enigmatic figures of postwar British politics. The son of a Liberal MP, he spoke of himself as a 'Liberal'; yet, ironically, the Liberals were the only major party he never joined. As a Conservative in the 1960s, he helped draw up the leadership rules which led to the election of Edward Heath, but he then lost his seat after leading the campaign for homosexual law reform.

Berkeley had since become chairman of the United Nations Association (UNA), the British charity which acts as a kind of UN supporters' club. The UNA had a staff of around fifty or sixty people, and so always needed money. During his term as chairman, Berkeley hoped to make the UNA finances secure, and sought somebody who could raise about a quarter of a million pounds.

Berkeley seems to have decided immediately that Archer was exactly the man he was looking for. Rarely can anyone have been so convinced of another's abilities. He recommended that Archer be put in charge of that year's flag collection on UNA Day, in October, on the strength, he said, of 'the vigorous and imaginative ideas he had employed in Oxfam and in the National Birthday Trust and of the money he had raised for them'.[25]

There were no interviews, and no other candidates. Berkeley saw the job of flag-day organizer merely as a way to get Archer on board, before discussing more serious fund-raising. He was employed for three and a half days a week and for five months, at 'a fee of £1,000 with expenses of £500'. Pro rata, it was almost double his salary at the Birthday Trust, though Berkeley probably didn't know that. Many people, after all, were under the misapprehension that the NBT had been paying Archer £4,000 a year. Berkeley was so confident that Archer could raise several thousands more than the previous year's flag day that he was 'personally ready to guarantee his fee if that extra amount (£1,000) were not raised'.[26]

Jeffrey moved into the UNA headquarters on the eighth and ninth floors of a block on the Albert Embankment, opposite the Tate Gallery. Alembic House enjoys a wonderful panorama over the Palace of Westminster and down the Thames towards the City. Jeffrey quickly fell in love with the view, and the power and money it represented. Humphry Berkeley recalls one occasion when Archer took him up to a higher floor, which was then on the market. 'Why don't you buy it?' Berkeley later recalled Archer suggesting. 'He obviously had his eye on it.'[27] It was almost another decade, however, before Jeffrey realized his dream.

Archer brought to the UNA the same energy that had served him so well with Oxfam. He visited each of the UNA regions, and wrote to every branch. Pupils from the City of London school were marshalled into selling flags at local cinemas, while Harold Wilson's wife, Mary, agreed to be photographed buying her UNA flag from the actress Susan Hampshire. Despite the big names, and television coverage, Archer's flag day didn't actually raise that much more than the year before – £19,771 compared with £19,061 in 1966. He hadn't quite matched Humphry Berkeley's much-trumpeted expectations, or even raised the extra £1,000 the UNA chairman had offered to guarantee.

Berkeley made it clear that Archer had better do something to compensate for this disappointment. By now his contract had already been extended to organize a much more ambitious project, a fund-raising dinner at 10 Downing Street. Archer was given a much grander title: director of special projects. His salary was increased to the equivalent of £4,800 a year.

Humphry Berkeley had already persuaded Harold Wilson, the UNA's joint president, to host the occasion; the Prime Minister would greet the guests, appeal for contributions, and acknowledge each donation personally. Jeffrey Archer's job was to rustle up a decent guest list. It was obvious that Wilson would not be meeting many political sympathizers: Berkeley and Archer were going for wealthy businessmen – the richer the better.

Berkeley later explained how he gave Archer a list of names to approach – headed by Olaf Kier, head of the civil engineering company J. L. Kier, and Jack Cohen, founder of the supermarket chain Tesco. Archer visited both tycoons in person. To everyone's astonishment he returned from Kier with a donation of £50,000. 'Jeffrey was, without doubt, a very, very good talker in the sense of persuading people to give money,' noted Humphry Berkeley.[28] Then, as if to show it wasn't a one-off, Jack Cohen also promised £50,000.

Archer was again making influential contacts, and both Kier and Cohen would reappear later in his career. Neither came from a traditional British business background; both had built themselves from nothing – Kier was a Danish engineer who'd settled in Britain in 1922; Cohen was an uneducated Jewish East Ender. The latter became one of the models for Archer's Charlie Trumper in his 1991 novel *As the Crow Flies*, about a cockney barrow boy who ends up with a famous department store. Both men had more wealth than they knew what to do with, yet were keen for Establishment blessing. In short, they were 'new money'.

If Humphry Berkeley suggested some names, Archer got others from Chris Chataway. And John Roper, the UNA vice-chairman, remembers how Jeffrey did his own research. 'He went through the *FT* and *The Times* for people whose companies had gone public in the last five years. He chose people who were flush with money, who were on the way up, and likely to be flattered by the idea of being invited to Number Ten.'[29]

Many he invited to Downing Street fitted the same profile – first- or second-generation immigrants, often Jewish, who'd made their fortunes in Britain; several were in construction or property, and quite a few in retailing. Among the UNA diners were John Sunley of the Sunley property group; Sebastian de Ferranti of the engineering firm; the rising Gerald Ronson; Marcus Sieff of Marks & Spencer; Joe Hyman of Viyella; Bernard Delfont, the impresario; Joe Levy, another property man; Michael Sobell of GEC; Norman Wates of the building group. Like Kier and Cohen, several would play roles in Jeffrey's subsequent career.

The dinner, in April 1968, was a resounding success. 'When I went to see the PM at Number 10,' Archer told the *Evening Standard*, 'he thought the whole thing would raise £10,000. The Chairman thought it was worth £50,000. I thought we'd get £500,000 even before it started.'[30]

Few businessmen could resist a free meal in Downing Street, and, even if it was hosted by a Labour Prime Minister, the presence of Edward Heath and the Liberal leader, Jeremy Thorpe, gave the evening a non-partisan air. Treated to turtle soup, blue trout, roast Aylesbury duck and peaches in brandy, the diners promised an average of £5,000 a head – the equivalent today of £50,000. The UNA expected to raise for certain '£300,000, possibly £350,000'.[31] It wasn't as high as Archer's initial claims, but still an extraordinary figure from one event, especially at a time when such fund-raising methods were novel.

The UNA hierarchy was delighted, and recorded 'that this magnificent result was very largely due to the efforts of Mr Jeffrey Archer'.[32] At the AGM a few days later, Archer's work was praised repeatedly. Indeed, his success had received so much favourable publicity that some concern was expressed about 'the danger of fund-raising becoming the main image of the Association'.[33] Later, it transpired that the dinner at Number Ten had been slightly less profitable than initially expected – with 'a total of £208,000', though the UNA minutes added that 'Another £50,000 should materialize from intended gifts.'[34]

Archer's reputation as a dynamic charity fund-raiser had been restored. His reward was another year's contract with the UNA, worth the equivalent of £5,000 a year – far more than the £3,000 salary being paid to the association's director-general.

Yet, according to one former UNA official, Archer did not make as much from the Downing Street dinner as he should have done, and was lax in pursuing guests who hadn't yet promised anything. 'I said to Jeffrey sometime afterwards, "Are you following them up? They've got to be made aware it was a fund-raising dinner." . . . At least half a dozen never paid a penny.' He also feels that, once Archer had achieved one great success, he relaxed. 'I have to say that Jeffrey was exceptionally lazy,' is the official's surprising judgement. 'He was never involved in sustained hard work over time; he was only interested in talking to people. He floated around the office.' And there were times, it seems, when Humphry Berkeley thought it necessary to press his director of special projects to do more.

Archer's subsequent work for the UNA proved to be disappointing by comparison. He arranged further dinners, both in London and around the country; there was a film première in Leicester Square at which he renewed acquaintance with Princess Alexandra, and a UNA ball for which David Frost did the cabaret. These events raised only a few thousand pounds, and the 1968 flag day was £3,000 down on the year before.

At the start of 1969 Archer decided to set up his own fund-raising and public-relations business. Rather than the obvious name, Archer Enterprises, he chose Arrow Enterprises. He asked the UNA to let him terminate his contract two months early, but offered to carry on working for the association on a 'function to function' basis.[35]

The UNA agreed to let him leave early, but found his alternative plans 'not altogether acceptable'.[36] Arrow offered to look after the UNA's membership renewals and to organize a series of regional dinners, in return for a flat fee of £6,000, and 10 per cent of all profits after the first £6,000.[37] The UNA said they didn't like the idea of the commission element. The real problem, as we shall see, was that Humphry Berkeley had become deeply unhappy about Archer's behaviour while working for the organization.

But if the UNA wasn't willing to pay 10 per cent, another body was.

Shortly after the Downing Street dinner, one of Archer's GLC colleagues, David Baker, introduced him to Ernest Wistrich, who had recently been appointed director of the European Movement, the main body campaigning for Britain to join the Common Market. Over lunch, Archer agreed to raise £50,000 for the organization. 'Hair will grow on my palm before he does,' Wistrich remembers a colleague saying, as he rubbed his hand.[38]

'What I need from you is to book the Guildhall and the three party leaders,' Archer then explained to Wistrich. That was no problem, since, whatever else they might have disagreed about, Harold Wilson, Edward Heath and Jeremy Thorpe were all committed to joining the EEC. However, Wistrich says he told Archer they didn't have enough money to pay for his services. 'He said, "All right, pay me 10 per cent." '[39]

Wistrich duly booked the three party leaders, and Archer recruited wealthy business guests in the same way he had for the UNA event – and many of the same names. This time he asked donors to sign seven-year covenants, which were a much less painful way of giving money, and had great tax advantages. Archer was on to a winner, since most industrialists were already impatient for Britain to join the Common Market.

The dinner, held in July 1969, was another triumph. Several contributors wrote out cheques for five figures – including eleven donations of £25,000 each, according to one account. And while the total reported in the press, £700,000, was an exaggeration, even the true figure, around £450,000, was a huge boost to the organization.[40]

At the last moment, however, the European Movement had been forced to agree not to pay him on commission. Harold Wilson had learned of the arrangement, and it is a sign of how upset he was that he later devoted half a page of his memoirs to the issue:

> A few days before it took place I decided to withdraw, as I had heard that ... Arrow Enterprises, which was in charge of the fund-raising activity, had been promised 10 per cent of the proceeds. Recalling all the thousands of voluntary workers who organized functions, for charities and other worthwhile activities, I revolted against this form of professionalism. I particularly disliked the principle that if either of the other two party leaders or I succeeded, through our eloquence, in persuading some rich fellow-diner to contribute £10,000 to the cause, the fund-raising organization concerned would benefit to the extent of £1,000.[41]

Jeremy Thorpe endorsed Wilson's objections. So, instead of giving Archer 10 per cent, the European Movement paid him a flat fee. This just happened to be about £45,000 – about a tenth of what the occasion had raised.

Financially, the European Movement dinner proved to be Archer's breakthrough. He was now making money on a grand scale; £45,000 in 1968 would be worth almost half a million pounds today. His experiences with Oxfam, the National Birthday Trust, the UNA and now the European Movement had taught him to ignore small projects, no matter how promising. The effort ought to be put into attracting big names and wealthy donors. 'I want to build this into doing one really great function a year,' Archer declared. 'I have had many offers, but I don't want to work on small ventures.'[42]

Yet Archer was never happy doing just one thing at a time. Besides politics and fund-raising, he still hoped to become a journalist. During the summer of 1969 he persuaded the *Sunday Times* sports features editor, John Lovesey, to let him do some reporting. 'I was subjected to an onslaught,' says Lovesey, who remembers Archer taking him to a lavish lunch at a London club, and introducing him to several distinguished friends, including the Shadow Cabinet minister, Geoffrey Rippon. 'He was very anxious to make an impression on his wife as a literary man,' Lovesey recalls. Eventually the paper let him do three athletics reports; they were published, but the *Sunday Times* wasn't convinced. 'He didn't write well enough,' says Lovesey, 'and there were a lot of objections from people in the NUJ.'[43]

Archer also tried to help with ITV's coverage of the 1968 Olympics. Chris Chataway had agreed to front ITV's coverage live from Mexico City (assisted, incidentally, by Adrian Metcalfe), and he persuaded his producers to employ Archer as his assistant. In the end, however, ITV couldn't afford the air-fare, and Jeffrey was confined to London. Frank Keating, one of the producers, remembers him hanging round the ITV Olympics operation 'like an extremely cheery, boringly keen office boy'.[44] But, frustrated with nothing much to do, Archer inevitably got in the way, and it didn't go down too well when he started advising people, including the experienced presenter in London, Leonard Parkin, how to do their work.

Keating and his colleagues decided they had to find a job to keep Archer out of their hair. 'Then we had this idea to put Jeffrey in a studio – his eyes lit up at that – in case the satellite went down, so that someone could then interview him.' Archer worked furiously hard, preparing for the moment when his expertise might suddenly be called upon. 'He filled exercise books of notes,' says Keating; 'he scribbled and scribbled, and had lots of bright ideas.'[45] Yet, so far as anyone can remember, the satellite always held up, which was unusual in those days. Jeffrey's work went to waste.

The former editor of ITV's *World of Sport*, John Bromley, also remembers Archer badgering him to do a 'Rugby slot' for the Saturday-afternoon programme. Archer wanted to pop up before the soccer results and do a summary of the day's games. 'He was searching desperately for exposure,' says Bromley. 'He said things like "I'll come up in vision and Eamonn [Andrews] will cut to me."'[46]

Archer also approached ITN and tried to become a sports correspondent there. 'I've never seen a greater case of self-confidence,' says the former ITN editor Nigel Ryan, 'never known cheek like it.' Ryan explained that there wasn't a vacancy, and that in any case he didn't think Archer had the necessary journalistic credentials. 'I could be a general reporter,' Archer persisted. The ITN editor pointed out patiently that there were probably forty or fifty people better qualified to be ITN reporters than him. Archer seemed 'completely unfazed' by this, Ryan remembers, and, to his interviewer's surprise, he dropped into the conversation the suggestion that Ryan might be interested in becoming a director of Arrow Enterprises. However innocently intended, Archer's remark was open to misinterpretation. Ryan politely showed him the door.[47]

If Jeffrey's attempts to become a journalist foundered, the business contacts he'd made through his big charity dinners were starting to bear fruit. One of them, the engineering contractor Olaf Kier, agreed to support a long-standing pet project of Archer's – opening an art gallery. Kier's wife, Bente, and his son-in-law, Peter Fawcett, invested £7,500 in the company and became directors. Two of Archer's fellow Tory politicians joined them: Geoffrey Rippon, who became chairman, and Brian Batsford, an MP and GLC alderman who also ran his family's publishing company and was 'the most knowledgeable of us all,' according to Rippon.[48]

The Archer Gallery opened in Grafton Street, Mayfair, at the end of October 1969, with a glittering reception. The guest of honour was the Conservative leader, Edward Heath, who was presented with a specially commissioned portrait of his yacht, *Morning Cloud*. And everyone who was photographed talking to Heath was sent a copy of the picture as a souvenir.

The gallery concentrated on modern art. Its opening exhibition featured a collection of sculpture by Leon Underwood, an English sculptor and painter whose work is now thought to have been underrated during his lifetime. In the 1920s Underwood had taught both Barbara Hepworth and Henry Moore, with whom he is often compared, but had never achieved the same recognition. Archer became a kind of patron for the artist, who was then seventy-eight and enjoying something of a critical renaissance. Underwood allowed his work to become virtually a permanent feature of the gallery. 'It shows Jeffrey Archer's ability to get people to do things for him that they don't always do for other people,' Rippon has said, noting that Underwood 'didn't much like art dealers and was very, very reluctant ever to put his work on the market'.[49]

*Arts Review* praised the 'lateral thinking' of the gallery's manager, Marie Bennigsen, and her 'perceptive eye for off-beat, untrendy art'.[50] Financially though, the Archer Gallery lost about £1,800 a month. After little more than a year, Archer and his colleagues sold the business to Watches of Switzerland, who retained the name and kept Jeffrey on as a director. The rise in property values ensured that the profit from the sale slightly outweighed their running losses. 'I got my money back,' Rippon says.[51] Peter Fawcett feels the site was too large to sustain, and the project was 'a little too ambitious perhaps . . . maybe we started in too high a gear'. It might have worked, he thinks, if the gallery had set up initially in Chelsea, rather than in the West End.[52] It never reached the stage, enjoyed by successful galleries, of artists queuing up to show their work.

'It was one of my rare failures,' Archer would later confess. He acknowledges, however, that the gallery 'did enable me to buy a lot of good sculpture and paintings. In fact I estimate my Russell Flint costs me a penny a day for life.'[53] Leon Underwood's first major painting, *Venus in Kensington Gardens*, more often called *Venus in the Park*, was another fine work he acquired cheaply. It is a highly personal picture, featuring a nude sitting in a park café among Underwood's art-school colleagues, his wife and friends. The Tate Gallery had apparently offered to buy the painting for £25,000, but Underwood was angry with them for postponing an exhibition of his work. As Archer later recalled:

> It was a painting I really loved and I had said I would give every-thing I owned to have it. He asked me how much I had in my bank account. At that time it was £820. He said, 'The painting's yours.' Later his son came round to see me and told me to give it back. But Leon Underwood told me to ignore his son.[54]

Archer says he later offered it back to the artist. Underwood refused, but asked Archer to leave the painting to the Tate Gallery when he died. It would later play a part in Archer's first novel, *Not a Penny More, Not a Penny Less*, and would enjoy pride of place in Archer's office, hanging behind his desk.

But by the end of 1969 Archer was fully absorbed in more pressing matters than art dealing: his fund-raising business was taking off, and then there was also serious politics.

# I I

# The Lincolnshire Poacher

Of all the stages on the slippery pole of a political career, securing a parliamentary seat is the most important, and often the most difficult and unpredictable. Qualities that later on may secure advancement in government may mean little to the activists of a local constituency party who choose an election candidate.

Archer began the quest for a seat almost immediately on leaving Oxford, and quickly gained a place on the Central Office list of potential candidates. It was an ideal moment to try. The Labour landslide of 1966 had cleared out a lot of sitting Tory MPs, and left a large number of promising seats without candidates. Safe and marginal constituencies like to pick their nominees well in advance of a general election, which meant that, despite his success with the GLC, Archer had to act promptly. Unlike many budding politicians, who usually begin by contesting hopeless constituencies, Archer seems from the very start to have been interested only in places likely to return him to Parliament. Not for him the drudgery of fighting a hostile mining town and losing by thirty thousand votes.

One of the first seats he tried, Billericay in Essex, not far from Havering, turned him down. Another Labour marginal, Reading, was more promising. In March 1967 the local party placed Archer on the final short list after he had promised to live in the constituency if chosen. Then, suddenly, he withdrew, telling officials it would be difficult to move to Reading, since Mary wasn't due to complete her doctorate for another two years.[1] It seems an odd thing to say when Reading is so near London and the working arrangements of postgraduates are so flexible. He also declined interest from Newark – 'for personal reasons', he said.[2] Most twenty-six-year-olds would have been delighted to win selection for such good Conservative prospects, but perhaps Archer was gambling on winning a much safer seat. If so, with hindsight his strategy was absolutely correct.

Archer was a serious contender for at least five seats between 1966 and 1969. They included Rugby and York (again Labour marginals) and two other constituencies where he could exploit his Somerset background. In Wells, close to Weston-super-Mare, they chose a local right-winger, Robert Boscawen. Neighbouring Bridgwater would have been even more suitable, since it included Oare, where Jeffrey had been christened. Archer felt his initial speech to Bridgwater Tories was the best he had yet delivered, and the agent, Peter Killmister, recalls that his rousing style of delivery had a considerable impact. Jeffrey won support from younger members of the party, and people were particularly impressed by Mary. 'I can remember thinking, "My goodness! A raven-haired beauty and a double first as well!"' says Killmister.[3] But Jeffrey narrowly missed the final short list, and Bridgwater went instead for a more senior local figure, the future Defence Secretary, Tom King. By the autumn of 1969 Archer's best two prospects of getting into Parliament had both gone; so had most other safe seats as the Tories geared up for an election expected in 1970.

In the meantime Archer had also pursued another important political opportunity: applying to work in the office of the Conservative leader, Edward Heath. At that time, Heath's political secretary, Douglas Hurd, was looking for a deputy to assume some of his heavy workload. One version has it that initially Hurd was inclined to appoint him, until the Tory Chief Whip, Willie Whitelaw, intervened to say Archer wasn't at all suitable. Heath's parliamentary private secretary (PPS), Jim Prior, remembers Archer 'was very disappointed not to get the job. In breaking the news to him, I asked what he was going to do. "I haven't decided yet," he replied, "but either become an MP or make a million."'[4]

Nevertheless, Archer maintained good relations with Hurd, who was establishing something of a reputation as a writer. The future Foreign Secretary was then working on a political thriller about a Foreign Office minister who becomes a spy for the Chinese, and whose constituency is Louth in Lincolnshire. (Hurd's fictitious local party, incidentally, includes a very bossy lady called Mrs Thatcher.)[5] By pure coincidence, shortly after Hurd's book was published in 1969, Sir Cyril Osborne, the real-life MP for Louth, suddenly died, causing a by-election.

Archer decided to go for the seat, though it was a long shot. He barely knew where Louth was: his nearest local connection was his mother's sister, Eileen, in Leeds, about sixty miles away. Geoffrey Rippon told him the selection process would at least be good experience when a more promising seat came up. Yet history shows that candidates often win the nominations they least expect.

The old Louth constituency, stretching south from the mouth of the Humber, was roughly pear-shaped, with a small bite taken out for Grimsby, a separate seat. It was a large area, covering almost 400 square miles, and measuring thirty-three miles from one end to the other.

It was also one of the most diverse parliamentary seats. At its heart lay Louth itself, dominated by St James's church, said to have the tallest spire of any parish church in England. The town's Georgian architecture and narrow streets have remained largely untouched by developers, and in 1969 the 11,000 population was roughly the same as in Victorian times. It still boasts its own cinema and, remarkably for such a small community, two weekly newspapers.

To the west lies the rich farmland of the Lincolnshire Wolds, which contrasts starkly with the terrain located eastwards towards the coast – flat, reclaimed marshes. The character of 'the Marsh' is described in the wonderful names of its small villages – Theddlethorpe and Grimoldby, Saltfleet and Somercotes, Grainthorpe and Marshchapel. Across the open landscape the villages stand out for miles, dominated by their churches.

The town of Louth and its surrounding countryside comprised the southern half of the constituency. The northern half was effectively the hinterland of the port of Grimsby. This included Grimsby's sister town, Cleethorpes, a declining seaside resort created by the Victorian railway-builders.

The constituency also extended around the northern side of Grimsby to industrial Immingham. And whereas Louth is one of the most attractive towns in England, Immingham, with its oil refineries and chemical plants, must be one of the most unpleasant. Though Immingham's population accounted for only a tenth of the Louth constituency, the town had grown rapidly since the war, and its economic importance was increasing. Immingham wasn't just chemicals and eyesores: it also spelt prosperity and expansion.

Agriculture, fishing, docks and petrochemicals; Wolds and Marsh; seaside resort, council estates, cattle markets and quiet country villages: few parliamentary constituencies enjoyed the variety of Louth. But its size and diversity presented great difficulties for its politicians. People living near Louth itself got London editions of the national papers, while the Grimsby area received copies printed in Manchester. Though everyone swore allegiance to Lincolnshire, the southern agricultural area around Louth saw itself as part of the East Midlands, while Immingham and Cleethorpes had the feel of northern England.

Louth's MP since 1945, Sir Cyril Osborne, had enjoyed a reputation for being one of the most right-wing Conservatives, fighting the tide of 1960s liberalism. He fought to keep hanging, resisted the relaxation of the laws against homosexuality, tried to stop coloured immigration and race-relations legislation, and opposed the Common Market. Yet Osborne could not be categorized as a right-wing Neanderthal: on economics he was quite to the left of his party. He also made frequent business trips to Moscow when such things were treated with suspicion, taking the view that the Soviet Union should be liberated economically.

When a previous MP for Louth, Thomas Wintringham, died in 1921, local supporters simply put his wife, Margaret, forward as a replacement (the woman whose secretary had been the Archers' landlady in Mark). Some Louth Conservatives suggested they should follow the Wintringham example in 1969, and nominate Lady Osborne in Sir Cyril's place. She would have been a popular choice, both in and outside the party, but she turned the offer down. 'The last paragraph of the very generous and kind letter that she wrote to us said, "You want a man,"' the Conservative chairman, Jack Vincent, later revealed.[6]

The BBC 24 Hours programme made a fascinating film about how Louth Tories chose their candidate – revealing a lot about the whole nature of such contests and showing how little the progressive 1960s had advanced into Lincolnshire. But if Lady Osborne's assertion that Louth needed a man seems ridiculous now, what followed is all the more absurd. 'A very quick decision was taken that it was doubtful whether a lady would be acceptable,' Jack Vincent explained on the programme. 'I think a Member of Parliament should be a man. I'm perhaps prejudiced, but I'm certain most of my members felt the same thing – including the ladies.' Lady Osborne's letter suited Vincent perfectly. 'Because she was so respected and so popular throughout the constituency, they attached great weight to her thoughts in this matter.'[7]

The twenty-two-strong selection committee considered about 250 names from the Central Office candidates list, together with several local Tories. After ruling out women, they also decided that the man they selected should be married, and that the ideal age-range should be thirty to fifty, with twenty-eight and fifty-five as absolute limits. Jeffrey Archer scraped in at twenty-nine.

The twenty-five men on the preliminary short list were invited to visit Louth in the first weekend in October.

They included a number of distinguished figures. Most prominent was John Davies, about to step down as the director-general of the CBI. There were several former MPs, including David Walder, who'd lost his seat at High Peak in Derbyshire and who, appropriately enough, had written a novel, *The Short List*, about a selection process and by-election.[8] Also on this real-life short list were Ian Gow, Margaret Thatcher's future PPS, and Sir Anthony Meyer, the back-bencher who challenged her for the party leadership in 1989.

The former local party vice-president, Clixby Fitzwilliams, remembers the initial response from Jeffrey quite well:

> A telegram arrived from New York to say Jeffrey Archer couldn't make the 10.00 appointment, but that a helicopter would arrive on Cleethorpes beach at 11.00 . . . In the end he came by train. He had certainly been in America, though I don't think it was quite so pressing as he had made it out to be.[9]

Only nineteen of those invited actually turned up at the Kingsway Hotel in Cleethorpes. In turn, they were given fifteen minutes to speak and another fifteen to answer questions. Archer was among the first on the schedule. He made much of his TV experience, and stressed the importance of good presentation. When asked about farming, he cited the similarities between Lincolnshire and his own rural Somerset, and explained that he'd been brought up on a farm, which was an approximation of the truth. As for Cleethorpes, that was very like his own Weston-super-Mare. He also explained how both his parents had served as councillors. But Archer hadn't done the homework that an ambitious candidate would do nowadays. He seemed totally unaware that the seat also contained Immingham, or what kind of place it was. Nevertheless, Trevor Knight, a young Immingham councillor, marked 'outstanding' against Archer's name. The agent, Peter Walker, in contrast, felt it was 'really and truly almost a lift of a Peter Sellers speech – "We must go forward into the future not backward into the past," . . . it was a *tour de force* of presentation that said very little.'[10]

The selection committee had no trouble whittling the names down to three. As a national figure, John Davies had to be included. The CBI man had performed badly, but the panel assumed this was because he was a businessman and not used to this kind of thing. David Walder was chosen for his experience as an MP for a similar kind of seat. And the third name, much to his own astonishment, was Jeffrey Archer.

On the Monday immediately afterwards, 6 October 1969, the three contenders appeared before the sixty-strong executive at Louth's imposing Victorian town hall. Again, a fifteen-minute speech was followed by questions. This time the candidates were asked to bring their wives, who were invited to say a few words. And most people concur with Jack Vincent's assessment that 'the wives played quite a part in the final choice'.[11] Joyce Osborne had been heavily involved in constituency activities, and Louth Tories were looking for a similar female figure – someone with style, willing to open bring-and-buy sales, coffee mornings and garden parties.

John Davies's wife, Vera, did not impress. She obviously wasn't keen to play any part in the constituency, and came across as 'very toffee-nosed', says one official. She had dressed as if going to Ascot, and had to remove her white glove as she arrived on the platform and shook the chairman's hand. 'Can we go and find a cup of coffee in this God-forsaken town?' she exclaimed in front of the agent's wife after her husband had spoken; this did not endear her to people. While the members had no objection to Elspeth Walder, they loved Mary Archer: she was attractive, very young (at twenty-four), and obviously extremely clever. They did not seem worried that she had her own academic career to pursue. 'Mrs Archer put me in mind of Lady Osborne, many years ago, when her husband first started,' said one committee member.[12] Peter Walker takes a minority view, however, in saying Mary's role has been exaggerated. 'Anyone who suggests she tipped the balance,' he insists, 'is talking through their hat.'[13]

What is striking about the selection of the candidate is what little part policies played in the process. Louth Conservatives weren't looking for a man with particular opinions on anything, but wanted a good MP, who would be energetic and diligent in looking after his large constituency. All three contenders were well to the left of Sir Cyril Osborne, at least on those issues on which Sir Cyril had made his name, such as immigration and the EEC. There was no reflection of the left–right Tory disputes at Westminster. Not once was Archer asked about the subject liberal Tories dread at selection meetings – hanging. Nor did anyone enquire about Enoch Powell or race, which were big issues at that time; but then Louth hadn't seen much immigration. Even local fears about the Common Market were raised only a few times. This is probably just as well for Archer, for on each of these emotive questions he had views very different from Sir Cyril's, and, inasmuch as they had any opinions, Louth Tories generally reflected the position of their former MP. Instead, they wanted to know what each man would do for the seat, whether he would live there, how often he would visit, and how he would get his message across. They wanted a local figurehead.

Naturally, for a farming seat, they did ask Archer about agriculture. 'He made an absolute cobblers of the question,' Peter Walker remembers. 'He blustered and waffled.'[14]

John Davies, on the other hand, made a very 'erudite speech', says Clixby Fitzwilliams, 'on the importance of oil throughout the world'.[15] But the CBI man suffered the severe disadvantage of being perceived as the 'Central Office candidate', backed by Edward Heath. Everyone assumed he was being groomed to join the next Tory Cabinet. But constituency parties guard their independence in choosing candidates – it is, after all, the only significant decision they ever have to make, and it doesn't occur that often. Nothing is more likely to cause a backlash than the suggestion that somebody is being imposed on them, and Fitzwilliams actually stopped supporting Davies when the president of the National Farmers' Union (NFU) sent a telegram urging the party to pick him. Others felt that Davies would be a poor constituency MP and by-election campaigner. 'The ladies felt that in a constituency like ours it's very necessary to canvass,' Jack Vincent explained. 'They just couldn't see Mr John Davies canvassing in the way that it would be necessary, particularly in the winter months.'[16]

On the first round of voting, Archer and Davies tied on twenty-two votes each, and David Walder was eliminated. So it all depended on how the Walder supporters divided. Trevor Knight, the Young Conservative chairman from Immingham, got up and said Archer would be ideal for attracting young voters like himself, in preference to a candidate sent by Central Office who'd been earmarked for higher things. But there were many with reservations. Wasn't Archer too young, too London-orientated and too flashy? 'A lot of the discussion afterwards,' says Peter Walker, 'was on how could we have a young man who was so gauche and knew nothing about agriculture, against an urbanite who raised the question of how long he was going to be a member.' Walker believes the crucial intervention came from the party president, Donald Webb, who was also a local NFU official. 'He said, "Why should we expect this man to know anything about agriculture? He's young and vigorous." And the crunch was, "He comes from a family with a history of public service." . . . It was largely about "Why are we arguing about detail? He looks right and he sounds right. If he doesn't know about farming, if we can't teach him, who can?" [17]

After about three and a half hours, Jack Vincent went to find the two rivals waiting anxiously outside. Archer was invited back into the hall and presented as the executive's nominee, to be endorsed formally at a full meeting of the association a week later. He had won by a margin of just three: twenty-nine votes to twenty-six.

Davies went on to become MP for Knutsford and quickly joined the Cabinet in 1970, only to discover that he was not really suited to politics. It must have been galling, however, to lose the nomination for Louth to a man barely half his age. 'The truth is that I was not worthy to be a candidate in his place,' Archer said many years later. 'He lost with a dignity I have never since seen equalled in public life.' [18]

There had been a degree of adventurousness about the Louth party's decision. They recognized they were taking a gamble with Archer. Few of them had ever met anyone like him before. 'It was like inviting a pop star to dinner, choosing this slick young man and his pretty wife,' says Pat Otter, a local journalist. 'An element of Carnaby Street and the Beatles had been transferred into rural Lincolnshire. Here was a man who actually knew the Beatles!' [19]

It was a remarkable achievement for Archer. It is unusual for any politician to secure a safe seat while still in their twenties; boundary changes permitting, he was set up for life. To a large extent, however, Archer had been chosen on a negative vote, as he later admitted: 'Those who were not wanting John Davies were looking for an alternative, and I appeared to be the alternative in every way.' [20] And, of course, they liked Mary. But then, having surprised everyone by winning the nomination, Jeffrey very nearly lost it again.

The following day, when news of Archer's selection broke, the UNA chairman Humphry Berkeley sprang into action. He immediately wrote to Edward Heath; to the Tory chief whip, William Whitelaw; and to the new party chairman, Anthony Barber, complaining about Archer's time at the UNA. Berkeley enclosed a collection of documents in support.

Berkeley's concerns had first arisen the year before, in the summer of 1968. One day the UNA finance officer, a certain Charles Dickens, had approached him and expressed anxiety about Archer's expense claims.

They were much more than anything he'd been asked to approve before, and Dickens was worried about what the auditors might say. When he asked to examine the paperwork, the UNA chairman was astonished.

The first bill Berkeley noticed was for a date he wouldn't easily forget: the day in April 1968 when he himself had resigned from the Conservative Party over race-relations policy. Archer's claim, Berkeley later said, was for 'lunch with two millionaires' at the Rib Room of the Carlton Tower Hotel (a favourite Archer eating-spot), but the UNA chairman immediately suspected it was incorrect. Berkeley remembered vividly how that morning, with reporters flocking to his flat, he'd invited Chris Chataway out to lunch. Chataway already had a lunch engagement – with Jeffrey Archer – so the three men went out together, to the Carlton Tower.

After seeing Archer's bill, Berkeley immediately rang the Carlton Tower Hotel to check whether they still had a record of the lunch. Surprised to learn they did, he gave them the receipt number and asked if they could say who paid it. The answer, he later related, was himself, Mr H. J. Berkeley, on a cheque from Barclay's Bank, 137 Brompton Road.

Berkeley soon assigned his personal assistant to spend several days quietly examining all Archer's other expenses. In all, according to Berkeley, he found incorrect claims from sixty or so separate occasions.

In particular, Archer appeared to have repeated the Carlton Tower mistake with another lunch involving himself, the UNA treasurer, Lord Luke and Jack Cohen, the founder of Tesco. *Private Eye* later reported that another disputed lunch had been with Dr Michael Hooker, who ran the fund-raising consultants Hooker–Craigmyle. This was for £8 4s 4d for the meal, together with eighty miles' travelling expenses at 9d a mile. 'Dr Hooker has told the UNA that he paid for the lunch, and even sent a chauffeur-driven car to collect Archer from County Hall . . . and deliver him back afterwards.'[21] Hooker, a former Conservative candidate, would later confirm that the *Eye* account was correct.

In September 1968 Archer had told the UNA director-general, John Ennals, that discrepancies in his expenses might be explained by 'their hurried presentation'.[22] And a year later the Louth Conservative chairman, Jack Vincent, concluded the errors were simply a matter of careless-ness and working under pressure.[23] These explanations seem a little strange when one considers that during the very same period Archer's colleagues on the GLC were so impressed with his diligence in filling in expenses and his mastery of the council's complicated claim forms that they were willing to pay for his services.

Humphry Berkeley's recollection of the number of disputed claims and the total amount involved, which, some years later, he put at £1,000 – well over a quarter of Archer's annual salary – may well have been an exaggeration. In October 1968, according to *The Times*, Archer agreed to repay the UNA £82; he himself would not confirm this figure but later said the sum had been 'trivial'.[24] When asked many years later about the amount of the refund, Archer's solicitor said that his 'recollection is that the sum involved was a little under £150'.[25]

The UNA chairman's second allegation to Edward Heath and Central Office in 1969 was arguably just as serious: that on an official form Humphry Berkeley had been named as a partner in Archer's business, Arrow Enterprises. When Berkeley discovered the error, he made Archer sign the following declaration: 'I hereby indemnify Mr Berkeley from any of the effects of his having been held out by me as a partner in the venture during the period from May 10, 1968, to December 10, 1968.'[26]

Berkeley had actually presented these allegations to the director of organization at Conservative Central Office, Sir Richard Webster, in 1968, a year before Archer was chosen to fight Louth. The UNA chairman had argued that Archer's behaviour was so serious that he should be struck off the candidates' list. No action had been taken then, but, since Berkeley had only recently resigned from the party, one can perhaps understand this reluctance to follow his advice.

Even before Archer was selected in October 1969, disquieting stories had reached one or two ears in Louth – the daughter of one official, who lived in London, had passed on details of Jeffrey's habit of doing GLC councillors' expenses for commission. Now came Berkeley's more serious allegations that Archer had overstated his own claims.

Archer's selection was due to be confirmed at a gathering of the whole party membership a week after the original selection meeting. The evening before, he was summoned to an emergency session with Louth party officials, who interrogated him at length about the UNA chairman's claims. 'They ranged from the trivial to the unbelievable,' says a former official, Henry Sharpley.[27] Archer's business colleague Geoffrey Rippon, a member of the Shadow Cabinet, added his support by arguing that the affair was 'a storm in a teacup'.[28] Moreover, Humphry Berkeley was not the kind of person likely to win favour in a place like Lincolnshire, and the local party felt he was motivated by personal jealousy as he had lost his own parliamentary seat in 1966. Archer offered to resign, but Louth officials wouldn't have it.

Berkeley remained determined to unseat Archer, however, and enlisted the support of Anthony Barber's predecessor as party chairman, Edward du Cann, while staying overnight at du Cann's home in Somerset. Du Cann wrote to both Barber and the chief whip, Willie Whitelaw, suggesting that the writ for the by-election should be delayed. But since du Cann was on bad terms with the party leadership, his opinion was not likely to carry much weight either.

It was several weeks, however, before any hint of the allegations reached the newspapers. Humphry Berkeley gave a copy of his dossier to a friend, William Rees-Mogg, the editor of *The Times*, who assigned a young reporter, John Clare, to investigate the charges. Clare says he then went through the report with Berkeley – 'mostly a collection of photostats of expenses claims' – to assess the strength of the evidence, but felt obliged to obtain Archer's response. Unable to get hold of him on the phone, the journalist travelled up to Louth and learned that Archer planned to return to London by train first thing the next morning. Clare got to Louth station before the candidate arrived, but, when he tried to introduce himself, he recalls that 'Archer got very agitated and walked away from me'. They eventually boarded the train together.[29]

As they sat talking *en route* for King's Cross, Archer at first denied everything, says Clare. But with the Berkeley dossier in front of him in the carriage, Clare systematically went through the allegations. 'It was clear,' Clare says, 'from Archer's response to each of these rather trivial allegations that each was true. He didn't really pretend otherwise . . . I was quite clear in my mind that what Berkeley said was true.' And Archer was getting increasingly upset until the point, says Clare, that he burst into tears and 'begged me not to write the story'. His reason, the journalist recalls, was that although his constituency officers were 'men of the world' and might not mind, the publicity 'would upset his wife'. Clare thinks Archer hoped that, if he showed how distressed he was, he might be persuaded to drop the matter. Clare explained he had no choice but to proceed.[30] Then, having failed with the soft approach, Archer threatened the newspaper with legal action.

Clare delivered his report to Rees-Mogg, but, to his surprise, it only appeared in *The Times* in a greatly truncated form. Rees-Mogg, a former

Conservative candidate, may have felt some sympathy for the aspiring politician. Perhaps he thought it would be wrong to ruin a promising career on the basis of offences that some people might regard as relatively trivial.

Apart from the press, the other big danger for Conservative officials was that Berkeley's allegations would be leaked to the opposition parties by UNA staff. But here Archer was greatly assisted by the internal conflict raging within the UNA between Berkeley and the organization's director-general, John Ennals.

As an enemy of Berkeley, Archer fell into the Ennals camp, even though Ennals was a left-wing socialist (and brother of the Labour minister David Ennals). Indeed, when Jack Vincent asked Archer for two employers' references, Archer suggested Ennals and Frank Hooley, the Labour MP who was chairman of the UNA Finance Committee. At one point Jack Vincent and Clixby Fitzwilliams even went to see Hooley at the Commons – producing the strange spectacle of Tory constituency officials asking a Labour MP to give a clean bill of health to their by-election candidate. 'His advice was not to see Humphry Berkeley,' says Fitzwilliams, 'and that it was a personal feud.' They returned to Louth and 'reported it was a storm in a tea cup and that Labour wouldn't make much of it'.[31]

Nevertheless, Anthony Barber asked Jack Vincent to come back to London and listen to Humphry Berkeley present his case in person. After two hours, the Louth chairman remained convinced that the charges were 'a lot of rubbish'.[32]

Yet Vincent had been placed in a problematic position by his previous support for John Davies: it would have been difficult for him to start querying Archer's candidature, especially after a visit to Central Office, the very body that was thought in Louth to have been promoting John Davies. Publicly Vincent argued that Archer had simply made careless mistakes through pressure of work.

Berkeley's charges finally appeared in the press in mid-November 1969, at the start of the by-election campaign. Barber immediately told Archer he had two options – 'either not to proceed with his candidature or to take appropriate legal action to refute the allegations'.[33] For Archer, it meant only one choice, and he issued a writ at once, suing Berkeley for libel and slander and thereby discouraging anyone from raising the issue during the rest of the campaign.

Nowadays Jeffrey Archer would not have survived a day as a by-election candidate. At the slightest whiff of scandal, journalists would have begun investigating; copies of Berkeley's correspondence would have surfaced in every national newsroom. With the intense scrutiny by-elections now receive from press and television, it would have been impossible even for Archer to continue.

As it was, the Humphry Berkeley row had remarkably little impact on the voters of Louth, where Archer began his campaign by forecasting a majority of more than 10,000 – a rash promise when the best Sir Cyril Osborne had ever attained in twenty-four years was 8,803, in 1959. His last majority, in 1966, had been only 4,092.

It was still an era of political public meetings, and Archer held nearly thirty in all. The biggest star to come and support him was the Shadow Chancellor, Iain Macleod; other speakers included Jim Prior and Chris Chataway, who had recently returned to Parliament by winning a by-election in Chichester. The pattern was to concentrate on a different cluster of villages each night, with successive meetings at 6.45 p.m., 7.30 p.m. and 8.15 p.m. – a brisk, sharp speech from Jeffrey, no time for questions, then he was off. The speakers would then leapfrog each other from one village hall to the next. It took great coordination and effort, but the voters still expected it.

One curious aspect of Archer's campaign was that his posters were red, rather than the usual Tory blue. Red was the traditional Conservative colour in that part of Lincolnshire, after the hunting colours of the local aristocrats; and the present local MP, Sir Peter Tapsell, still sports a splash of red on his election rosettes.

Archer's leaflets stressed his supposed farming background, and the local press regularly mentioned that he was a television commentator. This caused some voters to mistake him for Geoffrey Archer, a well-known reporter who had just left the local ITV station, Anglia. But if Jeffrey Archer picked up votes from people thinking he was a local TV presenter, then, in a neat twist, Geoffrey Archer would inadvertently turn the tables many years later. In the mid-1980s (by which time he was ITN's defence correspondent) Geoffrey Archer published a series of thrillers, undoubtedly gaining readers who mistook him for his namesake.

Archer treated the campaign like a marginal, and seemed nervous about the result, but a Conservative seat was hardly likely to produce a shock during an unpopular Labour government. The thing everyone remembers about the three-week contest was the atrocious weather –

wind, rain, hail, snow, icy roads. It was 'crucifyingly cold', says Archer's agent, Peter Walker.[34] On polling-day, 4 December, it snowed heavily. The result was declared in Louth town hall the following lunchtime:

| | |
|---|---|
| Jeffrey Archer (Conservative) | 16,317 |
| Bruce Briggs (Labour) | 5,590 |
| John Adams (Liberal) | 5,003 |
| Sir George Fitzgerald (Democratic) | 1,225 |
| CONSERVATIVE MAJORITY | 10,727 |

Archer proclaimed himself the 'Lincolnshire poacher', having more than doubled the Tory majority and achieved a swing of 14.3 per cent from Labour.[35] He had fulfilled his initial campaign promise, with a winning margin of more than 10,000.

Jeffrey Archer had secured a place in Parliament before the age of thirty, but his libel suit against Humphry Berkeley dragged on for another three years. It was finally concluded with a brief High Court hearing in February 1973, when Archer settled just as the case was about to come to trial. In a deal brokered by the journalist and future Cabinet minister, Jonathan Aitken, Humphry Berkeley did not have to retract a single word or make any public apology; his only concession was to agree that neither side should ever disclose the terms of the settlement. Archer was left to pay both Berkeley's costs of around £17,000 and his own legal bill, which was thought to be even higher.

Archer's original writ had saved his candidacy, and silenced discussion of the allegations during the by-election campaign. But it had cost him almost £40,000 – about twice the total parliamentary salary he earned during his five years as an MP.

Berkeley stuck by his allegations to the very end, and refused to retract a single detail. None the less, the UNA chairman had come under some pressure to withdraw, most notably during an extraordinary episode involving a Nobel prize.

Around the middle of 1970, the UNA public relations officer, Colin Harris – an ally of Berkeley's – took a mysterious phone call. It came from a man calling himself Thyssen, who claimed to be acting on behalf of the UN Secretariat in New York. He said he'd been sent to London by the secretary-general, U Thant, to gather details about Humphry Berkeley, with a view to his nomination for the Nobel peace prize. Thyssen wanted Harris to compile a dossier of Berkeley's achievements as UNA chairman, and could he also meet Harris as a matter of urgency?

Thyssen was reluctant to visit the UNA office, and suggested instead that they meet in the foyer of the Savoy Hotel that same evening.

Thyssen was in his early thirties, quiet, soberly dressed and rather nondescript. Harris's first impression was that he did not have the image, confidence and manner of a senior UN emissary. And despite his name, he had no obvious Germanic features and was quite English in speech and appearance. Harris also noted that Thyssen appeared nervous and ill at ease, as if anxious not to prolong the meeting any more than necessary. He gave Thyssen the report he'd requested, but the UN official didn't seem interested and barely glanced at it. Instead, he took great pains to impress upon Harris that an absolutely essential prerequisite for anyone even to be considered for nomination for the Nobel prize was that there should not be the slightest whiff of scandal or controversy hanging over them.

'I understand,' he reportedly went on to say, 'that Mr Berkeley is involved in some kind of legal dispute. This could be most unfortunate, as the existence of any outstanding legal action would ruin his chance of nomination for the peace prize. I think it's something you may want to pass on to Mr Berkeley.' Having made his point, and with nothing further to say, Thyssen got up and left. He gave Colin Harris no means of contact, not even a business card.

A few days later Harris was phoned out of the blue by Jeffrey Archer. 'I gather you've had a call from a chap called Thyssen about Humphry and the Nobel peace prize,' he apparently said. 'It would be a great pity if Humphry's chances were to be thrown away as a result of this libel business. Don't you think that, as a close friend whom he trusts, you ought to have a word with Humphry about settling the matter?'

Nothing more was heard from the mysterious Thyssen, who vanished without trace. When Harris told Berkeley about him, the UNA chairman checked with the UN in New York, which denied having any employee of that name. Harris and Berkeley concluded that Thyssen was a hoax, an out-of-work actor, perhaps, who needed the money, but had neither the heart nor the talent to play the part convincingly. If indeed it was a deception, it was a very elaborate one.

As for poor Humphry Berkeley, he was never a serious contender for the Nobel peace prize. That year, it went instead to an American food biologist.

# 12

# The Dash for Cash

The blurbs on his book covers invariably repeat Jeffrey Archer's proud claim that he was the 'youngest member of the House of Commons when he won the by-election at Louth in 1969'.[1] Archer has made the boast in numerous interviews; it's still in the potted biography he sends people, and he has even said it under oath in court. It's been repeated hundreds of times in newspaper, television and radio stories, even by experienced political journalists who should know better. For it's not true.

Jeffrey Archer was elected an MP on 4 December 1969, at the age of 29 years and 233 days. Earlier that same year, in April, in a much more famous by-election, Bernadette Devlin (now McAliskey) had won the Mid Ulster seat on the day before her twenty-second birthday. As was widely reported, she was the youngest person to be elected MP for half a century. Devlin was seven years and eight days younger than Archer.

Could Jeffrey Archer instead claim to be the youngest *British* MP in 1969? No. Two Labour MPs already had better claims to that: John Ryan, who had been elected for Uxbridge at the 1966 general election, was fifteen days younger than Archer, while Les Huckfield, who won the Nuneaton by-election in March 1967, was almost two years his junior.

Even so, at the time he was chosen as candidate, Archer could at least have had hopes of becoming the youngest *Conservative* MP. But then even that title was snatched from his grasp when only five weeks before the Louth poll, the Tories won another by-election, in Swindon. The town's new MP, Christopher Ward, was more than two and a half years younger than his colleague from Louth. With Devlin, Ryan, Huckfield and now Ward already installed on the green benches, Jeffrey Archer could merely claim to be the fifth most junior member of the Commons. It's a record hardly worth mentioning.

The claim of being the youngest MP has been another of Jeffrey

Archer's fantasies, a plausible-sounding assertion. Fortunately for him, people forget quite when Bernadette Devlin or Les Huckfield were elected, and don't even remember John Ryan or Christopher Ward. Everyone takes Jeffrey's word for it.

For his first four months in the Commons, Archer remained on the GLC and continued attending important council meetings. This, and his outside business interests, may partly explain why it took so long before he delivered his maiden speech. Most freshly elected MPs are eager to speak as soon as possible, no matter what the subject, to make their mark with their colleagues; not Archer. Apart from one or two minor interventions, he waited four and a half months, until five days after his thirtieth birthday, to make his first speech in the House. It's surprising for a man with such energy and vitality, but in all the chambers to which Archer has belonged – County Hall, the House of Commons and the House of Lords – his speeches have been comparatively rare. But when he does choose to pronounce, his words are usually well prepared.

In fact Archer had planned to speak four weeks earlier, in a debate on drugs. He briefed himself by visiting junkies around Piccadilly Circus with Caroline Coon, the director of Release, the drugs-help group. 'While I am adamant that only the sternest sentences are good enough for pushers,' Archer was quoted as saying, 'I am in favour of greater leniency and tolerance towards addicts.'[2] It was a surprisingly liberal view for a Tory MP at that time, and certainly not the sort of thing one would have heard from Sir Cyril Osborne. On the day of the debate, however, Archer got flu, and pulled out.

His maiden speech was finally delivered during the debate on Roy Jenkins's 1970 Budget. Surprisingly perhaps for an Opposition MP, he congratulated the Chancellor – for cutting taxes – though he must have been teasing when he praised it as a 'non-electioneering Budget', since many Labour MPs feared that Jenkins had not cut taxes enough, given that an election was imminent.[3]

It proved to be Archer's only speech during that Parliament, for Harold Wilson called the poll four weeks later. Also just in time, Archer announced that he'd bought a home in his constituency, in the village of Brigsley, six miles south of Grimsby, though it was several months before he moved in. The imperilled East Lincolnshire railway was the main local issue of the new campaign. Labour trebled its by-election vote with a new candidate (and indeed gained the highest vote the party had ever achieved in Louth) and Archer's majority fell slightly, but it was still a comfortable 9,256.

He was now returning to Westminster under a Conservative government, following Edward Heath's surprise victory. The chairman of the Archer Gallery, Geoffrey Rippon, was now in the Cabinet, first at Technology and then looking after the EEC negotiations, while Archer's mentor, Chris Chataway, was the new Minister of Posts and Telecommunications. Jeffrey might have entertained some hope that Chataway would again make him his personal assistant, or PPS in parliamentary terms. Just as in Bridgwater, Tom King beat him to it.

In any case, Archer was not desperate for immediate preferment. His political career was already well ahead of schedule, with what looked to be a safe seat for life. During the rest of 1970 Archer made only one more substantial speech in the Commons – on whether Lincolnshire should be transferred from the Anglia ITV region to the stewardship of Yorkshire Television. It was a highly emotive issue given the traditional animosity of many Lincolnshire people towards their Yorkshire neighbours. The MP whom some voters had mistaken for an Anglia reporter supported the East Anglian station's attempt to preserve its boundaries. It was the beginning of a long, and later highly controversial, association between the Archers and the TV company.

During his first twelve months in the House, Archer had delivered just two speeches; *Hansard* shows he also made three short interventions in debates, and asked five oral questions. He was a surprisingly inactive MP, but his low Commons profile is partly explained by what Adrian Metcalfe describes as Archer's 'Dash for Cash'. 'He was quite open that for his political career to prosper he should have sufficient capital to become a serious politician,' says Metcalfe. 'He wanted to sustain his lifestyle and have a proper political office.'[4] For the time being, business came first.

Arrow Enterprises had begun in 1969 in a small office in Lincoln's Inn Fields, though it transferred to the top floor of Grafton Street when the Archer Gallery opened later that year. Archer's shrewdest move, however, was not in his office location, but in his choice of business partners. Sir Noel Hall agreed for his name to be added to the Arrow notepaper, but the most important catches were two retired generals who were both fellow governors of Dover College. The generals, who were good friends of each other, were delighted when Archer asked them to come and work for him. With their meagre army pensions, they were glad to have the extra income, but also pleased to be doing something more interesting than the worthy jobs normally taken by retired army officers.

They brought the Establishment clout that Archer needed. Sir Gerald Duke, the chairman of the Dover governors, had recently retired as engineer-in-chief to the British army, while Sir William Oliver had served as the British representative to the great Expo '67 fair in Montreal. More important still, as a former British High Commissioner to Australia, Sir William had excellent contacts with Buckingham Palace. One of his first achievements for Arrow Enterprises was to get the Queen Mother to open the new Institute of Chartered Accountants hall in the City of London.

'The two generals were sensational,' says Adrian Metcalfe. 'Oliver made sure everyone was looked after – he knew the royals. Duke was good on planning events. They were thrilled to death. Here was this bouncy young man who pulled off extraordinary coups. They were fearless in playing their part in ventures, but they were clever.'[5] Archer was exploiting their names and rank, of course, but they understood perfectly well what he was up to, were happy to play along with it, and quietly enjoyed mixing with show business. And their gravitas and connections were the perfect balance to Jeffrey's impulsive energy.

It was all rather fun, and the generals ensured that the office ate well. 'They never slummed it there,' says Gerald Duke's son Peter. 'It was always a matter of principle that they had a reasonable hamper-type lunch . . . a good bottle of wine and good food prepared at home and brought into the office.'[6]

For most of 1970 the generals were busily helping with the biggest fund-raising event Archer had yet attempted – indeed, one of the most ambitious charity shows ever staged in Britain. It was the occasion which, by his own admission, confirmed his reputation as a fund-raiser, but gained him both admirers and critics in abundance.

Early in 1969 Archer had received a summons to visit the London flat of Earl Mountbatten of Burma. Mountbatten had noticed the success of the fund-raising dinner for the European Movement, and asked Archer to suggest money-making ideas for a charity he presided over. The United World Colleges was an organization founded by Kurt Hahn, the German refugee who had been headmaster of Gordonstoun. He was developing a network of schools around the world for sixteen- to eighteen-year-olds, designed to be character-building and, in Mountbatten's words, to provide 'an opportunity for future leaders to get to understand each other'.[7] The initial school had been Atlantic College, near St Donats on the South Wales coast, and Mountbatten wanted to raise a million pounds to set up several more colleges worldwide.

Archer's initial suggestion was audacious: a big concert featuring a double bill of Bob Hope and Frank Sinatra. 'Lord Mountbatten had got them within a fortnight,' he explained later. 'That's his attitude: you put up any idea and he can conquer it.'[8]

The idea evolved into a plan to hold two separate concerts, on the same night at different locations – the Albert Hall and the Royal Festival Hall. The venture was quickly dubbed the 'Night of Nights'. For most of 1970 both his parliamentary duties and the Archer Gallery took a lower billing, as Archer devoted most of his effort into putting the programme together. Occasionally he would travel down at weekends to see Mountbatten at his country home, Broadlands. Archer finally managed to book the Albert Hall on a night which Sinatra and Hope could both manage, but only after persuading Eric Morley to give up an evening of rehearsals for that year's Miss World contest. With Hope and Sinatra pencilled in for that venue, he tried to line up Richard Burton, Elizabeth Taylor and Leonard Bernstein for the simultaneous show at the Royal Festival Hall. But Mountbatten soon realized that the double event was a bad idea. Bernstein didn't like the thought of being in competition with the Sinatra/Hope concert; according to Mountbatten's diary, the conductor 'feared that when Sinatra and Hope heard there was going to be a rival show the same night they would start trying to get out of their engagement'.[9]

The plans were changed: now Hope and Sinatra would appear at one venue, the Royal Festival Hall, but the idea of a double event was retained when it was decided to run the same show twice in the same evening. As a bonus, Mountbatten persuaded Sir Noël Coward to act as compère. A colleague warned Archer that Coward was a sick man, however, and sure enough, with just five days to go, Sir Noël's secretary rang Archer to say he'd been taken to hospital with pleurisy. That evening the MP phoned Mountbatten for a frantic consultation. The two men agreed they should set their sights higher, not lower, and Jeffrey was asked to draw up a short list.

The Arrow staff sat in the Grafton Street office mulling over various names – Maurice Chevalier, Marlene Dietrich and Bing Crosby. 'We spoke to Maurice Chevalier,' says one of Archer's former staff, 'but he was in hypochondriac mood. We tried Dietrich but couldn't find her. Bing Crosby was actually staying at the Savoy, but he and Sinatra had had a tiff.' Then someone had an inspiration. How about the former Hollywood star Grace Kelly, now Princess Grace of Monaco? She hadn't appeared on stage since marrying Prince Rainier in 1956.

Archer rang Mountbatten back. The princess was a wonderful idea, Mountbatten thought, and he promised to ring her if Jeffrey could get hold of her number and arrange a time. Archer's secretary, Judy Horlington, rang the palace in Monte Carlo, and asked to be put through to the princess's office. 'Speaking,' she was astonished to hear. Archer then took the phone and told Princess Grace to expect a call from Mountbatten later that evening. When the earl rang, she immediately accepted his invitation to come over to London and host the Night of Nights.

When Archer flew to Monaco the next morning to iron out the details, he found the principality in mourning for General de Gaulle, whose funeral was taking place that day. Princess Grace explained that in the circumstances she wasn't really in the right mood to host a concert, but she would still come, since it was all to help children who might fall into bad ways. She seems to have misunderstood the purpose of Mountbatten's colleges: often the pupils had rather privileged backgrounds, and in many cases their parents paid for them to go. Frank Sinatra sent his private jet to collect the actress, with whom he'd once appeared in *High Society*.

Mountbatten opened each show with a long, tedious speech about the United World Colleges, before handing over to Princess Grace. She in turn introduced the other stars. Bob Hope performed for an hour in the first half, aided by David Frost and Miss World, who had small walk-on parts; Sinatra sang after the interval. Curiously, there was no big moment when all three stars appeared together. The first concert, which started at 9.00 p.m., was watched by Princess Alexandra and her husband. For the second, at 11.30 p.m., Archer's royal go-between, Sir William Oliver, welcomed Prince Charles and Princess Anne.

'It's a cheap evening for Anne and me, as we haven't paid,' Prince Charles joked.[10] Then, when it was all over, at about two in the morning, the prince and his sister invited the stars, Mountbatten, Archer and 270 guests back to St James's Palace for a party which continued until 4.30 a.m. Mountbatten was presented with a magnificent ice-cream cake, intricately decorated with Bob Hope and Frank Sinatra's faces in the middle, and a blank space where Noël Coward's features had hurriedly been covered over at the last moment. It had been made by Wall's, who had the Festival Hall's ice-cream concession and had agreed to donate the evening's profits to the World Colleges. The cake was the idea of the Wall's public-relations officer, Michael Stacpoole, and it was the start of a long friendship with Archer.

The following Sunday, highlights of the concerts were transmitted by the BBC, which featured the event on the front cover of the *Radio Times*. Sinatra's performance was repeated five weeks later on Boxing Day.

However, the Night of Nights was far from a critical triumph. The *Evening Standard* critic wrote of 'a slight feeling of disappointment' as Bob Hope told old jokes and Frank Sinatra forgot his words. And Princess Grace, he said, 'could hardly be described as anything more than dazzlingly ornamental'.[11]

Though it wasn't a sell-out, the occasion was reckoned to have made almost £200,000. Seat prices had ranged from five to fifty pounds. Archer's lucrative deal for television rights earned £25,000 from the BBC, while foreign networks contributed more. Immediately after the event, however, Archer came in for considerable criticism for his practice of taking a percentage commission. 'Mr $4\frac{1}{2}$%', boomed a headline in *The Sun*, rather underestimating Archer's normal rate. The young impresario threatened to take the paper to the Press Council. He was getting a flat fee, he said:

> We never take a percentage from our work for charity. What we do is charge a fee for the work involved. In this case the fee will probably be around £4,000. When you consider that the operation will raise around £150,000 to £175,000 for the United World Colleges Fund that is hardly extortionate.[12]

Yet, two weeks earlier, Archer had told another paper:

> If you raise £450 for someone, and take £45, then that's supposed to be all right. But if you raise £450,000 and take £45,000, that's supposed to be wicked. People still think it a crime to make money through charity. Not *sensible* people though. Not business people.[13]

Despite his denials, Arrow Enterprises had certainly proposed percentage deals in the past; unsuccessfully to the United Nations Association, and successfully to the European Movement, at least until the arrangement had to be changed because of Harold Wilson's objections.

Lord Mountbatten wrote to congratulate Archer on the success of the evening, although he was also upset that the Night of Nights hadn't generated more extensive press coverage. 'What went wrong with the British public-relations aspect?' Mountbatten asked. The only publication with a generous spread of pictures was the French magazine *Paris Match*. Even then Mountbatten was furious that the journal had made the 'ghastly' statement that his colleges were for 'difficult' children.[14]

Ever since his Oxfam days, Archer had suffered from not being able to repeat a fund-raising triumph for the same body. The second event for the United World Colleges took place the following March and had Leonard Bernstein conducting the Vienna Philharmonic Orchestra at the Albert Hall. It was 'a glorious performance', *The Times* said, but it hardly covered the organizer in glory.[15] Guided by Mountbatten's advice and his own optimism, Archer set prices far too high, and only about half the seats were taken. The sparse audience was rather embarrassing, since it included both the Queen Mother and the Prime Minister, Edward Heath, who later entertained the stars and main guests in Downing Street. This time Archer also had problems selling the television rights.

Kurt Hahn's sister-in-law, Lola, was particularly upset that the Bernstein concert flopped; the failure marked the end of Archer's work for Mountbatten and the United World Colleges.

Arrow's next big event, a concert for the mental-health charity MIND, proved to be an even bigger disaster. He'd approached MIND's campaign director, David Ennals, the former Labour minister, who had sat briefly with Archer in the Commons (and was the brother of John Ennals of the UNA). At the age of sixty-seven, Marlene Dietrich was willing to make her first appearance in London for more than six years. Would MIND be interested in having it as a fund-raising show? Ennals naturally said yes, but shrewdly stipulated in the contract that MIND would be guaranteed £10,000, no matter how well the concert did. Thereafter the profit would be divided on a percentage basis. Reluctantly, Archer agreed. 'Instead of the concert being a flaming, brilliant success,' says Ennals, 'it was quite difficult to sell the tickets.'[16]

In the presence of Princess Alexandra, Dietrich 'carried it all off like a dream', said the *Evening Standard*.[17] She even sang 'Naughty Lola', no doubt for Jeffrey's benefit. The *Daily Telegraph* noted how it was a 'surprisingly young audience', without revealing why: only about a third of the seats had been sold, and the Theatre Royal, Drury Lane, was filled near to capacity only when MIND gave away hundreds of tickets to nurses.[18] Again, it didn't help that Archer had pitched the prices too high – up to fifty pounds each. 'Knock some noughts off, Jeffrey, and let's be practical,' one colleague remembers telling him, but the advice was ignored.

If the income was disappointing, the outgoings were disastrous. Dietrich had demanded a hefty fee and the best hotel accommodation, and she enjoyed a lavish lifestyle; then there was the cost of her minders and musical backing, and the expense of hiring and staffing the theatre. Archer lost badly, since he also had to pay the £10,000 guaranteed to MIND.

Another failure was Arrow's work for the National Society for Cancer Relief. Archer had been recruited to the charity by its president, Michael Sobell, an industrialist he'd met through the UNA Downing Street dinner in 1968. Archer proposed that, to mark the society's diamond-jubilee celebrations, it should establish the Lillian Board Cancer Appeal, in memory of the Olympic runner who had died in 1970. The appeal was promised a gala concert along the lines of the Night of Nights, involving 'Miss Barbra Streisand and another stage personality of international reputation'. But Archer was unable to book them, and his contract was cancelled.[19] The charity had hoped to raise £1 million for a cancer clinic, but the appeal eventually closed after reaching only a third of its target.

Archer seemed to be losing his touch as an impresario. But he made a final effort at pulling off the two most ambitious musical fund-raising projects one could possibly imagine – bringing Elvis Presley to Britain for the first time, and reuniting the Beatles on stage.

To entice Elvis, Archer and Sir William Oliver flew to Las Vegas and booked into the hotel where the star was performing, having only just resumed doing live shows. Archer's mission was leaked to the press, however, and a reporter got through by phone from London. 'What makes you think I have been seeing Mr Presley?' a familiar clipped voice demanded. Then, it suddenly switched to an American accent: 'I think you have got the wrong Mr Archer. I am not the person you think I am. You must have got me muddled with someone else.'[20] But

Presley's manager, Colonel Tom Parker, was adamant that his star would stay on that side of the Atlantic.

Archer's attempt to bring the Beatles back together involved long discussions with their manager, Allen Klein. He and Klein drove round the southern English countryside in the white sheepskin-lined Rolls Royce in which John Lennon was said to have made love to Yoko Ono. They were viewing possible sites for a giant open-air concert: Lord Montagu's estate at Beaulieu in Hampshire was among the places considered. Then Archer decided to hold his great Beatles comeback concert at Wembley, and even went as far as booking the stadium and arranging compensation for disturbed local residents. The effort was wasted. The problem wasn't the venue but the acrimony between the individual Beatles.

Despite these show-business moves, Archer carried on with more traditional fund-raising for the European Movement. With Edward Heath's election and the death of General de Gaulle in France, the prospects of Britain joining the Common Market suddenly looked good. It would be the Heath government's great historic achievement, but, as Geoffrey Rippon began negotiations, initial opinion polls suggested public opinion was hostile to the idea of joining the EEC. Rippon told the European Movement's director, Ernest Wistrich, that politically there was a limit to how much the government itself could campaign for Europe; an independent effort was needed to transform public opinion.

Geoffrey Rippon held an informal lunch at the Cabinet Office, and invited several key players – Wistrich; Lord Harlech, the chairman of the European Movement; Jeffrey Archer; and the financial whiz-kid Jim Slater. Slater had made millions from his investment business, Slater Walker, in conjunction with Rippon's Cabinet colleague Peter Walker. After this meeting, Wistrich says, Slater recommended the names of about 'forty up-and-coming young rich men who wouldn't mind making a mark for themselves'.[21] Archer was to spend the next few months approaching the names on Slater's list.

Archer told potential donors they were doing 'something to shape British history', Wistrich says.[22] He was pushing at an open door, for, despite public scepticism, most businessmen were convinced that only membership of the Common Market would halt Britain's relative decline.

Ernest Wistrich reckons that this new phase of Archer's work raised about £1.5 million for his organization. Now the money came upfront in straightforward donations, rather than in seven-year covenants as before. Archer once again took 10 per cent commission, amounting to about £150,000 in all.[23]

Nevertheless, Ernest Wistrich is effusive in his praise for Jeffrey Archer's work. 'I'd paid fees previously to other fund-raisers without even getting the fees back,' he says.[24] The money was used for wide-ranging pro-European propaganda: press advertisements, pamphlets, leaflets, give-away newspapers, T-shirts, and posters showing young children waving flags emblazoned with the slogan 'Say Yes to Europe'. It also paid for opinion polls, and for a team of more than 300 trained speakers to preach the benefits of EEC membership. The European Movement's efforts between 1970 and 1973 did coincide with a signifi-cant shift in public opinion towards Europe. 'If Jeffrey Archer hadn't been there,' says Wistrich, 'it would have been impossible to run the campaign. Archer's money was absolutely crucial.'[25] In fact the funds he raised lasted several years, and later helped fight the 1975 referendum which confirmed Britain's membership of the EEC. It is quite possible that future historians will conclude that this fund-raising was the most politically significant act of Jeffrey Archer's career.

His work for the pro-European cause naturally aroused hostility from anti-marketeers. Particularly embarrassing publicity was caused by a large donation from Michael Sobell of GEC. A former colleague of Archer's distinctly remembers the day Sobell sent a cheque for £300,000; Jeffrey couldn't stop waving it proudly around the office, he recalls. It was intended just as the first instalment of a £600,000 donation the industrialist had promised the campaign.

In the 1972 New Year's Honours List, Sobell was given a knighthood. A few weeks later an obscure anti-EEC pamphlet suggested that Sir Michael had bought his elevation with this donation to the European Movement, and that Archer had acted as the middleman. The allegation was repeated in the *Spectator*, and then raised by the Labour MP Willie Hamilton, who quoted the magazine in the Commons:

'Mr Archer did, I understand, arrange a substantial donation of around £600,000 to the European Movement from Sir Michael Sobell last year. The honour, as I have noted, was given for "charit-able services".'[26]

It was unfortunate, perhaps, for the European Movement that Sobell's donation was pledged in two parts. The first £300,000 cheque had arrived in April 1971, but the second, expected a year later, never turned up. Once the controversy had arisen, it would have been difficult for Sir Michael to send it. And by then, of course, his knighthood was secure.

Willie Hamilton failed, however, to get Archer's conduct referred to the Commons Committee of Privileges, and Edward Heath denounced the allegations as 'a succession of nasty innuendoes based on a series of unfounded and completely irresponsible statements'.[27] But the controversy undermined Archer's reputation with his parliamentary colleagues, bolstering the impression that he was an ambitious hustler.

At the start of 1971, after selling the art gallery, Archer acquired a new base, close to Westminster, where he could combine business and politics. He bought the lease on three floors of offices above a café at 27–31 Whitehall, just down from Trafalgar Square and opposite the Whitehall Theatre. The address was quickly renamed Arrow House, and a sign above the door still bears the name. His former Dover College pupil Julian Dakowski remembers getting a message from Jeffrey at the Commons asking him to redesign the décor, and arrange modern furnishings: 'He said, "Right, I've got this office; it will be very good for you. I can't pay you anything, but it will make your name." '[28]

At one point Adrian Metcalfe, who'd just got a job with the American TV network CBS, took a small space in Arrow House, and observed his friend working at close hand. 'Jeffrey always had a completely clean desk,' he says, 'and he was the first person I knew who had a pocket calculator – a very large one, of course. He'd come in every morning with a piece of white paper with ten words on it – his current projects. He'd spend whatever time it took to work through those projects, doing deals and talking to people. Then the afternoon would be spent on political business.'[29] In practice, however, Arrow Enterprises took up most of his attention; to look after his parliamentary duties, Archer took on some able young assistants.

From early 1971 much of his constituency work was handled by a Cambridge graduate with political ambitions of his own. David Mellor was studying to become a barrister, but needed outside work to pay his way through bar finals and pupillage. It was comparatively rare in those days for politicians to employ researchers, and Mellor had written to every MP he thought might be interested. Archer took him on, and paid him reasonably generously. When Mellor left, in 1973, he was replaced by another aspiring Cambridge graduate, Richard Ryder. It is a mark of Archer's abilities as a talent-spotter that, twenty years later, both would be sitting round the Cabinet table – Mellor as Chief Secretary and then Heritage Secretary, and Ryder as Chief Whip – though their erstwhile employer would remain disappointed not to be there with them.

During his five years in the House, Archer earned a reputation as a lively personality, but hardly established himself as future Cabinet material. 'Though he was very aspirational, he didn't have the patience to master issues,' says a former colleague. 'He liked the idea of politics, but never addressed himself seriously to topics. He couldn't avoid appearing frivolous.' One Conservative who knew Archer well cites his behaviour on the famous night in October 1971 when the Commons voted to take Britain into Europe. As MPs gathered in the Harcourt Room at Westminster, they knew it was a momentous occasion; there was a buzz in the air that they were taking part in history. Archer, too, was excited – but for different reasons. 'Jeffrey kept rushing round telling people how much money he'd won betting on the precise majority,' his colleague recalls.

Yet it would be wrong to ignore Archer's record as an MP. What is most striking was that he was never frightened to rebel against his government, at a time when back-bench dissent was much less common than it is today. The main issue upon which he distinguished himself as an independent spirit was the proposal to impose admission charges on public art galleries and museums. Archer became the most outspoken Tory rebel in a struggle which lasted three years. On several occasions he joined one or two other Tories in the Opposition lobby. This resistance brought Archer into conflict with Margaret Thatcher, who, as Education Secretary, was responsible for the arts, although the actual debates were usually handled by her deputies.

What worried Archer was not the principle of charges, but imposing them on people who could not afford them: deterring children with entrance fees, he argued, might mean that their interest in art or history was never sparked. 'I cannot, under any circumstances, agree to charge the young and the old for admission to museums and art galleries,' he insisted. It was a 'moral question'. The government had 'proposed something which is eminently unfair', and the Tories were undermining their election commitment to be 'the civilized party'.[30]

Archer gained high praise from Labour MPs who hitherto had dismissed him as an upstart and had regularly heckled him with cries of '10 per cent!' 'In a sense, he has helped to save the soul of the Tory Party,' the Labour MP Norman Buchan suggested.[31] 'It was one of the ablest speeches I have heard from the back benches on either side for a long time,' said the long-standing Labour MP George Strauss.[32] In a later debate Archer even came close to disowning his party. 'In my opinion, there is no excuse whatever for making the old pay the charges,' he declared in 1972:

> The people who have the most spare time and the least money are
> the people the Government have decided to hit hardest. If this is
> what Conservative caring is about, and at the last election I thought
> we did care, I made a bad mistake.[33]

Archer voted against his whips after delivering a stout defence of back-benchers' rights to rebel. He feared the day when MPs 'shall be nothing but a bunch of puppets pretending to represent our constituents'.[34] Margaret Thatcher was later forced to make several concessions, partly in response to the campaign waged by Archer and his fellow dissidents, and also by museum curators. Pensioners would now be exempt; there would be one 'free day' a week; and museums and galleries would be allowed to keep some of the takings. The charges were eventually abolished when Labour came to power in 1974.

It was not on this issue alone that Archer was defiant. A study of dissent in the 1970–74 Parliament by Philip Norton (who coincidentally belonged to the Louth Young Conservatives at the time) shows Archer to have been among the most rebellious of all Conservative MPs.[35]

He attacked the abolition of free school milk – another notorious Thatcher measure. He advocated free TV licences for old-age pensioners. He lobbied for the withdrawal of VAT on theatre tickets. He campaigned vigorously against Peter Walker's unpopular reorganization of local government, which transferred part of the Louth constituency from Lincolnshire to the new Humberside (as well as creating the unpopular Avon). He joined the Opposition in urging ministers to do something for workers who lost unemployment benefit when they were laid off by strikes elsewhere. And he joined Labour in condemning French nuclear tests in the Pacific when the government preferred to turn a blind eye. 'I was hoping so hard that I should be able to get through three months without voting against my party,' he teased on the latter occasion.[36] He seemed to revel in being a rebel.

During the first two and a half years of the 1970 Parliament, Archer delivered only twelve speeches in the Commons chamber. It is considerably to his credit, however, that on all but two occasions he attacked government policy. Archer wasn't prepared to waste time making the kind of fawning speeches often heard from ambitious young Tories and indeed often from Lord Archer himself nowadays. Nor was he frightened to criticize ministers face to face; he bravely told Margaret Thatcher, for instance, that one of her answers was 'not a satisfactory reply'.[37] But then Archer could perhaps afford to rebel. He was not yet desperate for office – indeed Adrian Metcalfe says he doesn't think Archer 'would have accepted a PPS's job' at that time.[38] He had a safe seat, and the issues on which he caused trouble were not ones likely to lose votes or upset the constituency party in Louth. Neither were they fundamental matters of economic or foreign policy. Moreover, Archer probably knew enough political history to appreciate that the Tory rebels of one generation are often the leaders of the next – from Disraeli through Churchill, to Eden and Macmillan.

Archer would regularly cite the number of occasions on which he'd defied the Conservative whips. 'I voted against the party and was quite prepared to be the party rebel,' he later explained. 'It didn't seem worth toeing the party line in order to end up as Parliamentary Secretary for Sewage. I could never keep my mouth shut for the sake of my career.'[39] He was delighted when, at one point, his voting record was almost as disloyal as Enoch Powell's. Of course Archer was rebelling on very different issues from Powell: he generally veered to the left of his party, just as his father had in Stepney more than sixty years before. Archer was also a sponsor of the left-wing Tory pressure group PEST (the forerunner of the Tory Reform Group), while the *Daily Telegraph* got so upset over the pinkish nature of one Archer speech that it suggested he 'could be prosecuted under the Trades Descriptions Act for calling himself a Conservative'.[40]

On the great issue which still divides his party – Europe – Archer's credentials were never in doubt, especially after he'd raised so much money for the European Movement. (He also organized the big celebration banquet at Hampton Court when Britain finally entered the EEC in January 1973.) Nevertheless, before casting his vote in the big Europe debates, Archer made a show of consulting his constituents. This was only wise, perhaps, given that many farmers and fishermen in Louth had deep anxieties about how the EEC's agricultural and fisheries policies would affect them.

Capital punishment has always been an equally emotive issue, especially for grass-roots Tories. It was 'barbaric and obscene', Archer felt, but he skilfully coupled his opposition to hanging with demands that murderers be given much longer prison sentences.[41]

On race issues, Archer was a great admirer of Martin Luther King and usually took a liberal line, which is perhaps not surprising given that his foster-sister, Liz, is half-black. On the other hand, he argued it was a great tragedy when the 1970 South African cricket tour to England was cancelled under the pressure of anti-apartheid protests.

Archer always seems to have taken a rather American approach to politics. One suspects that, had he lived in the USA, the Jeffrey Archer of the late 1960s and early 1970s would have been a fairly liberal Democrat. John F. Kennedy, after all, was his great romantic hero. The fictional Florentyna Rosnovski, the Prodigal Daughter of his fourth novel, is also a Democrat.

Jeffrey Archer has never been an ideological politician, or a great policy thinker. To him, politics has always been about people and power. Ernest Wistrich tells a story about having tea with Archer sometime before his election to the Commons, and talking about their respective political ambitions. Wistrich has not forgotten the moment he asked Archer what his specific policies were. 'Jeffrey's typical disarming response was: "Whatever will get me in."'[42]

# 13

# Aquablasted

One Saturday in the summer of 1973, when I was fifteen and starting to take an interest in politics, my father pointed to an article in *The Guardian*. 'It's about this Tory whiz-kid,' he said. (I remember this, because I'd never heard the term before.) 'He's an MP who's become rich making money for charity and taking 10 per cent.' Thus was seeded my interest in Jeffrey Howard Archer.

With fascination I devoured Terry Coleman's profile of this energetic and thrusting MP – 'the sort of man who says "Pass the butter" with enthusiasm'. I learned of his frantic lifestyle, of the property deals over breakfast, and the sixteen hours a day spent making money. I read for the first time the stories of the million he'd helped raise for Oxfam, of how he arranged for the Beatles to dine with Harold Macmillan, of the fund-raising concerts, and of disputes about expenses at the UNA. How did he cram everything in, I wondered, on top of politics? Apparently, he was now a millionaire – though the profile never said so – or at least very well-off. 'I've no need to work ever again in my life,' Archer told Coleman. 'I can now, aged thirty-two, just sit in this room and talk to you for the rest of my life.'[1]

Over the years, Jeffrey Archer had steadily been accumulating the trappings of wealth. He'd had a Coutts bank account since Oxford, of course. Then, in 1970, he bought a cherished car number – ANY 1 – which he'd suddenly spotted on a Jaguar in the street. 'I went up to the owner who was sitting in the parked car and offered to buy it. I explained that I really wanted his registration number. He didn't seem that surprised, and agreed to sell it.' Archer then transferred it to a bronze MGB he now owned, and sold the Jaguar. 'I'm not saying how much I paid for it, but I didn't make a loss on the deal.'[2] The plate later appeared on Archer's E-type Jaguar and then on a blue Daimler. He had also acquired pictures through his ownership of the Archer Gallery – including the Underwood, a Dufy and a Russell Flint.

As well as owning the office in Whitehall, in 1972 Archer had moved his family (their first son, William, was born in May that year) from a small property in Lancaster Mews, near Paddington station, to a five-bedroom £100,000 Georgian-style house in The Boltons, an exclusive oval-shaped street in South Kensington. He also appeared to be so well off that he no longer needed the £3,250 he earned as an MP. 'I donate all my parliamentary salary to charity,' he said.[3]

In January 1973 he acquired another badge of prosperity when he became a member of Lloyd's; it was the beginning of an important association between the Archers and the insurance market. At that time, new members had to show realizable assets of £50,000. He had approached Roger Moate, a young Tory MP who was a director of the Alexander Howden insurance agency and involved in the Lloyd's syndicates run by Ian Posgate. 'Jeffrey expressed an interest in joining those Posgate syndicates, and I then made the introduction,' says Moate.[4] Posgate was winning a reputation (and the nickname 'Goldfinger') from the phenomenal returns he was making on his insurance business, and Archer would be eternally grateful to both men. 'He went to tremendous lengths some years later to say thank you for the introduction because it had been so helpful,' recalls Moate.[5] Quite *how* helpful, we shall see later.

By the summer of 1973 many observers assumed that Archer had already made his first million, and he said nothing to contradict them. Indeed he has since claimed to have been a millionaire at that time.[6] Yet, in reality, it was only the appearance of wealth: people who worked closely with Archer confirm he was nothing like as rich as he seemed. While his work for the European Movement had raised several hundred thousand pounds, there had been a number of failures involving much effort, little reward, and often financial losses – including the Archer Gallery, the Lillian Board appeal, and the Marlene Dietrich concert. And his unsuccessful libel action against Humphry Berkeley had cost almost £40,000. 'It's easier now for a young man to make a million than ever before,' he claimed.[7] In truth, however, Archer wasn't finding it easy: the Dash for Cash was running into trouble.

Towards the end of 1971 Archer redirected the work of Arrow Enterprises. Persuading show-business stars to perform for charity involved much bother, and the uncertainty of selling tickets. And, while dealing with world-famous entertainers might be glamorous and generate enormous interest, the publicity wasn't always favourable. Analysis of Arrow's financial position is difficult because the business never filed any accounts at Companies House, as it should have done. Jeffrey decided that from now on he'd remain in the world of entertainment, but drop the charity bit, and only pursue activities that would make more money. The two generals withdrew from Arrow, and Jeffrey went his own way.

'My company mainly finances films, plays and TV shows,' he would explain, though it's difficult to find any evidence that a film, play or television production was ever assisted by Archer.[8] But it wasn't for want of trying. He met the theatre producer Robert Stigwood, to float the idea of promoting some pop records. He held discussions with a TV producer, Ted Francis, who was seeking funding for a film he was hoping to make based on a book by a writer called Pete Kingsley. He even dabbled with televised boxing. With the backing of Jim Slater's company, Slater Walker, Arrow offered what now seems the absurdly low sum of $190,000 for the TV rights for the world heavyweight fight between George Foreman and Ken Norton in Venezuela, but then Slater Walker pulled out. And while looking for such projects to finance, he had negotiations with a young American banker based in London called Michael Altmann, who was assistant vice-president in charge of film finance for the First National Bank of Boston.

Archer was getting increasingly desperate to find a way to make some quick money. He observed some of the up-and-coming whiz-kids to whom he'd gone for charity donations in the past: John Sunley, now a squash partner, had made his fortune in property; Jim Slater from financial speculation. Perhaps he should try their techniques.

Not long after coming down from Oxford, Archer had begun to take an interest in the stock market. The man who took over his first London flat in Cadogan Place, Michael Buckley, recalls being woken at six o'clock one Saturday morning. 'He'd been given a share tip,' says Buckley, and wanted to know 'how do you buy shares?' Buckley told him how one used a stockbroker. 'Give me his number,' Archer demanded, apparently ignorant of the fact that one couldn't buy shares at the weekend. The eager young investor was soon busily playing the market through Buckley's broker, Frank Watts, who worked for the City firm Rowe Rudd.[9]

A colleague from his days at the UNA in 1967 and 1968 remembers how Archer was constantly asking round the office for good investment tips. And Adrian Metcalfe recalls how 'He went through a phase of being very interested in shares, talking to all the great men of the time.

"What do I go for?" "Do I move out of this?" Jim Slater was always ringing him up and saying "You should go into 'X' and move out of 'Y'." [10]

Soon the temptation of making a quick killing came to obsess Archer. He began dealing in the commodities market – in sugar, cocoa and copper – and made several business trips to Nigeria. As Archer would later explain in one of his short stories: 'since the discovery of oil in Nigeria there seemed to be no shortage of income and certainly no shortage of people willing to spend that money on behalf of the government.' [11] He worked closely in Nigeria with Eli Calil, a wealthy Lebanese Christian businessman whom he'd first met at Oxford. Calil had extensive business interests in the country, most notably a firm called Nigerian Oil Mills, which made a fortune from crushing groundnuts into oil. Archer acted as a consultant in Lagos; his status as an MP would no doubt have been helpful to firms seeking to persuade the Nigerian government to grant lucrative contracts.

Before long it wasn't just Slater who was being tapped for investment advice, but also his American contact at the First National Bank of Boston. Michael Altmann was a rising star – a graduate of the Harvard Business School and one of the first Jews to be employed by his bank. But Archer's contact with Altmann was something he'd regret for the rest of his life, for it trapped him in an elaborate share swindle which forced him out of Parliament and pushed him to the edge of bankruptcy.

Today, writing from his new home in Israel, Michael Altmann refuses to discuss the affair. He has 'no wish', he says, 'to revive a past episode in which both our friend, the Lord Archer, and I myself, were unfortunate victims'. [12]

Altmann may not be as innocent as he suggests. Certainly the Royal Canadian Mounted Police didn't think so when later they accused him in court of being part of a conspiracy to 'defraud' his bank of $435,000. [13]

Both Altmann and Archer might well have avoided the notorious Aquablast affair had it not been for an accident of personal circumstance. During the autumn of 1972 Altmann was renovating his London home in Cavaye Place, close to the Archers' house in The Boltons. The Boston banker was living temporarily with an English friend, John Kennedy, at his flat in Regent's Park. Kennedy had been involved in a wide range of activities in his time, from running a Fleet Street photo agency in the

1950s, to managing the entertainer Tommy Steele and then the comedian Sid James.

For several months Kennedy had been immersed in a project which appeared to have the potential to make millions. He and two colleagues had agreed to pay a German inventor, Curt Wymann, $25,000 for the rights for what was meant to be a revolutionary anti-pollution device for cars, which came to be known as the 'Wymann idler-adjuster valve'. Wymann claimed his invention would both cut carbon-monoxide emissions and reduce petrol consumption. It was a simple brass gadget, about three inches long, which looked rather like a spark-plug and could easily be fitted into a carburettor in about ten minutes, even on old cars. Each valve, it was reckoned, would cost no more than three pounds to make.

Kennedy seemed to be wheeling and dealing in all directions. On the one hand he was negotiating with Curt Wymann in Munich to buy the rights to his extraordinary device. At the same time he and two colleagues were in discussions with a respected American businessman in Geneva who knew the motor industry and might help finance the valve's development. Robert C. Mitchell was a former president of Chrysler International, part of the mighty car corporation. He now agreed to manufacture the valve through a Canadian firm of which he had just become a director, and which was quoted on the Toronto and Montreal stock exchanges. The company was called Aquablast, after its main activity, an industrial cleaning system it had developed.

The buzz about the Wymann valve seemed exciting. At a time when the West was suddenly waking up to the environmental problems of air pollution and also the depletion of oil reserves, it looked almost too good to be true. And, of course, it was.

John Kennedy lives today in Palm Springs, California, though he regularly returns to England to visit his wife and daughter. In recent years he has achieved considerable success as a sculptor, and his work has been exhibited in Mayfair. Though he was never formally charged with any offence, in 1977 he was named in court in Toronto as being at the very heart of the Aquablast scandal, one of at least eight co-conspirators in what was then one of the biggest fraud cases prosecuted in Canada. His version of how Jeffrey Archer was sucked into the affair has to be treated with scepticism. But some details are not disputed.

It was inevitable, Kennedy argues, that during Michael Altmann's stay in Regent's Park the American banker would overhear his frantic, excited discussions about the development of the Wymann valve and the search by the chosen manufacturer, Aquablast, for new investors.

Kennedy says he remembers Altmann coming home one evening and swearing about the fact that Archer had been calling him for the last few days, pressing him for share tips. According to Kennedy, Altmann kept telling Archer he hadn't any investment advice to give. 'Then Michael Altmann said, "The only thing I know is that a friend whose flat I'm staying in is very excited about this new nozzle." He mentioned Aquablast, and said it was quoted on the Toronto stock exchange.' According to Kennedy, Archer called Michael Altmann back and said he'd just bought some Aquablast stock. 'Altmann was furious,' Kennedy recalls: ' "He's fucking mad," he said.'[14]

Yet it wasn't a simple matter of Altmann mentioning that he had overheard Kennedy's phone calls. Altmann also persuaded his own bank to invest $430,000 in Aquablast debentures, and he showed Archer the documents to prove it. It was this fact, and a naïve belief in bankers' judgement, which convinced the MP that Aquablast was a sound investment. The prosecution alleged later in Canada that both Kennedy and Altmann were part of a conspiracy to defraud gullible investors; neither Kennedy nor Altmann, however, were ever prosecuted themselves.

It was October 1972. Over two or three weeks, in dribs and drabs, Archer got Frank Watts to acquire a total of more than 51,500 Aquablast shares, paying around 330p each. Several times Watts told Archer to be careful, warning him the company might not be a good buy. 'There were some signs that I thought were deeply suspicious,' Watts says.[15] Archer wouldn't have it: he was certain he was on to a winner – he had had a tip from people in the know. The fact that Aquablast shares had risen rapidly from 230p to 330p in only a few weeks bolstered his confidence. In all, at this stage, Archer invested about £170,000.

In order to buy this first batch of shares, Archer had taken out a second mortgage on his house in The Boltons, said at the time to be worth well over £100,000. The very fact that he had to borrow like this, of course, was a sign that Archer was not nearly as wealthy as he led people to believe.

Having acquired the rights to the Wymann valve, an asset they might pass off as valuable, several Aquablast executives then set about selling hundreds of thousands of Canadian dollars' worth of shares that they owned. Although the company was a small operation, it had the appearance of a big international concern, with three offices in Canada, and others in Cleveland, Ohio, and in London and Geneva. The firm also hired an innocent London public-relations expert, who paid £250 a year for the Aquablast share price to appear in the daily listings in the *Financial Times*, thus boosting the firm's credibility. The PR man was then asked to promote the company to financial journalists. Any doubts Archer might have had about his investment would have been allayed by articles in the *Financial Times* and the London *Evening Standard*. The Wymann valve, they said, could cut the carbon-monoxide emissions of an idling engine by 65 per cent. The device was 'already selling well in Germany', the *Evening Standard* reported, adding that in one town it had been fitted to local police cars. The *Standard* warned, however, that the 'share price now looks to take an awful lot on trust'.[16]

Archer's confidence would have been reinforced a few days later when Michael Altmann brought an Aquablast representative called Manny Silverman round to his home in The Boltons. In court, Silverman would later turn Queen's evidence, and admit to being at the very heart of the Aquablast conspiracy. It was his job, Silverman confessed, to supervise the operation to persuade innocent European investors to buy company stock.

A short man, who was then in his mid-forties, Silverman was a Canadian businessman who lived in Europe, flitting between his flat in London, a chalet in Switzerland and a villa near Monte Carlo. His smart suits, his long cigars, his Mercedes and his Porsche all presented the image of financial success that Archer himself was striving for. In reality, Manny Silverman had long been a share promoter who made his money pushing dubious Canadian stock in Europe, where the markets were much less tightly regulated. Silverman offered brokers or bankers who helped him place the stock unusually high rates of commission, sometimes as much as 20 per cent of the transaction price. The Aquablast scheme was carefully synchronized. As soon as Silverman knew that somebody in Europe intended to buy a certain number of shares, he quickly told Aquablast's bosses in Canada to release exactly that number on to the market from their personal holdings. This ensured that Aquablast directors were likely to profit from the deal, rather than other shareholders who might want to sell.

Archer met Silverman several times, and, according to his own evidence later in court in Canada, was won over by the share promoter's brilliant salesmanship.

He told me that the shares would reach as high as twenty-five dollars, the reasons being that the Wymann valve had been tested both in Germany and in Britain, and was about to be tested in the United States, and when the report came out these shares would go through the roof, and I would be wise to buy more.[17]

As well as the First National Bank of Boston's interest in Aquablast, Archer was impressed to learn that two Swiss banks had also invested in the enterprise. 'This,' he later said, 'gave me the confidence to believe that although Mr Silverman may not be a brilliant financier, and indeed I wasn't, that banks of such status would not be involved in something that was not safe.'[18]

The meetings with Silverman had persuaded Archer to buy more Aquablast shares. But by now, as he later explained, he had 'come to the limit on my own finances'.[19] He was so excited by the company, however, that he tried to convince various friends to come in with him, or to lend him money to invest. Among those he approached was an investment banker, Colin Emson, a friend to whom Jeffrey had once sublet the first and second floors of the Archer Gallery building in Grafton Street. Emson was highly sceptical:

> I said to him, 'You're a force, an impresario, why do you need to piggyback, to put your money into somebody else's enterprise?' He told me what Aquablast was, and how it got rid of petrol fumes and how there would soon be legislation on emissions, and I said, 'I used to motor-race, and quite honestly I don't believe any of this.' He said, 'I know this is a major concern for the government and I'm in the House of Commons and it's going to take off. It's an opportunity not to be missed.'[20]

Archer urged Emson to invest in Aquablast too: he would underwrite any losses that the banker might make, in return for a share of the expected profits. Emson flatly refused, and insisted that if Jeffrey was absolutely determined to invest in the company himself it should be only a small amount. 'I said, "Jeffrey, just put in five grand." He was actually quite rude to me about that. It was one of our minor fallings-out.'[21]

Rebuffed by Emson, Archer contacted a young businessman he'd met earlier that year while raising funds for the European Movement. Anthony Bamford was only twenty-seven, but already well on his way to a promising career. He had just been named Young Exporter of the

Year for his work for his father's firm, J. C. Bamford & Co., the Staffordshire company which makes JCB excavators. Without telling Bamford anything about his earlier purchase of Aquablast shares, or the mortgage he'd raised to pay for them, Archer seems to have put forward a similar proposal to the one offered to Colin Emson.

Instead of investing himself, Anthony Bamford decided to lend the MP the money to buy 50,000 shares – £172,000, a sum which Bamford had himself borrowed. In return the businessman was promised 30 per cent of the profits. The loan would not be needed beyond Christmas, six and a half weeks away, by which time Archer expected to have sold the shares at a handsome profit. 'My own conviction was, and that was what was agreed, that we would not be in Aqua very long,' Archer later explained.[22] Bamford couldn't possibly lose on the deal, the MP assured him, since if anything went wrong Archer would still owe him the money. After discussing it with his stockbrokers, Kitcat Aitken, Bamford insisted that the shares be held in joint names; he also demanded that they be bought through his brokers, rather than Frank Watts, and held by them as security.

What Archer was doing, of course, was insider trading. He was buying on the basis of what he thought was inside information from Michael Altmann, John Kennedy and Manny Silverman, who had told him about forthcoming research reports which the rest of the market did not know about. Surprisingly, perhaps, insider trading was completely legal in those days, and widely practised in financial circles, though it was regarded by many people as highly unethical. If challenged, Archer might have taken the view a journalist expresses in the play he later wrote, *Exclusive*: 'It's not considered to be insider trading if the shares subsequently *fall*. That's just thought to be lack of judgement.'[23]

Manny Silverman meanwhile must have been delighted that, while he was paying brokers and investment managers generous commissions for this kind of hard selling, here was a respectable MP willing to procure other people's capital for absolutely nothing. In all, Manny Silverman managed to dump 600,000 Aquablast shares in Europe, but Jeffrey Archer was by far his biggest individual catch, having bought 101,500 shares for almost £350,000 – an average of 345p each.

Archer's optimism about the Wymann valve was not completely without foundation. A report by the British Motor Industry Research Association had described the gadget's ability to cut pollution as 'excellent', and German reports too were good. But when the Ontario Research Association concluded that results were 'not promising' and did 'not merit . . . further expense', this was kept from investors.[24] So too was the even more alarming news that no patent could be taken out in America because the valve was too similar to an existing invention.

The 350p Archer paid for some of his shares proved to be close to the highest price the stock reached. By the end of December 1972, as Archer was preparing the Hampton Court banquet to celebrate Britain's entry into the EEC, the price had dropped to 250p. So much for the idea of being able to sell before Christmas at a good profit: he was already £100,000 in deficit.

Through January 1973 the price fell steadily. Growing more anxious by the day, Archer contacted Altmann and Silverman and asked for a meeting to find out why the shares were dropping. The two men turned up at Archer's home one Sunday morning in late January or early February, accompanied by the Aquablast director Robert Mitchell. 'I made it very clear that my whole financial life rested on this share, that I couldn't let the risk continue any longer. I wanted to put my shares on the market,' Archer said.[25] By now the shares were down to 170p – half what he had paid for them. Even if he had managed to sell them, it would have left him with serious financial problems.

Silverman and Mitchell tried to reassure their investor. Once new test results had been announced in America the price would start to rise again. If he tried to sell his shares, they said, there was a danger the price might collapse overnight. If he was that concerned, then Silverman would buy some of his stock back from him; when Archer later tried to pursue this offer, Silverman was 'always evasive', he said.[26]

It must have been agonizing for Jeffrey to pick up the *Financial Times* each morning and look at the Aquablast price, especially as Mary knew nothing about the investment. It usually moved in units of 5p, and generally downwards an average of about 10p a week. Every now and then there was an encouraging jump upwards – up 65p one day, for instance – but the gains quickly disappeared. Two or three times a week Archer would consult Altmann on the phone. Silverman he could never find: he was abroad somewhere – in Switzerland or Monte Carlo. As he later told a Canadian court, Archer's mental anguish grew by the day:

> There reached a point where I was going to lose a large amount of money selling and my only hope was that these men were telling the truth . . . There is a mental stage where one starts to have to

believe in oneself even if one deep down under thinks perhaps these men are not honest men; one has to hope that there is a degree of honesty in it which will bring you out alive.[27]

If one believes John Kennedy's version of events, Archer's share purchases were not his responsibility, but simply the result of Altmann accidentally overhearing his phone calls about Aquablast. Kennedy's claim is that he was simply a hopeful entrepreneur, and Altmann a hapless conveyor of overheard information. Yet in court in Canada the prosecution later alleged that Kennedy asked Manny Silverman to pay him $22,500 commission for arranging Archer's purchases. And Archer testified to the court that both Kennedy and Altmann made every effort to persuade him to hold on to his stock.

By Easter 1973 the price was down to 155p. Even if Archer had managed to sell, the loss would have been crippling. It was simply too much to hope that the price would return to the level he had bought at, and that he might recoup his losses. At one point, Archer says, he met Kennedy and was persuaded that the wise thing to do would be to wait. 'When the announcement came then I would be safe,' he was told.[28] By this, Kennedy was referring to two important American test results from official bodies in New York and Michigan.

Unravelling the facts of what happened in the Aquablast affair, and who is culpable, is almost impossible, as both Scotland Yard and the Royal Canadian Mounted Police later discovered. It involved businessmen, companies and financial institutions in several countries, and transactions incomprehensible to the layman, which were often channelled through secret Swiss bank accounts.

In his heart of hearts, Archer must have known that he was all but ruined financially. There was no way he could repay the £350,000 he'd borrowed to buy shares that were now worth only a fraction of their former value. Yet not an inkling of his financial plight ever appeared publicly. Archer carried on giving the impression that his business was thriving, and that he was well on the way to being a millionaire, if not one already. Privately, however, it was no longer a question of making his first million but of getting back to solvency. In desperation, Archer was frantically looking round for a scheme – any scheme – that might save him from financial and political disaster. As Anthony Bamford demanded his money, Archer assured him he would make it back through property deals.

Archer's attention had turned to Centre Point, the famous 388-foot-high office block, built in the early 1960s, which towers above Tottenham Court Road tube station in London. Centre Point and its owner, Harry Hyams, came to symbolize everything that was deplorable about the early-1970s property boom. Hyams, who also owned several other empty London office blocks, insisted he wanted a single tenant for Centre Point, and property values were rising so fast that he could afford to let the block remain empty rather than go to the trouble of letting it floor by floor to separate tenants. Centre Point was such a potent symbol, representing the supposed greed of property speculators, that Edward Heath threatened Hyams with financial penalties if he didn't let the building. The Environment Secretary, Peter Walker, even considered whether the government should take over the site.

Archer's plan was politically astute as well as potentially lucrative, and it was extremely simple. If Hyams wouldn't let individual floors, then Archer would. Working in conjunction with Town and City Properties, he offered to rent the whole building from Hyams at his asking price of £1,250,000 a year. Archer then confidently expected to more than recoup this annual outlay by subletting the building in small parts; he had already lined up one tenant for half the block, and he calculated he might make a profit of more than £400,000 a year from the whole venture. He himself planned to have the most prestigious office at the top, looking out over London. While many people regarded Centre Point as an eyesore, he considered it to be 'a beautiful building', and it looked to the outside world as if the MP had become obsessed with it.[29] He had – but not quite for the reasons that people thought.

'The deal he is now working on so secretly will certainly, from all reports, put him well into the millionaire class,' reported the *Sunday Times*.[30] Far from it: the weekend that article was published, Aquablast shares stood at 100p. Even if he could have sold at that price – which seems unlikely – his loss would have been £250,000, making Archer insolvent. Jeffrey was hardly a tycoon contemplating which model of luxury yacht to purchase: he was a drowning man hoping to be rescued by a cruise liner. Centre Point was the only vessel that might conceivably save him.

In the end, after five months' negotiations, Harry Hyams rejected Archer's offer. He declared that he himself would now let the building floor by floor, though it was some years before he did. Now it would only be a matter of time before Archer's insolvency was exposed. Now, surely, was the moment for a little modesty about his business achievements. Yet just a few days after the collapse of the Centre Point deal came his bold declaration to Terry Coleman that 'I've no need to work ever again in my life.' The following Monday, Aquablast shares were at 55p – a sixth of the price Archer had paid.

For more than eight months the MP had been in fevered discussions with Silverman and Altmann, seeking some reassurance – any reassurance – that things might still turn out all right. As it became clearer that his investment was doomed, he clung to the slight possibility, the slim chance, that Silverman was right, and that the shares would suddenly pick up. One day in late 1973 even those faint hopes were extinguished when a Scotland Yard detective appeared in the Arrow office in Whitehall. 'Archer was surprised that anybody had the audacity to walk in on him without an appointment,' says former Detective Inspector Clifford Smith, who confirmed the MP's worst fears. 'He was still full of confidence. He wasn't crying in his soup or anything. He was putting on a brave face,' says Smith. 'There was this front about him. Even if there was a shock, he didn't portray that.'[31]

Privately Archer must have known that now the police were involved there was probably no chance of ever getting his money back. By the end of 1973 Aquablast shares were no longer even quoted in the *FT*. It hardly mattered: by now they were almost worthless.

Anthony Bamford proved to be remarkably patient, though Jeffrey didn't see it quite like that. At the start of 1973, when it had become obvious that there wasn't going to be a quick profit, he had insisted that Archer pay 10 per cent interest on the money, simply to compensate for the interest Bamford himself was paying on the loan he'd taken out. Yet it was difficult for Bamford to press for his money, both because he might not get it and also because it was personally embarrassing, and any public action would expose his own rash judgement in backing Archer's investment. If Bamford insisted on calling in the loan, then Archer would almost certainly have followed his father sixty years before and been declared bankrupt. Since bankrupts are not allowed to sit in the Commons, he would have had to resign his seat.

As Edward Heath's government limped through the miners' dispute and the consequent three-day week into 1974, Bamford and his solicitor met Archer and finally threatened legal action unless the money was repaid immediately. The threats were made against a backdrop of political upheaval and the February 1974 election, when the Tories lost power, though Archer's majority in Louth actually rose by almost 500 votes. The bad news for the MP was that the new Labour government didn't have a majority in the Commons, and so a second election looked certain within months. Had either party secured a working majority in Parliament, he might well have survived as member for Louth.

Perhaps not wishing to upset Archer's chances, or provide any whiff of scandal for the Tories, Anthony Bamford had waited until after the election before starting the process of declaring Archer bankrupt. On 11 March he issued a High Court writ demanding repayment of his original loan of £172,162, plus £23,017 in interest. Archer failed to contest the action at first, so three weeks later judgement was entered against him. Remarkably, it was almost another four months before any of this reached the press.

More astonishing, his wife knew nothing about the proceedings either. On Friday 17 May, seven months pregnant with their second child, Mary Archer was at home organizing a party for their first son, William, whose second birthday it was. Suddenly Jeffrey came back and delivered the dreadful news. 'I felt weak at the knees,' Mary said later, 'but there was nothing else to do except carry on with the party. When you are told something like that, a sense of unreality takes over, and you are carried along in a state of shock which preserves you from the worst anxiety.'[32] Six days later Jeffrey was served with a bankruptcy notice, the next stage towards becoming bankrupt.

Yet even in July he was still thrashing round for some clever venture that would bring salvation. Could Elvis help perhaps? In a last, desperate attempt to bring the singer to Britain for the first time, Archer had dinner with Presley's manager, Colonel Tom Parker. If he staged two concerts at Wembley – one for charity and the other purely commercial – Archer calculated he might make £250,000 profit: more than enough to satisfy Bamford. Elvis, however, stayed put.

Details of Archer's plight finally appeared in the papers later that month, after a judge rejected an appeal against the bankruptcy notice. The MP was immediately summoned to Louth for urgent discussions, first with his constituency chairman, Henry Sharpley, and then with other officials. Sharpley advised Archer that with the second election pending he had no option: the honourable thing would be to stand down as their candidate – in effect, to resign. The MP agreed without protest, and the decision was announced on 22 August 1974. In 1969 Jeffrey Archer might not have been the youngest MP elected to Parliament, but now, five years on, aged thirty-four, he was certainly one of the youngest MPs ever to relinquish his seat.

After an uneasy start, most Conservative officials in Louth had come to respect their MP, and they were sorry to see him go. One or two of the women had tears in their eyes, and some members pressed their colleagues to find a way to keep him on. 'I didn't want him to step down,' says Clixby Fitzwilliams, who remembers that Jack Vincent, the former chairman, was particularly hard-line about the issue. The deciding factor was that Bamford might push Archer into bankruptcy at any moment – encouraged, they believed, by his father. 'Bamford senior was furious that his son had been duped,' Fitzwilliams says.[33] 'I still feel he should have stuck it out,' says another supporter, Trevor Knight. He recalls how Tories in Immingham were so upset that 'one old-age pensioner, a retired plate-layer, tried to start a collection to help him out, until we explained just how much money was involved'.[34]

The problem was, of course, that the crisis had blown up at the worst possible moment politically. The danger was that, if Archer was elected and then declared bankrupt, he would have been disqualified as an MP, and it would have caused a difficult by-election. It was simply impractical for Louth Conservatives to offer voters a candidate who in all likelihood would only last a few months in Parliament.

'It was a foolish investment and I was a fool to get involved,' Archer conceded.[35] 'I can't expect people to have trust and respect for a man who has behaved so stupidly. So I am doing the honourable thing.'[36] In later life he would readily admit he had been the victim of 'my own stupidity, and my own greed, and my own arrogance'.[37] His only consolation was that the Scotland Yard detective, Clifford Smith, publicly made it clear that Archer was not 'implicated in any way' in the fraud.[38]

In truth, Jeffrey Archer's resignation from Parliament may well have been a godsend for him in the long term. It probably rescued the boy who wanted to be Prime Minister from years of frustration on the Tory back benches, with scant prospect of ministerial reward. After almost five years as an MP, Archer was going nowhere. Nobody seriously tipped an ascent to the top of the political ladder. 'I had reached the point where I had nearly decided to give up the idea of office in the party anyway,' he later admitted.[39] 'I realized there would never be a career for me there,' he said of the Commons on another occasion.[40] Though his subsequent political career has also been one of thwarted ambition, one suspects that by resigning in 1974 Archer may actually have gone further in politics than he would have done by hanging on as MP for Louth.

Later, Archer would claim that, while contemplating his next move, he received a note from a man in Yorkshire who had lost £52,000 in Aquablast. In his case it was his entire life savings. 'And he wrote on the bottom of his letter: "And there's a difference between us, Mr Archer. I'm sixty-seven and will never come back. You're thirty-four and have a chance."' [41]

Above all, Archer's background made him determined to do his utmost to avoid bankruptcy. 'Coming from a middle-class, prudish family,' he later explained, 'that is equivalent to murder, equivalent to bigamy.' [42]

# 14

# The First Penny

The four-hour train journey up to Scotland gave him the chance to work uninterruptedly, to put the fruits of his imagination on to paper. Three weeks after announcing his resignation from Parliament, Jeffrey Archer found a welcome break from the troubles of Aquablast and the threat of bankruptcy with Michael Hogan's wedding in Kirkcudbrightshire.

Hogan sent his future brother-in-law, Martin Henderson, to collect the guest from Dumfries station. The train came and went, but there was no sign of Jeffrey at the ticket-barrier. Henderson feared that Archer had missed it, but before giving up on him he ventured on to the platform to check. He found Jeffrey crouching way down at the end, scribbling away furiously, resting his papers on his suitcase.

No interruptions, Archer insisted. He was writing a novel, he explained, and wanted to get his thoughts down straight away. 'I have to say I didn't treat this very seriously,' Henderson recalls. 'One took it with a great pinch of salt that he was writing a book.' He drove Archer to the small cottage where he was to stay that evening. 'We picked him up the next morning. He told us he'd been up all night writing,' says Henderson.[1]

Adrian Metcalfe, another wedding guest, vividly remembers long discussions with Archer around that time. Jeffrey was naturally feeling low, he says. He had no money to pay off his huge debt, but was determined not to go bankrupt. 'Nobody's returning my calls any more,' Metcalfe recalls him saying. 'The property deals haven't worked. All I can think of is to write a best-seller and make a film. That's the only way I, myself, with nothing, can make capital.'[2]

Metcalfe says he was astonished. '"Jeffrey, you can barely spell," I said, "let alone write." "That doesn't matter. I can tell stories."' The two friends discussed a plot based on Jeffrey's experiences, and devised various characters, and Metcalfe says he even suggested *Not a Penny*

*More, Not a Penny Less* as a provisional title. 'It was a game really,' Metcalfe adds. The game would create one of the most successful writers in the history of British publishing.[3]

But Metcalfe was right, in a way. Though Jeffrey's mother, Lola, had been a journalist, and had often nurtured dreams of becoming a wealthy author, he himself had little experience of serious writing. There had been the 'thesis' he'd produced while at Vicar's Hill, of course; the sports column for *Cherwell*; and a handful of athletics reports for the *Sunday Times*. But these hardly suggested great literary potential. At school he hadn't even managed to pass English-language O-level, though his lifelong love of theatre might help when it came to devising plots and building dramatic tension and climaxes.

In fact Archer was not really thinking of writing as a long-term career: his first inclination had been to return to his old dream of becoming the next David Frost. 'I would really like to become a TV political interviewer because of my parliamentary experience,' he said.[4] However, he was turned down for a PR job with a television company, and the nearest he had got to broadcasting stardom at that stage was a few sessions as a Sunday-night phone-in host on the London radio station LBC.

He was thinking of his story more as an 'exorcism' than a means to pay off his debts; he concluded that the only way it might be a serious financial proposition was if it were produced as a television series or a film. In building his plot around the story of his own financial misfortune, Archer acknowledged that he had been inspired by the film *The Sting*, one of the hits of the previous year. People who saw early versions of the synopsis of *Penny* say it read more like a film treatment than a book proposal. Among those whom Jeffrey approached was the TV producer Ted Francis:

> He rang me one evening at my office in St Martin's Lane and said, 'I want you to send all your people home. I want to come round to talk to you uninterrupted, unobserved.' He arrived with a sheaf of longhand notes and shut the sitting-room door. 'You're not to interrupt, though you may take notes.'[5]

When Francis asked who the author was, Archer said it was a friend. 'When he'd finished, I said it would make a fabulous film or TV series. Then he confessed he had written it. I laughed. "You can't even write your name and address."'[6]

The film producer David Niven Jnr was another whom Archer contacted with the proposal. 'My recommendation was that he write the story as a novel and then resubmit it, as studios are more prone to purchase a published work than just an idea.'[7]

Archer knew that he wouldn't be able to write at home, because of the distractions of Mary and the boys – two-year-old William and baby Jamie, who'd been born at the height of the crisis in June. As a solution, he turned to his old friends from Brasenose, Sir Noel Hall and his wife, Elinor. Lady Hall remembers Jeffrey telling her, 'I have something I want to do. I have to get away from London and get a little peace and quiet, get away from the kids.'[8] He was blunt about what he required. Since Sir Noel's retirement the year before as principal of Brasenose, the Halls had been living at their country home, 'Homer End', in the village of Stoke Row, about twenty miles south of Oxford, and Lady Hall recalls that Jeffrey stayed with them for about six weeks during the autumn of 1974.

He came down early one Monday and quickly adopted his regular routine: writing all morning, a brief lunch at the local pub, then writing again until about six o'clock. In the early evening he'd usually have a drink with the Halls, reading them what he'd written that day, and then often he'd go for dinner with friends in Oxford.

Late on Friday afternoons, Elinor Hall remembers, Jeffrey would return to spend Saturday and Sunday with his family in London, where work on the book continued. 'At weekends Mary edited it with him, because he'd never written before,' says Lady Hall.[9] 'Mary turned *Not a Penny More* from a fairly rough manuscript into a book,' says a close friend of Archer's. 'Mary took his appalling grammar, punctuation, sentence construction, and edited it.' His wife was more heavily involved in Jeffrey's first story than in any since then, and on its publication was credited 'for the hours spent correcting and editing'.[10]

Mary had shown her own literary promise some time before Jeffrey, in fact, when in 1971 she had won a BBC short-story competition. Her winning entry was based on a journey she'd once taken on the London underground. Mary found the only other passenger in her carriage was a transvestite sitting opposite. The story related how, instead of ignoring her unusual fellow passenger, as most people would, she struck up a conversation with him.[11]

But in spirit *Not a Penny More, Not a Penny Less* was very much Jeffrey's work, and written from the heart. In sum, it's a literary revenge on the crooks who had stolen his money, and Archer says that while writing it he sometimes snapped pencils in anger as he recalled his sheer stupidity. The tale involves four men – an American maths don at Oxford, a Harley Street doctor, a French art-gallery owner, and an upper-class twit – who between them are swindled out of a million dollars – roughly the amount Archer had lost – when they each invest in an oil company on the basis of what they think is hot inside information.

It was written with Hollywood in mind. 'I knew I had to make money, and to make the sort of money I needed to clear my debts I had to make it ideal American film-company material.'[12] Indeed, Archer later claimed he had particular actors pencilled in for each role. 'I was very cynical about how I wanted the thing constructed, I sat down and said, "When I write about this man, it will look like Hoffman, and when I write about this man, it will look like Steiger." '[13] And it was deliberately set in glamorous places likely to appeal to film producers – Monte Carlo, Boston, Ascot, Oxford and Mayfair (where, readers learned, prostitutes cost twenty pounds in Shepherd Market [14]).

Broadly speaking, Jeffrey Archer's novels fall into two categories – capers and sagas – and *Penny* is the greatest caper of them all, as the four men battle to get their money back. Which, of course, they do. Each uses his own specialism – the art world, medicine, academic life – to devise his own elaborate sting.

The book is sprinkled with fictional appearances by names and characters from Archer's life. Michael Hogan appears as an economist, for instance. Frank Watts, the stockbroker who bought Archer's initial Aquablast stock for him, now helps buy shares in Prospecta Oil, though once again he advises against the investment. To top it all, who should turn up as one of the main crooks but a chap called Silverman – Bernie Silverman, however, not Manny.

Not everyone was pleased with their new roles. When the journalist Nick Lloyd read of himself being 'hunched over the inevitable triple gin with a faint suggestion of tonic', he light-heartedly threatened to sue if Jeffrey ever made any money out of the book.[15] The Scotland Yard detective Clifford Smith, who helped Jeffrey with some of his research, was so annoyed to appear in print with brilliantined hair and a 'shabby suit' that he says he withdrew his name from the credits.[16]

Adrian Metcalfe found his name (though not his character) divided between the main villain, Harvey Metcalfe, and the Harley Street doctor,

Adrian Tryner. In later editions Tryner's name was changed to Robin Oakley, after a friend of Jeffrey's who was then political correspondent of the *Sunday Express*, and who had commented on an early draft. Many years later, when Oakley became famous as the BBC's political editor, Tryner was reinstated.

The art-gallery owner is Jean-Pierre Lamanns, the name of the man who actually ran the Archer Gallery after Jeffrey sold it. Henry Sharpley's son, Roger, who also saw an early version, appears as a Boston banker. The American don, Stephen Bradley, takes his surname from Bill Bradley, Jeffrey's old American friend from Oxford, but his academic brilliance was based on Mary Archer. The fictitious Bradley also has two sons, William and James, who are two years apart, and play small roles in the plot. Archer's own cherished painting, Leon Underwood's *Venus in the Park*, even makes an appearance.

Away from his writing-table, Jeffrey still had political and financial affairs to sort out. Six days after Michael Hogan's wedding, he returned to Louth to say farewell. 'I came here wanting to hold high office, and thinking that this constituency was merely a means to an end,' he admitted at one of his last engagements, a dinner-dance for the opening of a village hall. 'What I found was that I fell in love with the constituency and people, and that working for them gave me more pleasure than I could have imagined.'[17]

The constituency cottage in Brigsley was already up for sale; Archer wanted £25,000, but eventually settled for £23,000. It was twice what he had paid for it three years earlier, but the proceeds simply helped pay off an enlarged second mortgage he had taken on the property.

Anthony Bamford, meanwhile, seemed determined to pursue Archer to the end. Michael Hogan had travelled to the Midlands to spend half an hour with Bamford's solicitor, exploring the possibilities of a compromise. The trip was at Mary's instigation and, Hogan suspects, without Jeffrey's knowledge. 'I came away with a very clear picture that Anthony Bamford was not about to withdraw,' he says.[18]

But then, the day after the October general election, Archer and Bamford suddenly reached a crucial understanding. The businessman agreed not to pursue his bankruptcy action for the time being, while Archer dropped his appeal against the High Court judgement that he owed Bamford £195,000, and thus acknowledged his debt. The following April, Bamford formally withdrew his action from the High Court when Victor Mishcon, Archer's solicitor, devised a repayment schedule.

But Archer's financial troubles were far from over. In October 1975 his other main creditor, Williams & Glyn's Bank, began court action to recover the £238,000 he owed it. By this time, interest charges meant that the cost of Archer's investment in Aquablast had climbed to more than £400,000.

Today Archer is proud – 'overproud', he once confessed – of the fact he never actually went bankrupt.[19] In fact he's quick to take legal action against people who mistakenly say he did. Undoubtedly he was saved by the quiet, persuasive diplomacy of Victor Mishcon. 'Mishcon's genius stopped him going bankrupt,' Adrian Metcalfe believes. 'If there's one person Jeffrey owes an enormous debt to, it's Victor Mishcon.'[20]

The lawyer had been recommended by Peter Palumbo (now Lord Palumbo), one of the many up-and-coming business friends Archer had picked up during his fund-raising days. Archer has said that Palumbo also agreed to pay Mishcon's fees for the first twelve months. 'Without that gift,' he claims, 'I'd have gone under. I'd have been too broken to work out the business side *and* pay it all back.'[21] Palumbo, however, denies doing this.[22]

On the surface, Mishcon and Archer seemed an odd match. Victor Mishcon was a Labour politician, and, like Archer, he had served on the Greater London Council and the ILEA, though they never sat simultaneously (the lawyer had lost his seat on the day Jeffrey was elected). When asked about their political incompatibility, Archer once quoted the late Tory minister Iain Macleod as saying that a politician could get 'far more straight and honest advice from a man from another party'.[23] Mishcon came to guide and advise Archer in much the same way as several previous older father-figures – John Steadman, Tim Cobb, Noel Hall, Gerald Duke and William Oliver. It proved to be the most valuable relationship of all; Archer has since described the lawyer as one of the three great influences in his life (the others being his old English master, Alan Quilter, and Adrian Metcalfe).

In the face of the bankruptcy proceedings, Mishcon's initial tactic was to appeal against the court judgement, arguing that no money was due to be repaid at that time. Then he managed to convince Anthony Bamford that bankrupting Archer was not the best way to get his money back. 'He was playing the long game,' says Adrian Metcalfe, 'saying: "My client is not the man to run away from his responsibilities."'[24] Bamford was persuaded that in time Archer would discover a new way of making money and would repay his debt.

Jeffrey Archer has often remarked that it was during this period that he discovered who his true friends were – that people he thought he could rely on quickly dropped him, while others, whom he knew much less well, showed surprising loyalty. About some friends, though, he had no doubts. Adrian Metcalfe lent Jeffrey all his savings – more than £15,000 – to help with day-to-day expenditure. Michael Hogan, who made Archer a director of one of his companies, also lent him around £10,000. 'I didn't expect to be repaid, quite frankly,' Hogan says. 'I thought he would make the money back, but perhaps over twenty years.'[25] And Lola lent her son £3,000.

Before the crash, Archer had often given the impression of being much wealthier than he really was; since then he has been just as guilty of exaggerating the extent of his impoverishment. 'I have now only £18 left in the world,' he told one newspaper.[26] Later he would speak of 'days when I couldn't afford the bus-fare to work, so I had to walk'.[27] These stories, and an often-repeated Archer tale about how he considered becoming a dishwasher at the Dorchester, should all be taken with bucketfuls of salt. Above all, Archer has blurred the important distinction between being in debt and being in poverty.

Archer always talks about debts of £427,000. This included the £195,000 he owed Bamford and the £170,000 overdraft (plus interest) he'd taken with Williams & Glyn's Bank to buy the first batch of Aquablast shares.

Yet talk of being in debt to the tune of £427,000 is misleading, since it implies that the rest of Archer's previous business activities had generated no income or wealth to set against it. Although Arrow Enterprises was never a gold-mine, Archer had certainly acquired some valuable assets over the years.

First, he retained Arrow House in Whitehall, and he continued to use or let the premises until the lease expired in the mid-1980s. Second, Archer possessed several valuable works of art, though these were surrendered to his bank as security for the money he owed. Nevertheless, his financial position was never so dire that he had to sell these assets. True, Archer did sell his Daimler, but even then he managed to hang on to his cherished car number, ANY 1.

More valuable still was the Archers' home in The Boltons, then estimated to be worth well over £100,000. At first, Archer said the property was up for sale along with the cottage in Brigsley, and he spoke of acquiring a two-bedroom flat in Putney in its place. But he and his family were still living at 24a The Boltons more than two years after he announced his resignation from Parliament.

Quite apart from the £30,000 or so that Archer was lent by friends and relations – a considerable sum by the standards of the mid-1970s – the family also enjoyed the salary Mary was now earning as a university don, and her additional income from foreign lecture tours. But perhaps the biggest asset in the Archer portfolio was the income from his membership of Lloyd's.

Ian Posgate, the man who ran Archer's syndicate – number 128 – says that, as soon as news of his plight appeared in the press, the Lloyd's chairman, Paul Dixey, wanted to demand Archer's resignation. 'I said, "No member of Lloyd's has to resign until they are about to be declared bankrupt,"' Posgate recalls. 'He said, "It says in the papers that he's worth negative." I said, "That applies to a lot of members of Lloyd's."' Posgate adds, however, that he made Archer promise that if he were about to be declared bankrupt he would resign from Lloyd's ten minutes beforehand. Jeffrey readily agreed.[28]

In 1975 and 1976 Archer ceased underwriting, but Posgate's help in allowing him to retain his formal membership of Lloyd's meant he received his large cheques for the two previous years, 1973 and 1974, far quicker. 'If he had resigned,' Posgate says, 'then Lloyd's would have taken that money and held it and only released it very much later . . . In 1973 and 1974 he might have made £100,000 – it went a long way towards feeding the family – it was certainly tens of thousands. During that period I made Jeffrey quite a lot of money, and he's always been kind to me.'[29]

There was to be a neat piece of symmetry a decade later, when the two men's positions were reversed and Posgate was in trouble. In 1985 the man once known as 'Goldfinger' was trying to get back into Lloyd's underwriting following his suspension over involvement in the Alexander Howden scandal. Archer was among several referees who wrote to the Lloyd's appeals committee to recommend that Posgate be reinstated.

An office in Whitehall, an expensive art collection, a home in South Kensington, an income from Lloyd's and friends able and willing to lend £30,000: none of these is a normal attribute of the poverty-stricken. Of course Archer's net assets were negative, and it would be wrong to underestimate the seriousness or size of the debts arising from Aquablast, but this was not the kind of poverty his mother had known, for instance, when she gave birth to her first Jeffrey and barely had the rent to pay for their lodgings in Whitley Bay. It was more the sort of indebtedness that influential people often fall into, without letting it ruin their life-styles. Most revealing was Mary Archer's comment many years later that they 'couldn't afford to send our children to private schools for a time'.[30] For two years William had to attend a state primary school in Cambridge (where Mary had moved with the boys to take up a univer-sity teaching appointment) – not what most would consider an example of poverty.

Above all, Jeffrey Archer had what most ordinary people don't enjoy: good contacts. He still moved in the right circles. It was this that made it possible for him to get his first novel published. Initially Archer seems to have enlisted every friend and contact he could think of. One was his former parliamentary colleague John Selwyn Gummer, who had a back-ground in publishing and had written a few books himself. Gummer passed on a forty-page synopsis of *Penny* to his literary agent, Hilary Rubinstein, who rejected it. 'It was the most expensive mistake I ever made,' Rubinstein says, 'though not the most embarrassing. I didn't care for the flavour of it.'[31]

Archer's important breakthrough, however, came at a party towards the end of 1974, when he met Elise Smith, an American woman living in London. On hearing of Jeffrey's writing, she advised him not to give away all the rights to his book, in the way that Charles Webb (who wrote *The Graduate*) had done. It was vital to get himself a good agent. Did she know of anybody? Yes, she did as it happened: an American friend called Deborah ('Debbie') Owen. Once again Jeffrey Archer had managed to plug himself into the right network just when he needed it.

Here again, though, there might be problems of political incompati-bility, for Debbie Owen was married to the Labour MP David Owen, a junior member of Harold Wilson's new government – although it's hard to think of any significant political issue on which the left-wing Tory ex-MP and the right-wing Labour minister differed, either then or now.

Acquiring a literary agent isn't like signing on with a solicitor or a hairdresser: the agent has to be convinced of an author's potential. This was particularly true of Debbie Owen. Since taking over her agency three years before, she had been determined to keep it small enough to run from the Owens' home on the Thames in Limehouse. She had a strict, self-imposed limit of just twenty-five writers. This, Owen felt, gave her more time to cultivate the career of each of her clients, and enabled her to get to know each of them much better.

As ever, Jeffrey Archer had decided he must have the best, and Debbie Owen, he'd quickly concluded, was it. Adrian Metcalfe says he 'laid siege' to Owen in much the same way as he had to the equally hesitant Mary Weeden a decade before.[32] He invited her round to Arrow House in Whitehall, and opened a bottle of champagne, not knowing the drink was a favourite of hers. The sheer style and the fact he was willing to go to that kind of expense at a time when he was supposed to be penniless particularly impressed her.[33] She'd heard all the stories, of course – about Jeffrey's fund-raising and the controversy over his UNA expenses – but it was also a good sign that someone like Adrian Metcalfe should stick by him so loyally.

Debbie Owen received the manuscript of *Penny* early in 1975 – though at that stage it was still more of 'a glorified film script' – and took it away to the family's country home, an old rectory in Wiltshire.[34] Despite Archer's wooing, her initial inclination was to pass it on to an English agent in New York, Toby Eady. But then, almost by accident, David Owen himself intervened. Relaxing by the fire one Friday evening, seeking some light reading after a heavy week in London, and curious about another politician, he picked up Archer's text.

> As I read the manuscript I found myself chuckling and turning the pages avidly. When I finished that same evening I told Debbie that I did not think she would want to return the manuscript and that it was amazingly good for a first novel.[35]

Her husband's warm reaction convinced Debbie Owen she ought to keep Archer for herself. Owen says her initial gut instinct was to sell *Penny* first in America, simply because Archer was so controversial in Britain. The book had been written with the States in mind, of course – both the main hero, Stephen Bradley, and the leading crook, Harvey Metcalfe, are Americans – and Debbie Owen was well placed to sell such a transatlantic book, having grown up in the small, closely connected world of New York publishing, where her father, Kyrill Schabert, had founded Pantheon Books. He was 'the movie version of the old-time publisher', says one old friend, 'a nice elegant man'. The Schaberts would welcome dozens of writers and literary types to the family home at weekends, and Debbie herself had spent four years in American publishing before coming to England.

Some weeks after David Owen had found himself chuckling over Archer's work, the couple entertained two old friends, David and Susan Watt, in Wiltshire. David Watt was political editor of the *Financial Times*, while Susan worked as London editor for the American publishers Doubleday. Her job involved seeking out and then editing promising British authors who might appeal to the American audience. That weekend Debbie Owen passed Watt the Archer manuscript, simply for advice on whether she was right to try America first. 'She came down the next morning,' says Owen, 'and said she'd been up half the night reading it, and said, "Could I *please* get in touch with Doubleday about the book?"' Owen naturally said 'yes'.[36]

'It had an honest and angry emotion about it which carried one along,' Susan Watt recalls, 'and it had a great pace about it.'

> It also presented a picture of a part of British life which I thought Americans would find interesting . . . I recognized it wasn't a perfect novel, but it did have that quality of emotion which, if you think back to the sorts of novels that might have been published twenty years ago, was rare . . . Jeffrey was prepared to put his emotion, his anger, his pain on the line, and I think that was worth publishing.[37]

Doubleday accepted *Penny* and paid an advance of $12,000, almost entirely on the strength of Susan Watt's recommendation. Watt was assigned to edit the book herself, but says, 'I don't remember I did that much to it.'

> We spent a certain amount of time on development of the plot. I still think *Not a Penny More, Not a Penny Less* had some of the flaws you might associate with any first novel, but actually it's a tremendously lively and racy tale. It doesn't pause for characterization, and it was of course written in red-hot anger, and that comes out . . .[38]

As Archer pursued the story of his fictitious share fraud, both Scotland Yard and the Mounties (the RCMP) in Canada were proceeding against the characters behind the Aquablast conspiracy. The police forces agreed that any prosecutions would take place in Canada, and three men – John Pullman, Roger St Germain and Robert Keyser – were arrested and charged with several offences. Three more suspected conspirators turned Queen's evidence – both Manny Silverman and Robert Mitchell, who had directly dealt with Archer, and Ronald St Germain, who was already serving eight years for conspiracy to murder in a totally unconnected case. In November 1975 Archer flew to Toronto to give evidence in a preliminary court hearing.

The day before he was due to testify, Archer met the prosecution lawyer, Doug Hunt. While chatting, Archer reiterated how he was determined not to go bankrupt and would pay off all of his debts; he would eventually bounce back, he asserted. 'I still wear Savile Row suits,' Hunt remembers Archer saying. 'They may be five years old, but they're the best.'[39]

In his twenty minutes or so on the witness stand, Archer told the court how he'd come to lose more than £350,000. A star prosecution witness, he was just the sort to impress a jury: a respectable British politician who was the biggest individual victim of the fraud. Moreover, his testimony helped to corroborate the evidence of both Mitchell and Silverman, since he'd had dealings with both men. 'He was an important witness to show the conspiracy was international in scope,' says George Wool, the policeman in charge of the Mounties' investigation.

> It confirmed that the target was European investors. He was possibly the best witness I've ever seen. When he testified he didn't have to hesitate. Most people in court measure their words very carefully, especially business types. He was testifying from the heart – he was very, very effective. When they tried to cross-examine, there was nothing to suggest he was mistaken. He was meticulous and precise – a politician through and through.[40]

The Aquablast case didn't finally come to full trial in Toronto until March 1977. The one-time president of the company, Robert Keyser, and a former Toronto stock salesman, Roger St Germain, both pleaded guilty to several offences: conspiring to defraud investors through bribes to stockbrokers, prearranged trading, deceitful business transactions, and misleading information. Keyser got an eighteen-month jail term, while St Germain was sentenced to six months' imprisonment and fined 25,000 Canadian dollars. Both men were 'small fish', reckoned Doug Hunt. Jack Pullman, a bigger catch, refused to be so easily hooked and pleaded not guilty. Pullman was a former associate of the American Mafia boss Meyer Lansky, but he was acquitted after a fourteen-day trial – largely, it seems, because the main evidence against him came from self-confessed conspirators.

Archer was not called to give evidence at the full trial, since by then it was no longer disputed that a fraud had been committed.

After giving his evidence in November 1975, however, Archer had spent another day in Toronto, meeting one or two people in connection with his book, and seeing what the city's shops had to offer. At lunchtime on the day after his court appearance the prosecution team – George Wool, his deputy Larry Park and the lawyer Doug Hunt – went out to fetch some food. As they returned to Hunt's office at the Attorney General's department, they found a uniformed officer from the Toronto metropolitan police waiting to speak to Wool.

The policeman had with him one of George Wool's business cards. It had been produced, he said, by an Englishman who claimed to be in Toronto giving evidence in a major fraud case. The man had said he was a former British Member of Parliament, the officer explained, and that his name was Jeffrey Archer. The ex-MP, now at the police station, had been arrested at a department store on suspicion of stealing three suits to the value of 540 Canadian dollars. Wool confirmed that he did indeed have such a witness, and that he had given evidence in a fraud case.

The incident had occurred earlier that morning at Simpson's, then one of Toronto's biggest shops. After having been stopped by two store detectives while walking out of the shop, Archer had been handed over to the local police. Craig Carle, the officer who came to the store to arrest him, recollects the incident very clearly, particularly since it was strange for anybody to be accused of stealing something so conspicuous. 'I remember the three suits; I remember him saying he was a very important witness in a case,' Carle says. 'I remember him being in a hurry to catch a plane.'[41]

Robert Hutchison, a reporter on the *Toronto Globe*, says he happened to be in George Wool's office when Wool rang the police station where Archer was being held. 'I remember it almost as if it were yesterday,' he says. Hutchison's memory is that Wool and his colleagues were understandably anxious that the incident would affect Archer's credibility if he were needed at full trial.[42] The Scotland Yard detective Clifford Smith got a telephone call from George Wool asking his advice on what to do about the situation.

It was all a terrible misunderstanding, Archer insisted. Because of the unfamiliar layout of the store, he hadn't realized that he'd left the premises. The police obviously sympathized with his pleas and advised

Simpson's not to press charges. Unlike his father in Toronto in 1918, Archer was not brought to court but freed from custody.

But a decade later photocopies of an internal Simpson's document relating to the Archer incident began circulating in Fleet Street, and provoked considerable interest. Dated 18 November 1975, the day after Archer had given evidence, it was a standard company form apparently completed by two Simpson's store detectives, Marcel St Jean and Yens Yorken. What was impressive was the level of detail it contained, setting out Archer's full name – Jeffery [sic] Howard Archer; address – 24a The Boltons, London; date of birth – 15/4/40; height – 5′ 10″; weight – 165 lbs; and even the colour of his eyes – blue – and hair – brown. It stated that he had taken suits worth $225, $140 and $175, but the only part of the form that remained blank was the space for a signature which would have acknowledged that he had indeed taken the goods. Across the bottom of the document was typed, 'charges withdrawn at request of 52 Detectives', a reference to division no. 52 of the Toronto police.[43]

Reporters began investigating the case in some detail, while *The Star* desperately tried to buy the original document from the Simpson's employee who claimed he had lifted it from the shop's files. Paul Foot, then working for the *Daily Mirror*, even travelled to Toronto to speak to many of the individuals involved, only to find that nearly everyone – the Simpson's management, their former store detectives, and the Toronto police – was reluctant to talk. Foot returned after three days without enough evidence to persuade his editors it was worth running a story. After all, the document wasn't signed and might simply have been a forgery. Someone might have been trying to frame Archer – perhaps somebody involved in the Aquablast trial. Moreover, when Foot's office approached first his solicitors on his behalf and then Archer himself, they both declared, in similar terms, that he had never been 'involved in any such incident'.[44]

Despite the deal with Doubleday in America, and the sale of *Not a Penny More, Not a Penny Less* to Sweden, Spain and Japan, Archer still had no publisher in Britain. The famous story – repeated endlessly by Jeffrey – is that Debbie Owen sent *Penny* to no fewer than seventeen different London houses, and all seventeen rejected it. (One should treat the number with scepticism: seventeen seems to be Archer's favourite figure, and is often the number of drafts he claims for each novel.) But the book was certainly rejected by most, if not all, of the leading British publishers, including Collins and Weidenfeld & Nicolson. The chairman of the Bodley Head, Sir Hugh Greene, better known as a former director-general of the BBC, rather liked it, but was overruled by his colleagues. Another publisher, Hodder & Stoughton, expressed interest, but felt it needed a ghost-writer. 'I refused,' says Owen. 'I said, "It just is too close to the author's heart for it to have a ghost-writer." '45

At one point Debbie Owen had given up looking for a London buyer, hoping that success overseas would make British publishers reconsider. In December 1975 she began again, and approached Macdonald Futura, André Deutsch, Michael Joseph and Jonathan Cape. Her letters included a sheet of glowing testimonials from salesmen at Doubleday, some of whom made the parallel with *The Sting*, though Debbie Owen's preferred comparison was with another popular film of the period. 'This is a word-of-mouth book,' Owen suggested, 'which should have the same snowballing effect that *Jaws* had if given good promotion and in-house backing.'46

Jonathan Cape was perhaps the most unlikely of firms to be asked to publish Jeffrey Archer. Indeed, the firm's then managing director, Graham C. Greene (Sir Hugh's son), admits that if he had been an agent working for Archer he would never have bothered with Cape, who were 'rather an upmarket literary imprint'.47 Tom Maschler, the chairman and driving force at Cape, had been the charismatic whiz-kid of British publishing in the 1960s, the man who was seen at all the trendiest parties, and had quickly earned a great reputation as a literary talent-spotter. Joseph Heller, Edna O'Brien, John Fowles, Ian McEwan, Martin Amis, Julian Barnes, Bruce Chatwin and Salman Rushdie had all been nurtured by Maschler over the years, and today he boasts of having published no fewer than seventeen Nobel laureates. 'If you go through our catalogue,' he once said, 'you will not find anything that I call crap.'48 Even so, Cape had occasionally published thrillers, including Ian Fleming's James Bond books, Len Deighton and John le Carré, but they tended to be stylish thrillers.

But the chosen readers whom Tom Maschler asked to look at the manuscript seemed to be no more impressed than the rest of British publishing. 'We had two indifferent reports on it, mediocre reports,' says Maschler, but he remained intrigued by Archer's personal story:

Jeffrey Archer was writing this book in order to make the money ... to bail himself out of a con he'd been involved in. Extraordinary. And I thought that was so fascinating that I read it.

And I actually liked it. I thought it was charming, engaging and so on.[49]

Archer was paid an advance of only £3,000. He took a close interest in every aspect of the book's publication, and insisted, for example, that the British hardback edition should have 'fewer lines per page, bigger, bolder print, and more pages' than the Doubleday version in the States.[50]

The big risk, of course, was using so many real names, and so a former parliamentary colleague, Leon Brittan, earned £153 by reading the book for libel. Could Albert the doorman at Claridges object to the implication he was a crook? Jeffrey had shown the relevant part to Albert, and he had had no objections. Might not a reference to Lord Lichfield be taken to imply 'that he attempted to have intercourse with Anne Summerton', the leading female character?[51] The passage was changed. Archer had to spend several weeks tracking down the real characters he had mentioned to ensure that they didn't object. Most were amused or flattered.

When it came out initially in America, in April 1976, *Penny* sold 20,000 copies in a month, which was extremely good for a first novel. Though it hadn't sold enough to reach the best-seller lists, Doubleday went to a third printing.

'Absorbing reading,' said the *Toronto Globe*. 'The book will make Archer an enviable pile of money.'[52] Another Canadian paper wrote of 'an astonishing gift for storytelling and plot manipulation'.[53] The American *Library Journal*, however, felt it had 'about as much substance as a soap bubble', though conceded that 'it is quite entertaining'.[54]

That spring Warner Brothers bought the film rights to *Penny* for £125,000. The deal had been in prospect for several months, and now, even before his first book was published in Britain, Archer claimed that he had again made a million. 'In America, what I have done would be hailed as a remarkable achievement,' he told an American women's magazine, 'to have in 18 months gone from penniless back to million-aire.'[55] He was being premature; nor had he been a millionaire before. 'Three weeks ago I paid off the last of the debt,' he claimed in June 1976. Again this is curious, since years later he would always say it took seven years and three months to clear what he owed.[56]

In truth, his debts were nowhere near settled, and it was only towards the end of 1976 that a new debt-repayment programme was devised which finally satisfied Bamford, Williams & Glyn's Bank, and Archer's various smaller creditors. Again he was greatly assisted by the generosity of a loyal friend, who had found *Penny* a 'compelling read' and was confident that Archer's writing would see him through.[57]

Colin Emson, the investment banker, who makes a brief appearance in *Penny* as an economist, had warned Archer four years earlier that Aquablast was risky. After the crash, when his prospects as a writer were starting to look promising, Archer came to Emson, apologized for ignoring his previous advice, and asked for an advance against his future book royalties. Emson refused him, but instead went through Archer's financial position in great detail, and devised an ingenious deal involving the house in The Boltons.

Emson offered to buy the property from Archer, with a view to living there himself. But he proposed that, instead of paying off the mortgage with the proceeds, Archer should continue with the mortgage and carry on making monthly repayments, even though the house would now belong to Emson. This bizarre arrangement meant that Archer could instead use the funds to pay off a significant proportion of each of his debts, as a sign of his good faith to his creditors. Using his expertise as a banker, Emson had negotiated the deal at a meeting to which Victor Mishcon invited each of Archer's creditors. 'I only put up the money on condition that everybody agreed,' says Emson. 'It was the core settlement, involving five or six people, and all organized by Victor Mishcon.'[58] Nevertheless, Emson was taking a risk: if Archer had defaulted, the banker stood to lose both the property and the money he had paid for it.

When *Penny* was published in Britain, in September 1976, reviewers went so far as to compare it with the French playwright Molière in its farcical comic qualities, and with Frederick Forsyth and Len Deighton in Archer's obsession with factual detail. 'The writing, especially the dialogue, is bad beyond belief,' said the *Daily Telegraph*, though *The Observer* described it as 'delightfully old-fashioned' and a 'most exhilarating début'.[59]

'As much your achievment [*sic*] as mine,' Archer inscribed a copy he gave Tom Maschler, displaying characteristic poor spelling. The first run of 4,000 sold reasonably well, and the novelist badgered Maschler for a reprint, complaining that Hatchards bookshop had no copies left and 'they say they have been asking for them for two weeks'.[60] Earlier the publishers had responded to a complaint by a Mr J. M. W. Hogan that he couldn't find the book in three other London bookshops.[61] Cape probably didn't realize that Mr Hogan was Jeffrey's old friend Michael.

'The money just keeps pouring in,' Archer boasted, not long after he and his family moved out of The Boltons.[62] From now on, Mary and the boys would be based in Cambridge, where she had just been given a university fellowship in chemistry, and the family were lent a flat in Grange Road, by Trinity, one of the two colleges at which she taught (the other was Newnham).

Jeffrey, meanwhile, had suddenly acquired his dream property – the one he had set his heart on eight years before while working for the United Nations Association. A flat had become available covering three-quarters of a floor at Alembic House; its large, L-shaped panoramic room overlooking the Thames had been used for several films, including *The Naked Runner* and *A Touch of Class*, and the property had once belonged to John Barry, the composer of the James Bond music, whose personalized 0077 telephone number Archer has retained ever since. Jeffrey saw it as the ideal location for conducting big-money business deals. (What he may not have known is that Alembic House has also supposedly been occupied by the intelligence service, MI6, at one time.)

People would soon come to describe Jeffrey's flat as a 'penthouse', although it was only the tenth of fourteen floors. But for now, as he looked down on the Houses of Parliament, it certainly felt as if he was back on top.

# 15

# What Shall We Tell the First Lady?

The phone call came out of the blue, from a millionaire Canadian businessman who'd been educated at Oxford. Robert Opekar announced that he'd just read *Penny*, and loved it. He'd also heard about Jeffrey Archer's financial misfortunes, and felt badly that they had been caused by Canadians, especially Manny Silverman, whom he knew slightly. Would Jeffrey like to go and spend two months at his luxury home on the beach in Barbados? The house was empty; Opekar himself managed to get there for only about three weeks a year; Archer would be looked after by the butler, Sobers, and four or five other servants. The Canadian imposed only one condition: that Archer must use his time there to write another novel.

How could he decline? Archer had started planning a second book even before *Penny* had been published in Britain. He took himself away to Opekar's villa in Barbados during the summer of 1976, and discovered that the Caribbean was an ideal location in which to work. He quickly adopted a routine: 'Up at 4 a.m., write in longhand and then read it on to a tape-machine. Sleep from 2 p.m. until seven, the hottest part of the day. Up at 7 p.m. to transcribe the tape, all the while correcting. At nine in the evening – a sensible time – a typist comes in.'[1] The first version took him forty-two days, he said, and he then went through eight or nine further drafts.

This second book, even more than the first, was directed at the American market, and was again written with a film in mind (though none has ever been made). *Shall We Tell the President?* was quite blatantly based on Frederick Forsyth's *Day of the Jackal*, published in 1971, about a plot to kill General de Gaulle. 'Frederick Forsyth started all this, brilliantly,' Archer would later admit. 'I simply thought Kennedy would add authenticity and credibility.'[2] The book's publicity material was equally frank about his inspiration.

Archer's treatment of the theme involved an attempt to kill the

President of the United States, and was set in what was then the future, 1983. On its own, this idea might not have worked, but Archer hit upon a brilliant twist: the President was Teddy Kennedy, thus raising the spectre that all three brothers might die at the hand of assassins.

Teddy Kennedy has never made it to the presidency, of course, but in some other respects Archer's novel proved prophetic. Though the book was only completed shortly after Jimmy Carter entered the White House in 1977, Archer foresaw that in 1980 Kennedy would mount his only serious bid for the office and would challenge Carter in the Democratic primaries: in real life Carter won, though not convincingly, whereas in Archer's version Kennedy emerges triumphant.

Again inspired by Frederick Forsyth's use of detail to add authenticity, Archer did an enormous amount of research. He advertised in the student newspapers at Harvard and Yale, and took on three young Americans to help him. An ad in the *Washington Post* stated that a British author wanted to employ somebody who knew the workings of the FBI, and offered the enticement of several weeks in the Caribbean. Around forty people applied, including a reformed burglar; the job went to Paul Lamberth, a former FBI agent.

Lamberth says he surveyed several locations for the story, including a spot on the George Washington Parkway next to the Potomac River, where two fictional FBI men die in a car crash, and a Spanish restaurant in Georgetown. 'We also drove over and discussed the normal traffic routes and patterns that real-life characters would have been likely to use in scenes from the book.' At times the research seems to have been a little too thorough, and the book includes too many tedious descriptions of car journeys. Although they worked closely for several weeks, Lamberth has no recollection of Archer ever mentioning his own brief police career, but he does recall the author's surprise that the agent should ever have resigned from the FBI. 'He admonished me to aspire to become the FBI director, nothing less. He seemed to me a man who felt anything was possible.'[3]

Lamberth also introduced Archer to other FBI men, and arranged an interview with the new director, Clarence Kelley, at which Archer explained that he wanted his detail to be as accurate as possible, going so far as to include the names of real, serving FBI staff. So Archer was assigned to Nick Stames who was told 'to help as much as you can without revealing state secrets', he says. 'I suggested he ought to put a Greek in it, as I'm of Greek extraction.' Archer not only based some of the book in the American-Greek community, but he even included a precise portrait of Stames himself. 'My background was accurate, the names of the secretaries and my children. The character Nick Stames in the book is exactly me. He even noticed I had a little lapel-pin with the Greek and American flags entwined.'[4] Paul Lamberth also claims Archer included his own written description of another agent, Grant Nanna, 'without changing a single letter or punctuation'.[5]

In Archer's story, the FBI learns that a US senator is involved in a plot to kill Kennedy, and it has only six days to find out who it is. The assassination is planned for the Ides of March (echoes of *Julius Caesar*), and there's a touch, too, of Bob Woodward and Carl Bernstein's best-seller about Watergate, *All the President's Men*, when the FBI hero visits the Library of Congress to comb the *Congressional Record* for clues about the villain's identity. Woodward and Bernstein's book had been released as a film shortly before Archer wrote *President*.

Archer and Debbie Owen had set their sights much higher with this second novel. In America they wanted an advance of $250,000 – an extraordinary sum for a writer who was all but unknown. His first publishers, Doubleday, wouldn't pay that amount; *Penny* had sold well, but it hadn't been a best-seller. Five other houses also said 'No'.

So Debbie Owen turned to another long-standing American publishing friend, Tom Guinzburg, the president of Viking, whom she saw on one of his regular business trips to London. Her father was an old friend of Guinzburg's, and Tom himself had twice tried to employ Debbie in New York.

> She said she had a manuscript I might like. 'Can you read it while you're here?' She would be curious as to my reaction. I read it in a night, called her up and said, 'Here's what's wrong with it. If we took out all that extraneous Kennedy stuff, which overwhelms you with Kennedy romanticizing, the plot's OK. He's clearly a good storyteller.'[6]

Owen then arranged for Guinzburg to meet the author for dinner while he was in Britain. When the publisher learned that Archer and Owen wanted $250,000, he wasn't dismissive. 'I didn't consider it too much of a gamble, as I thought the book had real commercial possibilities. I was convinced we could make a much better book out of it.'[7]

Debbie Owen clearly thought the same thing, for she also wanted Guinzburg to assign a colleague, Cork Smith, to work on the novel. She rated Smith as 'one of the few really great editors' in America.

I was very adamant that Cork edit it, and I said, 'You can have it, the book, so long as you promise me that Cork will edit it,' because I knew from my days at Lippincott that he was just a unique editor, had edited Thomas Pynchon and all sorts of wonderful authors, and I knew that Jeffrey was very happy to learn at the feet of a really good editor . . . Jeffrey is a born learner, and he really, really wanted to get better and better at his writing.[8]

Tom Guinzburg was equally keen that Cork Smith should work on the book, and he dispatched the manuscript back to the editor in New York. Throughout American publishing, Smith is acknowledged as one of the finest editors in the business. Though most of his work has been with 'literary' authors, such as Robertson Davies, Muriel Spark, John Wain and Thomas Keneally, he's never been averse to dealing with the different and exacting demands of commercial fiction.

A gentle, courteous man, Cork (short for Corlies) Smith has the air of a Harvard professor, and some say he ought to have taught literature at an East Coast university. Smith was certainly a contrast to the brash, young, non-academic Englishman whose work Tom Guinzburg wanted him quickly to assess. 'I thought it was a viable commercial novel that needed work. But the one question was: "How will this sit with Jackie Onassis?" Guinzburg said he'd take care of that.'[9]

Cork Smith and Tom Guinzburg weren't considering Jackie Onassis's feelings simply out of courtesy. The problem was that John Kennedy's widow now worked for Viking as a part-time editor. When her appointment was made, a year earlier, it had been hailed as a crude publicity stunt, but Guinzburg regarded Onassis as an important asset, not just for editing books but also, he planned, in capturing new writers. It would be hard, he calculated, for even the most arrogant, reclusive author to refuse a call from the former Mrs Kennedy.

Guinzburg warned Owen that Jackie Onassis might present a problem. 'I said there's no way we could do this book if Mrs Onassis is made uncomfortable by the prospect.' Archer quickly agreed, Guinzburg says, that Viking should drop the idea if she found it distasteful, and he was impressed that he didn't suggest that the publisher should try to persuade her if necessary.[10] Yet Guinzburg also knew that the success of Archer's story depended entirely on the allure of the Kennedys. Nobody would have cared much, for instance, about a plot to kill Gerald Ford or Jimmy Carter.

Guinzburg's friends say he adored Jackie Onassis, and his determination not to upset her was personal as much as professional. On returning to New York, he entered her office and shut the door behind him. Only two people attended that meeting, and since Onassis is now dead we must rely on Guinzburg's account. It is worth relating at length:

I said, 'I've got a problem with a manuscript.'

'How?' she asked.

'It's a caper-thriller novel by an Englishman named Jeffrey Archer.'

She said, 'Tell me about it.'

I said that 'Like many of these things, this has a gimmick – an assassination plot.'

'What are you getting at, Tom?'

'In this case it's Ted, and the year's 1983.'

It was just as though I'd hit her; she winced. She muttered something about, 'Won't they ever stop?' And I didn't say anything.

Then Jackie visibly collected herself and said, 'Is it really a pretty good book?'

I said, 'It can be. There's a lot of extraneous Kennedy stuff and we can move it out, but it depends on that situation; it really does.'

She thought again for a few more seconds. 'Will somebody else take this if we don't?'

'Oh, sure they will.'

Then she said something really very sweet: 'I know how many books you've turned down, because you are always so protective of me and of the President, and I know that you've been absolutely terrific. Maybe the time has come when you ought to make a little money. Why should someone else always make the money?'

Then she paused again and said, 'I wouldn't have anything to do with editing or publishing or whatever?'

'Of course not. Once you and I have finished this conversation we don't have to discuss this book again, and you don't have to have anything to do with it.'[11]

Guinzburg says that most of that meeting is still 'pretty vivid' in his mind. The other books Onassis referred to were non-fiction exposés of the assassinations of John and Bobby Kennedy.

The former Viking president says he then rang Archer's agent to tell her that Jackie Onassis didn't object, and to confirm he would pay $250,000 for the book, thus outbidding one or two American rivals. To smooth things still further, Guinzburg also wrote to Stephen Smith, Teddy Kennedy's brother-in-law (and a friend of Guinzburg's), to tell him about the novel, stressing that the 'plot has a satisfactory solution'.[12]

In the late 1970s the aura of the Kennedy family still had a powerful effect on American public life, and the publication of a book by a British author which used another Kennedy presidency to such commercial ends was to provoke enormous controversy. For now, however, the critical task was to get Archer's manuscript into a state fit for publication. This was where Cork Smith came into his own.

Jeffrey flew to New York and spent three weeks working intensively with Smith. 'I thought it was a good yarn which was full of holes, but that's what we were working on,' Smith says, with a 'good deal of just plain working on the prose itself'.[13]

Like other editors who have worked with him, Smith is keen to refute the common view that he and other editors really write Archer's books:

> It is totally false what has been written. It's said he doesn't write it in the first place. It's absolutely untrue ... The general way it would go is I would say something like 'It's confusing, this sentence. Why don't you try something like this?' Then he'd say, 'No, that doesn't work either. How about this?' Then we'd settle on a third alternative. That would probably be Jeffrey's.[14]

Smith and Archer found a spare office at the Viking headquarters on Madison Avenue, sat side by side, and went through the manuscript page by page. The editor had already written notes on his copy of the text and had also prepared longer comments on a pad. If a sentence needed changing, they'd do it there and then. But if it was a question of rewriting a whole section, then Jeffrey would take elaborate notes, work on the passage that evening, and bring in the result the following day. Smith admired the fact that Archer was willing to work so hard: if he promised to redraft something that night, he always delivered it the next morning.

'We spent one whole day on one scene,' Cork Smith remembers: 'what for Jeffrey amounted to a sex scene. This was in bad shape – I think because Jeffrey was embarrassed by it. The dialogue went terribly wooden. He rewrote it with my help, mostly the dialogue – what they say to each other as the great act is being performed.' Smith regards Archer as a bit of a Victorian when it comes to describing sexual relations: 'He's really writing nineteenth-century stuff.'[15]

Archer has always acknowledged his debt to Cork Smith. 'I learnt and learnt and learnt. I was determined to learn everything I could steal from him,' he later admitted, explaining that one of Smith's best tips was 'Horse under the Picture': one should avoid stating the obvious – showing a picture of a horse, for example, and then adding the caption 'A Horse'.[16]

Smith describes his work as 'heavy editing'. He remembers that Archer 'had no particular pride about it. He didn't feel he was being savaged. He felt that whatever was being done was being done to make the book better – not as an ego trip by his editor.'[17]

Tom Guinzburg, meanwhile, had more than recovered the advance he'd paid. Six months before publication, the American paperback rights for *President* were auctioned in New York, and went for $425,000, half of which was due to Archer and half to Viking. In June 1977 the producer David Niven Jnr paid $250,000 for an option on the film rights, which he still owns.

In Britain, Debbie Owen again sold the book to Jonathan Cape, who paid an advance of £10,000. Even though Tom Maschler thought privately that the book was 'rather mediocre',[18] he promised a minimum first print run this time of 10,000 copies.[19] Owen emphasized that Jeffrey had to be consulted over 'jacket, copy, etc.', stressing that 'I don't need to tell you how important this is to him.'[20] The *Sunday Express* agreed to serialize the book over three weeks, while Coronet bought the paperback rights for £20,000. Cape boasted that the book had earned a million dollars even before one word had been published.

In America, Viking's initial print run was 75,000, and Jeffrey flew over for a promotional tour of twelve cities. Initial reviews were quite encouraging. 'One of the most gripping hair-raising plots ever disclosed in a novel,' said one Florida newspaper. 'The dialogue is brilliant,' it added.[21] 'A first-rate thriller,' another paper concluded, while a third said 'the author grabs the reader early and never lets go'.[22] But any satisfaction Archer and Viking might have felt was suddenly shattered by critics in heavyweight journals.

The *Washington Post* reviewer, Ron Nessen, a former press secretary to President Nixon, pilloried the book with a long list of factual errors; the publishers should withdraw all copies within fifty miles of the capital, he warned – 'Otherwise, it's likely to be laughed out of the bookstores.' He noted that the publisher's publicity suggested that the book invited comparisons with *Day of the Jackal*. 'It does,' Nessen agreed. 'And it loses. Badly.'[23]

It was the review in the *New York Times*, however, which raised the real storm. 'Clumsily plotted, indifferently written, wantonly silly,' was the verdict of the cultural editor John Leonard, who claimed the book 'has nothing on its mind but money – for Jeffrey Archer and for the publisher'. But the most piercing barb was left to the very end: 'There is a word for such a book. The word is trash. Anybody associated with its publication should be ashamed of herself.'[24]

Most *New York Times* readers probably hadn't a clue whom Leonard meant by 'herself'. But it was glaringly obvious to Tom Guinzburg and his distraught colleagues at Viking, though Leonard later said that he had in mind Debbie Owen as well as Jackie Onassis. 'There was nothing wrong with him saying it was a trashy book, and he didn't like it. That's OK,' Guinzburg says. The problem was the harsh attack on Onassis. 'It was so gratuitous, so unnecessary, so wounding.' Guinzburg tried to speak to his famous editor, but she didn't answer. He also tried to contact John Leonard, hoping to get a retraction. 'We called him, we sent telegrams, but he never acknowledged them.'[25]

It was a couple of days, however, before the story really erupted, when it was picked up by the *Boston Globe*, in the Kennedys' home patch. Guinzburg was quoted as saying that, when he first told Onassis about the book, she 'didn't indicate any distress or anger'.[26] This remark seems to have upset the former First Lady at least as much as John Leonard's review.

Archer, meanwhile, was touring newspapers and local radio stations, and called in from Los Angeles, offering to return to New York to try to placate Onassis. He was upset that his book should have caused such offence: ironically, he had always been a great fan of JFK, and Jackie Kennedy had even contributed to his Oxfam Gift Drive in 1964.

The novelist could also argue that his book was not that offensive. Teddy Kennedy himself hardly features after the opening chapter, and is not even told about the plot on his life until it has been foiled – hence the title, *Shall We Tell the President?*

That was not how the Kennedys saw it, though. Stephen Smith had already told Guinzburg that publication was an 'act of venal commerce and in basic bad taste'.[27] Jackie Onassis announced her resignation from Viking. 'When it was suggested that I had had something to do with acquiring the book and that I was not distressed by its publication, I felt I had to resign,' she was quoted as saying.[28] Guinzburg assumes she had come under extreme pressure from the Kennedy clan; her relations with the family had been strained since her marriage to Aristotle Onassis.

Suddenly, Jeffrey Archer's name and book were all over the front pages of the American press, rather than hidden away amidst the ads in the review sections of each paper. It was the sort of coverage which is impossible to buy. 'I must admit the publicity did no harm,' Archer said.[29] Viking even tried to turn Leonard's scalpel-wielding review to their advantage, and took a half-page ad in the same paper. Under the heading 'What they call "trash" in the *New York Times*, the rest of the country seems to like', it quoted numerous more favourable critics.[30] 'I think we thought it would all help sales, to tell you the truth,' Guinzburg confesses. 'But I think Viking and the Viking people lost their stomach for it. We were all so upset and overwhelmed by the unfairness of the situation – that one man's comment could do so much.'[31]

Tom Guinzburg says he was 'heartbroken' over the grief he had caused Jackie Onassis, though it's thought that when she later read the novel she found it quite harmless. The row about the book also further strained relations with his British bosses in the Pearson Group, which owned Viking. Around twelve months later he was sacked from the company his father had founded. Guinzburg says Jeffrey Archer was sympathetic when he heard the news. 'I think he really felt bad about it, particularly when I was fired. He called and said, "What can I do to help?"'[32]

At this point in the narrative, after Jeffrey has published his first novel about US politics, and upset a former First Lady, let us catch up with the story of Jeffrey's American half-sister, Rosemary Brainerd. Until the first edition of this book was published, Jeffrey Archer probably didn't even know of her existence. Now, with this revised account, he will be even more surprised – and rather pleased, I suspect – to learn what became of her. This aspect of the Jeffrey Archer story is more incredible than almost anything he himself has ever dreamt up.

After getting her marriage to William Archer annulled by the New York Supreme Court, Florence Brainerd quickly married again. Her new husband, Arthur Turner, who had helped her through the legal action, was business editor of the *New York Times* and later managing editor of the *Baltimore News*. Turner formally adopted his wife's baby girl and she became Rosemary Turner, and before long the Turners had two more children from their own marriage, both boys.

Unlike Jeffrey Archer's other siblings, Rosemary grew up in very comfortable circumstances. Her family were wealthy and prominent members of Washington and Maryland society, but emotionally she did not have a happy upbringing. Her step-father, Arthur Turner, did not give her the same love and affection that he devoted to his own sons; often she would be sent off to her room on the third floor. Relatives and friends seemed to treat Rosemary as if she wasn't quite legitimate – even though her mother had married William 'Grimwood' in perfectly good faith. America has always been a more puritanical society than Britain, and feelings were much more strict in the 1920s and 1930s. It was nothing really open or explicit, just the occasional throwaway remark or thoughtless deed. But it hurt.

Rosemary went to a high school in the US capital and then to the local George Washington University, where she studied journalism, three decades before her English half-brother Jeffrey tried to become a reporter on the *Sunday Times*. But Rosemary never used her reporting and writing skills professionally. In the summer of 1939 she met an up-and-coming lawyer who was already well-known for his prosecution work. Brien McMahon came from Connecticut but had Irish Catholic roots: the strange spelling of Brien was a shortened version of O'Brien. Aged thirty-five, short, stocky and with a ruddy complexion, McMahon was always impeccably dressed. He had served as Assistant Attorney-General and fought several celebrated cases in the 1930s against both gangsters and hard-line coal owners. And in twenty briefs before the US Supreme Court, McMahon had never lost.

In February 1940, after an eight-month courtship (and ten weeks before Jeffrey was born in London), the couple married. The ceremony at St Matthew's Catholic cathedral was a major event in the Washington social calendar, with extensive coverage in the local press. The guests at the city's high-class Mayflower Hotel included the former world heavyweight boxing champion, Jack Dempsey.

But Jeffrey Archer's half-sister knew she wasn't just marrying a brilliant lawyer. Brien McMahon was both aggressive and highly ambitious – too ambitious for his own good, some felt. Within five years, at the age of just twenty-seven, Rosemary McMahon had also become a senator's wife. In 1944 her husband had returned to his home state of

Connecticut, and, fighting his first election, had beaten an isolationist Republican with surprising ease. At forty-one, McMahon was one of the youngest members of the Senate, widely tipped for an even more glittering political career ahead.

It was on the great issue of the day, the newly discovered power of atomic energy, that McMahon really made his name: a *Newsweek* cover even called him 'Mr Atom'.[33] In 1946, the so-called McMahon Act set up the US Atomic Energy Commission, and despite being a freshman senator, McMahon was chosen ahead of more senior rivals to become chairman of the Congressional Joint Committee on Atomic Energy. The senator's interests also extended to nuclear weapons, and when Stalin tested his first atomic bomb in 1949, McMahon urged a six-fold expansion of American spending on its nuclear arsenal, and rapid development of the much more powerful hydrogen bomb. If the Russians got the H-bomb first, McMahon warned, then catastrophe was inevitable. The thing to do, he argued, was to 'blow them off the face of the earth, quick, before they do the same to us – we haven't much time.'[34]

Yet McMahon wasn't simply a cold warrior; he also advocated mutual disarmament, overtures to the Soviet Union and a world programme of foreign aid. In domestic politics McMahon was known as a liberal Democrat: a strong critic of the vehemently anti-Communist Joe McCarthy, he was never frightened to support American trade unions, and he boasted a strong voting record on civil rights.

The mid-term elections of 1950 were bad news for the Democrats, but Jeffrey's half-sister joined her husband on the campaign trail for the first time, and he easily secured re-election from Connecticut. Now McMahon had his eyes on a higher prize still. Every Presidential election has its 'will he? won't he?' questions but 1952 probably had more than most, particularly for an outsider contemplating whether to join the race. Would the unpopular President Truman go for a third term? Would the intellectual governor of Illinois, Adlai Stevenson, be persuaded to run? Most important, would General Eisenhower be a contender, and if so, for which party?

In January 1952 Eisenhower declared he would run – as a Republican – while Harry Truman still hadn't revealed his plans. Later that month Brien McMahon allowed supporters to put his name down for the Democratic primary in Illinois, but then four days later withdrew saying he'd prefer President Truman to win another term. In May, after

Truman had withdrawn and Stevenson was still reluctant, McMahon re-entered the contest. He had 'neither the right nor the desire' he told supporters, 'to discourage those who believe I am worthy of this honour'. But he himself would not wage 'a widespread personal campaign'.[35]

It seems strange today, in our present era of two-year, eighteen-hours-a-day presidential campaigns, and intense television coverage, that in the 1950s it was not vital to campaign for a party nomination. Fewer states held public primaries, but instead chose their nominee in closed caucuses, while the final party nominating convention could easily pick another name altogether.

While the boy who would later write novels about presidential elections was in his first year at Wellington School, he surely cannot have known that his half-brother-in-law was running for the White House, or that his thirty-four-year-old half-sister might become First Lady. If the senator completed the long trail to the White House, one Washington paper wrote, then 'Mrs McMahon will be one of the youngest, most attractive First Ladies in history'. Asked how she'd cope with White House receptions, Rosemary called them a 'necessary duty', adding that they 'are something that have to be done, but I don't see how anybody would like them'.[36]

Brien McMahon was playing a game as tricky as any fictional power-hungry politician in an Archer novel. Realistically the Connecticut senator was never a serious contender in 1952, and his name doesn't feature much in accounts of that year's campaign. His real hope was to be picked as the Democrats' vice-presidential nominee; in addition, he was putting down a marker for future years. But McMahon had a major difficulty: he was quite seriously ill with spinal problems caused by lung cancer. Several weeks spent in hospital stopped his bid gaining any momentum. Even so, when the Democrats met in Chicago in July, McMahon's supporters set up a campaign headquarters at the Hilton hotel. Connecticut's sixteen delegates nominated McMahon as 'a favourite son' on the first ballot, before he made them switch to Adlai Stevenson, who had only just agreed to challenge Eisenhower, and eventually lost.

Brien McMahon himself was too ill to attend the Chicago Convention, and had to watch the coverage on television from his hospital bed. Four days later he was dead. Struck down at the relatively young age of forty-eight, he had been denied perhaps another twenty-five years in politics, and five or six more attempts at the presidency. Brien and Rosemary knew it would never have been an easy target, especially since a Roman Catholic had not yet been elected to the White House.

Fifteen months after Brien McMahon's death, Rosemary married one of his closest friends, the Belgian ambassador to Washington, Robert Silvercruys. Her second wedding was an even more glittering occasion than the first. The new First Lady, Mamie Eisenhower, was among the guests, and the event got front-page coverage in the Washington press. And Rosemary hadn't just acquired a new husband, but also a new title. For Silvercruys was a Belgian baron, and she therefore became Baroness Silvercruys, thirty-nine years before her half-brother was elevated to become Baron Archer of Weston-super-Mare.

Just as Jeffrey would one day become one of the great London political party-givers, Baroness Silvercruys became a popular hostess of 1950s and 1960s Washington. Rosemary was noted for her fashionable French gowns, and the local papers often described her as one of the 'most beautiful women' in the capital.[37] Presidents, senators and Supreme Court judges would dine at the ambassador's mansion on Foxhall Road. And long before Jeffrey made his brief trip to see LBJ in the Oval Office, Baron Silvercruys and his wife were regular guests at the White House. Rosemary's friends included a succession of First Ladies – not just Mamie Eisenhower, but also Jackie Kennedy and Lady Bird Johnson.

Baron Silvercruys retired from the embassy in 1959, but the couple stayed in America, dividing their time between Washington, where Rosemary often held small bridge parties, and a holiday home in Nantucket.

The baron lived until 1975. Rosemary's mother, Florence, the former wife of William Archer, died a year later. Rosemary herself succumbed to cancer in 1986, at the age of sixty-nine.

Rosemary had only one child, by her first husband. Patty McMahon also took an interest in politics, and during the 1960s worked for the Senate Foreign Relations Committee. Married for a second time, and now called Patty Fox, she lives more than eighty miles from Washington in a remote part of Maryland. When I approached her in February 1996, she knew only a little about the sorry marriage between her grandparents, William Archer and Florence Brainerd. Gradually I revealed the whole amazing story, starting with everything I had learnt about William Archer, his first wife Alice, and the granddaughter now living in London, Val Haynes. I then moved on to the history of Lola and her first son, David Brown, before explaining how William Archer's final child had been born as late as 1940. I moved through the events of Jeffrey's life, and as I reached his time at Oxford the name suddenly clicked. 'Oh my God,' Patty exclaimed. 'I don't believe it! I've read all his books!' Her mother, Rosemary, had read them too, she says, though she cannot have realized, of course, that the author was her half-brother.[38]

Perhaps the most fascinating lesson of this biography concerns the power of genetic inheritance. In spare moments Jeffrey's American half-sister wrote fiction too, though Rosemary never had anything published. 'If she wasn't married,' one Washington paper said of Senator McMahon's wife in 1949, 'she would be pegging away at a typewriter turning out readable, sellable stories.'[39]

More interesting still is that these two children of William Archer should have shared an interest and involvement in high-level politics. And few British novelists have written as much about Washington as Jeffrey Archer; after *Shall We Tell the President?* two more of his novels would primarily be set in the US capital, a town where Rosemary, her two husbands, and many of their closest friends, were some of the biggest players.

Patty Fox believes that her father might just have become President McMahon one day. Political careers are perilously unpredictable, of course, but in 1960 another New England Democrat senator with Irish ancestry, John F. Kennedy, became the first Catholic to be elected to the White House. Had Brien McMahon lived longer, it is not inconceivable that Jeffrey Archer's half-sister might have become First Lady instead of her friend, Jackie Kennedy.

Brien McMahon's daughter, Patty, tells a particularly poignant story. Shortly after the senator's death in 1952, her mother, Rosemary, received a sympathy call from JFK's father, Joseph Kennedy. 'Papa Joe said to mother, "Well, now that Brien's gone, I guess I can let Jack loose."' The notoriously ambitious patriarch of the Kennedy clan seemed to be suggesting that McMahon's death had cleared another obstacle from his son's path.

'You can just imagine,' Patty adds, 'how my mother felt about that.'[40]

# 16

# The Making of a Best-Seller

With two books now under his belt, Jeffrey was again cheerfully boasting about how much he was now making, and getting angry with journalists who suggested he might once again be exaggerating. 'Oh yes, I'm not rich,' he said sarcastically, waving an arm around his flat:

> That's not a Manet. That's not a Henry Moore. If you picked that up and took it under your arm to Sotheby's they'd give you a cheque for £27,000. But I'm not rich. This flat doesn't exist. And you can get Henry Moores on hire, of course.[1]

Jeffrey had resumed underwriting at Lloyd's, and gave Mary £100,000 so that she could also become a Lloyd's name, and acquire a degree of financial independence from her husband. Jeffrey even spoke of becoming a tax exile, though one suspects this was mainly a political dig at the then Labour government. In any case, Mary insisted she wanted to continue working in Cambridge.

There were soon echoes of unfortunate Archer claims from the past. He need never write another word, he said: now he could simply survive on the interest from his newly acquired fortune. 'That is, assuming you could live off £50,000 a year.'[2]

His creditors must have found it all hard to swallow. For, by his own later admissions, it would still be another three years after that rash claim before Jeffrey Archer's Aquablast debts were finally settled.

And, despite the large sums of money, the publicity and the talk of Hollywood films, Jeffrey Archer still hadn't published a real best-seller. Both *Penny* and *President* had sold well, but they were only moderately successful. In the UK neither had made the *Sunday Times* best-seller list, while in America *President* had spent just one week in the charts in the *New York Times*.

His first two books were also short by Archer's later standards – at around 220 pages in their first editions, they were about half the length of his subsequent novels. Archer decided his next book would be his first serious work: a novel which would establish his name as a great writer, and a blockbuster which would be physically bigger than his first two works combined. Whereas *Penny* and *President* had both been set during the course of a few days, this was to be a saga, covering sixty years and running to more than five hundred pages.

'The project I am now working on will, hopefully, have at least two sequels and take me well into the eighties,' he claimed.[3] The first part of this proposed trilogy would take almost two years to complete, and involve four of the most highly respected editors in the English language. But the effort paid off. With *Kane and Abel*, Jeffrey Archer leapt from being a middle-ranking writer with an unusual background to an international best-seller. The near-bankrupt became 'bankable', to borrow the awful word used by his publicity people: *Kane and Abel*, he later admitted, was 'the one that cleared the debts'.[4]

Again, Archer wrote his first draft in the Caribbean, though not at the Opekars' house. He returned to the relentless, daily grind of writing every word by hand, for more than forty days non-stop. 'By the end I'm a walking zombie. After that it's not so bad, but the first draft is sheer agony – there's not one moment of the day I enjoy.'[5]

As a storyteller, Archer always compares himself to Charles Dickens, whose books were published in serial form as he wrote them, without thinking ahead to how the rest of the story would proceed. So it was, Archer later explained, when he sat down each day to write *Kane and Abel*: 'I had absolutely no idea where the next page was going to go. I never knew where the next chapter would go. I had no idea what the end would be.'[6]

*Kane and Abel* is the story of two men from very different backgrounds who are born on the same day in 1906. William Kane is a traditional and rather dull Boston Brahmin, from a distinguished banking family. The more interesting character, Abel Rosnovski, is born in poverty in rural Poland, but eventually makes his fortune in the United States. A misunderstanding embroils the two men in a long-standing feud, and they try to destroy each other as they fight for control of Kane's bank.

At the front of his work, Archer acknowledges 'the two men who made this book possible. They both wish to remain anonymous, one because he is working on his own autobiography and the other because he is still a public figure in the United States.'[7]

Abel Rosnovski appears to have been modelled on a Polish-American businessman, Henryk 'Rick' Kwiatowski, whom Archer met while staying in the Bahamas. They had been introduced by a close friend of Archer's, Victoria Campbell Kirsten, an upper-middle-class English-woman who divides her life between New York and the Bahamas, where her father was once the British governor. According to Kwiatowski, Archer spent two weeks as his guest at his home in Nassau, interviewing him about his life-story. On one occasion, Kwiatowski remembers getting rather upset about Archer's methods: 'While we were talking I stretched my leg, and I saw that under my dining-room table was a recorder. He hadn't told me. I didn't like that.' Kwiatowski says that, when challenged, Archer's reply was: '"When someone knows that they're being recorded they talk differently," and he was right.'[8]

Like Abel Rosnovski, Rick Kwiatowski was born in Poland but fled to the Soviet Union, only to end up in a Russian labour camp. From there he escaped to the United States, where he made a fortune through his company, Kwiatowski Aircraft, converting Boeing 707s to AWACS early-warning aircraft for the Pentagon. Kwiatowski also became a director of the airline TWA, and of Hilton International Hotels. The parallels with Archer's Abel Rosnovski are clear, for Rosnovski makes his millions with the Baron Group of worldwide hotels. The fictional Abel Rosnovski, however, was sent to Siberia after the First World War, whereas Kwiatowski was hauled off to his labour camp in 1939. And while Archer's character fled from the Soviet Union via Turkey, the real-life businessman escaped through Iran.

According to Kwiatowski, Archer originally intended to write his saga about just one figure. The book was to be about the age-old American dream of the penniless immigrant who makes it in the New World. But Kwiatowski says his conversations with Archer at his home in Nassau were regularly interrupted by phone conversations with the famous New York banker John D. Rockefeller Jnr. 'Rockefeller was calling me up, talking about whether they were going to finance TWA or not, and he [Archer] overheard these conversations.'[9] Kwiatowski believes Rockefeller himself may have become a model for William Kane, though he says Jeffrey never met him. Later the *Washington Post* suggested another model – Paul Cabot of the State Street Investment Company, who was a former treasurer of Harvard University.[10] This too seems possible, since the fictional William Kane is meant to be related to Boston's famous Cabot family. His surname, of course, had already been used by Orson Welles in his classic film *Citizen Kane*, about a megalomaniac millionaire newspaper publisher.

Both Kane and Abel display the typical Archer characteristics – bull-dozing ambition and determination, and cool efficiency and calculation as they pursue their obsessions with power and money. It's a simple exploration of the Archer philosophy of life: by his own admission, he's 'fascinated by people who get to the very top and why they do'.[11]

An underlying message of the book, which applies to both the main characters, is that 'Money Buys Everything'. And Archer returns to the familiar theme of a quick profit earned on the basis of inside information. While working as a young waiter in a New York hotel, Abel concentrates on those tables occupied by the most prosperous-looking business-men, hoping to pick up lucrative tips:

> The man who picked up the bill thanked Abel for his attentive service, and turning so that his friends could hear him, said 'Do you want a tip, young man?'
>
> 'Thank you, sir,' said Abel.
>
> 'Buy Woolworth's shares.'
>
> The guests all laughed. Abel laughed as well, took five dollars from the man and thanked him. He took a further two thousand four hundred and twelve dollars profit on Woolworth's shares during the next six months.[12]

Elements of Archer's own life and character, of course, are woven into both heroes. The nine-year-old William Kane makes a large profit from the latest school craze of collecting matchbox labels. Systematically – and Archer's heroes, like him, are always systematic and well organized – he writes to the chairman or president of each match-making com-pany, asking for samples. Each letter contains a typical piece of Archer flattery – 'PS: Yours are one of my favourites.'[13] The young Kane then sells his impressive collection just before the market in labels collapses. When the book was published, Archer claimed that his real model – the American Rockefeller figure – had actually done this with cheese labels at the age of seven. Then a *Sunday Telegraph* reporter pointed out that Jeffrey had told a very similar story about himself two years before – also involving cheese labels. 'So who was the real cheese-label king?' the journalist wondered. Surely they hadn't both made money selling cheese labels?[14]

Archer seemed to be developing a condition rather similar to the one that later appeared to afflict President Reagan when he couldn't distinguish between events in his own life and scenes he had acted in films or had seen on the screen. It is made more confusing by the fact that, some years later, Lola Archer also told the cheese-label story about Jeffrey. Perhaps he did actually collect cheese labels as a boy, or maybe she was simply repeating a story she heard from her son.

Equally intriguing are other autobiographical parallels. Initially Abel is brought up by a poor peasant family; only in his teens is it revealed that he is the illegitimate son of Baron Rosnovski, and he meets the half-brother who has enjoyed an aristocratic upbringing at the castle. The coincidence here – the similarity with the lives of Archer himself and of David Brown – is all the more striking since when Archer wrote the book he may not have known about his long-lost brother.

By far the most tantalizing parallel concerns the character of Henry Osborne, the novel's main villain. Osborne claims to be a Harvard graduate and marries William Kane's widowed mother, relieving her of much of her money, after representing himself as a hero from the First World War. 'He had a fund of splendid stories about Europe and the life he had led there as a young lieutenant preserving the honour of America on the Marne.'[15] As Mrs Kane's private investigator later explains:

> Enquiries show that Mr Osborne was never at Harvard nor was he an officer in the American armed forces. There was a Henry Osborne at Harvard who was five-foot-five, sandy-haired and came from Alabama. He was killed on the Marne in 1917. We also know that your husband is considerably younger than he claims to be and that his real name is Vittorio Togna.[16]

After a period as a Chicago city councillor, Osborne spends time in prison accused of fraud. Despite the slightly different sequence of events, the similarities with William Archer are uncanny. Could Jeffrey conceivably have known that stealing a dead man's identity, falsifying his age and qualifications, concocting war stories, marrying women for their money, spending time in jail on fraud charges, and service in local government were all features of his own father's dishonest career?

One of the research team who had worked on *President*, Natalie Wexler, a Harvard graduate, was asked to draw up a chronology from 1906 to the late 1960s. Archer insisted that she should go through sixty years' worth of newspapers day by day, but she took the short cut of using library almanacs.[17] Archer then wove details from her chronology into his text.

Archer was fully aware of the commercial potential of setting his novel in America. 'I'm very honest about that, that's where the market is,' he admitted. 'But it's more than that. I adore America. I wish I'd been born there.'[18] Yet this time Debbie Owen sold the book first in Britain.

She told Tom Maschler that Archer wanted an advance of £50,000. It was five times what Cape had paid for *President*, and Maschler says he had never paid any writer more than £20,000 before. 'I thought, "What do I do?" For the first time in my life I had actually hit upon a commercial writer – not a John Fowles sort of thing, but an overtly commercial writer.'[19] Maschler knew *Kane and Abel* would sell well, even though he himself wasn't all that impressed by Archer's story. 'The opening's slow,' he wrote to Graham C. Greene, and it was 'less-well written' than Archer's two previous works:

> However, there is no doubt that it is infinitely more commercial than either book and I must confess that with all its weaknesses (and there are many) I found it extraordinarily readable. If we hadn't published Jeffrey before I doubt whether we would want to take him on with this book. But since we have and, furthermore, recognized his potential (which in a sense has been fulfilled and could well be more so) I am naturally reluctant to give up at this stage.[20]

Another Cape reader also recognized the commercial potential: 'extremely readable,' he advised, '& highly predictable – but will sell & sell & sell'.[21]

Cape decided to take the risk and pay the £50,000 demanded. Maschler has described how he rang Owen to tell her the good news. 'And she says, "Oh!", and I said, "What do you mean, 'Oh'? Aren't you pleased?" And she said, "I'll have to talk to Jeffrey about it." '[22]

Maschler and Greene quickly concluded that Debbie Owen and Jeffrey Archer had already decided to go to a more commercial publisher and had expected Cape not to agree to the advance they had asked for. 'It was clear that she had already offered it to somebody else,' one Cape source recalls, 'and had obtained £50,000 from them.'

'She called back three days later,' says Maschler, 'and she said, "Jeffrey wants to know if you really like it." And I said, "That is too much,

Deborah! Forget it! I mean, really, you can have the money, but I'm not going to pretend to Jeffrey that it's really good!"'[23] So ended Jonathan Cape's relationship with Jeffrey Archer.

Debbie Owen admits that Tom Maschler has good reason to be cross with her (an anger which still smoulders). 'I think his criticism of me that I wasn't more direct is absolutely justified,' she confesses. 'I should have been bold enough to go in and say, "Tom, Jeffrey is really *very* unhappy here. It's not working. Would you release us?"' Owen concedes she did expect Cape to offer less than the £50,000 asking price, and that she would then have announced that Archer wanted to go elsewhere. She wasn't as brave as she should have been, she says, because Maschler is 'very, very emotional' and would have reacted badly, especially considering he had been the only British publisher willing to take the initial gamble on Archer.[24]

'Irrespective of how much money,' says Debbie Owen, 'I knew that Jeffrey could not stay at Cape. He was too exasperated at the less than vigorous hard-cover selling.'[25] In particular, Archer noticed the contrast between how his publishers had promoted the hardback edition of *Shall We Tell the President?* and the extraordinary effort made by Coronet, who had bought the paperback rights from Cape. It was not surprising, therefore, that Archer should have sold the hardback rights in his new book to Coronet's parent company, Hodder & Stoughton, which also offered him £50,000.

When they discovered the identity of Archer's new publisher, Cape executives felt badly treated by the affair. Debbie Owen had specifically forbidden them from talking to Alan Gordon Walker, who ran Coronet, about how much he might offer for the paperback rights. So they had had to consider the £50,000 demanded without knowing how much they might be able to lay off to Coronet. Hodder, of course, were under no such restriction, since Coronet was their own business. Moreover, Debbie Owen explains that Archer's career owed a lot to Alan Gordon Walker, who had become a close friend while publishing him in paperback.

The two men had in fact first met at Oxford, when Archer called on Gordon Walker's room-mate at Christ Church one day to persuade him to take part in university athletics. Over subsequent years they maintained distant contact, with the occasional lunch, but the relationship blossomed only once Gordon Walker brought out the paperback edition of *Penny* in 1977. It was partly fuelled by a common interest in politics, though from contrasting points of view. The publisher's father, Patrick

Gordon Walker, had been Foreign Secretary in the 1964 Labour government, and Alan Gordon Walker was a keen Labour supporter, though with no political ambitions of his own.

Archer seems peculiarly attracted to the relatives of Labour Foreign Secretaries. Debbie Owen's husband, David, had by now secured the same position under Jim Callaghan, and Jeffrey would later advise Susan Crosland, the widow of another Labour Foreign Secretary, to start writing fiction. On a more serious point, it's notable how often Archer's career has been furthered by Labour supporters – among them Adrian Metcalfe, Frank Hooley and Victor Mishcon.

'My assumption was Jeffrey would have written something which would not be terribly good,' Alan Gordon Walker says of *Penny*, explaining that he initially read the manuscript for much the same reason that David Owen had: 'out of curiosity, as Jeffrey was somebody that I knew'. When he was pleasantly surprised and bought the paperback rights, Coronet sold 100,000 in the first couple of months – 'which for us was quite a big quantity'.[26] More important, it carried on selling, even though there was very little promotion.

Archer and Alan Gordon Walker began playing squash together, for an hour once a week. It wasn't just a matter of friendship, though – of being at Oxford together or of common interests. With the paperback of *President*, Coronet had moved into a much higher gear, with a hard-marketing approach which involved its new sales manager, Eddie Bell, trying to push the book in new outlets such as supermarkets. 'He liked the enthusiasm and commitment of Coronet,' says Gordon Walker, 'and the way we had decided he would be one author on which the company grew, and we and he grew together.'[27]

Gordon Walker believes it was extremely difficult for Archer to leave Cape, as he is normally quite a loyal person. Yet it seems that Archer felt Hodder was more his type of company. The people there seemed more dynamic; they were of his generation. 'For an Archer to succeed,' Gordon Walker argues, 'he had to be in a publisher that supports commercial writers.'[28] With its outstanding 'literary' reputation, Jonathan Cape had never seemed a comfortable home for him. Archer was probably aware of the jokes flying round the office about how 'this guy thinks he's the new John Fowles'. It appears that Archer secretly wanted Tom Maschler to think of him as being in the same league as the great prizewinners he'd published. Maschler tells of the extraordinary conversation he had one day at Archer's flat. 'Jeffrey said to me, "I've read *The*

*French Lieutenant's Woman* three times. Do you think that if I were to read it another dozen times, I would have a chance of winning . . ." I thought he was going to say the Booker Prize, but I was wrong; he went on to say, ". . . of winning the Nobel prize one day?" I said, "Jeffrey, you don't understand. Sorry, Jeffrey, but it doesn't really work like that." '[29]

Outwardly at least, Maschler was magnanimous about Archer's departure, assuring him that '*Kane and Abel* will be a stunning success and I am proud of you for having brought it off so marvellously.'[30] Jeffrey too was generous, and sent a small gift to Maschler with a handwritten note: 'I shall never be too proud to come back and say I was wrong.'[31]

Almost as soon as the deal with Hodder was struck, Archer flew to New York. Under the terms of his previous contract with Viking, Archer was obliged to offer them first refusal on the American rights to *Kane and Abel*. 'Jeffrey said at the time he'd give it on very favourable terms,' says Tom Guinzburg, 'and that he was embarrassed by what had happened. He felt he owed us one.'[32] Cork Smith says he wrote an internal memo advising, 'this book has the makings of a best-seller, but I don't see how we can be the publishers', while Guinzburg's bosses in London made it clear that, after the Jackie Onassis episode, they had no enthusiasm for it. And when Guinzburg, Archer's champion, was suddenly sacked, the author lost interest in Viking.

Yet, by one of those strokes of luck which pepper Archer's career, he managed none the less to retain his American editor. Shortly after Guinzburg's departure, Cork Smith left the company to turn freelance, and Jeffrey became one of his first clients. Debbie Owen arranged for him to edit *Kane and Abel* on the basis, Smith says, of a 'small advance plus $2\frac{1}{2}$ per cent of what he got from America'.[33] It was a shrewd deal: Smith reckons that over the years he's made more than $100,000 from the book.

This time the two men worked in the library on the top floor of the Metropolitan Club on Fifty-Ninth Street, where Archer usually stayed when he was in New York. In the quiet, sepulchral surroundings of a typical gentlemen's club, amid the leather armchairs, desks and an old-fashioned globe, they toiled, Smith says, for more than a month, 'slugging away at this great script'.[34] They were rarely interrupted by other club members.

The editing 'involved a lot of cutting', Smith recalls – possibly as much as one-fifth of the manuscript. In characterization, Archer's traditional weakness, Smith thought the figures in *Kane and Abel* were a considerable improvement on his previous novels – 'as close to 3D,' he says, 'as you're going to get. But their actions and reactions are still predictable.'[35]

Over the following months, as the book evolved, Archer sent the story to friends: Jim Slater, for instance, was asked to check for financial accuracy. It was also tested on a group of supposedly ordinary people chosen to represent the typical reading public: among them, a traffic warden, a nurse and a university professor. Gradually their reactions and comments were taken on board. Jeffrey's foster-sister, Liz, noted how in an early draft Kane and Abel met each other about a dozen times. 'She said, "You know they only ought to meet once," and I said "Silly girl!" And I lay awake all night realizing she was right, and it took me the best part of six weeks to rewrite every section where they met, because she was absolutely right: the magic was to be that they would meet once.'[36] In fact Archer never quite fulfilled this, and they meet four times in all.

It was a long process, and Cork Smith was only the first editor. Back in London, Archer was introduced to the man who would soon come to play an even more important role in his literary career, Hodder & Stoughton's senior fiction editor, Richard Cohen. Numerous people deserve recognition for Jeffrey Archer's success as a writer – not least Debbie Owen, Tom Maschler, Alan Gordon Walker, Eddie Bell and Cork Smith – but nobody, apart from Jeffrey himself of course, has been more responsible than Cohen for the words on his pages. Over the next thirteen years, from 1978 to 1991, Cohen would edit seven of Archer's books: five novels and two collections of short stories.

On the 'literary' page of the satirical magazine *Private Eye*, Cohen is known as 'the Reverend', on the grounds that he looks like an Anglican vicar, though he bears a Jewish name and is actually a Roman Catholic. After Downside and Cambridge, Cohen did some teaching and then worked as a magazine sub-editor before moving into publishing. For many years he achieved distinction as a fencer: he won gold and bronze medals at the 1970 Commonwealth Games in Edinburgh and, unlike Archer, also competed in the Olympics (in 1972, 1976 and 1984). A common passion for sport helped cement the relationship with Archer, and Cohen soon joined Alan Gordon Walker on the early-morning squash rota.

Over the years, the myth has developed that Richard Cohen actually writes Jeffrey Archer's books. Indeed, inadvertently Cohen himself has perhaps been partly responsible for encouraging this idea. On social occasions his audiences may have read a little too much into the editor's jokes about 'saving the British public from Archer's original words'. When teased about writing Archer's stories, the Cohen smile or clever response may only fuel the myth. Archer undoubtedly owes Richard Cohen a great debt: his contribution has been significant, but the basic plots and storylines belong to Jeffrey. Archer remains the author.

One suspects that if Cohen did actually *write* Jeffrey Archer's books, they'd have rather more literary merit. Cohen is widely respected as an editor of serious fiction, and won high praise in the two years he ran the Cheltenham Festival of Literature. 'An intellectual with a feeling for commercial publishing,' is how his friend Alan Gordon Walker describes him.[37]

And Cohen feels his Archer work has given him something of a two-edged reputation. On the one hand he basks in the glory of having helped make Archer a best-selling author and multimillionaire. At the same time Cohen is dismayed at the thought that he might forever be known simply as the man who rewrites Jeffrey Archer. Intellectually, he regards Archer as a much less demanding job than many of his authors. Much of it is such obvious editing it doesn't require that much effort.

Cohen is not everyone's cup of tea, however. Some people find him difficult to work with, but Archer soon discovered he had just the approach he wanted, with a determination to squeeze every possible improvement out of his author. British editors are generally less demanding than their American counterparts, and more inclined to leave an author's manuscript untouched. This was particularly true in the past. Richard Cohen was an exception; Archer found him even more exacting than his American editor, and willing to be rude to achieve his ends, when necessary. 'He's as good as Cork Smith,' Archer said. 'He's as demanding, as agonizing, as annoying. He never gives in if he thinks you're wrong on something, he'll go on and on nagging you.'[38]

'He remains his own man,' Cohen once said of Archer. 'He is not academically trained and in several ways is very humble about his writing, but at every stage of editing it's he who decides what goes in, however much he takes from other people.' And Cohen confesses that he himself is hard on writers: 'I once said to an author, "I think my job is to stretch you to the point where you almost lose your temper with what I'm asking of you." '[39] 'He's a tough bastard,' Archer later admitted, in a rare use of crude language:

He drives me and drives me. He never writes a word – that's not his job; but he guides, guides, guides the whole time – he's never satisfied. He doesn't have a lot to do with the plot – I believe he thinks that's my strength. He'll get me to build characters – build, build, build, the whole time. He knows he's right. He'll go on and on at me; he won't give in.[40]

Richard Cohen put about three weeks' work into editing the early drafts of *Kane and Abel*. Then, much later, he had two further exhaustive sessions of about a week each, going through the proofs and, later, the revised proofs. With further editorial help from Alan Gordon Walker, the story of how the novel reached its final text was almost a saga in itself.

Having been rejected by Viking in New York, Debbie Owen put the US rights up for auction. The successful bid, of $250,000, came from the Linden Press, part of Simon & Schuster. 'I loved it,' says the then boss of Linden, Joni Evans. 'It was thrilling. Very commercial. So simple.'[41]

Although Evans thought the title *Kane and Abel* was corny, most of her colleagues disagreed with her; and Archer himself was immensely proud of it. Despite this difference of opinion, Joni Evans took to Jeffrey from their very first meeting:

He sat down and said, 'Young lady, I've waited seventeen minutes in your waiting-room. Nobody keeps me waiting seventeen minutes.' I liked his brashness. He was so determined to be number one. He was willing to put in the hours. I didn't have other authors like that.[42]

Linden was a small imprint, producing no more than twenty books a year. It had been created especially to cope with Joni Evans's personal situation. She had recently married Dick Snyder, the president of Simon & Schuster, and, rather than have his wife working directly under him, he had decided to hive off a small section of the company. And so Evans ran the Linden Press – for the most part on her own. The small size of the company meant that her authors got individual attention, and, despite the efforts of Cork Smith and Richard Cohen, she felt *Kane and Abel* still needed substantial rewriting.

Archer returned to New York, and to a full-time slog which took several more weeks. To avoid the distractions of the Linden office, they worked from Joni Evans's own apartment at the top of the St Moritz Hotel, overlooking Central Park, with a view to rival that of Archer's own flat in London. They were joined by a young editor from Linden, Jonathan Coleman. 'He wasn't over in New York to fool around,' says Coleman, who is now a full-time writer himself. 'He was very lively and very irreverent, and that fits with Joni's and my personalities.'[43]

Joni Evans agrees: 'The editing process with Jeffrey was as much fun as with anyone I've ever worked with.' The three of them would negotiate their way through the manuscript page by page – arguing, suggesting, rephrasing, cutting, adding, experimenting, altering, polishing, constantly 'heightening the ante' as she puts it. One important task was to keep fleshing out the characters – particularly the women. 'We had a lot of work to do, but it was enhancing work.' Coleman, the most junior of the trio, would sometimes be treated as a kind of whipping-boy. 'Jonathan, can't you think of something!' Archer would bark.[44]

'We're both, I would say, "heavy" editors, rather than light editors,' says Jonathan Coleman. 'So we asked a lot of him, and we argued about things, and we talked them back and forth, and we'd spot inconsistencies. But he never showed any unwillingness to work on things.'[45] And both acknowledge how Archer would happily credit them for their contributions. '"That's Joni's idea," he'd say.'[46] The editors on both sides of the Atlantic would feed their changes to each other, so that, apart from small differences in spelling and terminology, the British and American editions were largely the same.

All Archer's editors on *Kane and Abel* – Richard Cohen and Cork Smith, Joni Evans and Jonathan Coleman – stress that, though the book was heavily edited, the final product was Jeffrey's. 'It wasn't like other people were doing his work for him,' observes Evans. 'He was the talent – an extremely gifted storyteller.'[47] 'He did the rewriting,' insists Coleman, 'but I'd like to think we helped him advance it forward, in terms of what he was trying to do. I mean, he wasn't trying to write a literary masterpiece.'[48]

*Kane and Abel* was published in Britain in September 1979, and within two weeks reached number one in the *Sunday Times* best-seller list; it was the first time any Archer book had appeared on the list at all. Boosted by the publicity for this new novel, the paperback edition of *President* appeared on the chart for the first time too.

Despite this success in Britain, it was not for another six months, when the book was published in America, that Archer and his team realized they had produced a real best-seller on an international scale. By mistake, copies of the American edition were released early in the Miami area. Joni Evans remembers the day vividly:

> My sales people called my office and said, 'This book is just taking off.' . . . I remember calling Dick and saying, 'I'm getting these calls.' He said, 'Let me look.' I remember him calling back and saying, 'My God! This book is exploding!' It was based on word of mouth. People hadn't heard of his other books. It sold without Jeffrey. It was just the way Jeffrey wrote.[49]

But, as ever, the critics were generally less enthusiastic. 'A story about a battle between two millionaires from disparate backgrounds is not a bad idea,' concluded the *Washington Post*. 'But in Archer's clumsy hands it's a mess. He piles cliché upon cliché.'[50] Fortunately his paperback publishers were later able to ignore that verdict in favour of another review from the same paper, which described Archer as 'a storyteller in the class and style of Alexander Dumas'.[51]

It barely mattered what the critics said: the important verdict was in the shops. The months of effort – the rewrites, the 'seventeen drafts' – had all been worth it: *Kane and Abel* spent twenty-nine weeks on the *New York Times* best-seller list of America's top fifteen hardbacks.

When Simon & Schuster sold the American paperback rights to *Kane and Abel*, it finally marked Archer's joining the small group of authors whose work has made them seriously rich. The company's rights director, Susan Kamil, had distributed the manuscript to all the leading US paperback houses, then carefully picked the best date to conduct an auction by telephone.

Fawcett, the publishers of Archer's two previous books, had the right to make an opening bid, and had already offered $325,000. Kamil sat in her office waiting for bids from other houses. At 9 a.m. sharp, Simon & Schuster's own imprint, Pocket Books, offered $350,000. Every few minutes, as the auction went in rounds, Kamil spoke to each of the six publishing houses involved, and by mid-morning the price had topped half a million dollars, as Bantam Books bid $550,000. By lunchtime the price stood at $750,000, and Bantam improved on that again at 3.10 p.m. with a bid of $775,000.

Soon publishers began to reach their ceilings. Berkeley and Warner both dropped out after Pocket Books bid $800,000; then Avon offered $825,000. In the next round Pocket Books withdrew, while Avon in creased their bid to $950,000, within sight of the million-dollar mark. Bantam now gave up as well, leaving a straight contest between Avon and Fawcett. Did Avon want to improve their offer before Fawcett were allowed to bid again? No, they didn't.

It was all down to Fawcett. The company's editor-in-chief, Leona Nevler, had to decide whether Archer would join those few writers whose books had sold for a million dollars. Susan Kamil later described the tension in the Simon & Schuster rights department:

> Leona put down the telephone, and fifteen minutes later called back and said, 'We wish to top', which brought the auction price to over a million dollars. It was fantastic. The entire place went crazy. There isn't any such thing, you have to understand, as decorum, when this is going on. Joni was screaming. I was screaming. Whoever else was in this office, six editors were clapping and applauding, and carrying on and opening champagne and sending flowers and celebrating, and it was a wonderful moment.[52]

Jeffrey knew nothing of this. It was late at night in England when they rang with the news: the American paperback rights for *Kane and Abel* had gone to Fawcett for $1,045,000.

This was an extraordinary figure for an English writer who was still relatively unknown in America, but Fawcett easily recouped their outlay. The paperback edition sold 2.5 million copies in America over the next ten years. And for just one week it finally fulfilled Jeffrey's ambition, to be number one in the *New York Times* best-seller list.

# 17

# Is There Money Still for Me?

In athletics, his hero had been Chris Chataway; in politics, John F. Kennedy; in television, David Frost. Now, as a writer, Jeffrey Archer made no secret of the literary giants upon whom he modelled himself. As he talked to journalists about Dickens and Fitzgerald, about Maupassant, Galsworthy and Graham Greene, the suggestion seemed to be that, with only a little more perseverance, Archer, too, would be up there with the Nobel prize-winners and classic masters. 'Graham Greene is well worth setting up as someone to fight,' he asserted, while both himself and Scott Fitzgerald were two of a kind:

> Fitzgerald isn't a great writer, he's a great storyteller. My writing is entertainment. I'm a storyteller; at the end of the day there are only ten great storytellers and 1,000 great writers. So I'm not worried.[1]

He loved telling people how his editor, Cork Smith, had worked with writers such as Thomas Pynchon:

Cork is a great man. He edits me the way Maxwell Perkins edited Scott Fitzgerald; it makes your book better to have a man of that calibre look at it. After we had finished *Kane and Abel*, Cork said to me, 'Well, young man, what more do you want in life?' I told him I would like to be able to write one book which gained me respect all over the world as a writer. He said, 'You'll never do it, never in your life.' I sat there, broken-hearted. Then he walked to the door, touched the handle, turned and said, 'But of all the men I have worked with, you are the greatest storyteller.' I wept. It was one of the greatest moments of my life. He knew Steinbeck, Hemingway, knew them all; and he acknowledged me above all the great giants.[2]

Smith had never edited Steinbeck or Hemingway, of course, but the implication was obvious. It might have been destiny, as Jeffrey, after all, had been christened in the tiny Somerset church made famous in *Lorna Doone*, and later he had the same Dover landlady who had once looked after Auden and Isherwood. So in 1979 it was only fitting that his writing success should have enabled him to move to a home and village which had been made famous by the English poet Rupert Brooke, who died during the First World War at the age of only twenty-eight. Grantchester will be for ever associated, of course, with one of the best-known couplets in the English language:

>                                          yet
> Stands the Church clock at ten to three?
> And is there honey still for tea?[3]

The Old Vicarage, Grantchester, was where Brooke had rented rooms between 1910 and 1912, though his famous poem with the name of the house was dashed off later, while feeling homesick in Berlin.

Brooke and Archer were rather similar in some ways. Brooke was a popular rather than a classical writer, and also like Archer he was a romantic patriot who liked looking back fondly to an England that probably never existed.

Of the vicarage, the poet once wrote to his cousin, 'This is a lonely, dank, ruined, overgrown, gloomy, lovely house: with a garden to match. It is all five hundred years old and fusty with the ghosts of generations of mouldering clergymen. It is a fit place to write my kind of poetry in.'[4] In fact the house itself was built around 1683, though there had been a cleric's home on the site as early as 1380. In the middle of the back garden, between the house and the river, stands a two-storey Victorian folly.

The house cost £180,000, but it was in a terrible condition; the wiring and plumbing had to be gutted, and it was several months before the Archers could move in. Julian Dakowski, whom Jeffrey had recently employed to redesign the interior at Alembic House, was asked by Mary to help renovate the kitchen, but overall the Archers tried to restore both house and garden to how they had looked during Brooke's day. The folly was turned into offices: Jeffrey's upstairs, and Mary's on the ground floor.

Archer made it clear that his new home would not replace the flat in London, but complement it. The acquisition underlined the Archers' domestic situation: for three years they had effectively led separate lives during the week, with Mary in Cambridge and Jeffrey in London, but spent their weekends together. Mary was rarely seen at the flat, and during all the years Jeffrey has lived in Alembic House her name has never appeared on the electoral roll, even though it would be perfectly legal to register in both places.

The new owner of The Old Vicarage was entering a busy period as a writer. He spent several weeks studying cases at the Old Bailey, and then flew to Barbados to write a play based on a murder trial, once again borrowing Robert Opekar's villa. After he'd completed *Another Witness*, however, Archer had difficulty finding a producer, and it was only eight years later, during more appropriate circumstances, that a revised and retitled version finally reached the stage.

Archer also spent several days working with Cork Smith in New York on a revised version of *Not a Penny More, Not a Penny Less*, which came out in the autumn of 1980. At the same time, BBC Radio 4 transmitted a seven-part dramatization of the book, starring Francis Matthews and Lesley-Ann Down, with Stratford Johns as the American crook, Harvey Metcalfe. Jeffrey himself was the narrator. As a result of this publicity, and Archer's growing success, *Penny* finally spent a few weeks on the best-seller lists in 1981, five years after it was first published.

In 1980, Archer also wrote some children's books. He persuaded Octopus, owned by Paul Hamlyn, to publish *Willy Visits the Square World*, the story of two boys, Willy and Jamie, who live with their parents in Cambridge and embark on a space adventure. A second book, *By Royal Appointment*, published around the same time, relates the story of the King and Queen of Littleland and their attempts to find the fastest car in the kingdom.

By chance, the man who had commissioned Archer for Octopus, Colin Clark, then moved to become head of children's books at his main publishers, Hodder. They produced Archer's third children's story, *Willy and the Killer Kipper*, in 1981. Again it involved Willy and his brother Jamie.

Archer's account is that this venture into children's storytelling was simply a family affair, to placate his sons. 'My two children, at that time eight and six, were grumbling that everyone was telling them that I was a writer, but of course they couldn't read any of my books. So I sat down and wrote a book for them.' 'I only wrote a limited edition,' Archer added, 'and I refuse to allow it to be reprinted.'[5] While by the standards of his best-sellers it may have seemed to Archer to have been a limited edition, former staff at Octopus recall a print run of at least 15,000 copies. 'No way was it a limited edition,' says Graham Marks, the art director for the book: 'Octopus didn't do that sort of thing. They were a highly commercial outfit, a mass-market publisher.'[6] Children's books were a new venture for Octopus; their list was mostly non-fiction adult books. They were blatantly using Archer's name to sell a new product, in the hope that people who loved his novels would also buy his children's books as gifts.

Archer took his children's writing seriously, but he managed to alienate most of the Octopus people with whom he worked. 'He was very bumptious and tended to treat you as a member of his staff,' says Marks. 'I always felt that I had to do things because he was Jeffrey Archer that I wouldn't have had to do for other authors: jump into taxis and rush round to that flat.' Marks remembers having to take samples of various artists' work so that Archer could decide which illustrator he preferred. 'It was almost like we were on Jeffrey's team, when in fact it was basically the other way round . . . I found him an extremely unpleasant man, and working for him on these books was tough work really, because he's quite a hard taskmaster, but you couldn't actually tell him the truth, because they were crap.'[7] 'Had they not been by Jeffrey Archer,' says one Octopus editor, 'I don't think they would have been seriously considered.'

Yet at one point Archer got very angry that the publishers didn't seem to be giving his books the same publicity they were giving those of another children's writer, Michael Bond, the creator of Paddington Bear. Bond had written a new set of stories about an armadillo called J. D. Polson, and as part of the marketing campaign Octopus made a terracotta model to display in shops. When Archer dropped into the office one day and spotted a prototype of the model, he flew into a rage. Why didn't his books merit a model too? Archer picked up the armadillo as if to hurl it at one of the Octopus staff.

Derek Matthews, the illustrator Archer selected, says, 'It was suggested that I should bear in mind his sons.'[8] He was given a photograph of the family, and in the second Willy story the two boys and their parents bear a striking resemblance to the Archers, though Matthews only ever met Jeffrey.

'He saw himself as the next great children's novelist,' says one former Octopus executive. 'He was deadly serious about it.' Yet, unlike his adult fiction, the books were commercial failures, and ended up being remaindered. The tales have the air of bedtime stories which have been scribbled down. It was a very personal project, and Archer surprised his publishers by delivering manuscripts which were handwritten. Graham Marks believes he was using the books to prove 'that he could do it by himself – that was the feeling I got'.[9] Despite being heavily edited at Octopus, the stories still weren't very good, and contained flaws such as a car with 'green wheels, yellow upholstery and striped wheels'.[10]

'A golden opportunity missed,' is how Derek Matthews views it now. 'He didn't put the same amount of effort into these books as he puts into his ordinary books . . . He rather threw it away on these, and I can't quite work out why. They were a bit *too* ordinary.'[11] Archer seems to have been under the common misapprehension that anybody can write children's books; that if your own kids love your stories then so will everyone else's.

Nowadays Archer rarely mentions his brief spell as a children's author: it's consigned to the same closed drawer as his other failures. Indeed, he was most upset when *The Times* mentioned *Willy and the Killer Kipper* in a diary item in 1992. Today the books are difficult to find, and it came as some relief to this author eventually to locate second-hand copies. I can't imagine that the Bodleian Library at Oxford University even gets many requests for any of Jeffrey Archer's adult books, and it had been with some embarrassment that I had gone in and requested a copy of his *Willy and the Killer Kipper*.

If Archer's children's stories had failed to sell, he could at least console himself with the success of his first collection of short stories for adults. *A Quiver Full of Arrows* first came out in Britain in the autumn of 1980.

One story, 'The Luncheon', concerns an impoverished writer who offers to take a film director's wife out for a meal, only for her to choose an expensive restaurant and then pick the dearest items on the menu. As the lunch progresses, he gets increasingly worried about whether he has enough to pay the bill. It was a reworking of a story with the same title and a very similar plot by Somerset Maugham, and Archer acknowledged in the book that his version had been 'inspired' by Maugham.[12]

Archer also admitted at the front of the volume that only one of his stories was 'totally the result of my own imagination'.[13] 'The Coup' was inspired by a business trip Archer made to Nigeria in the mid-1970s, when he found himself stuck in his hotel during an attempted military take-over. 'The Hungarian Professor' is almost entirely factual; it recounts an episode from Archer's visit to the World Student Games in Budapest in 1965. It would be interesting to know who, if anyone, inspired 'One Night Stand', a story of two English friends, Michael and Adrian, who find themselves equally smitten by Debbie, a divorcée they both meet at a party in New York. Rather than quarrel over her, they agree that whoever returns to America first shall get the first chance to try to sleep with her.

The stories flit across the usual range of Archer interests – works of art, cricket, and meals in fine restaurants – and are populated with punctilious characters bound by reassuring daily routines. A nineteenth-century diplomat, Sir Alexander Heathcote, rises each day 'to eat one boiled egg cooked for precisely four minutes, two pieces of toast with one spoonful of Cooper's marmalade, and drink one cup of China tea'; whereas the modern-day Sevenoaks commuter Septimus Horatio Cornwallis leaves home at 7.55 each morning after 'one soft-boiled egg, two pieces of toast, and two cups of tea'.[14] In a hundred years, civilized British society has lost a spoonful of marmalade, but gained an extra cuppa.

The English edition of *A Quiver Full of Arrows* was dedicated to 'Robin and Carolyn' – the political correspondent Robin Oakley and his wife. In America, *Quiver* came out two years later, with the stories in a slightly different sequence, and without the one about cricket, presumably because Americans might have found it hard to comprehend. Here Archer discovered a trick he was to repeat with nearly all his subsequent works: there is nothing to prevent an author dedicating the same book to different friends in different countries. It enabled him to thank a lot more people. For the American edition of *Quiver*, the Oakleys' dedication was replaced by one to Archer's close friend Victoria Campbell Kirsten, with whom he was often seen on social occasions in New York. Kirsten had helped with some of the research for the collection.

Archer has said short stories 'are the form, I must confess, I most love writing'.[15] *Quiver* prompted some of his best reviews from critics in the quality press. 'I consider his novels to be scarcely readable rubbish,' wrote Peter Tinniswood in *The Times*. 'These short stories, however, are a completely different matter. They are stylish, witty and constantly entertaining.'[16] 'All these stories are skilfully constructed and well plotted,' declared Martin Seymour-Smith of the *Financial Times*. 'This is highly professional writing . . . and this writer improves with each book.

He has an exceedingly refreshing good humour, and his capacity to convey deep feeling is by no means common.'[17]

The positive reaction was particularly significant given that *Quiver* involved far less editing than Archer's novels. Both Richard Cohen and Cork Smith worked on the stories, but it was nothing like the formidable task they'd completed before. It was a 'routine editing job', says Smith. His recollection is that the work was performed by post, since the stories were 'very self-contained'.[18]

Cork Smith had much more trouble, though, with Archer's next novel, *The Prodigal Daughter*, the sequel to *Kane and Abel*, in which Abel's daughter, Florentyna, becomes the first woman President of the United States. Much of the early part of the book is familiar to anyone who has already read *Kane and Abel*, and recounts the early years of Florentyna's life. Cork Smith was particularly annoyed by Archer's proposal to take ninety pages from *Kane and Abel* and repeat them verbatim in the new novel.

Smith got involved with *Prodigal* only after Richard Cohen had done an initial edit. The manuscript was sent to him in New York, and then he and Archer worked together when Smith and his family flew to England for a holiday in the spring of 1981. Jeffrey invited them to stay at The Old Vicarage, and he and Smith spent several days in the folly ploughing through the manuscript in their usual manner. Smith refused to touch the ninety pages taken directly from *Kane and Abel*, and he thought it outrageous that Jeffrey proposed to recycle them. 'He said, "What's wrong with that?" I said, "That's plagiarism."' Archer insisted there was nothing wrong with plagiarizing himself, but Smith persisted, arguing it was a disservice to people who had already read *Kane and Abel*. 'You're selling something over again,' Smith recalls saying. 'I'm not sure I ever convinced him there was anything wrong with it. "Who's gonna sue me?" he asked. I said, "A reviewer would kill you on this." I don't think he was morally persuaded this was wrong. What persuaded him was the question of a reviewer.'[19]

In the end, Cork Smith left Joni Evans to resolve the dispute. She agreed with Smith. 'He was plagiarizing himself. He had every right to, but it just couldn't be done.'[20] So when Archer, Evans and a young editorial colleague, Marjorie Williams, began the next stage of revision, this time at Evans's new home on East Sixty-Second Street in New York, they spent much of their time reworking the repeated part of the story. Frequently it was simply a matter of turning sentences round, or describing scenes from the viewpoint of a different character. The outcome was far from satisfactory, especially for a reader who goes directly from the first book to the sequel: long passages appear tediously familiar. In the end, however, only one or two critics mentioned it.

Florentyna was the first substantial female figure to appear in an Archer novel, and he was fully aware of the likely problems. 'He's not good at writing about women,' Mary Archer once remarked. 'He's never been terribly interested in women as characters.'[21]

The story goes that Archer wrote to a number of prominent US politicians and asked them whom they tipped to become the first woman President. Among those supposedly approached were Gerald Ford's former Vice-President, Nelson Rockefeller, and the former Attorney-General and ambassador to Britain, Elliot Richardson. Both men are said to have mentioned a young woman they had employed called Janet Brown. She became both Archer's main researcher, and a model for Florentyna. Yet one should perhaps treat this story with scepticism. More significant is that Brown had been featured as one of a group of up-and-coming Washington high-flyers in *Changing of the Guard*, a book by the respected American commentator David Broder, which Jonathan Coleman had edited for Simon & Schuster. Brown says Coleman sent her the galley proofs of *Kane and Abel*, and asked her to contact Archer.

Once she realized it wasn't a joke, she was enthusiastic about the idea. She worked hard, and made him work hard. Brown saw her role both as immersing Archer in the unfamiliar world of American politics and also as helping him appreciate what issues would be important for an ambitious American woman politician.

Just as Natalie Wexler had for *Kane and Abel*, Janet Brown drew up a year-by-year summary of the important events and social trends over the span of Florentyna's life. She also wrote out her own autobiography up to the age of twenty-nine, to help Archer understand what it was like for an American girl in the 1950s, '60s and '70s. Jeffrey himself saw his story as something of a guide to the political process: 'I wanted schools to be able to say to their students, if you want to be President of the United States, just read *The Prodigal Daughter*.'[22]

Janet Brown spent her evenings and weekends devouring articles and books, highlighting everything she thought Archer ought to read. 'I was just trying to flag things and say, "These things are particularly important." . . . In some cases I ripped a book apart and sent him just chapter two.'[23]

She was very like Archer in some respects. David Broder wrote of the 'Janet Brown faith that, damn it, it doesn't have to be second-rate and it won't be around here'.[24] One suspects, however, that she did far more research than Archer had intended or required. She was also something of a safety net; she read through his early drafts not just to check for factual errors but for a feminine perspective. 'Is there anything that struck you as illogical for a woman politician to do?' she recalls him asking.[25]

Unlike most of Archer's researchers, Janet Brown was never offered payment, and did not expect it. One small acknowledgement, however, came in the story, where she became Florentyna's main political aide and eventually White House chief-of-staff. When the book was launched in the States in 1982, she was paraded in the media as a possible real-life Florentyna, even though she is a Republican, not a Democrat. She appeared on network television programmes and was pressed about her own ambitions. No, she had no plans to run for office, let alone the White House. Today Brown still lives in Washington, running the body which organizes the famous TV debates during presidential elections, and she still keeps in touch with Archer.

But what a pity it was that Jeffrey was never in a position to call on the advice of somebody who would have been ideally qualified to comment on the intricacies of Washington politics: his half-sister Rosemary, who was still alive at the time.

*Prodigal* was no better received by heavyweight reviewers than any of Archer's previous three novels. 'Trashy,' said the *London Review of Books*; 'plodding style and shallow characterization,' declared the *Washington Post*.[26] Florentyna is too dull, too perfect an individual to make a really interesting novel (she never tells lies – not even in a good cause), yet the public bought the book in their millions. Archer took particular satisfaction in the fact that a book about the first American woman President, written by an Englishman, reached number one in the *New York Times* on Independence Day. It was top of the paper's chart for only a week, but spent a month at number one in *Publishers' Weekly*. In all, *Prodigal* featured for almost as long in the American charts as *Kane and Abel* had. Archer proudly took copies of the American and British lists with *Prodigal* at number one and displayed them in the hall of his London flat, waiting to greet visitors as they emerged from the lift.

The subject-matter of *Prodigal* was an obvious one for a novel, and people wondered why nobody had tackled it before. Archer had hit on the right topic at a perfect moment. Margaret Thatcher's resolute conduct of the Falklands War in the weeks before publication prompted many Americans to consider the possibility of a woman as their Commander-in-Chief. Only two years later the Democrat Geraldine Ferraro became the first woman to appear on a US presidential ticket.

Jeffrey Archer had originally planned *Kane and Abel* and *Prodigal* as the first two parts of a trilogy; the third part, *Madam President*, was to cover Florentyna's time in the White House. It's said that Archer even began work on the third book, but abandoned the idea. He still managed to produce his trilogy, however. By the mid-1980s his second novel, *Shall We Tell the President?*, set in 1983, had obviously been overtaken by events. So in 1985 he revised the book and replaced the original assassination target, Edward Kennedy, with Florentyna Kane, shunting the setting forward to the late 1990s. It was a neat move, not least because it made the book less offensive to the Kennedy family.

The American edition of *Prodigal* was dedicated to two of his US publishers, Tom Guinzburg and Leona Nevler. The dedication in the British version, however, was to 'Peter, Joy, Alison, Clare and Simon', who were leading members of staff at Hatchards bookshop in Piccadilly.[27] It was a sign of the effort Archer put into selling his books, and of how he cultivated important bookshop staff. 'Peter' was Peter Giddy, Hatchards' managing director, while 'Simon' was Simon Bainbridge, the shop manager. Archer got to know the Hatchards people so well that he sometimes asked their advice about his manuscripts. After he'd ceased working for the shop, Simon Bainbridge helped research an Archer novel, and co-edited a collection of political short stories with him.[28]

At the time, it was reckoned that if Hatchards backed a book it could sell thousands more. Particularly coveted was a place on the circular table at the shop entrance. 'To get a book on that front table was vitally important,' says Derick Bostridge, a former Hodder sales director. 'It was as important as a television interview practically. You could watch people spend hundreds of pounds there on books. It was amazing.'[29]

Archer got so involved in selling his books that former Hodder staff say he sometimes behaved as if he worked for the company. Together, Archer and the Hodder/Coronet sales force took book marketing into a whole new league, particularly in paperbacks. Unlike most authors, Jeffrey Archer immersed himself in the minutiae of bookselling. 'He actually bothered to learn the rules, and tried to make it work for him,' says Derick Bostridge. 'I can think of no other author who's made it through the sheer, real, hard graft of going round, talk, talk, talking to anybody who would listen, and making it so quick.' Bostridge adds that, 'from a publisher's point of view, that is what you dream for'.[30] 'He was somebody who was always interested in what's happening,' says the then Coronet boss, Alan Gordon Walker. 'He wanted to meet the reps and the sales director and get involved in every part of the process.'[31]

Archer promised Hodder salesmen he would do anything to promote his books, any time, anywhere. Local radio and television producers loved him as an interview guest who was always guaranteed to be lively and controversial. He'd do book-signing sessions not just in big city stores but also in ordinary shops in smaller towns; he might sign fewer books there, but the visit would create much more of a splash in the local media. He loved telling people that Graham Greene had been only seventeenth in the *New York Times* when he had been top. 'You know why? Because he won't go out and promote his books like I do. I can't understand it.'[32] Archer especially relished the kind of hard sell that other authors found distasteful. He would appear at Hodder sales conferences and deliver a brilliant, funny speech, reminding the reps about how he'd worked his way back from near bankruptcy, and rousing them to go out and sell his new novel like they had never sold a book before. Afterwards he'd buy the reps a drink in the bar and spend time chatting to them. It sounds simple, but it was something most big authors didn't do. The reps felt he was professional; he gave a buzz and excitement to their work.

In advance of publication, reps would be given proof copies of his new book and be encouraged to read it to help generate an air of anticipation about the launch. Two months before it came out, Archer would do a pre-publication book tour, a series of receptions in about eight cities, where he would give a short talk (tailored to each location) about his new title, and then talk to local bookshop staff. From *Prodigal* onwards the launch date for every new novel was always June or July – just in time to catch the summer-holiday market, before picking up a steady Christmas trade through the autumn.

Archer also imported some political skills from his previous career: he went out of his way to learn the reps' names, noted their home phone numbers, and treated some of them like long-lost friends when he met them again. While he was visiting their patch, he would take them to dinner in a good restaurant. Sometimes the whole sales team would be invited for drinks at Alembic House, and on one occasion, during a Hodder sales conference in Cambridge, Archer threw them a champagne buffet in the garden at Grantchester. They felt he bullied them at times, but they admired the effort he put in. 'I worked harder for him than other authors,' admits Gordon McChesney, Coronet's flamboyant rep in the North-West. 'You felt you wanted to push hard. He sent letters to the reps telling them to get out there and sell the book: "200,000 is not enough, you've got to sell half a million." They were photocopied, but with a hand-written PS.'[33] McChesney consistently sold more Archers than any other salesman, and when he finally retired, after twenty-nine years with Hodder, Jeffrey made a surprise appearance at his leaving dinner.

Hodder reps were constantly kept on their toes. Wherever Archer travelled, he would pop into shops to check that his books were there. He would see whether any editions had sold out, or tell the local manager that they ought to be displayed more prominently. Sometimes he would rearrange the display himself.

He became obsessed with his sales figures. Most authors wait for their half-yearly royalty statements, or ask the occasional embarrassed question. Not Archer. He insisted that at least once a week somebody from Hodder ring him with the latest details, quizzing them for more information. Which areas were selling best? Why was this figure down? What new orders had come in? Had W. H. Smith reordered yet? Archer wanted to know not just about his most recent hardback, but about all his paperback titles too. By the mid-1980s, he had established one of the strongest backlists of any top-selling author. The paperback editions would often be repackaged with new covers whenever a new hardback novel came out, and the backlist was given special promotion when a new Archer was being publicized.

In 1983, for instance, *Prodigal* was the top-selling paperback in Alex Hamilton's annual survey of fast-sellers for *The Guardian*, with sales of 1,170,000 in Britain and the Commonwealth; in the same year Coronet also sold 549,000 copies of the three previous Archer novels, each of which would have earned a high placing in Hamilton's list had not the survey been confined to new paperbacks.[34] Each new book created a new cohort of Archer fans, who would then devotedly buy each previous title. 'The thing I'm most proud of,' said Archer, 'is that 86 per cent of people who have read one of my books have read all five.'[35] It's not clear where this figure came from, and it may be an exaggeration, but the general thrust was true, for he had generated a loyal fan club, several million strong. Many of them didn't read a lot of other writers, and two-thirds were women.[36]

By 1982 Archer was telling people he was paying the taxman £1,000 a day, implying an income of around £600,000 a year. He was profiled in the Sunday colour supplements; he appeared on television chat shows; he chose his favourite records for the BBC's *Desert Island Discs* (including 'Oh Lord It's Hard to be Humble When You're Perfect in Every Way'). And one day, while jogging across Westminster Bridge, he was ambushed by the Somerset cricket team and a track-suited Eamonn Andrews declaring, 'This is Your Life!' Yet despite the millions he was now making, despite the Henry Moore sculpture on the coffee-table and the Russell Flints on his wall, and despite his rapidly spreading fame and the recognition worldwide, Archer still hadn't managed to achieve the success he really craved.

Even though he no longer needed to sell film or television rights to secure his financial future, it nevertheless annoyed him deeply that none of his novels had yet been filmed. Although Warner Brothers had acquired the rights to *Not a Penny More*, they had done nothing with them, and around 1981 the rights were picked up by Charles Joory, an Iraqi-Jewish businessman based in Hong Kong. The Hollywood director Mel Frank agreed to make the film, and even drafted a screenplay which was then rewritten by others in London. However, Joory knew little of how the film industry worked, and he got embroiled with a succession of investors, producers and writers. Although he put thousands of dollars into the project, nothing came of it except a protracted legal dispute.

As Debbie Owen's expertise was mainly in publishing, Archer secured the services of Dennis Selinger, a film agent who typically represented actors rather than writers, numbering Roger Moore, Michael Caine and Oliver Reed among his clients. Selinger found Archer frustrating, since the novelist would often pursue his own production deals at the same time. For instance, the writer struck up a friendship with the American director Otto Preminger, after the two men met on a plane. Preminger was quoted in the paperback edition as saying that *Kane and Abel* was 'one of the best novels I have ever read', and he caused a flurry of excitement when he turned up to the launch party in Archer's flat.[37] 'Now, you be kind to Otto,' Jeffrey was heard telling guests as they arrived.[38] Preminger's enthusiasm came to nothing, however, though his widow says he did seriously consider a film of the book.

Stories then began appearing in diary columns saying that Steven Spielberg was taking an interest in Archer's work. It was also reported that Jeffrey had turned down an offer of $250,000 from Spielberg to write the book to accompany his blockbuster film ET. 'I thought about it and realized it was not my sort of book,' Archer said. 'I am a storyteller myself, not just a wordsmith, and although the money was good, I didn't need it that badly.'[39] Despite the reports, Dennis Selinger says the young Hollywood director never seriously considered Archer's work: 'Jeffrey did get in touch with Spielberg, but I doubt very much if he was interested, as Steven Spielberg very much likes to create his own properties.'[40] In the end, Selinger sold an option for Kane and Abel to Michael Grade, then director of programmes at London Weekend Television, who planned a co-production with NBC of America. After LWT's option expired, Grade bought the rights a second time when he moved to Embassy Television in Hollywood.

Grade is reported to have paid £300,000 to televise Kane and Abel, but Archer wasn't much bothered about the sums involved, and sold the rights to Prodigal Daughter to the BBC for one pound. He and Selinger knew that the real impact of dramatizing any of his novels would be to boost his book sales. But the process of getting a film made was too slow for Archer. He had started writing seven years earlier with Hollywood specifically in mind, yet by 1982 the only production of any Archer work had been a Radio 4 serialization of Penny.

A strong sense of show business seems to run through the Archer veins, having first manifested itself during his schooldays. He not only wanted the world to see his work on screen, he also felt the urge to perform himself. If only given the chance, Archer believed, he could be a world-renowned television personality. 'I want my own talk show,' he said in 1977. 'I want to be the serious David Frost.'[41] 'I've tried by talking to one or two people in high places in the BBC and ITV,' he said two years later, 'but nothing has come of it yet. I look on this as a failure.'[42]

In 1981 he gave it another try. When the two main channels announced the start of breakfast television in the UK, Archer asked an old BBC contact whether he could present the BBC's new show. Chris Capron, who'd made the 24 Hours film about the Louth by-election, was now head of BBC TV Current Affairs. Like Paul Fox many years before, Capron suspected Archer might be right in claiming he'd do a good job; he certainly had enough confidence. But more established stars like Frank Bough had much stronger claims.

Earlier, in 1976, no doubt hoping it would help his ambitions as a television performer, Archer had even become a member of Equity. The actors' union is notoriously difficult to join (particularly so then), but Archer was allowed in on the strength of his work for BBC and ITV sport in the late 1960s, since sports commentary is a qualification for Equity membership. He has remained a paid-up member ever since, though Equity officials seem a little embarrassed about the fact. The actors' union card would enable Archer to pursue one of his most extra-ordinary ambitions – to become a Hollywood actor.

Archer cajoled Otto Preminger into letting him audition for a part in his film *The Human Factor*, based on the Graham Greene spy novel. Archer was then filmed in a bedroom scene in London, running through a conversation with a succession of actresses who were trying for the female part.

'It was more of a joke than anything,' says the director's widow, Hope Preminger.[43] It seems Otto Preminger was auditioning the actresses while caressing Jeffrey's ego. The part he was trying for – as a British agent – eventually went to Nicol Williamson.

'I remember sitting with him in a theatre watching the rushes,' says Hope Preminger. 'And he turned to me and said, "I guess it's back to politics," or something like that.'[44]

# 18

# Ham–Salad Days

A biographer can learn a lot from the pages of *Who's Who*: not just from what people say, or don't say, about themselves, but also from how their entries change. From 1978 to 1981 Archer's description read, rather self-deprecatingly, 'author and has-been politician'. Then in 1982 the 'has–been' disappeared, and he became simply an 'author and politician'.[1] Jeffrey was bouncing back.

Leon Brittan, the Tory MP who'd checked his early manuscripts for possible libel, was among the first to invite Archer to address a political gathering, with his local party in Cleveland and Whitby. Word quickly got round among grass-roots Conservatives elsewhere that Archer was a good speaker, a little out of the ordinary. With his growing fame and popularity as a writer, he soon proved to be much more of a crowd-puller with local activists than the average Cabinet minister.

The invitations began flowing in: to coffee-mornings, women's lunches, association annual dinners, fund-raising auctions and, of course, by-election campaigns. Jeffrey accepted them all, adding a touch of glamour to politics; he was a name people had heard of, and a face they were starting to recognize. And, after each Conservative gathering, the author happily stayed behind to sign the copies of his books which he usually took along to sell. Hodder allowed him a larger discount than they normally gave to bookshops, and the profits of Archer's private Tory sales went to party funds.

Quite unlike any other guest speaker, Jeffrey would hector local Tories to get out and roll up their sleeves for the party, just as he was doing. He was blunt to the point of rudeness. In his home town of Weston, for example, he accused local Conservatives of being 'far too fat and far too lazy' to do anything.[2] 'Sit down, you silly woman!' he harangued a lady in Worcestershire who stood up during a raffle at the wrong moment.[3] Yet somehow Jeffrey got away with it: most Tory women were charmed rather than offended.

Yet there was an underlying political current to his popularity, too. In working his way back from the brink of ruin to new fame and wealth, Archer epitomized what Margaret Thatcher's Conservative Party stood for in the 1980s: hard work, enterprise, making money, and succeeding against all the odds.

Archer was delighted to join the so-called 'rubber-chicken circuit', though it was the number of Conservative ham salads he had to consume that he always joked about. It was tiring work, often monotonous, and at his own expense, but he reckoned it was worth it. He still had hopes of returning to politics full-time, but had been advised by Leon Brittan that any promotion to an official position would first have to be earned.

At the end of a successful meeting, Archer would ask his Tory audience if they had enjoyed themselves. 'Yes!' they shouted. Were they sure? 'Yes!' Then could they do him a small favour? Would they please write to Mrs Thatcher and tell her what a wonderful evening they'd had together? The letters began pouring into Downing Street from constituency associations around the country, each relating what a marvellous time they'd had with Jeffrey Archer, and saying how much he'd done to raise their spirits. Number Ten wasn't fooled: officials realized the mail wasn't entirely spontaneous. Equally, though, it couldn't be ignored. 'They came in kind of waves,' says one former official; 'they clearly had some kind of little push behind them.' People wouldn't write just because a speaker told them to, however: they must have been genuinely enthused. The Geoffrey Howes and John Selwyn Gummers would never rouse so many grass-roots members to write letters of praise and commendation, no matter how much they asked them to.

Archer quickly found himself in demand for other purposes too. Was he interested in standing for Parliament again? He later claimed to have been approached by twenty or thirty different constituencies, including one of the safe seats in Lincolnshire, but he said he had no wish to return to the Commons – at least not for now. 'I have no political ambitions any more,' he even claimed in 1982, at a time when it still sounded half-convincing.[4]

There was also speculation that Archer might join the new Social Democratic Party (SDP), formed in 1981 when David Owen and his associates in the 'Gang of Four' broke away from Labour. Archer was an obvious target for the new party. During his five years as an MP he'd always shown himself the kind of left-wing Conservative the SDP was keen to attract. The link through Debbie Owen fuelled the speculation, of course, and when her husband became leader of the Social Democrats, in 1983, Jeffrey (and others) teased people that it was only Debbie Owen's commission on his literary earnings which kept the new party going financially.

Press stories even appeared saying that Archer was being courted by the SDP to stand for Parliament. One can guess the source of these. Pat Otter of the *Grimsby Evening Telegraph* remembers the time, shortly before *The Prodigal Daughter* was published, when Archer rang and suggested he might be interested in selling a story to the nationals. Did he know that a former Tory MP was being approached by the SDP to fight Louth? The journalist was familiar with Jeffrey's ways of handling the press:

> I said, 'Do you mean you?' He said, 'It would certainly be a good story, wouldn't it?' 'Is it true?' I asked. 'Not in so many words. But what do you think of it as a story?'[5]

Not much, Otter replied, and he left it to others to feed Jeffrey's tale to Fleet Street. When they did, Archer was happy to declare his lack of interest. 'To the Social Democrat who spoke to me, I had to say that I remain a firm Conservative and a firm supporter of Mrs Thatcher.'[6]

Yet, while rejecting offers to stand again for Parliament, Archer couldn't resist one political campaign in 1984: for the rectorship of Glasgow University. Officially the rector acts as the students' representative and chairs the university court. It's a prestigious job, having been held in times past by prominent figures ranging from Benjamin Disraeli and William Gladstone to the television newsreader Reginald Bosanquet. But, as a Conservative standing on a Scottish campus, Archer wasn't given much of a chance.

He faced a diverse list of opponents – Michael Kelly, the Labour lord provost of Glasgow; Rikki Fulton, a traditional Scottish comedian; Matt Lygate, who'd been convicted of a bank robbery committed in the cause of Scottish independence; Menzies Campbell, the Liberal QC and former athlete (and Archer's team captain on the one occasion he ran for Britain); and the PLO chairman, Yasser Arafat. In an early (and extremely unscientific) opinion poll carried out for the Glasgow student newspaper, Archer was a poor fourth, scoring just 9 per cent.[7]

Jeffrey was never going to win, but his efforts ensured that the Conservative cause wasn't humiliated. Traditionally, candidates were not meant to campaign but that had changed the previous time round,

16. The Beatles had no option but to support Oxfam's 1963 Hunger Million campaign after Archer and Nick Lloyd (second from left) had announced the group's backing in *Cherwell*, though the group did little more for Oxfam than pose for this picture.

17. With Harold Macmillan at the 1964 Oxfam lunch from which the Beatles suddenly withdrew. One of the Beatles' staff had forgotten the engagement.

18. Sir Noel Hall and the Beatles at Brasenose College in 1964. From the left: Nick Lloyd, Paul McCartney, George Harrison, Archer, Hall, David Stockton (college dean), Ringo Starr and John Lennon. This picture, which appeared in the *Daily Mail*, is in fact two photos – note the join to the left of Sir Noel.

19. On a flying visit to the White House in 1964, where President Johnson signed a collection of Churchill's speeches for Oxfam.

20. Oxford had a surplus of good sprinters in 1965, and it looked as if Jeffrey might have the embarrassment of not making the Varsity team during his year as president. So he took up hurdling to guarantee his place.

21. Wedding day, 1966. Back row: Adrian Metcalfe (best man); Harold Weeden (Mary's father); Lola Archer; Jeffrey; Mary; Doreen Weeden (Mary's mother); 'Wings' Watson (Jeffrey's stepfather). Front: Jeffrey's 'foster' sister, Liz Fullerton, and Mary's sister, Janet. The marriage certificate incorrectly described Jeffrey as a 'research graduate'.

22. Campaigning with Mary and his hero Chris Chataway in his 1926 Bullnose Morris, during the 1967 GLC election.

23. Mary saw her scientific career as a means of insulating herself from Jeffrey's troubles. She played an important role in editing Jeffrey's first novel, and was a successful writer before he was, winning a BBC short-story contest in 1971.

24. Edward Heath opens the Archer Gallery in 1969. With them is the sculptor and painter Leon Underwood, for whom Archer became something of a patron.

25. Louth Town Hall steps. Archer always claimed he was the youngest MP after winning the Louth by-election in 1969 at the age of twenty-nine. In fact he was only the fifth youngest.

26. A hospital visit with Lord Mountbatten to see Noël Coward, who had to withdraw from the 1970 Night of Nights. Mountbatten and Archer quickly arranged for Princess Grace of Monaco to take Coward's place.

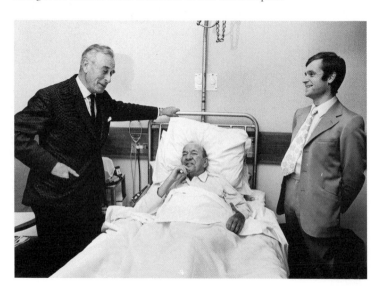

27. Mary swimming for charity in Louth in 1970. Louth Tories were keen to have a 'good constituency wife', and Mary almost certainly clinched the nomination for Jeffrey.

28. Swinging to the left. As an MP, Archer was well to the left of the Conservative Party and often rebelled against the Heath government.

29. Mary with their two sons, William, born in 1972, and James, two years younger.

when Bosanquet had defeated the Scottish Nationalist politician Margo MacDonald. It was Archer's first election since Louth, exactly ten years before, and he took it almost as seriously. He spent much of the three-week campaign in Glasgow, operating from a suite in the Grosvenor Hotel, meeting as many students as he could. He promised to be 'a working rector', with regular surgeries 'so that students could express their grievances'.[8] Perhaps the only slip occurred when someone asked about student housing. Archer promised to consult a ministerial friend at the Scottish Office. A good reply, it seemed, until it was pointed out that student housing is looked after not by the Scottish Office but by the Department of Education in London.

Archer 'charmed the pants off people', says John Nicolson, a prominent Glasgow debater who ran Matt Lygate's campaign.[9] He was particularly impressive in a big confrontation held at the Glasgow Union debating society. The ancient Union chamber can be an intimidating arena for any speaker, far more hostile than the more genteel Oxbridge Unions; Glasgow students think little of hurling fruit or half-eaten pies at speakers they dislike. That night the hall was overflowing, with a far bigger audience than for many years. 'We all thought Archer would be hammered,' Nicolson recalls, but he delivered a 'sizzling speech'. He warmed his audience with jokes they hadn't heard before, and a brilliant put-down of one student who tried to trip him up.[10]

In the final ballot Archer did better than forecast. Under the single-transferable-vote system, he survived to the last three candidates, polling 859 votes, compared with 1,641 for Fulton and 2,590 for the winner, Michael Kelly. A consolation prize came a few months later – an invitation to become president of the Glasgow University Dialectic Society, another student debating club.

Archer's return to political life was symbolized by the publication of his fifth novel, in the summer of 1984. If *The Prodigal Daughter* had taught aspiring presidents how to reach the White House, then *First Among Equals* was a step-by-step guide on how to become Prime Minister. It covers the careers of four rival MPs elected to Parliament in 1964 – two Conservative and two Labour. As they clamber up the political ladder, and are occasionally forced to step down a rung or two, Archer recounts their interlocking career advancement and scheming, their business failures and successes, their personal lives and, in two cases, their adultery.

His publishers naturally trumpeted *First Among Equals* as 'The Book he was Born to Write'. It was the first time Archer had drawn on his experience in Parliament (and, cheekily, he even mentioned his own Louth by-election at one point). Alan Gordon Walker's brother, Robin, a civil servant, was paid a small fee to check that the workings of Whitehall were accurately portrayed, and the political correspondent Robin Oakley was among several Westminster friends also asked to spot errors. Nevertheless, a surprising number of mistakes survived into the final text, including obvious aspects of parliamentary procedure.

Understandably, perhaps, Archer was best at describing Tory politics. His knowledge of how the Labour Party works bordered on the infantile at times; he failed to understand, for example, that members of the Communist Party cannot join Labour.

The story also suffered from a lack of contrast between the main characters, particularly with regard to their politics. Reflecting perhaps Archer's own pragmatic outlook, none of his four MPs was ideologically committed. Both his Labour MPs were fairly right-wing, while the politics of his two Tories were also difficult to differentiate. This was particularly surprising given that the book was written in the early 1980s, when Margaret Thatcher and Tony Benn were in the ascendancy and the gulf between left and right in British politics was greater than at any time since the Second World War. It may reflect the fact that Archer was also writing for an American audience, who might have found a committed left-winger uncongenial.

The Tory MP Simon Kerslake is obviously the man closest to Archer:

> The Americans would have described him as 'an achiever', while many of his contemporaries thought of him as pushy, or even arrogant, according to their aptitude for jealousy.[11]

A left-of-centre Conservative from a middle-class background, Kerslake attends a minor public school and then Oxford. Equally telling, he almost has to resign when he faces bankruptcy after speculating on an investment that goes wrong. Elizabeth Kerslake, his wife, was clearly modelled on Mary; she pursues an independent career as a leading gynaecologist, and finds it hard to balance the conflicting demands of medicine and politics.

The ultimate prize, however – the premiership – goes to Raymond Gould, a Denis Healey–Roy Hattersley type of Labour intellectual from a working-class background in north Leeds.

Archer was taking a risk with *First Among Equals*, jeopardizing the following he'd built up in the United States and other overseas markets. For the first time he was writing entirely about a British subject, for while *Penny* had been based in England, it was carefully crafted to feature American characters and foreign locations. Archer's American fans would know far less about the workings of the House of Commons than a British audience would about Congress. His American publisher, Joni Evans, had severe concerns about this when she bought the book, but to her credit she never tried to dissuade Archer from pursuing the idea.

Cork Smith was the book's first editor, but his role was much diminished. He was now running a small publishing imprint, and no longer had time to sit down with his author as before. Paid a set fee of around $10,000, it was his last contribution to any Archer book. 'I think we had kind of worn each other out,' he says.[12]

Since working on the short-story collection, *A Quiver Full of Arrows*, Richard Cohen had established himself as Archer's main editor. He and his author had developed a routine. Over a period of four to six weeks they would meet every day for two intensive sessions of two hours each, morning and afternoon, working through the text almost line by line, discussing amendments, additions and improvements. Every evening, or early the following morning, Archer would sit down alone and do what Cohen called his 'homework', redrafting long sections or writing new passages. Once this initial edit was complete, the whole manuscript would be retyped for Joni Evans to read for the first time. Archer and Cohen agreed they didn't like Joni to see anything until they had spent several weeks working on the manuscript.

The sheer weight of editorial work involved in a Jeffrey Archer novel was illustrated by an hour-long television documentary, *Best Seller?*, made by the director Mike Ockrent. It went into great detail about how *Equals* was written, edited and then marketed, and Ockrent shot sequences in the Bahamas, New York and London. It is easily the most revealing programme ever made about Jeffrey Archer, but it was only ever transmitted in the HTV television region, and by a few small stations in America.

Although there was obviously a large element of reconstruction for the benefit of Ockrent's camera, the film still has an authentic feel. One scene shows Cohen and Archer at Alembic House, ten months before publication. Jeffrey sits in a cricket sweater, with a pot of about twenty of his favourite blue pencils on the table in front of him. The camera cuts away to show his leg jiggling furiously beneath the table, and then a uniformed maid enters, carrying a large glass of orange-juice. The two men are heard debating a name for an aristocratic character. Archer's original choice is Clarence. No, that's wrong, Cohen says – 'almost a Monty Python name for a lord'. How about Adrian? No, Jeffrey doesn't like Adrian, and then throws up other possibles: 'James, Simon, Nigel.' No, definitely not Nigel, they both agree. 'It's a wanky name,' Archer says.[13] Considering the thousands of Nigels who must read his books, it's perhaps just as well that Ockrent's film never had a big audience.

When Archer turned up in New York with his new manuscript for Joni Evans, she felt her earlier worries might have been misplaced. 'Wait till you read the first chapter,' she remembered him saying. Then, with boyish Archer enthusiasm, he sat down and recited the opening section to her. Hearing it read aloud, Evans felt reassured: it didn't sound too bad. But when she took Jeffrey's text home to enjoy it in comfort she was 'slightly horrified'.

> It was impossible to follow. It wasn't as smooth or as polished. I didn't feel it had the kind of draft workmanship that usually Jeffrey does, and I was quite alarmed about it, frankly.[14]

Evans rang Debbie Owen and explained her worries, thinking a fellow American might be more sympathetic. Owen reassured her that she was absolutely right to be anxious. She agreed that Jeffrey was being too confident, that he simply didn't realize how much more work needed doing.

As Evans began going through the manuscript in detail, she had a call late one evening from Richard Cohen. According to the New York editor, Cohen had heard about her anxieties from Owen:

> I had the best phone call of my life. 'Joni, poor darling, oh my God,' he said. And so the two of us colluded, if you will, in the most kind way. And Richard said, 'Put that manuscript down! Put it down! Jeffrey shouldn't have let you see it at this point!' Usually Richard goes through the process first before I see the book, and so he said, 'You're seeing it at much too rough a stage. It must be alarming you, poor child. Just relax. Go to sleep.'[15]

Although Cohen and Archer had already gone through one long editing spell together, his English editor assured Evans that they'd always planned to do more work before she saw the manuscript. Evans even suggested it might help if she flew to London and joined Cohen in working with Archer. Cohen put her off the idea, arguing it would be much better if she came 'totally fresh' to the 'revised script' later on.

The initial American editing took place at Joni Evans's farm at Pound Ridge, a large country house with two live-in housekeepers in Westchester County, about forty-five minutes from Manhattan. Evans was joined by a young colleague, Marjorie Williams, while Archer was accompanied by Andrina Colquhoun, whom he had appointed his personal assistant.

Colquhoun, then in her early thirties, was an attractive, blue-eyed blonde from an aristocratic 'deb' background; she laughed a lot and clearly enjoyed life. Brought up by her stepfather, Peter Meyer of the Meyer Montague timber company, she was wealthy in her own right, but attracted to men of power. She first came to public attention through her friendship with Lord Lucan, for whom she waited in vain at the Clermont Club on the night he disappeared under suspicion of murder. She was a photographer by profession, but as Archer's PA she often acted as his hostess at the flat and as his escort on outside social occasions.

There was one change that Joni Evans had to consider at some length before she dared broach it with her author. Could he possibly introduce an American character – perhaps through one of the politicians' wives? 'Just for the translation purposes,' she suggested, 'making things easier for us to understand'. It would help make the book more accessible to the US audiences, and David Owen, of course, was only the most obvious example of an unusual number of British politicians who have American wives. Archer resisted the idea, arguing that if the book was good enough it didn't need 'an American sex scene in order to sell the thing. I think that's absolute drivel and I'll have nothing to do with it.'[16] In the end they compromised, and Raymond Gould acquired an American mistress.

Evans still felt the book didn't work for a US audience, partly because there were too many characters. 'I was thinking it was so complicated for an American to get what was going on. We had to simplify it . . . You're talking about British politics for an American. It was unsolvable, a maze. He understood that we could not leave it the way it was.'[17] Her solution was straightforward: produce a simpler edition of the story for the American market.

Traditionally, there have often been minor differences between the British and American editions of the same novel, particularly in commercial fiction. But Joni Evans's solution to the *First Among Equals* problem involved radical surgery. The Queen featured more heavily, and much of the action involving parliamentary procedure was either cut or explained.

The most glaring change was that the two books had different endings. Rather than finish with Raymond Gould, the Labour politician, in Number Ten, as in the original story (a rather generous gesture on Jeffrey's part), in the American edition the victor was the middle-class Tory 'achiever', Simon Kerslake. Evans decided that Kerslake was a much more attractive figure than Gould, especially for an audience which might find a Labour Prime Minister a rather alien idea.

Cork Smith says that it's 'significant' that it should have been so easy to switch the closing section in this way, and that it says a lot about Archer's work. 'In a well-made novel the ending may surprise us but in retrospect you realize it seems inevitable. From a literary point of view that [being able to change the ending] is a flaw.'[18]

The most complicated change, however, was that the four main characters in the British edition were distilled to three for America. Andrew Fraser, the Scottish Labour MP who defects to the SDP, was reduced to a minor role. He was the most obvious candidate for the chop, especially since Americans might have had trouble coping with the idea of a third political party. And not only was Fraser's character too similar to Simon Kerslake's, his right-wing Labour politics were too close to those of Raymond Gould. Removing him, however, was inevitably more complex than simply cutting out all the passages in which he featured. The original plot involved a whole series of interactions between Fraser and each of the other main figures, and somehow all of these had to be reworked. Several episodes from Fraser's career in the British version were simply reassigned to other players in the US edition.

At times Joni Evans and Marjorie Williams thought it was an impossible task. They spent several weeks rethinking the whole plot, working out the implications of Andrew Fraser's elimination. Evans compares the process to solving a puzzle where everything has to fall exactly into place. 'We kept blocking it and it didn't come out the same way,' she says.[19] After several weeks, everyone realized the book still wasn't right. Rather than face another long session in Westchester, all four flew to a villa Archer had found at Lyford Cay near Nassau in the Bahamas, to complete the work. The party included Andrina Colquhoun, who cooked meals for the team.

The weather was superb, of course, but Archer simply wanted to get on with the book, and Evans and Williams had to fight each day just to get a few minutes outside. ' "Jeffrey, the sun is out," we'd say. "Not yet, young lady." It would be a perfectly gorgeous day,' Evans recalls, 'and Jeffrey would insist we kept working.'[20] As they toiled away inside, the two editors found themselves playing parts. Joni Evans found this much easier to tolerate than her younger partner did. Though Archer usually accepted their suggestions in the end, they had to suffer his continuous mock contempt: 'If you knew anything about narrative, young lady, then . . .' and, 'What you have suggested to me, young lady, is perfectly terrible, but I see the need for a line here, so . . .' Then Jeffrey would slowly enunciate each word as he wrote out the new text in his rather childish handwriting.

While the American editors were working on their version of the book, Richard Cohen was in constant touch to discuss possible changes to both editions. Once the British proofs were ready, Cohen spent another week or two making further improvements with Archer, and yet more time when a revised set of proofs became available. But editing can't go on for ever. 'There's only so much you can do,' Cohen once explained. 'The book is slotted in for publication on a certain day and the bird must fly.'[21]

With *The Prodigal Daughter* and now *First Among Equals*, Debbie Owen and Archer had offered his publishers, Hodder & Stoughton, an extraordinary arrangement whereby they would pay the author an advance of just one pound. It was a trick that Archer claims to have picked up from Arthur Hailey, whom he'd met in the Bahamas. When the chairman of Collins, Ian Chapman, heard of the deal, he rang up and offered to double it. Hodder paid up with a flourish, presenting Archer with one gold sovereign. The other side of the coin, though, was that Archer was granted an unusually high royalty: $17\frac{1}{2}$ per cent on his hardbacks and 15 per cent on paperbacks – well beyond the normal range. 'I have decided that at this stage of my career I would much prefer to be earning from percentage on the book – from royalties – rather than have a high advance,' Archer explained, though the formula did not extend to America.[22]

The launch of the book in Britain in July 1984 involved an even more unorthodox move. The *Mail on Sunday* paid Archer £90,000 to serialize the whole of *First Among Equals* in four consecutive, pull-out magazine sections. The idea was not new – Charles Dickens, Wilkie Collins and other Victorian writers had regularly issued their novels in serial format – but it was said to be the first case in modern times of a new novel being completely serialized like this.

The expected gain for the newspaper was obvious: a rise in circulation at a time when it was still trying to establish itself after its troubled launch two years before. For the author and publisher, however, it represented far more of a gamble. It was possible, on the one hand, that the promotion and publicity attached to such a serialization would encourage new readers to pick up Archer for the first time, and that they would prefer the convenience of a book to having their novel spread across several newspapers. On the other hand, it was equally possible that readers would opt to pay £1.32 for four copies of the *Mail on Sunday* rather than seven times that amount for a new hardback. On top of that, Hodder & Stoughton were annoyed that Archer had negotiated the *Mail on Sunday* deal without their consent, and they questioned the whole legality of the venture under the terms of their contract with him. Booksellers were also concerned.

Hodder relented when the *Mail on Sunday* promised to spend £500,000 on promoting the serialization, and further reassurance came with advance orders of 104,000, including 2,000 copies for W. H. Smith at the Brent Cross shopping centre in north London. This was a record for Hodder, though many of the orders had been placed before the *Mail on Sunday* deal was arranged. The 130,000 print run was also a company record.

Though *Equals* was the second-highest hardback best-seller of 1984 (albeit well behind *The Growing Pains of Adrian Mole*), British bookshops seemed disappointed at first, with many smaller stores reporting lower sales than anticipated. But George Greenfield, the literary agent who originally sold the serialization idea in principle to Associated Newspapers, before Archer was chosen as the author, later insisted that, 'No one in the trade could reasonably claim that the *Mail on Sunday*'s serial version had in any way inhibited the novel's book sales.' He cited Hodder's figures. While *The Prodigal Daughter* had sold 40,000 copies in Britain in the first three weeks after publication – and a further 50,000 abroad – *First Among Equals* sold 60,000, and another 56,000 overseas. And the paperback edition of *Equals* issued the following year was particularly successful, with more than a million copies ordered before publication day; it outsold *The Prodigal Daughter* by 20 per cent.[23]

For Archer, then, another commercial experiment had paid off. As for the *Mail on Sunday*, it experienced a rise of 100,000 in circulation, and held on to much of the gain afterwards, though it was less than it had hoped for. Frederick Forsyth's publishers, Corgi, vetoed a similar serialization for his next book, and the newspaper tried the idea only once more, with Graham Greene's novella *The Tenth Man*. 'It was quite good for the *Mail on Sunday*,' the paper's former editor, Stewart Steven, claims – 'though not as good as it was for Jeffrey Archer.'[24] Indeed, Saatchi & Saatchi's campaign – involving billboards, radio and television, and leaflets delivered to 3 million homes – featured the novelist rather more prominently than it did the newspaper: he even presented the TV ad himself. Archer had thought it through carefully: while only 8 per cent of the population would buy the newspaper, almost everyone – including the other 92 per cent – would see the national advertising. 'Out of those 92 per cent, we only need 1 per cent to double my last record,' he calculated.[25]

In the United States, *First Among Equals* also performed strongly. Joni Evans could feel that her effort had been worthwhile. The book spent sixteen weeks on the *New York Times* best-seller list, including two weeks at number one. It was not quite as successful as Archer's two previous novels in the USA, but this was a striking achievement given the subject-matter. A year later, the paperback edition reached number one as well.

The fact that for the first time Jeffrey Archer had dared to write about British politics seemed to underline his yearning to make a more substantial political contribution than his circuits of the constituency associations. Although his London flat looked down on the Palace of Westminster, Archer claimed not to have returned to the House of Commons for the previous decade: 'I've never put a foot inside the place since I left.'[26] All requests to dine or drink at the House were politely declined.

Yet, increasingly, the author kept in touch with the political life below his flat, issuing invitations to enjoy his panoramic view. Politicians and political commentators were invited to his monthly all-male lunches, where they'd find themselves mixing with prominent figures from other fields: the comedian Ernie Wise, the football manager Lawrie McMenemy (who had managed Grimsby when Archer was MP for Louth), or King Constantine of Greece. He also began holding the

Christmas parties which soon became an institution, and spread to three separate nights. His friend Michael Stacpoole takes credit for devising the combination of shepherd's pie with Krug champagne – an expensive, sophisticated drink with cheap, simple food. 'More Krug?' the host would famously enquire. When guests asked the way to the lavatory, 'Straight down the passage,' they were told – 'just past the Picasso.'

'I totally rule out ever returning to the Commons,' Archer insisted, while dropping the most unsubtle of hints.[27]

> I want to do something worth while for my country, for Margaret Thatcher. I've been working very hard earning my spurs and there are rumours that Margaret is going to offer me something.[28]

Rumours? Well, perhaps not before he said that, but certainly there were rumours now. 'I'd love to get back into public life in a top job,' he declared.[29] And with each interview he carefully built up the momentum and pressure.

Margaret Thatcher let it be known that Archer was one of her favourite writers, along with John le Carré and Frederick Forsyth. She also admired him for the way he had overcome adversity, and for being, like her, a doer. The Archers became occasional guests at Chequers, but when, in July 1984, news of a lunch date with the Prime Minister reached the *Times* diary, Archer was furious. He threatened to take the newspaper to the Press Council, and 'the highest court in the land. Furthermore you have personally ruined my lunch with Margaret tomorrow.'[30]

Speculation grew during 1984 and 1985 that some reward was impending for Archer's work for the party – perhaps a peerage, or the Sports Minister's job, or a post at Central Office. The thought horrified traditional Tory grandees. One leading Conservative suggested that any such recognition would be dangerous for the party, as the press would inevitably dredge up embarrassing old episodes such as the United Nations Association expenses. The deputy leader, Willie Whitelaw, was particularly hostile to the idea of Archer's promotion – 'over my dead body', he is supposed to have said. Indeed, Whitelaw's hostility to the idea of promoting Archer was so well known that it prompted a rare example of Margaret Thatcher's sense of humour. On one occasion she deliberately raised the idea of sending Archer to the Lords, just for the fun of seeing Whitelaw explode with outrage. Whitelaw, of course, had been one of the Tories who had received a copy of Humphry Berkeley's damning UNA report back in 1969.

Archer was fully aware of this difficulty but he seems to have worked out a way to overcome it.

In September 1984 Margaret Thatcher received out of the blue a rather unusual letter, from a quite unexpected source. Like many of the messages that were pouring in from the constituency parties, it argued that Jeffrey Archer's drive, energy and ingenuity would be of great value to any political party, and indeed the country. If she decided to give Archer a job, the writer added, there would be no public complaint from him, even though the two men had once had serious, and public, differences. Nothing between them in the past, however, ought now to prevent Archer's future political progress.[31] The letter was signed by Humphry Berkeley.

It was a remarkably generous gesture by Archer's old enemy from the UNA, especially considering that Berkeley was also a political opponent (after leaving the Conservatives he had spent more than a decade with Labour and was now in the SDP). It was also an example of Archer's great ability to patch up old quarrels, as had been shown much earlier at the Oxford University Athletics Club.

The letter had not been written entirely on Berkeley's initiative. With the help of a mutual friend, the two men had met for lunch, and had subsequently developed a new friendship. Indeed, in the years that followed, towards the end of Berkeley's life, if journalists rang to ask about the old UNA dispute he would often refuse to help, explaining that, as a Christian, he believed in forgiveness. In turn, Archer gave considerable assistance to the charity Berkeley was then running: the Sharon Allen Leukaemia Trust. He signed a personal covenant to the trust, and helped with fund-raising events, such as an auction in his garden at Grantchester. When the trust later published a book of photos in aid of the charity, Archer agreed to write the captions, though he had Berkeley's assistance.[32]

Humphry Berkeley's most magnanimous move involved the former tenant of The Old Vicarage, Rupert Brooke. Berkeley's father, Reginald, had been living in Fiji when Brooke visited the Pacific islands in 1912, and had looked after the young poet. Rupert Brooke's thank-you letter was a family treasure; now Humphry Berkeley presented it to Archer.

Yet, despite placating his old arch-enemy, Jeffrey Archer was still nervous about his chances of political promotion: 'The thing I'm most frightened of is something coming out, after I've done all this work, that blows it, that gets Her angry.'[33]

# 19

# I'm a Deputy

Margaret Thatcher worked on the principle that it didn't matter too much who ran Conservative Central Office during the period after a general election. Leading up to an election, however, the position was vital; and only a close political ally could be trusted to plan the forthcoming campaign.

And so it was in September 1985 that Norman Tebbit became Conservative Party chairman, replacing the largely unknown and somewhat lightweight figure of John Selwyn Gummer. Friends say Tebbit had wanted the job for years. But there were problems. Less than a year before, he and his wife, Margaret, had been badly injured in the IRA bombing of the Grand Hotel in Brighton. Margaret Tebbit was now in a wheelchair, while he had spent weeks in hospital and still needed further treatment. Some wondered if Tebbit would ever recover the skills as a political bruiser which had earned him the nickname of 'the Chingford skinhead'.

On the evening of her ministerial reshuffle, Margaret Thatcher phoned Jeffrey Archer to offer him the unpaid job of deputy chairman. It was an irregular position, and carried no established list of responsibilities; in fact, for the previous year the post had been unfilled. As she explained in her memoirs, Thatcher's hope was that Archer would primarily:

> make those visits to the Party around the country which Norman's health precluded him from doing. Only someone with a high profile already could do this successfully and I decided that Jeffrey Archer was the right choice. He was the extrovert's extrovert. He had prodigious energy; he was and remains the most popular speaker the Party has ever had.[1]

Thatcher was always concerned about her ministers losing touch with the grass roots, and often told them so in Cabinet. Archer might help overcome this. His new title and status were not only rewards for all the work he'd done for the party so far: they were also intended to ensure he carried on with his constituency barnstorming. The Prime Minister also hoped that Archer might restore some of the charm and sparkle which the party had missed since Cecil Parkinson's resignation over the Sara Keays affair two years before.

Tebbit himself was not that excited about Archer's promotion: 'He will bring a touch of dash and style to the party,' he said, 'a rather different dash and a rather different style from my own.'[2] The new Conservative chairman said that one of Jeffrey's novels had been the first thing he read while recovering in hospital – it 'requires no mental effort', he explained.[3] The two men had worked together in the early 1970s, when as fellow back-benchers they had enjoyed heckling Harold Wilson and the Labour front bench.

As Tebbit later admitted, the appointment 'raised quite a few eyebrows', and Archer's energy and confidence 'did not initially overcome the caution of the old hands'.[4] Willie Whitelaw's well-known misgivings were confirmed almost at once. 'Unfortunately, as it turned out,' Mrs Thatcher would confess later, 'Jeffrey's political judgement did not always match his enormous energy and fund-raising ability: ill-considered remarks got him and the Party into some awkward scrapes, but he always got himself out of them.'[5]

The first scrape involved an interview in the *Sunday Mirror* – not the most sympathetic platform for a Conservative official. Archer told the paper that he had no fear of speaking his mind: 'If I get the sack for saying what no one wants to hear, I can always return to my million-pound job. And being in the middle of the big, big action will give me plots for ten new books.' He was asked about a recent comment of Mrs Thatcher's that people who complained about unemployment were 'moaning minnies'. 'It's my job to stop her saying things like that,' asserted Archer. And what did he think of Lord Gowrie, who had just resigned from the Cabinet, saying he couldn't afford to live on £33,260 a year? 'What a bunch of wallies some of those ministers . . .' Archer blurted out, before realizing he was about to put his foot in it again.[6]

It got worse. His most embarrassing gaffe came during an interview on Radio 4's Sunday-lunchtime programme *The World This Weekend*, just two days before the Conservative Party conference. The subject was unemployment, which had just reached a record 3,346,000. 'The truth is that many of the young are quite unwilling to move from their own areas. They are quite unwilling to put in a day's work ... I was unemployed with debts of £400,000. I know what unemployment is like, and a lot of it is getting off your backside and finding a job.'[7]

It seemed almost like a bid to out-Tebbit his chairman. They were among the most tactless comments delivered by a leading Tory since Tebbit's own remark, four years earlier, suggesting that unemployed people should follow his father's example and get on their bikes to look for work. But when Archer asserted that the Tories could not 'go into the next election with the same [unemployment] figures and expect to win', even Tebbit felt obliged to confess 'I do not altogether agree with him.'[8] Others in the queue of Tories seeking to distance themselves from their new deputy chairman included Kenneth Clarke, Stephen Dorrell (then still a back-bencher) and the former leader, Edward Heath.

Lord Young, the new Employment Secretary, made no secret of his irritation that his very first conference address, in which he planned to explain how unemployment would be tackled, might be overshadowed by Archer's remarks. Nevertheless, he still sought Archer's advice on how best to deliver his speech. 'Jeffrey Archer took me under his wing and heard me read it again and again with mounting desperation,' Young reveals in his memoirs. 'He tried to teach me about timing, about stressing words correctly, about waiting and pacing an audience.'[9]

Later, however, Archer could not resist telling the world how he had helped refashion Young's image. 'A great managerial brain, but could never win a seat,' was his less-than-helpful description.

> I asked him: 'Are you a poofter? With those silk ties and handker-chiefs and striped shirts, people will think you are.' So now he wears a dark suit and plain shirts and he looks great.[10]

Before the Tory conference was over, up popped another Archer gaffe. In an interview with a Young Conservative magazine, conducted some time before, he'd been asked about the government's presentation of its policies. 'It's been pathetic, hasn't it? Pathetic!' he told the reporter, before adapting that age-old political jibe: 'You wouldn't buy a used car from this government, would you?'[11]

The next blunder occurred on BBC Radio Ulster. 'I wonder if Ian Paisley would rather like to be the Prime Minister of the whole of Ireland?' he speculated.[12] The remark was meant to be tongue-in-cheek, but it might have jeopardized the Anglo-Irish talks which were then at a delicate stage.

Several Tories thought Archer should be sacked. The former head of Mrs Thatcher's Number Ten policy unit, Ferdinand Mount, described him as 'the most wince-provoking, hot-making mistake . . . he apparently cannot pose for a camera or answer a question without filling the room with almost palpable clouds of embarrassment'.[13] Archer was 'not to be taken seriously', said the Conservative MEP for Bristol, Richard Cottrell, who called him 'a plastic media non-person'.[14]

Conceding that his remarks on unemployment had been 'insensitive', the deputy chairman soon apologized for his earlier mistakes:

> It was my own fault. I'd been out of politics for ten, eleven years, and I'd forgotten that that sort of frankness would be taken out of context, and that was naïve of me, and that lasted for a couple of months . . . and so I've had to learn.[15]

From then on, Archer's media appearances became fewer, as he concentrated instead on his principal duty of keeping up morale in the constituencies. He'd spend two or three days each week out on the road, fulfilling almost the same demanding speaking programme he had managed before he became deputy chairman.

It was nearly always the same speech. Indeed, when a BBC team tried to make a short film about Archer's travels, he imposed one condition: that they record only one of his speeches. He feared that they'd assemble a sequence in which all the repeated lines were cut together. The Archer address invariably began with a series of self-deprecating jokes, most of which he was still delivering almost ten years later:

> Thank you for that interesting introduction. It doesn't compare with the introduction I had in Carlisle when the chairman rose and said, 'Those of you who have not heard Jeffrey speak before will be looking forward to hearing him speak now.' . . . [or] in Romford, where the chairman rose and said, 'Laydeez and gentlemen, [cockney accent here] I'd like to introduce to you Mr Jeffrey Archer, wot is well known for his debatable qualities.'[16]

Usually they'd hear highlights of the Jeffrey life-story: 'When I was three I wanted to be four. When I was four I wanted to be Prime Minister.'[17] They listened in admiration to how he'd foolishly lost all his money and then remade it.

Then came the ritual attacks on the Labour Party: 'They talk about cuts, I'll tell you about cuts. This government cut Arthur Scargill down to size.'[18] Margaret Thatcher would invariably be hailed as the greatest Prime Minister since Winston Churchill, and there followed an aggressive pitch exhorting the party faithful to slog their guts out for a third term of office: 'I want you to fight, every one of you, I don't want to see one of you complaining if we lose the next election, because it will be your fault.'[19]

Soon Archer had dreamt up a new gimmick to enlist their support. 'The Prime Minister cannot do it on her own ... I appoint each and every single one of you in this room deputy deputy chairman of the Conservative Party. Because we need every one of you.'[20] He even sold them thousands of blue badges he'd had printed, each declaring: 'I'm a Deputy Deputy'.

It was Jeffrey's act, taken round village halls, hotel banqueting suites and Conservative clubs, like a traditional northern comedian working the clubs. If he couldn't be an actor or a television star, this was the next best thing, with all the adrenalin of performing in public before an admiring audience. After his address, they'd often enlist him to draw the raffle or run a fund-raising auction. Sometimes he'd speak five or six times a day, with a party breakfast, a coffee-morning, a lunch, a tea and a dinner. Generally he attracted big audiences, often three or four hundred people in the healthier constituencies. It was tiring work, and incredibly repetitive, but he loved it.

Generally they loved him too; in fact many Conservative women – and his audiences were mostly women – adored him. At the end they'd flock round and ask him to autograph their books or lunch menus; friends would be pressed into snapping the occasion with their little Instamatics – creating souvenirs of the great day with their favourite author.

Not everyone was enthralled, though. Some found Archer's bumptiousness a little too much. He thought nothing of picking on individuals in the audience, and mocking them. 'Sheikh Yamani', he once called a man sporting a head bandage. 'Yes, you in the pyjamas,' he said when someone in a brightly coloured shirt wanted to ask a question.[21]

In London, Archer was allocated a small office at the Conservative headquarters in Smith Square, and quickly filled it with his own modern furniture: a smart black desk and stainless-steel chairs. He acquired a new secretary, Angie Peppiatt, and a personal assistant, David Faber, a grandson of Harold Macmillan, who had just left Oxford and written to ask for a job.

David Faber's arrival as his personal assistant marked the departure of Andrina Colquhoun. Newspaper gossip columns had speculated about the nature of her relationship with Archer, and, according to Nigel Dempster in the *Daily Mail*, 'A condition of the appointment of . . . Jeffrey Archer . . . as deputy chairman of the Conservative party is that he regularizes his personal affairs'.[22] Mary Archer visited her first Tory conference, and was spotted a little more often in her husband's company at the type of London social event where Andrina had often been seen at his side. Friends say he and his PA had grown fond of each other over the years, and that she would have liked to marry him. Certainly Archer's parting gesture was generous, as the MP Alan Clark recorded in his diary:

28 NOVEMBER 1985
At the Princes Gate traffic lights out of Hyde Park I drew up beside a black BMW, driven by a blonde, registered ANY 1. I looked sideways and saw browner, thinner in the face, but still with 'something' Andy Colquhoun . . .[23]

Archer had held on to his personal number-plate even during his most difficult financial times but now agreed to sell the plate and his BMW to her. The plate can still be seen on Andrina Colquhoun's car today, as she drives through the lanes near her country home in north Oxfordshire.

Disposing of the BMW was also good politics. Margaret Thatcher would hardly have been pleased to hear of him turning up at Tory Party dinners in a foreign vehicle, let alone one made in Germany. Jeffrey replaced it with a Daimler, and within nine months, presenting the Think Britain Awards, he was stressing how many British jobs would be created if we all bought more home-made goods.[24] (Years later, however, he bought another BMW.)

At Central Office, Archer attended many of the important meetings, and even chaired some of them. But he had few administrative duties, and his room saw little of the heavy paperwork found in the offices of other party officials. One former colleague says that in practice Norman Tebbit's personal chief-of-staff Michael Dobbs 'was more of a deputy chairman than Jeffrey Archer'. Dobbs, who later began his own career as a successful thriller-writer, was arguably much better qualified to advise on communications than Archer, having been both a journalist and in advertising with Saatchi & Saatchi. Tebbit had actually wanted to make Dobbs a deputy chairman too, but Thatcher disliked him, and would not agree to it.

In public, Archer was now more careful about his remarks – at least most of the time. 'They'll cheat at anything,' he said about the French, while the police had to deny his claim that they didn't bother to investigate frauds of less than £10 million.[25] But these were rare sightings of the celebrated Archer gaffe.

What was most notable was that Archer survived unscathed Mrs Thatcher's rockiest period in Downing Street, the January 1986 Westland crisis. It would have been easy for him inadvertently to contribute to the damage that Westland caused the government, since he was officially running Central Office at the time, while Norman Tebbit was in hospital. Wisely, he put his head down and kept quiet.

Despite claims to the contrary, Tebbit grew to like Archer. He admired his energy and enthusiasm, even if he didn't rate his abilities as a political strategist or thinker. They had breakfast together every Tuesday, when the chairman was grateful for his deputy's frankness. 'He was not afraid of Norman Tebbit,' says the former communications director Harvey Thomas, 'and he would answer him back. And of course Jeffrey, because he is so rich, is in such a safe position that no one can harm him, and this gave him the confidence to be entirely his own man.'[26]

The deputy chairman's constituency tours weren't just a matter of chivvying the party faithful, Tebbit says: 'he was coming back with some shrewd assessments'.[27] Archer had the great asset of appearing to be at one remove from the government, and people would often express grievances to him that they were too polite to raise with ministers.

On taking office, Norman Tebbit had quickly compiled a list of the sixty 'critical' seats in which the next election would be won or lost. These were not the most marginal constituencies – with a majority of 142, the party could afford to lose many of those – but those which the Conservatives had to retain to preserve a Commons majority. Archer was put in charge of the 'critical-seats campaign' which would give these decisive areas much more attention than they'd received before any previous election.

Working with Stuart Newman, a retired agent who'd been brought back for the project, Archer catalogued each constituency party's assets. Did it have an agent, a computer, decent offices and modern printing facilities? Was the local party publishing regular *In Touch* leaflets? Would it like more visits from government ministers? Did its members need any special training? And did it have enough funds? Resources were shifted towards the critical seats from areas where the result was more predictable. Archer also took charge of raising a separate war-chest specifically for these seats, and personally solicited at least half a million pounds from businesses and wealthy supporters.

This was on top of Archer's other financial help for the party. At the Conservative conference in October 1985 he had been entrusted with the traditional fund-raising speech before Margaret Thatcher spoke. He did it with typical gusto. Everyone was asked to wave a five-pound note above their heads, to the considerable discomfort of Cabinet ministers sitting on the platform. Archer also acquired his own niche as an auctioneer, and developed an astonishing ability to coax out absurdly high bids – many thousands of pounds, for instance, for a bottle of Commons whisky autographed by Margaret Thatcher, or a book signed by every living party leader. If an audience were behaving in a stingy manner, Archer would pretend to get angry, and insult them. 'Pathetic!' he'd yell, and it usually worked.

The deputy chairman was equally blunt with top businessmen. The former chairman of Guinness, Ernest Saunders, remembers sitting next to Archer at a lunch during the height of his company's notorious take-over bid for Distillers in 1986.

And he came out straight with the remark to the effect that he noticed that we didn't make any political donations to the Conservative Party and when were we going to, which I found a rather startling remark, until I sat next to Jeffrey Archer for a little longer, and then I became aware that it was just part of his style.[28]

On other occasions Archer was more subtle. He would often be guest of honour at one of the small, private lunches for perhaps a dozen wealthy donors organized by the highly secretive Conservative Board of Finance. No direct appeal would be made during the meal: the chance for a personal chat with Jeffrey Archer over good food and wine was the guests' reward for the handsome cheques they'd quietly given the party in the past.

Three days after his appointment as deputy chairman, Archer had set foot inside the House of Commons for the first time in eleven years. When Parliament was sitting he would now try to watch Prime Minister's Questions, partly to keep in touch with the pulse at Westminster, but for much of the time he stayed out of the political mainstream. For example, in the spring of 1986 he was not invited to join the small 'A-team' of senior ministers preparing the election manifesto.

Nevertheless, Archer couldn't resist telling people how close he now was to the Prime Minister, how much she valued his opinion, and how he could influence her on policy. Yet, when a BBC reporter asked him to cite examples, he was vague:

> It's a very interesting question because I can't answer it direct without giving two secrets away. I know that two things have happened. I couldn't prove that I personally made them happen, but perhaps tipped the extra inch – made her say, 'Yes, we should do that.' And there's one in the pipeline at the moment that she's taking very seriously and looking into herself.[29]

It was suggested in the press that Archer spoke to Margaret Thatcher once a fortnight, but sources from both sides say that the pair probably had no more than three or four one-to-one meetings during the whole of Archer's fourteen months in office. With senior Cabinet members constantly clamouring for her attention, Thatcher was simply too busy to see the deputy chairman regularly.

Instead, Archer was kept contented through frequent contact with Stephen Sherbourne, the political secretary at Number Ten. The two men would meet for breakfast at the Savoy every few weeks, usually on Wednesdays. After returning from a speaking tour, Archer might ring Sherbourne with 'intelligence' on what the constituencies were saying; this was highly valued, and would often be relayed to Thatcher by memo. Nevertheless, Archer's antennae were nothing like sensitive enough to spot the dangers of the poll tax, which was largely devised during his period at Central Office.

In September 1986, after a year in the job, it was seen as something of a snub to Archer when Margaret Thatcher appointed a second deputy chairman: her former Industry Minister, Peter Morrison. In the past the Conservative Party had sometimes managed with no deputy chairman at all, yet now there were two, and it was made clear that the Prime Minister regarded Morrison as the principal deputy, in charge of the day-to-day running of Central Office and party organization. Archer remained responsible for campaigning and the constituencies. Although he had lost out, the change was primarily to lighten the load on Norman Tebbit, and also to enable Thatcher to keep her chairman in line at a time when he seemed to her to be showing signs of being politically unsound.

After his gaffes the previous year, Archer had a very quiet party conference in 1986, but Conservative representatives could not escape his literary output. He basked in the attention surrounding Granada's ten-part production of *First Among Equals*, which had just started on ITV. After ten years in which none of his books had ever been dramatized, Archer fans were now in danger of being over-indulged. The year before, Anglia had run a two-hour version of his short tale 'Love Story'. Then, over three nights in one week in June 1986, the BBC ran a seven-hour US adaptation of *Kane and Abel*, starring Sam Neill and Peter Strauss, which had gone out in America the previous autumn. This was the same production for which Michael Grade had originally bought an option when he was at London Weekend Television five years earlier; he had later acquired the rights for CBS when he moved to Embassy Television in Hollywood. Grade had finally ended up buying the drama from CBS in his latest role as controller of BBC1. Archer cheekily claimed it had attracted more viewers than the Conservatives had votes at the 1983 election.[30]

Granada's *First Among Equals* – for which Archer was paid his customary token one pound – was a far superior production to the CBS version of *Kane and Abel*, and remained reasonably faithful to the British edition of the novel. The ITV company filmed alternative endings, however, and company executives chose the prime-ministerial victor only hours before transmission. As in Archer's British version of the book, it was the Labour MP, Raymond Gould.

The second episode of *First Among Equals*, broadcast on the first night of the Conservative conference in Bournemouth, included an incident in which Gould picks up a prostitute in Mayfair; he lies to her that he's a used-car salesman, and then they have sex in a seedy hotel near Paddington station. As the book relates:

> The room was small and narrow. In one corner stood a tiny bed and a threadbare carpet. The faded yellow wallpaper was peeling in several places. There was a washbasin attached to the wall; a dripping tap had left a brown stain on the enamel.[31]

The prostitute later discovers Gould's true identity, and blackmails him.

In the Granada adaptation, a *Daily Mirror* reporter approaches Raymond Gould about the girl's story. The MP threatens to sue for libel, and the paper drops the story. The original outcome in Archer's novel was even less convincing: Gould consults his lawyer, who advises him to ignore the girl's demands; the solicitor then admits to the *Mirror* reporter that the story is true, but successfully persuades him not to run it. 'Be thankful she hit on a fair journalist,' the lawyer tells Gould, 'because I expect he'll let this one go. Fleet Street are not quite the bunch of shits everyone imagines them to be.'[32]

And, with that rare sympathetic gesture from a tabloid newspaper, Archer's character survives unscathed.

# 20

# Jeffrey, Monica and Victoria

He may have been out of the spotlight, but the 1986 party conference must have been a difficult time for Archer. In the weeks beforehand, he'd had two strange phone calls from a woman called Debbie, and had heard the press were looking into a rumour about him. A few days before going to Bournemouth he'd contacted Peter Jay, the former British Ambassador to Washington, who was now working for Robert Maxwell at the Mirror Group, to ask what he knew of the gossip. During conference week itself the *Mail on Sunday* editor, Stewart Steven, also raised it with him. Steven presented it as a friendly warning, but he was also curious as to how Archer would react.

The editor of the *News of the World*, David Montgomery, later testified that twice during the latter half of September Archer had also rung him with anxious enquiries. Was the paper about to run 'a dirty story' on him?[1] Archer denied making any such calls.

The story finally broke on the night of Saturday 25 October in Montgomery's own paper, under the headline TORY BOSS ARCHER PAYS VICE GIRL. The *News of the World* showed a picture of Monica Coghlan, a prostitute who used the name 'Debbie', being 'offered an envelope crammed with £50 notes' by Archer's friend Michael Stacpoole, and it related how the novelist had told Coghlan, 'Go abroad as quickly as you can.'[2] The money was estimated to be £2,000, but Coghlan rejected it. Anyone reading the story would have thought that it implied that Archer had slept with Coghlan, but the newspaper was careful not actually to say this.

Over five pages, the *News of the World* told a complicated tale. Six weeks earlier, one of Coghlan's clients, an Asian lawyer called Aziz Kurtha, claimed to have seen Archer going with Coghlan to her hotel near Victoria station. Kurtha had tried to interest several Fleet Street newspapers in the story, and to get the prostitute to cooperate. Meanwhile the *News of the World* had found Coghlan themselves, and over four weeks taped six phone calls she made to Archer. When, at the prompting of the journalists, she told him that reporters were on to her, he consistently denied ever having met her, but eventually offered to help her financially to go abroad in order to get away from them.

The *News of the World* editor, David Montgomery, had been keen to stop his exclusive being lifted at the last minute by rival papers (a common habit of the tabloids). Making full use of the modern printing technology now available at News International's new plant in Wapping, he carefully planned a 'rogue' first edition carrying a very good (and very expensive) front-page story about a pregnant Irish woman who was tricked by her Arab boyfriend into carrying a bomb on to a plane. Only a few hundred copies were printed, for distribution to Fleet Street news-stands and the other Sunday newsdesks. They have since become collectors' items.

The decoy didn't prevent most of the other Sundays running the Archer story in later editions, though the paper's Wapping stable-mate, the *Sunday Times*, ignored it. The BBC mentioned it obliquely in their coverage of the morning press, but omitted the story from news bulletins.

Although the Archers knew about the story on Saturday afternoon, Mary didn't see a copy of the *News of the World* until the next morning. She sent one of the boys over the garden wall and down to the village paper shop, to avoid the reporters besieging the front gate.

Jeffrey, meanwhile, had driven from Grantchester to London at 1 a.m., as he couldn't get to sleep. Soon after dawn he had an hour-long meeting with his lawyer. Victor Mishcon, by now a peer, is reported to have asked him three questions. Did you sleep with this prostitute? No. Have you gone with any other prostitute? No. Do you still want to pursue a political career? Yes.[3]

Archer had several telephone conversations that day with Norman Tebbit at his holiday cottage on Dartmoor, and one with Margaret Thatcher at Chequers. With an election due in only a few months, she accepted his resignation. 'I have been silly, very foolish,' Archer conceded publicly. 'What else can I say?'[4]

Lord Mishcon said he was considering legal action, and issued a statement in which Archer admitted 'lack of judgement'. 'Foolishly,' he said, 'I allowed myself to fall into what I can only call a trap in which a newspaper, in my view, played a reprehensible part.' The Tory deputy chairman had offered to help Coghlan only because 'any publicity of this kind would be extremely harmful to me'. He insisted, 'I have never, repeat never, met Monica Coghlan, nor have I ever had any association of any kind with a prostitute.'[5] Clearly, the purpose and effect of Mishcon's statement was to deny the existence of any sexual relationship; Archer later explained when giving evidence in court that he had in fact met a prostitute on one occasion in quite different circumstances – as part of the research for one of his books.[6]

Things might have turned out differently had it not then been for the actions of another tabloid newspaper, *The Star*. Ironically, the paper had initially condemned the *News of the World* story: 'All the facts so far revealed,' *The Star* said, 'point to his being the victim of a particularly nasty set-up job' – adding that Archer had been 'totally honourable' for resigning so quickly.[7] Privately, however, the *Star*'s Australian editor, Lloyd Turner, was intrigued by the story. The next day he secretly managed to acquire transcripts of the *News of the World* phone calls from Coghlan to Archer, and assigned several reporters to follow up the story, hoping to answer the basic question of why the novelist had offered her the money.

As a result, the following Saturday *The Star* suddenly claimed its own 'exclusive' under the headings 'Poor Jeffrey' and 'Vice girl Monica talks about Archer – the man she knew'.[8] Superficially it looked as if the paper had interviewed Monica Coghlan, though closer inspection indicated that her quotes had been obtained only by speaking to her nephew, Tony Smith (who, it later emerged, had been paid £400). *The Star* was confident, however, that Smith was in close contact with Coghlan, since a lot of what he said tallied with the transcripts of her calls.

*The Star* went much further than the *News of the World* in suggesting that the prostitute had slept with Archer, and in doing so was challenging the denial he had issued through Lord Mishcon. And the paper then compounded its damage to Archer's reputation by saying that 90 per cent of Coghlan's clients 'demand a specialized field of sexual perversion'. 'One of them,' Tony Smith said, 'wanted to be dressed like Little Red Riding Hood, complete with suspenders. He had to be trussed up, and Monica would whip him on the floor of his room.'[9]

Archer quickly pounced. Having taken advice from both Mishcon and a leading QC, Robert Alexander, he issued libel writs against both the *News of the World* and *The Star*, and their respective editors. Archer and the two newspapers were heading for battle over what the judge would call 'as big a libel as has ever been tried this century'.[10]

At issue was what exactly had happened in Shepherd Market, Mayfair, and Victoria, late on Monday 8 September 1986 and in the early hours of Tuesday 9 September. The allegations came originally from Aziz Kurtha. A wealthy Asian who'd been born in Bombay and came to Britain in 1952, Kurtha was as intriguing as the man he wanted to expose. And he was similar in so many ways: smooth, charming and good-looking; a self-made multimillionaire, who collected modern art and sported a personalized number-plate. Indeed, he has sometimes been described as an 'Asian Jeffrey Archer'.

Since studying at the London School of Economics, where he was president of the students' union, Kurtha had dabbled in a wide range of activities – the law, academic life, journalism, television, business and politics. After nineteen years as a barrister, he'd just become a solicitor; he taught at, and was an examiner for, London University; he had published occasional articles in legal magazines and other journals. For three years he'd also presented the Channel 4 programme *Eastern Eye*; he had business and charity interests in Britain, Pakistan and the Gulf; and, after a spell in the SDP, he hoped to become a Labour MP after fighting an unwinnable council seat in Kew. The similarities between the two men did not stop there. In his youth Kurtha had acted on stage in the West End, while now, in his spare time, he was editing a collection of short stories. Above all, he showed a certain Archeresque naïvety about how his actions would be interpreted by the rest of the world.

Aziz Kurtha's remarkable tale, later repeated in court, went as follows. That night he had paid to have sex with Monica Coghlan – or 'Debbie', as she called herself – in room 6a at the Albion Hotel in Gillingham Street, not far from Victoria station. At around 12.30 to 12.45 a.m., just as he was about to drive Debbie back to her 'patch' in Mayfair, they saw a car – a Jaguar or a Daimler – flashing its lights at them. When Debbie got out and spoke to the driver, Kurtha said he suddenly noticed who it was.

> I said to her, beckoning to her, 'Do you know who this is?' and something like 'It's your lucky day' or 'You hit the bull's-eye' or 'jackpot' or something of that sort. The exact phrase I cannot recollect. But it was 'It's your lucky day.' She said, 'What do you mean?' and I said, 'Well, don't you know this is the deputy chairman of the Tory Party and that famous novelist, Mr Archer?'[11]

Debbie then went back into the hotel, Kurtha said, with the man he had identified as Archer.

Kurtha claimed to have noted the first three letters of the number-plate of the man's car – CUU – and the next day he approached *Private Eye*. The editor, Richard Ingrams, claims he quickly decided a jury would never believe Kurtha's word against Archer's, and one of his *Eye* colleagues, Paul Halloran, recommended he try one of the tabloids instead. Halloran introduced him to the *News of the World*, and Kurtha met their investigations editor, Eddie Jones, in the Wine Press in Fleet Street.

Later that week Kurtha found Coghlan through the Albion Hotel, had sex with her again, and then mentioned that *Private Eye* might be interested in running the story of what had happened. Had any newspapers contacted her? Kurtha wanted to know. Coghlan, who earned between fifty and seventy pounds per client, expressed reluctance to 'shop' one of them, especially if he was wealthy and influential, but wanted to know about the chances of being paid. Kurtha said she might get around £800 (about four nights' earnings for Coghlan).

Monica Coghlan had become a prostitute at seventeen in Manchester after she was sexually attacked, was forced to leave her flat, and fell into debt. Over eighteen years, in and out of the business, she'd collected numerous convictions, and had twice been in prison. Now thirty-five, she lived with her two-year-old son in a small bungalow in Rochdale. The boy would be looked after by relatives and neighbours as she travelled to London every week or so to spend several nights on the game. Basing herself at the Albion Hotel, she would meet regular clients by arrangement or solicit customers on the streets of Mayfair, then return to Lancashire when she had made enough money.

Coghlan may have had a difficult childhood, having left school at fifteen and spent time in an approved school, but Aziz Kurtha and several journalists quickly discovered that she was an intelligent woman, if also rather naïve. She appears to have had her own moral code: she maintained throughout that she had not wanted to grass on clients and that she was unhappy about lying to Archer. *News of the World* reporters later insisted that Coghlan never asked for any money, nor even for expenses. The prostitute said later in court that she had been paid £1,500 by the time of publication to cover expenses and loss of earnings, and a further £4,500 subsequently. She also earned £5,400 in photo fees from an agency introduced to her by the *News of the World*, though it was not connected with the paper. By Fleet Street standards, these were not large sums.

Aziz Kurtha continued to discuss the story with Eddie Jones for almost ten days, but grew increasingly anxious about how the paper was handling it. He wanted assurances that his own name would not be mentioned, an indemnity for any losses he might incur, and £10,000 to be paid to charities in Pakistan. But he was also worried about the methods the *News of the World* wanted to use to confirm it. When he discovered the paper was trying to contact Monica Coghlan independently, he suspected he was being double-crossed, and later approached the *Daily Mirror* instead.

Almost as soon as he'd heard Kurtha's story, Eddie Jones had assigned a freelance reporter, John Lisners, to track down Monica Coghlan for the *News of the World*. By Saturday, Lisners had found her at the Albion Hotel. Employing what he later conceded was 'subterfuge', he posed as 'a client who was a friend of Mr Archer's'. The reporter then showed her a photocopied photo of Archer, and Coghlan, according to the evidence Lisners gave in court, confirmed it was a man with whom she'd recently had sex.[12] Coghlan then gave Lisners her home telephone number.

Several days later Lisners contacted Coghlan in Rochdale, and they had dinner at a hotel in the centre of Manchester. The reporter then revealed who he actually was. Lisners' account was that Coghlan seemed scared, that she didn't want trouble, but he told her that if she helped the *News of the World* then they could stop other papers from bothering her. Coghlan spoke to Eddie Jones on the phone, and the next day Lisners even persuaded her to swear an affidavit outlining her account.

Over the next few days, Lisners and Jones kept in close touch with Coghlan, and before long, as is customary with tabloid scoops, the paper was escorting her constantly, moving her from location to location and keeping her away from her home, so that other journalists could not make contact. Lisners was joined in this operation by two colleagues: a female reporter, Jo Fletcher, included on the grounds that Coghlan might find it easier to deal with a woman, and Gerry Brown, an expert in tape-recording. They originally persuaded her to make just one call to Jeffrey Archer, and moved her to London to do so, just in case the politician suddenly agreed to see her. Clearly, the journalists recognized that they could not run the story on the evidence of Coghlan alone, but hoped that Archer might be foolish enough to say something to incriminate himself.

With Jo Fletcher sitting with her in a hotel bedroom and a tape-recorder rolling, the prostitute first rang Archer at 11.15 on the night of 25 September. He had already gone to bed (Archer usually retires early, around 10.30 p.m.). Coghlan began by telling him she was called 'Debbie' and had met him in Shepherd Market, and she explained that she'd been contacted by a man who'd seen them together:

> He's giving me a lot of hassle, you know. He's telling me who you are and he's been offering me money. I don't want anything to do with this. I just want this guy off my back.[13]

'You must have the wrong number,' Archer insisted more than once. With a note of desperation in her voice, Monica told how she was getting frightened and wanted 'this guy off my back'. At this stage she hadn't fully spelt out that she was a prostitute, but it was obvious what she was getting at.

ARCHER: Well, I'm awfully sorry. I don't know you, I don't know him. It's a ridiculous suggestion, and I suggest you go to the police.

COGHLAN: To the police?

ARCHER: I certainly would, if anyone suggested it was me, I wouldn't hesitate to go to the police.[14]

Later, people would wonder why Archer didn't actually go to the police himself. Nor, unlike his fictional Raymond Gould, did Archer at that stage consult a lawyer about the prostitute's approaches. As they listened to this and subsequent conversations, it always surprised *News of the World* journalists that Archer didn't consult any third party at this point.

In that first call, Coghlan went into detail about Shepherd Market, the offer of money, *Private Eye* and Kurtha. 'He's shown me a picture of you, and you know, as far as I'm concerned, it was you.' Again denying it was him, Archer advised her to keep well away from Kurtha, 'because it could get you into a court of law'. 'Can't you just sort of make a call and get this guy off my bloody back?' Coghlan pleaded. Archer asked for his number; she didn't have it, and he agreed Coghlan could ring him back with it.[15]

After that 'we let her go', says one of the *News of the World* reporters, and indeed that might have been the end of it. But some days later Coghlan rang the paper, saying she'd had a call from a reporter on the *Daily Mirror* asking to see her. Gerry Brown told the prostitute that, if she helped his Sunday paper instead, 'we'll try to prevent it degenerating into a circus'. Within an hour, one of the *News of the World*'s Manchester staff was at her home to take her away and stop the *Mirror* finding her. For the next three weeks *News of the World* people went everywhere with Coghlan; Jo Fletcher would frequently share Monica's bedroom and look after her young son.

The *News of the World* already had an excuse for a second call. Coghlan then told Archer she hadn't managed to get Kurtha's number because of the reporters 'hanging about' her home, and mentioned the *Daily Mirror*'s approach. Judging by her voice, Coghlan was on the point of tears. Archer was extremely sympathetic, and kept saying how sorry he was, but repeated that she must have the wrong man:

> I don' t know what to do about it, because it's – it's really nothing to do with me, and I'm just trying to help you. Get his name and I will get him off your back.[16]

He advised her, 'You'll have to say very firmly that you made a mistake, it certainly wasn't me, otherwise you will find it will never end.' If she spoke to the press her pictures would be all over the papers; and she certainly shouldn't reveal that they had spoken.

> Don't ever tell anyone you've phoned me. 'Cos they'll say, 'Have you been in contact with him since?' You say, 'I don't even know who he is.' They'll try every trick to get you to talk, and if you say you've phoned me they'll say – that will be tricky, so you've never phoned me.[17]

Her third call was made three weeks later, on the morning of Thursday 23 October. Monica explained that she'd been in Tunisia for two weeks, without adding, of course, that the *News of the World* had taken her there. She then gave Aziz Kurtha's full name to Archer for the first time, together with his phone number and the name of John Merritt, the *Mirror* journalist she'd previously spoken to. 'I think it's quietening down,' Archer reassured her. 'I hear from the people who have been in touch with me that it is, but I think you will have to stay out of sight for a bit more still, for which I'm very sorry.'[18]

Telling Monica she was 'very brave' and that he admired her, Archer promised to deal with the matter that day; but twenty minutes later Coghlan was on the phone again, claiming that *The People* had just approached her offering money. Archer again promised to sort things out, and agreed she should ring back at 10.30 that night, when he would tell her what he'd done.[19]

Later that day, the ever-vigilant Lord Mishcon fired off a letter to Kurtha warning him that if there was any 'further defamation of our client of any kind, for which you are directly or indirectly responsible, immediate steps will be taken'.[20]

Monica Coghlan performed remarkably well during the course of the six telephone calls she made to Archer, speaking to him for more than an hour. Not once did she let slip that she was in league with journalists from the *News of the World*, or give any indication that Jo Fletcher was sitting next to her, passing notes and mouthing suggestions of things to say. She probed and persisted with all the tenacity of a professional reporter, going back over the ground time and again in an effort to trip him up.

Coghlan rang Archer again at 10.55 p.m., a little later than suggested. He had 'done two things today which will frighten them', he assured her, including contacting two newspapers. It was when Coghlan once again described the pressure she was under that Archer made his extraordinary offer. Up until this moment, the *News of the World* had no story:

ARCHER: . . . Would it help if you went abroad again?

COGHLAN: I mean, you should know better than me, shouldn't you? All I know is that people from different newspapers and everything, have been trying to get hold of me, and I don't want to talk to them.

ARCHER: Well, I think that's very wise. What I'm saying is, if a friend of mine helped you −?

COGHLAN: A friend of yours?

ARCHER: − helped you financially to go abroad again, would that interest you?[21]

They discussed money. Coghlan mentioned a figure of 'about three hundred for the flight, something like that, for a bungalow, and spending money while I'm there', but kept stressing 'I'm not really after money.' When Archer enquired again, she said her last holiday had cost 'about seven'. They discussed a rendezvous for Coghlan to meet a 'friend' of Archer's the following morning:

ARCHER: He'll just pass you an envelope and go away.

COGHLAN: You must know somewhere in Victoria?

ARCHER: . . . A platform on Victoria station would be easy wouldn't it? . . . platform number three.

COGHLAN: What, on the station or the underground?

ARCHER: No, the station. Stand by the entrance to platform number three.

COGHLAN: The entrance.

ARCHER: At eleven o'clock.[22]

Coghlan wanted to know how the man would recognize her, and she suggested she should wear a green leather suit. 'And then,' said Archer, 'you'll just go abroad as quickly as you can, will you?' He suggested it should be for as long as possible.

ARCHER: I cannot under any circumstances come and see you, but I have a friend who will just pass the package over.

COGHLAN: Well, how do I know — he's, he's, you know, that he's a friend?

ARCHER: Well, he's going to see you in your leather suit, walk up and say, 'Are you Debbie?' You're going to say, 'Yes.' He's going to pass the package and walk away — forty-five, grey-haired, a little overweight.[23]

A minute later her journalist minders got Coghlan to ring back to ask for the man's name. Archer said she wouldn't need it:

ARCHER: He's just a friend, a very close friend who's very safe. You have absolutely no fears. I've known him —

COGHLAN: What's his first name then?

ARCHER: No — his first name is David.[24]

At that, the *News of the World* team assumed Archer was sending his young personal assistant, David Faber, and quite forgot his previous description of a rather overweight forty-five-year-old.

The events of that Friday morning on Victoria station are one of the most celebrated episodes in the history of tabloid journalism; it was a scene of the highest tension and the lowest farce. Gerry Brown had hidden a micro-cassette recorder and a tiny radio microphone in Coghlan's clothing, and he and his reporter colleagues positioned themselves at different points around the concourse to observe events. Also dotted around the station was a team of about six *News of the World* photographers, all disguised as railway passengers and carrying hidden cameras. It was the worst possible location for Archer to have chosen: rarely can an operation that was meant to be so surreptitious have been carried out so publicly.

The newspaper was anxious, however, that Archer might have been trying to trap *it*, not the other way round. Could police suddenly spring out and arrest Coghlan on suspicion of blackmail? If this happened, it was agreed that the journalists would quickly reveal themselves shouting '*News of the World!*' Coghlan had also been told that under no circumstances should she accept the money; instead, she should open the package, inspect it carefully, and remove any message that might be inside.

When Archer's emissary arrived, Gerry Brown was horrified. It wasn't David Faber but the novelist's old friend Michael Stacpoole, whom Brown knew quite well, having first met him about four years earlier. Stacpoole had even introduced the journalist to Archer, and the two men had discussed the possibility of Brown doing some research for his novels. Fearing Stacpoole might notice him, Brown darted off and hid in the Casey Jones burger bar; his colleagues were baffled.

At first Michael Stacpoole mistakenly approached another woman dressed in green. Then, once he'd made contact, he and Coghlan stood by the platform entrance for a couple of minutes while Stacpoole tried to persuade her to take the package. 'I don't really want the money, you can take it back,' she insisted. 'Tell him I'll ring him.'[25] Stacpoole begged Coghlan to come and talk, and they went for a drink. This was completely unexpected. So the whole *News of the World* circus – passengers with rucksacks and trolleys; men with their girlfriends; reporters taking mental notes; photographers snatching secret pictures – all slowly followed them. The only one who had a clue what Coghlan and Stacpoole were doing was Gerry Brown in the burger bar, listening to Coghlan's hidden microphone in his earpiece. Brown couldn't see where they were going, but, guessing from the strength of the radio signal, he deduced they were in the Grosvenor Hotel next door.

No sooner had Brown entered the lobby of the hotel than, in a moment of farce, he bumped into Stacpoole, who'd now left Monica Coghlan so as to make some phone calls. Brown bluffed that he'd come to see someone who'd not turned up, and the pair agreed to have a drink, whereupon Stacpoole blurted out that he was 'here to do a favour for a very important political friend. He's having a spot of bother and he wanted my help to smooth it out.'[26] Since he was 'being well paid' for the job, the drinks were on him. Eddie Jones and Jo Fletcher watched in bewilderment from elsewhere in the bar, trying hard to look like a couple of lovers.

In the meantime, Stacpoole had rung David Faber and asked him to come to the hotel at once. Faber appears to have known nothing about the arrangement with Coghlan. Archer was touring Lincolnshire that day, and had warned his assistant that Stacpoole might call; but that was not unusual since he was always ringing up. Faber was reluctant to come, but when he did turn up at the door of the bar, Stacpoole insisted he needed to speak to Archer urgently. Furtively, he told Faber that the man in the corner – indicating Gerry Brown – had told him that the Foreign Office was implicated in the recent plot to blow up President Samora Machel of Mozambique, and he must warn Archer about it at once. A puzzled David Faber accordingly rang the deputy chairman's carphone to say that Stacpoole needed to reach him urgently.

The *News of the World* now had an extraordinary story, with plenty of pictures, recordings, and names to go with it. It wasn't that Archer had slept with Coghlan – they could never prove that – but in its way it was something worse: a bizarre display of appalling judgement by the politician. He had been caught trying to give several thousand pounds to help a prostitute go abroad to stop the press contacting her. That Friday afternoon, David Montgomery decided to publish.

When Michael Stacpoole rang him the next day – Saturday – Gerry Brown told him they knew exactly what he'd been doing at Victoria station, and that Archer was dealing with a call-girl. 'Is that the greatest sin in the world?' Stacpoole responded.[27] With an air of desperation, he stressed how well-connected Archer was in Downing Street, and all the contacts Brown might get out of that.

Stacpoole had already told Archer what had happened at Victoria, but the politician didn't know the *News of the World* was going to run the story until just after 4 p.m. on Saturday afternoon. When he returned to Grantchester after a speech in Cambridge, Mary announced that Michael Dobbs, Norman Tebbit's right-hand man, needed to speak to him urgently. A frantic series of phone calls followed, involving Archer, Lord Mishcon and David Montgomery. 'I thought the least I should do before I ring the Prime Minister was ring you,' Archer told the *News of the World* editor. 'Do you think this is a story on which I should resign?' he asked. Montgomery responded that he could not advise him on the matter. 'David,' Archer insisted, 'I want to tell you there is no truth in it, so you have it on the record.' Montgomery promised to phone back once he'd spoken to his reporter. 'Can you ring quickly,' Archer pleaded, 'because my wife is here in tears, which is not making my life easy?'[28]

Montgomery passed Archer over to the journalist, John Lisners, who went through the details of what they were about to print.

> LISNERS: The essential point of the story is that you offered to pay money to a vice girl in return for her going out of the country, and not mentioning the fact that she might have seen you at a previous occasion.
> ARCHER: That is not true.[29]

Archer did confirm, however, that he'd been rung by a woman calling herself Debbie, and Lisners continued with his formal questions.

> LISNERS: Is it true that you offered to pay a girl called Debbie who telephoned you at your home money to go away on holiday?
> ARCHER: Certainly not.
> LISNERS: Fine. Second point. Is it true that you asked this girl Debbie not to say that she has never spoken to you [sic], that she would not recognize you, that she had never seen you?
> ARCHER: No, that is not true either.[30]

Archer tried to take the conversation 'off the record', but for the time being Lisners wanted to stay 'on the record', so that Archer could be quoted in his story.

> LISNERS: One further question I want to ask you is: did you send a friend of yours called Mr Stacpoole to pay her money in a brown envelope?
> ARCHER: No, I did not.[31]

Archer wanted to know what proof the paper had for its assertions. Lisners insisted they wouldn't run the story 'unless we have good evidence'.

> ARCHER: Well, I must say to you now, and I will say to your editor, that it is not true, and that I would issue a writ immediately.
> LISNERS: Fine. Well, Mr Archer, I have put the points to you and the very essential points are, again, I will repeat them again,

just in case you do want to comment on them, and this is on record. Did you or did you not organize money for a girl called Debbie to go away on holiday?

ARCHER: No, I did not.

LISNERS: You did not? You did not send a Mr Stackpole, Stacpoole, to see her?

ARCHER: No, I did not.

LISNERS: At platform number three at Victoria station?

ARCHER: No, you are just making it up now.

LISNERS: I am not making it up, Mr Archer, I am sorry.[32]

Speaking off the record, Archer conceded he'd taken several calls from 'Debbie' in which she'd talked about Kurtha, but he had insisted all along that he'd never met her. But, in eleven different responses to Lisners, Archer denied important elements of the *News of the World* story or the main thrust of it.

LISNERS: I don't think you have told us the whole truth all the way through, Mr Archer. I am sorry.

ARCHER: You will have to appear in court and say that.

LISNERS: Well, I am sorry about that.

ARCHER: And when you have broken my career I assure you you won't look very good in court.

LISNERS: I am sorry, I don't mean to break your career, I really don't.

ARCHER: Well, you are going to do it. Most unfairly.[33]

When it did eventually come to court, Archer would explain that he had made his denials because in the context any confirmation would be taken to support what seemed to be the overall line of the *News of the World* story – that he had slept with a prostitute. The phone conversations on the Saturday evening led John Lisners to conclude that Archer must be lying. The novelist later explained, however, that while he would have been prepared to speak more fully if he was not to be quoted, he realized that if he tried to explain his actions 'on the record', the headline the next morning would have been 'Archer admits his involvement with sex girl'.

In a subsequent conversation with David Montgomery, this time not for publication, Archer was more frank than with Lisners and pleaded with the editor to save his career:

David, all I can say to you, a lot of what you have got is true. I accept that totally. I don't know how to answer you, but I would beg you not to print it. And I will admit to you now that, if that article goes in, I am going to tell the Prime Minister it is true. I am going to resign and I am not going to sue you . . . I beg you not to put it in.[34]

It was reminiscent of Archer's tearful pleas to John Clare of *The Times* on the train from Louth seventeen years before, after the UNA expenses allegations had arisen. Once again he tried both threats and emotional appeals. Once more Archer's political future lay in the hands of a journalist:

Let me say to you one thing, and one thing clearly, so you know for the rest of your life. I believe I have an outside chance of being the chairman of the party if this dies. I believe I have an outside chance of doing some work in my life that I would be proud of, and I would like that privilege. I realize I have made a fool of myself, and I am telling you the truth about making a fool of myself.[35]

David Montgomery, who'd always been on friendly terms with Archer, seemed genuinely moved by his pleas. The editor promised to think about it for fifteen minutes and ring back. When Montgomery duly phoned to confirm that the story was going ahead, Archer said he'd just told Norman Tebbit he would resign if they printed. 'But it is true, Jeffrey, isn't it?' Montgomery asked. 'Every word of it is true?' 'Not every word is true, luckily. Luckily about a third of it is totally wrong,' Archer warned.[36]

As a final effort, he tried to contact the *News of the World*'s proprietor, Rupert Murdoch, but failed.

In the years that followed, the story of how Jeffrey Archer had offered £2,000 to a prostitute on Victoria station would become a favourite subject for satirists and comedians. Archer even had the dubious honour of becoming part of East End slang. While £20 had long been known as 'a score', £25 as 'a pony', and £500 as 'a monkey', the term 'an Archer' came to denote £2,000.

Monica Coghlan always said the wad of money she'd seen inside the envelope was all in £50 notes. After the débâcle at Victoria, *News of the World* journalists took her back to Wapping, and tried to work out exactly how much had been offered to her. They even took her to the cashiers' department to make comparisons with bundles of cash there. Having studied to become a lawyer, John Lisners thought it best to be cautious, and so he and his colleagues eventually decided to say it was just £2,000. This figure, repeated without question thereafter, would also be accepted by the novelist and his lawyer later in court.

But Monica claimed in court that the bundle was more than an inch thick, while Michael Stacpoole's recollection is that it was about three-quarters of an inch.[37] Either estimate suggests the sum was substantially more than £2,000.

# 21

# Spotless Reputation

Archer was fortunate. At that time, it used to take at least two years for a libel action to come to court, which would have meant that his case would not have been heard until the end of 1988. But *Archer* v. *Express Newspapers* reached the High Court in July 1987, little more than eight months after *The Star* had published its offending article.

He had asked to jump the queue, arguing in a sworn statement that 'I am prevented from any opportunity of resuming my political career.'[1] In fact, not long after a Boxing Day lunch at Chequers with Margaret Thatcher, Archer had returned to his former schedule of constituency visits and media interviews. He was right, however, in saying that he would not get his old post back, or any other political position, while the libel case hung over him. Mr Justice Boreham agreed that the 'circumstances were very unusual', and granted his application.[2]

Yet Archer had applied only to accelerate the case against *The Star*, not that against the *News of the World*. This was unfair, claimed Geoffrey Shaw, the barrister for Express Newspapers, the *Star*'s publishers: 'Since it was the *News of the World* who set this trap and forced Archer to resign, it seems very odd that the application for a speedy trial is not made against that paper. It was they who first destroyed him and one would expect he should seek redress against this paper first.'[3]

Despite Shaw's protests, dragging *The Star* into court first was a clever move by Archer's lawyers. *The Star* had gone much further in implying he had slept with Monica Coghlan, but at the same time it wasn't armed with the evidence that the *News of the World* had assembled, and it might not get much cooperation from its rival.

Initially *The Star* accepted the advice of its solicitors, Lovell, White & King, that it should settle with Archer out of court, since without help from the *News of the World* it could never hope to mount an adequate defence. When the *News of the World*'s editor David Montgomery heard that *The Star* was about to climb down, however, he was worried that it would make his own paper's position much more difficult. Montgomery demanded urgent talks with the *Star*'s editor, Lloyd Turner, and they held a quiet meeting at the Howard Hotel on the Embankment.

The two tabloid editors, from newspaper groups that were normally in cut-throat competition, reached a secret deal. It dramatically changed the whole course of events. Montgomery would give *The Star* full cooperation, including all his paper's files and, most crucially, access to Monica Coghlan, whom Jo Fletcher had been 'minding' at her home in Rochdale ever since the original story broke. This was a major concession, for many *News of the World* journalists felt bitter about *The Star*, believing that if it hadn't been for the paper's follow-up article Archer would not have bothered suing anyone. And Coghlan herself was less than happy to help *The Star*, since the paper had said she made £1,500 a week from prostitution, which she denied. Montgomery also promised to appear in court and admit that the implication of his original story had been that Archer had slept with Coghlan. In return, Lloyd Turner promised not to pull out but to fight the action all the way in court.

Now it was clear they were going to trial, the editors of *The Star* set a team to gather material on Archer. Two reporters, Allan Hall and Chris Anderson, were in effect asked 'to look for dirt'. In particular they were told to unearth evidence that would refute Archer's statement that he had never had any dealings with prostitutes. They also pursued the incident involving the three suits in Simpson's store in Toronto. Several leads sent anonymously to the paper – par for the course in such a high-profile case – were followed up fruitlessly. In the end their findings were of no use to the *Star*'s management and their lawyers.

*The Star* calculated that one of the vulnerable points in Archer's defence might be Michael Stacpoole, the emissary who'd tried to hand the money to Monica Coghlan. It was known that Stacpoole had gone to France only days after the story erupted, but nobody seemed to know quite where he was.

Then, one Friday night in the middle of May 1987, seven weeks before the start of the trial, Stacpoole was suddenly spotted in the Wine Press in Fleet Street, by one of the *Star*'s senior reporters, Don Mackay. Stacpoole explained he was briefly back in London to support his team Spurs in the Cup Final. Mackay rushed back to the office to raise the alarm and see if he could rustle up a subpoena to force Stacpoole to appear in court, but the in-house lawyer had already gone home. Chris Anderson followed Stacpoole to a café near Russell Square, but by the time Mackay had got the legal papers ready their quarry had vanished, and it was considered hopeless to try to comb the crowd at Wembley the next day. 'Had there been a will to serve a subpoena on him, he would have been subpoenaed,' says one of the reporters involved. 'There is no doubt they could have found him and done it, had there been a will.' The paper's behaviour was 'shambolic', he says – 'a curious policy of appearing to go through the motions without any real will'.

Some days later, Stacpoole made contact with *The Star* through Gerry Brown, the *News of the World* reporter he had so farcically bumped into at Victoria station. Don Mackay was quickly sent to Paris, where Stacpoole was living in a flat off the Avenue de la Grande Armée, opposite the American ambassador's residence. Stacpoole claimed to be in France working for his brother's computer rental company, and in all Mackay made three trips to see him.[4] The final time he was accompanied by a lawyer from Lovell, White & King (whom he introduced as a fellow journalist). After that, a senior editor, Nigel Blundell, made a fourth visit on his own. On each trip there were expensive lunches at a four-star establishment called L'Hôtel, with much wine consumed, in the hope that the more he drank, the more Stacpoole might reveal.

Stacpoole gave the impression that his relationship with Archer had gone rather sour. Was there any help he could give them, Mackay and his colleagues wondered. Could he even give them some idea of where they should look?

As his behaviour in the Grosvenor Hotel had shown, Stacpoole likes to appear important and loves intrigue. But he said nothing specific. 'He left huge, great, thudding, nine-ton-weight, Monty Python-type hints,' says one of those who visited him in Paris. 'He was all nod-and-wink stuff, that he knew more than he was letting on, if only we could get him to open up.' Stacpoole confirmed that the package he'd taken to Victoria station had been 'handed to him direct by Archer', but some of what he told the *Star* team seems to have been pure fantasy. According to notes of the meeting, he claimed he was writing a book about the case, which would be published in Paris a few weeks later. Stacpoole also promised to fly back to London the day before the court case opened, and, if not called as a witness, he would 'hold a daily press conference during the course of the trial, giving his views'.

Archer's long-standing friend seemed to enjoy playing games with the journalists. At one point he drew six lines on a napkin on the table, each one with a word or phrase on it – 'Leicester', 'Abingdon Road', 'Shepherd Market?', 'Party Conference', 'Jeffrey Archer', and 'Victoria' – and then later came up with a slightly different list: but it was impossible to work out what, if anything, it all signified.[5] As a result of this apparent tip, Allan Hall and Chris Anderson were sent on a fruitless trip to Abingdon Road, Leicester. In fact Stacpoole meant Abingdon Road in Kensington, where he had dinner with Archer one night.

Another problem was that, as the bar bill mounted, the journalists found it increasingly difficult to remember what Stacpoole had told them. Nor can it have helped that on one occasion Stacpoole himself had to pay the hefty restaurant bill, because Don Mackay's credit card had expired.

A crucial question was whether Stacpoole would be willing to return to England and testify at the trial. As the prosecution against William Archer had found way back in 1919, somebody living in France, or anywhere abroad, can't easily be compelled to appear in a British court.

At one meeting Stacpoole suggested that he might be willing to give the journalists a list of eight key questions they ought to ask, though they would have to find the answers themselves. A sum of £50,000 was mentioned. They also discussed the possibility of Stacpoole selling his story to *The Star* for £120,000. Another suggestion was that he should return to Britain to visit his sick mother, whereupon *The Star* would 'accidentally' spot him and issue a subpoena. That way Stacpoole might manage to preserve his relationship with Archer, since it would look as if he was being dragged into court against his will.

*Star* sources insist they never had any real intention of paying Stacpoole anything; they were just probing to see what his story was and whether it had any substance. What particularly worried them was that Stacpoole might be trying to set a trap on Archer's behalf, and that the novelist might accuse the paper of paying a key witness.

Stacpoole enjoyed the *Star*'s hospitality, but ultimately everything collapsed. The trips to Paris, the long drinking sessions and the expensive meals proved to be a waste of time, effort and money, and a fruitless diversion from preparing their case. Michael Stacpoole wouldn't help.

In any case it is unlikely that their lawyers would have wanted to put Stacpoole in the witness box, even if *Star* journalists had somehow managed to serve a subpoena. Calling any hostile witness is highly dangerous, and in Stacpoole's case it would have been especially risky. The *Star* could never have been certain of what he might say in court. Worse still, during cross-examination by Archer's counsel Stacpoole might then have revealed something highly damaging to the newspaper. If that happened, under court procedure the *Star*'s barrister would not have been able to re-examine him about the sudden new evidence that undermined the *Star*'s case.

While the journalists were desperately trying to get more facts, the lawyers – despite Lloyd Turner's agreement with David Montgomery – were discussing an out-of-court settlement. One potential deal was that the paper would pay £16,000 in damages, together with Lord Mishcon's legal bill. In addition, *The Star* would publish a front-page apology which, although it need not be grovelling, would have to say that 'substantial damages' had been paid. Foolishly, the paper rejected the idea.

In preparing Jeffrey Archer's case, Mishcon and his colleagues must have known they too faced a major problem. On the Saturday night the story broke, Archer had spoken to dozens of journalists who'd rung his home. Each time he'd begged them not to run with it, but only one agreed – Andrew Neil, the editor of the *Sunday Times*.

The political editor of *The Observer*, Adam Raphael, had written a report based on an unattributable conversation with Archer, saying that he 'is claimed by friends to have met the woman, 35-year-old Monica "Debbie" Coghlan, only once "very casually six months ago"'.[6] Similarly, Rupert Morris wrote in *Sunday Today* that Archer 'has told friends that he did meet the woman once, but denies sleeping with her'.[7] In newspaper terminology, 'friends' is often used as thin disguise for the person himself; both stories apparently contradicted Archer's subsequent statement that he had never met Coghlan, and the *Star*'s barrister would inevitably ask how these reports originated.

As the trial approached, Adam Raphael urged Jeffrey Archer to settle out of court. 'You realize, Jeffrey, do you, that if you give evidence about our conversation I won't be bound by confidence and if I then give my version it is bound to be very damaging to you?' Raphael claims to have told him.[8] Raphael would have had to testify that it was Archer himself who said he had met Coghlan six months before the story broke. The journalist says Archer reassured him, only two weeks before it got to court, that the case 'will all be settled'.[9]

Archer did indeed make a last effort to resolve matters, just a few days before the trial began, when he contacted Lord Stevens, the chairman of Express Newspapers. Archer now demanded a much higher figure than before – £100,001 – arguing that this was £1 more than the paper had recently paid the Liberal leader, David Steel, in a separate libel case concluded a few days before. In fact Steel had won only £10,000, but it was not the money that was the real sticking-point – it was the insistence that the accompanying apology should occupy most of the *Star*'s front page. Stevens expressed the view that his editor, Lloyd Turner, would never accept this. With that, all was set for a famous trial.

Jeffrey Archer's QC, Robert Alexander, was blessed with charm, a superb memory and quick reactions – Lord Denning had once described him as the best advocate of his generation. Later to become a peer and chairman of the National Westminster Bank, the fifty-year-old Alexander had recently chaired the Bar Council, and was reputed to earn £1 million a year (though he always denied it).

The *Star*'s counsel was almost as distinguished, though perhaps an unexpected choice. Michael Hill, a former chairman of the Criminal Bar Association, is known as a tough prosecutor – supposedly capable of making murderers weep – but he had little experience of libel. The *Star*'s solicitors had taken a gamble. They feared that a jury might initially be quite sympathetic to Archer, but took comfort from the fact that he himself was almost certain to give evidence. The hope, then, was that Archer might crack under Hill's fierce interrogation. Hill himself was initially very gloomy about the chances of winning, but grew more cheerful as the trial got nearer.

When the case opened in Court Thirteen of the Royal Courts of Justice in the Strand, on Monday 6 July 1987, all sides agreed that the hearing might overrun the week originally set aside for it. In the end it took almost three weeks. The case aroused intense interest, of course, and the court and its overspill gallery were packed each day well before proceedings began. It was sometimes so full that the judge, Sir Bernard Caulfield, invited press reporters to sit next to him on his bench. The public were there to observe representatives of some of the most disreputable professions in the land: lawyers, journalists, a politician and a prostitute. The case even involved a car salesman. All it lacked was an estate agent.

Robert Alexander opened with a quotation from Shakespeare's *Richard II*: 'The purest treasure mortal times afford is spotless reputation.'[10]

It was perhaps an unfortunate start, in the light of Monica Coghlan's later evidence about the state of her client's back.

For most of the opening day Alexander played the court tape-recordings of each of the six calls the *News of the World* had persuaded Monica Coghlan to make to Archer. Then he brought his client into the witness-box for the start of more than three days of questioning and cross-examination. Archer explained that he had responded to Coghlan's pleas only because he genuinely, though foolishly, believed her, and had sympathy with her story that she was under intense pressure from journalists.

Archer's first real obstacle came when the *Star*'s QC, Michael Hill, confronted him with the transcript of his Saturday-night telephone conversation with the *News of the World* reporter John Lisners. 'During which you lied and lied and lied, did you not?' suggested Hill. 'No, sir, and that is grotesquely unfair.'[11]

Hill then took Archer through each of his answers to Lisners' questions, in which he had repeatedly denied almost every aspect of the *News of the World* report. Archer responded that it was a matter of the context in which the questions had been put, and the fact that his words were 'on the record'; he also assumed at that stage that the story was based solely on his final conversation with Coghlan, and that the reporter was unaware of the previous five calls. 'When I was asked, was it true I had paid for a girl to go abroad, in its blank, blunt term taken out of context like that, Mr Hill, yes, it is true. In reality, over a five-week period with several conversations, it is not true and I stand by that.'[12] Facing continual hostile questioning, Archer lost his temper:

> I am innocent of this charge, and nothing you will say, however clever you are in the wording of out-of-context pieces, however clever you are in letting people know what 'on and off the record' means, there is only one thing that matters in this court of law, sir: I have never met this girl, I have never had sexual intercourse with her. And that is the truth![13]

As expected, Archer admitted talking to Adam Raphael on the Saturday night – among forty to sixty calls he got that evening. It was 'absolute bunkum' that he had said he had met Coghlan 'once only, very casually, about six months ago'. So, too, was the similar claim by Rupert Morris in *Sunday Today*.[14]

Now that Archer had discussed these confidential, off-the-record conversations in court, Raphael, as he had warned him, no longer felt it would be a breach of journalistic ethics to confirm Archer was his source. (As a result, Raphael became the target of a stinging editorial by Stewart Steven in the *Mail on Sunday*, which led to a separate libel action where the paper eventually apologized and paid substantial damages.) In court, the journalist explained where his *Observer* story came from:

RAPHAEL: Well, I said to him, 'How long have you known this woman?'

HILL: And he said?

RAPHAEL: And he gave me that particular quote, 'I once met her "very casually six months ago".' I then asked him further. I said, 'Where did you meet her?' And he wasn't willing to reply to that.[15]

Raphael pointed out that if Archer had insisted he'd never met Coghlan, then he would have put to him the obvious follow-up: 'Why on earth, if you've never met this woman, did you pay her off?'[16] Rupert Morris also stood by his story, though he was a little more willing to acknowledge he might have made a mistake.

Earlier, Archer had been greatly assisted in this particular dispute, and indeed other matters, by the testimony of his wife, Mary, who had never even visited a court before this trial. Robert Alexander had asked her about journalists' calls on that frantic Saturday night, and notably the conversation with Raphael:

Jeffrey certainly repeated, as he had throughout every telephone conversation, that he had never met Debbie, never had a sexual liaison with her or any other prostitute for that matter. But then in the middle of this particular conversation he said something that was so striking that I remember it very particularly. He said words to the effect: 'Well, if I did meet her, I don't know about it. If there is a photograph of me with her, I don't know about it.' I was fairly dumbfounded. I waited until the end of the conversation. I asked him who he had spoken to, that is when I think I recollect it was Adam Raphael, but I won't say on oath that it was. I said: 'What on earth made you say that? How can you say you have never met her and then you have met her?' I think I said it much in that tone of voice. Jeffrey said: 'Well, it's occurred to me that the

*News of the World* may have contrived some kind of meeting, at some kind of public function.'[17]

In some ways it was an odd decision to call Mary Archer, since she could hardly provide any direct evidence about Jeffrey's innocence. Yet her testimony may have proved crucial to the whole trial. Robert Alexander might have been influenced by his recent defence of Geoffrey Collier, the first City man to be prosecuted for insider trading. After Collier's wife had broken down in tears in the witness-box, he had escaped with only a light sentence.

Mary Archer described how she and Jeffrey had 'a happy marriage' and confirmed they lived what Alexander euphemistically called 'a full life'.[18] She'd been 'dumbfounded' on hearing of the *News of the World* story linking Jeffrey with a prostitute:

> Well, the thought of my husband consorting with a prostitute is preposterous. Anyone who knows him well knows that far from Jeffrey accosting prostitutes, if one accosted him he would run several miles in the opposite direction very fast; it would terrify him.[19]

One of the underlying currents of the case was the *Star*'s daily reporting of the proceedings, often on its front page. Its accounts were extremely hostile to Archer, and the paper would be accused of aggravating its original libel. The most prominent headline was 'You Lied and Lied and Lied', spread over half of the front page on the morning after Michael Hill had grilled Archer about his conversation with John Lisners. From the witness-box, Mary Archer rounded on the editor of *The Star*, Lloyd Turner, who, as a defendant, sat in the court every day. 'We all heard my husband say with equal conviction: "No, I did not, I have told the truth throughout." Mr Turner, your paper cannot keep a consistent line between one week and the next. How about that for your next headline?'[20] 'Very good, Mary, but no more speeches, if you *please*,' she was apparently told by one of the Archer team afterwards.[21]

Yet Mary Archer wasn't always so resolute. The day before, as she described how her husband had withstood 'an outrageous barrage of events', she had broken down in tears and had to be helped away by Jeffrey and an usher.[22]

The core of Jeffrey Archer's case was his alibi, but the actual details emerged for the first time only in Robert Alexander's opening speech. On the night when he had supposedly been seen by Aziz Kurtha,

Monday 8 September 1986, the author had enjoyed dinner at one of his favourite restaurants, Le Caprice in St James's in central London, with Richard Cohen and his wife, Caroline. It was to celebrate the publication earlier that year of his sixth novel, *A Matter of Honour*, which Cohen had once again edited. In fact the restaurant that night must have resembled a Jeffrey Archer social occasion, for several of his other friends also happened to be eating there, including Henry Togna and his wife. Togna, a businessman, is almost as close to Archer as Adrian Metcalfe and Michael Hogan. Another familiar face was the art dealer Chris Beetles, who supplies many of Archer's cartoons.

Richard Cohen had earlier testified that he and his wife had left Le Caprice at around 10.30 p.m. and that Archer had then gone back into the restaurant to chat to his other friends. None of these aspects of the alibi was disputed, and Archer even produced a copy of his credit-card slip.

The Tognas could help Archer account for his movements until almost midnight. And then Archer produced his trump card. He explained to the court that, around the time the Cohens left, yet another friend unexpectedly turned up at the restaurant: Terence Baker, one of his film agents. For about an hour and a half, Archer said, the two men sat at the bar discussing film rights to his novels, apart from a short break while Baker went to the lavatory and Jeffrey went to chat to the Tognas. Then, crucially, just before one o'clock – around the time he was accused of being with Monica Coghlan – Baker confirmed that Archer had actually driven him back to his home in Camberwell. One by one, Richard Cohen, Henry Togna and, most important, Terence Baker all came forward to support the alibi.

Michael Hill, however, suggested that the Baker element of the story had been concocted, and that Archer's account had significantly changed over time. First he pointed to a discrepancy as to when Archer had first asked Baker to give his evidence. The agent said Jeffrey had phoned him the day after the *News of the World* story, but the politician himself testified that he had not contacted Baker until 'about two weeks later'.[23]

The defence barrister also asked why this alibi was so different from accounts of Archer's movements which had been published in various newspapers a week after the original story broke. The fullest version, in the *Daily Express* on 3 November, quoted 'a friend':

> 'He had been in the presence of 40 other people at a function that night and then had other meetings he could confirm.'

After the function, Archer apparently met Tory chief whip John Wakeham to discuss Mrs Thatcher's impending ministerial reshuffle and then drove a colleague home in the early hours from Conservative Central Office.[24]

*Today* gave a similar account, attributing it directly to the novelist: 'Mr Archer says he was at a meeting with 50 people at the time the newspaper claims he met Miss Coghlan.'[25]

Both of the reporters who'd written these reports – Tony Dawe of the *Express* and Nick Constable of *Today* – stood by them in court, confirming that the details about a 'function' and a 'meeting' respectively had come from Archer himself. Constable even told the rather touching story of how he'd been the only journalist still waiting on a cold night outside the house in Grantchester, whereupon Archer had suddenly invited him in for a brandy, and had given him this account.

Questioned about these earlier reports, Archer insisted there was no discrepancy between the stories, since there had been fifty other people in the restaurant where he was eating with the Cohens: 'In the evening I was in a room with fifty other people, nine of whom, sir, will stand up and say so and prove it.' Had he told Tony Dawe he'd been at a function with fifty other people? Hill wanted to know. 'I think I said to all of them that I was at a place with fifty other people.'[26] As for the meeting with John Wakeham, his diary showed that this had occurred at 4.15 p.m., not late at night as the *Express* had suggested.

Then, towards the end of the trial, Mary Archer made a dramatic two-minute reappearance in the witness-box. In an affidavit which had emerged only during the trial, Monica Coghlan had claimed that her client's back 'did not have very good skin. It may have been dry or spotty.'[27] Archer was not asked to expose his back to the jury – it presumably being regarded as undignified – but instead his wife explained how he certainly did have distinguishing marks at the time in question. A recent summer holiday in Turkey had left 'a very white part around his midriff where his shorts or trunks were'. 'Were there any spots on his back?' Robert Alexander enquired. 'No, sir.'[28] It would be one of the most famous incidents of the whole trial.

The *Star*'s editor, Lloyd Turner, knew from very early on that he was in difficulty. After one session about three days into the trial, he happened to be walking down Fleet Street behind two of the jurors. One of them suddenly saw who was behind them, whereupon Turner heard him tell his colleague that 'We'll soon wipe the smile off his face.' Turner also felt that, even if he could convince those two jurors, the best his paper could achieve was an 11–1 verdict, judging by the behaviour of a grey-haired woman at the front of the jury. She kept smiling at Archer and seemed spellbound, as if he were reciting his latest novel.

What really torpedoed the *Star*'s case, however, was that neither of its two primary witnesses – Aziz Kurtha and Monica Coghlan – was a particularly attractive character. Despite his nineteen years as a barrister, Kurtha did not come across well. He was appearing against his will, brought to court under subpoena, which meant that the *Star*'s lawyers had no chance to sit down with him beforehand and go through his likely evidence. He admitted using a prostitute for sex, and trying to exploit the Coghlan story to damage Archer politically. There was also the disputed question of whether he wanted money for his story: Kurtha said the £10,000 he had mentioned would have gone to charity. But the most damaging aspect of Kurtha's testimony came when he revealed that he was colour-blind. The members of the jury seemed to snigger among themselves when he could only identify Archer's car as one of three colours – red, green, or brown. It was in fact dark grey. After Kurtha's evidence, Lloyd Turner wrote in his diary that they had lost the case.

Monica Coghlan was, of course, the only witness who could supply first-hand evidence that Archer had had sex with her. '*That* man,' she cried, when asked to identify whom she had slept with. 'The gentleman with the red tie on.'[29] She had no difficulty remembering him, she said, since the hotel room had been well lit, and 'I was lay [*sic*] on top of him the whole time.'[30] At the start of almost three days in the witness-box, Coghlan described the event in great detail:

We went into the room. He took his jacket off. I asked him for my present. He gave me a £50 note. As he gave me the £50, I suggested that if he took his time, if I took my time, made it last a bit longer, it was another £20, and he agreed and gave me another £20 note . . . Then we got undressed . . . He commented on how lovely I was. He was taken quite aback by my nipples.[31]

'He what?' asked a bewildered Justice Caulfield. The prostitute repeated herself, and explained that the whole act had taken ten minutes in all.

Because it was over so quickly, I suggested that he relax for a while and we try again. I got up. I cleaned him, washed him down with tissues and dried him.[32]

'And what?' Caulfield interjected. 'Took the Durex off first and then I washed him down and . . . I lit a cigarette and I laid down on the bed with him,' Coghlan went on. She asked the client what he did for a living. 'He told me that he sold cars.' (Monica Coghlan was never asked if she had read any of Archer's books, but the fictitious Raymond Gould, incidentally, told his prostitute the same thing.) With that, Coghlan said, her client suddenly leapt up, got dressed, and went off to move his vehicle. He never reappeared, she said.[33]

Coghlan's credibility as a witness could easily be undermined in court. She had two juvenile convictions for shoplifting and possessing cannabis, quite apart from a long criminal record for prostitution. She also confessed to not paying income tax and to fraudulent social-security claims. Like Aziz Kurtha, she also faced the nagging question of whether she had a financial motive. She had been paid £6,000 by the *News of the World*, but that, Coghlan insisted, was only to cover expenses and loss of earnings. Yet, if money wasn't her motive, why did she help the newspaper? The two reasons she gave – to show she was telling the truth, and to keep other reporters off her back – didn't sound convincing.

When Robert Alexander pushed her, Monica Coghlan had to admit, time and again, that she'd lied to Archer on the phone, that she'd been play-acting and practising deception. Several times she broke down and cried; on one occasion the judge even offered her some handkerchiefs. When Alexander again accused her of lying, she lashed out at him:

You're the liar and he's the liar. You're the one that's making vast amounts of money, not me. I'm penniless through all this. He can carry on. What's going to happen to me?[34]

When Alexander assured her that he didn't want to distress her, she turned on Archer as well:

Distress me? Do you know what I've been through, through that liar? Just because he's got power and money. Why are you doing this to me? Why are you doing it to your wife?[35]

Moments later she became hysterical. 'He knows that it's him,' she screamed. 'He knows it.'[36]

It didn't help *The Star*, however, that Coghlan, its main witness in court, was so willing to rubbish the paper's primary source for the disputed article – her nephew, Tony Smith. 'He's a compulsive liar and he romances a lot,' she said.[37] Coghlan repeatedly denied the quotations attributed to her in *The Star*, and condemned numerous other details in the article as 'false' or 'not true', including the claim that 90 per cent of her clients wanted 'kinky sex'. 'The only true part of it is I went to bed with Jeffrey Archer. The rest of it is fantasy from Tony.'[38] As Robert Alexander declared later, 'It must be the most astonishing defence in some ways ever conducted in a libel action. Their principal witness from the witness-box brands most of their story as fantasy.'[39]

Perhaps the most bizarre and damaging aspect of the *Star*'s case was not who appeared for the defence but the people who did not testify. Michael Hill called three *News of the World* journalists, including David Montgomery and John Lisners, but it was not their paper which was immediately on trial. With several other small walk-on parts, eight journalists appeared for the defence in all – nine if Aziz Kurtha is included. But no one came forward from *The Star* itself.

The paper's editor, Lloyd Turner, was due to appear as the very last witness, but during the trial there were long discussions within the defence team about whether this was wise. Turner himself knew that if he did give evidence he would almost certainly have to reveal his source for the *News of the World* transcripts he had secretly obtained and which had persuaded him to run his disputed story. But, overall, he felt he had a duty to the rest of Fleet Street to defend himself.

Turner was warned, however, that for three days Robert Alexander would make him defend not just the original article but all sorts of totally unrelated items he might have published, and even material in other tabloids.

Two days before he was due in the witness-box, Michael Hill and Lord Stevens decided Turner should not appear. They were worried that he was not a good performer and might come across badly under fierce questioning, without adding much to the defence. But Turner's silence did not look good. 'Even if he got into trouble in there, he should have stood up for the paper,' says one of the *Star* team who sat in court. 'It made it all look a bit slippery, a bit tawdry.' Nor did Hill call either of the reporters who had written the disputed article.

Jeffrey Archer's counsel, Robert Alexander, mocked 'the silent Mr Lloyd Turner' mercilessly. 'Does he have the power of speech?' he teased, speculating as to whether there was some 'physical infirmity' to prevent him from giving evidence.[40] Yet, legally, there was no logical reason for Turner to testify, since he himself had no direct evidence about whether Archer had slept with Monica Coghlan.

Moreover, had Turner and other *Star* journalists appeared, it might have assisted Alexander's overall strategy even more. As much as he could, Archer's counsel tried to turn the case into a trial of the ethics of tabloid journalism, and he almost admitted as much in his powerful closing speech:

> Members of the jury, as the case developed you may think that there came to be something more at stake in this action, and something that was directly and highly relevant to this action itself. Because if, as we suggest, this is a trumped-up charge against Jeffrey Archer, how did it come about? It came about, did it not, because of the methods adopted by certain people, such as Aziz Kurtha and certain Fleet Street journalists? . . . What we have to consider in this case is whether there are any boundaries, any limits to what can be tolerated of the press.[41]

If the jurors decided against *The Star*, Alexander promised, their award would 'have struck a blow for a fairer press, for a cleaner press and for a healthier society – and that will not be a bad thing either, will it?'[42]

Yet the speech for which the trial will mainly be remembered is the summing-up by Sir Bernard Caulfield, which was one of the most controversial judicial summaries in modern legal history. Ludovic Kennedy wrote that 'If there has been a more eccentric summing-up in any libel action in the past fifty years, I have not read of it,' while an editorial in *The Times* expressed surprise at the length of time the jury had taken to reach a decision considering its 'partiality'.[43] Caulfield, however, clearly didn't think much of the witnesses who had appeared for *The Star*, and his address simply reflected this.

Caulfield was clearly much taken with Mary Archer. When she appeared initially, Robert Alexander asked her how old she was. 'You should say, "How young are you?"' the judge interjected.[44] Later he referred to an 'elegant phrase' she had delivered.[45] But these were nothing compared with his concluding eulogy:

> Remember Mary Archer in the witness-box. Your vision of her

probably will never disappear. Has she elegance? Has she fragrance? Would she have, without the strain of this trial, radiance? What is she like in physical features, in presentation, in appearance? How would she appeal? Has she had a happy married life? Has she been able to enjoy, rather than endure, her husband Jeffrey? Is she right when she says to you – you may think with delicacy – 'Jeffrey and I lead a full life'?[46]

Then, of her husband Jeffrey, the judge asked:

Is he in need of cold, unloving, rubber-insulated sex in a seedy hotel round about quarter to one on a Tuesday morning after an evening at the Caprice? . . . It is possible even for the most happy, successful and respected married man to seek adventure in physical contact with persons who will not tell. Of course it is possible. But reflect, would you, upon the position.[47]

Caulfield wondered whether it was likely that Archer would wait outside a hotel for Kurtha to finish with Coghlan, as if to say 'After you, Aziz.' The jury would have to ask whether 'his taste is such that he can take his place in virtually a queue – it is only a queue of two – for the services that Debbie had to offer'.[48]

Jurors should be cautious, Caulfield warned, about witnesses who might be dishonest or have financial motives. And he had the court in laughter as he ridiculed Kurtha for his colour-blindness and his inability to tell the colour of Archer's car:

Aziz Kurtha has been, he said, a TV presenter. Not being able to recognize red, green or brown, he is hardly likely, is he, to be the presenter of *Pot Black*, or a commentator at the Crucible Theatre in Coventry [sic]? And if he did play snooker (if he could), you would not mind having a game with him, would you? And if you had a side-bet, would you not lay guineas to gooseberries you would win?[49]

Caulfield found it particularly surprising that none of the journalists had kept any of their notes of the events they were describing, especially when Archer had issued libel writs within only a few days of the *Star* and *News of the World* articles. Caulfield obviously found the novelist and his supporters to be far more credible in comparison with the newspaper's line-up. 'Archer snuffs any candle that is burning from this witness,' he pronounced dismissively at one point when assessing the relative merits of conflicting accounts.[50]

Caulfield was widely lambasted for his summing-up, and many legal experts thought it was a disgrace. An interesting comment came after his death in October 1994, in an obituary in *The Independent*. It accused him of 'the occasional irresistible and unresisted impulse to indulge in seemingly pompous hyperbole. This unhappily resulted in judicial pronouncements of questionable fairness and taste.' The judge had an 'emotional facet which was apt to lead him astray'.[51] This damning verdict on Caulfield came from a most unexpected source: the former Lord Chief Justice, Geoffrey Lane, a man not known for delivering rash remarks in the press.

The jury returned after four and a quarter hours. It took an agonizing five minutes for the room to settle, then another two for the judge to arrive. Mary sat taking deep breaths, clasping her hands in front of her. Jeffrey closed his eyes.

'Do you find for Jeffrey Archer or *The Star* newspaper?' the clerk demanded. 'Mr Jeffrey Archer,' replied the bow-tied foreman. 'Thank God,' Archer mouthed. 'What sum do you award by way of damages?' 'Five hundred thousand pounds.' 'Whew!' Archer was heard to exclaim. His wife patted him on the back; he kissed one of the legal team; Mary kissed Lord Mishcon. Onlookers cheered. And Mary wept. As they left the court, Jeffrey shook each of the twelve jury members by the hand. 'Thank you, thank you, thank you.' 'It's a pleasure,' one of them replied. Another asked for his autograph, and got it. 'The verdict speaks for itself,' Archer said later.[52]

The £500,000 award was a new British record. On top of that, Express Newspapers had to pay an estimated £700,000 to cover both sides' costs, though the precise figure was disputed for months. 'It's been quite an expensive day, hasn't it?' Lord Stevens was heard to comment as he welcomed the team for a drink back in his office. A few days later most of them reassembled in a private room at the St James's Club for what some called a 'Defeat Dinner'. Lloyd Turner and his wife were there, as were his assistant, Nigel Blundell; Michael Hill and his junior; and two solicitors from Lovell, White & King. David Montgomery also dropped in at one point. 'The attitude,' says one of those present, 'was "Let's have a massive piss-up even though we've lost a million pounds."' Towards the end, Michael Hill delivered a short speech saying Lloyd Turner was the most courageous editor he had ever met.

Privately, despite the bonhomie, many *Star* journalists had strong misgivings about the way the case had been handled. To start with, they were unhappy that their solicitors, Lovell, White & King, had actually been acting *for* Archer in responding to questions from the *Daily Mirror* the year before. They were disappointed, too, that Michael Hill had been nothing like as tough on Archer as they had expected, and had not grilled him on any of the contentious episodes of his past career. They also felt he had been far too soft with Mary. Hill himself had deliberately decided not to be too aggressive, so as not to alienate the jury and increase the possible damages.

Initially Lloyd Turner and Express Newspapers were determined to appeal. Michael Hill reckoned it would be fruitless to try to reduce the size of the damages, but he thought that Caulfield's summing-up gave them good grounds to ask for the whole case to be tried again. Indeed, the QC was more confident about securing a retrial than he had been about winning the original case. Gradually, however, they realized that it would be almost impossible to persuade Monica Coghlan to appear in court again. She felt very bitter about the way she had been treated in the witness-box, especially in comparison with Mary Archer. Even if she did agree to testify again, a retrial might not take place for another eighteen months or more, and Coghlan would have to be minded to ensure she did not disappear. Yet the case was hopeless without her.

Above all, Express Newspapers feared that a retrial might simply double their enormous legal bill and yet produce no better outcome. So, reluctantly, the idea of an appeal was dropped.

Three months after the High Court hearing, the *News of the World* settled their dispute out of court, paying Archer £50,000 damages and £30,000 costs. Following the *Star* verdict they had little option, especially after the paper's former editor, David Montgomery, had carried out his promise – albeit reluctantly – to admit in court that his readers would have drawn the conclusion that 'Jeffrey Archer had slept with a prostitute'.[53]

Jeffrey and Mary celebrated the *Star* trial verdict the following Sunday in Grantchester, with a garden party originally planned to mark their twenty-first wedding anniversary. The guest list seemed even more distinguished than usual – Michael Havers, the Lord Chancellor; David Mellor and Norman Lamont, both rising junior ministers; David and Debbie Owen; businessmen Sir Clive Sinclair and Sir Michael Edwardes; the actor Anthony Andrews; and Clive James, who for once was not late. Another Cabinet minister was also present, but he was too obscure to be noticed by reporters spotting faces at the gate – the new Treasury Chief Secretary, John Major. No one dared ask how many would have appeared had the case gone the other way.

Two months later Lloyd Turner resigned as editor of *The Star*, and the paper went further down-market for a while, in association with David Sullivan's *Sunday Sport*. As for Monica Coghlan, she eventually returned to the streets to pay off the heavy debts she'd accumulated, but her fame made work no easier. She appeared in court again, and was fined once more for soliciting.

After Michael Stacpoole returned from Paris, Archer continued to demonstrate how loyal he can be to his friends. Stacpoole has since told people that not only had Archer spent £24,000 paying for his nine-month holiday in Paris, but also that over the next two years the novelist employed his occasional services, at the rate of £1,000 a month.

In the early 1990s Stacpoole moved to Florida to work for a management consultancy firm called Integrated Control Systems, but in 1993 he fell out with the chairman, James Irwin, and was sacked. This left Stacpoole in some financial difficulty: he had spent $150,000 buying a house and now couldn't sell it. Stacpoole's story is that Archer generously stepped in and helped Irwin's company buy the house from him, though Irwin denies this. Despite this gesture, it wasn't long before the two men finally fell out. Aggrieved at the way he'd been treated by Irwin, Stacpoole thought it was particularly disloyal of his friend Jeffrey then to accept James Irwin's lavish hospitality. During the summer of 1994 Archer took his family and several friends – including Robin Oakley and Kenneth Baker – for a holiday off the coast of Turkey on Irwin's yacht.

That autumn Stacpoole decided that the time had now come to tell the story of his dealings with Archer. He approached several Fleet Street papers, including the *Sunday Mirror*, the *Express*, the *News of the World*, and the *Mail on Sunday*, in each case demanding a six-figure sum. There were long discussions about what Stacpoole had to say. One paper even went so far as to take him back to Paris to look up bank statements from his time there in 1986 and 1987. Ultimately, however, no paper would bite.

Having failed to sell his story, in 1995 Stacpoole moved to the Belgian port of Ostend. There he acquired the lease on the Bunny Bar, a night-club which specializes in nude dancing girls.

In the years since the libel trial, Jeffrey Archer has always maintained privately that he was simply the victim of mistaken identity. Some months after the trial, he approached several close friends with an astonishing letter he'd recently received. It came from a man in the north of England, who enclosed a photo of himself. He pointed out their striking resemblance, and the rather grainy picture did look just like Archer. The letter revealed that the correspondent was a salesman who drove a green Jaguar, and went on to explain how he'd been staying in London on business. Late one evening, desperate for sexual release, he caught sight of an attractive girl and followed her back to her hotel.

So it was quite clear what must have occurred, the letter said. The salesman apologized for all the trouble he had caused, and gave Archer full permission to publish the information to confirm his innocence. But he begged Jeffrey also to think of his own position: the salesman had a wife and four children, and their lives would be destroyed if the facts came out. He was revealing the information so that Archer could let Mary know the truth, and he left himself entirely in Jeffrey's hands.

Archer decided simply to show his letter to a few influential friends. It was best, he must have concluded, to let matters rest, not to let the letter-writer, who bore such a strong resemblance to him, suffer the kind of intense media scrutiny he had already endured.

# 22

# Mary, Quite Contrary

Without Mary, he might never have pulled it off. What they had once said of Archer's selection in Louth, people now declared about the libel action.

In 1969 she had travelled to Lincolnshire as the dutiful political wife. Every morning during the 1987 trial, she'd accompanied Jeffrey to the law courts in the Strand. The press and television had great fun as day by day she paraded a collection of elegant and expensive summer outfits, many bought at Aquascutum. She sat by his side in court, squeezing his hand, taking notes, wishing him well. When her turn in the witness-box came, she was happy to tell Michael Hill she could be rude if she wanted, and she sat glaring at Monica Coghlan when she testified.

And, as Mary Archer later related, the word 'fragrance' took on a whole new meaning afterwards. 'It escaped into gossip columns and dinner-table conversations, and pursued me round the world last month to the unsuitable venue of an international conference on electrochemistry in Hawaii.'[1] (It is conceivable that Justice Caulfield was actually inspired to use this phrase by reading Archer: a 'fragrant, silk-clad wife' appears in Penny.[2])

Jeffrey seemed to acknowledge his wife's contribution when he shared out his £550,000 damages from the two newspapers among various charities. Fifty thousand pounds went to Mary's old school, Cheltenham Ladies' College, and further sums were given to one of her former colleges, Newnham, and the Fitzwilliam Museum, of which she was a trustee. (Other beneficiaries included Jeffrey's disabled schoolfriend Geoff Bailey, Brasenose College and Ely Cathedral, which is thought to have received the largest amount – £100,000 – a particularly generous gesture given that Archer is sceptical about the existence of God.)

The 1987 libel case is often cited as a turning-point in Mary Archer's career. Until then she'd remained a quiet, industrious academic, finding it difficult to join her husband in public engagements, either because of

commitments elsewhere or through simple shyness. She'd found it hard
even to open summer fêtes in Louth, and when she attended parties at
Alembic House, she was heard muttering how she hated such events.

The flat on the Embankment has always been Jeffrey's in spirit −
brash and ostentatious, overflowing with expensive art and vulgar
icons of his writing success. Grantchester, on the other hand, is primarily Mary's home, furnished with tasteful coverings and fine English
oak antiques. There, Mary saw her garden grow; she enjoyed sewing
and playing the spinet, provided a home for the two boys and the three
family cats, and served as choirmistress for the local church. Her academic commitments were a short bike-ride away in Cambridge.

Since the trial, Mary Archer has become a public figure in her own
right. The change was highlighted on New Year's Eve 1991, when she
performed Tom Lehrer's comic song 'The Elements' on a Channel 4
alternative comedy show, and allowed herself to be photographed
sprawled across a grand piano, wearing a low-cut dress. She's produced
a CD of Christmas carols, appeared on *Desert Island Discs* and *Any
Questions*, modelled clothes, and, more importantly, taken up major
appointments in the City. Nowadays Mary Archer's life is based almost
as much in London as it is in Cambridge.

Mary Doreen Weeden was born in Epsom, Surrey, in December
1944, the second daughter of Harold Weeden and his wife, Doreen.
Her background seems to have been almost a caricature of the Surrey
stockbroker belt. The Weedens were well-off − much wealthier than
the Archers − and lived in a large house. Mary's father commuted
into London to work as a chartered accountant with a pharmaceutical
company, and at home in the evening he would sing songs with his
children round the piano. He also had a passion for model railways,
with an extensive layout in the attic. 'A firm but very nice man with
a slightly short fuse,' is how Mary's sister, Janet, has described him.[3]
It was a comfortable, untroubled background: Church of England,
Conservative-voting, very English and very middle-class. The Weedens
even kept three Labradors in kennels at the bottom of the garden.

When Mary was only four, so the story goes, she and several other
children were invited on to the stage during a Christmas pantomime.
What were they going to be when they grew up? 'I want to be an
expert,' she is supposed to have said. From early in life, Mary knew she
was brighter than others:

I remember on the bus, looking around at all those amazingly old, dull people staring into space as the bus jolted along the Epsom Road, wondering if they were thinking interesting things, or were they as dull inside as they looked outside? I think that's the reaction of a clever child.[4]

At school Mary was known as 'Weedlet', on account of her name and her thin, spindly appearance, but Harold Weeden pushed and encouraged his daughter. 'Like many women who've got fairly far in life, my father was a very important influence, both on me and my elder sister. He had very high, very uncompromising standards, and I think I was inculcated with those, and I always enjoyed work. I was always a boring, bookish girl.'[5] Her mother was shrewd, she's said, but slightly remote, and Mary thinks it's probably from her that she acquired her famous air of detachment. Doreen Weeden believed in making children stand on their own two feet, and at the age of eleven Mary was sent to London on her own to buy her new school uniform.

Her father was ahead of his day in believing that girls should be as well educated as boys. Harold Weeden sent both his daughters to Cheltenham Ladies' College, the epitome of the blue-stocking English girls' public school. Mary excelled academically. 'She was just the cleverest girl in the class,' says one fellow pupil, Lisa Jardine, who is now an English professor. 'And she was beautiful. It was quite maddening.'[6] She wasn't good just at science, but at arts subjects too, and she seemed to be blessed with a phenomenal memory. Jardine says that in all the time she knew her at school Mary never cried, not even when bashed on the shins during hockey. She still retains a strong image of her as she was about to enter a chemistry exam: 'Mary was sitting on a table, looking absolutely impeccable, with her fingers in her ears, looking at a chemistry textbook.'[7]

By the age of only sixteen, Mary Weeden had acquired A-levels and the tougher S-levels in maths, physics and chemistry, and had won a Nuffield science scholarship to St Anne's College, Oxford.

She went to Oxford in the autumn of 1962 to do a four-year chemistry course, aged only seventeen. Science generally requires harder work than arts degrees, but it wasn't all heavy toil: there was still time for singing with the Bach Choir, and for parties. A few days before the start of her second year, Mary fell in with the crowd on *Cherwell*, the Oxford University newspaper. It would change her life.

The paper's editor, Nick Lloyd, spotted this pretty young girl walking through the Union gardens near the *Cherwell* office. He nudged a colleague, and they went to chat her up. Within a few weeks Mary's face was on the front page, clutching a small kitten, beside the cheeky heading 'Poor Little Pussy!' Mary Weeden, so the paper explained next to another picture inside, had been trying to give away ten-week-old Priscilla. 'You see this kitten was going to be anaesthetized, so I took it in,' Mary was quoted as saying, with 'tears glistening in her eyes'.[8] It was only an excuse, of course, to run two nice pictures of a pretty girl.

'She was obviously a bit of a camp-follower,' says one of her *Cherwell* friends, and Mary quickly became part of the paper's social scene. She became first Lloyd's girlfriend, and then that of the paper's assistant editor, Jonathan Martin. Mary seems never to have written anything for the newspaper, but when Martin went to interview some politicians in London she accompanied him to take notes. Martin remembers a thank-you letter from George Brown, in which the deputy Labour leader asked him to pass on his regards 'to that pretty girl you brought to see me'.[9] In the winter of 1964 Mary also went on a *Cherwell* trip to produce a Paris edition of the paper. A front-page picture shows her on the Champs-Élysées with five colleagues copying the latest Beatles pose of leaping joyously into the air. The caption describes Mary merely as 'a mate'.[10]

So in two terms Mary Weeden's face had appeared more often in *Cherwell* than Jeffrey's. It indicates that, despite her apparent shyness and her rather sheltered Surrey and Cheltenham upbringing, Mary had a strong adventurous streak. The Paris trip was obviously something of a lark; one colleague even remembers Mary sleeping on the luggage rack on the boat-train. 'Underneath perhaps there's a wild woman trying to come out,' he suggests. Most female undergraduates with her background would have been highly embarrassed to appear as a kind of student-newspaper pin-up, or to be described as a 'St Anne's glamour girl' as the newspaper's gossip column did on one occasion.[11] Mary seemed to enjoy it.

In the autumn of 1964, by which time Mary was paired with Jeffrey, she even appeared on a radio programme that her former boyfriend, Jonathan Martin, made for the BBC. The hour-long broadcast, for the European English-language service, featured four young people discussing the future of Britain; Mary was meant to represent 'Oxbridge'.

Having beaten her future husband on to the front page of the university newspaper, Mary also seems to have reached the airwaves first.

Mary Weeden still came across as rather cold and undemonstrative, however. 'She'd got a barrier around her, and was almost self-contained,' says one former boyfriend. 'She's not the sort of person you would read very easily. She was very sweet, but not somebody who'd lay out her heart and soul for you.' Michael Hogan feels it was easy for Oxford people to get the wrong idea: 'She might have been shy in a group, but one-on-one she wasn't a bit shy. You don't want to confuse her being shy with being reserved.'[12]

And having fun with the *Cherwell* crowd wasn't allowed to interfere with her academic work. She would spend eight hours a day in the chemistry labs in her first three years, and up to thirteen hours in her final year. 'Mary was a very serious girl – extremely serious,' says Adrian Metcalfe. 'Yet in her own quiet way she was as ambitious as Jeffrey. She was so obviously going to get a first – it was beyond argument. The important thing was, Was she going to get an applauded first?'[13]

But why Jeffrey? Mary was clearly interested in men who were going places. 'She rather cultivated people she thought were likely to succeed,' observes one former Oxford friend. Nick Lloyd and Jonathan Martin both went on to successful careers in journalism – Lloyd as editor of the *Daily Express*, and Martin as head of BBC TV Sport. Another boyfriend, Nick Montagu, who was secretary of the Oxford Union, is now deputy secretary (the second-ranking civil servant) at the Department of Transport. Yet, even in comparison with these high-flyers, Jeffrey was far more ambitious, much livelier, and incredible fun. She also admired the fact that he seemed to have guts. 'Mary saw in Jeffrey a lot of things she would have liked to have had, but didn't have,' says Michael Hogan.[14] 'I was fascinated by him,' she's explained. 'He was something very unusual by my blinkered standards. I had hardly ever lifted my nose from a book, and here was this young man bounding around who knew about all sorts of things I didn't understand.'[15]

For Mary it wasn't love at first sight, but Jeffrey quickly grew on her, and they got engaged during her final year. 'I thought it would be an exciting and adventurous life,' Mary has said. Her parents were less keen. 'I think they found him a bit alarming, and they also thought, quite rightly, that I was too young to get married – I was twenty-one . . . But they liked him, and they always were very supportive.'[16]

Mary Archer always hated the idea of being a doting wife who would stand in the wings supporting her husband's career. 'It would be a complete waste of my own talents, such as they are.'[17] She wanted a marriage on equal terms. It would be wrong, however, to see Mary as an ardent feminist (in her twenties she once said she would rather vote for a man as her MP than for a woman).[18] But, suspecting that Jeffrey's life was likely to be something of a roller-coaster, she was determined to pursue her own academic career, seeing her profession partly as a 'back-stop' if things went wrong. That sense of independence was helped by Jeffrey's knowing absolutely nothing about chemistry.

The constant need to be her own woman is crucial in understanding how Mary Archer has withstood the successive crises of the last thirty years. And with each of her husband's scrapes she seems further to have 'insulated' herself, either by establishing financial independence or by making new career moves.

After a brief spell working at the Harwell nuclear lab near Oxford, Mary spent the first two years of marriage doing a PhD (on heterogeneous catalysis in solutions) at Imperial College. This was highly convenient, of course, since Jeffrey was by then working in London too. But in 1968 Mary got a teaching job at St Hilda's College back in Oxford, and they therefore began to spend much of the week apart. It set a pattern which has continued for nearly all their married life: in London and Oxford to start with; then in a triangle of London, Oxford and Louth; and more recently in London and Cambridge.

In 1972 Mary returned to London to work under Sir George Porter at the Royal Institution, where she became a pioneer in photoelectrochemistry, the conversion of the sun's radiation into electrical and chemical energy. She established the UK branch of the International Solar Energy Society, and also teamed up with a Canadian scientist, Jim Bolton, who at one time lodged in the Archers' home in The Boltons and is now a professor at the University of Western Ontario.

Although Mary Archer is widely acknowledged within her profession as a first-class scientist, she has never been a future Nobel Prize-winner, and has never become a full-time university professor. She has produced some original research, but perhaps not in sufficient quantity or quality. 'It's not absolutely the very, very top,' a colleague says of her published work, 'but it's certainly very good.' Since the late 1970s she and Jim Bolton have been working together on a *magnum opus*, a university textbook called *Photoconversion of Solar Energy*, on the ways of converting solar energy into other forms of energy, apart from heat. So far they've written more than a thousand pages, though Bolton says the book has turned out rather broader than they'd originally intended.[19] Jeffrey loves pointing out how many books he's written in the time it's taken Mary to prepare just one. He was once asked if he would read Mary's book when it was published. 'If I'm still alive,' he replied.[20]

'The attraction of opposites' is the scientific way in which Mary often describes their relationship.[21] 'They are completely, transparently different,' her sister adds, 'but their contrasting qualities complement one another.'[22] It's a common observation. 'Mary's very reserved,' says Michael Hogan, 'very cautious, extremely careful, whereas Jeffrey throws caution to the wind.'[23] Jeffrey became notorious for his gaffes when Conservative deputy chairman; he is guaranteed to give a lively television interview, and is an obvious sparky guest for *Any Questions* or *Question Time*. Mary, in contrast, thinks so carefully about what she's going to say on such occasions that she can end up saying nothing. She sometimes seems to have learned a little too much from her husband's mistakes.

Did she 'mind about being cleverer than Jeffrey,' Mary once discussed with Jonathan Aitken when he was a reporter on the *Evening Standard*. 'I don't think I am, except obviously in my own field. He'd get first-class degrees in the things he's really good at too.'[24] They represent two very different kinds of brain. Hers is an academic intelligence, whereas he had only a few O-levels. His intelligence is of the sharp variety, and involves a greater capacity for imagination and original thought than his wife. To Mary, with her scientific background, precision and factual accuracy are vital; to him, details are immaterial, and his wife has famously spoken of 'Jeffrey's talent for inaccurate précis'.[25]

More interesting than the glaring contrasts are the less obvious but important similarities. Both Mary and Jeffrey are chronic workaholics, and detest the idea of wasting time. 'I can relax only by doing something different,' remarks Mary, who says she is constantly aware of having only one life. Their younger son, Jamie, jokes about a family boat trip round the Greek islands on which his parents both spent the whole of each morning working in their cabins. 'In the afternoons Will and I had to persuade them to walk around an island, or to do some water sports, because they cannot sit and do nothing. They are similar in that respect.'[26]

Both Archers are puritanical types, and value courtesy; both hanker after organization, discipline and order. Jeffrey deplores lateness, and

Mary hates having her plans upset. Jeffrey sets out neat rows of pens on his table and writes for exactly two hours at a stretch, while Mary is constantly tidying the house and admits she can't leave home without emptying the waste-paper baskets. Despite great wealth, both are frugal. Mary constantly turns off lights to save energy, while Jeffrey notoriously checks his restaurant bills line by line. He also admits that, when catching taxis outside his flat, he'll walk 150 yards so as to avoid having to tour the one-way system and pay a higher fare.

Both are obsessive creatures; indeed Mary seems almost neurotic. In *Who's Who* she self-deprecatingly describes one of her pastimes as 'picking up litter', and is often seen walking round Grantchester with a plastic bag.[27] 'You get some very peculiar looks when you do it, but I do hate litter and I particularly hate to see it outside my own front door ... It becomes a kind of obsession. I find it very difficult to walk down the street without picking up rubbish.'[28]

Jeffrey boasts about the occasion when somebody wrote to complain about the number of factual errors in one of his novels. He contacted the reader to ask if he had ever written a book. On finding he had, Archer obtained a copy and had it combed for mistakes, until the moment of triumph when an error was spotted.

The couple find they prefer the same kind of people. 'I like doers not dreamers,' Mary says, and Jeffrey would agree.[29] They despise whingers. But they like different holiday locations and read separate types of book: in fact Mary admits that, if she wasn't married to him, she would never read Jeffrey's novels.

While her husband's misjudgements have become notorious, there have been occasions when Mary, too, has lacked basic common sense. The most notable example occurred while she was expecting their first baby, in 1972. Through foolishness and excessive devotion to her work, she nearly committed 'matricide' [sic], she says.[30] Being Archers, they had carefully planned to have their first baby during the summer vacation, but ten weeks early it suddenly started to arrive during the middle of a tutorial at Somerville in Oxford. Instead of doing the sensible thing and walking to the Radcliffe Infirmary next door, Mary treated the experience with a kind of scientific curiosity rather than urgency:

> I was losing the waters round the baby. And I knew very well
> what was happening. Only clever people can be this stupid, really.
> I went on teaching. And then I decided to go to the library to look

up what I should do next. Crazy, crazy. Anyway it said quite
clearly that this was quite a dangerous thing, you know, that labour
would ensue, and I cycled to the station and got on the train to
London, which was the next thing I was scheduled to do. So by
the time Jeffrey met me off the train I was well into labour.[31]

Squeezed into Jeffrey's tiny MGB, they raced from Paddington through
the rush-hour traffic to Guy's Hospital, where their son William was
born within minutes. Mary was told the baby would have only a fifty–
fifty chance of survival.

'He really worships the ground she walks on,' family friend Henry
Togna says of Jeffrey. 'He's so proud of her abilities.'[32] The 'education'
section of his *Who's Who* entry, for instance, declares 'by my wife since
leaving Wellington School'.[33] People remember how in the 1960s he
would talk of doing things which would impress Mary; one suspects,
for instance, that this accounts for his brief flirtation in 1967 with the
idea of going to London University. When John Clare of *The Times*
cornered him on the train from Louth in 1969, with accusations about
his UNA expenses, it wasn't so much what the constituency would
think that mattered, but how Mary would react.

The famous crises in Archer's life have naturally affected his wife
badly. After the Aquablast crash she had to see her doctor for depression,
had trouble sleeping, and developed a stress-related skin disease. 'I came
out in some of the most hideous kind of spottiness all round my face.'[34]
At twenty-nine, she felt her youth was over and that the rest of their
lives would be spent paying off the debt. It also dissuaded them from
having the third child they'd planned: Jeffrey wanted a girl called Lucy.
Yet now Mary talks of it as an experience she would not have missed –
showing herself again as the objective, disinterested scientist. Most reveal-
ingly, the big problem was not the shortage of money, or the fact that
Jeffrey faced such large debts: 'It was the loss of face I really minded.'[35]
Similarly with the Monica Coghlan episode. A friend suggests it wasn't
the thought that Jeffrey might have slept with a prostitute that would
have upset her, but the public humiliation.

On television in 1987, Mary Archer was asked about her attitude to
marital fidelity. 'If you mean strict sexual fidelity,' she responded, 'it
doesn't rank that terribly high on my scale of the importance of things,
in a quite objective sense.' Jeffrey agreed with her that loyalty is more
important.[36] Infidelity 'can be tolerated more than indifference', Mary

argued. 'That is the absolute killer for any marriage.'[37] She was also asked how she felt when the gossip columns suggested that Jeffrey was having an affair, clearly referring to the old stories of his relationship with Andrina Colquhoun. They were wrong, she said; 'I cannot see the point of gossip columns. I cannot see what they add to our lives.'[38]

'I think she changed virtually overnight in the libel trial,' says John Bryant, who has known the Archers for thirty years. 'She realized she could move out of her own patch.'[39] She also admits that it gave her a taste for performing publicly: 'It thrust me into the public eye and I suppose – it sounds awfully sanctimonious – I suppose I found that if I stayed there I would have a platform to promote worthwhile causes.'[40] Some believe that the whole balance of the relationship changed significantly after the trial. After twenty years in which she had so often boosted his standing and credibility, he could now help her to achieve more in her own right. Certainly, her strong latent ambition suddenly came into the open.

In fact Mary had already made the decision to leave academic life before anyone had ever heard of Monica Coghlan; she had resigned her Cambridge fellowship in the summer of 1986, several months before the News of the World story broke. With William away at Rugby School, and James about to go to Eton, she would suddenly have far more time and freedom. John Bryant remembers how in the old days he would be surprised to see Mary at one of Jeffrey's parties. 'Now it's unusual not to see her.'[41] Mary says the trial bound them together more strongly. They certainly see more of each other nowadays, and she now usually accompanies him on his long writing trips. Even so, they're often so busy they can only book social engagements through their respective secretaries.

In the last eight years Mary has sprouted almost as many branches as her husband. She was taken on as a scientific consultant to the Robert Fraser Bank, whose chairman was Jeffrey's close friend Colin Emson. For a basic retainer of two or three thousand pounds, she would be asked three or four times a year for advice on any deals with a scientific angle, and if she couldn't help she suggested someone who could. She became a director of Anglia Television, where she was asked to help overhaul the station's science output, and presented several programmes herself. (Years before, Yorkshire Television had also considered Mary as a science presenter, but had rejected her as not natural enough in front of camera.) She also joined the boards of two East Anglian local radio stations, and was appointed a trustee of the Science Museum. There was some writing, too, including a series of radio reviews for the *Sunday Telegraph* and a short book on Rupert Brooke and The Old Vicarage.[42]

Her most important new role, however, was in the City, with the insurance market, Lloyd's. She had been a Lloyd's 'name' since 1978, when Jeffrey gave her the necessary assets as her reward for her fortitude during Aquablast. Lloyd's had long been a bastion of male supremacy; it admitted female names only in 1974, and by 1987 no woman had yet been elected to the twenty-eight-strong Lloyd's Council, which regulates the market. That year Mary stood for election as a representative of the external names – the non-working members – but missed out by one place. When she stood again the following autumn she came top of the poll, though a female rival, Lady Rona Delves Broughton – who'd once unsuccessfully invested £100,000 in the film rights to *Penny* – complained of being overwhelmed by the Archer publicity machine.

Mary Archer joined the Lloyd's Council at the worst moment in the market's history. After decades of seemingly guaranteed profits, from which the Archers had done very nicely, a spate of accidents and natural disasters, combined with the long-term problems of pollution and asbestosis, meant that names suddenly faced enormous losses. The Archers themselves lost too, though not that badly, since the forty-two syndicates which between them they belonged to by 1989 were generally among the more profitable. The Labour MP Peter Hain also pointed out in the Commons in 1994 how fortunate the Archers had been in deciding to leave certain syndicates before they declared big losses.[43]

Thousands of other Lloyd's members, however, were in danger of financial ruin. Many had entered the market when property prices were high during the 1980s, when all they needed to show sufficient assets was a bank guarantee against their homes. When the Lloyd's Council established a new hardship scheme to help mitigate members' personal disasters, Mary Archer was an obvious person to serve as chairman (and that was the title she assumed, rather than chairwoman, chairperson or chair).

The Lloyd's Members' Hardship Scheme faced an awesome task. Its stated purpose was to ensure that names avoided severe financial embarrassment; one policy was to try to preserve the family home, provided it was worth no more than £150,000. Married names were also allowed to retain a net annual income of £17,600. Applicants to the scheme had, however, to cede to the committee control of all assets and income beyond these allowances and even any damages that might be gained by litigation over fraud in their syndicates. They naturally began to see Mary Archer and her colleagues not as allies but as hard-nosed debt-collectors.

With thirty-five staff at the Hardship Scheme's offices in Chatham in Kent, Mary had been asked to do a miserable, thankless job. She heard hundreds of tragic individual stories, often taking tearful phone calls, and, in a few instances, dealing with people who threatened suicide. Most names complained that they were being bled dry and treated too harshly, but some who had reached tough settlements earlier in the process complained about later applicants being let off lightly. There was great resentment, too, that those who happened to have rich spouses tended to lose much more. Another problem were 'filibusterers': names who applied to the committee without the slightest intention of reaching a settlement, in the knowledge that Lloyd's wouldn't force them to pay their debts as long as they were in negotiations with the scheme.

Mary Archer had been appointed, of course, because she herself was well known for having endured her own hardship and the prospect of bankruptcy. As a woman, she might also present a more compassionate, understanding image. But the history of her own troubles was hardly likely to placate desperate Lloyd's applicants when the Archers were now multimillionaires who had managed to pick relatively successful syndicates. As for feminine compassion, this is hardly something for which Mary Archer is well known at Lloyd's. 'Chilling', 'frosty', 'icy', 'cold', 'an ice maiden' – stricken members seemed to exhaust the thesaurus, but the most famous epithet was 'the poisoned cactus'.[44] 'Her glacial, charming style is not universally popular with most people she deals with,' says Tom Benyon, a Lloyd's victim and former MP. 'Not just the applicants – they don't matter – but the Lloyd's hierarchy, the staff. They thought it would be useful to do it without her.'[45]

At the end of 1994 Lloyd's reorganized the whole of its debt-collection strategy and the Hardship Scheme was abolished. A new Financial Recovery Department was designed to be much tougher on names who hadn't paid their debts. Mary was appointed to the committee of the new body, though her term on the Lloyd's Council has now ended.

Mary Archer has come across as cold not just in Lloyd's, but even sometimes with family friends who know her well. Her politeness, her cautious, carefully chosen diction, and the severe clothes she wears, all present an image of someone remote and unsympathetic. She herself explains that it is partly to do with being a scientist. 'Both by training and temperament I am a mental rather than emotional person. I'm afraid I'm devastatingly rational.'[46] She also confesses to a more masculine approach than most women: 'Feminine thinking is coloured by emotion and intuition. Mine is dispassionate and rational.'[47]

'A lot of people say that when they first meet her she can be quite chilling,' says Nick Archer (no relation), who has worked for Jeffrey as a political aide. 'But actually when you meet her there's quite a warmth and quite a sense of humour.'[48] Mary is happy, for example, to display disparaging *Private Eye* covers on the walls of the lavatory in Grantchester. When the alternative cabaret act Kit and the Widow gave a private performance for the Archers, she had no objection to jokes about people handing over £2,000 on railway stations. And it takes a certain humour to allow the pin-ups of Monica Coghlan that a television crew once spotted in William's bedroom.

'Unemotional' isn't the right term to describe Mary Archer: she is more complex. She admits, for example, to crying when she reads obituaries, even of people she doesn't know, and to often shedding tears when reading books or at the theatre. Much of her remote image seems to stem from a determination to guard her privacy. 'You can always have private space in your life and head,' she says. 'Nobody can invade that unless you invite them to, and I'm alarmingly good at keeping people out.'[49]

Mary's entry into public life was facilitated by the absence of her sons at boarding-school and then university. While it was Jeffrey's choice that William should go to Rugby, he clearly had reservations about James going to Eton; he once described it as 'that bloody school', and has admitted to having had a chip on his shoulder about Old Etonians.[50] 'It was Mary's idea that he should sit the exam, and when he won a guaranteed place I felt it would be unfair not to let him accept it.'[51]

Even before they went away to school, the boys had seen much less of their parents than ordinary children do. Jeffrey was usually in London during the week and sometimes away at weekends, as well as making regular trips abroad. Mary was based in Cambridge but often had to leave her sons with the nanny while she flew around the world to academic conferences at a time when her field, solar energy, was all the rage and attracted generous funding. During the mid-1970s, in fact, Mary was away more than Jeffrey. At the age of three, William was heard saying 'Daddy lives at home but Mummy lives in an aeroplane.'[52]

At William's christening, the academic Max Beloff, a friend of the

Archers, supposedly quipped, 'We must pray he has his mother's looks – and his mother's brains.' Yet William, or 'Will' ('Willy' was dropped when he was about thirteen), is said to be most like his father. He realized at Rugby that he wasn't good enough to follow Mary to either Oxford or Cambridge. Instead, he took the unusual decision to study art history and Spanish at Georgetown University in Washington DC, thus becoming the third generation of Archers to try their luck in America, and the second of William Archer's descendants, after Rosemary Turner, to go to university in the US capital. 'I went there partly to escape,' he admitted, after a school career dogged by having two parents so much in the public eye.

'I'm quite convinced Will will make his mark in the world,' says Henry Togna, to whom he writes letters in Italian. 'He's incredibly altruistic and has his head somewhat in the clouds.'[53] In Georgetown he chose to live in appalling conditions in a cold, damp flat above a take-away café, and, despite the family wealth, preferred to wear cheap clothes from second-hand shops. He spent one summer working with the refugees in northern Iraq, and after another vacation with Mother Teresa in Calcutta he came home saying he intended to emigrate and spend the rest of his life there.

Persuaded that this might not be the wisest course, Will Archer recently tried to develop a film script, having made a short black-and-white movie, $17\frac{1}{2}$ Minutes, while in Washington. Like his father, mother and grandmother, he has also taken to writing short stories. 'He writes beautifully,' says Togna. 'His father reckons he's a better writer than he is.'[54] When Will finished at university his father agreed he could live at home for a year while he found his bearings, but insisted he would then have to go out and get a proper job. At the start of 1996 he was trying to become a civil servant, with the Overseas Development Administration.

The Archers like to think they are quite strict about not spoiling their sons, and unlike many middle-class children, neither boy has had a car while he was a student. Indeed, when James or 'Jamie' asked for a convertible BMW for Christmas one year, his father complied by presenting him with a small toy model. Yet at Oxford Jamie appears to have been living in relative luxury. In comparison to the cold and cramped rooms endured by many fellow undergraduates, and indeed his brother in Washington, Jamie shared a large house with three wealthy friends. In 1994 a Cherwell reporter who made a quick tour of the three-storey home found not just an impressive collection of pornographic videos, but also a wide range of electronic wizardry, including a photocopier, a fax machine, a laser printer, satellite TV, a Nintendo entertainment system, four CD players, two mobile phones, an IBM computer and a laptop. Much of this equipment had been installed to run a T-shirt business the boys had just established. The house had also been generously furnished with items discarded by the Archers from their London flat, including six sofas. In addition, Jamie and his friends had the help of a Colombian woman who not only did their cleaning and laundry, but also provided breakfast in bed every morning.

James is the commercial one, Jeffrey has said, and the more streetwise.[55] Yet he is also the more academic of the two boys, and followed his mother in studying chemistry, and his father in going to Brasenose. He has also taken up Jeffrey's passion for running, and won an Oxford athletics blue in 1993 for the 800 metres. At one point he looked so promising a runner that Jeffrey arranged coaching from Sebastian Coe, but his career was subsequently hit by injury. One family friend remarks that James perhaps suffers from being neither one thing nor the other: he is not as strong athletically as his father, nor as good academically as his mother. Yet, as they enter adulthood, neither Archer son seems in danger of failing in life.

Mary could become as important a public figure over the next decade as her husband. In recent years she has applied to become High Mistress of St Paul's Girls' School in London; there has been talk of her becoming head of an Oxbridge college, or chairing a public body such as the Arts Council or the BBC. With John Major keen to appoint women to public positions, it can surely be only a matter of time before some 'Great and the Good' appointment arrives. If so, Michael Hogan thinks she will owe a lot to Jeffrey. 'Mary recognizes that she never could have done a lot of things she's done without Jeffrey's drive and push, and showing her the way, and introducing her to people. He's probably teaching her still . . . Equally, she has shown Jeffrey a lot of things. Both have brought a great deal to the other.'[56]

Many believe that the Archer marriage is stronger now than it was ten years ago. Few women can have had so much anguish heaped upon them so publicly – the scrapes, the financial problems, the gossip, the fantasizing, the personal embarrassment – and the fact that she remains at his side suggests that she still loves Jeffrey.

His life has been dominated by two intelligent, highly ambitious and strong-willed women – Lola for the first twenty-five years, and Mary for the next thirty. And one detects an inevitable tension between the two. When the existence of Lola's first son, David Brown, became public in August 1994 Lola was clearly upset that Mary didn't show much support: 'My daughter-in-law's secretary rang me, but not her. Just silence. Of course, Mary's so virtuous, so good. There's not so much as a clean divorce on her side of the family.'[57]

Mary Archer, just like Lola before her, must bear some responsibility for Jeffrey's recurring mishaps and misjudgements. 'It's tempting to see a young boy indulged,' says the Tory MP, Edwina Currie, 'first by his doting mother, and then by his wife.'[58] Some believe Mary has been far too tolerant of her Jeffrey, or 'Runner Bean' as she likes to call him. Instead of shrugging things off and giving him the benefit of the doubt each time, many spouses would have put their foot down much sooner. But then Mary Weeden always knew she faced a difficult ride, from the moment on their wedding day when Jeffrey's Bullnose Morris ran out of petrol between Brasenose and their hotel.

'I think,' she once said, 'I would find it a little monochrome, a little grey, to have a sort of a more conventional life with a more conventional husband.'[59]

# 23

## The Next Stage

As the courtroom drama drew to a close, Jeffrey was so nervous about the verdict that he found it impossible to watch and had to leave. That day the Archers had arrived amid journalists and television crews; a police cordon held back the crowds, some of whom had queued for five hours to get one of the few remaining seats. He knew his reputation was now on the line, at the mercy of ordinary members of the public. 'This case has already attracted much lurid publicity,' the judge warned the jury.[1] Would they take her word as the truth, or his? What would they make of the barristers' speeches? Above all, was the case convincing? Three weeks after one trial had ended at the High Court in London, another was about to unfold at the Theatre Royal, Bath.

Jeffrey Archer loves the theatre. It flows in the blood, as it did in his mother's. After his antics in the Weston Junior Arts Club, his direction of *L'Avare* at Wellington and his performance as Puck in Dover, he'd gone to Oxford hoping to get involved in OUDS, the Oxford University Dramatic Society. Archer often claims the American director Michael Rudman, then an Oxford student, considered him for a part in *Twelfth Night* before giving the role instead to Michael York, though Rudman himself denies this. But student drama at Oxford is a full-time commitment, and not even Jeffrey could have fitted in acting alongside his athletics, the Oxfam work, *Cherwell*, the Union and, of course, wooing Mary.

As a child, Archer had occasionally been taken to the Theatre Royal, Bath, and he was weaned as a teenager on Peter O'Toole at the Old Vic in Bristol. Later, at Oxford, he went on regular trips to Stratford. (It was on one of these, in fact, that he proposed to Mary.) He goes to plays once or twice a week, he claims, and he went almost every evening during the course of the libel trial. He boasts of a collection of theatre programmes several feet high.

As a young MP, he'd been active in the British Theatre Museum

Association, which had been looking for a permanent site to house its growing collection of theatrical archives and exhibits. Archer lobbied ministers, to no avail, to accommodate the museum in Somerset House. He also campaigned for theatre tickets to be exempt from VAT.

Arrow Enterprises had tried to get involved in financing drama, with little success, but later, after he restored his fortunes, Archer acted as an 'angel' for many London productions. By 1988, for instance, he claimed to have investments in seventeen different West End shows. The year before had seen Jeffrey Archer's chance to mount his very own play; his career was entering a new stage.

It might be logical to assume that *Beyond Reasonable Doubt* was based on Archer's experiences observing lawyers, witnesses, a judge and a jury during his own court case. In fact it was his great uncompleted piece of writing, which he'd been working on for almost as long as Mary had been completing her chemistry textbook. The original inspiration had come as a teenager while watching Charles Laughton and Marlene Dietrich in the film *Witness for the Prosecution*. 'I said to my mother, "Wouldn't it be wonderful if the lawyer had to defend himself in court?" That was all I really wanted to do. It wouldn't work as a novel, it had to be a play.'[2]

He'd written the first draft in the late 1970s at Robert Opekar's villa in Barbados, then revised it considerably in 1982. He spent several days in the public gallery at the Old Bailey to get the feel of a murder trial, and gave the script to a few lawyer friends, most notably the Attorney-General Michael Havers and the QC Gilbert Gray, to check for legal errors. Like his other works, it had gone through various drafts, but it still wasn't right. And he couldn't find a producer. By 1986 the only Archer work yet to have reached the stage was a short nativity play written for his sons' prep school.

After his resignation as Conservative deputy chairman in October 1986, Archer cancelled all political engagements and retired to Grantchester. Suddenly free, and with no book to work on, he turned once more to his courtroom play. The prospects of getting it staged now looked up.

Some months earlier Archer had been approached out of the blue by a London producer. 'I wrote to him saying, "Have you ever written a play?"' says Lee Menzies. 'I saw him later that week and bought an option on the play about two days later.'[3] When Menzies finally received the script of *Beyond Reasonable Doubt* he showed it to Tudor Gates, a television writer who had also written the successful West End play

*Who Killed Agatha Christie?* 'I was asked whether I thought there was any point in him taking it on as a project,' Gates recalls. 'I was working for Menzies anyway, doing another play. I took a look at it and my first view was it was not possible to salvage it.' Until that point, Gates says, Archer had failed to interest anyone in the work. 'In fact, I believe it was turned down by every producer in the West End.'[4] Archer's original version, Gates says,

> would have been laughed off the stage . . . It had such a ludicrous ending. I can quite understand why people turned it down. The ending was 'Do you find him guilty or not guilty?', and the fore- man of the jury opens his mouth, and the curtain comes down – which is about as ludicrous an ending as I've ever heard of.[5]

After mulling it over for a few days, Gates realized how the conclusion might be rewritten. He agreed to work on the script for Menzies, in return for £5,000 plus a 1 per cent royalty. As well as changing the ending, he reworked a lot of the dialogue. There were far too many long speeches consisting of old legal- and undergraduate-type jokes. 'It was extensive, but I kept what I could,' says Gates. 'I was in a tricky position. I mean, in effect I was rewriting the play, but at the same time I didn't want to offend Jeffrey Archer. I kept as much as I could of the dialogue intact.'[6]

Yet, in performing this operation, Gates wasn't acting as a kind of theatre version of Richard Cohen: he describes the work not as editing but as 'ghost-writing'. Remarkably, Gates never once spoke to Archer during the whole process; on submitting his revised script, he had ex- pected some feedback and resistance, but he was rather surprised to find that all his suggestions were accepted. Further revisions were made later by both Archer himself and the play's initial director, David Gilmore, but Gates believes his role was considerable: 'The story is certainly Archer's, but I made an important contribution,' he later maintained. 'It is substantially based on my edited version of Archer's original.'[7]

As is typical of such arrangements, Gates agreed to a clause promising never to disclose his work. He revealed his role in *Beyond Reasonable Doubt* only when he fell into a dispute over foreign royalties with Lee Menzies. Menzies disputes Gates's version of events almost entirely, sug- gesting he played only a minor rôle. 'What was performed on the stage was not written by Tudor Gates,' he says.[8]

*Beyond Reasonable Doubt* is an old-fashioned courtroom thriller, in which a QC, Sir David Metcalfe (that name again), defends himself at the Old Bailey against the accusation that he has poisoned his terminally ill wife, in order to inherit her money. The prosecution is led by his great barrister rival, Anthony Blair-Booth. (It was an intriguing name, given that the present Labour leader, Tony Blair, is a barrister and the maiden name of his wife – also a barrister and now a QC – is Booth; but Blair himself says this was coincidental – he was still relatively unknown when Jeffrey Archer wrote the play.)

As so often with Archer's works, the line between fiction and reality again becomes blurred. At one stage the main prosecution witness gets confused between the colours blue and green, rather like the colour-blindness Aziz Kurtha revealed during the libel case. There are tantalizing similarities between Archer and his leading man, Sir David Metcalfe, who, according to the stage directions, 'exudes endless energy'.[9] Sir David has also lost several hundreds of thousands of pounds through foolish share dealings:

SIR DAVID: I had invested in some shares on the advice of an old friend. The shares plummeted when the rumour of a take-over bid failed to materialize. Unfortunately, I found myself unable to pay the full amount when the account became due.

BLAIR-BOOTH: 'Rumour of a take-over bid', 'on the advice of an old friend'. Wouldn't it be accurate to say that government inspectors were sent in to go over the company books because they suspected 'insider trading'?

SIR DAVID: Yes, sir, but I knew nothing of it.

BLAIR-BOOTH: So *you* were not involved in the 'insider trading'?[10]

Even Tudor Gates, whatever the scale of his contribution, didn't manage to rid the play of all the old jokes, some of which had the flavour of a Middle Temple dinner, *circa* 1922. Some would also have been familiar to anyone who had ever heard Jeffrey speak: 'I should now like to introduce you to Sir David Metcalfe, who is well known to you all for his debatable qualities.'[11]

This mattered little, for Lee Menzies had no trouble attracting financial support for the production. His required investment of £250,000 was oversubscribed, with angels who included Marcus Sieff, Alan Coren, Peter Palumbo and Cecil Parkinson.

Archer's play opened in Bath with Frank Finlay, Wendy Craig and Andrew Cruickshank in the leading roles. His agreement with Menzies stipulated that on the poster and publicity material the playwright's name should appear in letters as big as Finlay's and not less than 75 per cent of the size of the title. Public interest was unlike anything the Theatre Royal had experienced before, with touts reported to be offering £10 tickets at £100. His agent, Dennis Selinger, remembers that when Jeffrey left the stage door with Finlay and Craig after the first performance the autograph-hunters 'immediately went to him not them'.[12]

The opening night was not a critical success, however. The play had not been sufficiently rehearsed, and the cast forgot their lines. The audience found the first act, based in a courtroom, difficult to follow. 'A damp squib,' declared the regional paper, the *Western Daily Press*. 'It is just the kind of play that you would find in a dim seaside rep in the '50s.'[13] Such as Weston-super-Mare, presumably.

Yet the provincial tour gave Archer, Menzies and the director, David Gilmore, the chance to make substantial improvements. Archer confessed that some of the initial criticisms were justified – 'I couldn't follow the first act myself' – and later revealed, 'I had to rewrite 25 per cent of it.'[14] To be fair, that is much of the purpose of a pre-London provincial tour – to test the play in front of an audience, without the attention of national drama critics, with a view to making adjustments.

Financially, the three-week tour (Bath was followed by Manchester and Brighton) was a great success. The publicity surrounding the real-life court case had guaranteed sell-outs everywhere. 'It opened with the biggest advance ticket sales that any play has ever done in the history of the English language,' Lee Menzies claims, perhaps with a touch of Archer hyperbole.[15]

On the opening night at the Queen's Theatre in London in September, the Duchess of York found some scenes so moving that she was in tears. Despite the extensive revisions, the critics were less moved. 'Mundane, flatly-written courtroom drama, retrieved from disaster by a few good performances' . . . 'run-of-the-mill' . . . 'This play is not very good. Nor is it very bad' . . . 'reminds me of a children's swimming pool: it is transparent and you can see the bottom of it in an instant' . . . 'theatrical equivalent of polystyrene, with no organic life of its own'.[16]

David Montgomery, who had now moved from the *News of the World* to edit *Today*, mischievously sent Monica Coghlan along as a guest reviewer. Gerry Brown and Eddie Jones accompanied her, along with a *Today* reporter as her ghost-writer. Coghlan kept threatening to walk out if Archer spotted her, but, surprisingly, nobody realized she was there. As they sat down to compose the review in a Chinese restaurant afterwards, there was only one problem: Coghlan couldn't decide if it was good or not, since she'd never been to the theatre before. 'It is really a very boring play,' her article concluded. 'It was obvious from the start how it was going to end.'[17]

Even Archer had admitted that his play would never have got anywhere had it been submitted anonymously. Yet, with his name, it was a phenomenal success; houses were full, and he was making more than £5,000 a week from his 7½ per cent royalty. Within a year, however, paying audiences for *Beyond Reasonable Doubt* at the Queen's dwindled, and some houses had to be bolstered by parties of Tory activists given free tickets.

In the long term, Archer was interested not just in his own plays but in staging others', and acquiring his own theatre. Over the previous four years he had bid unsuccessfully for three different West End venues; in April 1988 he finally bought a 60 per cent stake in the Playhouse for just over £1 million.

The 780-seat Playhouse Theatre had been built in 1882 on Northumberland Avenue, next to Charing Cross station, by a property speculator who had originally purchased the site in the expectation that the station would need to expand. Rebuilt in 1906, it is one of the most attractive theatres in London, but it had never enjoyed much commercial success and had a reputation as being 'unlucky'. From 1951 to 1975 it had been used by the BBC, mainly for recording radio comedies with audiences, such as *The Goon Show* and *Hancock's Half Hour*; it had also staged the first live broadcasts by both the Beatles and the Rolling Stones. Later the site lay empty for more than ten years. In the twelve months before Archer bought it, the building had been completely refurbished, but the previous owners were in great danger of running out of money.

Archer installed Lee Menzies as managing director and made David Gilmore his artistic director, though Gilmore admits that the title was a 'misnomer' and that he simply advised on scripts.[18] The former Lord Chancellor, Michael Havers, became chairman; he was a part-time playwright himself (and father of the actor Nigel Havers). Two distinguished actors, Alec McCowen and Tony Britton, also joined Archer's board.

The Playhouse general manager from that period, Mig Kimpton, says Archer treated his new acquisition like a 'toy'; it was either going to be the Playhouse or a Renoir, he recalls him saying. Initially, Kimpton says, Archer was heavily involved.[19] Jeffrey delighted in his new role of part-time impresario, and in meeting the directors, actors, agents and producers involved in Playhouse productions. 'I think of him as the "Tigger" of our troubled age,' says the director Patrick Garland. 'Unlike many theatre-owners, he was very much in evidence on the first day of rehearsals, and was friendly and welcoming to us all. He remained enthusiastic throughout, and made a strong appearance on the first night, warmly congratulating me and Eileen Atkins.'[20] Pat Macnaughton's first-night memories are a little different for a show she produced there. She claims Archer simply took over her party in the basement restaurant. 'He stood at the top of the stairs and when he saw a well-known face, he invited them down . . . Vast quantities of drink were consumed that I had not anticipated . . . I was ready to thump him by the end of the evening.'[21]

Meanwhile, Archer had also been writing another play of his own. This concerned another of the great professions involved in the Monica Coghlan case – the press. Archer saw the play partly as a modern, high-tech version of the film *The Front Page*, and also spoke of it 'doing for the newspaper world what the film *Wall Street* did for the world of money'.[22]

Originally to be called *Chronicle*, then renamed *Exclusive*, the play was based on a week in the life of a Fleet Street newspaper. Archer persuaded the editor of *The Times*, Charles Wilson – a good friend – to let him spend several days at Wapping sitting in on meetings, getting a feel of how the industry worked; he managed to be at the *Sunday Times* on the night of the Hillsborough football disaster, for example. John Bryant, the Oxford athletics colleague who was now deputy editor of *The Times*, checked the play for factual mistakes. Archer also spent time with the two *Mail* newspapers and *The Independent*. In the end, however, the paper portrayed in Archer's play was a middle-market tabloid – a cross between the *Mail* and the *Express*. And what did our man think of the fourth estate after seeing it working at close quarters? 'I've no time,' he declared, 'for the journalists who make it all up.'[23]

Lee Menzies, who again produced Archer's work, reckoned the play was superior to his previous one. '*Exclusive* was a far, far better play, an outstanding play,' he says. 'It had more depth, and it was a very well-written, beautifully constructed play.'[24] Archer was even more confident: 'I think it's the best thing I've ever written.'[25]

In fact, judging solely from the script and the views of those who saw it, *Exclusive* is probably Jeffrey Archer's worst-ever piece of writing, by quite a long measure. The characters are stereotypical; there is little insight into the workings of Fleet Street; and, most unusually for Archer the storyteller, it has almost no story, let alone tension. There is precious little wit or satire. And what seems most absent is drama.

*Exclusive* is possibly the best example of Jeffrey Archer's writing in the raw, so to speak. As usual, it went through several drafts, but, unlike his novels, it lacked the help of editors. Tudor Gates says he would have been happy to work on it – this was before his dispute – but Lee Menzies never asked him.

Nevertheless, the play attracted a very strong cast, including Paul Scofield and Eileen Atkins. When John Stride dropped out after an argument over script changes, Alec McCowen was suddenly available to take his place – a typical stroke of Archer luck. It also boasted a first-class director in his old Oxford friend Michael Rudman. When sent a copy of the script by courier, Rudman read it in one sitting, and then sent a card round by taxi to tell Archer he'd do it.[26]

After touring in Bath and Manchester, *Exclusive* opened in London in September 1989, at the Strand Theatre in the Aldwych; the stage at Archer's own Playhouse was too small for the set. In fact the elaborate set seems to have been the best thing about the production, comprising two revolving layers and dressed with computer terminals, wires, desks, Perrier bottles and rubber plants to look like a modern newspaper newsroom.

Archer suffered his worst-ever mauling from the critics in his thirteen years as a writer. 'Turgid and tepid,' Jack Tinker declared in the *Daily Mail*. 'Mr Scofield has never looked less comfortable on any stage.'[27] The verdict was almost unanimous: 'by the end of the first half, it would have taken a Molotov cocktail to wake up the audience' ... 'crushingly banal dialogue and predictable plotting' ... 'just embarrassingly bad'.[28] 'Nothing,' wrote the *Sunday Telegraph* reviewer, 'not even Archer's previous work, had prepared me for the elephantine dialogue, the asinine humour, the cardboard characterization, the general absence of zing.'[29] Only the *Daily Telegraph* offered the slightest speck of comfort: 'There is a degree of innocent pleasure to be derived from following the plot of *Exclusive*, thin and easily predictable though it is.'[30]

On opening night, Archer held a lavish party, with a constellation of showbiz personalities, Cabinet ministers and Fleet Street bigwigs. As they enjoyed their champagne and admired the newspaper-shaped cake, the playwright burst in, dressed as a paper-boy, and distributed copies of a special edition of the newspaper in the play, *The Chronicle*, which had been edited by John Bryant. Yet not even Jeffrey's closest editor friends would declare the production a success. 'The play lacked a real story and was not funny enough,' said Andrew Neil, the *Sunday Times* editor who had ignored the Monica Coghlan story.[31] Even Archer's old Cherwell chum Nick Lloyd, then running the *Daily Express*, diplomatically suggested that 'Fleet Street is a little more complicated than this play.'[32]

Perhaps it was to be expected that a play about newspapers would be rubbished by newspapers. But what is surprising is that Archer didn't use his work to take revenge on those who had done him down, as he had with *Not a Penny More, Not a Penny Less*. If he had, the play might have worked better. Within two months, houses at the Strand Theatre were down to around 35 per cent capacity. Long-term bookings were almost non-existent, and Archer agreed to waive his royalties. Lee Menzies announced the production would close a month later, and he has felt bitter about the critics ever since. 'The reviews on *Exclusive* had nothing to do with the play; it was a personal attack on Jeffrey . . . and the press thought, "Right, we're gonna kill it", and they did.'[33]

Despite the disaster with *Exclusive*, Archer's other play, *Beyond Reasonable Doubt*, was still on tour after a twenty-month run in London. It visited seventeen theatres in nine months. 'At the time, we broke seventeen house records,' says Menzies. 'And I don't think they've been broken since.'[34] The play was also licensed around the world – to Ireland, Australia, South Africa, Turkey, Greece and several other European countries. It is still performed regularly in amateur theatre. *Exclusive*, however, has not been staged since, and, unlike *Beyond Reasonable Doubt*, it has never been published. Despite discussions with the theatrical publishers Samuel French, it was decided not to issue the script. 'I don't think it does Jeffrey Archer's reputation any good to publish a play that's been so vilified,' says John Bedding, the company's managing director, with a touch of diplomacy.[35]

Before *Exclusive* went on stage, Archer had declared that 'If I wrote a book or a play that was a flop then I would never do it again.'[36] He has been true to his word. The critical pounding taken by *Exclusive* hurt him deeply. 'He was very damaged by the failure,' says one former colleague. 'It was a creative failure.'

At one point he'd discussed plans with Hodder & Stoughton to write a book based around his love of the theatre. It was envisaged as a semi-autobiographical work explaining how he'd first become interested in drama as a boy, and including the texts of his two plays, all lavishly illustrated with photographs and ephemera. When *Exclusive* flopped, the project was abandoned.

Archer still owned the Playhouse, though, and at the end of 1990 he struck up a promising partnership with the former director of the National Theatre, Sir Peter Hall. The deal was sealed very quickly. Hall was having lunch one day with a *Daily Mail* journalist, David Lewin, and mentioned that he needed a new home for his production company. Lewin passed the news on to Archer.

'What impressed me was the speed with which Jeffrey reacted,' says Lewin.[37] Archer cancelled other engagements and phoned the director to fix a meeting. Hall was taken aback to find Archer in a track suit when he arrived, but then discovered that the writer was about to go to Japan, and that this is his normal attire for long flights. The two men swiftly agreed that the Playhouse would henceforth become Hall's theatrical base, and that he would mount four plays a year there, including one Shakespeare, one modern revival and one new production. Archer would have no say in the selection, and he told Hall that his commitment was not to making money, but to good theatre. 'I said to the board that if I could declare at the end of Sir Peter's first term a ten pence profit I'd be a totally happy man, and if he loses the ten pence I shall ask him to pay for it.'[38] 'As long as it is only ten pence,' replied Hall, 'I will.'[39] Archer's friend Henry Togna says the new arrangement was 'as close to heaven as he could get. Here was the man he admired so much.'[40]

Yet in some ways it was an odd match, for Hall had never disguised his contempt for the Conservative Party, and in particular the Thatcher government's treatment of the arts. But he mounted several successful productions at the Playhouse – including *Twelfth Night*; Tennessee Williams's *The Rose Tattoo*, with Julie Walters; and Molière's *Tartuffe* – and they attracted good audiences.

Then, in November 1991, after Hall had been with the Playhouse for less than a year, Archer suddenly announced that he was selling. Three months later the writer/impresario Ray Cooney agreed to buy the theatre for £2.4 million. On paper this was more than twice what Archer had paid, but, given the investment he had put into the building, the heavy deficits on several productions, and the large debt he'd inherited, the novelist had lost heavily on the whole venture.

Archer had even brought in £500,000 worth of sponsorship from an insurance firm, MI Group – the first ever such deal for a West End theatre – which involved the venture's being officially renamed the MI Playhouse, and the company was allowed to use the building for daytime conferences. He also spent £200,000 on developing the downstairs catering area as a top-class restaurant, Shaw's, but it was probably a bad location for this. 'People were not going to spend £20 a head to have dinner,' says the former theatre manager, Mig Kimpton. 'You needed reasonable-quality fast food.'[41]

After four years the overall losses from Archer's stewardship stood at more than £1.5 million. Pat Macnaughton believes the basic problem was the way the theatre was managed. She says too much money was wasted, so the break-even level for each show was far too high. 'The theatre was appallingly run,' in her view. 'It was virtually impossible to get accountings; absolutely impossible to get weekly figures, which one normally expects as a co-producer.'[42]

For Sir Peter Hall, Archer's decision came as 'something of a shock. It seemed to me that he had invested so much in making the Playhouse a home for us – and we had built a large and loyal following at the theatre for him – that it was sad we could not continue there.'[43] Yet Hall's productions, though popular, had greatly added to the financial burden. 'They were costing three hundred grand or something ridiculous,' says Kimpton. 'He's not a cheap man to work with.'[44]

It wasn't just money that was a problem, Ray Cooney reckons, but the fact the Playhouse was taking up so much of Archer's time. 'The theatre was quite a handful, and he hadn't realized the personal commitment needed,' he says. 'You can't be an absentee landlord . . . The main reason he wanted to sell it was to get back into politics.'[45]

# 24

# Archer's Departures

On Channel 4 television in 1988, Jeffrey Archer told the world about his first sexual experience. It had happened while he was still living at home in Weston-super-Mare:

> I met a very mature girl. She was eighteen and I was eighteen and terribly immature, and I think we went up into Worlebury Woods and she taught me things that, you know, I just couldn't believe, and I enjoyed them![1]

What was surprising about this confession was that, although Jeffrey Archer has had a keen eye for women, he does not usually like talking or writing about sex. It is a remarkable feat for a modern author to achieve sales such as his without including detailed accounts of sexual intercourse. When Archer's stories do briefly touch on sex, the scenes are always mild: he writes more clumsily and seems rather embarrassed. Nor does Archer like to include descriptions of bloody violence, or language people might find offensive.

> I got sick and tired of people saying, 'You'll sell millions if there are raunchy sex scenes and lots of four-letter words and lots of violence,' and I went out of my way to prove that if you tell a story, and people enjoy the story, that they become irrelevant ... I do write scenes where people go to bed together or they fall in love ... but I've never found it necessary to join the rip-off-knickers brigade.[2]

One suspects this prudish streak is partly due to the influence of his mother, Lola, who reads each manuscript before publication. 'She rarely makes any comment,' he once said, 'but if I dared to put in a word like "damn", she'd draw a circle round it.'[3] The lack of sex and violence partly explains why Archer has had so little success in getting his books adapted as films, but equally it makes them more suitable for television

337

– especially for the American networks, who are notoriously worried about sex scenes, though keen on violence.

Archer's belief in traditional values, in both his writing and his characters, is exemplified in his sixth novel, *A Matter of Honour*, which was published in 1986 during his spell as Conservative deputy chairman. Originally to be entitled *The Czar's Crown*, it was an old-fashioned adventure story: Archer's first thriller since *Shall We Tell the President?* in 1977. Adam Scott is a true British hero, educated at Wellington (but the College in Berkshire, not the School in Somerset) and Sandhurst. Of particular interest is the subplot of Scott trying to restore his father's tarnished military reputation. (Fathers and honour are recurring themes in Archer's novels.) He is drawn into a chase round Europe trying to outwit the KGB, the CIA, and MI6, who are each vying to get hold of a Russian icon he has inherited in his father's will. The icon has the potential to wreck the balance of power between the superpowers. Archer and his publishers were brazen about the comparisons with John Buchan: he conceived of Scott as 'a 1980s version of Richard Hannay in *The Thirty-Nine Steps*', he claimed, 'because I believe heroes are coming back'.[4]

Archer's other model for Adam Scott – tall, handsome, honest and athletic – was his Oxford running friend Michael Hogan, whom he credited in an interview with 'total integrity and loyalty to a degree I've never seen in any other human being'.[5] Scott seems to prefer cold showers to sex, and early in the book rebuffs an attractive young woman who tries to climb into bed with him. 'The age of sex and violence in books is over,' Archer claimed, somewhat unconvincingly.[6]

By now, Richard Cohen had moved from Hodder to become publishing director at Hutchinson, but the two companies formally made a rather peculiar arrangement for him to edit Archer's latest book in his new employer's time. It was understood that Cohen would spend no more than two hours a day on the work, while Hodder's own copy-editor would check facts, consistency, spelling and punctuation. Neither Archer nor Cohen could spare the time to sit down together, as they had previously, so instead, the editor wrote comments and suggested amendments on the manuscript, and also drew up a further hundred pages or more of longer notes and possible improvements. In lieu of payment, Archer arranged for Cohen and his family to have a ten-day holiday at an expensive country-house hotel near Fort William.

That Archer should have gone to so much trouble to continue with his editor's services was surprising, given that he also seems to have been partly responsible for Cohen's leaving Hodder. The author had complained bitterly to the Hodder management following a *Sunday Telegraph* article about his writing in which the editor was quoted. Mary Archer 'helps him to put it into English', Cohen said, adding that after he had worked on a book 'finally you feel that literacy has been achieved'.[7] Cohen didn't deny the comments, but claimed they had been off-the-record, and so he didn't expect to be quoted. Archer had demanded that Hodder should discipline the editor – one version says he wanted the publishers to dismiss him. The company defused matters by telling Archer that it would be wrong to sack a man while he was representing his country (Cohen was fencing at the 1984 Olympics at the time). Not long afterwards, however, the editor was told that it would be highly unlikely that he would progress further in the firm and was led to understand that Archer's complaint was the reason. So Cohen left for Hutchinson.

This episode illustrates the influence and importance Jeffrey Archer had acquired within Hodder. Company bosses may have overreacted, treating Archer's grievance more seriously than they should have done. And so, bizarrely, while Richard Cohen left Hodder, he continued to edit the books of the man whose complaint had sparked his departure.

*A Matter of Honour*, like his previous book, *First Among Equals*, had an unusual serialization deal, and was reproduced in short extracts over several weeks in Eddie Shah's new newspaper, *Today*. The fee had originally been £125,000, but when Shah got into financial difficulties Archer agreed to take a 1 per cent share-holding in the paper instead.

By the novelist's usual standards, the critics were remarkably positive: 'Archer's best book', Mark Lawson declared in the *Sunday Times*. 'He gave me entertainment,' John Braine confessed, adding that Archer was a 'much better writer than John le Carré or Len Deighton'.[8] The reviews must have been particularly gratifying given the relatively small amount of editorial work the book had undergone.

In America, *A Matter of Honour* spent four months on the best-seller lists – about the same time as *First Among Equals*; though it never made number one, the sales figures were actually up on *Equals*.[9] In Britain the novel did even better, finishing as the second-highest best-seller of 1986. Archer's sales were boosted that autumn by a dramatization of the book on BBC Radio 4, as well as by that year's TV adaptations of *Kane and Abel* and *First Among Equals*.

An internal Hodder memo told staff never to discuss the Monica Coghlan case, yet, ironically, company salesmen say Archer's sales were considerably boosted both by the initial story, and by the libel trial which opened eleven days after *A Matter of Honour* came out in paperback. In 1987 he came top of *The Guardian*'s annual paperback chart for the second time, as the book sold 1.3 million copies, more than any of his previous paperbacks in their first six months.[10] More impressive still was the performance of the titles on Archer's backlist. At the start of 1986 Coronet claimed to have sold more than 8 million copies of his books in paperback, and that year they sold a further 1.25 million copies of his previous works.[11]

It would be five years, however, before Jeffrey Archer published another novel. With his political work and the libel case, as well as plays and the Playhouse, he was too busy. Short stories were another matter, since they require much less concentrated effort, and in 1988 Archer published his second collection, *A Twist in the Tale*. As the title suggests, each tale has an unexpected ending. Archer was delighted when the Hodder production director, Jamie Wilson, had the book designed so that in nearly every story the twist occurs on a left-hand page; this meant that readers found it only after turning the final page, and so weren't tempted to glance ahead.

In the longest story, 'A Perfect Murder', Archer again exploited his court experience: a man who has killed his mistress becomes foreman of the jury which convicts an innocent person for the crime. The story seems deliberately to tease readers with its apparent parallels with Archer's own trial, involving mistaken identity, arguments over the colour of a car and also, as in the Coghlan case, the significance of diary entries.

Two other stories in the collection, however, generated more serious controversy about the true inspiration for some of Archer's work.

The first dispute arose from an occasion four years earlier when the author had judged a short-story contest in Cambridge. The winning entry, 'Rita Chiquita', was written by Kathleen Burnett, an English literature specialist who lives in Trumpington, a mile from Grantchester. The story describes Rita's thoughts and rituals as she gets up in the morning. Only at the end do most readers realize she is a cat: 'Rita Chiquita arched her back, did a few dance steps on the spot – and purred.'[12]

Speaking at the award ceremony at Newnham College in 1984, Archer praised Kathleen Burnett's 'originality' and 'storytelling':

That is rare, very rare indeed. Kathleen told a story where she cons you all the way until the last line. It's a total con for five pages and it is the last line – very much in the tradition of Somerset Maugham and Maupassant, very much in the tradition of the great short-story writers. It's a con – from the first line it's a con – but it takes you right the way through to the last line. And then you just feel warm, and good, and you smile. And that takes some doing. I've tried to do it myself.[13]

Afterwards, Burnett recalls, Archer told her how he hoped to publish some short stories in about three years' time. She remembers him explaining that if her tale hadn't been published by then he would contact her to see if he could include it in his collection. Archer's account of this conversation is rather different: 'I did say, "Would you mind if I did my version of it?" and she made no objection at all.'[14]

When Burnett first spotted a hardback edition of *A Twist in the Tale*, she realized immediately what had happened, for the front cover featured a cat's face. Inside, she found Archer's story 'Just Good Friends', in which a female describes how she gets up in the morning and looks forward to breakfast. After eight pages, the subject then reveals herself: 'I began to lap up the milk happily, my tail swishing from side to side.'[15]

Quite apart from the same twist in both tales (or tails?) there are other similarities. Both stories' second paragraphs describe the cats' eyes getting used to the morning light; both creatures contemplate milk for breakfast; both stories mention their lovers and babies; and in both cases the denouement occurs when the cat enters the kitchen and greets her owner. On the other hand, there are differences: Burnett's story was written in the third person, whereas 'Just Good Friends' is in the first. 'Rita Chiquita' is solely about the cat, whereas Archer's story is much more concerned with the relationship between the pet and her owner.

Kathleen Burnett was so aggrieved that she wrote to Hodder & Stoughton, asking them to compare the stories. The reply came from Archer himself, explaining how he remembered 'with such pleasure your agreement on the night of the presentation at Newnham to allow me to try and tell the story in my own style'. He wouldn't have 'gone ahead without that agreement', he added. And he pointed out how at the front of the collection he had acknowledged her kindness with the words:

> Of these twelve stories gathered in my travels from Tokyo to *Trumpington*, ten are based on known incidents – some embellished with considerable licence. Only two are totally the result of my own imagination.
>
> I would like to thank all those people who allowed me to learn some of their innermost secrets.[16]

Burnett ignored Archer's offer to meet her, and instead complained to the publisher that the words quoted were not a proper acknowledgement of her work.

To this, Hodder executive Eric Major replied that 'there is no copyright in an idea, only in the way of its expression'.[17] Burnett was now furious, and wrote back saying 'That a judge should profit from a competitor's labours without that competitor's permission makes me, and I am sure would make others, highly indignant.'[18] Major suggested she should attend a meeting with himself, Deborah Owen and Archer, and even proposed a particular time; Burnett declined. This was perhaps foolish, for the fact that three such busy people were willing to see her suggests that they were concerned, and might have offered her compensation.

Burnett continued to fight by letter, arguing that she was entitled to both a named acknowledgement and a share of the royalties. Then she suggested that 'the matter would be highly newsworthy', adding that a journalist friend had already offered 'several thousand pounds' for details of her grievance.[19]

Archer now rolled out the legal artillery. His lawyers, Mishcon de Reya, wrote to Burnett saying her threat to go to the press was 'most improper'; Archer had 'no legal or moral obligation' to her whatsoever, they insisted. Mishcon also argued that the idea had 'been used by several writers in the past'.[20] (What they could have added, but probably didn't know, was that Archer himself had briefly used the same trick, of confusing a cat with a human, in *Shall We Tell the President?*)[21] Yet, as Burnett suggests, the lawyers' argument was rather undermined by the fact that at the prize-giving Archer had praised her 'originality'.

Advised that legal action for breach of copyright would be expensive and probably fail, Burnett let the matter drop, but it pained her to imagine how much Archer had made from her idea. *A Twist in the Tale* has probably earned him between one and two million pounds, and, as one of twelve stories in the collection, 'Just Good Friends' could be said to be worth £100,000 or more.

Appropriately, Kathleen Burnett's tale later had its own amusing twist. In 1991 she heard that Archer was judging another short-story competition, and quickly submitted an entry under her married name, hoping she might win the chance to confront him at the award ceremony. Sure enough, she did do well enough to be invited to the presentation, only to learn that she had come second to her sister! Archer, however, wasn't there: he had cancelled in favour of a more pressing engagement.

A second writer also complained that a story in the *Twist* collection was not entirely Archer's work. 'Clean Sweep Ignatius' concerns a Nigerian finance minister, Ignatius Agarbi, who is ostensibly trying to clean up corruption in his country. He visits a Swiss bank and demands the names and account numbers of all its Nigerian customers. The manager adamantly refuses, even when Agarbi puts a gun to his head. Whereupon the minister opens up his case to reveal several million dollars in cash, and asks to open an account.[22]

Virtually the same story had appeared in an obscure collection of speeches called *The Natives are Friendly?*, published in Britain in 1986.[23] The Nigerian author, J. K. Randle, says the anecdote was originally told at a seminar given by the World Bank. Randle's version takes just twenty-six lines, whereas Archer's lasts eight pages, but in essence the plots are exactly the same, though the names and dialogue differ.

Randle says he had sent a copy of his book to the novelist in the hope that, with Archer's business links with Nigeria, he might help promote it. When he later saw the story reproduced in *A Twist in the Tale,* he was 'enraged', he says. 'I've no doubt,' he protested, 'that Mr Archer has used my fictional story as a basis for his own work.' Archer responded that it was 'farcical' to suggest he had found the tale in Randle's book. 'I got the story from a Nigerian diplomat some two years ago,' he responded. 'I confirmed with him today the source of the story, and it is a true story.'[24] The Nigerian writer says he initiated legal proceedings in Britain, but, like Kathleen Burnett, he eventually decided the cost was prohibitive.

Randle, in fact, was not the only Nigerian prompted to take court action over the story. A former real-life finance minister, Major-General James Oluleye, began to sue Archer for libel on the grounds that people thought he was the character portrayed. 'Most of his friends now avoid him and view him as a saboteur and contributor to the economic adversities of Nigeria,' the writ argued, rather implausibly.[25] This action also seems to have fizzled out.

*A Twist in the Tale* sold astonishingly well, particularly since short stories are usually less popular than novels. In 1989 the paperback edition (the cat on the cover had been replaced by a cobra with a cat's tail) put Archer on top of Alex Hamilton's annual *Guardian* best-sellers chart for a third occasion. 'For the first time in British publishing history,' Hamilton reckoned, 'if you except the Bible, a book of short stories has sold more than a million copies in a year.'[26]

Archer had now been published exclusively by Hodder & Stoughton in Britain for a decade, and the company had benefited greatly from his popularity. It was reckoned around 1987 that Archer accounted for more than one in six of all Coronet's paperback sales. If Hodder were looking a little too dependent on one author, he assured them they need not worry. 'I am a man who believes intensely in loyalty,' Archer told *The Author* magazine in the spring of 1990. 'To begin with,' he said of Hodder and Coronet, 'I think they thought, "When he becomes famous, he'll leave us." But I couldn't think of anything more horrid.'[27] Until then Archer had indeed been loyal to most of the people who had assisted his career, although Tom Maschler at Cape was one exception. With hindsight, however, his words sound just like the expressions of confidence that football-club chairmen traditionally declare in their managers just before they sack them.

Around the very time that these professions of loyalty were published, Jeffrey Archer parted company with Debbie Owen. For fifteen years she had been his literary agent, and if credit is ever apportioned for Archer's success as a writer she would deserve to be head of the queue. It had been Owen who had ensured that Archer's career progressed steadily upwards, especially in the initial stages, and that each book was more successful than the last. On the other hand, her labours had been well rewarded. With the traditional agent's commission of 10 per cent, she must have earned at least a million pounds from Archer's writing, and possibly much more.

Jeffrey Archer had in fact already been holding direct financial negotiations with his American publishers without Owen. He felt he no longer needed his agent, and obviously concluded that he might as well keep the commission for himself. 'He had put an alternative arrangement to me,' Owen says, 'which I did not want and told him so.' Archer's plan was apparently to handle contracts in Britain and America himself, while Owen would continue to look after the rest of the globe. She refuses to confirm this, beyond saying that 'I like to represent an author round the world.'[28] Owen adds that 'it was an amicable parting', without the need for lawyers, and she even marked his going with an 'Archer Departure Party' on board a boat on the Thames.

Privately, though, it must have been a serious blow to her, especially as she felt that Archer could soon make enormous sums in the States. 'We knew that there were going to be some very big offers coming from America,' she says.[29] It was a setback also to David Owen, whose political office was financed by his wife's literary income, and who was adjusting to the failure of his new Social Democratic Party, a breakaway from the original SDP.

The split with Owen marked a significant turning-point both in Archer's literary career and, some believe, in his character. 'It was so unlike Jeffrey,' Joni Evans says. 'Jeffrey was such a loyal author. The three of us were such a spirited team – Debbie Owen, Jeffrey and myself. When I found out, I was stunned. I couldn't believe it. I called him up.' Evans believes the move indicated a new, harder, money-orientated attitude by Archer towards his book deals. 'He just changed somehow; he wasn't the same. I remember feeling there was a major sea change around that time.'[30]

Having wrested responsibility for his book contracts from Debbie Owen, Archer seems nevertheless to have been in two minds about how to handle them. 'I have been looking at three or four agents,' he announced, 'and I expect to appoint a new one within a month or so.'[31] Yet, around the same time, a curious quarter-page ad appeared in the publishing trade magazine *The Bookseller*.

### PA/AGENT WANTED BY NOVELIST

Novelist, published in twenty languages, requires high powered Personal Assistant who can cope with foreign contracts, collect monies due and still answer fan letters. Probably worked in Rights Department of leading publishers or literary agent.

The starting salary will be around £15,000, according to experience.

Applicants were asked to send CVs to 'Mr Charles Palmer' at Flat 11,

75 Warwick Square.[32] The then voters list, however, shows no Charles Palmer at that address, but does reveal an Iona Palmer, the name of one of Jeffrey Archer's secretaries.

No appointment seems to have resulted from the ad. Instead, Archer began consulting a seasoned literary agent, George Greenfield, who had recently retired from running the Farquharson's agency, and who had been the brains behind the *Mail on Sunday*'s serialization of *First Among Equals*. Greenfield says Archer called him occasionally 'for advice on little technical points, like copyright'; others suspect he is being rather modest about his role.[33] To handle most of the foreign-translation rights for his backlist, Archer also employed Vanessa Holt, who was just setting up her own agency.

His Japanese business, however, was placed in the hands of a Tokyo literary fixer, Tom Mori, an ebullient character with strong American links who is famous for his bulk. Ever since the publication of *Not a Penny More, Not a Penny Less*, Archer's books had been phenomenally successful in the Japanese market, and had made him one of the most popular English people in Japan (along with Margaret Thatcher). His publishers, Shincho-Sha, say that the lack of sex and violence compared with other foreign authors may account for Archer's particular appeal among Japanese women. His books have regularly reached number one in Japan, and Tom Mori reckons he ranks at roughly tenth among his country's best-selling writers.

Within three months of leaving Debbie Owen, Archer had hit the American jackpot that both she and he had expected. In the summer of 1990, he flew to New York, booked a suite in a major hotel, and had audiences, rather than a formal auction, with several major American publishing houses. What he was particularly seeking was a big multinational firm who could publish him on a world scale. Simon & Schuster, who had handled his six previous books in America, were not among those to pay homage in the Archer suite.

That Archer would leave Simon & Schuster had been expected well before he left Debbie Owen. The firm felt that only the 'A league' of the twenty or so blockbuster writers was worth the kind of eight-figure advance that Archer now wanted, and though they had paid seven-figure, million-dollar-plus, sums for his recent books, Archer was only in the 'B league'. While his latest story collection, *A Twist in the Tale*, had sold better than expected, his novels had been in steady decline ever since *Kane and Abel*. Simon & Schuster executives thought it was unlikely

Archer could regain his early-1980s popularity; indeed, one goes as far as to say that he had 'one book in him, which was *Kane and Abel*'.

Yet one particular personal factor had suggested that the company would still try to keep their author. The Simon & Schuster president, Dick Snyder, had now divorced his wife, Archer's old editor, Joni Evans, and was especially concerned that, given their personal rapport, Archer might want to follow Evans to Random House, where she now worked. So Simon & Schuster had offered Archer more than for any previous book – in the region of $2.5 million. It strained the limit of what they felt he was worth, but was nothing like enough.

Archer didn't go to Random House, in fact, but to Rupert Murdoch's recently acquired conglomerate, HarperCollins, the product of a merger between the American company Harper & Row and the British firm William Collins. Their advance would astonish the New York publishing community, which was already reeling from the $12.3 million that Dell had just paid for Ken Follett's next two books. Yet that was modest compared with Jeffrey Archer's new deal, which covered two novels and another set of short stories. The price was $30 million.

The contract involved world rights (excluding Britain, the Commonwealth and Japan) in both hardback and paperback. Financially, Jeffrey Archer had suddenly moved into a completely new orbit.

The $30 million figure soon leaked out, but many in publishing assumed it was exaggerated, and that $20 million was a more likely sum. Other publishers expressed astonishment and anger that HarperCollins were willing to pay even $20 million for a writer who was not in the American top twenty-five and widely thought to be in commercial decline. Archer's contract seemed ridiculous, for instance, in comparison with the latest signed by Tom Clancy, who was then America's best-selling author. Clancy had just accepted $10 million for one book – the same rate as Archer – but was expected to sell four or five times as many hardbacks as the English novelist. The Archer deal was an early example of the reputation HarperCollins has earned in recent years for paying writers much more than most people think they are worth.

Industry estimates (including Simon & Schuster sources) put the market value of three Archers at about $7 million; outsiders all agreed HarperCollins could never recoup their $30 million outlay from book sales alone. But, unusually, the HarperCollins deal also included film, television and audio rights, and the company hoped that these would make the contract worthwhile, especially if developed by other parts of the Murdoch empire, such as the Twentieth Century Fox film studios and Fox Television. 'News Corporation now has the ability to exploit a property in every type of medium one can think of,' a HarperCollins spokesman explained.[34] To seal their commitment to Archer, HarperCollins paid $1 million to the Simon & Schuster paperback imprint, Pocket Books, for every title on his backlist. Now all his output in the United States and over much of the globe was committed to Rupert Murdoch's media empire. It did not seem to matter that this was the same empire whose *News of the World* had broken the Monica Coghlan story.

The $30 million contract symbolized the radically changing international scale of modern publishing. It seemed to have gone crazy: a small number of worldwide conglomerates were chasing best-selling authors largely for prestige purposes, as an expression of their own importance and corporate clout. With a big name on their lists, so the theory went, HarperCollins salesmen would find it easier to get bookshops interested in the company's lesser-known authors. The problem with this theory was that Jeffrey Archer wasn't that big a name in the United States.

The Archer deal in fact had serious repercussions for American publishing, and inevitably prompted other writers to demand much larger advances. Shortly afterwards, Barbara Taylor Bradford secured a very similar contract. 'Taylor Bradford's deal was much bigger because of the Jeffrey Archer deal,' says one close observer. 'That's the insidious thing about all this.'

It was now clear why Archer had suddenly dropped Debbie Owen. Originally, it seems, HarperCollins had offered Archer a $20 million contract, without going through Owen, and this had prompted him to test what other American publishers would pay. Had she remained as his agent, Owen would presumably have been entitled to 10 per cent commission, yet this must have seemed unreasonable to Archer when HarperCollins had come straight to him. It was much cheaper to pay George Greenfield a fixed fee to sort out contractual details; Greenfield in turn recommended a New York entertainment lawyer, Mort Leavy, who drew up the legal documents, and also charged a flat sum. New York lawyers are never cheap, of course, but employing Leavy (and Greenfield) was considerably less costly than paying the commission Debbie Owen would have earned from Jeffrey's sudden bonanza.

In Britain, however, Archer's next book was still pledged to Hodder

& Stoughton, under his now traditional arrangement of a one-pound advance on $17\frac{1}{2}$ per cent royalties.

*As the Crow Flies* is a seventy-year saga, in the *Kane and Abel* genre, of business and family rivalries, though with elements of caper too. It tells the life-story of Charlie Trumper, who rises from being an East End barrow boy to own a Harrod's-like department store – 'the biggest barrow in the world' – and eventually becomes Lord Trumper of Whitechapel. (Of course, the book was published around the time when Archer himself was hoping for a peerage.) Archer sets several episodes in America and Australia, no doubt with an eye to his international audience, and the novel is unusual in that he often allows a chapter to be narrated by one of the leading characters, and then the next chapter by another player, so that the same incidents are seen through several different pairs of eyes.

Apart from the fact that both Archer's own father and his fictitious Charlie Trumper hail from the same area of the East End, there are other autobiographical parallels. Trumper's disreputable father dies when Charlie is seventeen (Archer's died when he was fifteen). His hero is streetwise and uneducated, but, like Jeffrey himself, marries a more academically intelligent woman who pursues her own career (as an art dealer and auctioneer). Trumper even enrols secretly for an evening degree course at London University, the same institution to which Archer himself applied after Oxford.

The chief villain of the story, Guy Trentham, is almost as intriguing a character to students of Archer's family background as Henry Osborne was in *Kane and Abel*. Not only is Trentham a bogus war-hero with a criminal past, he is also discovered to have fathered a long-lost daughter in Australia. Much of the book follows both this daughter – Cathy – and Trumper's adopted son, Daniel, in lengthy research which eventually establishes that Guy Trentham is father to both of them. Often they use exactly the same sources used by this author in exploring the true identity of William Archer: an old gravestone, a historic newspaper report, immigration lists, phone books, criminal records and even medal rolls from the First World War. The parallels are uncanny.

Archer explained that '*As the Crow Flies* is based roughly on four people I've met, known and had the privilege of listening to their wicked stories.'[35] Marcus Sieff of Marks & Spencer and Sir Charles Forte were two of his models, but the most important was Sir Jack Cohen, the founder of Tesco. 'The last chapter is virtually Jack Cohen's life,' Archer confessed. 'It is true. At the age of seventy he was fed up with his whole bloody empire and he went back to his barrow because it was there he could meet people, and not people who'd call him "Sir".'[36] Meanwhile, the professional aspects of Charlie Trumper's wife, Becky, were based on Melanie Clore, a young auctioneer who helped him research the world of auction houses and checked the manuscript, and by whom Jeffrey seems to have been smitten. 'Go and see her at Sotheby's; she's devastating,' he said. 'She flirts with them. I could watch her for ever.'[37]

*As the Crow Flies* was the last Archer book to be edited by Richard Cohen. When Cohen had worked on the previous book, *A Twist in the Tale*, his employers, Hutchinson, had been paid a small royalty; for this work he was paid the royalty himself, because he did the work in his own spare time. Cohen probably put more effort into *Crow* than into any of Archer's previous books. This was partly because – at 250,000 words – it was longer than anything Archer had written before, and also because Cohen knew that with this novel neither Cork Smith nor Joni Evans would be supplementing his work in America. His dedication to the achievement of literacy was considerable: his comments in the margin were typically about half as long as Archer's original text on each page. He also prompted Archer to write an extra 50,000 to 60,000 words – the equivalent of a short novel. This additional material was mainly to flesh out the character of the villainous Ethel Trentham, who pursues a long feud with Charlie Trumper. And Archer was still making radical changes to his manuscript right up to the last moment.

By comparison, the contribution of Ed Breslin, HarperCollins's editor in New York, was minor. Many of his suggestions were simply to amend cockney dialect that Americans might not understand, and he says he had only one significant editorial meeting with his author. While Archer was visiting Chicago, Breslin flew there and they spent several hours going through the text in the British Airways lounge at O'Hare airport. The American editor came to admire Archer's professionalism, however, and says he took the cries of 'Breslin, you pathetic creature!' in good spirit – unlike many of his colleagues. 'Some at HarperCollins didn't like that, or understand it. People heard this and asked why I was not offended. But it was imbued with such affection,' he says. 'The wink from Jeffrey was pronounced, but half the Americans missed it.'[38]

In recent years Archer's editors appear to have spent increasing amounts of time correcting factual errors. The novelist's normal procedure in writing a book, he often explains, is to get the story on to the page, without worrying about detail, in the knowledge that inconsistencies can be sorted out later. 'When you're going and you're going and you're going, the last thing you want to do is stop,' he says. 'The first draft is getting the story down – the story, the story, the story – and the second draft you can check the facts.'[39] Archer will often farm out the manuscript to young researchers who are told to go away and check the details. His editors, and in particular the publishers' copy-editors, are meant to act as a final factual safety net. Archer even warns his copy-editors – much to their irritation – that he has put deliberate mistakes in the text to test them.

With *Crow* the fact-checking process broke down. Richard Cohen did as much as he could, keeping an eye on details and basic chronology; Ed Breslin despatched a long, amusing memo of amendments; and Hodder's outside copy-editor, Morag Robinson, produced a list of corrections said to have been almost as fat as the manuscript. But between them the editors still missed a lot – which isn't surprising given the sheer volume of factual inaccuracies. Several months after the book was published, a *News of the World* journalist, Ray Chapman, wrote to Archer pointing out dozens more errors. The book suggested, for instance, that the D-Day landings and the battle of El Alamein were in the First World War instead of the Second.[40] Other mistakes included a marchioness who suddenly became a duchess. As a result, Archer invited Chapman to join his fact-checking team in future.

The novelist always liked to encourage a friendly rivalry between his British and American publishers – over who could design the best cover, for instance, or who had the better quality paper. But with *Crow* there was a new edge to this competition, since if Hodder didn't perform then Archer held the sanction of defecting to HarperCollins in Britain as well. 'That was something lurking in the background,' admits one of those who looked after the book for his British publisher. 'If they ever sort of missed a trick, that was obviously the cosh that Jeffrey particularly held over Hodder's head.'

By now Hodder & Stoughton were in considerable financial difficulty. Over the previous decade, Archer had become the firm's most lucrative asset. 'It was like, when I started in publishing, James Bond and Ian Fleming had been for Pan,' says the former managing director, Michael Attenborough. 'Given the strength of the backlist, he would have been our largest invoice-value author.'[41]

This gave Archer considerable clout; Hodder staff knew that his departure might be the final blow which forced the firm to succumb to a take-over bid, like many other family publishing firms. Just as he had originally gone to Hodder twelve years earlier to unite his British hardbacks and paperbacks under the same roof, it now seemed logical that one house should handle all his titles on both sides of the Atlantic. Moreover, Archer no longer felt the same personal ties to Hodder now that his three closest friends at the firm – Richard Cohen, Alan Gordon Walker and Eddie Bell – had all left. Of these, Bell was the most significant.

When the hardback edition of *Crow* came out in July 1991, it failed to make number one in the *Sunday Times* best-sellers list, beaten into second place by Jilly Cooper's *Polo*. It was a heavy blow. Not since *Shall We Tell the President?* fourteen years earlier had any Archer novel failed to make British number one. The author was quick to assign blame. 'He was thoroughly pissed-off not to be top of the best-sellers list with *As the Crow Flies*,' recalls the Hodder chairman, Philip Attenborough (Michael's brother). 'Jilly Cooper most unfortunately stayed number one. He was putting us on our mettle . . . I think he was in Australia and sent us a cheerful fax. It was blunt and to the point. He wanted to be number one, which he regarded as his place.'[42] Sales of the paperback edition of *Crow* a year later were well down, too. According to the *Guardian*'s end-of-year paperback survey, for example, *Crow* sold only 758,000 copies – a phenomenal figure by the standards of most writers, of course, but extremely disappointing for Jeffrey Archer. Over roughly the same period five years before, *A Matter of Honour* had sold nearly twice as many.[43]

Archer was also worried by the uncertainty over Hodder's future, and was aggrieved that company executives didn't take him into their confidence about what they were doing. The author felt he was entitled to be consulted about such matters when they would clearly affect him, and also considering that his output accounted for such a significant share of Hodder's business.

Archer had been particularly annoyed not to be consulted when the company quietly began searching for a buyer, around 1988, since he himself would have been interested. 'If a sale was to come up, I wanted to be told,' he said later. 'I wanted a part share. It was worth about £60 million then, so obviously I could not have bought it outright. I would have needed help.'[44] When he learned of the company's search, Archer immediately rang Philip Attenborough and offered to make a significant investment himself. Attenborough replied that he was grateful, but that the answer was probably 'No' – a decision his board endorsed. They were worried it would cause complications inside the company, and might upset other leading authors.

Archer remained annoyed both that he'd been kept in the dark and also by the dismissive response to his offer. 'He was terribly offended,' says one former Hodder executive. 'He felt he had a special relationship and ought to be the first in the know.'

# 25

# The Bell Boys

It was a Monday morning, the last day of September 1991, when Philip and Michael Attenborough answered the summons to an urgent meeting at Alembic House. Jeffrey Archer's fax from Australia had given the brothers ample warning of what lay in store; it clearly wouldn't be a comfortable occasion for any of them. 'Even before we got to the meeting,' says Michael Attenborough, 'Phil and I realized that the longer term with Jeffrey was most uncertain.'

The author began, as often before, with pleasantries about cricket, before moving on to more difficult territory: why his latest novel, *As the Crow Flies*, had failed to make number one. When Archer had finished explaining how unhappy he was with Hodder's performance with the book, he delivered the news the brothers had feared. After thirteen years, and seven of the most commercially successful books in the history of British fiction, the time had come for him to leave Hodder. 'It was done in typical style by Jeffrey,' says Michael Attenborough. 'He declared his intentions and expressed a determination that it would be a totally non-acrimonious parting, which it was.'[1]

It was agreed that both sides would keep quiet about Archer's decision for another year, until Coronet had published the paperback edition of *Crow* the following summer. But internally the news quickly leaked out, and not even the return to Hodder of his favourite editor, Richard Cohen, a few months later, could prevent the inevitable: Archer would now join HarperCollins in Britain as well as in the USA. What the Attenboroughs and their colleagues must have found particularly hard to swallow was that the prime mover behind the author's defection was their former sales director at Coronet, Eddie Bell.

In 1990 Bell had returned from HarperCollins in America to run the firm's British publishing arm. A large, rough-spoken, cigar-smoking, jovial, but tough Presbyterian Scot, Bell was brought up in the bleak town of Airdrie, east of Glasgow, where his mother was one of the first women Labour councillors. After leaving school at sixteen, he became a whisky salesman, and then moved on to selling greetings cards, before the crucial turning-point in 1970 when he heard that Hodder needed a new paperback rep in the West of Scotland. 'Who the fuck are Hodder?' he remembers asking.[2]

Eddie Bell may have known nothing about books to start with, but he rose rapidly within Hodder. His success coincided with the emergence of Coronet as a paperback imprint, and a new awareness of the importance of marketing within publishing in the late 1970s. Bell's advancement also reflected the growing importance the industry attached to people with a commercial rather than an editorial background. He earned a reputation as a rough bully who ruled his sales team by fear – hence his *Private Eye* nickname, Eddie 'McBastard' Bell. 'I was a hard man in the early days,' he once conceded. 'Awful. But a lot needed changing very quickly . . . I wasn't loved, but I never set out to be loved.'[3]

Jeffrey Archer and Eddie Bell had prospered together at Coronet, and each admired the other. 'Archer wanted to be involved in everything and he needed somebody to stand up to him,' Bell said. 'I could do that, and we became (and are) dear friends.'[4] It was Bell whom Archer would ring if he found a bookshop where his novels weren't on sale, or were poorly displayed. 'If that happens,' Bell once explained, 'I get the sales manager in and give him a bollocking. I have told the sales force that if I go into a shop and find Jeffrey's books out of stock, I will fire the local rep.'[5] Yet even his critics acknowledge that Eddie Bell has other qualities besides aggression. 'He has got the charisma and vision that few publishers have,' says a former colleague. 'He's inspirational, and has the sixth sense you need – seeing what is around the corner that's about to hit us.'

HarperCollins people remember that when Bell arrived in New York to set up the firm's new paperback division, in 1989, he boasted how Archer would be his trump card, and that he could spring his old friend from his existing publishers. It wasn't just a question of proving himself to his new employers: it was also revenge for the miserable way Bell felt he had been treated by the old-style English gentlemen who ran Hodder. He resented the fact that even after reaching high positions they had still called him 'the salesman from Glasgow'; it was meant amiably enough, but it hurt. Bell's departure in 1985 had been particularly unpleasant: 'I told them I was very likely to join Collins. They made me an alternative offer which they automatically assumed I would accept. When I didn't,

I was marched to the door and driven home.'[6] According to one former colleague, 'He saw Jeffrey as one of the ultimate goals to say to these people, "Take that, you awful upper-class prats! I've got my own back – I've got Jeffrey Archer!"'

HarperCollins's negotiations for Archer's British rights were handled personally by Bell and his boss, George Craig, and lasted several months. 'Everything was kept very secret,' says one close observer, who says that Archer was seen very much as 'Eddie's man'. The details were hidden even from senior members of management who might usually be expected to know them. Once agreement had been reached, Craig and Bell held a celebration dinner with the author at the Frankfurt Book Fair. It must have been galling for Hodder executives that, while their stand was still displaying Archer's latest title, *As the Crow Flies*, the whisper quickly spread that Eddie Bell had finally got his man.

The deal was in effect an amendment to the 1990 contract with Harper-Collins in America. It was reported to be worth anything from £1.7 million to £10 million, though the actual figure was probably nearer the bottom end of the range. Archer also took the unusual step of personally paying his old publishers more than £1 million for the rights to his backlist – including *Crow*, which Hodder had only just issued in paperback themselves – and then sold them to HarperCollins. The new company also paid Hodder a few thousand pounds for the page layouts of each title, which saved the expense of typesetting the paperbacks again from scratch. The HarperCollins editions had new covers, but the inside pages were identical.

It had helped considerably in winning Archer's signature that Bell had lured a steady trickle of other Hodder staff to HarperCollins over the years; internally they became known as 'the Bell Boys'. Furthermore, the managing director of the HarperCollins trade division, Jonathan Lloyd, was a long-standing squash partner of Jeffrey's. And the fact that HarperCollins had recently acquired Margaret Thatcher's memoirs was an added attraction for Archer. Indeed, it particularly tickled him that his new editor, Stuart Proffitt, was also in charge of Thatcher's book. Yet Proffitt was an odd choice to edit a best-selling commercial author, partly because most of his previous work had been serious non-fiction. 'Until Jeffrey Archer,' says one HarperCollins source, 'Stuart had always been a highbrow editor. He has serious talent, but no experience of the popular end of fiction.' But colleagues thought it important that Proffitt should do Archer's books, since he had recently taken the top editorial job in the company.

In editing Archer's next novel, *Honour Among Thieves*, Proffitt was helped by a bright, youthful-looking assistant, Robert Lacey (and a third editor in America, Rick Horgan). But, unlike the days of Cork Smith, Joni Evans and Richard Cohen, there were no sessions when they all worked together for weeks on the text, and certainly no trips to the Caribbean. Indeed, Eddie Bell firmly believes that a book can be over-edited. Nobody at HarperCollins had the time for that kind of intense treatment anyway, and Archer himself was busy with other things.

In some ways *Honour Among Thieves* was an Americanized version of his 1986 novel *A Matter of Honour*. (The book was originally to be called *Scapegoat*, and the title *Honour Among Thieves* had already been used for one of Archer's stories in *A Twist in the Tale*.) Again it involves a hero, Scott Bradley, trying to make amends for his father's disgrace. Instead of chasing round Europe with a valuable Russian icon, Bradley is trying to retrieve the original of the American Declaration of Independence, which has been stolen at the behest of the Iraqi dictator Saddam Hussein, who plans to burn it on 4 July 1993, Independence Day. Like his three previous caper/thrillers – *Penny*, *President* and *A Matter of Honour* – the plot relies heavily on people masquerading in a range of implausible disguises. More than ever before, Archer was changing the manuscript right up to the last moment (he even tried to make further changes ten days after submitting the 'final' version, but Eddie Bell says he wouldn't let him). Some late, topical additions were planned, however: blank spaces were left until the final draft to be filled with references to up-to-date events (including the Waco siege, which occurred only a few weeks before publication). It was one of the first books officially to be published on a Sunday – Independence Day 1993 – the day the plot reaches its climax.

It was also probably the first novel to include President Clinton, who had been in office for less than six months when it came out. By a further stroke of Archer luck, the weekend before publication Clinton became embroiled in America's most serious conflict with Saddam since the Gulf War two years earlier, and ordered a missile attack on Baghdad. Archer joked that the US ambassador had told him 'we'd like 50 per cent of the royalties', as once again the distinction between fact and fantasy seemed to be curiously blurred.[7]

HarperCollins went to extraordinary lengths to promote the hardback edition of *Honour Among Thieves*. Indeed, the pressure their salesmen put on bookshops to order advance copies and mount window displays became something of a joke within the book trade. The company spent £150,000 on advertising in Britain alone – roughly a pound for every copy eventually sold. W. H. Smith at Heathrow alone ordered a record 5,000 advance copies: many novelists would be happy to sell that number worldwide. At their British sales conference, the HarperCollins marketing director appeared in a Bill Clinton mask; Archer was presented with a cake designed like the book-jacket; the sales reps received gifts of dollar bills, and were promised bonuses in US currency if they exceeded their targets.

Eddie Bell was determined to succeed with *Honour Among Thieves* in Britain, where Hodder had so markedly failed with *Crow*. The personal stakes were raised further when, ten days before *Thieves*' publication, Hodder published John le Carré's latest thriller, *The Night Manager*. But Archer won the British best-seller contest easily. Just two weeks after publication, he deposed le Carré from top spot in the *Sunday Times* best-seller chart, and then stayed there for five weeks. The book spent four months on the list altogether.

In the United States, however – and it was primarily an American book – Archer still wasn't making the same impact on the best-seller charts that he had in the early 1980s. The picture is complicated: in terms of numbers, *Honour Among Thieves* sold at least as many hardback copies in America as any previous Archer, but his position *relative* to other top-selling authors was now much weaker. Over the previous decade the whole nature of the American book market had changed: discounting, book clubs and a relative fall in price compared with softcover books meant that best-selling hardcovers were selling in far greater quantities. Jeffrey Archer was nowhere near the premier league of best-sellers in America, whereas in the days of *Kane and Abel* and *The Prodigal Daughter* he had been on the fringes of the top ten. In sport, music, films, television and books, the American entertainment industries increasingly concentrate on big-name blockbusters. By the early 1990s, star writers such as Tom Clancy, Stephen King, John Grisham and Danielle Steel could expect to sell hardbacks in the millions. Archer sold just under 300,000 copies of *Honour Among Thieves* in America in 1993, but even this was exceeded by English rivals such as Ken Follett and John le Carré.[8]

In Britain too there are growing signs that Archer's position in the market is weakening. The paperback edition of *Thieves*, published in 1994, fared particularly badly. In the annual *Guardian* fast-seller survey, Archer came only sixth – his worst position so far. His sales of 656,000 were less than half his peak figure, recorded by *A Matter of Honour* in 1987.[9] This must have been especially disappointing for HarperCollins, since the paperback had been issued in March, giving an extra three months for sales compared with his previous books, which had usually come out in June or July. Moreover, the book had been promoted with the bonus of a free copy of his 1980 short-story collection, *A Quiver Full of Arrows*.

Despite the enormous pressure on the sales force, and the huge sums invested in promotion, many insiders say that Archer has been a financial disaster for HarperCollins. One highly informed observer describes the company's $30 million three-book contract in 1990 as 'without exaggeration the worst deal ever made in American book publishing'. In loss-making terms, it easily surpasses the $8 million that Simon & Schuster paid for Ronald Reagan's memoirs: of the $30 million advance, it is estimated that about $24 million remains unearned in royalties. Nevertheless, one should keep things in perspective; it is not that Archer has suddenly become unpopular. Far from it. 'He is still one of the leading authors in the world,' says one former HarperCollins executive. 'It's just that we have overpaid for him.'

'The great mistake that Eddie Bell made,' another source explains, 'was that he was convinced he could make a fantastic amount of money out of film rights, and Archer has always been famously unfilmable, and was yet again unfilmable.' There was talk of a huge Japanese TV/movie deal, worth as much as $9 million, but it never happened. Eddie Bell even appointed a specialist in TV and film rights, Cresta Norris, one of whose main tasks was to sell the Archer titles, but there appears to have been little interest, even within the Murdoch empire itself. More than five years after he first moved to HarperCollins, no film deal had been announced, though Eddie Bell remains optimistic. 'My prediction is we are going to see a number of Archer books in movies,' he asserts. 'There's a lot of interest.' And several of his short stories, he adds, may be adapted for television.[10] What is perhaps surprising is that no one appears to have suggested to Archer that, given that so much money has been invested in him, he might make his plots more filmable. Nobody would dare, says one former company insider.

This is a sign of the unusual relationship the author enjoys with his publishers. HarperCollins staff are expected to meet every Archer demand – even the seemingly trivial. 'On tour he has to have a feather pillow wherever he stays,' says someone who worked with him in America. 'Sales people have to lift his luggage. He needs a cellular phone everywhere to make calls. People are told, "Don't speak to him unless you're spoken to."'

In the USA, top-selling authors are usually accompanied on tour by people known as 'media escorts'; these are local guides – usually women – who are employed by the publisher to meet the author at the airport, and then drive him or her round the usual itinerary of newspaper offices, television and radio interviews, literary lunches, and signing sessions. At their annual party at the American Booksellers' Association convention, escorts traditionally vote on their most disagreeable client in the previous twelve months, and award them the Golden Dartboard or the 'Author From Hell' award. In 1992 Archer won the title with ease, after the way he behaved on his trip to promote *Crow* the previous summer. 'He does have a good sense of humour,' says one escort, 'but he has a cruel side and a very nasty side, and he wouldn't have won this award had he been a nice person.'

Archer always insists on absolute punctuality, and blames the escorts if he runs late. On the other hand, arriving early is almost as bad an offence, says one guide:

> He makes you arrive on the exact dot of time. If he has to spend more than thirty seconds at an interview waiting, he's very upset. You've wasted his time . . . Never mind that you might have to find a parking place, or something. You can't arrive early and you can't arrive late, which puts a great deal of pressure on us when we're going from place to place.

Many escorts tell of the novelist's rudeness to ordinary people, such as hotel staff. Archer even boasts, they say, of how an escort once almost hit him, and seems proud of the fact that few want to work with him again. 'What Jeffrey likes to do is push it to the limit. He likes to get a reaction. He likes it when people give it back to him, but unfortunately we are in a position where we can't do that.' Another observes that 'Basically, what he does is put you down. He'll call you "stupid". He'll say, "You don't know what you're talking about. You're so silly. This is a silly thing to do. Why are you doing this?"'

Experienced Archer-handlers agree that the worst thing is to let him bully you. 'His way of dealing with people was to intimidate them, to belittle them,' says a former HarperCollins executive in America. 'If he can sense there's fear, if he can get you off balance, he'll go for you.' In the USA HarperCollins staff due to work with the writer are now warned about what to expect, and advised how best to cope with him.

One tip is to take lightly everything he says. But this sounds easier than it is. It may be possible for senior executives to ignore or laugh at his insults and barked commands, but not salesmen who've been told how many thousands of his books they must sell. 'Most of them were so petrified by the target they had to make that they couldn't take it as a joke,' says one observer. 'He would happily bellow down the phone at someone very, very junior, who had no power to do anything about anything, was seriously terrified by his rage, and was completely blameless anyway.'

This is something of a contrast from Archer's early days as a writer, when many people in the book trade – both sales reps and shop managers – rather liked him. They admired the brazen way he went about promoting his titles compared with other authors, the effort, and the detailed interest he took in their side of the business: he remembered their names, enquired after them, and was always eager for the latest sales figures. He would also give the salesmen small gifts: those at Hodder all received Asprey wallets on one occasion, though they lived in fear thereafter that Archer would suddenly demand to see that they were using them. In recent years, however, the author has become heartily unpopular with much of the industry, as his enthusiasm has turned into a less attractive style: incessant demands, arrogance, rudeness, and continuous pressure to maintain the sales momentum.

On the other hand, it is perhaps to Archer's credit that he is still so willing to put so much effort into selling his books. In the days when Hodder paid him unusually high royalties, there was a direct financial return from every book sold. With the new HarperCollins arrangements, Archer can hope to get no more than his huge advances. Yet Eddie Bell's tough, aggressive approach and the harder salesmanship of HarperCollins seem to have rubbed off on him. With such large sums of money involved, much of the fun seems to have gone, as the whole Jeffrey Archer industry has acquired a new intensity and unpleasantness.

'The sales people at HarperCollins loathed him – absolutely loathed him – because he was so awful to booksellers,' says one former company manager:

> There was always this terrible sort of dichotomy of you wanting to have a successful book-signing, but you're cringing because Jeffrey's going to be terribly rude to this incredibly important bookshop manager; fussing about what he would and would not drink, what he would and couldn't use to write with; referring to the sales rep as a 'waste of space', being very abusive and unpleasant.

One former bookshop manageress says Archer is 'one of the worst authors you could ever have in a bookshop, and I would never have him again in a shop that I had anything to do with'. She adds, 'He is a nightmare, and I've come across some nightmares in my time, and he is the worst without a shadow of a doubt.' Another manager to use the word 'nightmare' is Willie Anderson, who has welcomed Archer to John Smith's bookshop in Glasgow five or six times: 'He just comes in and takes over. He's very demanding. Books have to be passed to him in a certain way and at a certain time.'[11] One W. H. Smith manager, Richard Brown, felt the wrath of Archer's tongue at a literary evening in Aylesbury in 1994. Brown hadn't been contacted in advance by HarperCollins, and the author wasn't due to sign any books, but on his own initiative the W. H. Smith man took along fifty paperback Archers and five copies of the latest hardback, *Twelve Red Herrings*. The novelist was furious with Brown when he discovered so few copies of his recent book were on sale. 'He was expecting 200 hardback books and he was incredibly rude to me, and you don't expect that from somebody of his calibre,' says Brown.[12] 'I believe it's polite to introduce yourself to somebody or acknowledge someone when you arrive. Yes, he may be a lord and worth a lot of money, but that doesn't mean he can dress people down. He was pretty rude to his driver and testy with a few other people as well.'[13] Even Archer admitted to his audience that evening that 'I'm far too abrasive.'[14]

The former Hatchards general manager, Geoffrey Bailey, now with Waterstone's, acknowledges that Jeffrey Archer can be rude, but also reveals a considerate side: 'He was very supportive of me when I was made redundant after twenty-two years by Hatchards,' he says. 'He was one of the first to write and say how horrified he was – he must have read about it in the trade press – and he also wrote to congratulate me when I got the job at Waterstone's.'[15]

Whatever his personal conduct, one aspect of Archer's approach has been welcomed by British bookshop managers – his hostility to book clubs, who buy cheaply in bulk, and then sell to their members at big discounts. In 1982 he delighted the Booksellers' Association conference by announcing that he would not allow *The Prodigal Daughter* to be published in a book-club edition. This took some courage, since book-club copies had accounted for more than half the British hardback sales of his previous book, *Kane and Abel* (60,000 out of 110,000). He took the same stand over his subsequent Hodder titles. 'It doesn't help the shopkeeper who's trying to make a living,' he argued. 'My first interest is in the bookshop. They've been very good to me over the years.'[16] Archer promised in 1990 that he would 'not, repeat *not*, allow a new novel of mine to go to a book club'.[17]

He was not being entirely altruistic, however. Book-club editions pay authors only a tiny fraction – often less than a fifth – of the royalty received from sales in shops. Not surprisingly perhaps, once royalties had effectively become irrelevant under the HarperCollins contract, Archer allowed a simultaneous book-club edition of *Thieves* in 1993; since then, however, he has again opposed book-club editions which are published at the same time as copies for shops.

A good illustration of Archer's special – almost inviolate – status at HarperCollins concerned a small book the company produced in the autumn of 1994. *The First Miracle* was a short story, based around the Nativity, which he had originally included in his 1980 compilation *A Quiver Full of Arrows*. Designed for the Christmas market, the new book was illustrated with several paintings by Craigie Aitchison. Some were previous works of his, and weren't always appropriate; others had been produced specially. Archer is a fan of Aitchison's, and was particularly keen to publish the book because it enabled him to acquire more Aitchison originals.

HarperCollins put the book forward as one of their ten paid entries for the 1994 Booksellers' Association Christmas catalogue, which had a print run of 4.5 million copies; such publications are always an important advertising medium for publishers. But the independent panel which approves entries to the catalogue rejected *The First Miracle* because the story had been published before. In protest, HarperCollins withdrew all ten entries, for which they had paid more than £21,000. In their commitment to one leading author, they were willing to undermine the Christmas sales of nine others.

One close observer goes so far as to describe Jeffrey Archer's relationship with HarperCollins as similar to that of a Third World country and its bankers: the financial commitment is so great that banks are afraid to do anything about it. 'The greater the debt HarperCollins got into, the more petrified HarperCollins people were of him. Instead of saying, "Right, you've got to come up with the goods. You've been given all this money", their attitude towards him was cowering.'

Staff at HarperCollins say the financial pressures are now so intense that the job of working with Archer has become a poisoned chalice. 'Because so much has been paid for these books, they're always edited in a tearing hurry,' says one source. 'The idea is to get the company's money back as fast as you can.' When the manuscript arrives late, instead of publication being delayed, the timetable is simply accelerated.

Archer's outside commitments – politics and charity work – inevitably mean that he devotes less attention to his writing nowadays. While everything is done in a great rush, he also has a habit of making extensive changes at proof stage, but never hesitates to express his anger if things go wrong. If an error is spotted in his books, as far as Archer is concerned the responsibility lies with his personal fact-checkers, or the editor and copy-editor at the publishers, for not finding it earlier. Yet his recent manuscripts have contained so many mistakes that Archer's editors now face a horrendous task. One recalls how he found that with one book:

> The facts were so wrong it was just hair-raising. I was worried because I was working at speed. I was also embarrassed to tell him they were wrong. With a lot, you could change a date or something, but others were more difficult. I spent hours and hours going to libraries, but the list of mistakes was so long it made you wonder about everything. I was so worried I hadn't spotted something major.

When the *News of the World* journalist Ray Chapman found numerous errors in *Crow* in 1992, Archer didn't blame himself, but the staff at Hodder. Archer promised Chapman he could check future manuscripts – a task he was willing to perform unpaid – yet he had to pester Archer's office to obtain a draft of *Honour Among Thieves*, and even then it arrived only at the last moment. Errors which the journalist spotted were nevertheless printed in the hardback edition, presumably because there had not been time to correct them. Chapman soon became disillusioned. He never managed to talk about his corrections with Archer himself, but invariably had to deal with his secretary. 'If a person's not prepared to discuss with me points and details, and his secretary seemed to know more about it than he did, I was beginning to think, "Well, hang on a minute, why won't you discuss it?"' Archer had succeeded in alienating somebody who was willing to help him avoid potential embarrassment. 'I was just treated very off-handedly,' says Chapman. 'Quite frankly, my opinion now is "Up Yours!"'[18]

Archer's third book of stories, *Twelve Red Herrings*, was published by HarperCollins in 1994. Despite falling sales of his recent novels, Archer's short stories again sold remarkably well in Britain, and the book was the fourth-best-selling fiction hardback of 1994.[19] In 1995, however, the paperback edition sold barely half the figure for *A Twist in the Tale*, six years before.[20] Rather than amuse readers with an unexpected twist to each tale, as in his previous collection, his editor, Robert Lacey, suggested adding a misleading red herring to each story – hence the title. Yet there had been considerable problems in assembling the tales. 'The first and longest story was so bad it was unsalvageable,' says one source. 'It didn't hang together.' The story was withdrawn.

At a party at the HarperCollins headquarters in Hammersmith, Archer pointed out how *Twelve Red Herrings* marked the fulfilment of his original contract with the company. Turning to Eddie Bell, and hinting of the hard negotiations that lay ahead, Archer suggested that perhaps he should now contact his old friend Jonathan Lloyd. Though apparently meant in jest, the point was obvious to everyone present, for Lloyd had just been sacked by Bell after more than twenty years with Collins, and was now acting as a literary agent. The underlying suggestion was that if HarperCollins didn't come up with a new contract, Archer might ask Lloyd to try elsewhere.

Then Archer turned to a clown who had been hired to perform party tricks and was tossing balls into the air. 'Jeffrey took the three balls,' says Eddie Bell, 'and juggled with them in front of everybody, and then threw them to me and said, "Let's see if the chairman can juggle with them." I got up and juggled and headed one to the clown and said, "Let's see if Jonathan Lloyd can juggle them."'[21]

Such teasing about Jonathan Lloyd was nothing new to Bell and Archer. When both men were with Hodder and Lloyd was with Collins, the position had been reversed, and the publishers were always aware of the possibility that Archer might turn to his squash partner if they failed to perform. But the humour and repartee hid genuine tensions. Having lost so much money on the first book deal, HarperCollins was unwilling to pay the novelist the same again. But Archer wasn't actually joking. Jonathan Lloyd did subsequently contact several of the big publishing conglomerates to ask if they'd be interested in a three-book contract for the author. The asking price was $40 million.

But no one seems to have taken Lloyd's approaches seriously. One top publisher says the figure was so outrageous that it wasn't even worth having a meeting. Ultimately HarperCollins knocked Archer down to $23 million for a second package of two novels and a collection of short stories. The press hailed the deal as a great coup for Archer, and, given the money he had again squeezed out of his publishers, in a way it was. Yet, compared with the big 1990 deal, he was getting quite a lot less for much more. Not only was the money $7 million lower, but this time the contract was for world rights, including the Japanese market, which Bell estimates is now worth about 15 to 20 per cent of Archer's global sales. In short, the new deal includes every possible right to his books, worldwide. 'I own his life,' Bell claims mischievously – 'totally.'[22]

Everyone in publishing expected Archer would eventually re-sign with HarperCollins, partly because the company has acquired the habit of paying top authors much more than other firms do. Losing Archer to another house would have been both an enormous blow in terms of corporate prestige and also a personal embarrassment for Eddie Bell. Colleagues also suspect that Bell would have had another consideration, too.

'I can swear on my children's head that I did not know Jonathan Lloyd was acting for Jeffrey,' says Bell, who adds that he finds it hard to believe.[23] But others within HarperCollins say Archer was quite frank about the fact that Lloyd was sniffing around on his behalf. Privately they acknowledge that his choice of agent was perfect. Had Archer actually signed a contract elsewhere, Lloyd's reward would have been considerable. The man who had been sacked by Eddie Bell might not have taken the customary 10 per cent commission, but even a few per cent, or a flat fee, would have been a handsome return.

'Jeffrey Archer knew Eddie Bell would rather pay the money than have an Archer deal go through Jonathan Lloyd,' says one of the people close to the negotiations. 'Bell could not accept the thought of Jonathan Lloyd collecting all that commission from Archer.'

For most of 1995 Archer worked hard on the first part of his new contract, the next blockbuster novel. And never had an Archer book been so widely trailed in advance. 'I think I've written the first novelography,' he boasted excitedly. 'It's *Kane and Abel* with knobs on.'[24] Supposedly eighty per cent true, it would tell the story of the rivalry between two world-wide media barons, Dick Armstrong ('the son of an illiterate peasant') and Keith Tremlett ('raised in a mansion on the other side of the world').[25] They were quite openly based on Robert Maxwell and Archer's own publisher, Rupert Murdoch, but the idea was not quite as original as Archer seemed to think. As Murdoch himself must have known, a rather similar book called *Family Business* had been published in 1988, with a Maxwell character called Piers Molinski and a Murdoch double – albeit female – by the name of Yarrow McLean. *Family Business* had actually been written by the publisher's wife, Anna Murdoch.[26]

Despite writing about two such colourful figures, Archer seems to have had trouble gathering interesting material on his subjects. It cannot be easy basing a fictional character on one's own publisher, though Archer reckoned Murdoch would 'probably be flattered by my depiction'.[27] Maxwell should have been easier, of course, since he was dead, but Archer didn't find him so. Coincidentally, HarperCollins were also due to publish an account by Tom Bower of the events leading up to Maxwell's mysterious death in 1991. Before publication in January 1996, Archer was keen to get an advance peek at Bower's manuscript to borrow some anecdotes. The novelist even rang Bower, claiming that he had already consulted the biographer's agent. Bower, who did not believe him, refused to help.

Originally Archer called his new novel *The Proprietor* – along the lines of *The Godfather*. Then it became *The Proprietors* (plural) but HarperCollins in New York were not happy with the title; for Americans a 'proprietor' is someone who runs a small shop or garage, not a multimillionaire media tycoon. Hastily, Archer tried to come up with a new title, and even appealed through Murdoch's *Sunday Times* for ideas, offering a case of Krug for the best. The winner was *The Fourth Estate*, though Archer was still uneasy with this too; he went round asking friends whether they thought readers would know what the term meant. In the absence of anything better, *The Fourth Estate* it remained.

# 26

# His Way with the Kurds

It was Jeffrey's fifty-first birthday: Monday 15 April 1991. That evening he enjoyed a celebratory meal in Grantchester with Mary and Jamie, who was home for the Easter holidays from Eton. After dinner they watched television, where Jeffrey was due to appear in a BBC *Panorama* programme about John Major.

What caught their eye, however, was the *Nine O'Clock News* beforehand, and a report on the terrible plight of more than 800,000 Kurds trapped, in the aftermath of the Gulf War, on Iraq's mountainous northern border with Turkey. The Archers were deeply moved as the pictures showed an old man burying his young grandson beneath a pile of stones. 'There was I, replete after a meal with my own 16-year-old son, and here was another family in the midst of such terrible tragedy.'[1] While they were enjoying themselves in the comfort of The Old Vicarage, in Kurdistan refugees from Saddam Hussein's genocide were dying in their thousands from cold, starvation and disease.

It was Jamie who prompted his father to respond.

> My son said, 'Why don't we do something?' I said the Government would do something, but he said, 'No, I mean we should hold a concert.' I said, 'You can't clear television schedules in two or three weeks to make way for a concert. It can't be done.' James looked at me and I shall never forget this, he said, 'Well, at least have a try, Dad.'[2]

The model, of course, was the Live Aid concert at Wembley organized by Bob Geldof in 1985, which had raised some £48 million for starving people in Ethiopia. But Live Aid had taken six months to arrange. Archer believed that, to capitalize on the sense of public outrage, a concert for the Kurds should be the climax of a campaign that lasted no more than a month.

Ever since his re-emergence in public life in the late 1970s, Jeffrey

Archer had regularly been involved in small charity events. This, however, was on a completely different scale. It would be his first major fund-raising exercise in twenty years. And the story of his efforts to help the Kurds would encapsulate many of Archer's best and worst qualities. On the one hand he brought to the Kurdish appeal his compassion, energy and unquenchable self-belief; yet at the same time his efforts suffered from his customary lack of attention to detail, bad judgement, and the tendency to exaggerate his own achievements.

In organizing his concert, Archer had one great advantage compared with the large charity events of his younger days: his prominence and personal contacts now ensured he could quickly get through to almost anyone. One of the first people he telephoned was Sir Paul Fox, the managing director of BBC Television. Fox, who was about to retire from the BBC, had been one of the moguls of British broadcasting in the 1960s, '70s and '80s. Archer had kept in touch with Fox – as he skilfully does with numerous powerful figures – ever since he had tried unsuccessfully to become a *Panorama* reporter twenty-five years before. They weren't exactly friends, Fox says, but he would sometimes be invited to Jeffrey's Christmas parties. If anyone could quickly organize a big event for the Kurds, he thought, it was Archer. 'It's always been Jeffrey's great skill that he *is* an operator, at the highest level,' says Fox. 'If he wants to get things done he can get them done.'[3]

Fox suggested that to assemble the necessary pop stars Archer should immediately call Harvey Goldsmith, the rock promoter who had helped organize Live Aid. Archer concurred, since by his own admission he knew little about modern music and had to ask Jamie which groups would have the most appeal.

As it happened, even before Archer called him, Goldsmith had been contacted by several entertainers offering to help the Kurds, including Peter Gabriel and Sting. 'I was getting these signals from different directions, so I knew there was the enthusiasm behind it to make it work,' he said. The first thing, Goldsmith insisted, was to decide on a date: 'I knew that 12 May looked promising because there were quite a lot of bands working. What we had to do was to get them to come in with us.'[4] One of the best locations, the indoor Wembley Arena, was already booked on that night for the rap singer MC Hammer. Goldsmith persuaded the artist's promoter to hand over the venue for a Kurds concert, on the understanding that MC Hammer would be part of the line-up.

While Bob Geldof's Live Aid had been an independent charity, Archer decided that with so little time he needed to work with an existing aid organization. He consulted a number of possible groups before ringing another old friend, John Gray, the director of public affairs at the British Red Cross. Archer had helped Gray's previous charity, the National Children's Home, on several occasions after the two men had originally been introduced by the former Speaker of the House of Commons, George Thomas.

John Gray says he can remember vividly Archer's call that Thursday afternoon: '"John, it's Jeffrey. What are we going to do about the Kurds? . . . Can you come round to my flat tomorrow? Bring with you a lot of people that can make things happen, because," he said, "I've got a wonderful idea to raise a lot of money to help the Kurds."'5

The timing of Archer's call was perfect: the British Red Cross at that moment was especially open to a big idea. John Gray had been appointed by the new director-general, Mike Whitlam, only seven weeks earlier, to help shake things up. The charity was still lumbered with a stuffy, sleepy, old-fashioned image, and Whitlam and Gray believed that a rock concert for an urgent cause would 'put the Red Cross on the fund-raising map as never before, and enhance our profile with the British public'.6 Indeed, a few days before Archer called, Gray had written to about ten impresarios to suggest just such a fund-raising event to help the victims of the Gulf War. There was no response.

Around the time Archer first rang the Red Cross, he also contacted one of the few singers he knew, Chris de Burgh. De Burgh was enthusiastic, and suggested that a song he'd written some time before might catch the spirit of the occasion. The title, 'The Simple Truth', was soon adopted for the whole campaign, and the singer donated all his royalties. Archer then spent a day at the BBC helping produce a video, matching de Burgh's soundtrack with the powerful news pictures from Kurdistan which had prompted him to act in the first place.

Ten days after first seeing the emotive BBC film report, Archer and his colleagues launched the Simple Truth appeal in London. They now had the backing of the leaders of the main political parties, and John Major promised £10 million on behalf of the government. The goal was to double that, and every member of the public was asked to donate five pounds.

Harvey Goldsmith had soon signed up Tom Jones and Lisa Stansfield to join MC Hammer at Wembley. Other performers – including Rod Stewart, Paul Simon, Gloria Estefan, Sting, Sinead O'Connor, New

Kids on the Block, and Peter Gabriel – volunteered to perform at a series of nine simultaneous concerts across three continents: four in America; two in Holland; and others in Manchester, Switzerland and Australia.

Archer, meanwhile, turned his office in Alembic House over to Simple Truth. He was joined by two young Kurds based in London, Broosk Saib and Nadhim Zahawi, former flatmates and business associates who had long been campaigning for Kurdish refugees. Archer dubbed the two friends Bean Kurd and Lemon Kurd (though people never knew which was which). He also took on several public-relations people recommended by Margaret Thatcher's advertising guru Sir Tim Bell, and paid their wages personally. Later, Archer would claim to have spent £100,000 of his own money on the whole campaign, and to have worked nineteen hours a day for six weeks. 'He was up at four in the morning,' says Zahawi. 'We'd get to the office at seven or seven thirty and he'd already done three hours' work. It was amazing.'[7]

One initiative was a series of letters faxed from Archer's office to the chairmen of major public companies, appealing for donations. Most of his work, though, consisted of personal diplomacy. Nadhim Zahawi arranged a programme of visits to the London ambassadors of every EC country, as well as those of America, Australia and Japan. On each occasion Archer asked them to match the £10 million donated by Britain. The climax of the diplomatic tour came eight days before the Wembley event, when Archer made a one-day round trip by Concorde to New York to see the UN secretary-general, Javier Pérez de Cuéllar. Archer promised him that at least £10 million of the money raised would be channelled through the United Nations.

The Simple Truth appeal faced political problems from the start. Other charities, particularly those already helping the Kurds, resented the way the Red Cross had adopted Archer's idea without consulting the Disasters' Relief Committee, which coordinates crisis appeals. Some people within the British Red Cross itself were unhappy that the Kurdish project cut across the society's existing efforts in the Gulf as a whole, and believed it was wrong to focus so much attention on the plight of just one group. There was concern too, that Simple Truth might divert effort and attention from the annual British Red Cross Week, scheduled for the days leading up to the Wembley event. And the International Red Cross was worried that the show conflicted with its own classical music concert, planned for the same weekend.

Nevertheless, with its international reputation and contacts, the British

Red Cross was probably better placed than most charities to exploit Simple Truth to the full, and Red Cross societies overseas helped sell the television rights in at least thirty-five other countries, including Russia and Japan. The event seemed to strike a chord in Australia and Europe, and especially in Scandinavia; it was difficult, however, to arouse much interest in America.

Considering how quickly it had been arranged, the Wembley concert was a big success. Archer was seen greeting the Princess of Wales, before he and Mary sat through the evening with John and Norma Major. Chris Tarrant presented BBC2's live coverage, which lasted almost five hours, and linked Wembley with the other nine concerts worldwide, in an operation involving twenty-three different artists. The television output was regularly punctuated with short film reports from Kurdistan by Charles Wheeler and other broadcasters.

But not everything ran smoothly. People in the audience at Wembley were each asked to donate a five-pound note, and the performers and other celebrities were urged to autograph their fivers. Unfortunately the signed notes were accidentally banked along with the ordinary donations, and were dispersed through the banking system before anybody realized. The Red Cross appealed for the public to check their wallets and hand in any autographed notes they found, but only three were ever returned (including John Major's).

Simple Truth transformed the British Red Cross, just as Oxfam had been galvanized by the Hunger £Million campaign in 1963. Until then, the organization had been a 'sleeping giant', in John Gray's words, 'and suddenly it awoke to an opportunity. I often say to Jeffrey that if we hadn't had the Simple Truth concert, or something of that magnitude, we would never be in the situation where we are today.'[8] From 70,000 individual donors in 1991, the charity now has around 600,000.

At a press conference six weeks later Jeffrey Archer held up a placard proclaiming the total he and the British Red Cross claimed to have made: £57,042,000. It was the second-highest sum ever announced by a British appeal, surpassing Bob Geldof's £48 million from Live Aid, and exceeded only by the £67 million raised by Sport Aid in 1986. 'I don't know how many lives we saved,' said Archer. 'I do know it's been the most worthwhile cause of my life.'[9]

According to the Red Cross, the Simple Truth income broke down as follows:[10]

| UK: | £ |
|---|---|
| British government | 10,000,000 |
| Individual and corporate donations | 3,167,000 |
| Commercial activities and TV sales | 665,000 |
| FOREIGN: | |
| Governments | 31,468,000 |
| Individual and corporate donations | 11,742,000 |
| TOTAL | 57,042,000 |

Of that total, almost £26 million could undoubtedly be attributed to Simple Truth (comprising £10 million from the British government, almost £12 million from private foreign sources, and £3.8 million raised from British donations and commercial activities). What proved to be much more controversial was the £31,468,000 – more than half the total – which Archer and the British Red Cross claimed to have raised from eleven foreign governments. This, the charity said, was the result of his personal diplomacy. But Archer has never revealed which governments gave this £31 million, let alone *how much* they each donated. Moreover, none of it was ever handled by the Simple Truth appeal; instead, it was sent directly to the UN.

Just as there are doubts about just how much Archer contributed to the Oxfam campaign in 1963, so the question is prompted about whether it is really accurate to attribute these funds to the Simple Truth venture at all. Many observers suspect that governments had already earmarked many of these contributions for the Kurds anyway, and that the money was not given specifically because of Archer's efforts. John Gray cites the example of how the novelist supposedly persuaded the Japanese government to contribute:

All I know is that he used to come back from one of his journeys, or one of his meetings, and say, 'The Japanese ambassador has said he will get the government to give 10 million, or 5 million.' I remember that very powerfully, and we had no reason to doubt that, none at all . . . Now it's quite likely the Japanese government were going to give money anyway, but the button was pressed to have it linked to that particular appeal, and that happened in about ten countries, I believe.[11]

Colin Adamson of the London *Evening Standard* later contacted the Japanese and several other governments – including those of the United States, Germany, France, Australia, Italy, Spain and Switzerland – but could not find a single one which confirmed it had given money to Simple Truth. Nor did the UN High Commission for Refugees have any record of donations made in the name of Simple Truth. According to a spokesman, 'We have a very careful and detailed accounting system which tells us how much came from each government. The name Simple Truth does not appear anywhere on our accounts.'[12] 'I suspect they [the governments] probably would have given money anyway,' says John Gray. 'What Jeffrey did was to push the urgency – and it was urgent then – and he did that highly successfully, and he may have got more money than they would have given normally.'[13]

Archer said he had correspondence in his possession from each foreign government and the United Nations to support his claims. 'I have received a letter . . . from the UN confirming they have received £36 million from governments in response to Simple Truth,' he said.[14] (This was the £31 million from overseas governments, plus the half of the British government's donation which went to the UN.) But he refused to release copies of these letters, claiming to have 'guaranteed complete confidentiality to those who sent them'. He added that disclosing the figures would only produce an international league table of donations which would be a 'pointless exercise which could open the door to prejudice and misinterpretation'.[15]

Nevertheless, it seems strange that not one of Archer's eleven overseas donor governments has ever acknowledged giving money to Simple Truth, especially since a lot of foreign administrations are rather less restricted by official secrecy than Britain's. Indeed, one would expect foreign politicians to trumpet the fact in the way John Major did. 'Maybe with hindsight,' Archer said, 'I should have said to every single person promising money to pledge it under the name Simple Truth. But what I said was please give to the Kurds. After all, they were the ones who really mattered. Maybe I made a mistake.'[16]

By claiming that he and Simple Truth had raised so much money, Archer had raised expectations and created a serious problem for himself. Less than four months after the Wembley concert, the rumbling began as to why so little of the £57 million seemed to have reached the three-quarters of a million refugees in Kurdistan. Twice Archer postponed a trip to the region to discover how much money had got there.

One problem was that only £7 million of the £57 million total was administered by the Simple Truth organizers and the British Red Cross. They provided details of how it had been distributed to other charities such as Oxfam and Christian Aid, and also explained how, within a week of Wembley, it had been sent in direct aid: 18 lorries, 4,000 tents, 49,000 blankets, and large quantities of medicine and food.

Another £37 million – the donations from governments, plus £1 million from the British Red Cross – went straight to the United Nations. This was a sure recipe for delay and waste. The UN had a Memorandum of Understanding with Saddam Hussein on the way in which they could operate in Iraqi Kurdistan; this was due to expire at the end of 1991, and the UN were constrained by fears that it might not be renewed. Moreover, UN bodies are scrupulous about dealing at official exchange rates, which in the case of the Iraqi dinar was around thirty times the market rate. This meant that in effect the Kurds were getting only one-thirtieth of the possible benefit. John Gray admits he will never be certain whether all the Simple Truth money sent to the UN actually got to Kurdistan. 'I can never answer that. I just hope that, as an organization, the UN were able to deliver the goods. I think there will always be a question there, because the UN never publish their accounts . . . I don't think it will ever be resolved.'[17]

In October, one British aid agency involved in helping Kurdistan – the Kurdish Disaster Fund – wrote to Archer asking what had happened to the money. Three weeks later, having had no reply, they vented their frustration in a full-page ad in *The Guardian* which took the form of an open letter. 'Dear Mr Archer, Kurdish children are still dying,' it declared:

> Mr Archer, our people are puzzled.
> So much money and yet, for nearly a million Kurds still stranded in the mountains, or camped in the ruins of their family homes, not nearly enough help has reached them.
> Why not? They don't understand and neither do we.[18]

With the harsh mountain winter only weeks away, shelters promised by the UN High Commissioner for Refugees had not yet arrived. There were fears, too, that a lot of the money had gone into the general UN fund for humanitarian aid for the whole region, not just Kurdistan. Above all, the open letter raised the worrying possibility that some of the funds might have gone to the Iraqi Red Crescent, which was effectively controlled by Saddam Hussein. 'Mr Archer, £57 million is a lot of money,' the open letter pleaded:

> It was enough to have solved our people's problems.
>
> We know that you – and the British Red Cross – have acted honourably and impeccably throughout.
>
> You must be as concerned as we are, that the Kurdish refugees have seen hardly any of the huge sums of money raised in the West in their name.[19]

'It's a very hard question to answer,' Archer admitted, when asked why so little money had reached Kurdistan. 'The honest answer is I don't know. But I'll do everything I can to find out.'[20] Three days later, at a British Red Cross presentation in Westminster, he addressed a sceptical audience of journalists and aid workers, but managed only to increase the uncertainty. It would later be reported that much of the relief supplies had been plundered by Iraqi troops, and even by Saddam Hussein and his family.[21]

Archer and the British Red Cross had become victims of their over-enthusiasm. They were bound to face criticism when it became obvious that nowhere near £57 million had reached the Kurds. Even the Kurdish leader Massoud Barzani, normally a diplomatic man, said Archer should have 'got more involved' in ensuring the Simple Truth funds got to his people.[22] Many Kurds were astounded at Archer's naïve faith in the UN.

In January 1992 Archer finally embarked on his long-awaited trip to Kurdistan, travelling via Turkey. He was carrying a letter from John Major to Massoud Barzani, which seemed to confer a semi-official status on his mission, though the Foreign Office insisted it was a private visit. Any misgivings the Kurdish leadership may have felt about the way the Simple Truth money had been handled were heavily outweighed by their gratitude that a political figure of some stature and influence was interested in their plight.

Deep snow on the narrow mountain passes delayed the journey for almost three days. Still dressed in jacket and tie, Archer was determined to deliver John Major's letter to Barzani: bad weather wasn't going to stop him. 'He got out of the car,' Nadhim Zahawi recalls, 'and started digging snow off the mountain and pushing the cars, the ones that were slipping, up the hill.'[23] Shoving, shouting, gesticulating, cajoling, scolding, demonstrating how it should be done, the man who'd failed in his teenage attempt to become an army officer tried to get the convoy of Kurds and British journalists to obey his orders:

> 'Right, I want you in here. Yes I'm talking to you! Are those wheels straight? Good. Now you. Jump up here and push . . . Yes, push! Harder, man, push harder! Good. Through you go. Go, I said! Now you. Off the road, please. Very good. We're winning, you know. Splendid people the Kurds. But no leadership. That's the problem.'[24]

Massoud Barzani had sent an escort – a man Archer quickly nicknamed 'The Commander' – to bring the party through. He was a senior figure – an effective, though quiet, man – but Archer couldn't understand why he didn't do more to get things moving. 'Right, Commander,' he cried. 'Let's get this sorted out!'[25]

'Jeffrey Archer started complaining to him,' says one observer, Tom Hardie-Forsyth – '"Why don't you give orders and start shouting?" Archer got a lot of backs up by barking orders. He didn't appreciate the vast difference in culture.'[26] The military methods drummed into Jeffrey on the Halifax parade-ground in 1958 did not endear him to senior Kurdish officials. Several complained to British reporters about his rudeness.

The convoy had to turn round at one stage, whereupon Archer demanded that American military forces should fly him by helicopter to Barzani's headquarters in Sulaymaniyah. 'They would have done, if he'd been nice about it,' says Hardie-Forsyth, a former British officer who had recently resigned over government policy towards Kurdistan and was now an adviser there.[27]

Yet, everywhere Archer went, thousands of people greeted him, with banners saying things such as 'Thanks Sir Gefry Archor'. As he visited refugee camps and the flattened city of Halabja, he was genuinely shocked; at one point a crowd of women, all dressed in black, rushed up waving photos of husbands they hadn't seen since the day they had suddenly disappeared eight years before.

Archer also addressed public rallies. He promised to press the British government and the UN to extend the allied exclusion zone in northern Iraq south from the Thirty-Sixth to the Thirty-Fifth Parallel, and also for the lifting of sanctions against the Kurdish part of the country.

At some meetings, attempting a little Kurdish, he tried to get the crowd to chant 'Long Live Kurdistan!'; due to a slight mispronunciation, however, his words came out as the equivalent of 'Bastard Kurdistan!' Fortunately most Kurds were more bewildered than offended.

The biggest event was held in a large open-air amphitheatre where several thousand people turned up, mainly to hear Massoud Barzani. As the Kurdish Democratic Party leader introduced Archer, the crowd began shouting his name, and there was the occasional burst of friendly gunfire. Basking in the adulation, Archer punched the air and called for a 'Free Kurdistan'.

This was politically embarrassing, since independence went beyond the demands of the Kurds' own leaders, who were asking for no more than semi-autonomy. The news certainly did not please the Foreign Office, since British diplomats then had to assure the Turks that Archer was not signalling a change in government policy. Britain is firmly opposed to the creation of an independent Kurdish state and the break-up of Iraq, in the belief that this would only increase instability in the region.

In contemplating their future, the Kurds and their supporters in the West have long discussed ways of achieving greater economic self-sufficiency, particularly through the oil and gas reserves which lie beneath their soil. The issue was reawakened by the fact that Kurdish refugees desperately needed heating-fuel, and yet there was untapped oil right under their feet. Early in 1992 Archer was drawn into negotiations to help the Kurds develop these natural resources on a large scale.

The whole issue is fraught with difficulties: legal, technical, financial, logistical and political. First, the Kurds in northern Iraq have suffered a double blockade, both from the UN sanctions against Iraq and from Saddam Hussein's own economic restrictions on his Kurdish population. Even without these obstacles, the rugged terrain would still make it extremely difficult to transport the technology to tap the reserves. Then, even in the unlikely event that refineries and pipelines could be installed in Kurdistan, they would be an easy target for Saddam Hussein.

On the other hand, the oil and gas beneath Kurdish territory could produce handsome rewards. It is not just a question of easing the terrible conditions of Kurdish refugees: in the long term, the revenues would be a vital step towards Kurdish semi-autonomy or independence.

Archer acted as an intermediary in a long chain designed to link Kurdish leaders with an American oil company. His friend Henry Togna says that Jeffrey approached him, knowing he had oil contacts, to ask if he knew anybody who might help. Tom Hardie-Forsyth says Archer

30. Andrina Colquhoun, his former personal assistant.

31. Monica Coghlan is offered a packet of £50 notes by Archer's emissary, Michael Stacpoole, at Victoria station in 1986. The gift was said to be £2,000, a deliberately cautious estimate by the *News of the World* on legal grounds. Both Coghlan and Stacpoole agree the wad was at least three-quarters of an inch thick.

32. Coffee for journalists waiting outside the Old Vicarage after the *News of the World* broke the Monica Coghlan story. Despite their troubles the Archers staged this scene three times for the benefit of photographers who had missed it earlier!

33. Archer bought a controlling interest in the Playhouse Theatre for more than £1 million in 1988, but sold the building four years later because it was taking up too much of his time and losing money.

34. Archer's long-lost brother, David Brown, at his second wedding in 1988. Brown, who is six years older than Jeffrey, finally met Lola again when the relationship became public in 1994.

35. By January 1996 Archer had still not made contact with Brown, but he had taken great pleasure in buying the original of this Jak cartoon.

"Actually I'm a third cousin of Jeffrey Archer, but we try to keep quiet about it!"

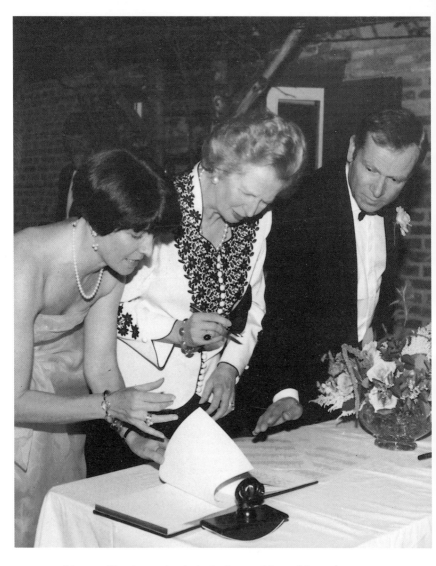

36. Margaret Thatcher at the Archer's silver wedding celebration in 1991. Few Tories remain as close to both Thatcher and John Major, and Archer has acted as a go-between.

37. Archer was always much better at Rugby than cricket. He occasionally coaches mini-Rugby and referees a few minor matches each season.

38. Mary's silver wedding present to Jeffrey, a grotesque installed on the folly in Grantchester.

39. Dr Archer enjoying the limelight in television cabaret in 1991.

40. Visiting Kurdistan in 1992 to investigate what happened to the £57 million he claimed to have raised from the Simple Truth Campaign. Behind Archer's right shoulder is Broosk Saib, the Kurdish aide with whom he made almost £80,000 profit dealing in Anglia TV shares in 1994.

41. Weston peer. Baron Archer of Weston-super-Mare of Mark in the County of Somerset, with his mother in 1993.

42. Questioned by the author for BBC 2's *Newsnight* during the 1993 Newbury
by-election.

also contacted him in the spring of 1992, offering to introduce 'some business friends' who might be able to resolve the deadlock over Kurdish energy resources. Hardie-Forsyth consulted Massoud Barzani, who asked him to explore the matter further with Archer.

To handle the deal, Henry Togna set up a Panamanian company called SETCO – Systems Engineering and Technology Co. – which was in turn a subsidiary of a firm called Gulf Resources. The chairman of Gulf Resources, Hani Salaam, is a wealthy Lebanese entrepreneur who had once employed Togna in America, and now played a critical part in the Kurdish negotiations.

The spring and summer of 1992 saw a series of meetings involving Hardie-Forsyth, Archer, Togna and Salaam. These were sometimes held at Alembic House, and on other occasions at Henry Togna's hotel in Jermyn Street, near Piccadilly Circus. On one occasion Hardie-Forsyth even travelled to Kurdistan with an oil engineer to carry out a preliminary geological survey.

Tom Hardie-Forsyth says he was encouraged to pursue the idea because he was led to believe that SETCO had heavyweight support, both financial and political. They talked of receiving 'the quiet nod from the US State Department', he says, and indications that Washington would be willing to lift sanctions to help the scheme.[28] This tacit approval, they maintained, had been obtained through two former American ambassadors with good contacts in the Middle East: Robert Oakley and Ed Djerejian.

It appears that SETCO also claimed to have the support of the American oil giant Occidental, which already had extensive business links with Gulf Resources. 'They made the Occidental and State Department claims on numerous occasions,' says Hardie-Forsyth, who adds that Archer suggested that he believed the scheme would also be likely to get British approval.[29]

Eventually Hardie-Forsyth persuaded the main Kurdish representatives in London, Latif Rashid and Mohsin Dizayee, to come to Alembic House to conclude a preliminary deal with Archer and his colleagues. There, the SETCO directors produced a draft mandate, which they hoped would ultimately be signed by the rival Kurdish leaders, Massoud Barzani and Jalal Talabani. It proposed to grant SETCO 'exclusive authority to explore for, produce, export and sell oil, gas and other mineral resources situate on, under and within the area known as Kurdistan . . .' No money was mentioned in the document, but it stipulated that all subsequent contracts which arose from the agreement would last 'for not less than twenty-five years'.[30]

However, the Kurds felt that SETCO's proposed terms were excessively onerous. Apart from its exclusivity, the agreement covered other minerals as well as oil and gas, and lasted too long. Togna argues that the proposed agreement was 'standard industry practice' and reasonable given the high risks involved: 'We tried to get them to give us an exclusive mandate so that we could send a team in to do some initial research.'[31]

The Kurds were also perturbed about the lack of solid evidence for the political and corporate support that SETCO claimed; they were equally puzzled as to why meetings took place in Togna's hotel or Archer's flat rather than at a company office. When they asked for some documentary proof that the scheme was supported by Occidental and Washington, Hardie-Forsyth says Archer got upset that his word was being doubted. 'Jeffrey Archer insisted it was all bona fide . . . They said it was too sensitive to produce a piece of paper saying that they were fronting for Occidental, and got uppity when questioned about it.'[32] Togna agrees that the question of proving their backing was a significant obstacle.

As negotiations broke down, Hardie-Forsyth decided to explore SETCO's claims for himself and spoke to two American diplomatic contacts. They denied any knowledge of SETCO, he says, and were adamant that the US would never lift sanctions for such a venture.

Henry Togna, on the other hand, explains that it is a complicated issue and inevitably delicate, given sanctions. Officially, he concedes, the State Department did say it was not sensible to continue talking to the Kurds, but he adds that SETCO were also getting unofficial signals from Washington that made them feel it was worth devoting time and money to the project. In particular, they had been given certain information which could only have been released with official approval.[33]

However, when the former US diplomat Robert Oakley heard that he was being cited in support of SETCO's claims, he sent a terse fax from Washington to Archer's associate, Hani Salaam:

Erroneous reports circulating in London Kurdish circles have reached key people here. These reports allege that I have said Occidental Petroleum has a concession for N. Iraq which has been approved for operation by the State Department as an exemption to the UN sanctions. State Department is taking steps to correct these reports, stating that: 1. it has no knowledge of an Occidental concession; 2. there has as yet been no application by the Kurds for sanctions relief with respect to oil and gas operations; 3. if and when such an application is received, it will be considered, but it is up to the UN to approve or disapprove . . .

My credibility (and yours) seems still to be intact with the State Department, but barely . . . Perhaps there is an explanation for the extreme distortion, but the main point is to set the record straight.[34]

Oakley says it was being claimed that he had helped to arrange a deal involving the State Department and Occidental, when all he did was advise Hani Salaam on the political climate in Washington and on the chances of a deal being approved. Salaam 'was an old friend', Oakley asserts, whom he had known since he was posted to the US embassy in Beirut in the early 1970s. 'Somebody was exaggerating,' he adds. 'I'm not necessarily sure it was Salaam, but others.'[35]

Tom Hardie-Forsyth was rather less diplomatic, and wrote to John Major threatening to reveal details of Archer's negotiations. 'The whole business,' he warned, 'has deeply hurt some of the prospects of the Kurdish democratic experiment with which I am intimately involved.'[36]

Jeffrey Archer and his colleagues insist he merely acted as a sympathetic intermediary, to help the Kurds make contact with an oil company. When challenged by Tom Hardie-Forsyth a year later, Archer said he hadn't had much to do with the proposed deal. 'I was never part of it,' he said, and then added rather confusingly, 'but I was part of it, you're quite right.'[37] His colleagues had mainly been responsible, he argued, not him, and it was Hani Salaam who dealt with Robert Oakley and Occidental.

In a document which emerged later, attached to a copy of the proposed mandate, Archer was described as chairman of SETCO and Togna as its president. Archer said he was unaware that his name had been used in this way, adding that if the chairmanship of SETCO had been offered to him he would have turned it down.[38]

'Jeffrey Archer would never, ever profit from the Kurds,' says his young Kurdish associate Nadhim Zahawi. 'The Kurds came to him for help; he pointed them in the right direction, but there was never, ever, any way that he would actually get involved in any financial reward or any type of reward.'[39] And although Kurdish officials in London were clearly unhappy about the terms they were offered, they do not criticize Archer.

The Foreign Office, meanwhile, remained unconcerned about the affair. The Overseas Development Administration had studied the prospects for oil in Kurdistan, but British diplomats dismissed the possibility of exploiting the reserves, and were therefore not very interested in Archer's dealings through SETCO. When Kurdish representatives told the Foreign Office they didn't think they were being offered a good deal, they were advised not to worry since nothing would happen anyway.

In January 1994 Jeffrey Archer made a second visit to the region. This time he had persuaded the government to allow an official to travel with his party. The Foreign Office again maintained it was a private visit, but felt that the presence of one of their people enabled them to keep an eye on Archer, as well as being a useful way of showing the Kurds that Britain was still concerned about them. But Archer was ungrateful when the Middle East desk offered him a briefing beforehand: 'I don't need a briefing on the Kurds,' he told them. 'I brief *you* on the Kurds.'

Archer seemed to have learned little about dealing tactfully with the Kurds either. 'He's so incredibly impatient,' says one of those who travelled with the group and witnessed Archer's frustration at the restrictions *en route*. 'When the cars going through south-eastern Turkey were searched for about the twenty-fifth time, he started getting out and shouting at a Turkish conscript of eighteen or nineteen. He's a man who could get himself shot. He doesn't have any caution ... His attitude was: "Let's get these stupid people out of the way. Let's get on."'

On this second visit, accompanied by his eldest son, Will, he addressed the Kurdish parliament and read out a letter from John Major reaffirming Britain's support for the safe havens in northern Iraq. 'We know the phrase that Kurds have no friends but the mountains,' he told the newly elected assembly. 'This is no longer true. You have friends all over the world and I am proud to be the Englishman chosen to tell you that.'[40]

But yet again Archer couldn't help adopting the air of an imperial governor. 'My Kurds', he would describe them to accompanying reporters; and to the Kurds the press were 'my senior journalists'. In Irbil, Archer met Marigold Curling, a London pathologist who was in the Kurdish capital to give evidence at the trial of a man accused of murdering her daughter Rosanna and two other members of a BBC film crew. Archer told Curling it was a great pity that the trial coincided with his visit, since 'all my journalists' were writing about it. 'It looks like you've stolen my thunder,' Curling recalls him saying.[41]

Despite Archer's undiplomatic behaviour, and the trouble he has caused to Britain's relations with Turkey, the Foreign Office look favourably on his efforts overall. 'Much of his energy on the whole is rather good,' says one British diplomat. 'He's been a help in that he kept it in the media; that's what keeps us there and keeps the Americans there . . . Anything that keeps it on top of the agenda is only helpful. I think the emotion he has about it is genuine.'

Archer is undoubtedly immensely popular in Kurdistan: he returned from his second visit through the red channel at Heathrow because of the many fine gifts with which he had been showered. Ordinary Kurdish refugees seemed almost as enthusiastic to greet 'Lord Archie' or 'Lord Arthur' in 1994 as they had been in 1992. 'Mr Archer is a dear,' proclaimed one of the welcoming banners. 'See how they love me,' Jeffrey boasted to his entourage.[42]

The novelist has promised to work for the Kurds for the rest of his life, and since the Simple Truth appeal the region and its people have continued to be important to him. Nadhim Zahawi and Broosk Saib have both stayed on close terms, with the latter sometimes acting as Archer's butler on social occasions. Zahawi became a close friend of Jamie Archer, and Jeffrey helped his successful campaign to become a Conservative councillor in Wandsworth in 1994. The Kurdish part of Iraq was also a setting for Archer's 1993 novel, *Honour Among Thieves*. And, since he became a peer in 1992, almost half of Archer's interventions in the House of Lords have involved Kurdistan or Iraq.

Indeed, few other British parliamentarians have taken as much interest in the Kurds as Archer has since 1991, and the Kurds are grateful for an advocate who can raise their concerns with the Foreign Secretary or the Prime Minister. Because of this, they are willing to forget the SETCO episode.

'He has drawn attention to the fate of the Kurdish people in political and media circles,' says Latif Rashid, the most senior Kurd in London, who took part in the SETCO talks. 'We appreciate what he's done for us.'[43]

# 27

# Stand and Deliver!

He had a special task to perform, Jeffrey Archer explained to journalist friends in Blackpool that week. As Michael Heseltine was still recovering from the heart attack he'd suffered that summer, the Industry Secretary couldn't deliver his traditional barnstorming conference speech. And quite frankly, as Archer intimated during the usual round of Conservative receptions and parties, no other member of the Cabinet was up to the job. Yet somebody needed to lift the spirits of the party loyalists and bring the audience to their feet. He would have to do it himself.

What better occasion than that traditional Tory cauldron of anger, passion and raw prejudice – the annual law and order debate? They cheered as he walked to the rostrum. 'Home Secretary – Michael, if I may,' he began jokily. And then, adopting a more serious tone, with half-moon spectacles perched on the end of his nose, he declared:

> I'm sick and tired of being told by old people that they're frightened to go out at night; they're frightened to answer their doors day or night; they're even frightened to walk through parks and fairways that their parents and their grandparents took for granted.

Retired people had the right to live 'in dignity and not in fear', he cried, and then condemned 'our ridiculously loose attitude towards bail'. The Home Secretary, Michael Howard, was on the platform listening, preparing to unveil a package of tough anti-crime measures. As he reached his climax, the one-time Metropolitan policeman looked up. 'Michael,' he demanded – 'stand and deliver!'[1]

The Conservative audience roared, and stood, and smiled, and applauded, and cheered, and felt good. Michael Howard clapped politely; the speech had ostensibly been intended to help him, but Archer had come dangerously close to upstaging the Home Secretary, and had only increased the pressure on him to 'deliver' something substantial. 'It was hard for Michael Howard after that,' admits Archer's then political aide, Nick Archer.[2]

The peer had taken more than twice the time allowed for floor speakers – nine minutes instead of four – but this included sixteen separate bursts of applause, which, he explained later, added up to almost three minutes. Towards the end the audience were clapping almost every sentence, and when he finished, the beaming Archer got a forty-five-second standing ovation as he walked along the front row clasping hands. He'd spent a month working on the speech, rewriting it again and again just like one of his novels. His words had been crafted brilliantly: a clever mix of humour, populist pandering and serious policy. And, while others spent the conference speculating about challenges to the leadership, Archer had pointedly included a resounding endorsement of John Major.

As intended, his address was one of the highlights of the conference. Surprisingly perhaps, commentators did not observe how singularly inappropriate it was, in a debate on crime, to cry 'Stand and deliver!', the call of the eighteenth-century mugger, the highwayman. But Archer's demand was not directed solely at Michael Howard. The underlying, unstated message, of course, was that it was also time for the Prime Minister to 'deliver' him a job.

It was seven years since he'd resigned as Conservative deputy chairman –'wilderness years', he called them – and Jeffrey Archer felt he had earned redemption. There can scarcely have been a constituency association that he hadn't visited, and a map in his office highlighted each location. He prided himself, too, on never missing a by-election, and he claimed to the author in Newbury in May 1993 that he had contributed to the last sixty-seven by-election campaigns – though by the next one, in Christchurch, three months later, this figure had mysteriously shrunk by a dozen or so. Neither number was right, for he certainly missed the Richmond campaign in January 1989, which seven years later was still the last by-election the Conservatives had won.

Even though Archer had won his libel actions against both *The Star* and the *News of the World*, there was no question, in the aftermath, of his returning to Central Office. Even if the jury had concluded that Archer had never slept with Monica Coghlan, he had still made the admitted misjudgement of trying to give her money to go abroad. If Archer had been appointed to any political post, it would only have attracted critical media attention. Far better, they thought in Downing Street, to let things cool down for a while.

There were still press rumours, of course. For example, during the autumn of 1988 several papers suggested that Margaret Thatcher might appoint Archer ambassador to the United States. The speculation was led by Trevor Kavanagh, the political editor of *The Sun* and a good contact of Archer's. He quoted the chairman of the British branch of the US Republican Party, John Woods, as saying the appointment would go down well in Washington. Woods, who is also a friend of the novelist, maintains that the suggestion was first floated with him by contacts in both the Reagan White House and the State Department. There was 'a certain logic behind that idea', he argues, for Archer was not only close to Margaret Thatcher and well known in America, he was also on good terms with several leading US politicians.[3] Yet the prospect of the novelist becoming ambassador to Washington seems farfetched. Given Margaret Thatcher's worries about Archer's gaffe-making, it is hard to believe she would have entrusted him with the one international relationship she prized above all others.

When Thatcher's leadership ran on to the rocks in the autumn of 1990, Archer was particularly well placed, having already established excellent relations with one of the favourites for the succession – the Chancellor of the Exchequer, John Major. The two men had first met before Major's election as MP for Huntingdon in 1979, when the retiring member, David Renton, invited Archer to speak at an inaugural dinner for his successor. Their friendship developed quickly, aided by Grantchester's being only twenty-five minutes' drive from Major's home in Huntingdon.

It was perhaps to be expected that the two men should get on, since the parallels between them – both personal and political – are striking. Both were born to fathers who were already old at the time – Archer's was sixty-four and Major's sixty-three – and who died when their sons were still teenagers. Archer and Major both came from lower-middle-class backgrounds, with strong streaks of show business, but had parents who were determined to give them a private education. Yet neither boy made much of the opportunity, and both left school with a handful of O-levels and little prospect of university. Like Archer, John Major spent several years after leaving school simply drifting, but with vague political ambitions.

Perhaps the most significant similarity is that both men regarded themselves as outsiders when they became active in the Conservative Party in the 1960s. They resented the aristocratic and upper-middle-class party élite who'd been to the leading public schools and felt they had the right to govern. Both have been the victims of snobbery about their relatively humble backgrounds, their meagre qualifications and their lack of formal education. Archer himself once revealed how:

> I didn't like in my youth that there were these people with double-barrelled names who seemed to be living in a different world to the one I did, and when you went up to London there were even more of them with their noses in the air. I so much agree with John Major that snobbery must be got rid of – I think a lot of it has been got rid of – but I hate it in every form.[4]

Both started as councillors in London in the late 1960s, and both gained seats in eastern England, but Major and Archer were drawn together not just by their backgrounds, but also by a common type of Conservatism. Neither is an ideological politician; both began their careers on the left of the party, and then found themselves drawn to the right by the force of Thatcherism, particularly on economics.

Accounts of John Major's career often credit Norman Tebbit with being the first person publicly to predict he might become party leader.[5] In fact Jeffrey Archer was almost a year ahead of his old Central Office boss. In October 1986 *Private Eye* quoted the journalist Julie Burchill as saying that Archer had told her John Major was 'the coming man . . . a possible future leader even'. The *Eye* thought this was such a preposterous idea – Major was then an obscure social-security minister – that they assumed Burchill was mistaken, and that Archer had actually tipped John Moore, the then Transport Secretary and a rising political star, who subsequently disappeared virtually without trace.[6]

Archer himself likes to tell the story of an occasion in the mid-1980s when he and John Major were both invited to lunch at Chequers by Margaret Thatcher. One of the waitresses requested Archer's autograph, whereupon he asked her if she knew who the man standing next to him was. When the embarrassed woman admitted that she didn't, Archer reportedly advised, 'You'd better get his autograph because he will live here one day.'[7]

Once John Major reached the Cabinet in 1987, as Chief Secretary to the Treasury, the two men saw more of each other. They would watch cricket together at Lord's, and Major joined the group of people whom Archer asked to read his draft manuscripts. Later, while Chancellor of the Exchequer, John Major performed a small ceremony in the back garden in Grantchester, reopening the folly which Archer had just restored.

The then Chancellor even seems to have given his friend tax advice. 'He was very helpful,' Archer said in 1993. 'When I was about to sign my three-book contract, I let him see it . . . Of course, he wasn't looking at the publishing clauses. He was Secretary of State at the Treasury, so his advice was about spreading out the money, from a tax and inflation standpoint.'[8] It is an astonishing claim. The Chancellor of the Exchequer, responsible for filling the government's coffers, was apparently telling his multimillionaire friend how to contribute less tax.

During the two weeks that shook British politics – the 1990 Tory leadership crisis – John Major was absent for much of the early drama, recovering at home in his constituency from an operation on a difficult tooth, and reading an early draft of *As the Crow Flies*. The day before the first leadership ballot, in which Michael Heseltine challenged Margaret Thatcher, Archer visited John and Norma Major in Huntingdon, and stayed until late afternoon. They enjoyed a lunch of moussaka and jelly, and then, according to Archer, he mentioned the unthinkable: that Thatcher might be forced out.

> When I brought it up and said, 'You know, there's just an outside chance she won't win. Have you thought about that?' And he said, 'Oh, no!' He was fairly confident she would win. And I said, 'Which would mean you should consider standing as Prime Minister.' And he said, 'One has to put a lot of thought in before you take on that job.' . . . He said, 'You've got to think of the way it will react with your family and your own life – whether it's worth sacrificing everything to do the job.'[9]

Two days later, after Thatcher had indeed fared badly against Heseltine, Archer was again close to the centre of events. The problem arose of how to get her nomination paper for the next ballot to John Major in Huntingdon, so that he could again second her candidature. Downing Street officials insisted it would be improper to use a government car, since the poll was purely a party matter. Thatcher's political secretary, John Whittingdale, mentioned the problem to Archer, who immediately volunteered the services of his driver. On arrival at Major's house, the chauffeur waited for more than an hour and a half while the Chancellor held fevered discussions with Number Ten over whether his signature would still be needed. (Incidentally, the fact Major didn't sign for so long lends credence to the theory that he was reluctant to support Thatcher again.) Eventually it was agreed that Major might as well sign anyway.

Jeffrey Archer himself was addressing a party meeting in south London that night, and when his driver finally returned with the signed form Archer went to bed with the document on his bedside table, intending to deliver it to Number .Ten first thing the next day. He couldn't get to sleep, however, and at around 1 a.m. he got dressed and took it round to Downing Street:

> I handed the envelope to Peter Morrison [Thatcher's PPS] and he took it and tossed it to one side, and carried on with the conversation. The significance is the tossing aside. If she had been standing – rip it open, check the names, get it into a file, see the chairman of the '22 gets it. 'Do we want to ring Cranley Onslow now?' They did none of those things. The decision that she should bring it to an end had been made.[10]

Thatcher announced her resignation later that morning. A few days later, Archer presented her with a first edition of Dickens's *A Tale of Two Cities* to commemorate her departure. By then he had already transferred his allegiance to John Major's campaign, and was given the specific role of liaising with the several Fleet Street editors he counted among his friends. This involved both passing on information from the Major camp and gleaning intelligence that had been picked up by the newspapers about whom various Tory MPs were supporting. 'At that time he was probably one of the best sources for any Fleet Street editor,' says John Bryant, who was then in charge of the short-lived *Sunday Correspondent* and spoke to Archer every day during the contest.[11]

Archer also found himself bearing a message from Margaret Thatcher to John Major that 'I do hope his campaign is going well.'[12] It was the first open sign that she wanted her Chancellor to win, and it was not the last time that Archer would act as a go-between for the leaders old and new.

An out-going Prime Minister has the privilege of a resignation honours list, to reward those who have been of political assistance over the years. Archer was pencilled in for a peerage on Margaret Thatcher's original list, and the fact was soon leaked to the press. But after Thatcher's nominees had been vetted by the Political Honours Scrutiny Committee (consisting of Lords Pym, Shackleton and Grimond) his name had disappeared. Archer's former UNA antagonist Humphry Berkeley told Grimond he would raise no objection, but the three peers apparently felt that his elevation would not go down well among colleagues in the Upper House.

Archer was one of several nominations to be queried, in fact; it appears that, in the tussles between the committee and Thatcher's office, his peerage was sacrificed to ensure honours for other candidates that were also challenged, such as his friend the property developer Peter Palumbo, who did go to the Lords. Strictly speaking, Thatcher could have tried to override the Scrutiny Committee by submitting her list directly to the Palace, but this would have embarrassed the Queen. Instead, she was persuaded it was best to omit Archer, knowing that John Major was likely to reward him later.

Whereas Jeffrey and Mary Archer had previously been regular Boxing Day guests of the Thatchers at Chequers, now they joined John and Norma Major for their first New Year's Day there in 1991. But, despite speculation, Archer was omitted both from the regular honours announced that morning and from the two other lists that John Major issued between then and the April 1992 election.

During that campaign Archer supplemented his usual constituency tours with regular assistance at the Prime Minister's evening meetings, where he acted as the warm-up man, delivering his usual polished, joky performance before introducing his party leader. He also coached various 'celebrities' who were booked to support the PM – actors from soap operas, for instance, or industrialists such as Sir Alistair Grant, the chairman of Safeway. He would listen to their proposed speeches and then help rewrite them, suggesting improvements (often quite radical ones). Although these celebrities had 'no terrors about an audience', says the Conservative vice-chairman, Sir Geoffrey Pattie:

> They were quite alarmed because, for once, they were doing their own lines, as opposed to somebody else's. And so they needed quite a bit of gentle taking to bits and putting together again . . . Jeffrey's got this kind of ability. I mean, he can say rude and direct things to people in a moderately cheerful way, and they will take it from him.[13]

The 1992 campaign was a difficult one for the Conservatives, and throughout it they were widely expected to lose. Though Major himself was always confident of victory, Archer was a welcome, upbeat presence amid the general gloom of the Tory high command, where there was widespread speculation about the possibility of defeat.

After his surprise victory, John Major created a new government ministry under the stewardship of his and Jeffrey's close friend David Mellor. The Department of National Heritage took over responsibility not just for the arts and sport but also for the proposed national lottery. There was press talk of Archer being made Minister of State there – which would have been an amusing twist, given that Mellor had once worked for him – but there is no evidence that Major ever considered this seriously.

Yet two months later, in June 1992, Archer finally achieved a life peerage. This time it had been harder for the Political Honours Scrutiny Committee to block the nomination, since, unlike Thatcher, Major proposed him as a Conservative working peer. It was also easier to justify because of Archer's fund-raising work for the Kurds. Yet Archer had never been a great supporter of the Lords, and has always been unhappy with titles. 'I'd get rid of hereditary peers,' he later said. 'I'm anti-Establishment . . . I'd have a system for keeping the ones that work. I'd get rid of those that don't work.'[14] The slightly ridiculous title he chose – Baron Archer of Weston-super-Mare of Mark in the County of Somerset – could be seen as a way of cocking a snook at the Establishment he was joining.[15]

As when he entered the Commons in 1969, the new peer was in no hurry to make an impact on the second chamber. Partly because of a long backlog of ennobled Cabinet ministers who took precedence, he couldn't take his seat until October, and then it was another two months before he delivered his maiden speech, on overseas aid.

Archer's contributions since have been no more frequent in the Lords than they were in the GLC or the House of Commons. By June 1995 Archer had made only nine speeches in the chamber. He had started as a fairly diligent attender, but during the 1994–5 session turned up on only 95 days out of 142.[16] He has also made regular use of the peers' gallery in the Commons, where he often watches John Major during Question Time and most of the important debates.

Jeffrey Archer's relationship with John Major is rather different from that with Margaret Thatcher. He is fifteen years her junior, but three years older than the Prime Minister. With Thatcher, Archer was one of the many dynamic 'likely lads' she liked to have around, whom she admired for their energy, 'can-do' attitudes and lively, entrepreneurial ideas. With Archer and Major, however, it is more a case of contemporaries, chums and equals.

Yet in many ways Archer has played a similar political role for both premiers: a source of blunt and unofficial advice, a 'plain man's opinion', independent of both Central Office and the whips. He is a cheerful, loyal figure off whom they have been able to bounce ideas – a sounding-board and occasional contributor for the big set-piece leaders' speeches. For example, when John Major practised his 1992 and 1993 conference addresses, Archer sat at the back of the private ministerial rehearsal room advising on which lines worked and which didn't.

Equally, political correspondents have found Archer of great value, in that they believe they are hearing the same opinions he is offering the Prime Minister. He is also an excellent source of political gossip – though it is rarely malicious – and he loves making journalists think that through him they are on the 'inside track'. 'I was only talking to the Prime Minister about you this morning,' one reporter recalls Archer saying. The journalist knew it was most unlikely to be true, of course, but the possibility was still flattering, and it contained the added implication that Archer and Major spoke frequently.

There is a danger, though, of exaggerating the strength of Major and Archer's relationship. 'He was not in as much as sometimes people were led to believe,' according to a former member of the Downing Street staff who says the two men tended to meet on social rather than political occasions. Even then he has not been one of the Prime Minister's closest personal friends: these tend to be people that Major and Norma have known since his early days in Brixton and his time in banking, and very few of them are prominent politicians.

A few weeks before Margaret Thatcher left Downing Street, the Archers were among a select group of twelve people invited to her sixty-fifth birthday celebrations; the friendship has continued out of office and the former Prime Minister has been a weekend guest in Grantchester. Both Margaret Thatcher and John Major attended Jeffrey and Mary's 1991 silver wedding anniversary party, but for their famous Christmas bashes, things are carefully arranged so that the two Prime Ministers don't turn up on the same night. In June 1993, when Thatcher famously let it be known that, contrary to common belief, she was still backing Major to lead the party into the next election, Jeffrey was – in his words – the 'messenger boy', entrusted with conveying the news to both Number Ten and the outside world.[17] Archer has also travelled with Thatcher on her lucrative lecture trips to Japan, and helped to promote her memoirs when they were published in the autumn of 1993. Jeffrey isn't always a welcome face, however. On one occasion when their mutual publisher, Eddie Bell, suggested Archer might introduce her at a big sales conference in America, she quickly rejected the idea, suggesting that she had seen enough of him lately.

In 1993 Archer was to assist another forceful woman who fascinates the world but feels bitterly that she's been pushed out of her rightful place: the Princess of Wales. Jeffrey Archer has always had ambivalent feelings towards the royal family. On the one hand, he's never been a great champion of the monarchy as an institution, but, on the other, he finds himself drawn to its aura and mystique. In the 1960s he worked with several royals in his charity fund-raising work, from Princess Alexandra at the National Birthday Trust to Lord Mountbatten on the Night of Nights. Despite his hatred of snobbery and protestations about being 'anti-Establishment', he is proud of the fact that his chauffeur once worked for the Sultan of Brunei, while Diana Bowes-Lyon, his secretary until recently, is a great-niece of the Queen Mother.

In December 1993 Archer was due to conduct a fund-raising auction at a lunch for one of his favourite charities, the Headway National Head Injuries Association. Diana was also due to speak, as patron of the organization, but it was expected to be a routine event for Archer. The afternoon before, however, the peer had calls from both Kensington Palace and Downing Street warning him that this would be no ordinary occasion. John Major's private secretary, Alex Allan, invited the peer to Number Ten and told him that Diana would use her speech for a personal statement. The Prime Minister, then preoccupied with the Irish peace process, wanted Archer to ensure it was not too much of an ordeal for her.

It wasn't until Archer paid a special visit to Diana the next morning that he learned what she was to say. A year after the announcement of her separation from Prince Charles, she now intended to scale down her public life considerably. Archer agreed to warn the Headway organizers that she was going to announce something important, and got them to rearrange the timetable so that his auction preceded her speech. Having raised £6,000 for a carriage clock she had donated, Archer then handed the platform over to the princess. After her speech he delivered a few words of thanks; as intended, they prompted a standing ovation, and an opportunity for her to slip away.

The *Daily Telegraph* reported Archer indirectly as saying that Diana had chosen the occasion specifically because she knew he would be conducting the function.[18] This was ludicrous. As Archer later admitted, he just happened to be there on an occasion she had already chosen. But since then Jeffrey and the princess have maintained contact through her work as vice-president of the British Red Cross. Archer also arranged for Diana to join a Red Cross excursion on the first passenger train through the Channel Tunnel.

The years of the Major administration have been probably the most troubled period endured by a peacetime government this century, as ministers have reeled from crisis to scandal and Europe has caused the Tories to be more divided than at any point since the 1930s. At times, things have been so grim that Cabinet ministers have been strangely unavailable to defend the government on radio or television. Archer has willingly batted for John Major when nobody else would. With no departmental responsibilities, he was able to speak on any subject. Equally, he could be more frank than any minister, but could be disowned by the government if necessary. From early morning on Radio 4 to late at night on *Newsnight*, he has regularly given his full support to John Major.

Earlier, in 1990, Archer achieved his long-standing ambition of a television show of his own. *Behind the Headlines* was a 'talking heads' programme, half an hour long, which went out on Thursday afternoons on BBC2. He and a Labour co-presenter – Paul Boateng initially, then Tony Banks – were meant to be deliberately provocative and partisan as they jointly questioned two expert guests on a succession of topical issues. Though Archer did not come across badly to the viewer, his Labour partners sometimes managed to dominate the discussion. In a debate about the Maastricht Treaty in December 1992, for instance, Tony Banks was left arguing with the guests while Archer hardly uttered a word; and when he did speak he seemed uncomfortable with the heady constitutional issues his colleagues were chewing over.[19]

Archer worked hard for each programme, and set aside Thursday morning to prepare for the show, diligently reading the briefing papers and cuttings prepared by BBC researchers. 'Jeffrey had to be briefed like mad,' says one of the programme team, 'and he did read it all. But he doesn't take it in – that's the trouble . . . In a sense we had to look after him, and had to think more for him than we certainly did for Tony.' Unlike Tony Banks, another producer recalls, Archer would stick to the briefing material and the suggested questions fairly rigidly, making little attempt to ad lib. 'He was not a good presenter, in the sense that he basically had to learn everything off pat. If he didn't absolutely commit it to memory, he couldn't improvise.' After four series of *Behind the Headlines* between 1990 and 1993, and around three dozen editions, the programme was brought to an end – to Archer's great disappointment.

The peer was increasingly frustrated that he wasn't doing enough. His life of writing, promoting books, media appearances, charity functions, constituency visits and the House of Lords was hardly fulfilling to a man of his ambition. He was in danger of remaining a footnote in history – the court jester, cheer-leader and political party-giver of his day. In 1992 Archer moved up three levels within Alembic House and took a lease on the thirteenth and fourteenth floors combined. He spent almost £2 million refurbishing his magnificent new, genuinely penthouse apartment. New furniture was specially built – each item slightly larger than normal, to reflect the grand scale of the location – and a marble staircase leads up to Jeffrey's study on a gallery overlooking the main room below. The new flat meant that his Krug parties were more lavish than ever, as Archer became established as the great political host – the Emerald Cunard, Lady Londonderry or Sibyl Colefax of the 1990s, or the Baroness Silvercruys, perhaps, of London. As with the great Tory hostesses of the interwar era, ministers, businessmen, editors, entertainers and even the odd archbishop flocked to his salon. Indeed, it was hard to find anyone at an Archer party who wasn't powerful or famous. And while privately some Cabinet members would admit they weren't really admirers of Archer, they were grateful at least for the way he welcomed their wives on such occasions. Jeffrey was revelling in the thick of politics, but was without power.

During 1993 he started making it clearer than ever that he no longer wanted to be a bit-player: he wanted to be centre-stage. He went further. Amid speculation that Sir Norman Fowler was likely to retire after two not very successful years as Conservative chairman, Archer was quite unabashed that he wanted the job when it became available. His supporters began stressing how he could transform Conservative finances – now deeply in the red – and Archer's campaign intensified early in 1994 when Fowler announced that he intended to leave Central Office.

Jeffrey and his young political aide, Nick Archer, decided to separate Archer-the-writer from Archer-the-politician. 'To be taken seriously as a politician,' says Nick Archer, 'the two sides had to be drawn apart.'[20] Jeffrey had already acquired a new gravitas with the half-moon spectacles which became a regular feature from around 1990. And his power base was the constituencies, where his appointment as chairman would have gone down well. A straw poll of 100 local party chairmen for the *Sunday Express* showed that forty-two of them wanted Archer to run Central Office – more than supported any other contender.[21] Indeed, Nick Archer suggests that if the Conservative Party were more democratic, and allowed ordinary members to elect the chairman, Jeffrey would have got the job long ago. He is probably right.

Jeffrey Archer had set his heart on the chairmanship, and publicly refused to contemplate any lesser position. In practice, however, he probably would have taken any job, though it was difficult to see him filling most ministerial posts. His temperament was not suited to the demanding paperwork of the daily red boxes, to handling bright civil servants or the grinding detail of many ministerial briefs. In a junior government job, with no major responsibility to call his own and confined to the Lords, Archer would inevitably have become bored. The exception, of course, would have been the Department of National Heritage, which seemed almost tailor-made for Archer's interests in sport and the arts. His work promoting the Manchester Olympic bid in 1993 was an example of the kind of prestige role he might play. And after the heritage minister Iain Sproat had mishandled the plans for the D-Day commemorations in the spring of 1994, it even looked as if there might soon be a vacancy.

Archer could also have been an ideal 'Lord Lottery' – a ministerial salesman to front the government's new money-raising scheme for the arts and sport which was due to be launched later in the year. Arguably no one was better qualified for the job, since Archer had publicly supported the idea of funding the arts with a lottery ever since his days on the GLC.

National Heritage was probably his best chance of a political job. Several sources close to John Major agree that Archer was never a serious contender for the party chairmanship, especially in the run-up to a general election. Although Archer comes across well on television and radio, and has learned to tame his inclination to say the first outrageous thing that comes into his head, he would inevitably have come under pressure from journalists and opponents hoping to provoke a headline-making gaffe. And while he might be inspirational in the constituencies, and a superb fund-raiser, Archer has never been the kind of political strategist needed to plan a campaign. Nor did he display an acute grasp of policy issues, at a time when politics was increasingly dominated by complex arguments over Europe, the economy and Ireland. Above all, with so many senior Tories deeply hostile to the idea of his appointment, Archer could never have fulfilled the principal task of a party chairman – uniting the party. The dangers were simply too great.

Indeed, Jeffrey came close to illustrating the risks in his famous 1993 'Stand and deliver!' speech. It would be a clever trick, he thought as he prepared his address, to ask the hall, 'Hands up, all of you who have been burgled in the last few years!' When he mentioned this line to colleagues beforehand, they were horrified and talked him out of it. The television pictures might well have provided one of the great moments of conference history – hundreds of Tories showing that, after fourteen years of Conservative rule, they'd been victims of crime. The propaganda value of Archer's dramatic gesture could have been enormous – at least to the Labour Party.

# 28

# Grave Error

At a lunch at Lloyd's of London in the mid-1980s, Jeffrey Archer told his fellow diners a story about himself. He had telephoned his bank one day, to ask if he could go round and see all his money. What did he mean by '*see*', the manager had enquired nervously. Well, it was quite simple: Jeffrey just wanted to drop by and look at the cash sitting in the vault. After all, didn't the bank have a legal duty to produce a customer's deposit on demand? The bewildered official went away to consult, and returned saying it wouldn't be possible. They didn't actually hold several million pounds in cash.

It was something only Jeffrey Archer could have done, and only he would tell the story afterwards. And it was, of course, a less than subtle way of reminding his listeners how much he was worth. But Archer has always been strange about money. Many wealthy people are notorious, for instance, for never having any cash, but during the libel trial Archer revealed how he keeps wads of fifty-pound notes in a safe in his flat.[1]

There was a time, some years after his financial crash, when Archer was *nouveau riche* once again, when he loved telling people of his wealth. When asked by a journalist in the early 1980s whether he was really worth £1 million, Jeffrey indicated that it was in fact much more, as he silently raised his fist and slowly opened it to reveal five splayed fingers.[2] As the 1980s progressed, his annual income was measured in terms of the number of Cabinet ministers his tax bill could pay for – from seven in 1983 to eight in 1984 – 'and I have told my Prime Minister the eight which I have chosen' – until in 1986 he was paying more tax ('£800,000, he said') in a year 'than the entire Cabinet earn put together.'[3] 'Last time I was in my bank,' he once joked, 'there was a piece of paper asking, "Is your income more or less than £20,000?" I told them, "Some days it is, some days it isn't." '[4]

The *Sunday Times*'s annual surveys of Britain's richest people have estimated Archer's wealth in recent years at £25 million.[5] Unless he has been quietly squandering a lot of his money, or is still investing un-wisely, this is probably a substantial underestimate. His eight books before joining HarperCollins must have reaped at least £25 million between them. The two recent deals with his new publisher amount to $53 million – well over £30 million – although much of that money has not been received yet, since the payments are spread over some years. In addition, he must have made considerable income and capital gains from his investments. A more realistic estimate of Archer's riches – if an approximate one – would be of the order of £40 to £50 million.

While much of his money has been invested in property, another substantial chunk has gone into his personal collection of paintings, drawings and sculptures. His interest in art, he says, was sparked ini-tially by a visit to the galleries in Bristol with a teenage girlfriend from Weston. Subsequently, after he married Mary, Jeffrey paid twenty-five pounds for two paintings by the artist Brian Davies which he spotted in a pavement display in the King's Road, Chelsea. These initial purchases, on the spur of the moment, led to more planned col-lecting. 'I went to the curator at the Royal Academy and at the Royal Watercolour Society, and asked for the names of the half dozen or so most promising young artists. I chose some I liked and started from there.'[6] Later, of course, he acquired several works cheaply through running his own gallery. Today Jeffrey Archer boasts one of the most valuable private art collections in the land, which some estimate could be worth around £10 million. The London flat contains mostly the modern works: a small Picasso drawing of two doves; a plate of sau-sages, chips and ketchup by Sandy Guy; four Dufys; two Lowrys; and works by Sutherland, Pissarro, Sisley, Braque, Matisse, Miró and Vuillard. Some of these works Archer has even had reproduced on personal postcards. Older portraits and landscapes are housed in Grantchester, where the garden is adorned by a couple of bronze nudes by Sydney Harpley.

Archer often visits auctions with a long-standing friend, Godfrey Barker, the gallery correspondent of the *Daily Telegraph*, but he bids only occasionally. He can get better prices, he believes, by bargaining with galleries, where he generally starts by offering half the asking price. Sometimes he deals directly with artists themselves. The summer exhibition at the Royal Academy is another favourite hunting-ground. Archer rarely sells, and when he dies his son William (an art-history graduate) will be allowed his pick of the collection, which now numbers more than 400 works. But most of them, he promises, will be left to his old Oxford college, Brasenose.

Apart from art, Jeffrey Archer's other great investment is in first editions of books, and he claims to have complete sets of Dickens, Henry James, Hemingway and Scott Fitzgerald. But there are few of the other indulgences often associated with self-made multimillionaires – no yacht, no racehorses, no helicopter or plane, no foreign villas and no drug habit. He is generous, however, with charitable requests, and claims to respond even to hardship pleas from individuals. 'I send £100 automatically to every letter that interests me and I think is genuine,' he once claimed. 'About 50 per cent of all the people who write to me get money. I give about £100,000 a year that way.'[7]

As well as his spurned offer to take a substantial stake in Hodder & Stoughton, Archer has attempted to invest in one or two other literary businesses. In 1983, for instance, he tried to buy the magazine *Punch*, before it folded. And around the time he joined HarperCollins he tried to buy his favourite bookshop chain, Hatchards, which his new publishers then owned. He offered £9.5 million, but was heavily outbid by Dillons, to the dismay of many Hatchards staff.

Despite his disastrous investment in Aquablast, Archer is still unable to resist a tempting bit of speculation. In 1986, for instance, he gambled £400,000 on a plot of land on the other side of the world without even seeing it – sixty-two acres near Auckland in New Zealand. In effect, Archer was betting on New Zealand winning the next America's Cup yachting competition, since by tradition the reigning champions are always entitled to host the next contest. Archer's plot overlooked the harbour where New Zealand would probably hold the event if given a chance, and so it stood to soar in value. Initially Archer was to be disappointed, as a strongly fancied Kiwi side failed to win the race in 1987. The land slowly appreciated in value anyway, and then in 1995, when New Zealand finally lifted the trophy, Archer looked set to make a handsome profit.

Archer has sometimes claimed that he hasn't dealt in the stock market since his 1974 crash. 'Shares just don't appeal to him,' says Adrian Metcalfe. 'He said after Aquablast, "I will never, never, never buy a share again."'[8] Archer told Bristol Conservatives in 1987, 'I get so involved in politics and books that I don't want to be involved in anything else . . . I have a happy life without waking up at night worrying about the Stock

Exchange.'⁹ This seems strange, for, two years before, Archer had invested heavily in one particular public company.

In July 1985, after the Burton Group had announced a take-over bid for Debenhams, he spent roughly £1.6 million on 500,000 Debenhams shares, in two separate purchases. Archer then sold them again about a month later, after Burton had won a takeover battle, but any profit he made on the deals can only have been a small one.

The mid-1980s had seen increasing worries about dishonesty in the City of London, and Jeffrey Archer was a public advocate of cracking down on offenders. 'If they have broken the law, they must go to jail,' he insisted in 1987.

> Why should a man in the north of England get five or six years for stealing silver and someone in the City who makes a quarter of a million pounds overnight out of other people's money not be punished? I hope there will be arrests, and the law tightened up even more than it has been. We were led to believe that everybody who worked in the City had standards and codes they would not break. That was a myth.¹⁰

Yet his own approach to share deals was a little puzzling. Around the time of his appointment as Conservative deputy chairman in September 1985, Archer arranged to see Anthony Hilton, the City editor of the *Evening Standard*. Over lunch at Le Caprice, the multimillionaire explained how difficult he found it to get good advice on investment. Hilton, he presumed, must regularly come across a lot of price-sensitive information, especially about imminent take-overs. How about an arrangement? Archer suggested that if Hilton supplied the tips he would invest the money, and they could split the profits. The journalist was astonished at how blatant the proposition was, particularly coming from the newly appointed Conservative deputy chairman; indeed, at first he wondered if his leg was being pulled. But Archer quickly added that Hilton must tell him if he thought the idea was remotely unethical, as then, of course, they couldn't possibly go ahead. Hilton suggested they might indeed have a problem, especially if anything appeared in *Private Eye*. It did.

The theme of making a killing from inside information recurs throughout Jeffrey Archer's writing. The four men in *Not a Penny More, Not a Penny Less* foolishly invest in a hot tip, just as Archer had done with Aquablast, and one of the heroes of his 1979 saga *Kane and Abel* successfully plays the stock market by eavesdropping on business con-versations while working as a waiter.[11] Much later, in the first story in his 1994 collection *Twelve Red Herrings*, the narrator ends with the following advice:

> You should look up the new stock in the *FT* around the middle of next year, and buy yourself a few, because they'll be what my father would have called 'a risk worth taking'.
>
> By the way, Matthew advises me that I've just given you what's termed as 'inside information', so please don't pass it on, as I have no desire to go back to jail for a third time.[12]

But the most astonishing passage of all relating to insider dealing occurs in Archer's 1987 play *Beyond Reasonable Doubt*, where the QC, Sir David Metcalfe, is heard phoning his stockbroker:

> SIR DAVID: Did you get the shares? *(He listens.)* Good. *(He listens again.)* The bid will be announced on Thursday. My source is impeccable. Naturally, I shall want you to sell within the account. *(He listens.)* That gives you a clear ten days . . . The sum is larger this time because the source is even more reliable. I don't see how anyone could describe me as an insider.[13]

Sir David's investments are made on the basis of 'advice from an old friend' about a take-over bid. Selling 'within the account' means that the QC intends to sell his shares before the end of the fortnightly accounting period, so that both deals are settled on the same day and, if he makes a profit, he will not have to part with any money. This fictional episode bears strong similarities to the extraordinary events of January 1994, when Archer himself was involved in buying a large batch of shares in Anglia Television – though not for himself – at the time when the company was considering a take-over bid. Stranger still, just as in his play, Department of Trade and Industry inspectors were then brought in to investigate suspicions of insider trading.

Jeffrey Archer's links with Anglia Television go back more than twenty-five years, to the 1969 Louth by-election when a number of voters mistook him for an Anglia reporter called Geoffrey Archer. As an MP he had supported the company's unsuccessful struggle with York-shire Television for the Belmont ITV transmitter. And in 1987 Mary Archer had been an obvious choice when the then Anglia chairman, Lord Buxton, was looking for new directors. Not only was the board short of women, but she also provided valuable links with Cambridge University, as well as political contacts and scientific expertise.

In November 1993 Anglia's future as a medium-size ITV company was suddenly thrown into doubt when the National Heritage Secretary, Peter Brooke, announced that from the start of 1994 companies would be allowed to own two major ITV franchises. Medium-sized ITV stations such as Anglia were suddenly prey for the bigger fish, and the final days of 1993 and early weeks of 1994 saw frantic take-over activity and speculation. From mid-December Anglia's share price rose steadily.

A few weeks after Brooke's statement, Archer was telephoned by Simon Wharmby, a stockbroker from a City firm, Charles Stanley & Co. Wharmby didn't know Archer, but had been put on to him by his colleague Frank Watts, the broker who had arranged the original Aquablast purchase for Archer in 1972 (after advising against it). Simon Wharmby and Frank Watts were a kind of partnership, and had moved together through four different stockbrokers. Wharmby was ringing Archer to suggest a new investment: it was almost as speculative as Aquablast, though not in shares. It involved an operation to recover silver bullion from a British transport ship, the *John Barry*, which had been torpedoed in the Arabian Sea off Oman in 1944. The salvage team was assembling a syndicate to invest $4 million in bringing the treasure to the surface.

Archer quickly told Wharmby he wasn't interested. This may have been because, ten years earlier, he had put money into a similar venture, to recover gold bullion from a German U-boat believed to have been sunk in the Caribbean, but the wreck could never be found. As events turned out, Archer would have done well from Wharmby's proposition, since it proved highly profitable, and would have been far less embarrassing than the course he did take. Archer did note the broker's number, though.

About two weeks later, on the morning of Thursday 13 January 1994, Archer telephoned Wharmby. Could he arrange a more conventional deal, for shares in Anglia Television? How many were available at that moment, he wanted to know, and at what price? Wharmby was delighted to gain such a distinguished client, and, despite warning that shares might be scarce amid the current take-over talk, he quickly discovered that a batch of 80,000 was on the market. But the price was too high for Archer, who then specified that he needed about 25,000 shares at 485p. Wharmby quickly found what Archer wanted, and the deal went through at 10.25 a.m.

Contrary to most later accounts of the episode, sources at the brokers say that Archer had made it clear from the very start that the purchase was intended for a third party. 'We never thought that we were dealing for him,' says Charles Stanley's managing director, David Howard. 'At an early point in the first conversation that day Archer said, "I'm buying these for somebody else. Is that all right?" or some conversation like that.'[14] That 'someone else' later turned out to be Broosk Saib, the Kurdish aide Archer had acquired during the Simple Truth campaign, and Charles Stanley executives believe that Saib was in the room with Archer during the initial calls. But rather than give Saib's usual address of 28 Heath Rise, Kersfield Road, Putney, the peer asked that the deal should be in the name of 'B. Saib Esq., c/o J. Archer, Alembic House, 93 Albert Embankment, London SE1 7TY'.

It was an unusual arrangement, though not unprecedented. The finance director of Charles Stanley, Peter Hurst, soon queried why the firm was doing such a large deal for an unknown customer, only to be reassured by Archer's involvement. Crucially, if anything had gone wrong, David Howard says that 'We would have held Lord Archer personally responsible for the money ... We were relying on Lord Archer's bona fides in accepting the order, even though the deal was made in the name of Saib.'[15] When Charles Stanley checked afterwards, they discovered that this was the first time Saib had ever used this strange arrangement with Archer.

Archer told Wharmby he would be interested in buying more Anglia shares for his associate if they became available. Just before 2 p.m. the following day, Friday, the broker arranged a second purchase, for a second batch of 25,000, again at 485p.

Whereas the fictional Sir David Metcalfe had tried to buy and sell shares within the fortnightly account period, Archer faced a problem if he wanted to avoid committing any money. The two days on which he had made the Anglia purchases – 13 and 14 January – were the very last days of the account, which gave him no time to sell again at a profit. To overcome this, Archer asked for the shares to be purchased for 'new time', so that the transaction would be regarded as part of the following account period and settlement could be delayed by a fortnight. Before the practice of the account period was abolished later in 1994, this was a common service, though brokers usually levied a premium of 0.5 per cent. In this case it appears that Archer and Saib were never charged the extra levy.

Although not one of the top 'blue-chip' stockbrokers, Charles Stanley regularly deal for top politicians – Labour as well as Conservative. The managing director, David Howard, is the son of Sir Edward Howard, a baronet and former lord mayor of London who himself ran the firm in his day. Howard is also an active Conservative: a former councillor who once had parliamentary ambitions and had occasionally welcomed Archer to local party engagements. But Charles Stanley would have been an unwise choice for anyone hoping to deal in Anglia shares on the basis of inside knowledge. Three of the brokers' seven offices outside London are in East Anglia – in Ipswich, Cambridge and Norwich – which meant that the firm was more familiar with the TV station's affairs than with most quoted companies.

In September 1992 the Anglia board had adopted new rules on share transactions, in line with common practice for public companies. Directors, their spouses, relations and associates were henceforth prohibited from dealing in Anglia equity during the 'close' period between the end of the company's financial year on 31 December and the announcement of the annual results around mid-March. Mary Archer and each of the other Anglia directors were required to sign a copy of these rules to confirm that he or she would comply. They were also expected to tell their spouses and other relevant parties about them. These rules were not binding on Jeffrey Archer, of course; nor did they have the force of law. But the company had stated its position that, as the spouse of a director, he should not have been involved in buying Anglia shares at that time of year, even in normal times.

And January 1994 was far from normal. As early as 16 December 1993 the Anglia board had received a tentative take-over proposal from MAI, the media and financial-services group run by the Labour peer Lord Hollick, whose company Meridian already held the ITV franchise covering the region south of London and along the south coast. On 31 December Anglia directors were sent a memo and bankers' advice which outlined the MAI proposal and three other options. The board first discussed the MAI bid on 5 January, when they also dismissed a rival approach from LWT. Exactly a week later – on Wednesday 12 January – the directors considered a firmer offer from MAI, at 610p a share. Company executives held productive negotiations with Lord Hollick that afternoon, and called a special board meeting for the following

Sunday to consider the offer. Some board members were told that Wednesday evening about the emergency meeting, others early the next day – just when Archer ordered the first parcel of company shares.

The MAI offer was discussed by the Anglia directors on the Sunday, but according to the Anglia chief executive, David McCall, it was not finally clinched until the next day, Monday.[16] It was announced publicly at 8 a.m. on Tuesday 18 January, at not less than 637p a share. Two hours later Archer telephoned Simon Wharmby and instructed him to sell all Broosk Saib's 50,000 stock; the deal went through at 10.15 a.m. at a price of 646p. In all, the deals made £77,219 profit, after deducting commission and stamp duty. And neither Jeffrey Archer nor Broosk Saib had needed to move a penny of their own money.

Charles Stanley, like most stockbrokers, have a compliance department, whose duty is to examine all transactions the following day and spot unusual movements. Surprisingly, given the speculation about Anglia, and the company's regional presence, the Archer/Saib deals had been the only dealings in the TV company that they had conducted during the previous week or more. Once the take-over was announced, of course, these transactions looked suspiciously well-timed.

Charles Stanley's compliance officer, Eric Hurrell, referred Archer's purchases to his directors, who gathered informally in David Howard's office to discuss them, and to consider any possible link between the client and the company. Until that point neither Simon Wharmby, David Howard, Eric Hurrell nor anyone else within the brokers had been aware of Archer's family link with Anglia. Then a member of staff who worked closely with the brokers' Norwich office asked whether they realized that Mary was a director of the company. David Howard was immediately aware of the implications. 'My God,' he exclaimed. 'This is front-page stuff!'

In fact, even had they not known of the Mary Archer connection, sources at Charles Stanley say that the company would none the less have referred the deals to the Stock Exchange Surveillance Department, since the timings were simply too good. In any case, the Stock Exchange insists that it had already noticed the deals, though there has been a quiet dispute between the Exchange and the brokers as to who acted first.

It took four days for Charles Stanley to complete a report on the affair and send it to the Stock Exchange, which had also been compiling its own dossier. The Exchange almost immediately passed the matter to the Department of Trade and Industry, which has ultimate responsibility for policing share-dealing and initiating prosecutions. On Tuesday 8 February, having consulted Downing Street, the DTI appointed two outside inspectors: Hugh Aldous, managing partner of the accountants Robson Rhodes, and Roger Kaye, a QC and deputy High Court judge. Two days later, presumably unaware that he was being investigated, Broosk Saib deposited a cheque for £77,219.62 into an account at the NatWest Bank in Cromwell Road, west London.

During February and March the DTI inspectors stationed themselves in Aldous's office at Robson Rhodes in the City Road (funnily enough, the street where Archer was born). They summoned a succession of witnesses – including staff from Charles Stanley, Broosk Saib, and, on separate days, both Jeffrey and Mary Archer. Each was grilled thoroughly about every conceivable aspect of the affair. In deciding whether the peer had broken the law on insider dealing and ought to be prosecuted, the DTI inspectors must have probed several obvious questions. Had Archer learned from Mary Archer about the take-over? Why did he risk even the suspicion of insider trading for what was such a small amount by his standards? Why did Archer conduct the deals on behalf of Broosk Saib? Why couldn't Saib make them himself – particularly when it came to selling the shares, and no further financial risk was involved? Above all, why didn't Jeffrey consult Mary first?

Broosk Saib says he was born in Britain in 1962, soon after his parents came to this country from Iraq. The Saibs were known as big landowners in the area of Kurdistan around Sulaymaniyah, and his father, Fawzi Saib, served as vice-governor of the province of Baghdad and as chamberlain to King Faisal in the late 1950s. Broosk Saib's parents live in the same block of flats in Putney as he does, and the family is obviously wealthy. In the mid-1980s, when he was calling himself Broosk Jamil, Saib became involved in several property-related businesses: London Construction and Design, Broosk Interior Design, and Broosk Estate Agents, the last two of which were effectively owned by him. All three firms eventually went into liquidation – the two Broosk companies with debts of more than £220,000. Of this, £77,750 was owed to Saib himself and £27,500 to his close Kurdish friend, Nadhim Zahawi.

Despite these losses, Broosk Saib is evidently not poverty-stricken; within London Kurdish circles the Saibs are said to be worth millions. Broosk Saib himself owns several properties around London, including a small five-storey block of shops, offices and flats in the Fulham Road. Journalists who later gained access to details of his bank account discovered that some of the Anglia profit went to pay everyday expenses. But in September 1994 Saib took delivery of a new SL500 Mercedes sports car. It was worth around £76,000.

DTI enquiries into possible insider trading are carried out quite frequently, particularly after company take-overs, but the department appoints outside inspectors only when the allegations are particularly complicated, serious or sensitive. Though evidence is given on oath, as if in a court of law, and a record is kept of every word, the investigations are nearly always kept secret. Indeed, unless prosecutions result, it may never be publicly known that there has been an enquiry. So it might easily have proved with the 1994 enquiry into Lord Archer and Anglia.

But in June 1994 a freelance journalist, Martin Tomkinson, received a better tip-off than most journalists get in a lifetime. He was given just three pieces of information: that there was a DTI investigation, that it concerned a take-over, and that it involved Lord Archer. He was not given the name of the company. 'The person that helped me feared it would be swept under the carpet,' he says. 'I think they felt that if it wasn't brought to the press's attention it would never see the light of day.'[17] Tomkinson never saw any documents or met his informant: the tip-off came through a third party, though the journalist later realized that he had once met the source, quite fortuitously, in the distant past.

Tomkinson specializes in financial investigations, not just as a journalist but often for business clients too. Having once been in charge of the business pages of *Private Eye*, he needed little prompting to follow up the story. A quick trip to Companies House revealed to him that Mary Archer was a director of Anglia, and any financial observer would have known that the company had recently been taken over by MAI.

Tomkinson first mentioned his story, albeit only in general terms, to Dominic Prince, the City editor of the *Sunday Express*, though he didn't expect much interest. Prince never had a chance to pursue it anyway, for coincidentally he parted company from the newspaper the same day. Tomkinson considered going to *The Guardian* or the *Daily Mirror*, but he decided he wanted a paper which would both pay and which had clout. So in going to *The Times* the journalist quite deliberately chose an Establishment paper, though at first it was actually reluctant to pay him much, and he thought he might have to go elsewhere. Early on the morning of Thursday 7 July, *The Times* rang back and asked him to come to Wapping at once. By the evening, following an extraordinary development, the story was out.

That morning, Tomkinson rang MAI's external public-relations adviser, Maurice Barnfather, and said he understood the DTI was investigating dealings by Lord Archer in Anglia shares. Could Barnfather comment? Around lunchtime the PR man came back with a statement – approved by the DTI inspectors – confirming that 'Anglia was aware of the DTI investigation', and had cooperated with it, though they were not 'aware of the alleged transaction'.[18] So *The Times* had confirmation of an enquiry into Anglia, but not the Archer element.

Tomkinson then phoned the DTI and reported that Anglia had confirmed that there was an investigation, and he also mentioned Archer's involvement. He regarded it as pretty much a routine, obligatory call, and didn't really expect much response. But at 4 p.m. a DTI press officer rang back to say he was authorized to make a statement. 'It is long-standing practice,' the official began dictating, 'not to comment in such cases . . .' Tomkinson immediately expected the usual unhelpful DTI 'no comment'. He was quickly surprised:

> However, in this instance, in view of the statement made to the press by a company, we feel it right to confirm that, following a report from the Stock Exchange concerning certain transactions close to the announcement on 18 January 1994 of an agreed bid from MAI plc for Anglia Television Group plc, the Secretary of State appointed two inspectors on 8 February 1994 to investigate possible insider dealing contraventions by certain individuals, including Lord Archer.[19]

It was an extraordinary revelation. Quite unnecessarily, the DTI had corroborated the Archer element of Tomkinson's story. Without that statement, the only evidence he and *The Times* had for Archer's involvement was Tomkinson's leak, which wasn't enough on its own to run the story (though the journalist was confident of corroborating it through other means). There is a suggestion that the DTI had tried to get MAI to withdraw its lunchtime statement, though it would have been absurd for the company to do so. The decision to confirm Archer's name was then taken personally, by the Secretary of State, Michael Heseltine, after departmental lawyers told him there was no legal obstacle to doing so.

The same afternoon the City editor of *The Times*, Melvyn Marckus, made contact with Archer on his car phone, waking the peer from an afternoon nap as he was being driven back from speaking at a school prize-day in Gloucester. 'It is completely untrue,' said Archer. 'I did not buy any shares. I am not going to make a statement. That sort of accusation is libellous. Thank you.'[20]

The fact that news of the Archer investigation was now public destroyed any chance he might have had of a political job from John Major. Years of pounding the rubber-chicken circuit for the Conservative Party were obliterated by this latest development. 'He was completely shattered when this exploded,' says Adrian Metcalfe. 'He felt the whole thing had gone.'[21]

Conspiracy-theorists naturally suggested that Heseltine's decision was influenced by the pending ministerial reshuffle. Had he released Archer's name to stop him becoming Conservative chairman? The less well informed even pointed out that Heseltine himself was a contender for the job, but, since the Industry Secretary had made it very clear he wasn't interested, this theory doesn't stand up. Nevertheless, some in the Conservative Party cannot have been too distressed for the world to be reminded how bad Archer's judgement can be. Another theory was that John Major had allowed the peer's name to be released so as to explain why he wouldn't be getting a job. This is also highly implausible, since the Prime Minister could easily have omitted Archer from the reshuffle without offering an explanation. Moreover, the last thing Major wanted was yet another 'sleaze' scandal, especially one involving a personal friend.

Yet even Labour politicians asked why the DTI had confirmed Archer's name. The most probable explanation seems to be that Michael Heseltine feared accusations of a cover-up. This has to be viewed in the context of the feverish political climate of 1994, when new allegations about the conduct of Tory politicians seemed to surface almost every week. The Scott enquiry into selling defence equipment to Iraq had already shown that Heseltine can be stricter than most of his colleagues about standards of ministerial conduct. But he and his DTI officials seem to have overestimated the strength of the evidence *The Times* had for its story, and to have assumed that MAI and Anglia had actually confirmed the Archer element. Their thinking appears to have been that, since the story was going to break anyway, and in a serious newspaper, to be noncommittal about Archer might be perceived as protecting a political ally.

Michael Heseltine was, in fact, one of the members of the Cabinet to whom Archer was the least close, though this does not mean they were enemies: the Industry Secretary has attended the peer's parties, for instance. They were similar characters, of course, and the two most flamboyant Tory politicians of the Thatcher–Major era: both favourites of the constituency circuit, tub-thumping orators, self-made millionaires and highly ambitious. Yet, to the party's old-fashioned grandees, Heseltine and Archer have always been seen as rather vulgar – men who 'bought their own furniture' – politically risky and suspect.

Initially, however, none of the precise details of Archer's dealings in Anglia emerged, apart from a figure of around £80,000 profit. What was not yet understood is just how intimately Archer had been involved in Saib's deals. And at first he was treated with extraordinary sympathy by other newspapers and politicians. The general view was that poor Jeffrey and his chances of a job had been deliberately scuppered by a dirty-tricks campaign.

Archer's 'friends' quickly set to work trying to put the best gloss on events, and, as in the Monica Coghlan affair, their initial explanations proved to be highly misleading. Jeffrey, they claimed, had merely suggested to an acquaintance that certain ITV shares were a good bet in the prevailing climate. 'He told the inspectors,' one close source was quoted as saying, 'that he had advised a friend to buy shares in Yorkshire TV and Anglia because the industry shake-up made the shares look attractive.'[22] The typical press and political reaction was that, if this was all Archer had done, then he was being hounded unfairly. It was also reported that the enquiry was likely to clear him anyway, and his supporters quickly explained that this made it all the more imperative for Michael Heseltine to consider the inspectors' conclusions quickly, so that the peer might still have a chance in John Major's reshuffle.

For the time being the Prime Minister remained remarkably supportive. 'Jeffrey is a very long-standing friend of mine and will remain so,' he said. 'I do not know how the name first came into the public domain.'[23] Ten days after the *Times* story broke, John and Norma Major were among 150 guests at the Archers' summer party in Grantchester, where the two men were seen strolling through the garden together, the premier in shirtsleeves clutching a mug of beer. But the following week the DTI announced it had only just received the inspectors' report, and that Heseltine would need time to digest it.

The day after the report arrived on the Secretary of State's desk, John Major unveiled his ministerial changes, and the party chairmanship went to the largely unknown Jeremy Hanley. 'They chose a better man,' Archer had to say, adding that Hanley was 'the right man for the job'.[24]

Yet the new chairman turned out to be nearly as big a liability as many had feared Archer would have been; he was quickly dubbed 'The Gaffer' for a series of errors in his opening weeks and only lasted a year in the job. What must have been as bad for Jeffrey, however, was that his former job of deputy chairman went to his old rival from Central Office days, Michael Dobbs, who himself had since become a best-selling thriller writer. And at the Department of National Heritage – a more realistic possibility – the junior minister, Iain Sproat, kept his position.

'I had hoped to be speaking here this evening as a minister of the Crown,' Archer joked to a charity dinner that night, adding, with obvious bitterness, 'but I am actually speaking here courtesy of the DTI.'[25] Yet, just over a week later, the department announced that Heseltine had decided he 'should take no further action against any of the parties concerned'. He had taken the decision after passing the inspectors' report to a QC for an outside opinion. 'I am grateful to have been exonerated,' Lord Archer announced, though that was not the word the DTI had used.[26]

It appears that the two inspectors were extremely tough on Archer (the accountant, Hugh Aldous, is known as a hard investigator, and was scathing in a previous DTI enquiry into the House of Fraser). Aldous wouldn't comment about the Anglia investigation, but talking generally about DTI enquiries he remarked that 'It is an inspector's job to produce a report. If the Department of Trade and Industry with all its lawyers wants to let someone off it is up to them.'[27] Taking the advice of its outside QC, the DTI seems to have concluded that a prosecution was likely to fail. There was no hard evidence that Archer ever had any inside knowledge, especially when Mary insisted she had never told her husband about the take-over. And had it come to court Archer would have been able to cite newspaper tips from the period suggesting that Anglia was ripe for take-over.[28]

The record on insider-trading cases was not encouraging either: of the forty-six people charged since 1985, twenty-two had been convicted; and in 1993 all seven instances had resulted in 'Not guilty' verdicts. The authorities' normal rule is only to prosecute where there is more than a fifty per cent chance of conviction; in Archer's case, they presumably decided there wasn't enough evidence to be confident of this. There may also have been the consideration that Archer is a popular figure, and a jury might be especially sympathetic towards him.

As Archer returned from his family sailing holiday in Turkey in late

August, further facts began to emerge about the whole affair, however, thanks largely to persistent digging by reporters on the *Financial Times* and the *Sunday Times*.[29] It was revealed for the first time that, far from simply giving a friend advice to buy Anglia – as the Archer camp had been telling people – he had actually issued the order himself, and not once but twice. More precise details of the deals showed just how fortunate the timing had been, and eventually Broosk Saib's name became public. 'Yes,' Saib confirmed, 'I was involved in a private deal with Jeffrey. It was all perfectly innocent.'[30] The businessman denied he had been insider-dealing, but admitted that the money had not gone to help Kurdish refugees. 'I have bought a lot of shares in my lifetime,' Saib added, 'and I continue to do so.'[31] This, of course, only prompted the further question: if he had bought 'a lot of shares' before, why had he made this peculiar arrangement with Archer, and not used his previous brokers?

The pressure was once again on Archer, and Labour's industry spokesman, Robin Cook, called for the DTI inspectors' report to be referred to the Crown Prosecution Service for a second, independent opinion. 'One Tory politician,' Cook argued, 'should not sit in judgement on another Tory politician.'[32]

On 24 August 1994, for the third time in his career, Jeffrey Archer formally and publicly conceded that he had made a serious mistake. It was twenty years and a day since he'd resigned over Aquablast and confessed, 'I was a fool.' In 1986 he had admitted 'lack of judgement' as 'foolishly' he fell into a 'trap' over the Monica Coghlan episode.[33] Now, over Anglia, Jeffrey Archer was obliged to confess that he had made a 'grave error'. The admission came in a statement issued by his solicitor, Lord Mishcon:

> There have been no new facts mentioned by the media which were not known to and which had not been investigated by the Inspectors in the course of their very full Inquiry. The DTI who had the Inspectors' Report before them have stated in their decision that they have taken independent legal advice and have decided that no further action be taken against anyone involved in the Inquiry. They can accordingly be taken to have concluded, as Lord Archer has maintained throughout, that this transaction was not carried out with the benefit of any insider information. He realizes however that it was a grave error when his wife was a Director of

Anglia to have allowed his name to be associated with the purchase and sale of shares in that company on behalf of a third party (and from which he in no way benefited) and indeed his deepest regret is the embarrassment needlessly caused to Lady Archer in this matter.[34]

It was a model of legal obfuscation and public-relations window-dressing. On what basis could Mishcon say that the DTI 'can accordingly be taken to have concluded . . . that this transaction was not carried out with the benefit of any insider information'? That may have been true, but what appears more likely was that the DTI simply accepted that there was not enough evidence to mount a successful prosecution. The words 'allowed his name to be associated with' were a particularly favourable description of what Archer had done. They made his actions sound as if he had absent-mindedly drifted into the deals by accident. Archer had in fact contacted the brokers initially, had approved two share purchases, and had then ordered the sale of the shares a few days later. And, quite apart from specifying that his flat be used as Broosk Saib's mailing address, his reputation had been taken as a financial guarantee.

Strangely, Lord Archer seemed to have been almost as surprised by Mishcon's statement as everyone else. He was on tour in Australia at the time, promoting *Twelve Red Herrings*, and as he left a literary lunch in Melbourne he was confronted by a crowd of reporters and TV crews brandishing front-page headlines faxed from London. Archer stopped, read one of the articles, and was visibly taken aback. 'I didn't know there'd been a statement overnight,' he admitted.[35]

While Jeffrey acknowledged the enormous trouble he'd caused his wife, Mary Archer has said even less about the whole affair than he has. The Stock Exchange decided she had not behaved improperly, and her fellow Anglia directors accepted her assurances that she had not told her husband about the take-over. One brave reporter who dared ask Mary if she was going to resign as a director was told his question was 'impertinent'.[36] To leave the board then, of course, might have been interpreted as an admission that she or her husband was guilty of something. But four and a half months later, in January 1995, Mary Archer did indeed announce her resignation as an Anglia director. Anglia colleagues insisted she was under no pressure to go, and of course being a director did not hold the same status now that the firm was a subsidiary of MAI and no longer a public company.

In the months that followed his public apology, neither Archer himself nor Broosk Saib ever clarified matters. 'I would love to speak out and clear my name,' said Saib at one point, 'but I dare not at this stage.'[37] It was all very puzzling.

Jeffrey Archer had embarrassed not only his wife: his actions had also done little for the City's reputation for regulating the share market, and had further damaged the Conservatives at a time when they seemed to be overwhelmed by scandal. The new party chairman, Jeremy Hanley, with obvious frustration, accepted that the affair was 'unlikely to go away within the next couple of weeks. It has to be sorted out properly. But largely that is a matter for Lord Archer to decide.'[38] The former party treasurer and arch-Thatcherite, Alistair McAlpine, was characteristically much more blunt. 'To call this transaction . . . a "grave error" is, at least, a monstrous understatement.' McAlpine, a former colleague of Archer's at Central Office, quoted Oliver Cromwell's words to the Rump Parliament: 'Depart, I say, and let us have done with you. In the name of God, go.'[39]

The former DTI minister Alan Clark led several Tories in asking his old department to publish the inspectors' report. This was out of the question, the DTI maintained, since the evidence had been gathered on a confidential basis and not for publication. Labour responded that the DTI should therefore seek Archer's permission to publish; he surely would not refuse, they argued cleverly, if he was convinced the report 'exonerated' him. Michael Heseltine never tried to obtain such consent.

Senior Tories tried hard to keep their distance as the party attempted to forget the affair. Archer chose not to attend the 1994 conference in Bournemouth – despite having been a hit the year before – and had a good excuse in that, unusually, the House of Lords was sitting that week (and Archer attended, voted, and even spoke briefly). This meant, of course, that party bigwigs were deprived of the traditional social highlight of the week – Jeffrey's late-night champagne party. Worse still, he also cancelled his usual string of Christmas soirées, explaining that building work in Alembic House meant that only one lift was working, which would cause serious problems if it broke down.

By the time the Commons reassembled in late October, the Anglia affair seemed largely to have run its course. The Trade and Industry Select Committee did not think it worth pursuing, though several Opposition MPs maintained an interest, including the Labour member Dale

Campbell-Savours, who was required to leave the chamber for a day when he suggested that Archer was guilty of 'criminal activity'.[40]

Archer did not withdraw entirely from the public stage, however. He continued with his usual programme of charity auctions, local political meetings, and book-signings and other events to promote the three separate editions of his books that HarperCollins had published during 1994. But Archer steered clear of the Dudley and Islwyn by-elections, and for seven months he barely appeared in the press or on television or radio. The only exception was just after Christmas, when the whole family was involved in an accident when their new BMW careered off the M25 in Hertfordshire. The Archers were taken to hospital, but fortunately nobody was seriously hurt.

In the New Year, Archer went away for five weeks to Majorca to write his next book, the Maxwell–Murdoch novelography due to be published in the spring of 1996. While he was abroad, an extraordinary new element to the Anglia story emerged. It was revealed that a forty-one-year-old stockbroker at the City firm James Capel & Co., Karen Morgan Thomas, had purchased 10,000 Anglia shares at the start of January 1994 – nine days before the first Archer/Saib deal – and then sold them, at a profit of almost £22,000, after the bid was announced. What made the case interesting was that Thomas admitted she was an acquaintance of Archer's, having originally met him at a Conservative gathering twelve years before.

But the stockbroker vehemently denied ever having discussed Anglia with Archer. 'I utterly refute any suggestion that I was acting on the basis of insider information from Lord Archer or anybody else,' she said.[41] Her decision had been based on a tip in the *Sunday Times*, she insisted, and on advice from the media analyst at James Capel. 'I believe that I spoke briefly to Lord Archer on the telephone during the December 1993/January 1994 period,' she stated in an affidavit to try to prevent *The Guardian* publishing the story, 'but what I am absolutely certain about is that at no time did Lord Archer make any reference to Anglia shares or suggest that I purchase those shares.'

Thomas admitted making two calls to Archer around the crucial period. The first, she explained, had been in mid-December to thank him for 'a small Christmas present (a book)', while the second, in January, had been to enquire how his trip to Kurdistan had gone, and therefore occurred after she bought the shares.[42] Her solicitor called her relationship with Lord Archer 'an acquaintance, not a close friendship', though the gift suggests otherwise.[43] He also denied any romantic attachment.[44]

But in March 1995, the *Sunday Mirror* revealed that Thomas had phoned Archer on three more occasions.[45] The first of the new calls was on 24 January, four days after the stockbroker had sold her Anglia shares. She briefly rang Archer again on 10 June, and finally on 8 July 1994, the very day the Anglia story broke. This last call, it was explained, was because Morgan Thomas wanted to cancel a dinner she had arranged with the novelist that evening, as she didn't want to be photographed amid all the press interest.

Karen Morgan Thomas insisted she had told her bosses at James Capel about her Anglia purchase at the time. The deal was also examined by both the Stock Exchange and the regulatory Securities and Futures Authority but she had not been questioned during the enquiry into Archer. It wasn't until two months after the *Sunday Mirror* article that the DTI appeared to show any great interest in Morgan Thomas. In May 1995 Michael Heseltine asked Roger Kaye and Hugh Aldous to reopen their investigations into Anglia and in particular they were asked to look closely at her transactions. The inspectors questioned Thomas's old colleagues at James Capel and even her former secretary, but after another seven months' work, and several hundred thousand pounds expense, they concluded there were insufficient grounds to take action.

# Epilogue

Even by Archer standards, Anglia was a pretty bad mistake. Not only had he embarrassed Mary, and reminded fellow Tories how gaffe-prone he was, but it was also difficult to explain publicly. In previous scrapes there was always someone else to blame: with both Aquablast and the Coghlan episode he could portray himself as an unfortunate victim, either of crooked businessmen, or unscrupulous tabloid newspapers. But with the 1994 Anglia deals, Jeffrey had nobody to blame but himself.

Just as after previous crises, Archer switched his attention to writing. For most of 1995 he concentrated on his next novel, *The Fourth Estate*, and claims to have put more effort into it than into any of his previous works. 'I sweated night and day,' he later revealed. 'I hadn't become chairman of the party, I hadn't achieved what I wanted to do. I had something to prove. I really believed I'd got to make this novel the best thing I've ever done in my life ... I had failed on that side, I must compensate by working as I had never worked before.'[1]

It illustrated once again what is probably the greatest Archer quality: resilience, the determination to bounce back, a refusal to be defeated. He's survived not just the major disasters of Aquablast and Coghlan, but also a string of less well-known scrapes such as the débâcle at the Birthday Trust, the controversy over his UNA expenses, and, of course, the strange incident at Simpson's store in Toronto. Some even believe this extraordinary ability to recover each time has given Archer a dangerous sense of being indestructible; indeed, this may help explain why he behaved so foolishly during the Anglia affair.

Yet even before the final draft of *The Fourth Estate* had been submitted to the publishers, there were the first stages of yet another political comeback. Too many people depend on Jeffrey Archer for him to be allowed to disappear from politics altogether; not just the Tory party, which is desperately short of flamboyant, inspirational figures, but the press and broadcasting also need him.

John Major had first given Archer a green light to return in March 1995, less than a year after the Anglia story broke, with an astonishingly strong show of support in the Commons. 'Lord Archer is my friend,' he told MPs, 'has been my friend and will remain my friend in the future.'[2]

That summer Jeffrey repaid the Tory leader with a string of supportive interviews during the leadership election against John Redwood, and then returned to the by-election trail in Littleborough and Saddleworth. October saw the resumption of his famous late-night champagne parties at the Tory conference in Blackpool. By the time of the Conservative Women's conference in December, Archer was clearly angling for a job again, as he offered his latest constituency intelligence to Brian Mawhinney, and addressed the new party chairman as 'Sir'. He then delivered the fund-raising warm-up before the Prime Minister's speech to the Tory women. Archer knows that John Major still provides his best chance of preferment; it is asking too much that he could manage to be quite so close to a third successive Tory leader. None of those most likely to succeed Major – Michael Portillo, Kenneth Clarke or possibly Michael Heseltine – is anything like as well disposed towards him.

But John Major would be crazy to give Archer any political job. He possesses what must be by far the worst judgement in British politics. There are simply too many murky episodes in his past career – starting with the false degree claims that got him into Oxford. Archer is unfit to hold public office until he gives satisfactory answers to several simple questions about Anglia. Above all, why did he buy the shares for Broosk Saib when the Kurd could quite easily have used his own broker?

The fact that Archer has already made so much of a comeback since 1994 shows not just the failure of fellow Tories in holding him to account, but also the negligence of the media. Cabinet members and Fleet Street editors turned up to Jeffrey's parties in Blackpool each night – in some cases, both nights – as if Anglia had never happened. Many of the journalists cosily supping his champagne were the very people who should have been asking him tough questions about the Anglia deals.

Reporters have notoriously short memories; some are reluctant to probe because they've forgotten the detail. In other cases journalists are frightened to offend: Archer always provides a good, colourful interview, and if they're too aggressive, they fear, he might not come on their programmes again. One BBC TV producer was so determined to get Archer on to his early-morning television show that he volunteered not to ask him about Anglia. The novelist hadn't even raised the subject. More remarkable still have been the occasions when Archer has appeared on radio or television discussing the current state of the Tory party. Strangely, some of the toughest interviewers have failed to ask him about his own contribution to the party's sleazy image. Indeed, I am not aware of a single case of any journalist asking him about Anglia, though doubtless there must be one or two examples.

Archer's career is a shaming indictment of the standards of British journalism. The latest, particularly absurd, example occurred in September 1995 with the story of his £35 million book deal.

It all began when a *Mail on Sunday* reporter heard from a publishing contact that Archer had signed a new contract with HarperCollins. In fact, it seems the source was simply a bit slow and was referring to the 1994 deal. When the *Mail on Sunday* rang Archer, the novelist responded in a way which seemed to provide confirmation. Trying to find a figure to put on the deal, the *Mail on Sunday* reporter asked Archer whether it might be worth as much as £35 million. In typical aggressive style, Archer demanded how anybody could possibly imagine he would write for anything less. So it was that the story ran.[3]

When the *Sunday Times* newsdesk saw the first editions of the *Mail on Sunday*, they were eager to run it too. When they rang Archer he reacted just as he had to the *Mail on Sunday*, saying he simply couldn't deny it. Hollywood film producers, he advised the reporter, were so in love with the idea for his next book that they were prepared to pay millions. With apparent confirmation from the man himself, and no time to get a comment from HarperCollins, the *Sunday Times* also went ahead. And the fact that Murdoch's own paper had now run the story was taken as confirmation by everyone else.

The trouble was, the story was total rubbish. There was no new HarperCollins contract, and they weren't paying him £35 million. The 1994 deal still stood, and that was worth $23 million, or about £15 million, less than half the figure for his fictitious new contract.

HarperCollins were baffled and also deeply embarrassed, since the company was in the middle of making staff cuts. Yet the reports were difficult to deny: the extra-strict secrecy surrounding Archer's contracts meant that very few people could say for sure. George Craig in New York was ill, and Eddie Bell was on holiday. The story was only scotched on Bell's return several days later.

In three decades of following Archer's career, journalists seem to have learnt nothing. Thirty years on from reporting Archer's '£4,000 salary' at the National Birthday Trust, newspapers are as gullible as ever.

'I know I ought to resist him,' the politician Alan Clark once said, 'but I find him irresistible.'[4] Many can't bring themselves to treat his failings in a way they would other people's. Yet what makes Archer such a fascinating and complex character to study is that it's difficult to portray his life as all bad. Beside all his faults, Archer undoubtedly has positive, laudable qualities.

Quite apart from his obvious energy, imagination and refusal to give up, there's a generous and considerate side to his character. After finishing a book, for instance, he'll send cases of wine to his editors; he can afford it, of course, but so too can many other authors who would never think of such a thing. Archer will often be among the first to respond to others' misfortunes. When the former Labour leader John Smith suffered his first heart attack in 1988, Archer took time off from a speaking tour to visit him in hospital, and yet he hardly knew Smith. A Vancouver radio journalist tells of the time he and his wife came to London on holiday and took the opportunity to interview Archer at his flat. When the novelist later heard the couple had had all their money stolen, he whipped out a wad of cash and peeled off four £50 notes to lend them. But perhaps the clearest indication of Jeffrey's decent, generous side is simply the number of close, long-standing personal friends he has – very few of them public figures – who are genuinely loyal and fond of him.

Friends and colleagues try to explain some of the worst Archer excesses. Both Adrian Metcalfe and the former Conservative Communications Director, Harvey Thomas, believe his harsh, arrogant and rude side is largely a front to conceal his basic inner shyness. As for Archer's famous 'talent for inaccurate précis', Metcalfe argues he's not really telling lies, but that much of it is simply a tendency to romanticize:

> I think he is continually writing and rewriting his own life, in a sense – just giving it a more attractive shape in his head. 'I was the youngest MP – well, maybe there were one or two others younger, but, you know, I was sort of the youngest, or I was the youngest one that everybody was interested in' is really what he's saying.[5]

Compared with most individuals, and even allowing for his notorious setbacks, Archer's life has been a glittering success, with genuine achievements in several fields, worldwide fame, vast wealth and a thriving family. Yet by his own measure, being a globally successful writer has always been an unsatisfactory second-best. The two ambitions Archer most wanted to fulfil – to reach the top in either politics or some branch of show business – have eluded him, and probably always will.

Even if he could have overhauled the department in his brain marked 'judgement', Archer would always have been too lightweight a politician to have reached Downing Street or one of Her Majesty's great offices of state. What's so poignant, given what became of his half-sister Rosemary in Washington, is that Jeffrey has always recognized that his brazen style is too 'un-British', and would be better suited to America. 'If I was born today,' he once confessed, 'and wanted to go into politics, I would want to be born in the United States.'[6] Privately he has voiced his frustration with his friend, the US senator Bill Bradley, for not being more ambitious and running for the White House in 1992 at a time when the Democratic nomination was within easy grasp. One can easily see Archer thriving amidst the razzmatazz of the US campaign trail, where personality and money matter far more than ideas or policy. Given the successes of Ronald Reagan and Dan Quayle there is no saying how far he might have gone. On the other hand, his chequered past might not have withstood the media scrutiny that has brought down so many other US politicians: with much weaker libel laws, American journalists would have felt less constrained than their British counterparts.

Jeffrey has often spoken of his anxiety that his tombstone will simply say no more than 'best-selling author'; he could not bear to confine the rest of his life to writing books. His past career suggests he will find some new outlet for his energy and infectious enthusiasm; probably not even he knows what that might be (though the arts, sport, charities and the plight of the Kurds are obvious possibilities). But with a platform in the House of Lords, powerful contacts, wide recognition and popularity, and above all, money, Archer enjoys considerable assets which are not readily available to most ambitious people.

Historians are likely to see him as no more than a colourful side-character, a diversion from the main plot, a jester at the courts of Queen Margaret and King John. Politically, there are no great ideas or legislative achievements to his name. Even with his literary output, it must be doubtful whether many people will still be reading Jeffrey Archer books a hundred years from now.

But rather like his novels, Jeffrey Archer's life is worth relating simply as a good story. And the fact he has got so far reveals a lot about the world in which he lives.

# Notes

PROLOGUE

1. Margaret Thatcher, *The Downing Street Years* (London, HarperCollins, 1993), p. 422
2. The first was Jonathan Mantle, *In for a Penny* (London, Hamish Hamilton, 1988)
3. Julian Critchley, *Some of Us* (London, John Murray, 1992), p. 156
4. Letter from Mary Archer to author, 24 October 1994
5. Hugo Young, *One of Us* (London, Macmillan, 1989); Ben Pimlott, *Harold Wilson* (London, HarperCollins, 1992); John Campbell, *Edward Heath* (London, Jonathan Cape, 1993)
6. Joe Haines, *Maxwell* (London, Macdonald, 1988); Tom Bower, *Maxwell: The Outsider* (London, Aurum, 1988)
7. Campbell, op. cit., p. xi
8. Letter from Jeffrey Archer to author, 1 June 1992

CHAPTER I

1. *Weston Mercury*, 24 February 1956
2. *Bristol Evening Post*, 18 April 1990
3. *The Times*, 23 July 1994
4. *Weston Mercury*, 24 February 1956
5. *Army List*, 1900 to 1940
6. *Western Daily Press*, 18 September 1979
7. For example in *The Observer*, 10 June 1984; *Chicago Tribune*, 10 September 1985
8. *The Guardian*, 21 July 1973
9. *Colonial Office List*, 1920 to 1940
10. Marriage certificate of William Archer and Lola Cook, Scotland, 12 January 1939
11. William Cobbett, *Rural Rides* (London, Dent, Everyman edition, 1912), vol. 1, pp. 17–18 and 179
12. Ibid., vol. 2, p. 93
13. Marriage registry of Stepney parish church, 30 August 1857
14. *As the Crow Flies* (London, Hodder & Stoughton, 1991), p. 10
15. *London Post Office Directory*, 1858, 1862 and 1864
16. 1871 census, Mile End Old Town
17. *Eastern Post and City Chronicle*, 14 December 1907
18. Ibid.
19. *Eastern Post and City Chronicle*, 21 December 1907
20. *Eastern Post and City Chronicle*, 8 February 1908
21. *Eastern Post and City Chronicle*, 11 April 1908
22. Val Haynes, interview with author

**23**. *New York Times*, 1 April 1919

**24**. Transcript, *Grimwood v. Archer*, New York Supreme Court [NYSC], 21 November 1919, pp. 26–7

**25**. Ibid., p. 8

**26**. Ibid., p. 9

**27**. Public Record Office, Calendars of Prisoners, HO140/314 1914 CCT, 13 October 1914

**28**. Ibid.

**29**. NYSC transcript, p. 32

**30**. Ibid., pp. 24–5

**31**. Ibid., p. 81

**32**. NYSC summons, p. 3

**33**. Ibid., p. 4

**34**. Ibid., p. 5

**35**. Papers of the Supreme Court of the District of Columbia, case no. 32521, *US v. William Grimwood*, National Archives, Washington DC

**36**. Ibid.

**37**. Testimony, *Crown v. Grimwood/Archer*, Toronto, November 1918

**38**. *Daily Mail*, 7 February 1919

**39**. NYSC transcript, p. 46

**40**. Letter from W. Archer to F. Grimwood, 19 August 1919, NYSC papers

**41**. NYSC transcript, p. 11

**42**. NYSC summons, pp. 6–8

**43**. Letter from A. Archer to F. Grimwood, 10 February 1919

**44**. Death certificate of Alice Archer, 31 January 1953

## CHAPTER 2

**1**. Will of Arthur Edgar Cook, 1933, Somerset House, London

**2**. Steve Humphries, *A Secret World of Sex* (London, Sidgwick & Jackson, 1988), p. 94

**3**. *Daily Mirror*, 1 August 1994

**4**. Wendy Burchell, telephone conversation with Margaret Crick

**5**. Birth certificate of David Brown (Jeffrey Neville Howard), 24 April 1934

**6**. Ibid.

**7**. *Night & Day (Mail on Sunday* magazine), 28 May 1995

**8**. David Brown, interview with author

**9**. *Night & Day*, 28 May 1995

**10**. Marriage certificate of William Archer and Lola Cook, Scotland, 12 January 1939

**11**. David Brown, interview with author

**12**. Ibid.

**13**. Ibid.

**14**. Ibid.

**15**. Ibid.

**16**. *Night & Day*, 28 May 1995

**17**. Ibid.

**18**. Ibid.

**19**. Ibid.

## CHAPTER 3

**1**. Birth certificate of Jeffrey Howard Archer, 15 April 1940

**2**. Will of William Robert Archer, 1956, Somerset House

**3**. Jeffrey Archer election address, Louth by-election, December 1969

**4**. *Somerset Countryman*, October–December 1952

**5**. Ibid.

**6**. Gertie Tidball, interview with author

**7**. John Creber, interview with author

**8**. Mary Wall, interview with author

**9**. Cyril Dowzell, interview with author

**10**. Bert Allen, interview with author

**11.** *The Times*, 23 July 1994

**12.** *Bristol Evening Post*, 18 April 1990

**13.** W. H. Auden, 'Twelve Songs' (1936) in *Collected Poems*, ed. Edward Mendelsohn (London, Faber and Faber, 2nd edn, 1991), p. 140

**14.** *News of the World*, 15 July 1984

**15.** *Weston Mercury*, 9 February 1951

**16.** *Weston Mercury*, 18 June 1949; 4 January 1952; 19 January 1951; 26 February 1954

**17.** *Weston Mercury*, 13 August 1949; 15 August 1952

**18.** *Weston Mercury*, 28 May 1949

**19.** *Western Daily Press*, 14 July 1992

**20.** *Weston Mercury*, 16 July 1949

**21.** *Weston Mercury*, 12 November 1949

**22.** Michael Taudevin, interview with Margaret Crick

**23.** Michael Taudevin, notes written for author

**24.** Ibid.

**25.** *Daily Mail*, 15 June 1984

**26.** *Weston Mercury*, 25 March 1950

**27.** *Weston Mercury*, 15 April 1950

**28.** *Weston Mercury*, 29 April 1950

**29.** *Weston Mercury*, 2 September 1950

**30.** *Weston Mercury*, 9 March 1951

**31.** *Weston Mercury*, 13 April 1951

**32.** *Hello!*, 15 August 1988

**33.** *Weston Mercury*, 11 May 1951

**34.** *Weston Mercury*, 22 May 1953

**35.** *Weston Mercury*, 9 November 1951

**36.** *Weston Mercury*, 20 July 1951

**37.** *Weston Mercury*, 27 July 1951

**38.** *Weston Mercury*, 3 August 1951

**39.** *Weston Mercury*, 7 March 1952

**40.** *Weston Mercury*, 16 May 1952

CHAPTER 4

**1.** Leonard Isaac, *The Story of Wellington School 1837–1990* (Wellington, Friends of Wellington School, 1993), p. 114

**2.** John Nash, interview with author

**3.** Michael Taudevin, notes written for author

**4.** Jill Fisher (née Taudevin), interview with author

**5.** Taudevin notes

**6.** Fisher interview

**7.** Ibid.

**8.** Ibid.

**9.** *Evening Standard*, 26 September 1995

**10.** Taudevin notes

**11.** Richard Benson, telephone interview with author

**12.** Howard Preece, telephone interview with author

**13.** Jeffrey Archer, *First Among Equals* (London, Hodder & Stoughton, 1984), p. 328

**14.** David Bromfield, telephone interview with author

**15.** Nigel Coombes, telephone interview with Margaret Crick

**16.** Postcard from Archer to Jill Taudevin, 11 August 1955

**17.** *The Times*, 23 July 1994

**18.** Alan Quilter, telephone interview with author

**19.** *Wellington School Magazine*, December 1955

**20.** Geoffrey Matthews, conversation with author

**21.** *Sunday Express*, 7 October 1984

**22.** *Weston Mercury*, 28 December 1956

**23.** *Sunday Express*, 7 October 1984

**24.** Lucille Iremonger, *The Fiery Chariot: A Study of British Prime Ministers and their Search for Love* (London, Secker & Warburg, 1970)

**25.** Adrian Metcalfe, interview with author

**26.** *Wellington School Magazine*, December 1957

**27.** *Weston Mercury*, 30 March 1956

**28.** Letter from Lola Archer to the editor of *Woman's Hour*, 2 June 1954, BBC Written Archives Centre [WAC], Caversham

**29.** Letter from Lola Archer to Janet Quigley, 2 August 1954, BBC WAC

**30.** Note from Joanna Scott-Moncrieff to Kenneth Hudson, 5 November 1954, BBC WAC

**31.** Transcript of 'Running a Social Club for the Disabled', *Window on the West*, BBC West of England Home Service, 22 March 1955, BBC WAC, Ref: B/C WEHS 22/3/55

**32.** Letter from Robert Goodyear of the BBC to Lola Archer, 18 February 1955, BBC WAC

**33.** *Weston Mercury*, 16 August 1957

**34.** *Wellington Weekly News*, 11 September 1957; 22 January 1958; 17 September 1958

**35.** Preece interview

**CHAPTER 5**

**1.** *Oxford Mail*, 22 October 1965

**2.** Anne Lonsdale, former Oxford University external relations officer, telephone conversation with author

**3.** Letter from Archer to London Institute of Education, 22 May 1967

**4.** Assessment of Archer by Management Selection Ltd, 1 February 1966, National Birthday Trust Archive, Wellcome Institute, NBT/N6/1/1

**5.** *The Guardian*, 21 July 1973

**6.** *Isis*, 7 November 1964

**7.** Ibid.

**8.** *London Review of Books*, 15 September 1988

**9.** Letter from Geoffrey Grimes of Lovell, White & King to Bryan Rostron and Paul Foot of the *Daily Mirror*, 30 January 1986

**10.** *Open To Question*, BBC TV Scotland, 5 November 1985

**11.** John Golding, telephone interview with author

**12.** Ibid.

**13.** James McClarnon, telephone interview with author

**14.** Golding interview

**15.** Ibid.

**16.** Ibid.

**17.** Major-General Simon Lytle, telephone interview with author

**18.** Libel Trial Transcript, Day 1, 6 July 1987, p. 72

**19.** Janet Eldershaw, telephone interview with Margaret Crick

**20.** Libel Trial Transcript, Day 1, 6 July 1987, p. 72

**21.** Bill Johnstone, telephone interview with Margaret Crick

**22.** *Police Review*, 15 July 1960

**23.** Brian Morris, telephone interview with author

**24.** Ibid.

**25.** Lovell, White & King, op. cit.

**26.** Euan MacAlpine, telephone interview with Margaret Crick

**27**. John Steadman, interview with author
**28**. MacAlpine interview
**29**. Charles Neel, telephone interview with author
**30**. Michael Stevens, telephone interview with Margaret Crick
**31**. Steadman interview
**32**. Ibid.

CHAPTER 6

**1**. Tim Cobb, telephone conversation with author
**2**. Jean Tuckwell, telephone interview with Margaret Crick
**3**. Richard Rottenbury, telephone interview with Margaret Crick
**4**. Stephen Catt, telephone interview with author
**5**. *Daily Mail*, 25 July 1987
**6**. John Wise-Fone, telephone interview with author
**7**. Bruce Dakowski, interview with author
**8**. Catt interview
**9**. Rottenbury interview
**10**. *The Dovorian*, Christmas 1961
**11**. *Tit-bits*, 25 February 1961
**12**. *Health and Strength*, 1949
**13**. *Class List*, Dover College, Michaelmas Term 1962
**14**. *Reveille*, 23 November 1961
**15**. Joan Czarnowski, telephone interview with Margaret Crick
**16**. Ibid.
**17**. Daniel Dane, telephone interview with Margaret Crick
**18**. James Philbrick, interview with Margaret Crick
**19**. Maureen Gough, telephone interview with Margaret Crick
**20**. *Dover Express*, 6 July 1962

**21**. *The Dovorian*, Lent 1963
**22**. *The Dovorian*, Summer 1962
**23**. Penny Matthews, telephone interview with Margaret Crick
**24**. *Sunday Express Magazine*, 15 December 1985
**25**. *Dover Express*, 28 June 1963
**26**. John Holt, telephone interview with author
**27**. Julian Dakowski, interview with author
**28**. Bruce Dakowski interview
**29**. *The Dovorian*, Summer 1963
**30**. *Dover Express*, 28 June 1963
**31**. *Daily Mail*, 25 July 1987
**32**. Czarnowski interview
**33**. Diana Carruthers, telephone interview with Margaret Crick

CHAPTER 7

**1**. Ronald Burrows, telephone interview with Margaret Crick
**2**. Alexander Peterson, unpublished memoirs in the possession of his widow, Corinna
**3**. Anne Lonsdale, former Oxford University external relations officer, telephone conversation with author
**4**. Burrows interview
**5**. *The Dovorian*, Lent 1964. This article has particular value as a source as it was written only a few weeks after the events
**6**. Oxfam internal broadsheet, 5 December 1963
**7**. Richard Exley, interview with Margaret Crick
**8**. *Cherwell*, 22 January 1964
**9**. Geoffrey Parkhouse, telephone interview with author
**10**. *The Dovorian*, Lent 1964

**11**. Maggie Black, *A Cause for Our Times: Oxfam the First 50 Years* (Oxford, Oxfam and Oxford University Press, 1992), p. 83
**12**. Letter from Archer to Maggie Black, 2 December 1992
**13**. *Oxfam Bulletin*, February 1964
**14**. *Cherwell*, 30 November 1963
**15**. *Daily Mail*, 4 December 1963
**16**. Brian Sommerville, telephone interview with author
**17**. Sir Nicholas Lloyd, interview with author
**18**. Pat Davidson, telephone interview with author
**19**. Lloyd interview
**20**. Ray Coleman, *Brian Epstein: The Man who Made the Beatles* (London, Viking, 1989), p. 211
**21**. Sommerville interview
**22**. Jonathan Stockland, interview with Margaret Crick
**23**. Sommerville interview
**24**. *Daily Mail*, 12 December 1963
**25**. *Daily Mail*, 17 December 1963
**26**. Ibid.
**27**. *Daily Mail*, 1 January 1964
**28**. *Financial Times*, 2 January 1964
**29**. *Cherwell*, 22 January 1964
**30**. Gordon Rudlin, interview with Margaret Crick
**31**. Lady Elinor Hall, interview with author
**32**. David Stockton, interview with author
**33**. *Daily Mail*, 6 March 1964
**34**. *Cherwell*, 11 March 1964
**35**. Sommerville interview
**36**. Letter from Maggie Black to author, 30 January 1993
**37**. Bruce Ronaldson, interview with Margaret Crick
**38**. *Cherwell*, 5 February 1964

**39**. Mary Dicken (née Bircham), telephone interview with Margaret Crick
**40**. Thomas Champlin, telephone interview with Margaret Crick
**41**. Stephen Benson, telephone interview with Margaret Crick
**42**. Adrian Twiner, telephone interview with Margaret Crick
**43**. Dicken interview
**44**. John Webster, telephone interview with Margaret Crick
**45**. Burrows interview
**46**. White House Daily Diary, 19 December 1964, LBJ Library, Austin, Texas
**47**. *Daily Mail*, 21 December 1964
**48**. *Cherwell*, 20 January 1965
**49**. Letter from Michael Parrish of LBJ Library to author, 3 February 1994
**50**. *Daily Mail*, 23 December 1964
**51**. Andrew Bull, telephone interview with Margaret Crick
**52**. Report of the Oxford Union election tribunal, 13 March 1965
**53**. Minutes of the Oxford Union standing committee, 31 May 1965
**54**. Tariq Ali, telephone interview with author
**55**. *Cherwell*, 26 May 1965
**56**. Raymond Walters, telephone interview with author
**57**. Oxford Union public minutes, February 1964 to November 1965
**58**. *Isis*, 26 November 1965
**59**. *Isis*, 10 June 1965
**60**. Oxford Union public minutes, March to December 1965

CHAPTER 8

**1**. *Today*, 16 July 1994

**2**. Ronald Burrows, telephone interview with Margaret Crick

**3**. *Daily Mirror*, 30 October 1986

**4**. *Oxford Mail*, 13 June 1964

**5**. John Parsons, telephone interview with author

**6**. Ibid.

**7**. Mike Morris, telephone interview with author

**8**. Brian Donnelly, telephone interview with author

**9**. *Evening Standard*, 20 October 1993

**10**. Michael Hogan, interview with author

**11**. Adrian Metcalfe, interview with author

**12**. Ibid.

**13**. Agreement between the Universities of Oxford and Cambridge with respect to Inter-University Contests, 1936

**14**. Letter from G. Grimes of Lovell, White & King to Bryan Rostron and Paul Foot of the *Daily Mirror*, 30 January 1986

**15**. *Daily Mirror*, 30 October 1986

**16**. John Bryant, interview with author

**17**. Damien Knight, telephone interview with author

**18**. Andrew Ronay, interview with author

**19**. Knight interview

**20**. Tim Taylor, telephone interview with author

**21**. Gordon McBride, telephone interview with author

**22**. Tim Jones, telephone interview with author

**23**. *The Times*, 7 May 1966

**24**. Metcalfe interview

**25**. *The Observer*, 8 May 1966

**26**. Taylor interview

**27**. Jones interview

**28**. Metcalfe interview

**29**. *Who's Who 1995* (London, A. & C. Black, 1995), p. 47

**30**. *British Athletics 1965*, p. 24

**31**. *British Athletics 1966*, p. 42

**32**. *British Athletics 1967*, p. 39

**33**. Hogan interview

**34**. Sir Arthur Gold, telephone interview with author

**35**. Letter from J. Archer to 'Peter', dated 12 July 1966

**36**. Gold interview

**37**. *Who's Who 1995* (London, A. & C. Black, 1995), p. 47

**38**. Marriage certificate of J. Archer and Mary Weeden, 11 July 1966

CHAPTER 9

**1**. Andrew Ronay, interview with author

**2**. *The Times*, 8 December 1965

**3**. Report by Management Selection (MSL) to NBT, 24 November 1965, NBT Archive, Wellcome Institute, NBT/N6/1/1

**4**. NBT executive minutes, 8 February 1966, NBT/A1/8(1)

**5**. MSL assessment of Archer, 1 February 1966, NBT/N6/1/1

**6**. Adrian Metcalfe, interview with author

**7**. NBT executive minutes, 8 February 1966, NBT/N6/1/1

**8**. Letter from Sir Noel Hall to J. D. Walters, 23 February 1966, NBT/N6/1/1

**9**. Ibid.

**10**. Letter from J. D. Walters to Archer, 4 March 1966, NBT/N6/1/1

**11**. The £4,000 salary was mentioned, among other places, in the *Oxford*

*Mail*, 4 March; *The Times*, 7 May; the *Daily Express*, 8 August; the *Evening News* (London), 8 and 10 August; and the *Dover Express*, 12 August 1966.

12. Letter from Archer to M. Morley, 19 May 1967, NBT/N6/10/4

13. *Cherwell*, 2 March 1966

14. *Evening News* (London), 8 August 1966

15. Elspeth Chowdharay-Best (née Rhys Williams), telephone interview with Margaret Crick

16. Letter from Archer to Shell, 16 August 1966, NBT/N6/5

17. Letter from E. F. Westray of Shell to Archer, 24 August 1966, NBT/N6/5

18. Letter from Audrey Slaughter to Archer, October 1966, NBT/N6/5

19. Letter from Major Peter Clarke to Archer, 20 October 1966, NBT/N6/4

20. Letter from Archer to H. J. Heinz & Co., 14 November 1966, NBT/N6/7/1

21. Ibid.

22. Director-general's report to NBT executive, 4 January 1967, NBT/A1/8(2)

23. Ibid.

24. Ibid.

25. NBT executive minutes, 4 January 1967, NBT/A1/8(2)

26. Director-general's report to NBT executive, 4 January 1967, NBT/A1/8(2)

27. NBT executive minutes, 4 January 1967, NBT/A1/8(2)

28. Anthony Patten, telephone interview with Margaret Crick

29. NBT executive minutes, 4 January 1967, NBT/A1/8(2)

30. Anthony Fletcher, telephone

interview with Margaret Crick

31. Bernard Brook-Partridge, telephone interview with author

32. *Evening News*, 13 February 1967

33. For example in *West Country Lives*, BBC Radio Bristol, 21 July 1993

34. *The Times*, 16 March 1967

35. Letter from Archer to Walter Gilbey (NBT chairman), 1 May 1967, NBT/N6/1/2

36. *The Observer*, 16 April 1967

37. NBT executive minutes, 3 May 1967, NBT/A1/8(3)

38. Director-general's report to NBT executive, 22 May 1967, NBT/N6/2

39. Letter from Archer to Robert Maxwell, 8 June 1967, NBT/N6/5

40. Anthony Patten's report on director-general's work to date, June 1967, NBT/A1/8(3)

41. Ibid.

42. Ibid.

43. NBT executive minutes, 26 June 1967, NBT/A1/8(3)

44. Ibid.

45. Ibid.

46. Doreen Riddick, telephone interview with Bryan Rostron of the *Daily Mirror*

47. Letter from Walter Gilbey to MSL, 5 May 1967, NBT/N6/1/2

48. Letter from Doreen Riddick to Walter Gilbey, 27 June 1967, NBT/F2/6

CHAPTER 10

1. Alan Mouncer, telephone interview with author

2. Letter from Archer, 14 March 1967

3. Letter from Archer to Bryan

Cowgill of BBC Sport, 13 April 1967

4. Sir Paul Fox, telephone interview with author

5. Ibid.

6. For example, *Sunday Express*, 7 October 1984

7. NBT executive minutes, 3 May 1967, National Birthday Trust Archive, Wellcome Institute, NBT/A1/8(3)

8. NBT executive minutes, 26 June 1967, NBT/A1/8(3)

9. Letter from Archer to Sir William Fiske, 28 April 1967

10. Letter from Archer to Christopher Chataway, 3 May 1967

11. Michael Wheeler, telephone interview with Margaret Crick

12. Letter from Archer to Christopher Chataway, 3 May 1967

13. Geoffrey Seaton, telephone interview with Margaret Crick

14. Sir Christopher Chataway, interview with author

15. Bernard Brook-Partridge, telephone interview with author

16. Norman Munday, telephone interview with Margaret Crick

17. *Hansard*, 15 February 1971, vol. 811, col. 1425

18. Chataway interview

19. Sir Neil Thorne, telephone interview with author

20. Christopher Chalker, telephone interview with author

21. Letter from Archer to Hamish Hamilton, 20 January 1994

22. Seaton interview

23. Letter from Archer to M. Morley of Harris & Hunter, 19 May 1967

24. Letter from Archer to University of London Institute of Education, 22 May 1967

25. Minutes of UNA finance and general purposes committee (F&GP), 24 June 1967

26. Ibid.

27. Humphry Berkeley, telephone interview with author

28. Ibid.

29. John Roper, telephone interview with author

30. *Evening Standard*, 4 April 1968

31. Minutes of UNA executive, 30 March 1968

32. Ibid.

33. Minutes of UNA executive, 13 July 1968

34. Minutes of UNA F&GP, 8 June 1968

35. Minutes of UNA F&GP, 1 February 1969

36. Ibid.

37. Minutes of UNA F&GP, 8 March 1969

38. Ernest Wistrich, interview with author

39. Ibid.

40. *Evening News*, 30 July 1969

41. Harold Wilson, *The Labour Government 1964–70* (Harmondsworth, Penguin, 1974), p. 863

42. *Evening News*, 30 July 1969

43. John Lovesey, telephone interview with author

44. Frank Keating, telephone interview with author

45. Ibid.

46. John Bromley, interview with author

47. Nigel Ryan, telephone interview with author

48. Geoffrey Rippon, telephone

interview with Bryan Rostron of the *Daily Mirror*
49. Ibid.
50. *Arts Review*, 6 December 1969
51. Rippon interview
52. Peter Fawcett, telephone interview with author
53. *Sunday Times*, 3 June 1973
54. *Observer Magazine*, 22 August 1982

CHAPTER 11

1. Jeffrey Archer, letter to Reading Conservatives, 10 April 1967
2. Jeffrey Archer, letter to Newark Conservatives, 10 March 1967
3. Peter Killmister, telephone interview with author
4. James Prior, *A Balance of Power* (London, Hamish Hamilton, 1986), p. 54
5. Douglas Hurd and Andrew Osmond, *The Smile on the Face of the Tiger* (London, Collins, 1969)
6. *24 Hours*, BBC2, 4 December 1969
7. Ibid.
8. David Walder, *The Short List* (London, Hutchinson, 1964)
9. Clixby Fitzwilliams, interview with author
10. Peter Walker, interview with author
11. *24 Hours*, BBC2, 4 December 1969
12. *Daily Mail*, 8 October 1969
13. Walker interview
14. Ibid.
15. Fitzwilliams interview
16. *24 Hours*, BBC2, 4 December 1969
17. Walker interview

18. *Grimsby Evening Telegraph*, 30 June 1984
19. Pat Otter, interview with author
20. *24 Hours*, BBC2, 4 December 1969
21. *Private Eye*, 24 September 1971
22. Letter from Archer to John Ennals, 24 September 1968
23. *The Times*, 19 November 1969
24. Ibid.
25. Letter from Geoffrey Grimes of Lovell, White & King to Paul Foot and Bryan Rostron of the *Daily Mirror*, 30 January 1986
26. *The Times*, 19 November 1969
27. Henry Sharpley, telephone interview with Margaret Crick
28. *The Times*, 19 November 1969
29. John Clare, telephone interview with author
30. Ibid.
31. Fitzwilliams interview
32. *The Guardian*, 18 November 1969
33. *The Times*, 21 November 1969
34. Walker interview
35. *Grimsby Evening Telegraph*, 5 December 1969

CHAPTER 12

1. For example, *As the Crow Flies* (London, Hodder & Stoughton, 1991)
2. *Daily Mirror*, 12 March 1970
3. *Hansard*, 20 April 1970, vol. 800, col. 84
4. Adrian Metcalfe, interview with author
5. Ibid.
6. Peter Duke, telephone interview with author
7. *Daily Telegraph*, 17 November 1970

**8**. *Evening Standard*, 4 November 1970

**9**. *From Shore to Shore: The Tour Diaries of Earl Mountbatten of Burma, 1953–1979*, ed. Philip Ziegler (London, Collins, 1989), p. 192

**10**. *Evening Standard*, 17 November 1970

**11**. Ibid.

**12**. *Daily Express*, 18 November 1970

**13**. *Evening Standard*, 4 November 1970

**14**. Letter from Mountbatten to Archer, 7 January 1971

**15**. *The Times*, 16 March 1971

**16**. Lord Ennals, telephone interview with author

**17**. *Evening Standard*, 16 September 1971

**18**. *Daily Telegraph*, 17 September 1971

**19**. Minutes of National Society for Cancer Relief executive committee, 7 December 1971

**20**. *Sunday Express*, 21 February 1971

**21**. Ernest Wistrich, interview with author

**22**. Ibid.

**23**. Ibid.

**24**. Ibid.

**25**. Ibid.

**26**. *Hansard*, 1 March 1972, vol. 832, col. 427; this referred to *The Spectator*, 4 March 1972, and *Pride, Prejudice and Persuasion – a Study in the Manipulation of Public Opinion in Britain* (London, David Rendel Ltd, 1972)

**27**. *Hansard*, 16 March 1972, vol. 833, cols. 759–60

**28**. Julian Dakowski, interview with author

**29**. Metcalfe interview

**30**. *Hansard*, 21 June 1971, vol. 819, cols. 1032–4

**31**. Ibid., col. 1034

**32**. Ibid., col. 1050

**33**. *Hansard*, 18 October 1972, vol. 843, col. 330

**34**. Ibid., col. 375

**35**. Philip Norton, *Dissension in the House of Commons 1945–74* (London, Macmillan, 1975)

**36**. *Hansard*, 2 July 1973, vol. 859, col. 90

**37**. *Hansard*, 16 December 1971, vol. 828, col. 828

**38**. Metcalfe interview

**39**. *Daily Mail*, 13 September 1976

**40**. *Daily Telegraph*, 24 March 1973

**41**. Letter to *The Times*, 4 April 1973

**42**. Wistrich interview

CHAPTER 13

**1**. *The Guardian*, 21 July 1973

**2**. *Sunday Express*, 12 July 1970

**3**. *Sunday Times*, 3 June 1973

**4**. Sir Roger Moate, telephone interview with author

**5**. Ibid.

**6**. For example in *Hello!*, 22 August 1988

**7**. *Sunday Times*, 3 June 1973

**8**. Ibid.

**9**. Michael Buckley, telephone interview with author

**10**. Adrian Metcalfe, untransmitted interview with BBC2 *Newsnight*, 14 July 1994

**11**. 'The Coup', *A Quiver Full of Arrows*, Coronet, London, 1981, p. 40

**12**. Letter from Michael Altmann to author, 4 February 1994

**13**. Transcript of Aquablast preliminary hearing, Toronto, Canada, 6 November 1975, p. 6

**14**. John Kennedy, interview with author

**15**. Frank Watts, telephone interview with author

**16**. *Financial Times*, 4 December 1972; *Evening Standard*, 24 November 1972

**17**. Hearing Transcript, 17 November 1975, p. 285

**18**. Ibid., pp. 285–6

**19**. Ibid., p. 286

**20**. Colin Emson, interview with author

**21**. Ibid.

**22**. Hearing Transcript, 17 November 1975, p. 286

**23**. *Exclusive* (unpublished script), 1989, Act 1, Scene 3 (p. 35)

**24**. Hearing Transcript, 17 November 1975, p. 272

**25**. Ibid., p. 288

**26**. Ibid., p. 289

**27**. Ibid.

**28**. Ibid., p. 290

**29**. *Sunday Times*, 24 June 1973

**30**. *Sunday Times*, 3 June 1973

**31**. Clifford Smith, interview with author

**32**. *Woman's Own*, 7 June 1986

**33**. Clixby Fitzwilliams, interview with author

**34**. Trevor Knight, interview with author

**35**. *Grimsby Evening Telegraph*, 23 August 1974

**36**. *Daily Mirror*, 24 August 1974

**37**. Speech to Cheltenham Festival of Literature, 18 October 1992

**38**. *Daily Telegraph*, 26 August 1974

**39**. *Daily Mail*, 13 September 1976

**40**. *The Scotsman*, 7 January 1978

**41**. *On the Ropes*, BBC Radio 4, 7 June 1990

**42**. *Ian Wooldridge Interviews*, BBC1 South, 13 November 1981

## CHAPTER 14

**1**. Martin Henderson, telephone interview with author

**2**. Adrian Metcalfe, interview with author

**3**. Ibid.

**4**. *Sunday Express*, 22 September 1974

**5**. Ted Francis, interview with author

**6**. Ibid.

**7**. David Niven Jnr, fax to author, 16 January 1995

**8**. Lady Elinor Hall, interview with author

**9**. Ibid.

**10**. Jeffrey Archer, *Not a Penny More, Not a Penny Less* (London, Jonathan Cape, 1976), acknowledgements

**11**. *Evening Standard*, 23 April 1971

**12**. *Northern Echo*, 21 September 1976

**13**. *Women's Wear Daily* (USA), 20 May 1976

**14**. Archer, op. cit., p. 105

**15**. Ibid., p. 155; Sir Nicholas Lloyd, interview with author

**16**. Archer, op. cit., p. 49; Clifford Smith, interview with author

**17**. *Grimsby Evening Telegraph*, 21 September 1974

**18**. Michael Hogan, interview with author

**19**. Libel Trial Transcript, Day 4, 9 July 1987, p. 68

**20**. Metcalfe interview

**21**. *Sunday Telegraph*, 1 May 1974

**22**. Lord Palumbo, telephone conversation with author

**23**. Libel Trial Transcript, Day 2, 7 July 1987, p. 38

**24**. Metcalfe interview

25. Hogan interview
26. *Sunday Express*, 22 September 1974
27. *Grimsby Evening Telegraph*, 9 September 1976
28. Ian Posgate, telephone interview with author
29. Ibid.
30. *Independent on Sunday*, 14 February 1993
31. Hilary Rubinstein, telephone interview with author
32. Metcalfe interview
33. Deborah Owen, telephone interview with author
34. *Publishing News*, 23 April 1982
35. David Owen, *Time to Declare* (London, Michael Joseph, 1991), p. 230
36. Owen interview
37. Susan Watt, telephone interview with author
38. Ibid.
39. Douglas Hunt, interview with author
40. George Wool, interview with author
41. Craig Carle, interview with author
42. Robert Hutchison, telephone interview with author
43. Robert Simpson Co. internal report, 18 November 1975
44. Letter from G. Grimes to B. Rostron and P. Foot, 30 January 1986; Letter from Archer to P. Foot, 3 December 1987
45. Owen interview
46. Letter from Deborah Owen to Tom Maschler, 5 December 1975, Cape Archive
47. Graham C. Greene, interview with author

48. Talk to Society of Young Publishers, 28 November 1984
49. Ibid.
50. Memo from Susannah Clapp to Tom Maschler, 2 February 1976, Cape Archive
51. Libel report on *Penny* by Leon Brittan, undated, Cape Archive
52. *Toronto Globe and Mail*, 10 April 1976
53. *The Province* (Vancouver, Canada), 15 April 1976
54. *Library Journal*, 1 May 1976
55. *Women's Wear Daily* (USA), 20 May 1976
56. *Evening Standard*, 14 June 1976; *The Jamesons*, BBC Radio 2, 19 July 1994
57. Colin Emson, interview with author
58. Ibid.
59. *Daily Telegraph*, 16 December 1976; *The Observer*, 19 September 1976
60. Letter from Archer to Tom Maschler, 16 March 1977, Cape Archive
61. Letter from Peter Sampson of Jonathan Cape to J. M. W. Hogan, 25 January 1977, Cape Archive
62. *Daily Mail*, 11 January 1977

## CHAPTER 15

1. *Los Angeles Times*, 20 October 1977
2. Ibid.
3. Paul Lamberth, letter to author, 7 September 1994
4. Nick Stames, telephone interview with author
5. Lamberth, op. cit.
6. Tom Guinzburg, interview with author

7. Ibid.
8. Deborah Owen, telephone interview with author
9. Cork Smith, interview with author
10. Guinzburg interview
11. Ibid.
12. *Boston Globe*, 12 October 1977
13. Smith interview
14. Ibid.
15. Ibid.
16. *Evening Standard*, 1 July 1977
17. Smith interview
18. Talk to Society of Young Publishers, 28 November 1984
19. Letter from Tom Maschler to Debbie Owen, 20 April 1977, Cape Archive
20. Letter from Debbie Owen to Tom Maschler, 21 April 1977, Cape Archive
21. *News-Chief* (Tampa, Florida), 18 September 1977
22. *Gazette-Journal* (Reno, Nevada), 25 September 1977; *Buffalo Courier-Express*, 9 October 1977
23. *Washington Post*, 11 October 1977
24. *New York Times*, 10 October 1977
25. Guinzburg interview
26. *Boston Globe*, 12 October 1977
27. Ibid.
28. *New York Times*, 15 October 1977
29. *The Scotsman*, 7 January 1978
30. *New York Times*, 3 November 1977
31. Guinzburg interview
32. Ibid.
33. *Newsweek*, 4 June 1951
34. David Lilienthal, *The Journals of David E. Lilienthal, 1945–1950*, vol. 2, Harper and Row, New York, 1964, p. 585
35. Press release, 1 May 1952, McMahon papers, Library of Congress, Washington
36. *Washington Evening Star*, 27 January 1952
37. For instance, *Washington Evening Star*, 17 September 1953
38. Patty Fox, telephone conversation with author
39. *Washington Evening Star*, 17 April 1949
40. Patty Fox, telephone conversation with author

CHAPTER 16

1. *Yorkshire Post*, 24 January 1978
2. Ibid.
3. *Daily Mail*, 19 January 1978
4. Libel Trial Transcript, Day 1, 6 July 1987, p. 76
5. *Newsagent and Bookseller*, 4 January 1979
6. Speech to Cheltenham Festival of Literature, 18 October 1992
7. Jeffrey Archer, *Kane and Abel* (London, Hodder & Stoughton, 1979), acknowledgements
8. Rick Kwiatowski, telephone interview with author
9. Ibid.
10. *Washington Post*, 7 March 1980
11. *Telegraph Sunday Magazine*, 2 September 1979
12. Archer, op. cit., p. 193
13. Ibid., p. 69
14. *Telegraph Sunday Magazine*, 2 September 1979
15. Archer, op. cit., pp. 75–6
16. Ibid., pp. 156–7
17. Natalie Wexler, telephone interview with author
18. *New York Times*, 4 May 1980
19. Tom Maschler talk to Society of

Young Publishers (SYP), 28 November 1984

**20**. Letter from Tom Maschler to Graham C. Greene, 23 November 1978, Cape Archive

**21**. Anonymous and undated note to Tom Maschler, Cape Archive

**22**. Maschler SYP talk, 28 November 1984

**23**. Ibid.

**24**. Deborah Owen, telephone interview with author

**25**. Ibid.

**26**. Alan Gordon Walker, interview with author

**27**. Ibid.

**28**. Ibid.

**29**. Tom Maschler, interview with author

**30**. Letter from Tom Maschler to Archer, 8 December 1978, Cape Archive

**31**. Letter from Archer to Tom Maschler, 10 December 1978, Cape Archive

**32**. Tom Guinzburg, interview with author

**33**. Cork Smith, interview with author

**34**. Ibid.

**35**. Ibid.

**36**. Cheltenham speech, 18 October 1992

**37**. Gordon Walker interview

**38**. George Greenfield, *Scribblers for Bread* (London, Hodder & Stoughton, 1989), p. 39

**39**. Ibid., p. 174

**40**. *The Author*, spring 1990

**41**. Joni Evans, interview with author

**42**. Ibid.

**43**. Jonathan Coleman, telephone interview with author

**44**. Evans interview

**45**. Coleman interview

**46**. Evans interview

**47**. Ibid.

**48**. Coleman interview

**49**. Evans interview

**50**. *Washington Post*, 7 March 1980

**51**. Jeffrey Archer, op. cit.

**52**. *Best Seller?* (Quintet Productions for HTV, 1984)

CHAPTER 17

**1**. *International Herald Tribune*, 3 May 1980

**2**. *Sunday Times Magazine*, 4 July 1982

**3**. *The Poetical Works of Rupert Brooke*, ed. G. Keynes (Faber and Faber, London, 1946), p. 72

**4**. Quoted by Mary Archer in 'Rupert Brooke: The Old Vicarage, Grantchester', in Kate Marsh (ed.), *Writers and Their Houses* (London, Hamish Hamilton, 1993), p. 51

**5**. *Contemporary Authors*, new rev. series, vol. 22 (Gale Research Co., Detroit, Michigan, 1988)

**6**. Graham Marks, telephone interview with author

**7**. Ibid.

**8**. Derek Matthews, telephone interview with author

**9**. Marks interview

**10**. Jeffrey Archer, *By Royal Appointment* (London, Octopus, 1980), p. 10. My thanks to Miss Catherine Crick for spotting this

**11**. Matthews interview

**12**. Jeffrey Archer, *A Quiver Full of Arrows* (London, Coronet, 1981), author's note

**13**. Ibid.

**14**. Ibid., pp. 11 and 112
**15**. Speech to Cheltenham Festival of Literature, 18 October 1992
**16**. *The Times*, 13 November 1980
**17**. *Financial Times*, 1 November 1980
**18**. Cork Smith, interview with author
**19**. Ibid.
**20**. Joni Evans, interview with author
**21**. *Woman's Own*, 7 June 1986
**22**. *Los Angeles Times*, 19 August 1982
**23**. Janet Brown, interview with author
**24**. David Broder, *Changing of the Guard* (Harmondsworth, Penguin, 1981), p. 480
**25**. Brown interview
**26**. *London Review of Books*, 19 August 1982; *Washington Post*, 23 July 1982
**27**. Jeffrey Archer, *The Prodigal Daughter* (London, Coronet, 1983)
**28**. Jeffrey Archer and Simon Bainbridge (eds.), *Fools, Knaves and Heroes: Great Political Short Stories* (London, Bellew Publishing, 1989)
**29**. Derick Bostridge, telephone interview with author
**30**. Ibid.
**31**. Alan Gordon Walker, interview with author
**32**. *Sunday Times Magazine*, 4 July 1982
**33**. Gordon McChesney, telephone interview with Margaret Crick
**34**. *The Guardian*, 9 January 1984
**35**. *The Guardian*, 20 July 1985
**36**. *Telegraph Sunday Magazine*, 2 September 1979
**37**. Jeffrey Archer, *Kane and Abel* (London, Coronet, 1981)
**38**. *Evening News*, 11 September 1979
**39**. *Daily Mail*, 13 December 1982

**40**. Dennis Selinger, interview with author
**41**. *Los Angeles Times*, 20 October 1977
**42**. *Telegraph Sunday Magazine*, 2 September 1979
**43**. Hope Preminger, telephone interview with author
**44**. Ibid.

CHAPTER 18

**1**. *Who's Who* (London, A. & C. Black, editions from 1978 to 1982)
**2**. *Bristol Evening Post*, 21 January 1984
**3**. *Sunday Times*, 8 September 1985
**4**. *Sunday Times Magazine*, 4 July 1982
**5**. Pat Otter, interview with author
**6**. *Sunday Telegraph*, 28 February 1982
**7**. *Glasgow University Guardian*, 23 February 1984
**8**. *Glasgow Herald*, 18 February 1984
**9**. John Nicolson, interview with author
**10**. Ibid.
**11**. Jeffrey Archer, *First Among Equals* (London, Hodder & Stoughton, 1984), p. 9
**12**. Cork Smith, interview with author
**13**. *Best Seller?* (Quintet Productions for HTV, 1984)
**14**. Ibid.
**15**. Ibid.
**16**. Ibid.
**17**. Joni Evans, interview with author
**18**. Smith interview
**19**. Evans interview
**20**. Ibid.
**21**. *Sunday Telegraph*, 22 July 1984
**22**. *Best Seller?*

23. George Greenfield, *Scribblers for Bread* (London, Hodder & Stoughton, 1989), pp. 294–5. The fact that Hodder also published Greenfield's book gives one some confidence about these Archer sales figures
24. Stewart Steven, interview with author
25. *Channel 4 News*, 14 June 1984
26. *Mail on Sunday*, 10 June 1984
27. *Time Out*, 26 July 1984
28. *Daily Mail*, 15 June 1984
29. *Evening Herald* (Plymouth), 15 June 1984
30. *The Times*, 28 August 1985
31. *Sunday Express*, 8 September 1985
32. Gemma Levine, *Faces of the 80s* (London, Collins, 1987)
33. *The Guardian*, 20 July 1985

CHAPTER 19

1. Margaret Thatcher, *The Downing Street Years* (London, HarperCollins, 1993), p. 422
2. *The Times*, 4 September 1985
3. *Glasgow Herald*, 27 October 1986
4. Norman Tebbit, *Upwardly Mobile* (London, Weidenfeld & Nicolson, 1988), p. 242
5. Thatcher, op. cit., p. 422
6. *Sunday Mirror*, 15 September 1985
7. *The Times*, 7 October 1985
8. *Daily Telegraph*, 4 October 1985; *The Times*, 7 October 1985
9. David Young, *The Enterprise Years* (London, Headline, pbk edn, 1991), p. 169
10. *The Independent*, 22 January 1987
11. *The Crusader*, October 1985
12. *The Guardian*, 18 October 1985
13. *The Spectator*, 12 October 1985
14. *Western Daily Press*, 21 October 1994
15. *Open To Question*, BBC TV Scotland, 5 November 1985; *This Week Next Week*, BBC1, 4 May 1986
16. *This Week Next Week*, BBC1, 4 May 1986; *People* (US), 18 November 1985
17. *The Scotsman*, 18 April 1986
18. *This Week Next Week*, BBC1, 4 May 1986
19. *Cosmopolitan*, November 1985
20. *Los Angeles Times*, 19 January 1986
21. *People* (US), 18 November 1985
22. *Daily Mail*, 10 October 1985
23. Alan Clark, *Diaries* (London, Weidenfeld & Nicolson, 1993), pp. 124–5
24. *Daily Express*, 18 June 1986
25. *Cosmopolitan*, November 1985; *The Times*, 19 December 1985
26. Harvey Thomas, telephone interview with author
27. Tebbit, op. cit., p. 243
28. Untransmitted interview for *Panorama*, BBC1, *c.* September 1990; see also James Saunders, *Ernest Saunders and the Guinness Affair* (London, Arrow, 1988), pp. 165–6
29. *This Week Next Week*, BBC1, 4 May 1986
30. *The Times*, 24 June 1986
31. Jeffrey Archer, *First Among Equals* (London, Hodder & Stoughton, 1984), p. 72
32. Ibid., p. 84

CHAPTER 20

1. Libel Trial Transcript, Day 9, 16 July 1987, pp. 66–7

2. *News of the World*, 26 October 1986

3. See Adam Raphael, *My Learned Friends* (London, W. H. Allen, 1989), p. 6

4. *The Guardian*, 27 October 1986

5. Ibid.

6. Libel Trial Transcript, Day 3, 8 July 1987, p. 27

7. *The Star*, 27 October 1986

8. *The Star*, 1 November 1986

9. Ibid.

10. Libel Trial Transcript, Day 13, 23 July 1987, p. 40

11. Libel Trial Transcript, Day 8, 15 July 1987, p. 62

12. Libel Trial Transcript, Day 9, 16 July 1987, pp. 54–5

13. Tape of first call from Coghlan to Archer, 25 September 1986

14. Ibid.

15. Ibid.

16. Tape of second call from Coghlan to Archer, 2 October 1986

17. Ibid.

18. Tape of third call from Coghlan to Archer, 9.30 a.m., 23 October 1986

19. Tape of fourth call from Coghlan to Archer, 9.55 a.m., 23 October 1986

20. Libel Trial Transcript, Day 1, 6 July 1987, p. 42

21. Tape of fifth call from Coghlan to Archer, 10.55 p.m., 23 October 1986

22. Ibid.

23. Ibid.

24. Tape of sixth call from Coghlan to Archer, 11.21 p.m., 23 October 1986

25. *News of the World*, 26 October 1986

26. Ibid.

27. Transcript of call from Michael Stacpoole to Gerry Brown, 25 October 1986

28. Recording played in court, Libel Trial Transcript, Day 2, 7 July 1987, p. 16

29. Ibid., p. 17

30. Ibid., p. 18

31. Ibid., pp. 18–19

32. Ibid., pp. 19–20

33. Ibid., p. 22

34. Ibid., pp. 29–30

35. Ibid., pp. 30–31

36. Ibid., p. 36

37. Michael Stacpoole, interview with author

## CHAPTER 21

1. *Daily Telegraph*, 21 March 1987

2. Ibid.

3. *UK Press Gazette*, 30 March 1987

4. Notes of meeting between Michael Stacpoole, Don Mackay and Nick Atkins, L'Hôtel, Paris, 12 noon, 27 May 1987

5. Ibid.

6. *The Observer*, 26 October 1986

7. *Sunday Today*, 26 October 1986

8. Adam Raphael, *My Learned Friends* (London, W. H. Allen, 1989), p. 16

9. Ibid.

10. Libel Trial Transcript, Day 1, 6 July 1987, p. 3, quoting from William Shakespeare, *Richard II*, Act 1, Scene 1

11. Libel Trial Transcript, Day 2, 7 July 1987, p. 56

12. Ibid., p. 57

13. Ibid., p. 66

14. Libel Trial Transcript, Day 3, 8 July 1987, p. 16

**15**. Libel Trial Transcript, Day 8, 15 July 1987, p. 34

**16**. Ibid., p. 39

**17**. Libel Trial Transcript, Day 5, 10 July 1987, p. 1

**18**. Libel Trial Transcript, Day 4, 9 July 1987, p. 71

**19**. Ibid., p. 73

**20**. Libel Trial Transcript, Day 5, 10 July 1987, p. 2

**21**. *Sunday Times*, 1 November 1987

**22**. Libel Trial Transcript, Day 4, 9 July 1987, p. 74

**23**. Libel Trial Transcript, Day 5, 10 July 1987, p. 29, and Day 3, 8 July 1987, p. 52

**24**. *Daily Express*, 3 November 1986

**25**. *Today*, 3 November 1986

**26**. Libel Trial Transcript, Day 3, 8 July 1987, pp. 61–2

**27**. Libel Trial Transcript, Day 8, 15 July 1987, p. 25

**28**. Libel Trial Transcript, Day 10, 17 July 1987, p. 56

**29**. Libel Trial Transcript, Day 5, 10 July 1987, p. 61

**30**. Libel Trial Transcript, Day 6, 13 July 1987, p. 10

**31**. Libel Trial Transcript, Day 5, 10 July 1987, p. 64

**32**. Ibid.

**33**. Ibid., pp. 64–5

**34**. Libel Trial Transcript, Day 8, 15 July 1987, p. 3

**35**. Ibid.

**36**. Ibid.

**37**. Libel Trial Transcript, Day 6, 13 July 1987, p. 68

**38**. Ibid., p. 70

**39**. Libel Trial Transcript, Day 12, 22 July 1987, p. 10

**40**. Libel Trial Transcript, Day 10, 17 July 1987, p. 1

**41**. Libel Trial Transcript, Day 12, 22 July 1987, p. 3

**42**. Libel Trial Transcript, Day 12, 22 July 1987, p. 60

**43**. *The Times*, 28 July 1987; 25 July 1987

**44**. Libel Trial Transcript, Day 4, 9 July 1987, p. 71

**45**. Libel Trial Transcript, Day 5, 10 July 1987, p. 13

**46**. Libel Trial Transcript, Day 13, 23 July 1987, p. 2

**47**. Ibid., p. 3

**48**. Ibid., p. 4

**49**. Ibid., p. 13

**50**. Libel Trial Transcript, Day 13, 23 July 1987, p. 62

**51**. *The Independent*, 24 October 1994

**52**. *The Independent,* 25 July 1987

**53**. Libel Trial Transcript, Day 10, 17 July 1987, p. 20

CHAPTER 22

**1**. *Sunday Times*, 1 November 1987

**2**. Jeffrey Archer, *Not a Penny More, Not a Penny Less* (London, Jonathan Cape, 1976), p. 69

**3**. *Daily Mail*, 25 July 1987

**4**. *Sunday Times*, 29 December 1991

**5**. *Desert Island Discs*, BBC Radio 4, 17 April 1988

**6**. Lisa Jardine, telephone interview with author

**7**. Ibid.

**8**. *Cherwell*, 9 November 1963

**9**. Jonathan Martin, interview with author

**10**. *Cherwell*, 26 February 1964

**11**. *Cherwell*, 11 March 1964

**12**. Michael Hogan, interview with author

**13**. Adrian Metcalfe, interview with author

**14**. Hogan interview

**15**. *Woman's Own*, 7 June 1986

**16**. *Desert Island Discs*, BBC Radio 4, 17 April 1988

**17**. *The Archers: Not an Everyday Story of Country Folk*, BBC2, 18 August 1987

**18**. *The Sun*, 11 December 1969

**19**. Jim Bolton, telephone interview with author

**20**. *The Archers: Not an Everyday Story of Country Folk*, op. cit.

**21**. *Daily Telegraph*, 15 January 1986

**22**. *Daily Mail*, 25 July 1987

**23**. Hogan interview

**24**. *Evening Standard*, 27 September 1967

**25**. *Sunday Times Magazine*, 4 July 1982

**26**. *Sunday Times Magazine*, 10 July 1994

**27**. *Who's Who 1995* (London, A. & C. Black, 1995), p. 48

**28**. *Desert Island Discs*, BBC Radio 4, 17 April 1988

**29**. *Sunday Express*, 8 September 1985

**30**. *The Archers: Not an Everyday Story of Country Folk*, op. cit.

**31**. Ibid.

**32**. Henry Togna, interview with author

**33**. *Who's Who 1995* (London, A. & C. Black, 1995), p. 47

**34**. *Desert Island Discs,* BBC Radio 4, 17 April 1988

**35**. *Today*, 29 August 1994

**36**. *The Archers: Not an Everyday Story of Country Folk*, op. cit.

**37**. *Mail on Sunday*, 4 October 1987

**38**. *The Archers: Not an Everyday Story of Country Folk*, op. cit.

**39**. John Bryant, interview with author

**40**. *Sunday Telegraph*, 29 November 1992

**41**. Bryant interview

**42**. Mary Archer, *Rupert Brooke and The Old Vicarage, Grantchester* (Cambridge, Silent Books, 1989)

**43**. *Hansard*, 13 July 1994, vol. 246, col. 1126

**44**. *Tatler*, November 1992

**45**. Tom Benyon, telephone interview with author

**46**. *Mail on Sunday*, 4 October 1987

**47**. *Sunday Telegraph*, 1 May 1994

**48**. Nick Archer, interview with author

**49**. *Daily Mail*, 27 July 1987

**50**. *Daily Telegraph*, 25 April 1986

**51**. *Woman*, 10 October 1987

**52**. *Daily Mirror*, 29 August 1975

**53**. Togna interview

**54**. Ibid.

**55**. *The Independent*, 28 December 1993

**56**. Hogan interview

**57**. *Night & Day* (*Mail on Sunday* magazine), 28 May 1995

**58**. *Sunday Times*, 4 June 1995

**59**. *The Archers: Not an Everyday Story of Country Folk*, op. cit.

## CHAPTER 23

**1**. Jeffrey Archer, *Beyond Reasonable Doubt* (London, Samuel French, 1989), p. 1

**2**. *The Times*, 21 September 1987

**3**. Lee Menzies, telephone interview with author

**4**. Tudor Gates, telephone interview with author

**5**. Ibid.

6. Ibid.

7. *The People*, 18 August 1991

8. Menzies interview

9. Archer, op. cit., p. 26

10. Ibid., pp. 20–21

11. Ibid., p. 28

12. Dennis Selinger, interview with author

13. *Western Daily Press*, 20 August 1987

14. *Michael Aspel*, BBC Radio 2, 12 September 1987; *Western Daily Press*, 7 August 1989

15. Menzies interview

16. *Daily Telegraph*; *Daily Mail*; *Financial Times*, 23 September 1987; *Sunday Times*; *The Observer*, 27 September 1987

17. *Today*, 23 September 1987

18. David Gilmore, telephone interview with Margaret Crick

19. Mig Kimpton, telephone interview with Margaret Crick

20. Patrick Garland, letter to Margaret Crick, 10 January 1995

21. Pat Macnaughton, interview with author

22. *Woman's Own*, 14 August 1989

23. Ibid.

24. Menzies interview

25. *Sunday Express Magazine*, 17 September 1989

26. Michael Rudman, telephone conversation with Margaret Crick

27. *Daily Mail*, 20 September 1989

28. *Today*; *The Guardian*; *Financial Times*, 20 September 1989

29. *Sunday Telegraph*, 24 September 1989

30. *Daily Telegraph*, 20 September 1989

31. *Evening Standard*, 20 September 1989

32. Ibid.

33. Menzies interview

34. Ibid.

35. John Bedding, telephone conversation with author

36. *Today*, 12 August 1989

37. David Lewin, telephone interview with author

38. David Lewin notes of interview with Archer

39. *Daily Mail*, 17 December 1990

40. Henry Togna, interview with author

41. Kimpton interview

42. Macnaughton interview

43. Sir Peter Hall, letter to Margaret Crick, February 1994

44. Kimpton interview

45. Ray Cooney, telephone interview with Margaret Crick

## CHAPTER 24

1. Rushes of interview with Archer by Oliver James for Channel 4's *Network 7*, 9 March 1988

2. Ibid.

3. *News of the World*, 15 July 1984

4. *Daily Mail*, 3 July 1985

5. *The Times*, 8 October 1986

6. *Daily Mail*, 3 July 1985

7. *Sunday Telegraph*, 22 July 1984

8. *Sunday Times*, 19 July 1986; *London Standard*, 2 July 1986

9. Details supplied by Deborah Hoffmann of the *New York Times* and Morgan Roberts of *Publishers Weekly* (US); *Publishers Weekly*, 13 March 1987

10. *The Guardian*, 8 January 1988

11. See Coronet ad in *The Bookseller*, 22 March 1986; *The Guardian*, 5 January 1987

**12**. *Cambridgeshire, Huntingdon & Peterborough Life*, March 1984

**13**. Recording of BBC Radio Cambridgeshire Short Story Competition award ceremony, 23 January 1984

**14**. *Clive Anderson Talks Back*, Channel 4, 19 October 1990

**15**. Jeffrey Archer, *A Twist in the Tale* (London, Hodder & Stoughton, 1988), pp. 93–100

**16**. Letter from Archer to Kathleen Burnett, 29 March 1989

**17**. Letter from Eric Major to Kathleen Burnett, 27 April 1989

**18**. Letter from Kathleen Burnett to Eric Major, 10 May 1989

**19**. Letter from Kathleen Burnett to Eric Major, 13 August 1989

**20**. Letter from Mishcon de Reya to Kathleen Burnett, 17 August 1989

**21**. Jeffrey Archer, *Shall We Tell the President?* (London, Coronet, 1978), p. 124

**22**. Archer, *A Twist in the Tale*, pp. 49–56

**23**. J. K. Randle, *The Natives are Friendly?* (Winchester, Hambleside Group, 1986), p. 138

**24**. *Sunday Express*, 23 October 1988

**25**. *Daily Telegraph*, 14 August 1992

**26**. *The Guardian*, 11 January 1990

**27**. *The Author*, spring 1990

**28**. Deborah Owen, telephone interview with author

**29**. Ibid.

**30**. Joni Evans, interview with author

**31**. *Evening Standard*, 27 March 1990

**32**. *The Bookseller*, 23 February 1990

**33**. George Greenfield, telephone interview with author

**34**. *New York Times*, 10 July 1990

**35**. Speech to Cheltenham Festival of Literature, 18 October 1992

**36**. *Publishers Weekly* (US), 26 April 1991

**37**. *Sunday Times*, 9 June 1991

**38**. Ed Breslin, interview with author

**39**. Cheltenham speech, 18 October 1992

**40**. Jeffrey Archer, *As the Crow Flies* (London, Hodder & Stoughton, 1991), p. 500

**41**. Michael Attenborough, telephone interview with author

**42**. Philip Attenborough, telephone interview with author

**43**. *The Guardian*, 12 January 1993; 8 January 1988

**44**. *The Times*, 3 June 1993

CHAPTER 25

**1**. Michael Attenborough, telephone interview with author

**2**. Eddie Bell, interview with author

**3**. *Publishing News*, 28 February 1986

**4**. Ibid.

**5**. *Sunday Times Magazine*, 4 July 1982

**6**. Bell interview

**7**. Speech to *Kent Messenger*/Hatchards literary dinner, Maidstone, 6 July 1993

**8**. *Publishers Weekly* (US) supplement ('The Red and The Black'), 7 March 1994

**9**. *The Guardian*, 10 January 1995

**10**. Bell interview

**11**. Willie Anderson, telephone interview with author

**12**. *Bucks Herald*, 24 November 1994

**13**. Richard Brown, telephone interview with Margaret Crick

**14**. *Bucks Herald*, 24 November 1994

15. Geoffrey Bailey, telephone interview with Margaret Crick
16. *Cover Stories*, BBC Radio Scotland, 9 May 1994
17. *The Author*, spring 1990
18. Ray Chapman, telephone interview with author
19. *Daily Telegraph*, 31 December 1994
20. *The Guardian*, 19 January 1996
21. Bell interview
22. Ibid.
23. Ibid.
24. *Evening Standard*, 12 September 1995
25. HarperCollins catalogue, January–June 1996, London, 1995
26. Anna Murdoch, *Family Business*, Collins, London, 1988
27. *Evening Standard*, 12 September 1995

CHAPTER 26

1. *Radio Times*, 11–17 May 1991
2. *Today*, 10 May 1991
3. Sir Paul Fox, telephone interview with author
4. *Today*, 10 May 1991
5. John Gray, telephone interview with author
6. Red Cross presentation, 5 November 1991
7. Nadhim Zahawi, telephone interview with author
8. Gray interview
9. *Daily Mirror*, 20 June 1991
10. British Red Cross accounts of Simple Truth appeal, November 1991
11. Gray interview
12. *Evening Standard*, 16 December 1991
13. Gray interview
14. *Evening Standard*, 2 October 1991
15. *Evening Standard*, 16 December 1991
16. Ibid.
17. Gray interview
18. *The Guardian*, 2 November 1991
19. Ibid.
20. *The Observer*, 3 November 1991
21. See *Sunday Times*, 8 January 1995
22. *The Independent*, 19 November 1991
23. Zahawi interview
24. *Sunday Times*, 12 January 1992
25. Ibid.
26. Tom Hardie-Forsyth, interview with author
27. Ibid.
28. Ibid.
29. Ibid.
30. Proposed SETCO Mandate for Exploration, Production, Export and Sale of Oil, Gas and Mineral Resources, Kurdistan, 1992
31. Togna interview
32. Hardie-Forsyth interview
33. Togna interview
34. Fax from Robert Oakley to Hani Salaam, 9 September 1992
35. Robert Oakley, telephone interview with author
36. Letter from Tom Hardie-Forsyth to John Major, 8 June 1993
37. Telephone call from Tom Hardie-Forsyth to Archer, May 1993
38. *The Observer*, 2 April 1995
39. Zahawi interview
40. *The Guardian*, 10 January 1994
41. Unpublished report by Colin Adamson of the *Evening Standard*, 4 January 1994
42. *The Guardian*, 10 January 1994
43. Latif Rashid, interview with author

CHAPTER 27

1. Recording of BBC TV live conference coverage, 6 October 1993
2. Nick Archer, interview with author
3. John Woods, telephone interview with author
4. *West Country Lives*, BBC Radio Bristol, 21 July 1993
5. See *Daily Telegraph*, 5 October 1987
6. *Private Eye*, 17 October 1986
7. Nesta Wyn Ellis, *John Major* (London, Macdonald, 1991), p. 85
8. *The Independent*, 28 December 1993. The interviewer, Hunter Davies, as is his habit, showed the finished article to Archer, who raised no objection to this quotation
9. *Panorama*, BBC1, 15 April 1991
10. Edward Pearce, *The Quiet Rise of John Major* (London, Weidenfeld & Nicolson, 1991), p. 157
11. John Bryant, interview with author
12. *Daily Mail*, 10 July 1993
13. Sir Geoffrey Pattie, telephone interview with Margaret Crick
14. Recording of interview for *The Printer's Devil*, September 1995
15. *Daily Mail*, 10 July 1993
16. *Alphabetical List of Members of the House of Lords* (Information Sheet No. 3, Lords Information Office, 1996)
17. *Daily Mail*, 10 July 1993
18. *Daily Telegraph*, 4 December 1993
19. *Behind the Headlines*, BBC2, 3 December 1992
20. Nick Archer interview
21. *Sunday Express*, 19 June 1994

CHAPTER 28

1. Libel Trial Transcript, Day 4, 9 July 1987, p. 61
2. *The Observer*, 10 June 1984
3. *Glasgow Herald*, 18 February 1984; *Evening Herald (Plymouth)*, 15 June 1984; *The Listener*, 10 July 1986
4. *Daily Telegraph*, 13 June 1992
5. *Sunday Times Magazine*, 4 April 1993; 10 April 1994
6. *Daily Mail*, 4 November 1987
7. *Family Wealth*, April 1987
8. Adrian Metcalfe, untransmitted interview with *Newsnight*, BBC2, 14 July 1994
9. *Bristol Evening Post*, 31 October 1987
10. *Family Wealth*, April 1987
11. Jeffrey Archer, *Kane and Abel* (London, Hodder & Stoughton, 1979), p. 193
12. Jeffrey Archer, *Twelve Red Herrings* (London, HarperCollins, 1994), pp. 64–5
13. Jeffrey Archer, *Beyond Reasonable Doubt* (London, Samuel French, 1989), pp. 31–2
14. David Howard, telephone interview with author
15. Ibid.
16. David McCall, telephone interview with author
17. Martin Tomkinson, interview with author
18. *The Times*, 8 July 1994
19. Statement to *The Times* by DTI Press Office, 7 July 1994
20. *The Times*, 8 July 1994
21. Metcalfe, *Newsnight* interview
22. *Sunday Telegraph*, 10 July 1994
23. *Daily Telegraph*, 12 July 1994
24. *Richard Littlejohn – Live and Uncut*,

London Weekend Television, 22 July 1994

25. *The Times*, 22 July 1994
26. *The Guardian*, 29 July 1994
27. *Sunday Times*, 11 September 1994
28. For example, *Sunday Times*, 2 January 1994
29. Some of the most revealing items were in the *Sunday Times* of 21 and 28 August 1994 and the *Financial Times* of 3 and 19 September 1994
30. *Evening Standard*, 22 August 1994
31. *Financial Times*, 23 August 1994
32. Press notice from Robin Cook MP, 21 August 1994
33. *Grimsby Evening Telegraph*, 23 August 1974; *The Guardian*, 27 October 1986
34. Statement issued by Mishcon de Reya on behalf of Lord Archer, 24 August 1994
35. *The Observer*, 28 August 1994
36. *Financial Times*, 27 August 1994
37. *Evening Standard*, 26 August 1994

38. *Daily Telegraph*, 1 September 1994
39. *Daily Mail*, 10 October 1994
40. *Hansard*, 27 January 1995, vol. 253, col. 471
41. *Daily Telegraph,* 4 February 1995
42. Affidavit sworn by Karen Morgan Thomas, 3 February 1995
43. *Daily Express*, 4 February 1995
44. *The Times*, 4 February 1995
45. *Sunday Mirror*, 5 March 1995

EPILOGUE

1. Recording of interview for *The Printer's Devil* magazine, September 1995
2. *Hansard*, 23 March 1995, vol. 257, col. 484
3. *Mail on Sunday*, 3 September 1995
4. *The Guardian*, 15 June 1992
5. Adrian Metcalfe, untransmitted interview for *Newsnight*, BBC2, 14 July 1994
6. *Ian Wooldridge Interviews*, BBC1 South, 13 November 1981

# Index

# READ MORE IN PENGUIN

In every corner of the world, on every subject under the sun, Penguin represents quality and variety – the very best in publishing today.

For complete information about books available from Penguin – including Puffins, Penguin Classics and Arkana – and how to order them, write to us at the appropriate address below. Please note that for copyright reasons the selection of books varies from country to country.

**In the United Kingdom**: Please write to *Dept. EP, Penguin Books Ltd, Bath Road, Harmondsworth, West Drayton, Middlesex UB7 0DA*

**In the United States**: Please write to *Consumer Sales, Penguin USA, P.O. Box 999, Dept. 17109, Bergenfield, New Jersey 07621-0120.* VISA and MasterCard holders call 1-800-253-6476 to order Penguin titles

**In Canada**: Please write to *Penguin Books Canada Ltd, 10 Alcorn Avenue, Suite 300, Toronto, Ontario M4V 3B2*

**In Australia**: Please write to *Penguin Books Australia Ltd, P.O. Box 257, Ringwood, Victoria 3134*

**In New Zealand**: Please write to *Penguin Books (NZ) Ltd, Private Bag 102902, North Shore Mail Centre, Auckland 10*

**In India**: Please write to *Penguin Books India Pvt Ltd, 706 Eros Apartments, 56 Nehru Place, New Delhi 110 019*

**In the Netherlands**: Please write to *Penguin Books Netherlands bv, Postbus 3507, NL-1001 AH Amsterdam*

**In Germany**: Please write to *Penguin Books Deutschland GmbH, Metzlerstrasse 26, 60594 Frankfurt am Main*

**In Spain**: Please write to *Penguin Books S. A., Bravo Murillo 19, 1° B, 28015 Madrid*

**In Italy**: Please write to *Penguin Italia s.r.l., Via Felice Casati 20, I–20124 Milano*

**In France**: Please write to *Penguin France S. A., 17 rue Lejeune, F–31000 Toulouse*

**In Japan**: Please write to *Penguin Books Japan, Ishikiribashi Building, 2–5–4, Suido, Bunkyo-ku, Tokyo 112*

**In South Africa**: Please write to *Longman Penguin Southern Africa (Pty) Ltd, Private Bag X08, Bertsham 2013*

# READ MORE IN PENGUIN

## A CHOICE OF NON-FICTION

**Citizens**  Simon Schama

'The most marvellous book I have read about the French Revolution in the last fifty years' – *The Times*. 'He has chronicled the vicissitudes of that world with matchless understanding, wisdom, pity and truth, in the pages of this huge and marvellous book' – *Sunday Times*

**1945: The World We Fought For**  Robert Kee

Robert Kee brings to life the events of this historic year as they unfolded, using references to contemporary newspapers, reports and broadcasts, and presenting the reader with the most vivid, immediate account of the year that changed the world. 'Enthralling ... an entirely realistic revelation about the relationship between war and peace' – *Sunday Times*

**Cleared for Take-Off**  Dirk Bogarde

'It begins with his experiences in the Second World War as an interpreter of reconnaissance photographs ... he witnessed the liberation of Belsen – though about this he says he cannot write. But his awareness of the horrors as well as the dottiness of war is essential to the tone of this affecting and strangely beautiful book' – *Daily Telegraph*

**Nine Parts of Desire**  Geraldine Brooks
The Hidden World of Islamic Women

'She takes us behind the veils and into the homes of women in every corner of the Middle East ... It is in her description of her meetings – like that with Khomeini's widow Khadija, who paints him as a New Man (and one for whom she dyed her hair vamp-red) – that the book excels' – *Observer*. 'Frank, engaging and captivating' – *New Yorker*

**Insanely Great**  Steven Levy

The Apple Macintosh revolutionized the world of personal computing – yet the machinations behind its conception were nothing short of insane. 'One of the great stories of the computing industry ... a cast of astonishing characters' – *Observer*. 'Fascinating edge-of-your-seat story' – *Sunday Times*

# READ MORE IN PENGUIN

## A CHOICE OF NON-FICTION

**Time Out Film Guide**   Edited by John Pym

The definitive, up-to-the-minute directory of every aspect of world cinema from classics and silent epics to reissues and the latest releases.

**Flames in the Field**   Rita Kramer

During July 1944, four women agents met their deaths at Struthof-Natzweiler concentration camp at the hands of the SS. They were members of the Special Operations Executive, sent to Nazi-occupied France in 1943. *Flames in the Field* reveals that the odds against their survival were weighted even more heavily than they could possibly have contemplated, for their network was penetrated by double agents and security was dangerously lax.

**Colored People**   Henry Louis Gates Jr.

'A wittily drawn portrait of a semi-rural American community, in the years when racial segregation was first coming under legal challenge ... In the most beautiful English ... he recreates a past to which, in every imaginable sense, there is no going back' – *Mail on Sunday*

**Naturalist**   Edward O. Wilson

'His extraordinary drive, encyclopaedic knowledge and insatiable curiosity shine through on virtually every page' – *Sunday Telegraph*. 'There are wonderful accounts of his adventures with snakes, a gigantic ray, butterflies, flies and, of course, ants ... a fascinating insight into a great mind' – *Guardian*

**Roots Schmoots**   Howard Jacobson

'This is no exercise in sentimental journeys. Jacobson writes with a rare wit and the book sparkles with his gritty humour ... he displays a deliciously caustic edge in his analysis of what is wrong, and right, with modern Jewry' – *Mail on Sunday*

# READ MORE IN PENGUIN

## A CHOICE OF NON-FICTION

**Mornings in the Dark**  Edited by David Parkinson
The Graham Greene Film Reader

Prompted by 'a sense of fun' and 'that dangerous third Martini' at a party in June 1935, Graham Greene volunteered himself as the *Spectator* film critic. 'His film reviews are among the most trenchant, witty and memorable one is ever likely to read' – *Sunday Times*

**Real Lives, Half Lives**  Jeremy Hall

The world has been 'radioactive' for a hundred years – providing countless benefits to medicine and science – but there is a downside to the human mastery of nuclear physics. *Real Lives, Half Lives* uncovers the bizarre and secret stories of people who have been exposed, in one way or another, to radioactivity across the world.

**Hidden Lives**  Margaret Forster

'A memoir of Forster's grandmother and mother which reflects on the changes in women's lives – about sex, family, work – across three generations. It is a moving, evocative account, passionate in its belief in progress, punchy as a detective novel in its story of Forster's search for her grandmother's illegitimate daughter. It also shows how biography can challenge our basic assumptions about which lives have been significant and why' – *Financial Times*

**Eating Children**  Jill Tweedie

'Jill Tweedie re-creates in fascinating detail the scenes and conditions that shaped her, scarred her, broke her up or put her back together … a remarkable story' – *Vogue*. 'A beautiful and courageous book' – Maya Angelou

**The Lost Heart of Asia**  Colin Thubron

'Thubron's journey takes him through a spectacular, talismanic geography of desert and mountain … a whole glittering, terrible and romantic history lies abandoned along with thoughts of more prosperous times' – *The Times*

# READ MORE IN PENGUIN

## A CHOICE OF NON-FICTION

**Fisher's Face**  Jan Morris

Admiral of the Fleet Lord 'Jacky' Fisher (1841–1920) was one of the greatest naval reformers in history. 'An intimate recreation of the man in all his extraordinary complexity, his mercurial humours, his ferocious energy and bloodthirstiness, his childlike innocence, his Machiavellian charm' – *Daily Mail*

**Mrs Jordan's Profession**  Claire Tomalin

The story of Dora Jordan and her relationship with the Duke of Clarence, later King William IV. 'Meticulous biography at its creative best' – *Observer*. 'A fascinating and affecting story, one in which the mutually attractive, mutually suspicious, equally glittering worlds of court and theatre meet, and one which vividly illustrates the social codes of pre-Victorian Britain' – *Sunday Times*

**John Major: From Brixton to Downing Street**  Penny Junor

Within a year of a record-breaking general election victory, John Major became the most unpopular Prime Minister ever. With his party deeply divided and his government lurching from crisis to crisis, few thought he could survive. This absorbing biography uses interviews with family, friends, foes, Cabinet colleagues and the Prime Minister himself to uncover the real John Major.

**The Bondage of Fear**  Fergal Keane

'An important source for anyone trying to understand how South Africa achieved its transfer of power' – *Independent*. 'A first-class journalistic account ... likely to be the most memorable account of this terrible, uplifting time' – *Literary Review*

**The Oxbridge Conspiracy**  Walter Ellis

'A brave book that needed to be written ... Oxbridge imparts to our élite values which, in their anti-commerce, anti-technology, anti-market snobbery, make them unfit to run a modern economy. It is the Oxbridge élite which has presided over the decline of this nation' – *Financial Times*

# READ MORE IN PENGUIN

## BIOGRAPHY AND AUTOBIOGRAPHY

**Freedom from Fear**   Aung San Suu Kyi

This collection of writings gives a voice to Aung San Suu Kyi, human rights activist and leader of Burma's National League for Democracy, who was detained in 1989 by SLORC, the ruling military junta, and today remains under house arrest. In 1991, her courage and ideals were internationally recognized when she was awarded the Nobel Peace Prize.

**Memories of a Catholic Girlhood**   Mary McCarthy

'Many a time in the course of doing these memoirs,' Mary McCarthy says, 'I have wished that I were writing fiction.' 'Superb ... so heartbreaking that in comparison Jane Eyre seems to have got off lightly' – *Spectator*

**A Short Walk from Harrods**   Dirk Bogarde

In this volume of memoirs, Dirk Bogarde pays tribute to the corner of Provence that was his home for over two decades, and to Forwood, his manager and friend of fifty years, whose long and wretched illness brought an end to a paradise. 'A brave and moving book' – *Daily Telegraph*

**When Shrimps Learn to Whistle**   Denis Healey

*The Time of My Life* was widely acclaimed as a masterpiece. Taking up the most powerful political themes that emerge from it Denis Healey now gives us this stimulating companion volume. 'Forty-three years of ruminations ... by the greatest foreign secretary we never had' – *New Statesman & Society*

**Eating Children**   Jill Tweedie

Jill Tweedie's second memoir, *Frightening People*, incomplete due to her tragically early death in 1993, is published here for the first time. 'Magnificent ... with wit, without a shred of self-pity, she tells the story of an unhappy middle-class suburban child with a monstrously cruel father, and a hopeless mother' – *Guardian*